MECKLENBURG-LOWER POMERANIA

BRANDENBURG

EASTERN GERMANY

SAXONY-ANHALT

SAXONY

THÜRINGIA

BAVARIA

Rostock

Schwerin

Berlin

Potsdam

Magdeburg

Leipzig

Dresden

Erfurt

Nürnberg

Munich

D0375458

Putting Germany on the Map

LOCATED in the centre of Europe, between the North and Baltic Seas and the Alps, Germany covers an area of nearly 360,000 sq km (139,000 sq miles). Its neighbouring countries are Poland and the Czech Republic to the east, Austria and Switzerland to the south, France, Belgium, Luxembourg and Holland to the west, and Denmark to the north. The capital is Berlin. Its largest river is the Rhine. Germany is inhabited by over 81 million people.

KEY

--- National border

✈ Airport

— Motorway

— Major road

— Railway

⛴ Ferry terminal

--- Ferry route

0 km   100

0 miles   100

◁ **Grapevines stretching as far as the eye can see in the North Rhine-Palatinate**

INTRODUCING GERMANY

1 Introduction
The landscape, history and character of each region are described, showing how the area has changed through the ages. It also outlines the sights on offer for visitors.

GERMANY AREA BY AREA
In this guide, Germany is divided into 13 areas, each of which is covered in a separate section. The most interesting cities, towns, villages and sights in the area are marked on the Area Map.

2 Area Map
This shows the main roads and the general topography of the area. All sights are numbered, and there are also details on how to get there.

Boxes contain additional information about sights.

Colour coding at the edge of every page makes it easy to find each particular region.

3 Detailed Information
All major towns, places of interest and other tourist sights are listed in order and numbered according to the Area Map. Each entry contains information on important sights.

A Visitors' Checklist for each of the main sights provides practical information to help you plan your visit.

4 Major Sights
At least two pages are dedicated to each major sight. Historic buildings are dissected in order to show their interiors. Interesting towns or town centres have street maps with the main sights indicated and described.

How to Use this Guide

THIS GUIDE will help you to get the most out of a visit to Germany, providing expert recommendations as well as thoroughly researched practical information. The first section, *Introducing Germany*, locates the country geographically and provides an invaluable historical and cultural context. Succeeding sections describe the main sights and attractions of the different regions and major cities. Feature spreads, with maps and photographs, focus on important sights. Information on accommodation and restaurants is provided in *Travellers' Needs*, while the *Survival Guide* has useful tips on everything you need to know from money to getting around.

BERLIN

This section is divided into two parts: East and West. Sights outside the centre are described in the section *Around Berlin*. All sights are numbered and plotted on a map of the region. Detailed information for each sight is given in numerical order to make it easy to locate within the chapter.

Sights at a Glance describes, by category, buildings in a particular area: Historic Streets and Buildings, Museums and Galleries, Churches, Parks and Gardens.

2 Street-by-Street Map gives a bird's-eye view of each sightseeing area described in the section.

Stars indicate the sights that no visitor should miss.

Pages marked with red refer to Berlin.

A locator map shows where you are in relation to the city plan.

1 Area Map *For easy reference the sights in each area are numbered.*

A suggested route for a walk is marked with a broken red line.

3 Detailed Information *All the sights of Berlin are described individually. Addresses, telephone numbers, opening hours, admission charges and information on how to get there are given for each sight. The key to symbols is shown on the back flap.*

Picturesque landscape in Mecklenburg

Statue of a dancing figure, Stadtmuseum in Munich (see p204)

Mainz Cathedral (see pp336–7)

LONDON • NEW YORK • MUNICH
MELBOURNE • DELHI

Produced by Wydwnictwo Wiedza i Życie, Warsaw
CONTRIBUTORS Małgorzata Omilanowska, Marek Stańczyk,
Tomasz Torbus, Hanna Köster, Teresa Czerniewicz-Umer
CARTOGRAPHERS Kartographie Huber (Munich),
Magdalena Polak, Dariusz Romanowski
PHOTOGRAPHERS Adam Hajder, Dorota and Mariusz Jarymowiczowie,
Wojciech Mędrzak, Tomasz Myśluk, Paweł Wójcik
ILLUSTRATORS Lena Maminajszwili, Paweł Marczak,
Andrzej Wielgosz, Bohdan Wróblewski, Magdalena Żmudzińska
DTP DESIGNERS Paweł Pasternak, Paweł Kamiński
EDITORS Teresa Czerniewicz-Umer, Joanna Egert-Romanowska
PRODUCTION Anna Kożurno-Królikowska
DESIGNERS Ewa Roguska, Piotr Kiedrowski

Dorling Kindersley Limited
EDITORS Sylvia Goulding, Irene Lyford
TRANSLATORS Magda Hannay, Ian Wisniewski
DTP DESIGNERS Jason Little, Conrad Van Dyke
PRODUCTION Marie Ingledew

Printed and bound in Italy by Graphicom s.r.l.

First American Edition 2001
02 03 04 05 10 9 8 7 6 5 4

Published in the United States by DK Publishing, Inc.,
375 Hudson Street, New York, New York 10014

Reprinted with revisions 2002

Published in Great Britain by Dorling Kindersley Limited.

Library of Congress Cataloging-in-Publication Data
Omilanowska, Małgorzata.
 Germany / main contributor, Małgorzata Omilanowska.
 p. cm. -- (DK eyewitness travel guides)
 Includes index.
 ISBN 0-7894-6646-5 (alk. paper)
 1. Germany--Guidebooks. I. Title. II. Eyewitness travel guides.
DD16 .065 2001
914.304'88--dc21

00-069404

THROUGHOUT THIS BOOK, FLOORS ARE REFERRED TO IN ACCORDANCE WITH
EUROPEAN USAGE, I.E., THE "FIRST FLOOR" IS ONE FLIGHT UP.

See our complete product line at
www.dk.com

**The information in every
DK Eyewitness Travel Guide is checked regularly.**
Every effort has been made to ensure that this book is as up-to-date
as possible at the time of going to press. Some details, however,
such as telephone numbers, opening hours, prices, gallery hanging
arrangements and travel information are liable to change.
The publishers cannot accept responsibility for any consequences
arising from the use of this book, nor for any material on third party
websites, and cannot guarantee that any website address in this book
will be a suitable source of travel information. We value the views
and suggestions of our readers very highly. Please write to:
Publisher, DK Eyewitness Travel Guides, Dorling Kindersley,
80 Strand, London WC2R 0RL, Great Britain.

◁ Church in Bavaria nestled at the foothills of the Alps

CONTENTS

INTRODUCING GERMANY

Heraldic shield over the entrance
to the Nuremberg town hall

BERLIN AREA BY AREA

Renaissance doorway of the
Rathaus (town hall) in Gotha

DK EYEWITNESS *TRAVEL GUIDES*

GERMANY

Main contributors: JOANNA EGERT-ROMANOWSKA
AND MAŁGORZATA OMILANOWSKA

DK PUBLISHING, INC.

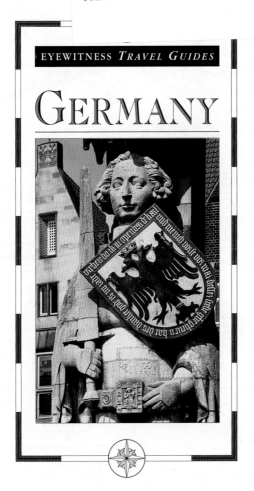

EYEWITNESS *TRAVEL GUIDES*

GERMANY

Mecklenburg Bay
Bergen
Lübeck Bay
Stralsund
Ribnitz-Damgarten
Rostock
Greifswald
Wismar
Güstrow
Anklam
Ückermünde
Schwerin
beck
Boizenburg
Ludwigslust
Neubrandenburg
Neustrelitz
Prenzlau
Baltic Sea

BERLIN
WIELKI BERLIN
Reinickendorf   Pankow
Wedding   Weissensee
Charlottenburg   Tiergarten   Mitte   Prenzlauer Berg
Friedrichshain
Wilmersdorf   Kreuzberg
Schöneberg   Treptow
Tempelhof   Neukölln
Schwedt
Steglitz

0 km   3
0 miles   3

lzen
Wittenberge
Salzwedel
Havelberg
Neuruppin
Eberswalde
Wolfsburg
Gardelegen
Stendal
Rathenow
BERLIN
Frankfurt am Oder
nschweig
Wolmirstedt
Brandenburg
Potsdam
Fürstenwalde
Magdeburg
Schönebeck
Luckenwalde
Eisenhüttenstadt
Halberstadt
Stassfurt
Dessau
Lutherstadt Wittenberg
Wernigerode
Aschersleben
Cottbus
Nordhausen
Lutherstadt Eisleben
Halle
Lauchhammer
Senftenberg
Sangerhausen
Marseburg
Riesa
Hoyerswerda
Leipzig
Erfurt
Weimar
Zeitz
Altenburg
Freital
Dresden
Bautzen
Görlitz
Gotha
Jena
Gera
Pirna
Freiberg
Zittau
Arnstadt
Rudolstadt
Chemnitz
Zwickau
Plauen
Hof
Coburg
Kulmbach
Bamberg
Bayreuth
langen
Fürth
Amberg
nsbach
Nürnberg
Regensburg
Eichstätt
Kelheim
Deggendorf
Neuburg
Ingolstadt
Passau
Landshut
Augsburg
Dachau
München
Rosenheim
Garmisch-Partenkirchen

Area Colours

■ Berlin

Eastern Germany

■ Brandenburg

■ Saxony

■ Saxony-Anhalt

□ Thuringia

Southern Germany

■ Munich

■ Bavaria

■ Baden-Württemberg

Western Germany

■ Rhineland-Palatinate & Saarland

■ Hesse

■ North Rhine-Westphalia

Northern Germany

■ Hamburg, Bremen, Lower Saxony

■ Schleswig-Holstein

■ Mecklenburg-Lower Pomerania

A PORTRAIT OF GERMANY

GERMANY IS A WEALTHY COUNTRY, *whose people are generally regarded as hard-working, determined and efficient. This view stems from the country's industrial might and the smooth functioning of its economy, but it overlooks other important aspects of Germany. These include its important contributions to art and culture, its breathtaking scenery and excellent tourist facilities.*

Contemporary Germany is far removed from the traditional, stereotyped view of the country. In the last 50 years, it has developed into a multi-ethnic, multi-cultural melting pot. Over 7 million of Germany's inhabitants are immigrants; the majority of these are Turks, with more recent guest workers arriving from the former Yugoslavia, Italy and Greece. In the city of Stuttgart, every third inhabitant is a foreigner; in Frankfurt it is one in four. Hamburg has more mosques than any other city in Europe and, in some schools in Berlin, German children are in the minority. Almost every town has a selection of Italian, Chinese, Greek and Turkish restaurants and cafés, testifying to the multi-ethnicity of its population.

The colourful Bavarian coat of arms

HISTORY AND ROMANCE

For many, the <u>river Rhine</u> epitomizes tourist Germany, particularly the romantic stretch between Mainz and Cologne. The country has far more than this to offer in the way of scenery, however. There is the ever-changing Baltic coastline, the sandy islands of the North Sea, the lakes of Mecklenburg, lonely castles perched on crags in Baden and Thuringia, mountain ranges including the Alps, the vast Bodensee lake, medieval cities and fairy-tale villages. Not all of the latter are original, as countless towns were destroyed by bombs during World War II, but many have been meticulously rebuilt to the original plans, and now it is difficult to tell the difference between the old and the new.

Verdant Alpine meadow against a backdrop of majestic, snowy peaks

◁ Alter Flecken – Freudenberg's quarter of traditional-style houses

Procession during the Plärrer Fest, a beer festival in Augsburg

TRADITIONS

Today's German nation has evolved over the past thousand years, mainly from various Germanic tribes, notably the Franks, Saxons, Swabians and Bavarians. Traditions and dialects have developed within regional ethnic groups that emerged as a result of historical alliances. There is no such thing as a single German tradition. Even the assumption that Germany is a country of beer-drinkers is belied by the large numbers of wine-lovers. These groups, along with consumers of stronger beverages, have given Germany a high position in the world league table for alcohol use. Nevertheless, drunks are rarely seen in Germany.

Bavarian scene on a beer glass

Various ethnic groups in the country are ascribed different characteristics. The people of Mecklenburg, for example, are seen as introspective, while Swabians are regarded as thrifty; the Saxons are seen as disciplined and cunning, while Bavarians are typified as a people bound by rustic traditions, quick to quarrel and fight. Indeed, one of the most pop-

A Bavarian dressed in regional costume

ular Bavarian men's folk-dances ends with them slapping each other in the face. Bavaria, of course, is home to the traditional Oktoberfest, a beer festival that brings millions of people to Munich every year from virtually all over the world.

The people of the Rhineland have a reputation for enjoying life. Their favourite season is the Carnival period, and they spend practically the entire year preparing for this week-long event. It begins on the last Thursday before Lent, with "town soldiers", helped by the huge crowds, storming the town hall. The town councillors surrender and power passes to the masked revellers. On the Monday, the Carnival proceeds through the thronged streets of the towns on the Rhine, and the pubs are busy until the end of Shrovetide.

Carnival is rooted in ancient rituals marking the banishment of winter. This custom was most common in the south of Germany, but it also reached the Rhineland, the Palatinate and Hessen. There is a special enthusiasm for the festival among the inhabitants of the former East Germany, where Carnival used to be banned, as it had been during the Third Reich.

ART AND CULTURE

Germany is a land of sagas and legends that tell of woodland spirits, beautiful princesses, magicians and sirens such as the Lorelei. These legends have had a strong influence on German art. An example is the German epic poem, the *Nibelungenlied*, which was written around 1200 on the basis of old legends. This poem was the inspiration for Richard Wagner's cycle of operas, *The Ring of the Nibelungen*, as well as for a trilogy of plays by Christian Friedrich Hebbel and a film by Fritz Lang.

Germans have won eight Nobel Prizes for Literature. The most recent prizewinner was Günter Grass, whose *Tin Drum* brought him world renown. More recently a film adaptation of the book was made by Volker Schlöndorff, which won the Golden Palm at the Cannes Film Festival. After a relatively stagnant period, the German film industry became revitalized around 1995 with a number of hits, albeit only at the national level. German cinemas are now always full and traditional cinemas are increasingly being replaced by multiplexes.

Germans read widely, even in today's age of television and the internet. Every year 70,000 new books are published in Germany and eight times that many titles are on sale. Germany is second only to the United States in the number of books published annually, while the number of bookshops per square kilometre is the highest in the world. The same applies to museums and art galleries.

Germany has over 2,000 national, provincial and local history museums,

The historical Frohnauer hammer forge near Annaberg in Saxony

as well as numerous church museums, folk museums and former royal palaces. This variety and choice owes much to the fact that, in the past, local dukes acquired collections of art in order to impress others and to demonstrate their wealth. The Bavarian dukes also built up extensive collections of machines, artisans' tools, musical instruments and minerals. As early as the 16th century, Munich was an international centre of the arts and the Grünes Gewölbe in 17th-century Dresden was one of the largest treasuries for storing fine art in Europe. Of the many art galleries to be found throughout Germany, the finest are in Cologne, Frankfurt, Stuttgart, Munich and Berlin.

Lorelei overlooking the Rhine

Music also flourishes in Germany. Most large cities have their own symphony orchestra and opera company and every year some 100 regional and local music festivals take place. Musical comedies are especially popular.

The imposing Schönburg Castle, near Oberwesel on the Rhine

SOCIETY AND POLITICS

The scars of World War II are more evident in Eastern Germany, although they are gradually disappearing there, too. Görlitz, Bautzen, Leipzig and Weimar have now acquired a splendour that was previously hidden behind the grim façade of East Germany. The mental, social and political scars of the war and subsequent division of Germany have, however, left deeper scars. Although reunification took place on 3 October 1990, unity among the people themselves has been longer in coming. East Germans are the poor relations: the region has high unemployment rates and its people tend to regard their western counterparts as arrogant and self-assured. The latter, for their part, claim that the inhabitants of the "new states" are jealous and ungrateful despite the billions of marks that have been poured into the region to equalize living standards.

The *Bundestag* in session in the old Reichstag building

Germany has almost always been divided regionally into states with fluctuating borders. The present-day states were, for the most part, created after 1945 while those in East Germany were not created until forty years later. In all cases, old territorial and historical ties were taken into account. That is the reason for their evocative names, such as the "Free State of Bavaria" or the "Free State of Saxony".

There are now 16 federal states, or provinces. North Rhine-Westphalia, Baden-Württemberg and Bavaria are the largest and are like economically powerful countries. At the other end of the scale, the tiny province of Saarland has only 1.1 million inhabitants, while the Free Hanseatic City of Bremen has fewer than 700,000. The former East German states are also relatively small but all play an important role in the *Bundesrat*, or Federal Council, where they are instrumental in enacting legislation. All laws, apart from those relating to the Federation as a whole, such as defence or foreign policy, require the agreement of the *Bundesrat*, which is made up from current local governments. Depending on the number of inhabitants, each federal state has from four to six votes.

The skyline of Frankfurt am Main, reminiscent of New York

A government with a major-ity in the *Bundestag* (parlia-ment) cannot always count on support in the *Bundesrat*, even if it has a majority there. Each state looks after its own interests and often makes alliances with other states to achieve its own aims, without regard for party loyalty. The complex working of German federalism is based on the compromises that this system makes necessary.

Bathers on the sandy beaches of Norddeich

DAILY LIFE

The traditional image of German women used to be summed up in the "three Ks": *Küche, Kinder, Kirche* (kitchen, chil-dren, church). As in other Western European countries, however, this stereotype no longer holds true. Although cookery is fashionable and there are countless TV cook-ery programmes starring celebrity chefs, for everyday meals, ready-prepared dishes are eaten, either at the work canteen or from the super-market. The German birthrate is declining, while the anti-authoritarian model of education that was intro-duced in the 1960s has to some extent relieved par-ents of many of the more onerous duties of child-rearing. As a result, many young people show little respect for their elders. The churches, for their part, are usually empty. Although the largest churches (Catholic and Protestant) have many adherents, the vast majority are not practising believers and limit themselves to the payment of church dues.

Germans speak of themselves as a high-performance society *(Leistungs-gesellschaft)*, which gives the highest rewards to those who devote almost all their energies to their careers. As a result, stress is often a factor in people's lives, from schooldays onwards. In Germany today there are increasing numbers of people who live alone.

Participant in a parade marking the Reunification celebrations

Single-person households are most common in the cities and even young people regard their careers as of paramount importance. Increasingly large numbers say that they are not interested in having a family.

Nevertheless, Germans enjoy mass events such as public holidays and pop-ular festivals. The country has the high-est number of public holidays in Europe and German workers have the longest annual holidays. Its citizens are Europe's most enthusiastic travellers, each year spending over DM 70 million on foreign holidays. When they return there is a tendency to long for the southern climes they have just visited – perhaps this explains why restaurants offering Mediterranean food are so popular.

The Bodensee, a popular tourist destination

Flora and Fauna

Black-headed gull

GERMANY IS A VAST country whose varied geography has given rise to a great diversity of flora and fauna. It is famous for its forests, many of mixed deciduous trees, including oak, beech and birch. Around 31 per cent of the country is forested.

The Alpine regions have a rich variety of wild flowers, with meadow species a particular feature in spring and summer. On the northern peat moors, heaths and heathers are common. Germany is home to a wide range of wildlife, including wild boar, lynx and marmots. Many valuable wildlife areas have now been placed under protection.

GERMAN WILDLIFE

The fauna of Germany is typical of central Europe, with a variety of wood-land, wetland and Alpine birds. Of the larger mammals, visitors are most likely to see deer, squirrels and foxes. Small populations of rarer species such as lynx and Euro-pean beaver exist, but these are threatened with extinction.

Alpine raven

COASTAL REGIONS

Germany's coasts vary considerably: the North Sea coast is predominantly flat with drained land, dikes and islands; the Baltic Sea coast is hillier with sandy inlets and cliffs. Together with differences in tides and temperature, these variations determine the variety of species found along coastal regions.

Cross-leaved heath *is a species of heath that is commonly found growing on the moors and peat bogs and in the damp coastal forests of northern Germany.*

Sea lavender *is one of the salt-tolerant species that grow along Germany's North Sea coast.*

Sea holly *is a beautiful thistle-like plant with an amethyst hue. It is commonly found growing in sand dunes.*

LAKES

Most of Germany's lakes are grouped in the northern part of the country, mainly in the Mecklenburg region, where they are divided from the south by the mountain ranges, rifts and valleys of the Central Uplands. However, the largest lake in Germany – the Bodensee (Lake Constance) – is situated in the south, on the border with Austria and Switzerland.

Yellow floating heart *grows in shallow, fertile water. Its habitats are disappear-ing but it still survives in the Rhine basin and on the lower Elbe.*

The white water lily, *with its elegant floating flowers and lush foliage, adorns lakes and reservoirs.*

Yellow flag *is a protected species of iris that is found amongst reeds and in damp woodlands, particularly in older, mixed species forests.*

Wild boars are mammals of the pig family, living in boggy forests. They feed mainly on acorns, beechnuts and the small animals that live in the ground cover of the forest.

Deer live in leafy and mixed forests and are one of the most common mammals seen in Germany.

Marmots live on vegetation growing in the high Alpine meadows. Rodents of the squirrel family, they sleep in burrows at night and whistle loudly when anxious.

Lynx are distinguished by small tufts of hair on the tips of their ears. These mammals are becoming ever rarer.

UPLANDS

Upland landscapes dominate the southern part of Germany, including Bavaria. Here, the climate is mild, and forests cover nearly a third of the region. In this picturesque and popular part of the country, winter-sports centres and spa resorts are common.

MOUNTAINS

Mountain ranges in Germany vary both in age and in height above sea level. Older, not very high mountains covered with forests predominate. The Bavarian Alps are higher and more recent. Here sub-alpine plants grow, with alpine plants at higher altitudes.

Beech is one of the commonest trees found in Germany's forests of mixed deciduous species.

Gentian, with its intensely blue trumpet-like flowers, is one of the most impressive plants to be seen in the Alps. It is pollinated by bumblebees.

Holly, the symbol of Christmas with its glossy leaves and scarlet berries, is found in forests of beech or beech and fir in the west of the country.

Edelweiss is a small flowering plant with flat, white flowers and grey-green woolly leaves. It grows high up in the Alps.

Hepatica is a protected plant in Germany. It blooms in early spring and the seeds of the blue, star-like flowers are distributed by ants.

Rhododendron hirsutum is a low, dense variety of rhododendron, one of a group of plants that grow at sub-Alpine levels.

German Literature

THE FIRST KNOWN examples of written German date from the 8th century. German literature flourished in the Renaissance, although it was mainly later writers who entered the world's canon of great literature. Goethe and Schiller, who wrote many of their most famous works in the *Sturm und Drang* (Storm and Stress) era, in the late 18th century, count among the greatest. Germany also produced many dramatists, poets and novelists in the 19th and 20th centuries. German writers have won eight Nobel Prizes for literature, awarded to Nelly Sachs, Thomas Mann, Heinrich Böll and Günter Grass among others.

Schleswig-Holstein

Gotthold Ephraim Lessing
(1729–81), the most famous German writer of the Age of Enlightenment, wrote dramas such as Nathan the Wise, *reviews of plays performed in Hamburg as well as essays on literary and cultural theory.*

Lower Saxony, Hamburg, Bremen

North Rhine-Westphalia

Erich Maria Remarque
(1898–1970) emigrated from Germany in 1931. His pacifist writings, including All Quiet on the Western Front *and* L'Arc de Triomphe, *brought him acclaim around the world.*

Hesse

The Brothers Grimm,
Jacob Ludwig Karl (1785–1863) and Wilhelm Karl (1786–1859), were university professors and philologists, but better known as writers of some of the world's favourite fairy-tales.

Rhineland-Palatinate & Saarland

Baden-Württemberg

Friedrich Schiller
(1759–1805) wrote about the concept of individual freedom in his great dramas, such as The Robbers *and* Wallenstein. *He also wrote ballads and songs, including* Ode to Joy.

0 km   75

0 miles   75

Thomas Mann *(1875–1955) was awarded the Nobel Prize in 1929. The best-known of his novels is* Buddenbrooks, *which chronicles the life of a Lübeck family.*

Gerhart Hauptmann *(1862–1946), dramatist, novelist and winner of the Nobel Prize in 1912, lived and worked mainly in Silesia. The Weavers is his most famous drama.*

Mecklenburg-Lower Pomerania

Theodor Fontane *(1819–98) was born in Neuruppin, although his literary activities were chiefly connected with Berlin. He was the author of realistic novels such as* Effi Briest, *and he wrote excellent theatre reviews.*

Berlin

Saxony-Anhalt

Brandenburg

Bertolt Brecht *(1898–1956), the great dramatist, poet and director, wrote* The Threepenny Opera, *and was a co-founder of the Berliner Ensemble theatre company.*

Saxony

Thuringia

Karl May *(1842–1912) was known around the world as the author of travel books but his great popularity stems from a cycle of stories featuring the Indian chief* Winnetou, *which he wrote in Radebeul.*

Bavaria

Johann Wolfgang von Goethe *(1749–1832) was the most highly acclaimed German poet and writer of the* Sturm und Drang *period. Born in Frankfurt, he spent most of his life in Weimar. His most famous work is* Faust.

Munich

Lion Feuchtwanger *(1884–1958) lived in Munich until his opposition to the National Socialists forced him to emigrate in 1933. He wrote in exile, alluding to contemporary events in his historical novels.*

Music in Germany

Richard Strauss

Gᴇʀᴍᴀɴ ᴄᴏᴍᴘᴏsᴇʀs have made an enormous contribution to the world's cultural heritage. Many great musical geniuses were born and worked here, including Johann Sebastian Bach and Ludwig van Beethoven. Today their work, and that of other German composers, continues to be performed to enthusiastic new generations of music-lovers in concert halls and opera houses around the world. In Germany, their work is celebrated regularly at hugely popular music festivals.

Renowned composer, Johann Sebastian Bach (1685–1750)

EARLY MUSIC

Dᴜʀɪɴɢ ᴛʜᴇ ᴇᴀʀʟʏ Middle Ages, music evolved in the courts and monasteries of Europe. The basis of sacred music was the Gregorian chant, which was introduced by Pope Gregory I in the late 6th century. An influential role in medieval court music was played by roving poets (*Minnesinger*), who sang love verses to a lute accompaniment. From the 14th century, German singing guilds known as *Meistersinger* emerged. Unlike the *Minnesinger*, these artistes adopted a settled lifestyle. In the succeeding centuries, both vocal and instrumental music continued to evolve, with many new forms appearing.

In the second half of the 17th century, interest in organ music developed and organ schools were established in many towns. One of the best

was in Nuremberg. This was directed by Johann Pachelbel (c.1653–1706), who worked in Vienna, Stuttgart, Erfurt and Nuremberg as a church organist. He is best known for his organ work *Canon*, a set of variations on a theme.

The first German opera, *Dafne*, was composed by Heinrich Schütz (1585–1672). Completed in 1627, the opera has unfortunately been lost.

THE 18TH CENTURY

A ʜᴜɢᴇ ꜰʟᴏᴡᴇʀɪɴɢ of musical talent took place in Germany during the 18th century, when divisions both in German politics and religion led to the development of several important artistic and cultural centres. The most

Georg Friedrich Händel (1685–1759)

renowned figure in German music in the 18th century was undoubtedly Johann Sebastian Bach who, until 1717, was associated with the Weimar court. From 1723 until his death, he was associated with Leipzig, where he was the choir master at the church of St Thomas. Bach's output as a composer is vast and embraces most of the musical forms known at that time. His Passions are today performed in many countries during Holy Week, and his Brandenburg Concertos are among his most frequently performed works. His sons – Wilhelm Friedemann, Carl Philipp Emanuel, Johann Christoph Friedrich and Johann Christian – also became acclaimed composers and made significant contributions to German classical music.

Georg Friedrich Handel was another great composer of late Baroque music. Before forging a prestigious career in England, he began as the cathedral organist in Halle, from where he transferred to the opera house in Hamburg. A friend of Handel and another important composer, Georg Philipp Telemann (1681–1767) was employed as conductor at many German courts. His work includes chamber music, operas and church music.

MUSIC FESTIVALS

The Bach festival in Leipzig's Church of St Thomas

Germany is a country of musical festivals, which are usually held in the summer and early autumn. Among the most popular are the festivals dedicated to the works of a single composer, such as Wagner in Bayreuth, Bach in various cities of Thuringia, Handel in Halle and Beethoven in Bonn. Apart from these specialized festivals, opera festivals with a broader repertoire are also popular. These include the outdoor opera festival in Berlin and the Sommerfestspiele in Xanten.

Son of a court musician and arguably the greatest figure in classical music, Ludwig van Beethoven (1770–1827) was born in Bonn, although he worked mainly in Vienna. Among his best-known works are his nine symphonies, as well as piano and violin concertos, two masses, various chamber works and the opera *Fidelio*.

The life of this great composer, is shrouded in legend. Succeeding generations have been fascinated not just by his music, but also by the fact that he began to lose his hearing at the age of 30. During his final years, when totally deaf, he composed from memory.

Statue of Ludwig van Beethoven

THE 19TH CENTURY

ROMANTICISM brought about the flowering of opera in Germany. One of the leading creators in this tradition was the composer Ernst Theodor Amadeus Hoffmann (1776–1822), whose opera *Undine* was staged for the first time in 1816 in Berlin. Carl Maria von Weber (1786–1826) rose to prominence following the success of his opera *Der Freischütz*, which was the first opera in the German Romantic tradition. Another

Composer Felix Mendelssohn-Bartholdy (1809–47)

major figure from this time was Felix Mendelssohn-Bartholdy, whose "Wedding March" from *A Midsummer Night's Dream* accompanies wedding celebrations around the world. As well as this famous piece of music, however, Mendelssohn left a legacy that includes five symphonies, piano music, chamber music and oratorios. In 1843, Mendelssohn founded Germany's first musical conservatory, in Leipzig.

The master of chamber music was Robert Schumann (1810–56), a poet and composer whose miniature works for piano, violin sonatas and song cycles all remain popular. The Hungarian composer Franz Liszt, who worked in Weimar from 1848 to 1861, also made a significant contribution to the evolution of German music.

In the second half of the 19th century, Richard Wagner was the major influence on German opera. During his early years, he composed traditional operas such as *Tannhäuser*. He later developed his own creative synthesis, integrating lyrics with the music. This found its finest expression in his Ring cycle, which was based on medieval sagas.

Wagner's ideas about musical theatre, including his use of *leitmotifs* (recurring phrases), were adopted by Richard Strauss (1864–1949), who composed many operas, symphonies and songs. The first bars of his symphonic poem *Zarathustra* became a guiding musical motif in Stanley Kubrick's 1968 film *2001: A Space Odyssey*. Johannes Brahms (1833–97) composed in traditional forms and was

Richard Wagner (1813–83)

Composer and pianist Johannes Brahms (1833–97)

unsympathetic to the progressive ideas of Wagner and Liszt. From 1872 to 1875, Brahms was the musical director of the *Gesellschaft der Musikfreunde* (Society of Friends of Music).

THE 20TH CENTURY

DURING THE 20th century, many contemporary composers continued the traditions of the earlier masters. One renowned figure was Paul Hindemith (1895–1963), whose work includes opera, ballet and concertos. His music was banned by the Nazis in 1933 and Hindemith emigrated to the USA in 1939.

Another important figure in German musical life was Carl Orff (1895–1982) whose best-known work is the oratorio *Carmina Burana*, based on 13th-century Latin and German poems found in a Benedictine monastery in Bavaria. The Austrian composer Arnold Schönberg (1874–1951) lived in Berlin during the 1920s and exerted great influence on German music.

Among the most important composers living and working in Germany today, mention should be made of Hans Werner Henze, Paul-Heinz Ditrich, Dieter Schnebel, Helmut Lachenmann and Georg Katzer.

German Painting

THE DIVERSITY IN German painting has its roots in the political and religious divisions that existed in the country in the past. The Old Masters working in the north, for example, were more likely to be influenced by the Netherlandish school, while artists working in the south leaned towards Italian styles. German art reached the peak of its individuality during the late-Gothic, late-Baroque and Expressionist periods – all periods when one of the chief characteristics of artistic style was strength of expression.

Emil Nolde (1867–1956), one of Germany's foremost Expressionists, painted landscapes of his native region. Pictured above is his North Friesian Landscape.

Schleswig-Holstein

Master Francke (14th–15th century) was the leading representative of the North German Late-Gothic style, working in Hamburg c.1410–24. He painted religious scenes and his works include St Thomas's Altar, of which this is a detail.

Bremen, Hamburg and Lower Saxony

North Rhine-Westphalia

Hesse

Peter von Cornelius (1783–1867) joined the Nazarenes during the anti-academic rebellion. He later became director of the academy in Dusseldorf and others. He painted the picture The Wise and Foolish Maidens at that time.

Rhineland-Palatinate and Saarland

Baden-Wurttemburg

Adam Elsheimer (1578–1610) was born in Frankfurt am Main but spent most of his life in Rome. His poignant landscapes, such as The Flight to Egypt shown here, greatly influenced the development of 17th-century painting.

Caspar David Friedrich *(1774–1840) was one of the most prominent exponents of Romanticism. He created poignant images, such as this* Traveller above the Sea of Clouds, *in which Man contemplates the power of Nature as created by God.*

Mecklenburg-
Lower
Pomerania

Max Liebermann *(1847–1935) is considered one of the leading representatives of Impressionism. His* Man with Parrots *was painted during his association with the Berlin Secession.*

Berlin

Saxony-Anhalt   Brandenburg

Lionel Feininger *(1871–1956) was born in the USA but spent much of his life in Germany. He lectured at the Bauhaus and painted Cubist-inspired scenes of architectural subjects, such as this* Gelmeroda IX.

Saxony

Thuringia

Albrecht Dürer *(1471–1528) is one of the best-known German painters. This great master of the Renaissance period was also an outstanding engraver and art-historian. His* Paumgärtners' Altar *was made for St Catherine's Church in Nuremberg.*

Bavaria

Munich

0 kilometres   80

0 miles   80

Wilhelm Leibl *(1844–1900) painted this scene of women praying in a village church in Bavaria,* Three Women in a Church, *which is regarded as one of the outstanding works of German Realism.*

Castles in Germany

Crest from the castle portal in Gotha

I N A NUMBER OF GERMAN regions, medieval castles are among the most characteristic features of the landscape. Some have survived only in the form of picturesque ruins, but many others, refurbished and modernized over the years, continue to be the main residence for the families for whom they were built. The most impressive grouping of great fortresses is to be found along the banks of the Mosel and the central Rhine, while, in the Münster area, you will see the most beautiful moated castles to have survived in the lowlands.

The Great Knights' Hall, where knights ate, drank and entertained, was a feature of every castle.

The 15th-century Michaels-kapelle

Marburg Castle *is one of the best-preserved fortresses in Hesse. At its core is a 12th-century building, but the castle's current appearance is the result of work carried out between the 14th and 16th centuries* (see p355).

The Royal Room was an apartment specially designated for the use of important guests.

The Wartburg *in Eisenach is one of the most important monuments in Thuringia, not only because of its excellently preserved architecture but also for its association with Martin Luther* (see pp176–7).

Heidelberg Castle *has survived as a picturesque ruin. A Gothic-Renaissance structure of imposing proportions, it continues to captivate with its commanding position and fascinating architecture* (see pp284–5).

Gardens were laid out in the 19th century in an area between the castle walls and the site of the farm buildings.

Raesfeld *is one of the most beautiful castles in Münsterland, a region of Westphalia that is renowned for its historic moated castles. The castle was extended in the mid-17th century for Alexandra II von Velen (see p374).*

19TH-CENTURY CASTLES

In the 19th century, many ruined castles in Germany were rebuilt in a wave of nostalgia for the Middle Ages. A number of completely new castles were built, which were modelled on medieval designs.

The Schwerin castle, *built on an island, has a 16th-century chapel, but the rest, dating from 1843–57, was inspired by the French castles along the river Loire (see p456).*

Lichtenstein castle *owes its fame to the novel* Lichtenstein *by Wilhelm Hauff and its beauty to the Romantic-style remodelling that was carried out in 1840–41 (see p301).*

Evangelical Chapel

The main entrance to the castle leads through a gate house – here in the form of a tower.

Wernigerode's *castle dominates the entire city. Despite later extensions, it has retained a late-Gothic tower, a beautiful staircase dating from 1495 and some valuable furnishings (see p136).*

BURG HOHENZOLLERN

The family seat of the Hohenzollern family, Burg Hohenzollern in Hechingen, is set on a clifftop in the Swabian Jura. The first building was established here in the 13th century and rebuilt many times over the years. The current medieval appearance is the result of work that was carried out in 1850–67 in the spirit of romantic historicism *(see p300)*.

Burg Eltz, *set high above the Mosel, is one of the most beautiful castles in Germany. Built between the 12th and 16th centuries, it has survived with very few alterations (see p331).*

German Scientists and Inventors

GERMANY IS POPULARLY regarded as a nation of practical people, so it is hardly surprising that the history books abound with the names of Germans who have made important contributions to technological progress and the development of science. They include Johann Gutenberg (c.1400–68), who invented printing with movable type, and Karl Benz (1844–1929) and Gottlieb Daimler (1834–1900) who developed the first petrol-driven car. In terms of Nobel Prize winners alone (and not counting those who received the prize for achievements in other fields), there is currently a total of 69 Germans. One of the most illustrious of these is physicist Albert Einstein (1879–1955).

1791 Alexander von Humboldt, a naturalist and geographer, discovers the presence of carbon dioxide in the air

c.1600 Johann Schult invents the dental mirror.

1645 Althanasius Kircher constructs the magic lantern – the first projector

1671 Gottfried Wilhelm Leibniz, philosopher and mathematician, is known for his important philosophical works and his (disputed) claim to have invented differential calculus

c.1709 Johann F Böttger produces the first European porcelain

1718 Jacob Leupold constructs the first decimal scale

1747 Andreas Marggraf succeeds in extracting sugar crystals from sugar beet

1600	1650	1700	1750	18

1600	1650	1700	1750	18

1609, 1619 Johannes Kepler discovers the principal laws of planetary movement

1669 Hennig Brand discovers phosphorus

1650 Otto von Guericke, researching air pressure and electrostatic phenomena, develops the vacuum pump

1694 Rudolph Jacob Camerarius discovers the existence of gender in plants, and explains the role of stamens and pollen in fertilization

1740 Johann Pott, porcelain pioneer, discovers manganese

1781 Martin H Klaproth, chemist, discovers uranium

1745 Ewald G Kleist invents the first electric condenser

GERMAN PHILOSOPHERS

German intellectuals have played a major role in the history of philosophy. Gottfried Leibniz (1646–1716), for example, was one of the most renowned exponents of modern rationalism. At the turn of the 18th and 19th centuries, Germany was a fertile source of new ideas, with the work of philosophers such as Immanuel Kant and Georg Hegel. Karl Marx and Friedrich Engels expounded materialism, while Friedrich Nietzsche developed his cultural and human philosophy. Martin Heidegger and Karl Jaspers were leading existentialists.

Georg Wilhelm Friedrich Hegel (1770–1831)

1813 Karl Freiherr von Drais invents the first two-wheeled vehicle – a kind of bicycle

1874 Otto Lilienthal constructs the first glider for engineless flights

1989 Wolfgang Paul and Hans Dehmelt receive the Nobel prize for research into nuclear and molecular physics and for their work in the 1950s developing the "Paul trap" – a device for capturing ions

1991 Erwin Neher and Bert Sakmann receive the Nobel prize for research into defining the process of communication between cells

1831 Justus von Liebig develops a new method of chemical analysis

1841 Julius Mayer formulates the principle of conservation of energy

1865 Rudolf J E Clausius formulates the second law of thermodynamics

1876 Nikolaus Otto invents the internal combustion engine

1882 Robert Koch discovers the tuberculosis bacillus (Nobel prize in 1905)

1987 Georg Bednorz and Karl A Müller receive the Nobel prize for discovering high temperature superconductivity in metal oxides

1922 The Nobel Prize is awarded to Albert Einstein, who developed the theory of relativity

1999 Günter Blobel is awarded the Nobel prize for discovering the process that determines the direction of movement and the location of proteins within cells

1850	1900	1950	2000

1850	1900	1950	2000

1885 Karl Benz and Gottlieb Daimler construct the first petrol-driven car

1918 Nobel Prize awarded to Max K Planck who founded the principles of quantum theory

1963 Nobel Prize awarded to Karl Ziegler for his work on industrial production of polymers

1886 Heinrich Hertz discovers radio waves

1903 Arthur Korn demonstrates how to transmit a photograph from a distance

1944 Nobel Prize awarded to Otto Hahn for discovery (with Lise Meitner) of the process of nuclear fission

1866 Ernest W Siemens develops the dynamo

1938 Ernst Ruska and Max Knoll construct the first electron microscope

1850 Wilhelm Bauer constructs a submarine

1841 Christian Schönbein discovers ozone

1941 Konrad Zuse constructs the Z3 calculator – the first digital "computer"

1826 Georg S Ohm shows that the ratio of a steady current to voltage is a constant

1901 Nobel Prize awarded to Wilhelm C Röntgen, for his discovery of X-rays and their uses

German Beer

ALTHOUGH FINE WINES are produced in Germany, beer is unquestionably the country's favourite alcoholic drink. Germans drink an average of 140 litres of beer annually and Bavarians lead the world in consumption, drinking an average of 240 litres each per annum. Beer is drunk on every occasion, but it tastes best in the summer when it is poured straight from a barrel at one of the numerous festivals or public holidays.

Hop flower cones

The **mass** *is a tankard that is used to serve beer in Bavaria. It holds a litre, but waitresses are used to carrying eight or nine such tankards at a time.*

GERMAN BREWERIES

Historic brewing facilities in Freising *(see p251)*

IN GERMANY most towns and the larger villages have a brewery. The country's oldest brewery, established in 1040, is the Weihenstephan Benedictine monastery in Freising, which is believed to be the oldest working brewery in the world. Many large breweries and consortiums produce beer that is known throughout the world, but beers produced by small operators, which are available only in a few regional pubs, are in no way inferior. When visiting Germany, do try the produce of small local breweries as well as the beer produced by the giants, such as Paulaner and Löwenbrau.

Logo of the famous Munich brewery, Paulaner

STYLES OF BEER

ONE OF THE MOST POPULAR STYLES of beer is *Pils* (short for *Pilsener*) a light, bottom-fermented beer of the lager type. Of the seasonal beers, it is worth trying spring beers such as *Maibock* or *Doppelbock*, and in autumn the strong beer that is brewed especially for the Oktoberfest. In the lower Rhine valley, *Altbier* is still produced; this is a top-fermented beer, prepared by traditional methods. In the south, *Weizenbier*, a wheat beer, is also produced. The Berlin version, *Berliner Weisse* (white beer), is served with fruit juice. Dark beers, such as *Dunkel* and *Schwarzbier*, also enjoy great popularity. Breweries have their own specialities. In Bamberg, they produce *Rauchbier*, which has a light smokiness; in Kulmbach it is *Eisbock*, which gains its thicker consistency through a freezing process.

Wheat beer, Berliner Weisse

Seasonal autumn beer, Bock

DRINKING BEER

The largest pub in the world, created during the Oktoberfest

IN GERMANY, BEER is served with a head. Pouring lager from a barrel is supposed to take about 10 minutes, so the head sinks to the regulation level and has a thick consistency. A small beer is normally 0.3 litre, a large one 0.5 litre. In Bavaria, however, a large beer is served in a *Mass*, a tankard holding 1 litre. When travelling in Germany, order the brew of the local brewery, ideally in a *Bierkeller* or *Bierstube* (pub) and, in summer, in a *Biergarten* (beer garden). The largest gardens are in Bavaria – Munich's *Hirschgarten* caters for 8,000 beer drinkers. The Oktoberfest, which is celebrated each year in Munich *(see p217)*, is the largest beer festival in the world.

HOW BEER IS BREWED

The method of brewing beer that is now virtually standard dates from the 19th century, when Czech brewers first produced bottom-fermented beers at lower temperatures. The method was perfected by Gabriel Sedlmayr. Each brewery has its secrets, but the initial stages of production are the same.

A climbing plant, hops are trained to grow up special supports

Mashing vat

Barley and hops

1 The main ingredients in the production of beer are barley, hops and crystal-clear water. Other grains, including wheat and rice, can also be used – for example Weizenbier is made from wheat rather than barley. The first stage of brewing is malting, when the grains are soaked and left to germinate. After a few days, these are dried and then milled.

2 The milled barley is mixed with warm water and placed in a copper mashing vat. During the mashing process, the starches in the grain turn into fermentable sugars. The mash is then filtered to separate out a liquid, known as the wort, from the mash.

3 The wort is put into a copper vessel with the hops and then cooked. Depending on the amount of hops added, the beer will be more or less bitter. Traditionally the hops are added to the vessel by hand, in carefully measured proportions. Sometimes, however, they are added, as required, during the cooking process.

4 The wort is filtered again, cooled and combined with yeast. Fermentation then takes place. At temperatures above 20° C (68° F), the liquid reaches "top fermentation", which takes 3–5 days. "Bottom fermentation", where the temperature is below 12° C (54° F), takes 7–10 days.

5 The young beer produced by fermentation is left to rest in special containers that enable a higher pressure to be maintained. During this resting stage, which can last from a couple of weeks to a year or even longer, the beer matures. The effect of resting the beer is to make it stronger. Resting takes place in metal or traditional wooden barrels.

6 The mature beer, which is ready to be sold, is then transferred to bottles or cans and pasteurized. This process removes micro-organisms that threaten the quality of the beer.

Traditional wooden barrels containing resting beer

Sport in Germany

SPORT HAS LONG enjoyed a significant role in German life both for active participants and spectators. The country regularly produces world champions in a variety of activities, including football, tennis and motor racing. Excellent facilities exist throughout the country for taking part in sporting activities, including sailing, swimming, climbing and skiing as well as in field- or track-based events. Southern Germany plays host to a variety of winter sports and competitions.

FOOTBALL

THE LARGEST SPORTS organization in the country, the German Football Association has over 6 million registered members in some 25,000 clubs. The national team has won the World Cup three times – in 1954, 1974 and 1990 – and the European Cup in 1972, 1980 and 1996.

One of the outstanding figures in German football is Franz Beckenbauer, who was a member of the team that won the European Cup in 1972 and the World Cup in 1974. He trained the team that took second place in the 1986 World Cup and first place in 1990. Beckenbauer was twice named the best footballer in Europe.

The best-known club is Bayern München, which has won the German Cup a record 16 times. Matches between teams in the elite *Bundesliga* enjoy a great following. League matches are held on Saturday afternoons while European Cup games are usually held on Wednesday evenings. The club teams include a

significant number of professionals from abroad. The 2006 World Cup will be held in Germany.

Competing in Hamburg's annual Deutsches Spring Derby

SHOW-JUMPING AND EQUESTRIAN EVENTS

SHOW-JUMPING is another sport at which Germany excels. Since it was introduced to the Olympic Games in 1912, German riders have won 32 gold, 18 silver and 21 bronze medals. Major equestrian events are held in Hamburg and Aachen in June. Hamburg's Derby Week is popular with racing fans.

The German Open in Hamburger Rothenbaum

LAWN TENNIS

THE GERMAN TENNIS Association is the largest in the world with over 2 million members, belonging to some 10,200 clubs. From the mid-1980s, Germany became one of the world's most successful tennis nations thanks to some outstanding players. In 1985, aged 18, Boris Becker was the youngest player to win the Wimbledon championships. He repeated his achievement in 1986 and 1989 and was runner-up to fellow-German Michael Stich in 1991. From 1987–91 Steffi Graf was ranked number one among the world's female tennis players.

ATHLETICS

DURING THE COLD WAR period, East and West German athletes competed against each other for the glory of their rival political systems as much as for the love of their sport. The extraordinary achievements of the East German athletes during that time have since been tarnished by revelations of systematic drug abuse. Since reunification, some athletes have managed to maintain their reputations, but the majority have not.

Germany's most important event, the International Stadionfest (ISTAF), is held each year in Berlin, as the climax of the season.

***Bundesliga* football match (Hertha BSC Berlin v FC Bayern München)**

FORMULA ONE

BACK IN THE 1930s, motor-racing was dominated by the famous "Silver Arrows", made by Mercedes-Benz. Formula One has been a decidedly German discipline since its beginnings in 1950. In all the events there have always been at least three German drivers taking part. The German Formula One Grand Prix is held each July at the Hockenheim-Ring, near Heidelberg. In most years there is a second Grand Prix at the Nürburgring circuit close to the Belgian border. This is dubbed the European Grand Prix or the Luxembourg Grand Prix.

Germany's leading Formula One driver, Michael Schumacher, won the World Championship in 1994, 1995 and 2000. He has also twice achieved second place and been twice in third place.

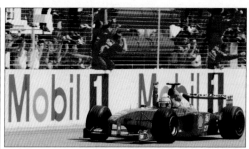

The Hockenheim race track near Heidelberg

Markus Eberle during the slalom in Ofterschwang in the Allgäu

SKIING

SINCE 1953, the last week of December and the first week of January have been dominated by the Four Ski Jumps Championship for ski jumpers. This classic event, which is held in Oberstdorf and Garmisch-Partenkirchen in Germany, as well as in Innsbruck and Bischofshofen in Austria, attracts several thousand spectators and millions of television viewers. German athletes have gained first place in this competition 15 times over the years.

As well as in the German Alps, which have the most popular ski resorts, excellent conditions exist for downhill and cross-country skiing in the less glamorous and less expensive Black Forest and the Harz Mountains.

CYCLING

CYCLING ENJOYS a great following in Germany. The Tour de France is broadcast simultaneously by two television stations, and ever-increasing numbers of people are taking part in the sport, both for pleasure and competitively. Success on the cycle track has long been a German tradition, but Jan Ullrich exceeded all expectations when he won gold in the long distance and silver in a time trial at the Sydney Olympics in 2000.

SAILING

KIELER WOCHE is the most important regatta in the world, according to Paul Henderson, the President of the International Sailing Federation. On 1 September 1881, five officers of the Emperor's navy held a yachting race in the Bay of Kiel, as it was then called. The following year 20 yachts competed while thousands of spectators watched from the shore. The championship went on to become an international event, which gained in prestige as the Emperor took part in each race from 1894 until 1914.

Today it is traditional for the president of the German Federal Republic to formally open the regatta (in the last week of June) in which thousands of yachts from many countries take part.

SWIMMING

SWIMMING, more than any other sport in Germany, has seen a decline in success since reunification and the subsequent cessation of competition between East and West. At the 1988 Olympics in Seoul, for example, Kristin Otto won 6 gold medals. In 2000, the reunified German team returned from Sydney having gained only three bronze medals. Two figures who rose to the top in the past are Michael Gross, who was a member of the West German team, and Franziska van Almsick, a member of the East German team.

Franziska von Almsick during the German Swimming Championships

GERMANY THROUGH THE YEAR

GERMANS LOVE to have fun and this is evident from the huge number of light-hearted events that are held throughout the year. Virtually every town has a calendar of festivals and fairs. These include folk festivals connected with local traditions – for example celebrating the asparagus or grape harvest.

A festival mascot

Many towns preserve the tradition of an annual fair – or *Jahrmarkt* – known in Westphalia as *Kirmes* and in Bavaria as *Dult*. Germany is also known for its music and film festivals, which attract an international audience, as well as for organizing major international trade fairs, such as the annual Frankfurt Book Fair.

Witches participating in the Walpurgisnacht celebrations in Thale

SPRING

SPRING IS an idyllic time to arrive in Germany. In the high mountains, conditions are still ideal for skiing, while in the valleys everything is already in bloom. In April and May the first spring fairs and festivals are held. Spring is also time for the traditional solemn observance of Easter and its associated celebrations. May Day, which is also International Labour Day, is marked both by traditional festivities and, in some cities, by demonstrations.

MARCH

Sommergewinn *(3 weekends before Easter)* Eisenach. The largest folk festival in Thuringia, linked with a fair.
CeBIT *(end of March)* Hanover. International trade fairs dedicated to information technology, telecommunications and automation.
Easter During Holy Week, Passion concerts are held throughout the country and colourful church services take place, particularly in rural Catholic areas. On Easter Sunday, in cities in the Luzyce region, horse races and a gala take place.
Leipziger Buchmesse *(end of March)* Leipzig. International book fair, with antiquarian books.
Thüringer Bach-Wochen Celebration of the life and works of Johann Sebastian Bach with concerts and lectures: held in Arnstadt, Eisenach, Erfurt, Gotha, Mühlhausen and Weimar.

APRIL

Kurzfilmtage Oberhausen. The International Festival of Short Films has been held here since 1955.

The International Dixieland Festival, held annually in Dresden in May

Hannover Messe *(2nd half of April)* Hanover. International industrial trade fairs.
Hamburger Dom *(April, August and November)* Hamburg. The largest folk festival in northern Germany, held three times a year.
Walpurgisnacht *(30 April/ 1 May).* On the witches' sabbath, witches gather on Brocken Mountain and in several other places in the Harz mountains.

MAY

Maibaumaufstellen *(1 May).* In Bavarian villages, maypoles are decorated with highly ornamental wreaths.
Rhein in Flammen *(1st Saturday in May).* Festival with firework displays, in towns in the Rhine Valley.
Hafengeburtstag *(7 May)* Hamburg. A huge festival with fireworks, regatta and a parade of sailing boats.
Ruhrfestspiele *(May–July)* Recklinghausen. Cultural festival with a number of concerts, performances and exhibitions.
International Dixieland Festival *(2nd week of May)* Dresden. A traditional jazz festival has been held here since 1971.
Blutritt *(Friday after Ascension)* Weingarten. A horseback procession carrying religious relics around the town – held here for 450 years.
Leineweber Markt *(end of May)* Bielefeld. Street theatre, jazz and folk concerts.

SUMMER

IN GERMANY the summer is a time of great open-air festivals and other outdoor events and activities. Nearly every town and village has its festival with a parade, street shows, concerts and fairs. In many places there are colourful illuminations and firework displays. Banquets and knights' tournaments are held in historic castles, while concert series are organized in palaces and castles with the tourist particularly in mind. In June, a number of classical music festivals take place, while July is a popular month for wine and beer festivals.

Yacht race during the annual Kieler Woche regatta in Kiel

JUNE

Spreewaldfest *(June)* Spreewald. Folk festivals are held throughout the summer in Lübbenau and other villages in Spreewald.
Fronleichnam. Observed in states with a Catholic majority. Magnificent processions take place in towns in Bavaria and in Cologne.
Christopher Street Day *(mid-June)*. Gay and lesbian parades held in many towns, including Berlin and Hamburg.
Kieler Woche *(3rd week in June)* Kiel. Huge yachting regatta with concerts and street fairs.
Open-Air-Saison *(4th week in June, beginning of July)* Berlin. Opera festival held on outdoor stages and in squares in the city.

A wedding couple during the Landshuter Hochzeit festival

Schützenfest *(June)* marks the traditional start of the hunting season. Celebrated in many north German cities.

JULY

Landshuter Hochzeit *(every 3rd summer: 2004; 2007)* Landshut. Re-enactment of the wedding feast of Georg, son of Duke Ludwig the Rich and Polish Princess Jadwiga. Costumed wedding procession and medieval tournament.
Love Parade *(2nd Saturday)* Berlin. A parade for fans of techno music, who dance throughout the day and night in all the city's discos and around vehicles equipped with sound systems.

Internationaler Johann-Sebastian-Bach Wettbewerb Leipzig. International music competition dedicated to Johann Sebastian Bach.
Schwörmontag *(penultimate Monday)* Ulm. Folk festival with a parade by the Danube.
Kinderzeche *(3rd Monday)* Dinkelsbühl. Ten-day folk festival commemorating the events of the Thirty Years' War (1618–48).
Richard-Wagner-Festspiele *(last week July/August)* Bayreuth. Festival dedicated to the works of Richard Wagner.

AUGUST

Zissel *(beginning of August)* Kassel. Picturesque folk festival with parades, markets and concerts.
Mainfest. Frankfurt am Main. Feast of the river Main.
Gäubodenfest *(mid-August)* Straubing. Folk festival with a market and beer tasting.
Rhein in Flammen *(2nd Saturday)* Koblenz. Huge firework display on the Rhine and a flotilla of illuminated passenger ships.
Wikingerfest *(even years)* Schleswig. Historical festival with costumed participants, tournaments and regattas.
Weindorf *(end August)* Stuttgart. Huge wine festival with wines served along with typical Swabian cuisine.

Performance of *Tannhäuser* at Richard-Wagner-Festspiele, Bayreuth

AUTUMN

AUTUMN IS a popular time for tourism in Germany, especially September and early October when many cities, including Berlin and Munich, organize cultural events and important festivals. The autumn is also the time when the most significant trade fairs and great sporting events take place. At this time, also, conditions in the mountains and countryside continue to be ideal for outdoor activities such as walking and cycling.

SEPTEMBER

Berliner Festwochen, Berlin. Lasting all month, this is a major series of cultural events, opera performances, exhibitions and various literary events.
Beethovenfestival, Bonn. A musical festival of the works of Beethoven in the city where he was born.
Heilbronner Herbst *(1st Saturday)* Heilbronn. Wine festival, including parades and firework displays.
Berlin-Marathon *(last Saturday)* Berlin. Marathon through the streets of the city centre, with runners in various age groups and the participation of the disabled in wheelchairs.
Oktoberfest *(last Saturday)* Munich. Beer festival held

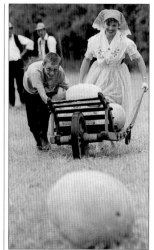

Pumpkin race during Dorffest

over 16 days, beginning with a parade through the city's streets. Ceremonial removal of the bung from a new barrel of beer brewed for the festival.
Plärrer *(May and September)* Augsburg. Festival held twice a year, considered one of the most important in Swabia.
Dorffest im Spreewald *(end)* Lehde. Folk festival.
Cannstatter Volksfest *(end September/beginning October)* Stuttgart. The second largest beer festival in the world.
Internationales Stadionfest (ISTAF), Berlin. The largest athletics event at the end of the season.

OCTOBER

Nationalfeiertag *(3 October)*. German national holiday, established after re-unification. Concerts, parades and meetings.
Frankfurter Buchmesse *(2nd week in October)* Frankfurt am Main. The world's largest book fair, which attracts publishers from around the world.
Freimarkt *(mid-October)* Bremen. Two-week folk festival beginning with a procession.
Liszt-Tage Weimar. Celebration of the life and work of Franz Liszt, with concerts at which world-class musicians are invited to perform.
Ost-West Jazz Festival *(end October)* Nuremberg. International jazz folk festival.
Colmansfest *(2nd Sunday)* Schwangau. Religious festival featuring hundreds of horses and decorated carriages.

NOVEMBER

St Leonard's Day *(1st Sunday in November)*. Folk festival in Bavaria, which is held in conjunction with horse parades.
Kasseler Musiktage *(beginning of November)* Kassel. One of Europe's longest-established classical music festivals.
Weinfest *(1st weekend in November)* Cochem. Festival celebrating the removal of the bung from the first barrel of young Mosel wine.
Martinsfest *(11 November)*. St Martin's Day is celebrated in northern Baden and the Rhineland with fairs and the essential roast goose. In the Rhine Valley, St Martin's Day signifies the beginning of the Carnival season.
Internationales Film-festival *(2nd week in November)* Mannheim-Heidelberg. Annual festival of short, documentary and educational films.

The International Book Fair in Frankfurt am Main

A major film gala held during Berlinale in Berlin

WINTER

DECEMBER IS synonymous with Christmas festivities. Every city has fairs where you can buy Christmas-tree decorations, delicacies and presents. In December, shops have longer opening hours and the skiing season begins in the Alps. January and February are a time for parties and balls (the Carnival season), with enjoyment reaching a peak in the last few days of the season. Then the fun continues all weekend from Thursday, reaching a height on *Rosenmontag* then diminishing on the last Tuesday of Carnival.

DECEMBER

Christkindelsmarkt and **Weihnachtsmarkt**. Christmas fairs are held from

The famous Christmas market in the city of Nuremberg

the beginning of the month until Christmas Eve. The most beautiful are in Baden-Wurttemberg and in Bavaria, while the most renowned is held in Nuremberg.
Christmas *(25/26 December).* Traditionally celebrated throughout Germany. A Christmas tree is considered essential, together with presents and delicacies.
New Year's Eve *(31 December).* The New Year is greeted at balls, opera galas, in restaurants, clubs, private houses and in the streets and squares of city centres.

JANUARY

Four Ski Jumps Tournament *(begins 1 January).* Renowned tournament for ski-jumping held annually in Garmisch-Partenkirchen.
Sechs-Tage-Rennen *(begins 1 January)* Berlin. Spectacular cycle races with associated events, held in Berlin Velodrome.
Grüne Woche *(last week)* Berlin. International trade fairs dedicated to agriculture, animal breeding and the food processing industry. Producers from all over the world offer specialities from their own national cuisines.

FEBRUARY

Berlinale–Internationale Filmfestspiele *(2nd and 3rd weeks)* Berlin. International film festival in which major stars participate.

Fastnacht, also known as **Fasnet**, **Fasching** or **Karneval** (Shrovetide). Carnival is celebrated enthusiastically in virtually every region of Germany. The most interesting events are held in the Rhine Valley, and particularly in Cologne. *Karneval am Rhein*, which marks the lasts three days of the Carnival, begins on the Thursday of the week before Ash Wednesday with a women's parade, known as *Weiberfastnacht*. On the Monday there is a superb costume parade, known as *Rosenmontagsumzug*.

Costumed revellers on the streets of Cologne during Carnival

PUBLIC HOLIDAYS

Neujahr *New Year* (1 Jan).
Hl. Dreikönige *Three Kings* (6 Jan: Bavaria, Baden-Wurttemberg, Saxony-Anhalt).
Karfreitag *Good Friday.*
Ostern *Easter.*
Maifeiertag/Tag der Arbeit *Labour Day.*
Christ Himmelfahrt *Ascension.*
Pfingsten *Pentecost.*
Fronleichnam *Corpus Christi* (Bavaria, Baden-Wurttemberg, Hesse, North Rhine Valley-Westphalia, Rhine Valley-Palatinate and Saar).
Mariä Himmelfahrt *Assumption of the BVM* (15 Aug: Bavaria, Saar).
Nationalfeiertag *Reunification of Germany Day* (3 Oct).
Allerheiligen *All Saints* (1 Nov: Bavaria, Baden-Wurttemberg, North Rhine Valley-Westphalia, Rhine Valley-Palatinate).
Weihnachten *Christmas* (25/26 Dec).

The German Climate

GERMANY LIES in a temperate climatic zone. In the north of the country, with marine influences predominating, summers tend to be quite cold and winters mild, with relatively high rainfall. In the eastern part of the country, however, the climate is more continental and this produces harsher winters and hotter summers. Germany's highest rainfall and the lowest temperatures are recorded in the Alps.

SCHLESWIG-HOLSTEIN

°C			
20			
10.5	12	13	
2.2	3	7	
-2			

Average daily maximum temperature
Average daily minimum temperature
Average daily amount of sunshine
Average monthly rainfall

☀	1.3 hrs	5.5 hrs	7 hrs	3 hrs
☔	80 mm	55 mm	92 mm	90 mm
Month	Jan	Apr	Jul	Oct

BREMEN, HAMBURG, LOWER SAXONY

°C	22	12.5	12	14
	3.2	3.5		6
	-2			
☀	1.3 hrs	5 hrs	6 hrs	3 hrs
☔	56 mm	48 mm	69 mm	55 mm
Month	Jan	Apr	Jul	Oct

NORTH RHINE-WESTPHALIA

°C	23	14	12.5	15
	4.5	3.6		6
	-1			
☀	1.5 hrs	5 hrs	6.5 hrs	3.7 hrs
☔	62 mm	54 mm	84 mm	55 mm
Month	Jan	Apr	Jul	Oct

HESSE

°C	24	14	13	14
	3	4		6
	-2			
☀	1.3 hrs	5 hrs	7.4 hrs	3.3 hrs
☔	44 mm	51 mm	63 mm	50 mm
Month	Jan	Apr	Jul	Oct

RHINELAND-PALATINATE, SAARLAND

°C	23	13	12	14
	3	4		7
	-1.5			
☀	1.3 hrs	5 hrs	7 hrs	3 hrs
☔	60 mm	53 mm	69 mm	65 mm
Month	Jan	Apr	Jul	Oct

BADEN WURTTENBERG

°C	23	14	13	15
	4	5		7
	-1			
☀	1.7 hrs	5 hrs	8 hrs	4 hrs
☔	60 mm	80 mm	95 mm	66 mm
Month	Jan	Apr	Jul	Oct

Flensburg, Schlesw, Ham, Bremen, Nienbu, Hanove, Münster, Paderborn, Götting, Dortmund, Düsseldorf, Kassel, Cologne, Siegen, Aachen, Bonn, Marburg, Fu, Koblenz, Frankfurt am Main, Mainz, Würzbu, Trier, Mannheim, Heidelberg, Saarbrücken, Karlsruhe, Stuttgar, Ulm, Freiburg im Breisgau, Konstanz

0 km 100
0 miles 100

THE HISTORY OF GERMANY

GERMANY IS *a country of cultural and religious contrasts. Regional differences in culture, language and traditions arose from the historical division of the country into many small states. Such differences have been further accentuated by the recent experience of generations of Germans who, until 1990, grew up under two conflicting social systems: capitalism and communism.*

EARLY HISTORY

In the 1st millennium BC, the basins of the Rhine, Danube and Main rivers were settled by Celts, who had been largely displaced by Germanic tribes by the 2nd century BC. In the 1st century BC the Roman legions waged wars with the Germans, and conquered the territories west of the Rhine. The settlements they founded there later developed into towns like Trier, Mainz, Cologne and Xanten. The Romans made numerous attempts to conquer the eastern regions between the Rhine and the Elbe rivers. They eventually reached the Elbe at the end of the 1st century BC, but the Germans, under the leadership of Arminius, also known as Germanus, defeated the Roman armies in the Teutoburg Forest in AD 9, and so ended their presence in this region. A system of fortifications, or *limes,* built in the 2nd century along the course of the Danube and the Rhine, divided the region into two: *Germania Romana,* the Roman province, and *Germania Libra,* free Germany. The free German tribes,

Heinrich I, from the house of Liudolf

notably the Goths, often entered into alliances with the Romans. In the 5th century, however, they took advantage of Rome's weakness to appropriate parts of the empire for themselves.

EARLY MIDDLE AGES

After the collapse of the Roman Empire, the area between the Rhine and the Elbe was ruled by the Franks, who gradually converted to Christianity from the 6th century. One of the most important figures in this process was the 8th-century missionary, St Boniface. When Charlemagne was crowned Emperor in 800, the territory of present-day Germany became part of the Frankish Empire. The Empire was partitioned by the Treaty of Verdun in 843, with the eastern part going to Ludwig the German. In the 10th century the kingdom, which was made up of numerous tribal states, passed to the house of Liudolf. Otto I, son of Heinrich I and the first king from this Saxon family, was crowned Emperor in 962 after several political and military victories, in particular his defeat of the Magyars.

TIMELINE

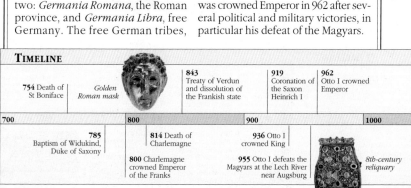

754 Death of St Boniface

Golden Roman mask

843 Treaty of Verdun and dissolution of the Frankish state

919 Coronation of the Saxon Heinrich I

962 Otto I crowned Emperor

700	800	900	1000

785 Baptism of Widukind, Duke of Saxony

814 Death of Charlemagne

800 Charlemagne crowned Emperor of the Franks

936 Otto I crowned King

955 Otto I defeats the Magyars at the Lech River near Augsburg

8th-century reliquary

◁ **Germany's Awakening**, a patriotic 19th-century work by Christian Köhler

CONSOLIDATING POWER

With Otto being crowned emperor, the dynasty of the Saxon house of Liudolf acceded to power. It gave the country three further rulers – Otto II, Otto III and Heinrich II. In the year 925 Otto I annexed Lotharingia (present-day Lorraine). On the eastern frontier he created two "marks", the Nordmark and the Ostmark, as buffer states designed to subjugate the Slav-populated regions east of the Oder River. After Heinrich II's death, the house of the Salian Franks took the imperial throne and used their authority to limit the power of the local feudal dukes.

Stained-glass window in Augsburg cathedral

THE INVESTITURE CONTROVERSY

In the 11th century the empire came into conflict with the papacy. Matters came to a head in the so-called "investiture controversy". Pope Gregory VII asserted the church's right to appoint bishops. Emperor Heinrich IV meanwhile, who had been relying on the support of the clergy he had appointed, called his bishops together and asked the Pope to step down. Pope Gregory VII excommunicated Heinrich.

The dukes of Saxony used the opportunity to appoint a king in opposition to Heinrich, and the Pope attempted to intervene in the dispute. Heinrich IV saw himself forced to march to Canossa in Italy, where the Pope had sought refuge, in order to stop his empire from falling apart. Doing penance in this way forced the Pope to withdraw his excommunication. However, the dispute did not end there, but continued for several years, finally ending with the Signing of the Concordat of Worms in 1122.

Enamelled Romanesque medallion, dating from c.1150

HOHENSTAUFENS AND WELFS

After the Salian dynasty died out in 1125 and the brief reign of Lothar III of the Saxon dynasty, another long drawn-out conflict broke out, between the houses of Hohenstaufen and Welf (known in Italian as Ghibellines and Guelphs). Imperial power went to the Hohenstaufens, while the greatest political victories were scored by Friedrich I Barbarossa (meaning "red beard"). He intended gradually to break up his subject principalities and to rule them under a feudal system. The 12th century also saw further expansion eastwards and northwards into areas inhabited by the northwestern Slavic tribes. From the start of the 13th

12th-century reliquary from the Welf family vaults

TIMELINE

1027 Coronation of Konrad II, first Emperor of the Salians

1138 Coronation of Konrad III, first Hohenstaufen Emperor

1155 Coronation of Friedrich I Barbarossa as Emperor

1000 | 1050 | 1100 | 1150

11th-century reliquary cross

1074 Beginning of Investiture Struggle

1077 Heinrich IV does penance at Canossa

1122 The Concordat of Worms

Portable altar from the vaults of the Welfs

century Barbarossa also conquered territories occupied by the Baltic peoples and the Estonians, which involved armed expeditions by the North German cities and orders of knights.

Friedrich II, crowned Emperor in 1220, was also King of Sicily and his Italian interests brought further conflict with the papacy. Ultimately his policies brought about the collapse of imperial power. After his death in 1250, his successor was unable to find any support, which led to the period known as the Great Interregnum.

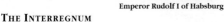

Emperor Rudolf I of Habsburg

13th century a system evolved by which only seven elector-dukes had the right to elect the emperor. These were the Margrave of Brandenburg, the Elector of Palatine (or the Bavarian dukes), the Duke of Saxony, the King of Bohemia and the Archbishops of Trier, Cologne and Mainz. Starting with Rudolf I of Habsburg, who was elected king of Germany in 1273, until 1438 the kings came from the rival houses of Habsburg, Wittelsbach and Luxemburg. After 1312, the same houses also competed for the title of Emperor. The most outstanding of the 14th-century rulers of Germany was Karl IV of Luxemburg, who resided permanently in Prague. In 1338 the electors had rejected the requirement for the Pope to confirm election results. In 1356 Karl IV issued the "Golden Bull" which underlined the federal nature of the state, and clarified the rules for electing its leader.

THE INTERREGNUM

The fall of the Hohenstaufens marked the end of the old imperial system. The absence of an overall ruler led to a breakdown in law and order, and resulted in the rise of the *Raubritter* (robber-barons). To protect their common interests, the trading cities set up alliances. The collapse of imperial power, and the decline in the power of the dukes thus gradually led to an increase in the power of the German cities.

From the beginning the imperial throne had been elective, with dukes electing the emperor from the male members of the dynasty. There was also no capital city, as the emperors moved from one city to another, thus spreading the costs of maintaining the imperial court among different duchies. In the

A "Minneteppich" – part of a medieval tapestry, depicting a variety of human traits and a griffin, the mythical beast

1250 Beginning of the Great Interregnum

1312 Heinrich VII crowned Emperor

Silver coin from 1369

200　　　　　1250　　　　　1300　　　　　1350

1273 End of the Great Interregnum and coronation of Rudolf I

1348 Prague University founded

1356 Golden Bull issued

1386 Heidelberg University founded

The Hanseatic League

THE GERMAN Hanseatic League, or Hanse, was only one of many guilds of traders or cities that existed in the Middle Ages, but its important historical role made it one of the best known. Established in the 13th century, it reached its peak in the 14th century and declined again in the 16th century. Over 160 cities, primarily the trading cities of northern Germany, but also including Baltic ports as far afield as Visby, Riga and Tallinn, joined the League. It exercised total control over trade from the Baltic in the east to England in the west. The Hanseatic cities were among the wealthiest in Europe, and crafts and the arts flourished there.

Madonna of the Roses
15th-century painting by Stefan Lochner of the Cologne School.

The Wise and Foolish Maidens
The flowering of art in the Hanseatic cities brought about works such as this portal of Magdeburg Cathedral.

Hanse ships, loaded with merchandise, entering the harbour

Revenue officials awaiting the cargo

Round wooden cranes with swivelling arms were used to unload ships. One example still survives in Lüneburg.

Crucifix in Lübeck Cathedral
This crucifix is one of only few painted wood-carvings made by Bernt Notke of Lübeck that have survived until today.

Cogs
Cogs – heavy, flat-bottomed sailing ships with limited manoeuvrability – were fishermen's and merchants' boats or navy vessels in the North Sea and the Baltic from the 12th to the 14th centuries.

Panoramic view of Lübeck
The vast port town of Lübeck was the largest Hanseatic city. This 15th-century woodcut shows a view of the city with its numerous church spires.

THE HANSEATIC CITIES

In the major Hanseatic cities, the most prominent buildings grew up around the *Markt* (market square) and along the streets that led to the port. The market square would contain the *Rathaus* (town hall), with its multi-functional interiors, and the equally splendid banqueting halls and ballrooms, such as the Gürzenich in Cologne. The main cathedrals in the cities were dedicated either to St Mary or St Nicholas. The gabled residential houses had narrow façades with distinctive portals. The townscape of the port areas was dominated by granaries, warehouses and numerous cranes. The cities were all enclosed and protected by solid fortifications.

Harbour officials in their offices

The Leichter was a harbour boat used to carry cargo from the ships to the warehouses.

Hamburg merchants

Russian merchants, recognizable by their distinctive clothing, are engrossed in intense negotiations.

***The town hall in Brunswick**, with its open upper arcades and statues of the Welfs, is one of the finest surviving Hanseatic secular buildings.*

***The Kröpeliner Tor** in Rostock (see p462) is one of 22 towers on the defensive walls around the medieval city centre.*

THE PORT OF HAMBURG

Hamburg, along with Bremen, Lübeck and Gdansk, was one of the leading Hanseatic cities. In the 14th century, it was the main centre for trade between the North Sea and the Baltic. This miniature, showing the port of Hamburg, dates from the 15th century.

Jan Hus being burned at the stake

THE HUSSITE WARS AND THE HABSBURG DYNASTY

The last king and emperor of the house of Luxemburg, Sigismund, brought an end to the "Great Schism" in the Western church that had persisted since 1378. The Council of Constance, which he called in 1414, led to the election of a single, rather than two rival popes. However, new religious controversy was provoked by the death sentence for heresy passed in 1415 on Jan Hus, a religious reformer from Bohemia. The ensuing Hussite Wars ravaged the northern and western regions of Germany.

From 1482 the imperial crown went to the Habsburgs, who retained it

Title page of the first German edition of the Bible

until 1740. Attempts at political reform in the second half of the 15th century failed. The most ambitious reformer was Maximilian I. He called an Imperial Tribunal in 1495 which set about transferring part of the king's authority to the judiciary; however, it did not result in any great practical changes, although it gave slightly more power to the *Reichstag*, the imperial parliament.

THE REFORMATION

Germany entered the 16th century as a country simmering with social conflict, gradually becoming steeped in the ideas of humanism, thanks to the writings of Erasmus of Rotterdam and others. The rise of Martin Luther, who in 1517 nailed his 95 Theses to the door of the Castle Church in Wittenberg, and who opposed the trade in

Lion-shaped water jug (1540)

indulgences conducted by the clergy, set the Reformation in motion *(see pp116–17)*. The idea of ecclesiastical reform propounded by Luther gained a growing following. His supporters included princes who hoped to profit from the secularization of church property, as well as other social classes that simply saw an opportunity to improve their lot. In 1519 Maximilian I died, and Karl V was elected to succeed him. Karl's interests were focused on Spain and the Netherlands, and he was unable to prevent the spread of Lutheranism.

TIMELINE

1419–36 Hussite Wars	**c.1450** The first printing press	*Maximilian I*		**1517** Luther's Theses and the start of the Reformation	**1540** The first stock exchanges are s[et] up in Augsburg and Nürnbe[rg]
1400		**1450**			**1500**
	1414–18 Council of Constance	**1438** Coronation of Albrecht II, first Emperor of the House of Habsburg	**1495** Edict banning the waging of private wars	**1522** The Knights' War	**1524–25** Peasants'

Urban life in Germany in the early 16th century, in a painting by Jörg Breu the Elder (c.1475–1537)

The unrest led to rebellions such as the Knights' War of 1522 and the Peasants' War of 1524, and these were followed by continuous religious conflict. In 1530 the Protestants set up the League of Schmalkalden, which was finally broken up by the Emperor in the war of 1546–7. These basically religious clashes ultimately led to the division of Germany into a northern Protestant part and a Catholic south, a situation that was sanctioned in 1555 by the Peace of Augsburg. This established the principle of *cuius regio, eius religio*, which meant that each ruler had the right to decide on the faith of the region, and the only option left for anyone of a different persuasion was to move elsewhere.

THE THIRTY YEARS' WAR

The second half of the 16th century was relatively stable for Germany, despite the religious conflicts. However, the influ-ence of the Counter-Reformation in the early 17th century ended this stability. The Protestant Union and Catholic League were established in 1608 and 1609 respectively. Unrest in Prague, where the states with a Protestant majority opposed the election of the Catholic Ferdinand II as king of Bohemia, began the Thirty Years' War. This religious war quickly spread throughout Germany, and also drew in Denmark, Spain, Sweden and France. Much of the country and many towns were laid waste, and vast numbers of people died. Finally, in 1648, the German states, France and Sweden signed the Peace of Westphalia in Münster, resulting in major losses of territory for Germany, mainly in the north. A new political system emerged, with the German princes enjoying complete political independence, under a weakened emperor and pope. The second half of the 17th century was marked by the rebuilding of towns and the hard work of restoring the ruined economic infrastructure.

A scene in the Thirty Years' War, in a painting by Wilhelm von Diez

1555 Religious Peace of Augsburg

1609 Establishment of the Catholic League

1608 Foundation of the Protestant Union

1618 Thirty Years' War breaks out

Monument to the Great Elector, Friedrich Wilhelm I

1550

1600

1650

546 chmalkalden ar begins

16th-century tile, depicting a falconer

1640 Accession to the Brandenburg throne by Friedrich Wilhelm I

1648 Peace of Westphalia ends the Thirty Years' War

Goethe in the Roman Campagna by Johann H. W. Tischbein (1787)

ABSOLUTISM AND
THE RISE OF PRUSSIA

In the second half of the 17th century and throughout the 18th century, Germany was a loose federation of small, politically weak states in the west, and much more powerful states in the east and the south – Saxony, which was ruled by the house of Wettin, and Bavaria, ruled by the Wittelsbachs. However, the rising star was the state of Brandenburg, ruled by the house of Hohenzollern, which from 1657 also ruled Prussia. In 1701 the Elector Friedrich III crowned himself King of Prussia (as Friedrich I), and subsequently the name "Prussia" was applied to all areas ruled by the house of Hohenzollern. During the 18th century Prussia became the greatest rival to Habsburg Austria. In 1740, Friedrich II, also known as Frederick the Great,

Portrait of Frederick the Great as successor to the throne

was crowned King of Prussia. Under his rule, Berlin became a major European city and a centre of the Enlightenment. In 1740–42, in the Seven Years' War, Frederick the Great took Silesia from the Habsburgs without major losses. In 1772 he took part in the first partition of Poland.

In the second half of the 18th century Germany produced a succession of great poets and playwrights – figures such as Gotthold Ephraim Lessing, Friedrich Schiller and Johann Wolfgang von Goethe.

THE NAPOLEONIC WARS, RESTORATION
AND REVOLUTION

From 1793 onwards the German states were involved in the Napoleonic Wars. After France's occupation of the lands west of the Rhine, a territorial reform was carried out by the Reichstag in 1801. This resulted in the secularization of most church property, and the total of 289 states and free cities was reduced to 112 larger states. States that gained from this reform supported Napoleon in his crushing defeat of Austria in the war of 1805–7. In 1806 the Holy Roman Empire of German Nations was dissolved, and Bavaria, Saxony and Wurttemberg were given the status of kingdoms. Napoleon defeated Prussia at Jena and the country was occupied by France.

TIMELINE

1701 The first king of Prussia is crowned	**1740–42** The Silesian War	*Leopold Hermann von Boyen, Prussian army general*		**1813** Battle of the Nations at Leipzig
1702–14 Germany joins the War of Spanish Succession				
1700	**1730**	**1760**	**1790**	
1706 Meißen porcelain factory opened		**1756–63** The Seven Years' War	**1803** Territorial reform of the German states	
1700 Academy of Sciences founded in Berlin	**1740** Frederick the Great crowned King of Prussia	**1806** Dissolution of the Empire	**1814–15** The Congress of Vienna	

The tide turned for Germany at the Battle of Leipzig in 1813, when Russia, Austria and Prussia defeated the French. After Napoleon's final defeat at Waterloo in 1815, the Congress of Vienna established a German Confederation under Austrian control. Its supreme body was the

Victory Report at the Battle of Leipzig by Johann Peter Krafft (1839)

Bundestag (federal parliament), which met at Frankfurt am Main.

The wars of liberation against Napoleon had led to a growth in nationalism and democratic awareness, as well as a desire for unification. In 1848 the March Revolution broke out in Berlin. Its main driving force was the urban middle class, but the revolt was finally put down by Prussian troops in 1849.

In the 1820s and 1830s, Germany underwent rapid industrialization, and the establishment of the Zollverein (customs union) in 1834 marked the first step towards a united Germany. Uniting Germany was the main goal of the Prussian premier Otto von Bismarck. Prussia's victories over Austria in 1866 and France in 1871 resulted in the proclamation of a German Empire on 18 January 1871.

Vase with portrait of Kaiser Wilhelm II

THE SECOND REICH

The Second Reich was a federation of 25 states, and its first Chancellor was Otto von Bismarck. The unification of Germany led to a widespread confrontation between the state and the Catholic Church (known as the "Kulturkampf"). The economy, however, flourished, due to the boom in industry, in particular mining, metallurgy, electrical and chemical engineering. This led to the rise of a workers' movement, inspired by the ideas of Karl Marx. In 1875 the workers' parties united and formed the Social Democratic Party of Germany (SPD). Although the party was banned between 1878 and 1890, it rapidly gained support, and a system of social welfare for workers was gradually introduced.

At the beginning of the 20th century, Germany was a powerful state with overseas colonies. Imperialist tendencies grew, and increased tensions in European politics, particularly in the Balkans, led inevitably to war.

Fighting on the Barricades in May 1848, a fanciful picture of the revolution in Berlin by Julius Scholz

1834 German Customs Union (Zollverein) is established	**1847** The Communist Manifesto is published	**1871** Proclamation of the German Empire with Prussian king as Emperor Wilhelm I	**1898** Construction of the German navy begins
	1848–49 The March Revolution		
1820	**1850**	**1880**	**1910**
	1844 Silesian weavers' uprising	**1870–71** Franco-Prussian War	**1890** Fall of Bismarck
Neo-Gothic chalice designed by K.F. Schinkel		**1866** Prussian-Austrian War	Abandoned, *bas-relief by Ernst Barlach*

Bismarck's Germany

THE ESTABLISHMENT of a Reich headed by the King of Prussia on 18 January 1871 ensured Prussia's prominent role over the following decades. The Chancellor was the Prussian Prime Minister Otto von Bismarck. Thanks to large reparations paid by France and a favourable economic situation, the economy flourished throughout the Reich. This in turn fostered the development of science and culture. The cities grew rapidly, and the housing shortage led to the development of huge *Miets-kasernen*, blocks of apartments for renting.

GERMANY IN 1871

   The Second German Reich

Kaiser Wilhelm I
Mosaics, depicting a procession of members of the house of Hohenzollern, decorate the vestibule of the Kaiser-Wilhelm Gedächtnichskirche (memorial church) in Berlin.

The Kaiser's Family Taking a Walk in Sanssouci Park
"Happy family" portraits such as this one were often painted for propaganda purposes.

The Reichstag
The monumental Reichstag (parliament building), was built in the centre of the capital, Berlin, by the architect Paul Wallot.

Members of Parliament   Heads of the federal states

A Steel Mill in Königshütte
Germany's economic progress was achieved through a high degree of industrialization. Adolf von Menzel's painting depicts a steel mill in Königshütte, Upper Silesia.

Officer's helmet
The characteristic spiked helmet worn by German soldiers was known as a Pickelhaube.

Ludwig II of Bavaria
The federal states, which made up the Reich, enjoyed complete autonomy. Their rulers, however, for instance King Ludwig II of Bavaria, patron of Richard Wagner and builder of "fantastic" castles and palaces, had little real political influence.

The Kaiser's wife, Augusta Victoria

Wilhelm, the heir to the throne

Mourning dress was worn by the women and black ribbons by the men as a mark of respect for the two previous Kaisers who had died in 1888 – the father and grandfather of Wilhelm II.

The Diplomatic Corps

Otto von Bismarck   **Kaiser Wilhelm II**

INAUGURATION OF THE REICHSTAG

This vast canvas by Anton von Werner (1893) shows the opening ceremony for the Reichstag after the coronation of Kaiser Wilhelm II on 25 June 1888 in the Kaiser's Palace in Berlin. The painter depicts the moment when the Kaiser delivers his speech.

Otto von Bismarck
Originating from a Pomeranian family of Junkers, the Prussian Premier and Chancellor of the Reich was one of the most prominent political figures of his time.

WORLD WAR I

When Germany entered World War I in 1914, the Kaiser's generals hoped for a quick victory, but their invasion of France was halted on the Marne. The war dragged on for the next four years, devastating much of Europe, and ending in Germany's defeat. The Allied offensive in the summer of 1918 forced Germany to the negotiating table – it also led to the November revolution in Germany. Within days the state monarchs were toppled from power, Kaiser Wilhelm II abdicated, and on 9 November 1918 a republic was proclaimed. The form of government had not been decided, and at first the political advantage was held by the socialists. But the Workers' Uprising in Berlin in 1919 was defeated.

Ein Volk, ein Reich, ein Führer!

Propaganda poster for Adolf Hitler

THE WEIMAR REPUBLIC

The Treaty of Versailles of 1919 imposed many unfavourable conditions on Germany. The country lost a great deal of her territory, mainly to Poland, France and Lithuania, and she was obliged to pay huge reparations, undergo partial demilitarization and limit arms production.

During the Weimar Republic, Germany was riddled with instability. The economy collapsed under the heavy burden of reparation payments and the onset of hyperinflation. Constant changes of government failed to stabilize the political situation, which led to the rise both of left-wing revolutionaries and of right-wing nationalists, and to a general dissatisfaction with the country's status after the humiliating Treaty of Versailles. It is perhaps remarkable that at this time German culture flourished.

Cover of a Socialist magazine attacking the book-burning

However, this was not sufficient to stave off the political disaster that led to the rise of the Nazi Party (the NSDAP or National Socialist German Workers' Party).

THE THIRD REICH

Adolf Hitler was appointed Chancellor by President Hindenburg on 30 January 1933 and immediately started to get rid of potential opponents. A fire that burned down the Reichstag served as a pretext for persecuting the communists,

A Berlin synagogue burning during Kristallnacht, 1938

TIMELINE

1914 World War I breaks out	**1919** Signing of the Treaty of Versailles		**1926** Germany accepted in League of Nations
	1921 Adolf Hitler becomes leader of the NSDAP		
1915	**1920**	**1925**	
	9 Nov 1918 Declaration of the Republic	**1923** Hitler's Putsch in Munich	**1926** Hitler Youth set up
Poster of Marlene Dietrich		**1925** Hitler writes *Mein Kampf*	

Poster of Marlene Dietrich

while in April 1933 a boycott of Jewish businesses began. Trade unions were banned, as were all parties apart from the Nazis. Books by "impure" authors were burned, and the work of "degenerate" artists was exhibited as a warning, marking the start of the persecution of artists and scientists, many of whom decided to emigrate. At the same time, Hitler attempted to present to the world a face of openness and success, particularly with the Berlin Olympics of 1936. Germany broke almost all the demilitarization conditions of the Versailles Treaty. The growth in arms production brought with it an improved economic situation, increasing Hitler's popularity. All his opponents who had not managed to emigrate were either killed or sent to concentration camps.

In 1935 the Nuremberg Laws were passed, which officially sanctioned the persecution of Jews. During the *Kristallnacht* (crystal night) of 9 November 1938, synagogues throughout Germany were burned and Jewish shops and homes were looted, resulting in streets littered with broken glass. Hitler's plans to conquer Europe were realized in March 1938, with the "Anschluss" (annexation) of Austria, then in 1939 German forces occupied Czechoslovakia. After obtaining peace guarantees from the USSR, Germany invaded Poland on 1 September 1939, thus starting World War II.

The centre of Dresden after Allied carpet-bombing

WORLD WAR II

The first two years of World War II were marked by one victory after another for the German Army, which managed to occupy half of Europe. Great Britain was the only country that succeeded in fending off Hitler. In 1941 the Wehrmacht occupied large swathes of the Soviet Union. Terror and genocide were instigated in all occupied territories. The decision to exterminate all Jews in Europe was taken at the Wannsee Conference in Berlin in January 1942. Attempts to oppose Hitler in Germany were crushed. The course of the war did not change until 1943, when on 31 January Germany suffered a major defeat in the Battle of Stalingrad.

The Allied landings in Normandy and the creation of the second front helped bring the war to an end. When Soviet forces reached Berlin in 1945 the city lay in ruins and the populace was starving. During five and a half years, 55 million people had lost their lives.

Pieta, sculpture by Käthe Kollwitz (1937–8)

1935 Enactment of law to build up army	**1938** Anschluss with Austria; occupation of Czechoslovakia	**1 Sep 1939** German invasion of Poland; the beginning of World War II	
30 Jan 1933 Hitler appointed Chancellor of the Reich	**9/10 Nov 1938** "Kristallnacht"	*The Enigma Code machine*	

1930	1935	1940	1945

Poster for the Berlin Olympics in 1936

1936 Berlin Olympics	**22 Jun 1941** Germany invades USSR		**30 Apr 1945** Hitler commits suicide as Soviet troops enter Berlin
1935 November laws sanction persecution of Jews		**20 Jan 1942** Wannsee conference	

Nazi war criminals on trial at Nuremberg

THE AFTERMATH OF WORLD WAR II

Germany's unconditional surrender was signed on 8 May 1945, ending the bloodiest war in human history. Peace negotiations began which were to shape the new face of Europe for decades to come. In fact, discussions on Germany's future had already taken place at the Tehran and Yalta Conferences, where the leaders of the Big Three Powers met. But it was not until the Potsdam Conference that the terms were finally agreed.

Germany lost large parts of its territory to the east, displacing the German population there. It was decided to demilitarize Germany. The four Allied powers – the USA, the USSR, Britain and France – divided Germany into zones of occupation which they would rule until democratic structures were in place. The main perpetrators of war crimes were tried in Nuremberg and sentenced to death. Unfortunately, tensions increased between the Western powers and the Soviet Union, rapidly escalating in the "Cold War", which was largely played out in occupied Germany. In

The Berlin Airlift in 1948–9

1948 the three western zones introduced a new currency, which led the Soviets to blockade the western part of Berlin. Thanks to the Berlin Airlift, which supplied the population with food and fuel, the blockade was abandoned. On 23 May 1949 the Federal Republic (Bundesrepublik) of Germany was established in the three western zones, and on 7 October 1949 the German Democratic Republic (DDR) was set up in the Soviet zone. West Berlin, as it was then known, became an enclave inside East Germany.

GERMANY 1949–90
▦ *Federal Republic*
☐ *DDR*

GERMANY DIVIDED

The German Democratic Republic was democratic only in name. It became one of the satellites of the Soviet Union, and as the westernmost outpost of the Eastern Bloc it was subject

Graffiti-covered section of the Berlin Wall

TIMELINE

						1973 West and East Germany accepted into U...
24 Jun 1948 Blockade of West Berlin starts	**1949** Federal Republic and DDR established	**1955** Federal Republic and German Democratic Republic gain sovereignty			**1968** Student riots	

1945	1950	1955	1960	1965	1970

4–11 Feb 1945 Yalta Conference **8 May** Germany capitulates *Konrad Adenauer*	**7 Jun 1953** Workers' uprising in East Berlin	**13 Aug 1961** Building of the Berlin Wall	**1972** Official relations established between East and West Germany; Munich Olympics

Reunification ceremony outside the Reichstag in Berlin in 1990

to great restrictions. Attempted protests, such as the Workers' Uprising of 17 June 1953 in Berlin, were ruthlessly suppressed. For many people the only solution was to leave the country. As the exodus of skilled workers to the West continued, on 13 August 1961 a wall with barbed wire was built to contain them. Many attempts to cross the frontier between the two Germanies ended in death. A highly efficient apparatus was set up in East Germany to watch over citizens' activities by the infamous Stasi secret police.

The first Chancellor of the Federal Republic of Germany, Konrad Adenauer, had Germany's integration into Western Europe as his main objective. Thanks to aid under the Marshall Plan, the economy rapidly recovered. Willy Brandt, first elected as Chancellor in 1969, pursued a policy of openness to the East, and recognized the German Democratic Republic.

REUNIFICATION

German reunification was made possible by a number of political events, in particular those going on in Eastern Europe. The Soviet premier Gorbachev's policy of *glasnost* led to the loosening of political constraints throughout the Eastern Bloc. Democratic changes in Poland set off a chain reaction. In 1989, people started to flee the German Democratic Republic en masse via its embassy in Prague and across the Austro-Hungarian border. Then, on 9 November 1989, the Berlin Wall fell and East Germans were free to leave. When, only three weeks later, Chancellor Helmut Kohl presented a ten-point plan for German reunification, few believed that it would happen, but the country was officially reunified on 3 October 1990. Since then, Germany has been undergoing a process of integration.

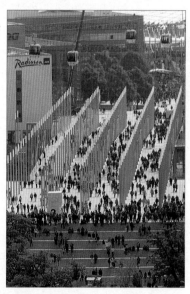
Crowds visiting the giant Expo 2000 exhibition in Hannover

1982 Helmut Kohl becomes German Chancellor

3 Oct 1990 Reunification of Germany

8 Nov 1989 Fall of the Berlin Wall

Helmut Kohl and Richard von Weizsäcker at the reunification ceremony

1975	1980	1985	1990	1995	2000

1994 Withdrawal of last Russian military units from Berlin

The Trabant, a trademark of East German industry

1998 Gerhard Schröder becomes Chancellor

2000 Expo 2000 World Fair in Hannover

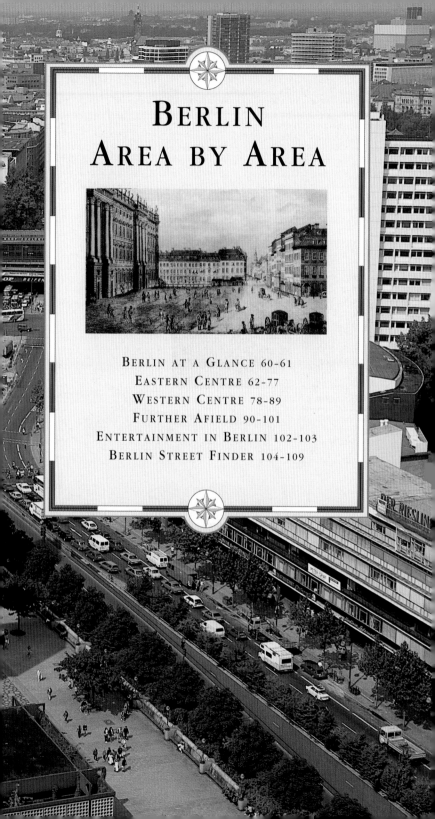

BERLIN
AREA BY AREA

Berlin at a Glance

SINCE THE REUNIFICATION of Germany in 1990, Berlin has become an increasingly popular destination for visitors. The following pages provide a useful guide to places of interest both in the town centre and the outskirts, including historic monuments such as Nikolaikirche *(see p76)*, museums, modern developments, such as the Potsdamer Platz, as well as places of recreation and amusement, such as the Botanical Gardens *(see p100)*. In the guide, we have divided central Berlin into two parts (east and west); these, however, do not correspond with the city's former partition into East and West Berlin.

LOCATOR MAP

WESTERN CENTRE

The Tiergarten was once a royal hunting estate but, after 1818, it was converted into a landscaped park by Peter Joseph Lenné (see p83) *with lakes and streams.*

The Gemäldegalerie (see pp86–7) *houses an exceptional collection of European masters, including Hans Holbein's* Portrait of George Gisze *(1532).*

The Kaiser-Wilhelm-Gedächtniskirche was almost totally destroyed by bombs during World War II. However it was rebuilt in 1963 to a design by Egon Eiermann (see p82).

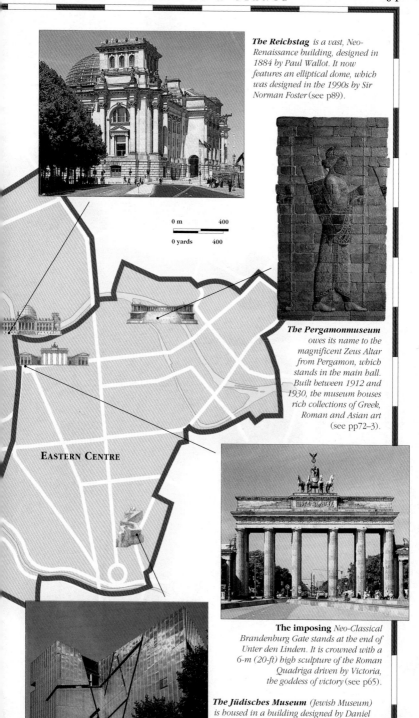

The Reichstag *is a vast, Neo-Renaissance building, designed in 1884 by Paul Wallot. It now features an elliptical dome, which was designed in the 1990s by Sir Norman Foster* (see p89).

The Pergamonmuseum *owes its name to the magnificent Zeus Altar from Pergamon, which stands in the main hall. Built between 1912 and 1930, the museum houses rich collections of Greek, Roman and Asian art* (see pp72–3).

0 m   400
0 yards   400

EASTERN CENTRE

The imposing *Neo-Classical Brandenburg Gate stands at the end of Unter den Linden. It is crowned with a 6-m (20-ft) high sculpture of the Roman Quadriga driven by Victoria, the goddess of victory* (see p65).

The Jüdisches Museum *(Jewish Museum) is housed in a building designed by Daniel Libeskind. It features a symbolic projection of a broken Star of David* (see p76).

EASTERN CENTRE

THIS PART of Berlin is the historic centre of the city, and includes the Mitte district and parts of Kreuzberg. Its beginnings date back to the

Relief on Schadow-Haus

13th century when two settlements were established on the banks of the river Spree. One was the former Cölln, situated on an island, and the other its twin settlement, Berlin. Berlin's first church, the Nikolaikirche, survives to this day.

This part of the city features most of its historic buildings, which are located mainly along Unter den Linden. It also includes Museumsinsel, the location of the vast Berliner Dom as well as of the impressive collection of museums that gives the island its name. These include the Pergamonmuseum.

During the city's partition, Mitte belonged to East Berlin while Kreuzberg was in West Berlin.

SIGHTS AT A GLANCE

Museums and Galleries
Alte Nationalgalerie ⑰
Altes Museum ⑮
Bodemuseum ⑲
Deutsches Technikmuseum
   Berlin ㉘
Jüdisches Museum ㉖
Märkisches Museum ㉕
Neues Museum ⑯
Pergamonmuseum ⑱
Topographie des Terrors ㉗
Zeughaus ⑦

Streets and Squares
Alexanderplatz ㉒
Bebelplatz ②
Nikolaiviertel ㉔
Schlossplatz ⑬
Unter den Linden ④

Churches
Berliner Dom ⑭
Deutscher Dom ⑪
Französischer Dom ⑨
Friedrichswerdersche
   Kirche ⑧
Marienkirche ⑳
St Hedwigs-Kathedrale ③

**Historic Buildings
and Monuments**
Brandenburger
   Tor ①
Fernsehturm ㉓

Humboldt-Universität ⑤
Konzerthaus ⑩
Neue Wache ⑥
Rotes Rathaus ㉑
Schlossbrücke ⑫

GETTING THERE
This part of Berlin is served by S-Bahn 1, 2, 3, 5, 7, 9, 75 and U-Bahn 2, 5 & 9. Bus 100 runs along Unter den Linden and Karl-Liebknecht-Strasse.

KEY

■ Street-by-Street map
   See pp64–5

■ Street-by-Street map
   See pp70–1

🚉 Railway station

Ⓢ S-Bahn station

Ⓤ U-Bahn station

Ⓟ Parking

0 m   400
0 yards   400

◁ **Personification of History** adorning the monument of Friedrich Schiller

Street-by-Street: Around Bebelplatz

THE SECTION of Unter den Linden between Schloss-brücke and Friedrichstrasse is one of the most attractive areas in central Berlin. As well as some magnificent

Eagle from Altes Palais

Baroque and Neo-Classical buildings, many of them designed by famous architects, there are also some restored palaces that are now used as public buildings. Of particular interest is the beautiful Baroque building of the Zeughaus (the former Arsenal), which now houses the German History Museum.

Neue Wache
Now serving as a memorial to all victims of war and dictatorship, this monument was designed by Karl Friedrich Schinkel **6**

Humboldt University
The university courtyard teems with life all year round. Second-hand book-sellers set up their stalls in front of the gate **5**

| 0 metres | 100 |
| 0 yards | 100 |

Unter den Linden
Replanted with four rows of lime trees in 1946, this is one of the most famous streets in Berlin **4**

Branden-burg Gate

Staatsbibliothek
Designed by Ernst von Ihne and constructed between 1903 and 1914, this impressive building houses part of the State Library collection.

Altes Palais

UNIVERSITÄTSSTRASSE
CHARLOTTENSTRASSE
UNTER DEN LINDEN
BEBEL-PLATZ
BEHRENSTRASSE

KEY

– – – Suggested route

★ **Zeughaus (Deutsches Historisches Museum)**
Minerva, goddess of wisdom, decorates this beautiful Baroque building ❼

LOCATOR MAP
See Street Finder, maps 1, 4 & 5

★ **Friedrichs-werdersche Kirche**
In this Neo-Gothic church, designed by Karl Friedrich Schinkel, is a museum devoted to the great architect ❽

Staatsoper Unter den Linden

Rotes Rathaus

Kronprinzenpalais
A magnificent portal from the dismantled Bauakademie building can be found the rear of the palace.

St-Hedwigs-Kathedrale
Bas-reliefs (1837) by Theodore Wilhelm Achtermann adorn the cathedral's supports ❸

STAR SIGHTS

★ **Friedrichswerdersche Kirche**

★ **Zeughaus**

Brandenburger Tor ❶

BRANDENBURG GATE

Pariser Platz. **Map** 4 A2, 15 A3.
Ⓢ *Unter den Linden.* 🚌 *100.*

THE BRANDENBURG GATE is the quintessential symbol of Berlin. A magnificent Neo-Classical structure, modelled on the Athenian Propylaea (the entrance to the Acropolis), it was constructed between 1778 and 1791. Its sculptured decorations were completed in 1795. A pair of pavilions, once used by guards and customs officers, frames its powerful Doric colonnade and entablature. The bas-reliefs depict scenes from Greek mythology and the whole structure is crowned by Johann Gottfried Schadow's famous sculpture, *Quadriga*. In 1806, during the French occupation, the sculpture was dismantled, on Napoleon's orders, and taken to Paris. On its triumphal return in 1814, it was declared a symbol of victory, and the goddess received a staff bearing the Prussian eagle and an iron cross adorned with a laurel wreath.

Throughout its history, the Brandenburg Gate has borne witness to many of Berlin's important events. Located in East Berlin, the gate was restored between 1956 and 1958, when the damaged *Quadriga* was rebuilt in West Berlin. Over the next 40 years it stood watch over the divided city, until 1989, when the first section of the Berlin Wall came down.

Frieze and sculpture, *Quadriga*, on the Brandenburg Gate

Bebelplatz **2**

Map 4 C2. Ⓢ & Ⓤ *Friedrichstraße.* 🚌 *100, 157, 348.*

ONCE NAMED Opernplatz (Opera Square), Bebelplatz was intended to be the focal point of the Forum Fridericianum – an area designed to mirror the grandeur of ancient Rome. Although the plans were only partly implemented, many important buildings were eventually erected here.

On 10 May 1933, the square was the scene of the infamous book-burning act organized by the Nazi propaganda machine. Some 25,000 books, written by authors considered to be enemies of the Third Reich, were burned.

Today, a monument in the square commemorates this dramatic event. A translucent panel inserted into the road surface provides a glimpse of a room filled with empty bookshelves, while a plaque bears the tragically prophetic words of the poet Heinrich Heine, written in 1820: "Where books are burned, in the end people will burn."

Relief on the façade of the Staatsoper (Opera House), Bebelplatz

St-Hedwigs-Kathedrale **3**

ST HEDWIG'S CATHEDRAL

Bebelplatz. **Map** 4 C2. Ⓢ & Ⓤ *Friedrichstraße.* 🚌 *100, 157, 348.* ⏰ *9am–9pm Mon–Fri, 9am–5pm Sat.*

THIS HUGE CHURCH, set back from the road and crowned with a dome, is the Catholic Cathedral of the Roman Archdiocese of Berlin.

The façade of St-Hedwigs-Kathedrale, with beautiful bas-relief sculptures

It was built to serve the Catholics of Silesia (part of present-day Poland), which became part of the kingdom of Prussia in 1742 following defeat in the Silesian Wars.

The initial design, by Georg Wenzeslaus von Knobelsdorff, was similar to the Roman Pantheon. Construction began in 1747 and the cathedral was consecrated in 1773, although work continued on and off until 1778. Later work was carried out from 1886 to 1887.

The cathedral was damaged during World War II and subsequently rebuilt between 1952 and 1963. The building received a reinforced concrete dome and its interior was refurbished in a modern style.

The crypt holds the tombs of many of the bishops of Berlin. It also contains a 16th-century Madonna and a Pietà dating from 1420.

Unter den Linden **4**

Map 1 C4, 4 A2, B2, C2, 5 D2. Ⓢ *Unter den Linden.* 🚌 *100, 157, 348.*

ONE OF THE MOST FAMOUS streets in Berlin, Unter den Linden starts at Schlossplatz and runs down to Pariser Platz and the Brandenburg Gate. It was once the route to the royal hunting grounds, which were later transformed into the Tiergarten.

In the 17th century, the street was planted with lime trees, to which it owes its name. Although the original trees were removed around 1658, four rows of limes were planted in 1820.

During the 18th century, Unter den Linden became the main street of the westward-growing city and gradually came to be lined with

WILHELM AND ALEXANDER VON HUMBOLDT

The Humboldt brothers rank among the most distinguished Berlin citizens. Wilhelm (1767–1835) was a lawyer and politician on whose initiative the Berlin University (later renamed Humboldt University) was founded in 1810. At the university, he conducted studies in comparative and historical linguistics. His brother Alexander (1769–1859), a professor at the university, researched natural science, including meteorology, oceanography and agricultural science.

Alexander von Humboldt

prestigious buildings, which have been restored in the years following World War II.

Since the reunification of Germany in 1990, Unter den Linden has acquired several cafés and restaurants, as well as many smart new shops. The street has also become the venue for interesting outdoor events. It is usually crowded with tourists and students browsing the book-stalls around the Humboldt Universität and the Staats-bibliothek (State Library).

Humboldt Universität **5**

HUMBOLDT UNIVERSITY

Unter den Linden 6. **Map** 4 C2. **S** & **U** *Friedrichstraße.* 🚌 *100, 157, 348.*

THE UNIVERSITY BUILDING was constructed in 1753 for Prince Heinrich of Prussia. The overall design of the palace, with its main block and the courtyard enclosed within two wings, has been extended many times. Two marble statues by Paul Otto (1883) stand at the entrance; these represent Wilhelm and Alexander von Humboldt.

Many famous scientists have worked at the university, in-cluding physicians Rudolf Virchow and Robert Koch and physicists Max Planck and Albert Einstein. Among its graduates are Heinrich Heine, Karl Marx and Friedrich Engels.

After World War II, the university was in the Russian sector and the difficulties encountered by the students of the western zone led to the establishment in 1948 of the Freie Universität.

Neue Wache **6**

Unter den Linden 4. **Map** 7 A3, 16 E2. **S** *Hackescher Markt.* 🚌 *100, 157, 348.* 🕐 *10am–6pm daily.*

DESIGNED BY Karl Friedrich Schinkel and built between 1816 and 1818, this monument is considered to be one of the finest examples of Neo-Classical architecture in Berlin. The front of the

monument is dominated by a huge Doric portico with a frieze made up of bas-reliefs depicting goddesses of victory.

In 1930–31 the building was turned into a monument to soldiers killed in World War I. Following its restoration in 1960, Neue Wache became the Memorial to the Victims of Fascism and Militarism. It was rededicated in 1993 to the memory of all victims of war and dictatorship. Inside is an eternal flame and a granite slab over the ashes of an unknown soldier, a resistance fighter and a concentration camp prisoner. In the roof opening is a copy of the sculpture *Mother with her Dead Son*, by Berlin artist Käthe Kollwitz.

Zeughaus **7**

Unter den Linden 2. **Map** 5 D2. 📞 *20 30 40.* **S** *Hackescher Markt.* 🚌 *100, 157, 348.* ⚫ *until 2004.*

THIS FORMER arsenal was built in the Baroque style in 1706 under the guidance of Johann Arnold Nering, Martin Grünberg, Andreas Schlüter and Jean de Bodt. A magnificent structure, its wings surround an inner courtyard. Its exterior is decorated with Schlüter's sculptures, which include masks of dying warriors.

Princesses Luise and Friederike in the Schinkel-Museum

Since 1952, the building has housed the German History Museum. It is currently closed for refurbishment but the collection is on display in the Kronprinzenpalais opposite (Unter den Linden 3; open 10am–6pm Tue–Sun).

Friedrichswerder-sche Kirche (Schin-kel-Museum) **8**

Werderstraße. **Map** 5 D2. 📞 *(030) 208 13 23.* **U** *Hausvogteiplatz.* 🚌 *100, 147, 157, 257, 348.* 🕐 *10am– 6pm Tue–Sun.* ♿ 🚻

THE FIRST Neo-Gothic church to be built in Berlin, this small single-nave structure with its twin-tower façade was designed by Karl Friedrich Schinkel and built between 1824 and 1830.

Schinkel's original interior was largely destroyed in World War II. Following its reconstruction, the church was con-verted to a museum. It currently houses the Nationalgalerie's permanent sculpture exhibi-tion. Highlights include a model of the famous sculpture by Johann Gottfried Schadow, depicting the princesses Fried-erike and Luise (later Queen of Prussia).

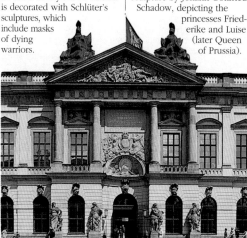

Part of the façade of the Zeughaus on Unter den Linden

Side elevation of the Französischer Dom, built for Huguenot refugees

Französischer Dom **9**
FRENCH CATHEDRAL

Gendarmenmarkt 6. **Map** 4 C2.
📞 *(030) 204 15 07.* Ⓤ *Stadtmitte or Französische Straße.* **Museum**
🕐 *noon–5pm Tue–Sat, 11am–5pm Sun.* 🏛 **Viewing Platform** 🕐 *11am–5pm daily* 🏛 **Church** 🕐 *noon–5pm Tue–Sun.* 🔔 *Sun 10am.*

ALTHOUGH THE TWO churches standing on opposite sides of Schauspielhaus seem identical, their only common feature is their matching front towers. The French cathedral was built for the Huguenot community, who found refuge in protestant Berlin following their expulsion from France after the revocation of the Edict of Nantes. The modest church, built between 1701 and 1705 by Louis Cayart and Abraham Quesnay, was modelled on the Huguenot church in Charenton, France, which was destroyed in 1688. The interior features a late-Baroque organ from 1754.

The structure is dominated by a massive, cylindrical tower, which is encircled by Corinthian porticos at its base. The tower and porticos were designed by Carl von Gontard and added around 1785. It houses the Huguenot Museum, which charts the history of the Huguenot community in France and Brandenburg.

There is a smart restaurant on the upper floor and on the top is a viewing platform offering a magnificent view. The 60-bell carillon in the tower can be heard every day at noon, 3pm and 7pm.

Konzerthaus **10**
CONCERT HALL

Gendarmenmarkt 2. **Map** 4 C2.
📞 *(030) 203 09 21 01.* Ⓤ *Stadtmitte.*

A LATE NEO-CLASSICAL jewel, this magnificent theatre building, known until recently as the Schauspielhaus, is one of the greatest achievements of Berlin's best-known architect, Karl Friedrich Schinkel. It was built between 1818 and 1821 around the ruins of Langhan's National Theatre, destroyed by fire in 1817. The portico columns were retained in the new design. Following bomb damage in World War II, it was reconstructed as a concert hall and the exterior was restored to its former glory. The Konzerthaus is now home to the Berlin Symphony Orchestra.

The whole building is decorated with sculptures alluding to drama and music. The façade, which includes a huge Ionic portico with a set of stairs, is crowned with a sculpture of Apollo riding a chariot pulled by griffins.

In front of the theatre stands a shining white marble statue of Friedrich Schiller, which was sculpted by Reinhold Begas and erected in 1869. Removed by the Nazis during the 1930s, the monument was returned

Sculpture from Deutscher Dom

Interior of the Konzerthaus, formerly the Schauspielhaus

to its rightful place in 1988. The statue is mounted on a high pedestal surrounded by allegorical figures representing Lyric Poetry, Drama, Philosophy and History.

Deutscher Dom **11**
GERMAN CATHEDRAL

Gendarmenmarkt 1. **Map** 4 C3.
📞 *(030) 202 26 90.* Ⓤ *Stadtmitte or Französische Straße.* **Exhibition**
🕐 *10am–6pm Tue–Sun.*

THE CATHEDRAL at the southern end of the square is an old German Protestant-Reformed church. Based on a five-petal shape, it was designed by Martin Grünberg and built in 1708 by Giovanni Simonetti. In 1785 it acquired a dome-covered tower identical to that of the French cathedral.

Burned down in 1945, the church was rebuilt in 1993, its exterior faithfully reconstructed and the interior adapted as exhibition space. On display is the popular "Fragen an die Deutsche Geschichte" ("Questions on German History"), which was formerly on show in the Reichstag building.

Schlossbrücke **12**

Map 5 D2. Ⓢ *Hackescher Markt.*
🚌 *100, 157, 348.*

THIS IS ONE of the city's most beautiful bridges, connecting Schlossplatz with Unter den Linden. It was built in 1824 to a design by Karl Friedrich Schinkel. Statues were added to the top of the bridge's sparkling red-granite pillars in 1853. These figures, made of white Carrara marble, were also created by Schinkel. The statues depict tableaux from Greek mythology, such as Iris, Nike and Athena, training and looking after their favourite young warriors. The elaborate wrought-iron balustrade is decorated with intertwined sea creatures.

The surviving Stadtschloss portal fronting a government building

Schlossplatz ⓭

Map 5 D2. Ⓢ Hackescher Markt.
🚌 100, 157, 348.

THIS SQUARE was once the site of a huge residential complex known as Stadt-schloss (City Castle). Built in 1451, it served as the main residence of the Brandenburg Electors. It was transformed from a castle to a palace in the mid-16th century when Elector Friedrich III (later King Friedrich I) ordered its reconstruction in the Baroque style. The building works, which lasted from 1698 until 1716, were overseen initially by Andreas Schlüter and then by Johann von Göthe and Martin Heinrich Böhme.

The three-storey residence, designed around two court-yards, was the main seat of the Hohenzollern family for almost 500 years until the end of the monarchy. The palace was partly burned during World War II but, after 1945, it was provisionally restored and used as a museum.

In 1950–51, despite protests, the palace was demolished and the square was renamed Marx-Engels-Platz under the GDR.

Now all that remains of the palace is the triumphal-arch portal that once adorned the façade on the Lustgarten side. This is now incorporated into the wall of the government building, the Staatsratgebäude, which was erected in 1964 on the square's south side. The building's decor features the remaining original sculptures, including the magnificent atlantes by the famous Dresden sculptor, Balthasar Permoser. Their inclusion was not due to appreciation of their artistic merit, but rather to their propaganda value: it was from the balcony of the portal that in 1918 Karl Lieb-knecht proclaimed the birth of the Socialist Republic.

In 1989 the square reverted to its original name. There have been ongoing discussions about rebuilding the palace, but no final decision has yet been reached. In 1993, how-ever, a spectacular model was built out of cloth stretched over a scaffolding frame.

Berliner Dom ⓮

Am Lustgarten. **Map** 5 D1.
📞 (030) 20 26 91 19. Ⓢ Hackescher Markt. 🚌 100, 157, 348. ⏰ 9am–7:30pm daily. 🎫 🕇 10am, 6pm Sun.

THIS PROTESTANT cathedral was built between 1747 and 1750 as a church and mausoleum for the Hohen-zollern family on the site of a Dominican church. Although it now has a central copper dome some 85 m (279 ft) high, the first Berliner Dom was a more modest design by Johann Boumann. It was remodelled in Neo-Classical style from 1816 to 1821 by Karl Friedrich Schinkel.

The present Neo-Baroque structure is the work of Julius Raschdorff, dating from 1894 to 1905. Following World War II damage, it has now been restored in a simplified form, including the dismantling of the mausoleum that once adjoined its northern wall.

The Neo-Baroque interior of the Berliner Dom

BERLIN'S BRIDGES

Despite wartime damage, Berlin's bridges are still well worth seeing. The Spree river and the city's canals have some fine, exemplary architecture on their banks, while many of the bridges were designed and decorated by famous architects and sculptors. Probably the most renowned bridge is the Schlossbrücke designed by Karl Friedrich Schinkel. Further south along the Kupfergrabenkanal, the Schleusenbrücke, dating from c.1914, is decorated with reliefs of the early history of the city's bridges and sluices.

The next bridge, heading south, is the Jungfernbrücke (1798), which is the last drawbridge in Berlin. The next bridge along is the Gertraudenbrücke. Where Friedrichstrasse crosses the Spree river is the Weidendammer Brücke, built originally in 1695–7 and subsequently rebuilt in 1923, with an eagle motif adorning its balustrade. On the Spree near the Regierungsviertel is the magnificent Moltkebrücke (1886–91). The bridge is guarded by a huge griffin wielding a shield adorned with the Prussian eagle, while cherubs dressed in a military fashion hold up lamps. On the arches of the bridges are portraits of leaders, designed by Karl Begas.

Ornamental feature of a bear on the Liebknechtbrücke

Street-by-Street: Museum Island

THE LONG ISLAND that nestles in the tributaries of the
Spree river is the cradle of Berlin's history. It was here
that the first settlements appeared at the beginning of the
13th century: Cölln is mentioned in documents dating
back to 1237, and its twin settlement, Berlin, is mentioned
a few years later, in 1244. The island's character was
transformed by the construction of the Brandenburg
Electors' palace, which served as their residence from
1470. Although it was razed to the ground in 1950, some
interesting buildings on the north side of the island have
survived, including the Berliner Dom (Berlin Cathedral)
and the impressive collection of
museums that give the
island its name,
Museuminsel.

LOCATOR MAP
See Street Finder, maps 4 & 5

Bode Museum
*A rounded corner of the
building, crowned with
a dome, provides a
magnificent end-piece to
the tip of the island* 19

Neues Museum
*Currently undergoing
reconstruction, this
museum will house an
impressive Egyptian
collection when it
reopens in 2005* 16

AM KUPFER–GRABEN

Alte Nationalgalerie
*The equestrian statue of
King Friedrich Wilhelm IV
in front of the building is
the work of Alexander
Calandrelli* 17

★ Pergamonmuseum
*The museum is famous
for its reconstruction of
fragments of ancient
towns, as well as the
original friezes from
the Pergamon altar* 18

KEY

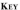

– – –   Suggested route

★ **Altes Museum**
The corners of the central building feature the figures of Castor and Pollux, heroes of Greek mythology ⓯

0 metres	400
0 yards	400

Lustgarten
A 70-ton granite bowl, the biggest in the world, was placed in the garden in 1828 ❺

LUSTGARTEN

STAR SIGHTS

★ **Pergamonmuseum**

★ **Altes Museum**

Altes Museum ⓯

Am Lustgarten (Bodestraße 1–3).
Map 5 D1. (030) 20 90 55 55.
Ⓢ Hackescher Markt. 100, 157, 348. ☐ 10am–6pm Tue–Sun.

DESIGNED BY Karl Friedrich Schinkel, this museum building is one of the world's most beautiful Neo-Classical structures, with an impressive 87-m (285-ft) high portico supported by 18 Ionic columns. Officially opened in 1830, the museum was purpose-built to house the royal collection of art and antiquities.

In the years that followed World War II, the museum building was used only to display temporary exhibitions. Since 1998, however, it has housed the Antikensammlung, with a magnificent collection of Greek and Roman antiquities.

Pericles' Head

Neues Museum ⓰

NEW MUSEUM

Bodestraße 1–3. **Map** 5 D1.
Ⓢ Hackescher Markt or Friedrichstraße.
100, 147, 257, 348. 1, 2, 3, 4, 5, 13, 53, 58. ● until 2005.

THE NEUES MUSEUM was built on Museum Island between 1841 and 1855 to a design by Friedrich August Stüler. Until World War II, it housed a collection of antiquities, mainly ancient Egyptian art. The rooms in the museum building were decorated to complement the exhibitions

they contained, while wall paintings by Wilhelm von Kaulbach depicted key events in world history.

The building was badly damaged in 1945 and reconstruction work has only recently started. When complete, the museum will house the collection of Egyptian art once again, serve as a venue for exhibitions and contain an information centre.

Alte Nationalgalerie ⓱

OLD NATIONAL GALLERY

Bodestraße 1–3. **Map** 5 D1. (030) 20 90 55 55. Ⓢ Hackescher Markt or Friedrichstraße. 100, 147, 257, 348. 1, 2, 3, 4, 5, 13, 53, 58. ☐ 9am-5pm Tue–Sun.

THE NATIONALGALERIE building, designed by Friedrich August Stuuler, was erected between 1866 and 1876. It was originally intended to house the collection of modern art that had been on display in the Akademie der Künst (Art Academy). After World War II, however, the collection was split up and part of it was shown in West Berlin, where the Neue Nationalgalerie was erected for this purpose (see p84). This building was then renamed Alte Nationalgalerie.

Following the reunification of Germany, the modern art collections were merged again. The more recent paintings are now shown in the Neue Nationalgalerie; 19th-century works are shown here. The building has been undergoing renovation since 1998, and the collection is awaiting its permanent home.

Arnold Böcklin's *The Island of the Dead* **(1883), Alte Nationalgalerie**

Pergamonmuseum ⑱

THE PERGAMONMUSEUM WAS BUILT between 1912 and 1930 to a design by Alfred Messel and Ludwig Hoffmann. It houses one of the most famous collections of antiquities in Europe and owes its name to the famous Pergamon Altar, which takes pride of place in the main hall. The three independent collections – the Museum of Antiquities (Greek and Roman), the Museum of Near Eastern Antiquities and the Museum of Islamic Art – are the result of intensive archaeological excavations by German expeditions to the Near and Middle East at the end of the 19th and beginning of the 20th century.

★ **Pergamon Altar** *(160 BC)*
This scene, featuring the goddess Athena, appears on the large frieze illustrating a battle between the gods and the giants.

Roman Mosaic
(2nd or 3rd century BC)
This ancient mosaic was found at Jerash, Jordan. A second part of it is in the collection of the Stark Museum of Art, Texas.

Non-exhibition rooms

First floor

The Goddesss Athena
This enchanting Hellenistic sculpture of the goddess Athena is one of many displayed in the museum.

Ground floor

Main entrance

Assyrian Palace
Parts of this beautifully reconstructed palace interior, from the ancient kingdom of Assyria, date from the 12th century BC.

Aleppo Zimmer
(c.1603)
This magnificent panelled room comes from a merchant's house in the Syrian city of Aleppo.

VISITORS' CHECKLIST

Bodestraße 1–3 (entrance from Am Kupfergraben). **Map** 4 C1, 5 D1. (030) 20 90 55 55. Friedrichstraße or Hackescher Markt. 100, 147, 257, 348. 10am–6pm Tue–Sun, 10am–10pm Thu. 1 Jan, Tue after Easter and Pentecost, 24, 25, 31 Dec. without flash.

GALLERY GUIDE
The central section of the ground floor houses reconstructions of ancient monumental structures, while the left wing is devoted to the Antiquities of Greece and Rome. The right wing houses the Museum of Near Eastern Antiquities; the first floor of the right wing houses the Museum of Islamic Art.

Façade of the Mshatta Palace *(AD 744)*
This fragment is from the southern façade of the Jordanian Mshatta Palace, presented to Wilhelm II by Sultan Abdul Hamid of Turkey in 1903.

★ **Market Gate from Miletus** *(c.AD 120)*
Measuring over 16 m (52 ft) in height, this gate opened onto the southern market of Miletus, a Roman town in Asia Minor.

★ **Ishtar Gate from Babylon**
(6th century BC)
Original glazed bricks decorate both the huge Ishtar gate and the impressive Processional Way that leads up to it.

STAR EXHIBITS

★ Ishtar Gate from Babylon

★ Market Gate from Miletus

★ Pergamon Altar

KEY

- Antiquities (Antikensammlung)
- Near Eastern antiquities (Vorderasiatisches Museum)
- Islamic art (Museum für Islamische Kunst)
- Non-exhibition rooms

The Bodemuseum designed by Ernst von Ihne

Bodemuseum ⑲

Monbijoubrücke (Bodestraße 1–3).
Map 4 C1. 🅒 (030) 20 90 55 55.
Ⓢ Hackescher Markt or Friedrichstraße.
🚌 100, 147, 257, 348. 🚆 1, 2, 3,
4, 5, 13, 53, 58. ⬤ until 2005.

THE FOURTH MUSEUM building
on Museuminsel was
constructed between 1897 and
1904. It was designed by Ernst
von Ihne to fit the wedge-
shaped northwestern end of
the island. The interior was
designed with the help of an
art historian, Wilhelm von
Bode, who was the director
of the Berlin state museums
at the time.

The museum displayed a
rather mixed collection that
included some old masters. Its
original name, Kaiser Friedrich
Museum, was changed after
World War II. Following the
reassembling of the Berlin
collections, all the paintings
were rehoused in the Kulturforum (see pp80–81), while
the Egyptian art and the
papyrus collection were
moved to the Ägyptisches
Museum (Egyptian Museum)
at Charlottenburg (see p92).

Following its current
refurbishment, the building
will once again house its
collection of coins, medals
and Byzantine art. It will also
be home to the reassembled
collection of sculptures, which
includes the works of Tilman
Riemenschneider, Donatello,
Gianlorenzo Bernini and
Antonio Canova. A copy of
the magnificent equestrian
statue of the Great Elector,
Friedrich Wilhelm, by Andreas
Schlüter, will once again take
its place in the old hall.

Marienkirche ⑳

Karl-Liebknecht-Straße. **Map** 5 E1.
Ⓢ Hackescher Markt. 🚌 100, 157.
⬜ 10am–4pm Mon–Thu, noon-4pm
Sat–Sun. 📷 1pm Mon & Tue.
✝ 10:30am Sun.

ST MARY'S CHURCH, or the
Marienkirche, was first
established as a parish church
in the second half of the 13th
century. Started around 1280,
construction was completed
early in the 14th century.
During reconstruction works
in 1380, following a fire, the
church was altered slightly,
but its overall shape changed
only in the 15th century when
it acquired the front tower. In
1790, the tower was crowned
with a dome, designed by
Carl Gotthard Langhans,
which includes both Baroque
and Neo-Gothic elements.

The Marienkirche was once
hemmed in by buildings, but
today it stands alone in the
shadow of the Fernsehturm
(Television Tower). The early
Gothic hall design and the

**Baroque altar in the Marienkirche,
designed by Andreas Krüger**

lavish decorative touches
make this church one of the
most interesting in Berlin. An
exquisitely carved alabaster
pulpit by Andreas Schlüter,
dating from 1703, is decorated
with bas-reliefs of St John the
Baptist and the personifications of the Virtues.

The Baroque main altar was
designed by Andreas Krüger
around 1762. The paintings
with which it is adorned
include three works by
Christian Bernhard Rode.

A Gothic font, dating from
1437, is supported by three
black dragons and decorated
with the figures of Jesus
Christ, Mary and the Apostles.

Rotes Rathaus ㉑
RED TOWN HALL

Rathausstraße 15. **Map** 5 E2.
🅄 & Ⓢ Alexanderplatz. 🅄 Klosterstraße, 🚌 100, 142, 157, 257, 348.

THIS IMPRESSIVE structure is
Berlin's main town hall.
Its predecessor was a much
more modest structure that,
by the end of the 19th
century, was inadequate
to meet the needs of the
growing metropolis.

The present building was
designed by Hermann
Friedrich Waesemann, and
the construction works went
on from 1861 until 1869. The
architect took his main inspiration from Italian Renaissance
municipal buildings, but the
tower is reminiscent of Laon
cathedral in France. The walls
are made from red brick and
it was this, rather than the
political orientation of the
mayors, that gave the town
hall its name.

The whole building has a
continuous frieze known as
the "stone chronicle", which
was added in 1879. The frieze
features scenes and figures
from the city's history and
traces the development of
its economy and science.

The Rotes Rathaus was
severely damaged during
World War II but, following
its reconstruction between
1951 and 1958, it became the
seat of the East Berlin
authorities. The West Berlin
magistrate was housed in the

Fernsehturm ㉓

THE TELEVISION TOWER, called by the locals *Telespargel*, or toothpick, remains to this day the city's tallest structure at 365 m (1,197 ft). It is also the second-tallest structure in Europe. The tower was built in 1969 to a design by a team of architects including Fritz Dieter and Günter Franke, with the help of Swedish experts. However, the idea for the tower originated much earlier from Hermann Henselmann (creator of the Karl-Marx-Allee development) in the Socialist-Realist style.

VISITORS' CHECKLIST

Panoramastraße **Map** 5 E1.
Ⓢ & Ⓤ *Alexanderplatz.*
100, 157. ◻ *Mar–Oct:
9am–1am daily; Nov–Feb:
10am–midnight daily.*

The television antenna
is visible all over Berlin.

Transmitter aerial

The metal sphere is
covered with steel cladding.

View from the Tower
*On a clear day the viewing platform
offers a full view of Berlin. Visibility
can reach up to 40 km (25 miles).*

**Concrete structure rising
to 250 m (820 ft)**

The concrete shaft contains two
elevators that carry passengers to the
café and viewing platform.

Tele-Café
*One of the attractions of
the tower is the revolving
café. A full rotation takes
about half an hour, so it is
possible to get a bird's-eye
view of the whole city while
sipping a cup of coffee.*

**The monumental, red-brick town
hall, known as the Rotes Rathaus**

Schöneberg town hall *(see p99).* Following the reunification of Germany in 1990, the Rotes Rathaus became the centre of authority, housing the offices of the mayor and the Berlin cabinet.

The forecourt sculptures by Fritz Kremer, which depict Berliners helping to rebuild the city, were added in 1958.

Alexanderplatz ㉒

Map 5 E1, F1. Ⓤ & Ⓢ *Alexanderplatz.* 100, 142, 157, 257.

ALEXANDERPLATZ, or "Alex" as it is called locally, has a long history, although it would be hard now to find any visible traces of the past. Once known as Ochsenmarkt (oxen market), it was the site of a cattle and wool market. It was later renamed after Tsar Alexander I who visited Berlin in 1805. At that time, the square boasted a magnificent monumental colonnade, which was designed by Carl von Gontard.

In time, houses and shops sprang up around the square and a market hall and urban train line were built nearby.

"Alex" became one of the city's busiest spots. Its frenzied atmosphere was captured by Alfred Döblin (1878–1957) in his novel *Berlin Alexanderplatz.*

In 1929, attempts were made to develop the square, though only two office buildings were added – the Alexanderhaus and the Berolinahaus, both by Peter Behrens.

World War II erased most of the square's buildings and it is now surrounded by characterless 1960s edifices, including the Forum Hotel (formerly Hotel Stadt Berlin) and the Fernsehturm. Now Alexanderplatz awaits its next transformation, to be based on the winning design chosen from a competition for the square's redevelopment.

Riverside buildings of the Nikolaiviertel

Nikolaiviertel ㉔

Map 5 E2. **U** & **S** *Alexanderplatz.*
U *Klosterstraße.* 🚌 *100, 142, 157, 257, 348.*

THIS SMALL AREA on the bank of the Spree is a favourite place for both Berliners and tourists. Some of Berlin's oldest houses stood here until they were destroyed in World War II. The redevelopment of the area, which was carried out by the GDR government between 1979 and 1987, was an interesting attempt to recreate a medieval village. Now, with the exception of one or two restored buildings, the Nikolaiviertel consists entirely of newly built replicas of historic buildings.

The **Nikolaikirche** was destroyed by bombing in 1945 and rebuilt in 1987. All that remains of the original structure, which was probably built around 1230, is the base of the two-tower façade of the present church, which dates from around 1300.

The only Baroque building in Nikolaiviertel to escape damage during World War II was the **Knoblauchhaus**, a small townhouse built in 1759 for the Knoblauch family. The current appearance of the building is the result of work carried out in 1835 when the façade was given a Neo-Classical look.

Ephraim-Palais was built in 1766 for Nathan Veitel Heinrich Ephraim, Frederick the Great's mint master and court jeweller. Parts of the original structure, which were saved from demolition, were used in the reconstruction.

Märkisches Museum ㉕

Am Köllnischen Park 5. **Map** 5 F2.
📞 *(030) 30 86 60.* **U** *Märkisches Museum.* **S** *Jannowitzbrücke.* 🚌 *147, 240, 265.* ⭕ *10am–6pm Tue-Sun.* 🎟 *(free Wed). Presentation of mechanical musical instruments 3pm Sun.*

BUILT between 1901 and 1907, this complex of red brick buildings was inspired by the brick-Gothic style popular in the Brandenburg region. The museum, founded in 1874, is dedicated to the cultural history of Berlin from the first settlements to today. The department "Berliner Kunst" (art), for example, presents a remarkable collection of paintings, sculpture, textiles, faiences, glass and porcelain. The main hall features the original Gothic portal from the sculpture *Quadriga*, which once crowned the Brandenburg Gate *(see p65).* A further collection in the same building is devoted to the Berlin theatre during the period 1730 to 1933. One of the galleries houses

some charming old-time mechanical musical instruments, which are played during special shows.

The museum has recently acquired exhibits from the former Museum Berliner Arbeiterleben which was located in Prenzlauer Berg. There are interior furnishings that would have typified a worker's *fin-de-siècle* flat.

Surrounding the museum, which is a branch of the Stadtmuseum Berlin organization, is the Köllnischer Park. The park is home to three brown bears – the official city mascots.

Jüdisches Museum ㉖

Lindenstraße 14. **Map** 4 C5.
📞 *(030) 25 99 33.* **U** *Hallesches Tor or Kochstraße.* 🚌 *240.* 🎟 *3pm Fri, 1 & 1:30pm Sat, 11 & 11:30am Sun (compulsory). Permanent exhibition opens in late 2001.*

THE BUILDING housing the city's recently opened Jewish Museum is an exciting and imaginative example of 20th century architecture. Designed by a team of Berlin-based architects led by Daniel Libeskind, an American of Jewish descent, the plan, shape, style, and interior and exterior arrangement of the building are part of a complicated philosophical programme. The museum's architecture itself conveys something of the tragic history of the millions of Jews who perished in the Holocaust. The zig-zag layout recalls a torn Star of David.

The interior arrangement is dominated by a gigantic empty crack, which cuts a swathe through the building. Several

The exterior of the Märkisches Museum, echoing a medieval monastery

corridors lead to a window-less Holocaust tower. Wooden posts fill a sloping square, evoking the empti-ness and isolation faced by thousands of German Jews who were condemned to a life in exile.

The collection focuses on Jewish history and art. Also on display are artifacts that were once part of everyday Jewish life in Berlin. A suite of empty rooms symbolizes lost Jewish culture.

The new steel-and-glass building of the Jewish Museum is accessible only through an underground passageway in the former Berlin-Museum building. This historic building is charac-terized by a Baroque façade dating from the reign of King Friedrich Wilhelm I. Both buildings will house a variety of exhibits relating to Jewish culture when the permanent exhibition opens in late 2001.

The austere, steel-clad walls of the Jüdisches Museum

Topographie des Terrors ㉗

Stresemannstraße 110 (enter on Nied-erkirchner Straße). **Map** 4 B4.
C (030) 25 48 67 03. **S** &
U Potsdamer Platz. 129, 248,
341. Oct–Apr: 10am–6pm daily;
May–Sep: 10am–9pm daily.

DURING the Third Reich, Prinz-Albrecht-Straße was probably the most frightening address in Berlin: here, three of the most terrifying Nazi political departments had their headquarters. The Neo-Classical Prinz-Albrecht palace,

which stands at Wil-helmstraße No. 102, became the head-quarters of Richard Heydrich and the Third Reich's security service. The school of arts and crafts at Prinz-Albrecht-Straße No. 8 was occupied by the head of the Gestapo, Heinrich Müller, while the Hotel Prinz Albrecht at No. 9 became the headquarters of the Schutzstaffel or SS.

After World War II, the buildings were pulled down. In 1987, however, in cellars that were once torture cells, an exhibition documenting Nazi crimes was mounted.

A new museum building, designed by Peter Zumthor, has been under construction on the site since 1998.

Deutsches Technikmuseum Berlin ㉘

Trebbiner Straße 9. **Map** 4 A5.
C (030) 25 48 40. **U** Gleisdreieck.
129. 9am–5:30pm Tue–Fri,
10am–6pm Sat–Sun.

THE TECHNICAL MUSEUM was first established in 1982 with the intention of grouping more than 100 smaller, specialized collections under one roof. The current collec-tion is arranged on the site of the former trade hall, the size of which allows many of the

Exhibition documenting Nazi crimes at the Topographie des Terrors

museum's exhibits, such as locomotives, water towers and storerooms, to be dis-played full-size and in their original condition.

Of particular interest in the collection are the dozens of locomotives and railway car-riages from different eras, as well as vintage cars. There are also exhibitions dedicated to flying, the history of paper manufacture, printing, weaving, electro-technology and com-puter technology. There are also two windmills, a brewery and an old forge. The section called Spectrum is especially popular with children as it allows them to try the "hands-on" experiments. A new hall for aircraft and engines will open at the end of 2001.

A special attraction of the Technical Museum is the Historical Brewery, which opened in 1995. The building was once used by the brewery Tucker Bräu for storing beer, but it was destroyed in World War II. Decades later, the brewery was rebuilt on four levels. Some visitors claim they can smell roasted malt.

One of dozens of locomotives displayed in the Deutsches Technikmuseum

WESTERN CENTRE

THIS PART OF BERLIN includes the areas of Tiergarten, Charlottenburg and parts of Kreuzberg, as well as a small section of Mitte, which used to belong to East Berlin.

Tiergarten, which was once a royal hunting estate, became a park in the 18th century. It survives as a park to this day, although in an altered form.

To the south of Tiergarten is the Kulturforum – a large centre of museums and other cultural establishments, which was created after World War II. The neighbouring Potsdamer Platz is now an ultra-modern development, built in recent years on the wasteland that formerly divided East and West Berlin.

Although the eastern part of Charlottenburg does not feature a great number of historic buildings, it is one of the city's most attractive districts, which, after World War II, became the commercial and cultural centre of West Berlin. Kreuzberg is a lively area that is now populated by immigrants, artists and affluent young professionals.

Detail from Theater des Westens façade

SIGHTS AT A GLANCE

Museums and Galleries
Bauhaus-Archiv **7**
Bendlerblock **8**
Gemäldegalerie **9**
Hamburger Bahnhof **17**
Käthe-Kollwitz-Museum **3**
Kunstgewerbemuseum **12**
Kupferstichkabinett und Kunstbibliothek **10**
Museum für Naturkunde **18**
Musikinstrumenten-Museum **14**
Neue Nationalgalerie **11**

Streets and Squares
Kurfürstendamm (Ku'damm) **2**
Potsdamer Platz **15**

Tiergarten **5**
Zoologischer Garten **4**

Churches
Kaiser-Wilhelm-Gedächtniskirche **1**

Historic Buildings and Monuments
Philharmonie **13**
Reichstag **16**
Siegessäule **6**

KEY

- Street-by-Street map *See pp80–81*
- **R** Railway station
- **S** S-Bahn station
- **U** U-Bahn station
- **P** Parking

GETTING THERE
This part of town is served by S-Bahn lines 3, 5, 7, 9, 75 and by U-Bahn lines 1, 2, 9, 15.

◁ **Mosaic in Kaiser-Wilhelm-Gedächtniskirche depicting a herald bearing the Prussian royal insignia**

Street-by-Street: Kulturforum

Sculpture by Henry Moore

THE IDEA OF CREATING a new cultural centre in West Berlin was first mooted in 1956. The first building to go up was the Berlin Philharmonic concert hall, built to an innovative design by Hans Scharoun in 1961. Most other elements of the Kulturforum were realized between 1961 and 1987, and came from such famous architects as Ludwig Mies van der Rohe. The area is now a major cultural centre that attracts millions of visitors every year.

★ Kunstgewerbe-museum
Among the collection at the Museum of Arts and Crafts you can see this intricately carved silver and ivory tankard, made in an Augsburg workshop around 1640 ⓬

Kupferstichkabinett
The large collection of prints and drawings owned by this gallery includes this portrait of Albrecht Dürer's mother ⓾

★ Gemäldegalerie
Among the most important works of the old masters exhibited in this gallery of fine art is this Madonna in Church *by Jan van Eyck (c.1425)* ⑨

Kunstbibliothek
The Art Library boasts a rich collection of books, graphic art and drawings.

REICHPIETSCHUFER

LANDWEHRKANAL

STAR SIGHTS

★ **Gemäldegalerie**

★ **Kunstgewerbe-museum**

★ **Philharmonie**

KEY

– – – Suggested route

Neue Nationalgalerie
Sculptures by Henry Moore and Alexander Calder stand outside this streamlined building, designed by Ludwig Mies van der Rohe ⑪

★ Philharmonie
Its exterior covered in a layer of golden aluminium, the Berlin Philharmonic concert hall is known all over the world for its superb acoustics ⓭

LOCATOR MAP
See Street Finder maps 1 & 3

Musikinstrumenten-Museum
This clavichord is part of a collection of musical instruments dating from the 16th to the 20th century ⓮

St-Matthäus-Kirche
This picturesque 19th-century church stands out among the modern buildings of the Kultur-forum.

0 metres 50
0 yards 50

Staatsbibliothek
Hans Scharoun designed this public lending and research library built in 1978.

Kaiser-Wilhelm-Gedächtniskirche ❶

THIS CHURCH-MONUMENT is one of Berlin's most famous landmarks. The vast Neo-Romanesque church was designed by Franz Schwechten. It was consecrated in 1895 and destroyed by bombs in 1943. After the war the ruins were removed, leaving only the front tower, at the base of which the Gedenkhalle (Memorial Hall) is situated. This hall documents the church's history and contains some original ceiling mosaics, marble reliefs and liturgical objects. In 1963, Egon Eiermann designed a new octagonal church in blue glass and a new freestanding bell tower.

Tower Ruins
The damaged roof of the former church has become one of the best-known symbols of Berlin.

Tower Clock

★ **Kaiser's Mosaic**
Kaiser Heinrich I, seated on his throne, is depicted in this elaborate mosaic.

Figure of Christ
This vast sculpture by Hermann Schaper once decorated the church altar. It survived World War II damage.

Main entrance

Main Altar
The massive figure of Christ on the Cross is the work of Karl Hemmeter.

STAR SIGHTS

★ **Kaiser's Mosaic**

Ku'damm ②

Plan 2 A5, 2 B4. 🚇 *Kurfürstendamm*. 🚌 *109, 119, 129, 219.*

THE EASTERN AREA of the Charlottenburg region, around the boulevard known as Kurfürstendamm (the Ku'damm), was developed in the 19th century. Luxurious buildings were constructed along the Ku'damm, while the areas of Breitscheidplatz and Wittenbergplatz filled up with hotels and department stores. After World War II, with the old centre (Mitte) situated in East Berlin, Charlottenburg became the centre of West Berlin. Traces of wartime destruction were removed very quickly and the area was transformed into the heart of West Berlin, with dozens of new company headquarters and trade centres being built.

Mother and Child, from the Käthe-Kollwitz-Museum

Käthe-Kollwitz-Museum ③

Fasanenstraße 24. **Map** 2 A5. 📞 *(030) 882 52 10.* 🚇 *Uhlandstraße or Kurfürstendamm.* 🚌 *109, 119, 129, 219, 249.* 🕐 *11am–6pm Wed–Mon* 🅰 🐾

THIS SMALL private museum provides a unique opportunity to become acquainted with the work of Käthe Kollwitz (1867–1945). Born in Königsberg, the artist settled in Berlin where she married a doctor who worked in Prenzlauer Berg, a working-class district. Her drawings and sculptures portrayed the social

A tranquil area within the Tiergarten

problems of the poor, as well as human tragedy and suffering. She frequently took up the theme of motherhood and war after losing a son and grandson in World Wars I and II.

This museum displays the work of Käthe Kollwitz and includes posters, drawings and sculptures as well as documents, such as letters and photographs.

Zoologischer Garten ④

ZOOLOGICAL GARDEN

Hardenbergplatz 8 / Budapester Str. 34. **Map** 2 B3, C3, 2 B4, C4. 📞 *(030) 25 40 10.* Ⓢ & 🚇 *Zoologischer Garten.* 🚌 *100, 109, 145, 146, 149, 245, 249.* 🕐 *Apr–Sep: 9am–6:30pm daily; Oct–Mar: 9am–5pm daily.* 🅰

THE ZOOLOGICAL garden is actually part of the Tiergarten and dates from 1844, making this one of the oldest zoos in Germany. It offers a number of attractions, including the monkey house, which contains a family of gorillas, and a specially darkened pavilion for observing nocturnal animals. A glazed wall in the hippopotamus pool enables visitors to observe these enormous animals moving through the water. The large aquarium contains sharks, piranhas and unusual animals from coral reefs. There is also a huge terrarium with an overgrown jungle that is home to a group of crocodiles. One of the best loved animals at the zoo is the giant panda named Bao-Bao.

Tiergarten ⑤

Map 2 C3, 3 D3, E3, F3. Ⓢ *Tiergarten or Bellevue.* 🚌 *100, 187, 341.*

ONCE A FOREST used as the Elector's hunting reserve, the Tiergarten was transformed into a landscaped park by Peter Joseph Lenné in the 1830s. A Triumphal Avenue, lined with statues of the country's rulers and statesmen, was built in the eastern section at the end of the 19th century.

World War II inflicted huge damage, but replanting has now restored the Tiergarten and its avenues are bordered with statues of figures such as Johann Wolfgang von Goethe and Richard Wagner.

Near the lake and the Landwehrkanal are memorials to Karl Liebknecht and Rosa Luxemburg, the leaders of the Spartakus movement who were assassinated in 1918.

Siegessäule ⑥

TRIUMPHAL COLUMN

Großer Stern. **Map** 3 D2. Ⓢ *Bellevue.* 🚌 *100, 187, 341.* 🕐 *Apr–Oct: 9:30am–6:30pm daily; Nov–Mar: 9:30am–5:30pm daily.*

THE TRIUMPHAL column, based on a design by Johann Heinrich Strack, was built to commemorate victory in the Prusso-Danish war of 1864. After further Prussian victories in wars against Austria (1866) and France (1871), a gilded figure representing Victory, known as the "Goldelse", was added to the top of the column. It originally stood in front of the Riechstag building but was moved to its present location by the Nazi government in 1938. The base is decorated with bas-reliefs commemorating battles, while higher up a mosaic frieze depicts the founding of the German Empire in 1871. An observation terrace at the top offers magnificent vistas over Berlin.

Siegessäule (Triumphal Column)

The captivating, streamlined buildings of the Bauhaus-Archiv

Bauhaus-Archiv ❼

Klingelhöferstraße 14. **Map** 3 D4, E4.
🎫 (030) 254 00 20. Ⓤ Nollendorf-
platz. 🚌 100, 129, 187, 341, 1, X-9.
⭕ 10am–5pm Wed–Mon. 🎫 (free
Mon.) ♿

THE BAUHAUS school of art,
started by Walter Gropius
in 1919, was one of the most
influential art institutions of
the 20th century. Originally
based in Weimar, this school
provided inspiration for many
artists and architects. Staff and
students included Mies van der
Rohe, Paul Klee and Wassily
Kandinsky. The school moved
to Berlin in 1932, but was
closed by the Nazis in 1933.
   After the war, the Bauhaus-
Archiv was relocated to Darmstadt. In 1964 Walter Gropius
designed a building to house
the collection but, in 1971, the
archive was moved to Berlin
and the design was adapted to
the new site. As Gropius had
died in 1969, Alexander
Cvijanovic took over the
project. Built between 1976
and 1979 the gleaming white
building with its glass-panelled
gables houses the archive,
library and exhibition halls.

Bendlerblock (Gedenkstätte Deutscher Widerstand) ❽

Stauffenbergstraße 13–14.
Map 3 E4, F4. 🎫 (030) 26 99 50 00.
Ⓤ Mendelssohn-Bartholdy-Park.
🚌 129, 142, 148, 341.
⭕ 9am–6pm Mon–Wed, 9am–8pm
Thu, 10–6pm Sat–Sun. ⬤ 1 Jan, 24,
25 & 31 Dec. 🎫

THE COLLECTION of buildings
known as the Bendlerblock
was built during the Third

Reich as an extension to the
German State Naval Offices.
During World War II they
were the headquarters of the
Wehrmacht (German Army).
It was here that a group of
officers planned their assassination attempt on Hitler on 20
July 1944. When the attempt
led by Claus Schenk von
Stauffenberg failed, he and
his fellow conspirators were
arrested and death sentences
passed. Stauffenberg, Friedrich
Olbricht, Werner von Haeten,
and Ritter Mertz von Quim-
heim were shot in the Bendlerblock courtyard. A monument
commemorating this event,
designed by Richard Scheibe
in 1953, stands where the
executions were carried out.
   On the upper floor of the
building there is an exhibition
documenting the history of the
German anti-Nazi movements.

Gemäldegalerie ❾

See pp86–7.

Kupferstichkabinett und Kunst-bibliothek ❿

Matthäikirchplatz 6. **Map** 3 F3.
🎫 (030) 20 90 55 55. Ⓢ & Ⓤ
Potsdamer Platz or Ⓤ Mendelssohn-
Bartholdy-Park. 🚌 129, 142, 148,
248, 348. **Kupferstichkabinett:**
Exhibitions 10am–6pm Tue–Fri,
11am–6pm Sat–Sun. **Studio gallery**
9am–4pm Tue–Fri. **Kunstbibliothek:**
Exhibits 10–6pm Tue–Fri, 11am–6pm
Sat–Sun. **Library** 2–8pm Mon, 9am–
8pm Tue–Fri. 🎫 ♿ 🚫

THE PRINT COLLECTIONS of
galleries in the former East
and West Berlin were united
in 1994 in the Kupferstichkabinett (Print Gallery), whose

collection includes around
2,000 engraver's plates, over
520,000 prints and 80,000
drawings and watercolours.
   The **Kunstbibliothek** (Art
Library) is not only a library
with a range of publications
about the arts; it is also a
museum with an extensive
collection of posters,
advertisements and other
practical forms of design.

Munch's lithograph *Girl on a*
Beach, **Kupferstichkabinett**

Neue Nationalgalerie ⓫

Potsdamer Straße 50. **Map** 3 F4.
🎫 (030) 20 90 55 55. Ⓤ & Ⓢ
Potsdamer Platz or Ⓤ Mendelssohn-
Bartholdy-Park. 🚌 129, 142, 148,
200, 248, 341, 348. ⭕ 10am–6pm
Tue–Fri, 11am–6pm Sat & Sun.
🎫 ♿

AFTER WORLD WAR II, when
this magnificent collection
of modern art ended up in
West Berlin, the commission
to design a suitable building to
house it was given to Mies van
der Rohe. The result is a
striking building with a flat
steel roof over a glass hall,
which is supported only by
six slender interior struts.
   The collection comprises
largely 20th-century art, but
begins with artists of the late
19th century, such as Edvard
Munch. German art is well
represented: as well as the
Bauhaus movement, the
gallery shows works by exponents of a crass realism, such

Karl Schmidt-Rottluff's *Farm in Daugart* **(1910), Neue Nationalgalerie**

as Otto Dix. The most celebrated artists of other European countries are included, as are examples of post-World War II art.

Kunstgewerbe-museum ⑫

Matthäikirchplatz. **Map** 3 F3. 📞 *(030) 20 90 55 55.* Ⓢ *Potsdamer Platz.* Ⓤ *Potsdamer Platz or Mendelssohn-Bartholdy-Park.* 🚌 *129, 142, 148, 248, 341, 348.* ⏰ *10am–6pm Tue–Fri, 11am–6pm Sat & Sun.* ⏺ *Tue after Easter, Whitsun, 1 Oct, 24, 25 & 31 Dec.* 📷 ♿ 🚫

THIS MUSEUM holds a rich collection embracing many genres of craft and decorative art, from the early Middle Ages to the modern day. Goldwork is especially well represented, as are metal items from the Middle Ages. Among the most valuable exhibits is a collection of medieval goldwork from the church treasures of Enger and the Guelph

treasury from Brunswick. The museum also takes great pride in its collection of late Gothic and Renaissance silver from the civic treasury in the town of Lüneberg. In addition, there are fine examples of Italian majolica, and 18th- and 19th-century German, French and Italian glass, porcelain and furniture.

Philharmonie ⑬

PHILHARMONIC AND CHAMBER MUSIC HALL

Herbert-von-Karajan-Straße 1. **Map** 3 F3. 📞 *(030) 25 48 80.* Ⓢ & Ⓤ *Potsdamer Platz or* Ⓤ *Mendelssohn-Bartholdy-Park.* 🚌 *129, 142, 148, 248, 348.*

HOME TO ONE of the most renowned orchestras in Europe, this unusual building is among the finest postwar architectural achievements in

Europe. Built between 1960 and 1963 to a design by Hans Scharoun, the Philharmonie pioneered a new concept for concert hall interiors, with a podium occupying the central section of the pentagonal hall, around which are galleries for the public. The exterior is reminiscent of a circus tent. The gilded exterior was added between 1978 and 1981.

Between the years 1984 to 1987 the Kammermusiksaal, which was designed by Edgar Wisniewski on the basis of sketches by Scharoun, was added to the Philharmonie. This building consolidates the aesthetics of the earlier structure by featuring a central multi-sided space covered by a fanciful tent-like roof.

Musikinstrumenten-Museum ⑭

Tiergartenstraße 1. **Map** 1 A5. 📞 *(030) 25 48 11 78.* Ⓢ & Ⓤ *Potsdamer Platz or* Ⓤ *Mendelssohn-Bartholdy-Park.* 🚌 *129, 142, 148, 248, 348.* ⏰ *9am–5pm Tue–Fri, 10am–5pm Sat–Sun.* **Wurlitzer Organ demonstration** *noon, first Sat of the month.* 📷 ♿

BEHIND the Philharmonie, in a small building designed by Edgar Wisniewski and Hans Scharoun between 1979 and 1984, the fascinating Museum of Musical Instruments houses a collection dating from 1888. Intriguing displays trace each instrument's development from the 16th century to the present day. Most spectacular of all is a working Wurlitzer cinema organ dating from 1929. Saturday demonstrations of its impressive sounds attract enthusiastic crowds. There is also an archive and a library.

The tent-like gilded exterior of the Philharmonie and Kammermusiksaal

Gemäldegalerie ⑨

Woman in a Bonnet by Rogier van der Weyden

T HE GEMÄLDEGALERIE collection is exceptional in the consistently high quality of its paintings. Unlike those in other collections, they were chosen by specialists who, from the end of the 18th century, systematically acquired pictures to represent all the major European schools. Originally part of the Altes Museum collection *(see p71)*, the paintings achieved independent status in 1904 when they were moved to what is now the Bodemuseum *(see p74)*. After the division of Berlin in 1945, part of the collection was kept in the Bodemuseum, while the majority ended up in the Dahlem Museum *(see p100)*. Following reunification, and with the building of a new home as part of the Kulturforum development, this unique collection has finally been united again.

★**Cupid Victorious** (1602)
Inspired by Virgil's Omnia vincit Amor, Caravaggio depicted a playful god trampling over the symbols of Culture, Fame, Knowledge and Power.

Madonna with Child (c.1477)
A frequent subject of Sandro Botticelli, the Madonna and Child are depicted here, surrounded by singing angels holding lilies to symbolize purity.

Circular lobby leading to the galleries

Birth of Christ (c.1480)
This beautiful religious painting is one of the few surviving paintings on panels by Martin Schongauer.

Portrait of Hieronymus Holzschuher (1529)
Albrecht Dürer painted this affectionate portrait of his friend, who was the mayor of Nuremberg.

Main entrance

The Glass of Wine
(c.1658–61)
Jan Vermeer's carefully composed picture of a young woman drinking wine with a young man gently hints at the relationship developing between them.

VISITORS' CHECKLIST

Matthäikirchplatz 8. **Map** 3 F3.
📞 *(030) 20 90 55 55.*
Ⓢ & Ⓤ *Potsdamer Platz.*
Ⓤ *Mendelssohn-Bartholdy-Park.*
🚌 *129, 142, 148, 248, 348.*
⏰ *Tue–Sun 10am–6pm.*
🚫 *first Tue after Easter and Whitsun, 1 May, 24, 25 & 31 Dec.*

Love in the French Theatre
This picture has a companion piece called Love in the Italian Theatre. *Both are the work of French painter, Jean-Antoine Watteau.*

★ Portrait of Hendrickje Stoffels (1656–57)
Rembrandt's portrait of his lover, Hendrickje Stoffels, is typical of his work in the way it focuses on the subject and ignores the background.

KEY

☐ German painting:
13th–17th c. (I–III & 1–4)
18th c. (XII–XIV & 23–28)
19th c. (20–22)

☐ Dutch painting:
14th–17th c. (IV–VI & 5–7)
& Flemish 18th c. (VII–XI & 8–19)

☐ French painting:
14th–17th c. (IV–VI & 5–7)
& Spanish 18th c. (XII–XVIII & 23–28)
& English 18th c. (20–22)

☐ Italian painting:
14th–17th c. (XV–XVIII & 29–41)
18th–19th c. (XII–XIV & 23–28)

☐ Miniatures

GALLERY GUIDE
The main gallery contains over 900 masterpieces grouped by period and country of origin. These are complemented by around 400 works in the study gallery on the lower floor and by a computerized digital gallery.

STAR EXHIBITS

★ **Cupid Victorious**

★ **Dutch Proverbs**

★ **Portrait of Hendrickje Stoffels**

★ Dutch Proverbs (1559)
Pieter Brueghel managed to illustrate more than 100 proverbs in this painting.

Potsdamer Platz ⓯

I N THE SHORT SPACE of a few years a new financial and business district has sprung up on what was the vast wasteland surrounding the Potsdamer Platz. It boasts splendid constructions designed by Renzo Piano, Arata Isozaki and Helmut Jahn. As well as office blocks, the area has many public buildings, including cinemas and a theatre, as well as a huge shopping centre (the Arkaden) plus a luxury hotel, restaurants and several bars.

The Sony Center, designed by Helmut Jahn, features a huge central courtyard with a roof perched on top like a hat.

The Sony Tower

POTSDAMER PLATZ

This office building, designed by Kollhoff & Timmermann Partnership, alludes to North German building traditions with its clinker brick wall cladding.

POTSDAMER STRASSE

ENTLASTUNGSSTRASSE

Arkaden, opened in autumn 1998, immediately became one of the city's favourite shopping centres.

LANDWEHRKANAL

The Daimler-Benz new head office was designed by Renzo Piano.

The Debis-Center office block, designed by Arata Isozaki, straddles a walkway.

0 metres		100
0 yards		100

The Reichstag, crowned by a dome designed by Sir Norman Foster

Reichstag ⑯

Platz der Republik. **Map** 1 B4, 4 A1, A2. [C] (030) 22 73 21 52. [S] Unter den Linden. [bus] 100, 248, 257. **Dome** [○] 8am–midnight daily. **Assembly Hall** [○] 9am–4pm Mon–Sun, holidays by appointment only. [tour] noon Tue (in English). [●] 1 Jan, 24–26 & 31 Dec.

BUILT TO HOUSE the German Parliament, the Reichstag was constructed between 1884 and 1894 to a New-Renaissance design by Paul Wallot. Capturing the prevailing spirit of German optimism, it became a potent symbol to the populace.

In 1918, from the Reichstag, Philipp Scheidemann declared the formation of the Weimar Republic. The next time the world heard about the building was in February 1933, when a fire destroyed the main hall. The Communists were blamed, accelerating a political witch-hunt driven by the Nazis, who then came to power.

With the onset of World War II, the building was not rebuilt, yet its significance reson-ated beyond Germany, as shown by a photograph of the Soviet flag flying from the Reichstag in May 1945, which became a symbol of the German defeat.

Following rebuilding work between 1957 and 1972, the Reichstag provided a meeting-place for the lower house of the German Parliament as well as a spectacular backdrop for festivals and rock concerts. After German reunification in 1990, the Reichstag was the first meeting place of a newly elected Bundestag. The latest rebuilding project, to a design by Sir Norman Foster, trans-formed the Reichstag into a modern meeting hall in which the first parliamentary meeting took place on 19 April 1999.

Hamburger Bahnhof ⑰

Invalidenstraße 50/51. **Map** 1 A2, B2. [C] (030) 20 90 55 55. [S] Lehrter Stadtbahnhof. [bus] 157, 245, 248, 340. [○] 10am–6pm Tue–Fri, 10am–10pm Thu, 11am–6pm Sat & Sun. [●] 1 Jan, Tue following Easter and Whitsun, 24, 25 & 31 Dec. [&][Ø][tour]

THIS MUSEUM is situated in a Neo-Renaissance building, formerly the Hamburg Railway station, which dates from 1847. The building stood vacant after World War II but, following refurbishment by Josef Paul Kleihues, it was opened to the public in 1996. The neon installation surrounding the façade is the work of Dan Flavin. The museum houses a magnificent collection of contemporary art, including the work of Erich Marx. The result is one of the best modern art museums in Europe, which features not only represent-ative art, but also film, video, music and design.

Jeff and Ilona **(1991), Hamburger Bahnhof**

Museum für Naturkunde ⑱
NATURAL HISTORY MUSEUM

Invalidenstraße 43. **Map** 1 E2. [C] (030) 20 93 85 91. [U] Zinnowitzer straße. [bus] 157, 245, 340. [train] 6,8. [○] 9:30am–5pm Tue–Sun. [tour]

OCCUPYING A purpose-built Neo-Renaissance building constructed between 1883 and 1889, this is one of the biggest natural history museums in the world, with a collection containing over 60 million exhibits. Although it has undergone several periods of extension and renovation, the museum has maintained its unique old-fashioned atmosphere.

The highlight of the museum is the world's largest dinosaur skeleton, which is housed in the glass-covered courtyard. The colossal brachiosaurus measures 23 m (75 ft) long and 12 m (39 ft) high. It was discovered in Tanzania, in 1909, by a German fossil-hunting expedition.

The adjacent rooms feature collections of colourful shells and butterflies, as well as stuffed birds and mammals. A favourite with children is Bobby the Gorilla, who lived in Berlin Zoo from 1928 until 1935. The museum also boasts an impressive collection of minerals and meteorites.

Brachiosaurus skeleton in the Museum für Naturkunde

FURTHER AFIELD

BERLIN is a huge city with a unique character that has been shaped by the events in its history. Until 1920 the city consisted only of the districts that now comprise mainly Mitte, Tiergarten, Wedding, Prenzlauer Berg, Friedrichshain and Kreuzberg. At that time the city was surrounded by satellite towns and villages that had been evolving independently over many centuries.

In 1920, as part of great administrative reform, seven towns, 59 parishes and 27 country estates were incorpo-

Detail from Schloss Charlottenburg

rated into the city, thus creating an entirely new city covering nearly 900 sq km (350 sq miles), with a population of 3.5 million. This metropolis extended to small towns of medieval origin, such as Spandau, as well as to private manor houses and palaces, towns and smart suburban districts. Although the 20th century has changed the face of many of these places, their unique characters have remained undiminished. Because of this diversity, a trip to Berlin is like exploring many different towns simultaneously.

SIGHTS AT A GLANCE

Museums and Galleries
Ägyptisches Museum ❸
Brecht-Haus ⓫
Bröhan-Museum ❶
Brücke-Museum ㉔
Gedenkstätte Berlin-
   Hohenschönhausen ⓯
Gedenkstätte Plötzensee ❾
Sammlung Berggruen ❷
Stasi-Museum ⓰

Places of Interest
Flughafen Tempelhof ⓳
Klein Glienicke ㉘
Köpenick ⓱
Muzeumszentrum Dahlem ㉒
Nikolskoe ㉗

Olympia-Stadion ❼
Pfaueninsel ㉖
Prenzlauer Berg ⓭
Strandbad Wannsee ㉕

Streets, Squares and Parks
Karl-Marx-Allee ⓮
Schlosspark ❹
Treptower Park ⓲
Victoriapark ⓴

Historic Buildings and Monuments
Jagdschloss Grunewald ㉓
Messegelände ❻

0 metres   400

0 yards   400

Neue Synagoge ⓬
Rathaus Schöneberg ㉑
Schloss Charlottenburg ❺
Schloss Tegel ❿
Zitadelle Spandau ❽

KEY

🟦	Central Berlin
⬜	Outskirts of Berlin
✈	Airport
▬	Motorway
▬	Main road
═	Secondary road
—	Railway line

MAP OF GREATER BERLIN

◁ **Façade of Schloss Charlottenburg**

Pablo Picasso's *Woman in a Hat* (1939), Sammlung Berggruen

displays more than 20 works by Paul Klee and paintings by other major artists – Van Gogh, Braque and Cézanne. The exhibition is supplemented by some excellent sculptures, particularly those of Henri Laurens and Alberto Giacometti.

Ägyptisches Museum ❸

EGYPTIAN MUSEUM

Schlossstraße 70. [(030) 20 90 55 55. [U] Richard-Wagner-Platz & Sophie-Charlotte-Platz. [S] Westend. 🚌 109, 110, 145, 1, X-21, X-26. ◯ 10am–6pm Tue–Sun.

THE TWO PAVILIONS on either side of Schlossstraße were built between 1851 and 1859 by Friedrich August Stüler, inspired by a design by King Friedrich Wilhelm IV. The eastern pavilion now houses the collection of the Egyptian Museum. Many sculptures, sarcophagi, murals and architectural fragments of various eras are on display. The greatest attraction is the fascinating collection from 19th-century archaeological digs by Richard Lepsius and Johann Ludwig Burckhardt in Tell al-Amarna. This was the capital of Egypt during the reign of Amenhotep IV (also called Akhenaten), a pharaoh in the 14th century BC. He revolutionized Egyptian religion and also brought about a radical change in the basic principles of representative arts. In a break from tradition he and his wife, Nefertiti, are shown more naturalistically with broad hips and swollen stomachs. The pharaoh is plainly depicted, but the queen is beautiful, as can be seen from other displays in the museum.

Figure from Ägyptische Museum (c.660 BC)

Bröhan-Museum ❶

Schlossstraße 1a. [(030) 32 69 06 00. [U] Richard-Wagner-Platz & Sophie-Charlotte-Platz. [S] Westend. 🚌 109, 110, 145, 1, X-21, X-26. ◯ 10am–6pm Tue–Sun. ● 24 & 31 Dec.

LOCATED IN A late-Neo-Classical building is this interesting, small museum. The collection was amassed by Karl H Bröhan who, from 1966, collected works of art from the Art Nouveau (Jugendstil or Secessionist) and Art Deco styles. The paintings of artists who were particularly connected with the Berlin Secessionist movement are especially well represented. Alongside the paintings are fine examples of other media and crafts including furniture, ceramics, glassware, silverwork and textiles.

Each of the main halls features an individual artist, often using an array of media. There is also a display of furniture by Hector Guimard, Eugène Gaillard, Henri van de Velde and Joseph Hoffmann, glasswork by Emile Gallé, and porcelain from the best European manufacturers.

Sammlung Berggruen ❷

Schlossstraße 1. [(030) 326 95 80. [U] Richard-Wagner-Platz & Sophie-Charlotte-Platz. [S] Westend. 🚌 109, 110, 145, X-21, X-26. ◯ 10am–6pm Tue–Fri, 11am–6pm Sat & Sun. 🎟 (free first Sun of the month.)

HEINZ BERGGRUEN assembled this tasteful collection of art dating from the late 19th and first half of the 20th century. Born and educated in Berlin, he emigrated to the US in 1936, spent most of his life in Paris, but finally entrusted his collection "Picasso and his Time" to the city of his birth. The museum opened in 1996, in what was once the west pavilion of the barracks, using space freed up by moving the Antikensammlung to Museum Island (see p70). The exhibition halls were modified according to the designs of Hilmer and Sattler, who also designed the layout of the Gemäldegalerie. The Sammlung Berggruen is well known for its large collection of paintings, drawings and gouaches by Pablo Picasso. In addition to these, the museum

Schlosspark ❹

PALACE PARK

Luisenplatz (Schloss Charlottenburg). ![U] Richard-Wagner-Platz & Sophie-Charlotte-Platz. ⓢ Westend. 🚌 109, 110, 145, X-21, X-26. **Neuer Pavillon** 📞 (030) 32 09 12 12. ☐ Apr–Oct: 10am–5pm Tue–Fri; Nov–Mar: 9am–5pm Tue–Fri, 10am–5pm Sat & Sun. **Mausoleum** ☐ Apr–Oct: 10am–5pm Tue–Sun. **Belvedere** 📞 (030) 32 09 12 85. ☐ Apr–Oct: 10am–5pm Tue–Sun; Nov–Mar: noon–4pm Tue–Fri, noon–5pm Sat & Sun.

THIS EXTENSIVE royal park surrounding Schloss Charlottenburg is a favourite place for Berliners to stroll. The park is largely the result of work carried out after World War II, when 18th-century prints were used to help reconstruct the layout of the original grounds. Just behind Schloss Charlottenburg is a French-style Baroque garden, constructed to a strict geometrical design with a vibrant patchwork of flower beds, carefully trimmed shrubs and ornate fountains adorned with replicas of antique sculptures. Beyond the curved carp lake is a less formal English-style landscaped park, the original layout of which was created between 1819 and 1828 under the direction of the renowned royal gardener, Peter Joseph Lenné.

Designed by Karl Friedrich Schinkel and completed in 1825, the Neo-Classical **Neuer Pavillon** is a charming two-storey building with rooms ranged around a central staircase. A cast-iron balcony encircles the entire structure.

The **Mausoleum** in which Queen Luise, wife of Friedrich Wilhelm III, was laid to rest, was designed by Karl Friedrich Schinkel in the style of a Doric portico-fronted temple. After the death of the king in 1840, the mausoleum was refurbished to create room for his tomb. The tombs of the king's second wife and those of Kaiser Wilhelm I and his wife were added later.

Built as a summerhouse for Friedrich Wilhelm II, with a mixture of Baroque and Neo-Classical elements, the **Belvedere** now houses the Royal Porcelain Workshop, with pieces from the Rococo period up to late Biedermeier.

Schloss Charlottenburg ❺

See pp94–5.

The Funkturm (radio tower) in Berlin's Messegelände

Messegelände ❻

Hammarskjöldplatz. ⓢ Witzleben. ![U] Kaiserdamm. 🚌 104, 149, 204, 219.

THE PAVILIONS of the vast exhibition and trade halls south of Hammarskjöldplatz cover more than 160,000 sq m (1,700,000 sq ft). The original exhibition halls were built before World War I, but nothing of these buildings remains. The oldest part is the Funkturm and the pavilions surrounding it. The building at the front (Ehrenhalle) was built in 1936 to a design by Richard Ermisch, and is one of the few surviving buildings in Berlin designed in a Fascist architectural style.

The straight motorway at the rear of the halls is the famous Avus, the first German autobahn, built in 1921. At one point adapted as a car-racing track, it now it forms part of the autobahn system.

Olympia-Stadion ❼

Olympischer Platz. ⓢ & ![U] Olympia-Stadion. 🚌 218.

OLYMPIA-STADION, originally known as Reichssportfeld, was built for the 1936 Olympic Games in Berlin. It was designed by Werner March in the Nazi architectural style and was inspired by the architecture of ancient Rome. To the west of the stadium lie the Maifeld and what is now called the Waldbühne. The former is an enormous assembly ground surrounded by grandstands and fronted by the Glockenturm, a 77 m (250 ft) tower, while the latter is an open-air amphitheatre. Stretching north is a group of sports grounds and swimming pools. The entire complex provided the infrastructure for Berlin to hold the Olympics. However, it also provided Hitler plenty of opportunities to use it for his own propagandist purposes.

French-style garden in the Schloss Charlottenburg park

Schloss Charlottenburg ➎

Detail from the main gate

T HE PALACE IN CHARLOTTENBURG was intended as a summer home for Sophie Charlotte, the wife of Elector Friedrich III. Construction began in 1695 to a design by Johann Arnold Nering. Johann Eosander von Göthe enlarged the palace between 1701 and 1713, adding the orangery wing. Further extensions were undertaken between 1740 and 1746 by Frederick the Great (Friedrich II) who added the east wing.

The palace was restored to its former elegance after World War II and its richly decorated interiors are unequalled in Berlin.

GALLERY GUIDE

The ground floor of the main building can only be visited by guided tour. The upper floor and the Neuer Flügel can be visited independently.

First floor

Ground floor

Museum für Vor- und Frühgeschichte

The museum is housed in a pavilion that served formerly as the court theatre, designed by Carl Gotthard Langhans.

★ Porzellankabinett

This exquisite mirrored gallery has walls lined from top to bottom with a fine display of Japanese and Chinese porcelain.

Main entrance

Monument to the Great Elector

Schlosskapelle

Only the pulpit in the court chapel is original. All the remaining furniture and fittings, including the splendid royal box, are reconstructions.

Palace Façade

The central section of the palace is the oldest part of the building. It is the work of Johann Arnold Nering.

Fortuna
*A new sculpture by
Richard Scheibe crowns
the palace, replacing the
original statue destroyed
during World War II.*

KEY

Official reception rooms

Sophie-Charlotte's apartments

Neuer Flügel or Knobelsdorff-
Flügel exhibition space

Friedrich Wilhelm II's apartments

Mecklenburg apartments

Friedrich Wilhelm IV's
apartments

Friedrich Wilhelm II's apartments

Frederick the Great's apartments

Eichengalerie
*This long gallery, lined with
huge oil paintings and
decorated with oak-panelling,
was completed in 1713.*

★ Galerie der Romantik
*The Romantic art collection
belonging to the Nationalgalerie is housed in the new
wing of the palace.*

STAR SIGHTS

★ Gersaint's Shop
Sign

★ Porzellankabinett

★ Gersaint's Shop Sign (1720)
*An avid collector of French painting,
Frederick the Great bought this and
seven other fine canvases by Antoine
Watteau for his collection.*

Hohenzollern coat of arms above the main gate of Spandau's citadel

Spandau ❽

Zitadelle Spandau Am Juliusturm.
🇨 (030) 354 94 42 00. 🇺 Zitadelle.
🕐 9am–5pm Tue–Fri, 10am–5pm Sat
& Sun. 📷

Spandau is one of the oldest towns within the area of greater Berlin, and it has managed to retain its own distinctive character. Although the town of Spandau was only granted a charter in 1232, evidence of the earliest settlement here dates back to the 8th century.

The area was spared the worst of the World War II bombing, so there are still some interesting sights to visit. The heart of the town is a network of medieval streets with a picturesque market square and a number of the original timber-framed houses. In the north of Spandau, sections of the town wall dating from the 15th century are still standing.

In the centre of town is the magnificent Gothic St-Nikolai-Kirche, dating from the 15th century. The church holds many valuable ecclesiastical furnishings, such as a splendid Renaissance stone altar from the end of the 16th century, a Baroque pulpit from around 1700 that came from a royal palace in Potsdam, a Gothic baptismal font and many epitaphs.

A castle was first built on the site of the Zitadelle Spandau (citadel) in the 12th century, but today only the 36 m (120 ft) Juliusturm (tower) remains. In 1560 the building of a fort was begun

here, to a design by Francesco Chiaramella da Gandino. It took 30 years to complete and most of the work was supervised by architect Rochus Graf von Lynar. Although the citadel had a jail, the town's most infamous resident, Rudolf Hess, was incarcerated a short distance away in a military prison after the 1946 Nuremberg trials. In 1986, when the former deputy leader of the Nazi party died, the prison was torn down.

Gedenkstätte Plötzensee ❾

PLÖTZENSEE MEMORIAL

Hüttigpfad. 🇨 (030) 344 32 26.
🇺 Jakob-Kaiser-Platz, then 🚌 123,
126. 🕐 Mar–Sep: 9am–5pm;
Nov–Feb 9am–4pm.

A narrow street leads from Saatwinkler Damm to the site where nearly 2,500 people convicted of crimes against

Memorial to concentration camp victims at Gedenkstätte Plötzensee

the Third Reich were hanged. The Gedenkstätte Plötzensee is a simple memorial in a brick hut, which still retains the iron hooks from which the victims were suspended.

Claus Schenk von Stauffenberg and the other main figures in the assassination attempt against Hitler on 20 July 1944 were executed in the Bendlerblock (see p84), but the rest of the conspirators were executed here at the Plötzensee prison.

Count Helmut James von Moltke, one of the leaders of the German resistance movement, was also killed here. He was responsible for organizing the Kreisauer Kreis – a political movement that gathered and united German opposition to Hitler.

Schloss Tegel ❿

Adelheidallee 19–21. 🇨 (030) 434
31 56. 🇺 Alt Tegel. 🚌 124, 133,
222. 🕐 May–Sep: 10am–noon &
3–4pm Mon. 📷 compulsory.

Schloss Tegel is one of the most interesting palace complexes in Berlin. The site was occupied in the 16th century by a manor house. In the second half of the 17th century, this was rebuilt into a hunting lodge for the Elector Friedrich Wilhelm. In 1766 the ownership of the property passed to the Humboldt family, and between 1820 and 1824, Karl Friedrich Schinkel thoroughly rebuilt the palace, giving it its current style.

Decorating the elevations on the top floor of the towers are tiled bas-reliefs designed by Christian Daniel Rauch, depicting the ancient wind gods. Some of Schinkel's marvellous interiors have survived, along with several items from what was once a large collection of sculptures. The palace is still privately owned by descendants of the Humboldt family, but guided tours are offered on Mondays.

It is also worth visiting the park in which the palace stands. On the western limits of the park lies the Humboldt family tomb, also designed by Schinkel. The tomb contains a

The elegant Neo-Classical façade of Schloss Tegel

copy of a splendid sculpture by Bertel Thorwaldsen. The original piece stands inside the Schloss Tegel.

Bertolt Brecht's study in his former apartment

Brecht-Weigel-Gedenkstätte ⑪

BRECHT-WEIGEL MEMORIAL

Chausseestraße 125. **(** (030) 283 05 70 44. **U** Zinnowitzer Straße or Oranienburger Tor. ▦ 157. ▦ 13. ◐ 10am–noon Tue–Fri, also 5–7pm Thu, 9:30am–1:30pm Sat, 11am–6pm Sun. ⬛ compulsory. Every half hour (every hour on Sun). ● Mon, public holidays. ▨

PLAYWRIGHT Bertolt Brecht was associated with Berlin from 1920, but emigrated in 1933. After the war, his left-wing views made him an attractive potential resident of the newly created German socialist state. Lured by the promise of his own theatre, he returned to Berlin in 1948 with his wife, the actress Helene Weigel.

In 1953, Brecht moved into Chausseestraße 125 and lived there until his death in 1956. His wife founded an archive of his work, which is located on the second floor.

Neue Synagoge ⑫

NEW SYNAGOGUE

Oranienburger Straße 30. **S** Oranienburger Straße. ▦ 1, 13. ▦ 157. ◐ 10am–6pm Sun–Thu, 10am–2pm Fri. ● Jewish festivals. ▨ ∅

CONSTRUCTION OF the New Synagogue was begun in 1859 by architect Eduard Knoblauch, and completed in 1866. The design was a highly sophisticated response to the asymmetrical shape of the plot of land, with a narrow façade flanked by a pair of towers and crowned with a dome containing a round vestibule. A series of small rooms opened off the vestibule, including an anteroom and two prayer rooms – one large and one small. The two towers opened onto a staircase leading to the galleries, while the main hall had space for around 3,000 worshippers. An innovative use of iron in the construction of the roof

The Neue Synagoge with its splendidly reconstructed dome

and galleries put the synagogue at the forefront of 19th-century civil engineering.

With its gilded dome, this fascinating structure was Berlin's largest synagogue, until 9 November 1938 when it was partially destroyed during the infamous *Kristallnacht*. The building was damaged further by Allied bombing in 1943 and was eventually demolished in 1958 by government authorities.

Reconstruction began in 1988 and was completed with due ceremony in 1995. The front of the building is now used for public exhibitions by the Centrum Judaicum.

Prenzlauer Berg ⑬

Sammlung Industrielle Gestaltung Kulturbrauerei entrance, Knaack-straße 97. **(** (030) 443 93 82. **S** Senefelderplatz or Eberswalderstraße. ◐ 2–9pm Wed–Sun.

TOWARDS THE END of the 19th century this was one of the most impoverished, densely populated districts of Berlin, which became a centre for anti-Communist opposition.

After 1989, however, artists, journalists and students began to gather here from all parts of Berlin, creating a colourful, vibrant community.

Schönhauser Allee is the main thoroughfare of Prenzlauer Berg. A former old brewery was transformed into the "Kulturbrauerei", a centre for cultural events. It also houses a museum – **Sammlung Industrielle Gestaltung** – with a collection of industrial designs from East Germany.

Heading along Sredzkistraße you reach Husemannstraße. At No. 12 was the former Museum Berliner Arbeiter-leben; its collection of period interiors has been transferred recently to the Märkisches Museum (*see p76*). Amid the greenery around Belforter Straße is a water tower built in the mid-19th century. Near-by, on Schönhauser Allee, there is an old Jewish cemetery dating from 1827. Among those buried here is the renowned painter Max Liebermann.

Fragment of Socialist Realist decoration from Karl-Marx-Allee

Karl-Marx-Allee ⓮

Map 5 F1. Ⓤ *Strausberger Platz or Weberwiese.*

THE SECTION OF Karl-Marx-Allee between Strausberger Platz and Frankfurter Tor is effectively a huge open-air museum of Socialist Realist architecture. The route to the the east was named Stalinallee in 1949 and chosen as the site for the showpiece of the new German Democratic Republic. The avenue was widened to 90 m (300 ft) and, in the course of the next ten years, huge residential tower blocks and a row of shops were built. The designers, led by Hermann Henselmann, succeeded in combining three sets of architectural guidelines. They used the style known in the Soviet Union as "pastry chef" according to the precept: "nationalistic in form but socialist in content", and linked the whole work to Berlin's own traditions. Hence there are motifs taken from famous Berlin architects Schinkel and Gontard, as well as from the renowned Meissen porcelain.

The buildings on this street, renamed Karl-Marx-Allee in 1961, are now considered historic monuments.

Gedenkstätte Berlin-Hohen-schönhausen ⓯

Genslerstraße 66. 🄲 *(030) 982 42 19.* Ⓢ *Landsberger Allee, then* 🚋 *5, 6, 7, 15, 17.* 🚌 *256.* ⏰ *1pm Mon–Thu, 11am & 1pm Fri–Sat.* 🈸

THIS MUSEUM was established in 1995 within the former custody building of the Stasi. The building was part of a huge complex built in 1938. In May 1945, the occupying Russian authorities created a special transit camp here, in which they interned war criminals and anyone under political suspicion. From 1946 the buildings were refashioned into the custody area for the KGB; in 1951, it was given over to the Stasi.

During a visit to the complex you can see prisoners' cells and interrogation rooms, two of which have no windows and are lined with rubber. Housed in the cellars was the "submarine" – a series of cells without daylight to which the most "dangerous" suspects were brought.

Forschungs-und Gedenkstätte Normannenstraße (Stasi-Museum) ⓰

Ruschestraße 103 (Haus 1). 🄲 *(030) 553 68 54.* Ⓤ *Magdalenenstraße.* ⏰ *11am–6pm Tue–Fri, 2–6pm Sat–Sun.* 🈸

UNDER THE German Democratic Republic, this huge complex of buildings at Ruschestrasse housed the Ministry of the Interior. It was here that the infamous Stasi (GDR secret service) had its headquarters. The Stasi's "achievements" in infiltrating its own community were without equal in the Eastern block.

Since 1990 one of the buildings has housed a museum that displays photographs and documents depicting the activities of the Stasi. Here, you can see a model of the headquarters, and equipment that was used for bugging and spying on citizens suspected of holding unfavourable political views. You can also walk around the office of infamous Stasi chief Erich Mielke.

Köpenick ⓱

Ⓢ *Spindlersfeld, then* 🚌 *167 or* Ⓢ *Köpenick, then* 🚌 *269, 360.* 🚋 *26, 60, 62, 67, 68.* **Kunstgewerbemuseum** *Schloss Köpenick, Schlossinsel.* ⬤ *closed for renovation until mid 2002.*

KÖPENICK IS MUCH older than Berlin. In the 9th century AD, this island contained a fortified settlement known as Kopanica. In about 1240 a castle was built on the island, around which a town began to evolve. Craftsmen settled here and, after 1685, a large colony of Huguenots also settled.

In the 19th century Köpenick recreated itself as an industrial town. Despite wartime devastation it has retained its historic character and, though there are no longer any 13th century churches, it is worth strolling around the old town. By the old market square and in the neighbouring streets, modest houses have survived that recall the 18th century, alongside buildings from the end of the 19th century.

At Alt Köpenick No. 21 is a vast brick town hall built in the style of the Brandenburg Neo-Renaissance. In 1906, a famous swindle took place here and the event became the inspiration for a popular comedy by Carl Zuck-mayer, *The Captain from Köpenick*.

Köpenick's greatest attraction is a three-storey Baroque palace, built between 1677 and

Office of the infamous Stasi chief Erich Mielke at the Stasi Museum

A reconstructed drawing room from 1548 in the Kunstgewerbemuseum

1681 for the heir to the throne Friedrich (later King Friedrich I), to a design by the Dutch architect Rutger van Langfield. Since 1963, the magnificent palace has housed part of the craft museum, **Kunstgewerbemuseum** *(see p85)*, but restoration work will prevent public access until 2002.

Gigantic wreath commemorating the Red Army in Treptower Park

Treptower Park [18]

Archenhold-Sternwarte, Alt-Treptow.
Ⓢ *Treptower Park.* 🚌 *166, 167, 177, 265.* **Archenhold Sternwarte** ☏ *(030) 534 80 80.* 📷 *compulsory 8am–3pm Mon–Fri; also 6pm Wed, 3pm Sat.*

THE VAST PARK in Treptow was laid out in the 1860s on the initiative and design of Johann Gustav Meyer. In 1919 it was where revolutionaries Karl Liebknecht, Wilhelm Pieck and Rosa Luxemburg assembled 150,000 striking workers.

The park is best known for the colossal monument to the Red Army. Built between 1946 and 1949, it stands on the grave of 5,000 Soviet soldiers killed in the battle for Berlin in 1945. The gateway, which leads to the mausoleum, is marked by a vast granite sculpture of a grieving Russian Motherland surrounded by statues of Red Army soldiers.

In the farthest section of the park is the astronomical observatory, **Archenhold Sternwarte**, built for a decorative arts exhibition in 1896. Given a permanent site in 1909, the observatory was used by Albert Einstein for a lecture on the Theory of Relativity in 1915. It is also home to the longest reflecting telescope in the world (21 m or 70 ft), and a small planetarium.

Beyond Treptower Park lies another park, Plänterwald, while the Spree river provides an ideal place for a riverside stroll or a trip in one of the rowing or pedal boats.

Flughafen Tempelhof [19]

Platz der Luftbrücke. Ⓤ *Platz der Luftbrücke.* 🚌 *104, 119, 184, 341.*

SITUATED BEYOND Kreuzberg, the Tempelhof was once Germany's largest airport. Built in 1923, the structure is typical of Third Reich architecture. The additions to the original structure were completed in 1939.

In 1951, a monument was added in front of the airport. Designed by Edward Ludwig, it commemorates the airlifts of the Berlin Blockade. The names of those who lost their lives during the Blockade appear on the plinth.

Viktoriapark [20]

Ⓤ *Platz der Luftbrücke.*
🚌 *119, 140.*

THIS RAMBLING PARK, with several artificial waterfalls, short trails and a small hill, was designed by Hermann Machtig and built between 1884 and 1894. The Neo-Gothic Memorial to the Wars of Liberation at the summit of the hill is the work of Karl Friedrich Schinkel and was constructed between 1817 and 1821. The monument commemorates the Prussian victory against Napoleon's army in the Wars of Liberation. The monument's cast-iron tower is well ornamented.

In the niches of the lower section are 12 allegorical figures by Christian Daniel Rauch, Friedrich Tieck and Ludwig Wichmann. Each figure symbolizes a battle and is linked to a historic figure – either a military leader or a member of the royal family.

Rathaus Schöneberg [21]

SCHÖNEBERG TOWN HALL

John-F-Kennedy-Platz.
Ⓤ *Rathaus Schöneberg.*

THE SCHÖNEBERG town hall is a gigantic building with an imposing tower, which was built between 1911 and 1914. From 1948 to 1990 it was used as the main town hall of West Berlin, and it was outside here, on 26 June 1963, that US President John F Kennedy gave his famous speech. More than 400,000 Berliners assembled to hear the young president say "*Ich bin ein Berliner*" – "I am a Berliner", intended as an expression of solidarity from the democratic world to a city defending its right to freedom.

While Kennedy's meaning was undoubtedly clear, pedants were quick to point out that what he actually said was "I am a small doughnut".

Japanese woodcut from the Museum für Ostasiatische Kunst

Museumszentrum Dahlem ②

Lansstraße 8, Dahlem. **(** (030) 20 90 55 55. **U** Dahlem Dorf. **==** 110, 183, X-11. **Museum für Indische Kunst**. **Museum für Ostasiatische Kunst, Ethnologisches Museum (formerly Museum für Völkerkunde), Museum für Kunst Afrikas & Nordamerika Ausstellung** ◯ 10am–6pm Tue–Fri, 11am–6pm Sat & Sun. ▨

DAHLEM'S FIRST museums were built between 1914 and 1923, but the district was confirmed as a major cultural and education centre after World War II with the establishment of the Freie Universität and completion of the museum complex. With many of Berlin's collections fragmented, a miscellany of art and artifacts was put on display here. In the 1960s the museums were extended and the new Museumszentrum was created to rival East Berlin's Museum Island.

German reunification in 1990 meant that the collections could be reunited and reorganized. Paintings were moved to the Kulturforum (*see pp80–81*), and sculptures to the Bodemuseum (*see p74*).

Five museums are now housed at Dahlem: the Ethnologisches Museum (Museum of Mankind); the Museum für Indische Kunst (Museum of Indian Art); the Museum für Ostasiatische Kunst (Museum of Far Eastern Art); the Museum für Kunst Afrikas (Museum for African Art) and the Nordamerika Ausstellung (Exhibition of Native North American Cultures).

Highlights include bronzes from Benin at the Museum of African Art, gold Inca jewellery at the Museum of Mankind, and Japanese woodcuts from Chinese Turkestan at the Museum of Far Eastern Art. The recently opened Exhibition of Native North American Cultures includes a collection of 600 ceremonial objects.

Jagdschloss Grunewald ②

Am Grunewaldsee 29. **(** (030) 813 35 97. ◯ May–Oct: 10am–1pm & 1:30–5pm Tue–Sun; Nov–Apr: 10am–1pm & 1:30–4pm Sat & Sun. ▨

JAGDSCHLOSS GRUNEWALD is one of the oldest surviving civic buildings in Berlin. Built for the Elector Joachim II in 1542, it was rebuilt around 1700 in a Baroque style.

In this small palace on the edge of the Grunewaldsee is Berlin's only surviving Renaissance hall, which currently houses a collection of paintings that includes canvases by Rubens and van Dyck, among others.

In the east wing is the small Waldmuseum, with illustrations depicting forest life and the history of forestry. Opposite the Jagdschloss, a hunting museum (Jagdmuseum) houses a collection of historic weapons and equipment.

Brücke-Museum ②

Bussardsteig 9, Dahlem. **(** (030) 831 20 29. **==** 115. ◯ 11am–7pm Wed–Mon.

THIS ELEGANT Functionalist building hosts a collection of German Expressionist painting linked to the Die Brücke group. It is based on almost 80 works by Schmidt-Rottluff bequeathed to the town of Dahlem in 1964. In addition to other works of art contemporary to Die Brücke, there are paintings from the later creative periods of these artists, as well as works of other closely associated artists. Nearby lie the foundation's headquarters, established in the former studio of the sculptor Bernhard Heliger.

Strandbad Wannsee ②

Wannseebadweg. **(S)** Nikolassee. **==** 513.

THE VAST lake Wannsee, on the edge of Grunewald, is a popular destination for Berliners seeking recreation. The most developed part is the southeastern corner where there are yachting marinas and harbours. Further north is one of the largest inland beaches in Europe, Strandbad Wannsee, which was developed between 1929 and 1930 by the construction of shops, cafés and changing rooms on man-made terraces. It is also pleasant to walk around Schwanenwerder island, with its many elegant villas.

Boarding point for lake cruises on the Wannsee

The Schloss Pfaueninsel designed by Johann Brendel

Pfaueninsel 26

Pfaueninsel. **(** (030) 805 30 42. **Ⓢ** Wannsee, then take 🚌 A16, 316. 🚢 Schloss Pfaueninsel. 🕐 Apr–Oct: 10am–5pm Tue–Sun. 🎗

THIS PICTURESQUE island, named for the peacocks that inhabit it, is now a nature reserve, reached by ferry across the Havel river. It was laid out in 1795 according to a design by Johann August Eyserbeck. Its final form, which you see today, is the work of the landscape architect Peter Joseph Lenné.

One of the most interesting sights on the island is the small romantic palace of **Schloss Pfaueninsel**. Dating from 1794, it was designed by Johann Gottlieb Brendel for Friedrich Wilhelm II and his mistress Wilhelmine Encke (the future Countess Lichtenau). The palace was built of wood, with a façade fashioned in the form of a ruined medieval castle. The cast-iron bridge that links the towers was built in 1807. The palace is open to the public in the summer months, when you can see the 18th- and 19th-century furnishings.

Other sights worth visiting include **James's Well**, which was built to resemble an ancient ruin. Towards the northeast corner of the island is the **Luisentempel** in the form of a Greek temple. Its sandstone portico was relocated to the island from the mausoleum in Schloss-park Charlottenburg *(see pp94–5)* in 1829. Nearby is a stone commemorating Johannes Kunckel, an alchemist who lived on

Pfaueninsel in the 17th century. During his quest to discover how to make gold, he discovered a method of producing ruby-coloured glass. Near the **Aviary**, home to multicoloured parrots and pheasants, is a tall fountain that was designed by Martin Friedrich Raabe in 1824.

Nikolskoe 27

Nikolskoer Weg. **Ⓢ** Wannsee, then take 🚌 A16 or 316.

ACROSS THE RIVER from Pfaueninsel (Peacock Island) is Nikolskoe. Here you'll find the Blockhaus Nikolskoe, a Russian-style *dacha* (country house) that was built in 1819 for the future Tsar Nicholas I and his wife, the daughter of King Friedrich Wilhelm III.

The house was built by the German military architect Captain Snethlage, who was responsible for the

Guests on the terrace of the Blockhaus Nikolskoe in summer

Alexandrowka estate in Potsdam *(see p124)*. Following a fire in 1985, the *dacha* was reconstructed. It currently houses a restaurant.

Close by is the church of St Peter and Paul, which was built between 1834 and 1837, to a design by Friedrich August Stüler. The body of the church is completed by a tower crowned by an onion-shaped dome, reflecting the style of Russian Orthodox sacral architecture.

Klein Glienicke 28

🚌 116. **(** (030) 805 30 41. 🕐 mid-Jun– mid-Oct: 10am–5pm daily. 🎗

THE PALACE in the palace-park of Klein Glienicke was built in 1825 according to a design by Karl Friedrich Schinkel for Prince Karl of Prussia. The charming park in which it is located was created by Peter Joseph Lenné. Beyond the Neo-Classical palace extends an irregular cluster of buildings, grouped around a courtyard, including a pergola and staff cottages. Passing by the palace, you approach the **Coach House**, also designed by Schinkel and now housing a restaurant. Nearby are an orangery and greenhouses designed by Ludwig Persius. Also by Persius is the **Klosterhof**, a mock monastery with pavilions, on whose walls are many Byzantine and Romanesque architectural elements from Italy. Towards the lake is the **Grosse Neugierde**, a circular pavilion based on the Athenian monument to Lysikrates from the 4th century BC. From here there are beautiful views across the Havel river and **Glienicker Brücke** (known under the East German regime as the bridge of unity). The border with West Berlin ran across this bridge where, during the Cold War, the exchange of spies was conducted.

Karl Friedrich Schinkel's Neo-Classical Schloss Klein Glienicke

ENTERTAINMENT IN BERLIN

With so much entertainment on offer, from classical drama and cabaret to variety theatre and an eclectic nightclub scene, it is possible to indulge just about any taste in Berlin. During the summer, many bars and restaurants set up outdoor tables, and the areas around Unter den Linden, Ku'damm and the whole of Kreuzberg and Prenzlauer Berg turn into one large social arena. The city really comes into its own at night, when its cocktail

Flute player

bars, cafés and bars are open all night and dancing goes on until dawn. The city has many night-life centres, each with a slightly different character. The younger generation favours Kreuzberg and Prenzlauer Berg, while Friedrichshain is more exclusive and Kreuzberg has a vibrant gay scene. The Mitte district offers a true mixture, with its opera house and classical theatre surrounded by lively bars.

PRACTICAL INFORMATION

THERE ARE so many things going on in Berlin that it can be difficult to find what you're looking for. Tourist Information Centres offer basic information, but the most comprehensive guides are the listings magazines *Tipp* and *Zipp*, which are published every other Wednesday. The daily *Berliner Morgenpost* publishes its supplement *bm Live* on Fridays, while *Ticket* comes out on Wednesdays, together with the *Tagesspiegel*. *Cinemataz*, the Thursday supplement to *Taz*, gives weekly cinema programmes. *Berlin Program* gives monthly lists of events, while *Berlin Magazin*, published by Berlin Tourismus Marketing GmbH, gives quarterly information. The most comprehensive information can be found in

the monthly *Kunstkalender*. It is also worth checking the free pamphlets and music publications that are on display in bars, cafés and by the entrances to public toilets.

TICKETS

THEATRE AND concert tickets can usually be booked up to two weeks in advance, and can be bought directly at the box offices or by telephone. Reserved tickets must be picked up and paid for at least half an hour before the performance. You can also pre-book tickets at special outlets all over Berlin: the best one in the city centre is the **Fullhouse Service**.

One agency that specializes in last-minute ticket purchase is **Hekticket Theaterkassen** on Hardenbergerstrasse, where you can get tickets on the day, even an hour before a show.

Cinema Zoo Palast, where many cinema festivals are held

These tickets are usually sold at a 50 per cent discount.

Students, seniors and the disabled are entitled to a 50 per cent discount on tickets, for which they must present proof of status.

THEATRES AND CINEMAS

BERLIN IS one of the most important towns on the theatrical map of Germany. One of its most famous theatres, the magnificent **Berliner Ensemble**, was once managed by Bertold Brecht. The **Deutsches Theater** offers an ambitious programme, while **Volks-bühne** stages works by young playwrights.

Berlin has many multiplex cinemas, offering a good selection of the latest films. The biggest, with 19 screens, is **CinemaxX** in Potsdamer Platz. Some of the films there

Prokoviev's *The Love of Three Oranges* staged at the Komische Oper

Whitsun Karneval der Kulturen in the streets of Kreuzberg

are shown in the original language. Next door is the ultra-modern **Imax** cinema whose huge curved screen is 27m (89ft) in diameter.

MUSIC AND DANCE

BERLIN HAS one of the finest orchestras in the world — the Berlin Philharmonic Orchestra, whose home, the **Philharmonie**, is also one of the world's most beautiful concert halls. The city boasts three opera houses: the **Staatsoper Unter den Linden** and the **Komische**

Oper are in the eastern part of city, while the **Deutsche Oper Berlin** is in the west. The three opera houses have ballet programmes built into their repertoires and these are performed largely by resident dance companies.

Apart from regular concerts, the city stages many festivals, such as Musik-Biennale and the Open Air Festival, as well as many concerts organized in churches and public parks.

ROCK, JAZZ AND POP

BERLIN IS always a popular destination for world-famous musicians, whose concerts are often held in the **Waldbühne**. Numerous music clubs offer daily opportunities to hear good music: favourite venues are **Quasimodo** in the western part of the city centre, **Schlot** in Prenzlauer Berg and **Junction Bar** in Kreuzberg. Good traditional jazz can be heard during the annual Jazzfest Berlin, and modern experimental work at the Total Music Meeting.

CHILDREN

THE CHOICE of entertainment for children and teenagers is huge. Special attractions include circuses, zoological gardens, Deusches Technik-museum *(see p77)*, **Museumsdorf Düppel**, **Teddy Museum** and **Kindermuseum Labyrinth**. An ascent to the rotating café at the top of the Fernsehturm (television tower) *(see p75)* is a great treat. Many restaurants provide play areas for children.

A glimpse of medieval life at the Museumsdorf Düppel

DIRECTORY

TICKET AGENTS

Hekticket Theaterkassen
Hardenbergstr. 29d.
Map 2 B4.
(*(030) 230 99 30.*

Karl-Liebknecht-Str. 36-38/ZDF-Shop.
Map 5 D2.
(*(030) 24 31 24 31.*

Fullhouse Service
Unter den Linden.
Map 4 B2.
(*(030) 262 05 15.*

THEATRES

Berliner Ensemble
Bertold-Brecht-Platz 1.
Map 1 C3.
(*(030) 28 40 81 55.*

Deutsches Theater
Schumannstr. 13a.
Map 1 C3.
(*(030) 28 44 12 25.*

Hebbel Theater
Stresemannstr. 29.
Map 4 B5.
(*(030) 25 90 04 27.*

Volksbühne am Rosa-Luxemburg-Platz
Rosa-Luxemburg-Platz.
(*(030) 247 67 72.*

CINEMAS

CinemaxX
Potsdamer Platz
Potsdamer Str. 1–19.
Map 4 A3.
(*(030) 44 31 63 16.*

Imax
Marlene-Dietrich-Platz 4.
(*(030) 26 06 62.*

MUSIC AND DANCE

Philharmonie
Herbert-von-Karajan-Str. 1.
Map 3 F3.
(*(030) 25 48 82 32.*

Deutsche Oper Berlin
Bismarckstr. 34–37.
(*(030) 341 02 49.*

Komische Oper
Behrenstr. 55–57.
Map 4 B2.
(*(030) 47 99 74 00.*

Staatsoper Unter den Linden
Unter den Linden 7.
Map 4 C2.
(*(030) 20 35 45 55.*

ROCK, JAZZ, AND POP

Junction Bar
Gneisenaustr. 18.
(*(030) 694 66 02.*

Schlot
Kastanienallee 29
(*(030) 448 21 60.*

Quasimodo
Katzlerstr. 12a.
(*(030) 312 80 86.*

Waldbühne
Glockenturmstr. 1.
(*(030) 23 08 82 30.*

CHILDREN

Museumsdorf Düppel
Clauertstr. 11.
(*(030) 802 66 71.*
Apr–Oct: 3–7pm Thu, 10am–5pm Sun and hols.

Teddy Museum Berlin
Kurfürstendamm 147.
(*(030) 893 39 65.*
3–6pm Wed, Thu, Fri.

Kindermuseum Labyrinth
Osloer Str. 12.
(*(030) 494 53 48.*
9am–1pm Mon–Fri, 2–6pm Tue–Fri, 1–6pm Sat, 11am–6pm Sun.

Tierpark Berlin
Am Tierpark 125.
(*(030) 51 53 10.*

BERLIN STREET FINDER

MAP REFERENCES given for historic buildings, hotels, restaurants, bars, shops and entertainment venues refer to the maps included in this section of the guidebook. The key map below shows the area of Berlin covered by the Street Finder. The maps include all major sightseeing areas, historic attractions, railway stations, bus stations, U-Bahn stations and the suburban stations of the S-Bahn. The names of the streets and squares in the index and maps are given in German. The word *Straße* (or *STRASSE, Str*) indicates a street, *Allee* an avenue, *Platz* a square, *Brücke* a bridge and *Bahnhof* a railway station.

KEY

Major sight	Bus terminus
Place of interest	Tram stop
Other building	Parking
S-Bahn station	Hospital with emergency dept.
U-Bahn station	Police station
Railway station	Church
Bus stop	Synagogue

Post office
Railway line
One-way street
Pedestrian-only street

SCALE OF MAPS 1–5

0 metres   250

0 yards   250

1:16 500

EASTERN GERMANY

Eastern Germany at a Glance

THE EASTERN region of Germany is immensely rich in tourist attractions. The imposing valley of the Elbe River, the beautiful lake district of Lower Brandenburg, attractive trails in the Harz Mountains of Saxony-Anhalt, the Thuringian Forest as well as the Erzgebirge and the Lusatian Mountains in Saxony all invite the visitor with their dramatic scenery and excellent recreational facilities.

Eastern Germany is rich in historic sights, too, ranging from the Baroque residences of Potsdam in Brandenburg to the grand architecture of Dresden and Leipzig in Saxony and the important cultural centre of Weimar in Thuringia. The most rewarding destinations in the region are featured here.

The Magdeburg Reiter, *in the market square, is the copy of one of Thuringia's most famous sights. The identity of the rider is not certain.*

Naumburg Dom *is a huge, well preserved Gothic cathedral (see pp140–141), one of Germany's greatest buildings. Splendid statues of its founders, Ekkehart and Uta, adorn the walls of the presbytery.*

Erfurt Dom *dominates the town-scape. A massive Gothic structure, the cathedral's three towers were built on the Romanesque foundations of an earlier church.*

SAXONY-ANHALT
(see pp132–47)

THURINGIA
(see pp170–87)

Weimar, *with its picturesque market square (see pp184–5) and historic buildings, was an important cultural centre for many centuries. Friedrich Schiller, Johann Wolfgang von Goethe and Johann Sebastian Bach all lived here.*

Sanssouci in Potsdam (see pp126–7), the enchanting Baroque summer residence built for Prussia's King Frederick the Great, stands on the site of former gardens and vineyards.

0 km   20

0 miles   20

LOCATOR MAP

Schloss Wörlitz is surrounded by a romantic landscaped park (see pp146–7) criss-crossed by a network of waterways open to pleasure boats.

BRANDENBURG
(see pp118–31)

The Völkerschlachtdenkmal in Leipzig (see pp152–3) was erected to celebrate the centenary of the battle fought by Prussia, Austria, Russia and Sweden against Napoleon's army in 1813.

SAXONY
(see pp148–69)

The Zwinger in Dresden (see pp164–5), Saxony's glorious palace and a Baroque jewel, was immaculately restored to its original glory after World War II destruction.

Meißen Porcelain

Figurine by J. J. Kändler

U NTIL THE early 18th century the only porcelain known in Europe was that imported from the Far East, and the Chinese jealously guarded the secrets of its production. Finally, in 1709, the Berlin alchemist Johann Friedrich Böttger, working on orders of August II the Strong, succeeded in developing a recipe which made it possible to produce genuine porcelain. A factory was set up in Meißen, and from 1713 it began to export its products to the entire European continent. Its first famous designers were Johann Joachim Kändler and Johann Gregor Höroldt.

The Porcelain Museum, opened in 1916, holds exhibitions and demonstrations illustrating the various stages in the manufacture of porcelain. The museum also runs courses on porcelain-making.

BÖTTGER STONEWARE

Johann Friedrich Böttger's first success in recreating Chinese ceramics came in 1707 when, with the assistance of Ehrenfried Walther von Tschirnhaus, he managed to produce stoneware almost identical to that produced in Yi Hsing. The stoneware was dark, varying in colour from red to brown.

These plates and bowls are typical examples of Böttger stoneware; its plain and simple lines were modelled on Far-Eastern designs.

The dark colour of the dishes is due to the use of red clays.

The "Yellow Lion" design, dating from c.1728, was used to decorate the first Meißen service.

Imari tree

The "Yellow Lion" was in reality a tiger.

FAR-EASTERN MOTIFS

Until the 17th century the only porcelain known in Europe came from the Far East, and the first items made from Saxon hard porcelain were initially strongly influenced by the Asian products. In Meißen, Chinese figurines and dishes were copied, adapting "European" shapes, but using Japanese or Chinese motifs for decoration. Special designs were created to adorn the services intended for the royal court. The oldest among these include the "Yellow Lion" and the "Red Dragon". New designs, inspired by European art, began to appear after 1730, and gradually replaced the Asian patterns.

PRODUCTION PROCESS

The process of porcelain production has not changed significantly over the centuries. The formula for "hard-paste" porcelain contains kaolin, quartz and feldspar. Each product is dried and fired, with glazed products being fired twice. The decoration can be applied before or after the glazing process. Hand-painted and gilded items are the most expensive.

Demonstration of the intricate art of hand-painting porcelain at the Meißen factory

TABLEWARE

In the second half of the 18th and in the 19th centuries, porcelain manufacturers developed their own designs. This proved so popular that some remain in production to this day. The best-known Meißen designs are the "vine-leaves" and the "onion" patterns, first introduced in the 18th century. Customers can thus still replace items in the services which have graced their family tables for generations.

This coffee pot and cup is decorated with the cobalt "onion" pattern, depicting stylized pomegranate fruits.

FINE-ART MOTIFS

A new type of decoration, which became popular in the second half of the 18th century, involved the accurate copying of famous paintings or etchings onto a vase, a pot or a plate. This type of decoration proved particularly popular during the Classicist period.

Decorator copying an etching onto a vessel

Vase decorated with a miniature of a painting by Antoine Watteau

SERVICES AND FIGURINES

Several outstanding sculptors and painters were employed in the Meißen porcelain manufacture to design unique services and figurines for the royal courts. The most famous among them are the services designed by Johann Joachim Kändler. He also created sets of figurines to adorn dining tables, vases and censers (containers for burning incense) for decorating the home, and large religious compositions for churches.

Figurine of August III

"Swan" Service Tureen

Europa, a figure from the "Four Continents" series, designed by J. J. Kändler

---

MARKS ON MEISSEN PORCELAIN

All porcelain manufacturers mark their products with their own symbols. The symbols are generally applied under the glaze, at the bottom of the piece. The Meißen factory initially used marks that imitated Japanese or Chinese writing; later, for a short time, letters were used, and from 1724 blue trademarks in the shape of crossed swords became the standard mark. The last three symbols below identify the respective court for which each piece of porcelain was produced.

K.P.F.

Königliche Porzellan-Fabrik, trademark used in 1723

K.P.M.

Königliche Porzellan-Manufaktur, trademark used in 1723–4

Trademarks used from 1724

Augustus Rex, the initials of **King August**

K.H.K

Königliche Hof-Küche

K.H.C.W.

Königliche Hof-Conditorei Warschau

Luther and the Reformation

Coat of arms

IN 1517, on the eve of All Souls' Day (31 October), Martin Luther nailed his 95 "theses" to the doors of the castle church in Wittenberg, condemning the practice of indulgences. His subsequent pronouncements, in which he criticized many aspects of the Church's teaching, made him the "father" of the Reformation movement in Germany and other countries. Luther's teaching gained the support of many of the princes, who in 1531 formed the Schmalkalden Union and started to introduce a new administration to the Church. This led to religious wars which finally ended with the Augsburg Peace Treaty, signed in 1555, which confirmed the religious division of Germany.

The Bible, *translated into German by Luther, was first published in one volume in 1534. One year later an illustrated, two-volume luxury version was published in Augsburg.*

The Schlosskapelle *in Hartenfels Castle, in Torgau (see p154), was built in 1543–4 and consecrated by Martin Luther. It is generally considered to be the first church built specifically for the Lutheran community.*

The baptism of a child is performed by Philipp Melanchthon.

The Last Supper, at the centre of the altar, stresses the importance attached by Lutherans to the sacrament of communion. The figures of the Apostles are portraits of the main church reformers.

Martin Luther, *the great theologian and religious reformer, initiator of Church reform and founder of Lutheranism, is depicted in this portrait by Lucas Cranach the Elder (1520).*

This group of faithful, listening to the sermon, includes members of Luther's family.

Luther's Room (Lutherstube), shown here, is part of Luther's House in Wittenberg (see p144). The famous reformer lived here with his wife and family.

Philipp Melanchthon, an associate of Luther's and the co-founder of Lutheranism, initiated a great educational reform. He was also known as praeceptor Germaniae, Germany's teacher.

REFORMATION ALTAR

The main altar of St Mary's Church in Wittenberg *(see pp144–5)* is one of the most important works of art of the Reformation period. The central picture was painted by Lucas Cranach the Elder (c.1539), the wings by his son, Lucas Cranach the Younger, before 1547.

Cup Bearer Serving at the Table is the title of a portrait by Lucas Cranach the Younger.

Protestant confession is taken by Johannes Bugenhagen.

Katharina von Bora, a former nun, became Martin Luther's wife in 1525. She lies buried in the Marienkirche in Torgau (see p154), in a tomb which survives to this day.

Sermon preached by Martin Luther, who points to the figure of the crucified Christ.

BRANDENBURG

THE PROVINCE *of Brandenburg is a lowland region criss-crossed by a dense network of rivers, canals and lakes. Quiet in part, it is also crossed by some of the main tourist routes to Berlin. Its most popular attractions are the historic sights of its capital city, Potsdam, and the Spreewald, where all day can be spent boating on the waterways of the Lusatian forests and villages.*

In early medieval times, the area that was to become present-day Brandenburg was the scene of violent conflict between various Germanic tribes. The latter conquered the region, and in 1157 created the margravate of Brandenburg. Its first ruler was Albrecht der Bär (Albert the Bear), from the house of Ascan. From 1415, Brandenburg was ruled by the Hohenzollern dynasty. It was quick to embrace the Reformation, which was officially adopted here as early as 1538. In 1618, Brandenburg merged with the duchy of Prussia through personal union. The region became entangled in the Thirty Years' War and suffered devastating losses; depopulated and plundered, it took Brandenburg many years to rise from the ashes. In 1701, the Great Elector, Frederick III, crowned himself King Frederick I, and the whole region now assumed the name of Prussia.

While Berlin remained the seat of power and a strong industrial and cultural centre, 18th-century Potsdam also played an important role: it was, after all, the favourite haunt of Frederick the Great. Other towns in the region were less significant – Brandenburg was, and still is, a fairly rural region. Reunification in 1990, however, has opened up the newly created land to Berliners and tourists alike.

Travellers in Brandenburg will encounter ancient tree-lined avenues that stretch to the horizon. The Spreewald, Brandenburg's lake district, is an oasis of tranquillity, ideal for boating and cycling. Brandenburg also has grand castles in Oranienburg, Branitz just outside Cottbus and Rheinsberg, Gothic churches and monasteries in Lehnin and Chorin and the towns of Brandenburg/Havel and Zelle.

Baroque palace in Rheinsberg, on the shores of the Grienericksee

◁ **A picturesque corner in the Babelsberg Palace in Potsdam**

Exploring Brandenburg

Brandenburg is ideally suited for gentle exploration by bicycle or car, and its proximity to Berlin allows the visitor to make a one-day excursion to the capital. A whole day should be allocated for visiting Potsdam and the castle of Sanssouci, and another day for a boat trip in the Spreewald. A visit to Cottbus can be combined with an excursion to Frankfurt an der Oder. The best time for a visit to Chorin is the summer when concerts are held there in the ruined monastery.

SEE ALSO:
- *Where to Stay* pp476-7
- *Where to Eat* pp505-6

Cecilienhof, the summer residence of the Hohenzollern family in Potsdam

Schloss Branitz in Cottbus

KEY

▬	Motorway
▬	Major road
▬	Scenic route
➤	River
⚶	Viewpoint

↑ *Pasewalk*

109

E28/11

PRENZLAU

Oder

104

C K E R M A R K

109

E28/11

8
CHORIN

158

**EBERSWALDE-
FINOW**

158

167

Oder

E55/10

1

RLIN

Poznań →

E30/12 **9**

FÜRSTENWALDE   E30/12

**FRANKFURT
AN DER ODER**

96

EISENHÜTTENSTADT

E55/13

87

S P R E E W A L D

11

10

02

LUCKAU

COTTBUS

E36/15

N I E D E R L A U S I T Z

13

SENFTENBERG

LAUCHHAMMER

↓ *Dresden*

Tourist boats on the Spreewald canals, near Lehde

GETTING AROUND

There are many flights to Berlin.
Brandenburg has an extensive
network of motorways – the
circular Berliner Ring joins with
the motorways A11 from Stettin,
A24 from Hamburg, Schwerin
and Rostock, A2 from Hanover,
A9 from Munich and Nurem-
berg, A12 from Frankfurt an der
Oder and A13 from Cottbus and
Dresden. Local roads and
country lanes in Brandenburg
are often narrow and twisting.
The outskirts of Berlin are well
served by the local train network, which provides frequent
links with many small towns.
There are also numerous local
bus services.

0 kilometres   20

0 miles   20

SIGHTS AT A GLANCE

Elbetal ❶

Road map D2. 🚉 *to Wittenberge or Bad Wilsnack.* 🚌 *Am Markt 5, Bad Wilsnack (038791-26 20).* ⓦ www.städtenetz.prignitz.de.

THE ELBE valley in the western part of Prignitz is an area of gentle rolling hills and unspoiled nature. Storks, increasingly rare in Germany, nest here to this day. When travelling around this parkland it is worth stopping at **Pritzwalk** to admire the late-Gothic Nikolaikirche (St Nicholas church). Another place of interest is **Perleberg** with its picturesque market square featuring an original 1515 timber-frame building, a sandstone statue of the French knight Roland (1546), now standing by the 1850 Town Hall, and the town's star attraction is the 15th-century Gothic Jakobskirche (church of St Jacob).

Bad Wilsnack owes its fame to the discovery of the therapeutic properties of the iron oxide-rich mud found in the surrounding marshes. Already known in medieval times, the town was an important place of pilgrimage. After a church fire, in 1384, three hosts displaying the blood of Christ were found untouched on the altar. The Gothic **Nikolaikirche** (church of St Nicholas), which survives to this day, was built soon after for the pilgrims.

Plattenburg Castle, in a scenic situation on an island, is also worth a visit. Combining late-Gothic and Renaissance architecture, it is used as a venue for concerts.

Chapel of the Holy Sepulchre in Heiligengrabe, near Wittstock

Wittstock ❷

Road map E2. 🚶 *13,700.* 🚌 🚌 *Markt 1, Wittstock/Dosse (03394-43 34 42).*

THE SMALL town of Wittstock was first awarded its municipal status in 1284. From the 13th century to the Reformation, Wittstock was the see of the Havelberg bishops. Although much of the town was destroyed, the original city walls remained almost completely intact, with one surviving gate – the **Gröper Tor**. All that remains of the former bishop's castle is the gate tower, which now houses a small museum. The town's star attraction is the Gothic **Marienkirche** with its late-Gothic reredos depicting the crowning of St Mary. It originated in the wood carving workshop of Claus Berg, probably after 1532. Other interesting features include the 1516 sacrarium and the late-Renaissance pulpit, dating from 1608.

ENVIRONS: Ten km (6 miles) to the west lies **Heiligengrabe**, with its Gothic Cistercian Abbey. One of its many

highlights is the 1512 **Chapel of the Holy Sepulchre** with an intricately sculpted gable and some charming timber-frame cloister buildings.

Neuruppin ❸

Road map E2. 🚶 *27,300.* 🚌 🚌 *Karl-Marx-Str. 1 (03391-454 60).*

THE TOWN of Neuruppin, in a scenic location on the shores of a large lake, the Ruppiner See, is mainly Neo-Classical in style, having been rebuilt to the design of Bernhard Matthias Brasch after the great fire of 1787. The only older buildings are the Gothic post-Dominican church and two small hospital chapels. Neuruppin is the birthplace of the architect **Karl Friedrich Schinkel** and the novelist **Theodor Fontane** *(see p23)*; both are commemorated by monuments.

ENVIRONS: The beautiful, albeit neglected palace of **Rheinsberg**, 25 km (16 miles) to the north, was converted from 16th-century Renaissance castle in 1734–7. In 1734–40 it was the residence of the Crown Prince, which now later became Frederick the Great, King of Prussia. Some 30 km (19 miles) northeast of Rheinsberg is the National Socialist concentration camp **Ravensbrück**, for women and children. It is now a place of remembrance.

Schinkel monument

Oranienburg ❹

Road map E3. 🚶 *30,000.* 🚉 🚌 🚌 *Bernauer Str. 52 (033 01-70 48 33);* ⓦ www.tourismus-or.de.

THE STAR attraction of the town is **Schloss Oranienburg,** the Baroque residence built for Louisa Henrietta von

The Gothic-Renaissance Plattenburg Castle, in the Elbetal

Nassau-Oranien, wife of the Great Elector Friedrich Wilhelm. Designed by Johann Gregor Memhardt and Michael Matthias Smids, it was built in 1651–5 and later extended to reach its present H-shape. It is surrounded by a grand park.

⬛ Schloss Oranienburg

Schlossplatz 1. ☎ *(03301) 38 63.*
◯ *8:30am–4pm Tue–Sun.*

Early-Renaissance palace in Caputh, north of Lehnin

ENVIRONS: Sachsenhausen, which is located northeast of Oranienburg, is now a place of remembrance and a museum. Opened in 1936 by the National Socialists, this concentration camp claimed the lives of 100,000 inmates.

⬛ Sachsenhausen

☎ *(03301) 20 00.* ◯ *Apr–Aug: 8:30am–5:30pm Tue–Sun; Sep–Mar: 8:30am–4pm Tue–Sun.*

Brandenburg/ Havel ❺

Road map E3. 🏘 *87,700.*
🚉 🚌 ℹ *Hauptstr. 51 (03381-194 33).* 🎭 *Havelfestspiele (Jun).*

BRANDENBURG is the oldest town of the region. It was settled by Slavs as early as the 6th century, and a mission episcopate was established here in 948. Scenically sited on the Havel River, it has preserved historic centres on three islands, despite wartime destruction. The oldest island is the **Dominsel**, with its Romanesque **Dom St Peter und St Paul**. This cathedral was constructed from 1165 to the mid-13th century. In the 14th century it was raised and given new vaultings. It contains numerous valuable Gothic objects, including the **"Czech" altar** (c.1375), the present main altar (from Lehnin, 1518) and the sacrarium of the same year. The most valuable treasures are on display in the **Dommuseum**.

Other sights worth visiting are the huge, 15th-century **Katharinenkirche** built by Hinrich Brunsberg, the **Gotthardkirche**, in the Altstadt ("old town"), with its Romanesque façade and Gothic interior, the Gothic Rathaus (Town Hall), with a statue of Roland from 1474, and the **Stadtmuseum**, a museum of local history and toy manufacture.

⬛ Dommuseum

Burghof 11. ☎ *(03381) 20 03 25.*
🌐 *www.brandenburg-dom.de.*
◯ *Mar–Oct 10am–4pm Mon–Fri, 11am–5pm Sat & Sun; Nov–Feb 10am–4pm Mon–Sat, 11am–4pm Sun; Jun–Sep 10am–noon Wed.* 🎫

⬛ Stadtmuseum

Ritterstr. 96. ☎ *(03381) 52 20 48.*
◯ *9am–5pm Tue–Fri, 10am–5pm Sat & Sun.* 🎫

Lehnin ❻

Road map E3. 🏘 *3,100.* 🚌
ℹ *Friedensstraße 13 (03382-76 50).*

VISITORS TO THIS small town mainly come to see the huge **Klosterkirche** (abbey) founded for the Cistercian order of Otto I, son of Albert the Bear. The church was built from the late 12th to the late 13th century, originally in Romanesque, then in early-Gothic style. Following the dissolution of the monastery, in 1542, the buildings fell into disrepair, but much of the abbey has survived.

⛪ Klosterkirche

Klosterkirchplatz. ☎ *(03382) 76 86 10.* ◯ *Oct–Mar 9am–noon & 1–4pm Mon–Fri; 11am–noon & 1–5pm Sat & Sun.*

ENVIRONS: Caputh, situated 23 km (14 miles) to the north, has an early-Baroque **Palace** built during the second half of the 17th century, as summer residence for the wives of the Great Electors. The interior has many original features, including a dining hall decorated with Delft tiles.

The Gothic "Czech" altar in the Dom St Peter und St Paul in Brandenburg

Potsdam ❼

AN INDEPENDENT city close to Berlin, Potsdam, with almost 138,000 inhabitants, is also the capital of Brandenburg. The first documented reference to Potsdam dates back to AD 993; it was later granted municipal rights in 1317. The town blossomed during the times of the Great Electors and then again in the 18th century. Potsdam suffered very badly during World War II, particularly on the night of 14–15 April 1945 when Allied planes bombed the town centre.

A sculpture on display in Park Sanssouci

Sightseeing in Potsdam

Potsdam remains one of Germany's most attractive towns. Tourists flock to see the magnificent royal summer residence, Schloss Sanssouci, to stroll around Neuer Garten (new garden) with its Marmorpalais (marble palace) and Cecilienhof, to visit the old city centre and the Russian colony of Alexandrowka, to be entertained in the film studios of Babelsberg and to take a walk around the parks of Schloss Babelsberg.

♣ Cecilienhof

Am Neuen Garten (Neuer Garten).
📞 *(0331) 969 42 44.* 🚌 *695.*
🕐 *Apr–Oct: 9am–5pm Tue–Sun;
Nov–Mar: 9am–4pm Tue–Sun.*
The Cecilienhof residence played a brief but important role in history, when it served as the venue for the 1945

Potsdam Conference *(see p129)*. Built between 1914 and 1917, the palace is the most recent of all Hohenzollern dynasty buildings. Designed by Paul Schultze-Naumburg in the style of an English country manor, Cecilienhof is a sprawling, asymmetrical, timber-frame building with inner courtyards and irregular breaks.

The palace remained a residence of the Hohenzollern family after they had lost the crown – the family stayed in Potsdam until February 1945. Today the palace is a hotel, where visitors interested in history are able to relax amid green shrubs. The large, scenic park

remains open to the public even when the rooms used during the Potsdam Conference are closed to visitors.

♣ Marmorpalais

Am Neuen Garten (Neuer Garten).
📞 *(0331) 969 42 46.* 🚌 *695.*
🕐 *15 May–15 Oct: 10am–5pm
Tue–Sun; 16 Oct–14 May: 10am–4pm
Sat & Sun (in winter only with guide).*
This small palace, situated on the edge of the lake, is a beautiful example of early Neo-Classical architecture. The palace is named after the Silesian marble used on its façade. The main part of it was built between 1787 and 1791 by Carl von Gontard to a design and under the direction of Carl Gotthard Langhans, on the initiative of King Friedrich Wilhelm II.

🎏 Alexandrowka

Russische Kolonie Allee/ Puschkinallee.
🚊 *92, 95.* 🚌 *138, 604, 609, 650, 692, 697.*
A visit to Alexandrowka takes the visitor into the world of Pushkin's fairy tales. Wooden log cabins with intricate carvings, set in their own gardens, create a charming residential estate. They were constructed in 1826 under the direction of the German architect Snethlage, for twelve singers of a Russian choir that was established in 1812.

🎏 Holländisches Viertel

Friedrich-Ebert-Str , Kurfürstenstr., Hebbelstr., Gutenbergstr. 🚌 *138, 601–604, 606–612, 614, 631, 632, 650.* 🚊 *92, 95.*
Just as amazing as the Russian colony of Alexandrowka is the Holländisches Viertel (Dutch quarter), part of a Baroque town built in the middle of Germany. Dutch workers arrived in Potsdam in

A view of the Baroque Dutch district known as Holländisches Viertel

the early 18th century and, between 1733 and 1742, a settlement was built for them on the orders of Friedrich Wilhelm I to plans by Johann Boumann the Elder. It comprised 134 gabled houses arranged in four groups. The houses were built from small red bricks and finished with stone and plaster details.

⛪ Nikolaikirche

Alter Markt. 🚌 601, 603, 692, 694, 🚋 91, 92, 93, 95, 96, 98.
🕐 2–5pm Mon–Fri, 10am–5pm Sat, 11:30am–5pm Sun.

This imposing church built in the late Neo-Classical style, is indisputably the most beauti-

The Nikolaikirche, with its dome resting on a colonnaded wall

ful church in Potsdam. It was built on the site of an earlier, Baroque church, which burned down in 1795. It was designed during 1828–30 by Karl Friedrich Schinkel and the building work was supervised by Ludwig Persius. The interior decoration and furnishings of the church date from the 1850s, but were mostly based on the earlier designs by Schinkel.

🏛 Marstall

Alter Markt. 🕐 (0331) 27 18 10.
🕐 10am–6pm Tue–Sun. 📷 🚌 601, 603, 692, 694. 🚋 91, 92, 93, 95, 96, 98.

This long Baroque pavilion, once used as royal stables, is the only remaining building of a royal residence. It was constructed in 1714 and currently houses a film museum devoted to the history and work of the nearby Babelsberg Film Studio.

🏛 Bildergalerie

Zur Historischen Mühle. 🕐 (0331) 969 41 81. 🚌 612, 614, 695.
🕐 15 May–15 Oct: 10am–12:30pm & 1–5pm Tue–Sun. 📷

Baroque paintings once owned by Frederick the Great, including Caravaggio's

VISITORS' CHECKLIST

Road map E3 🕐 (0331) 14 30 00. 🚉 Lange Brücke 🛈 Friedrich-Ebert-Str. 5; Brandenburger Str. 18 (0331-27 55 80) **FAX** (0331) 27 55 899 🎭 Hofkonzerte (May–Sep); Musikfestspiele Sanssouci (Jun).

Doubting Thomas, Guido Reni's *Cleopatra's Death*, as well as paintings by Rubens and van Dyck, are on show in the picture gallery situated next to Schloss Sanssouci.

Caravaggio's *Doubting Thomas*, on show in the Bildergalerie

POTSDAM

Alexandrowka ③
Bildergalerie ⑦
Cecilienhof ①
Holländisches Viertel ④
Marmorpalais ②
Marstall ⑥
Nikolaikirche ⑤
Park Sanssouci ⑧

KEY

🛈 Tourist information
🅿 Parking
🚉 Railway station

Park Sanssouci

THE ENORMOUS Park Sanssouci, which occupies an area of 287 hectares (700 acres), is one of the most beautiful palace complexes in Europe. The first building to be constructed on the site was Schloss Sanssouci, built as the summer palace of Frederick the Great. It was erected in 1747, on the site of a former orchard. Over the years, Park Sanssouci was expanded considerably and other palaces and pavilions added. To enjoy the park fully, allow at least a whole day.

Flower-filled urn, Park Sanssouci

Communs
Situated next to a pretty courtyard, this building has an unusually elegant character. It is now used to house palace staff.

★ Neues Palais
Constructed between 1763 and 1769, the monumental building of the Neues Palais is crowned by a massive dome.

Römische Bäder
Shaded by pergolas over-grown with greenery, the Roman baths include a Renaissance-style villa.

```
0 metres          200
0 yards           200
```

STAR SIGHTS

★ Neues Palais

★ Schloss Sanssouci

Schloss Charlottenhof
This Neo-Classical palace gained its name from Charlotte von Gentzkow, the former owner of the land on which the palace was built.

Lustgarten
The extensive park-land is made up of several gardens. The Lustgarten (pleasure garden) is nearest to the Orangerie.

VISITORS' CHECKLIST

Am Neuen Palais. ☎ (0331) 969 42 55. 🚌 606, 695. ⏰ Mid-May–mid-Oct: 9am–5pm; mid-Oct–mid-May: 9am–4pm (in wintertime, visit possible only with guided tour). 🎫 (free access to park). 🔲

Orangerie
This large Neo-Renaissance palace was built in the mid-19th century to house foreign royalty and other guests.

Neue Kammern
Once the orangerie of the Sanssouci Palace, this Rococo pavilion was later rebuilt as a guest house.

★ Schloss Sanssouci
A beautifully terraced vineyard creates a grand approach to Schloss Sanssouci, the oldest building in the complex.

Bildergalerie
Built between 1755 and 1764, this is Germany's oldest purpose-built museum building. The Baroque pavilion houses an art gallery.

Chinesisches Teehaus
An exhibition of exquisite Oriental porcelain is housed in the small, Rococo-style Chinese Tea House.

Friedenskirche
The Neo-Romanesque Church of Peace is modelled on the Basilica of San Clemente in Rome.

Paintings in the music room, in Schloss Sanssouci

♠ Schloss Sanssouci

Zur Historischen Mühle. **[** (0331) 969 41 90. **⬜** Apr–Oct: 9am–5pm; Nov–Mar: 9am–4pm. **Damenflügel & Schlossküche:** 15 May–15 Oct: 10am–12:30pm & 1–5pm Sat & Sun. **⬜**

This Rococo palace was built in 1745–7 by Georg Wenzeslaus von Knobelsdorff to sketches by Frederick the Great. Knobelsdorff and Johann August Nahl designed the interior. *Sanssouci* ("carefree") was the perfect name for the enchanting castle. The Damenflügel, the castle's west wing which was added in 1840 to house ladies and gentlemen of the court, and the Schlossküche (castle kitchen) can also be visited.

♠ Schloss Neue Kammern

Zur Historischen Mühle (Lustgarten). **[** (0331) 969 42 06. **⬜** 1 Apr–14 May 10am–5pm Sat & Sun; 15 May–15 Oct 10am–5pm Tue–Sun. **⬜ ⬜**

The Neue Kammern (new chambers) adjoin Schloss Sanssouci in the west, like the Bildergalerie in the east. As part of this ensemble it was originally built in 1747 as an orangery, to a design by Georg Wenzeslaus von Knobelsdorff who gave it its elegant Baroque forms. The building has an attractive roof with sloping ends and sides. In 1777 Frederick the Great ordered the building to be transformed into guest accommodation. The architect, Georg Christian Unger, left the exterior of the orangery largely untouched but converted the interior into

sumptuous suites and four elegant halls. The Rococo décor has been maintained, similar to that of other palaces and pavilions of Sanssouci.

▦ Orangerie Schloss

Maulbeerallee. (Nordischer Garten). **[** (0331) 969 42 80. **⬜** 15 May–15 Oct: 10am–5pm Tue–Sun; **viewing terrace ⬜** 1 Apr–14 May: 10am–5pm Sat & Sun; 15 May–15 Oct 10am–5pm Tue–Sun.

Above the park towers the Orangerie, designed in Italian Renaissance style and crowned by a colonnade. It was built to house guests, not plants, and served as guest residence for Tsar Nicolas and his wife, King Friedrich Wilhelm IV's sister. The Orangerie was constructed in 1852–60 for the king by Friedrich August Stüler, with the final design partly based on plans by Ludwig Persius. Modelled on the Regia Hall in the Vatican, the rooms were grouped around the Raphael Hall and decorated with replicas of this great Italian master's works. The observation terrace offers a good view over Potsdam.

▦ Chinesisches Teehaus

Ökonomieweg (Rehgarten). **[** (0331) 969 42 22. **⬜** 15 May–15 Oct: 10am–5pm Tue–Sun.

The lustrous, gilded pavilion that can be seen glistening between the trees from a

distance is the Chinese Teahouse. Chinese art was very popular during the Rococo period – people wore Chinese silk, wallpapered their rooms with Chinese designs, lacquered their furniture, drank tea from Chinese porcelain and built Chinese pavilions in their gardens. The one in Sanssouci was built in 1754–56 to a design by Johann Gottfried Büring. Circular in shape, it has a centrally located main hall surrounded by three studies. Between these are pretty *trompe l'oeil* porticos. The structure is covered with a tent roof and topped with a lantern. Gilded ornaments, columns and Chinese figures surround the pavilion. Originally a tea room and summer dining house, it houses today a collection of 18th-century porcelain.

▦ Römische Bader

Lenné-Str. (Park Charlottenhof). **[** (0331) 969 42 24. **🚌** 606. **🚋** 91, 94, 96, 98. **⬜** 15 May–15 Oct: 10am–5pm Tue–Sun.

The Roman baths, situated by the edge of a lake, form a picturesque group of pavilions which served as accommodation for the king's guests. They were designed in 1829–40 by Karl Friedrich Schinkel, with the help of Ludwig Persius. The gardener's house at the front stands next to a low, asymmetrical tower, built in the style of an Italian Renaissance villa. In the background, to the left, extends the former bathing pavilion, which is currently used for temporary exhibitions. The pavilions are grouped around a garden planted with colourful shrubs and vegetables.

Figure on the roof of
Chinesisches Teehaus

♠ Schloss Charlottenhof

Geschwister-Scholl-Str. (Park Charlottenhof). **[** (0331) 969 42 28. **⬜** 15 May–15 Oct: 10am–5pm Tue–Sun.

This small Neo-Classical palace stands at the southern end of Park Sanssouci, known as Park Charlottenhof. Built in

1826–9 for the heir to the throne, the future King Friedrich Wilhelm IV, this small, single-storey building was designed by Karl Friedrich Schinkel in the style of a Roman villa. Some of the wall paintings, designed by Schinkel in the so-called Pompeiian style, are still in place. There is also a collection of Italian engravings. The most interesting part of the interior is the Humboldt Room. The palace is surrounded by a landscaped park designed by Peter Joseph Lenné.

♣ Neues Palais

Am Neuen Palais. *(0331) 969 42 55.* ◯ *Apr–Oct 9am–5pm Sat–Thu; Nov–Mar 9am–4pm Sat–Thu.*

One of Germany's most beautiful palaces, this imposing Baroque structure, on the main avenue in Park Sanssouci, was built for Frederick the Great to initial plans by Georg Wenzeslaus von Knobelsdorff in 1750. Its construction, to designs by Johan Gottfried Büring, Jean Laurent Le Geay and Carl von Gontard, was delayed until 1763–9, after the Seven Years' War. The vast, three-wing, two-storey structure comprises over 200 richly adorned rooms and has many interesting sculptures. The south wing houses the kings' quarters and a small theatre.

THE POTSDAM CONFERENCE

Towards the end of World War II, the leaders of the Allies – Winston Churchill, Franklin Roosevelt, and Joseph Stalin – met in Schloss Cecilienhof in Potsdam. The aim of this conference, which lasted from 17 July until 2 August 1945, was to resolve the problems arising at the end of the war. The main participants changed, however, before it was concluded. Churchill was replaced by newly-elected Clement Attlee, and Harry S. Truman took over after President Roosevelt died. The conference set up the occupation zones, the demilitarization and monitoring of Germany, the punishment of war criminals and the reparations. It also revised the German borders. These decisions established the political balance of power in Europe, which continued for 45 years.

Atlee, Truman and Stalin in Potsdam

♣ Schloss Babelsberg

Im Park Babelsberg. *(0331) 969 42 50.* ◯ *Apr–Oct:10am–5pm Tue–Sun; Nov–Mar: 10am–4pm Sat & Sun.*

Built in 1833–5 for Prince Wilhelm (Kaiser Wilhelm I), by Karl Friedrich Schinkel, this extravagant castle ranks as one of his finest works. An irregular building with many towers and bay windows, built in the spirit of English Neo-Gothic, with allusions to Windsor Castle and Tudor style, it now holds the Museum of Pre-History.

♛ Babelsberg Film Studio

Großbeerenstr. *(0331) 721 27 50.* ◯ *17 Mar–8 Nov 10am–6pm Mon–Sun; Jul & Aug 10am–8pm.*

This amazing film park was laid out on the site where Germany's first films were produced in 1912. From 1917 the studio belonged to Universum-Film-AG (UFA), which produced some of the most famous films of the silent era, including Fritz Lang's *Metropolis* and some films with Greta Garbo. The *Blue Angel*, with Marlene Dietrich, was also shot at Babelsberg, but subsequently, the studios were used to film propaganda for the Nazis. The studio is still operational today, and the public can admire some of the old sets, the creation of special effects and stuntmen in action.

♛ Einsteinturm

Albert-Einstein-Str. ◯ *once every month, by arrangement with the Urania Society (331-200 27 81).* 694.

This tower, built in 1920–21 by Erich Mendelsohn, is one of the finest examples of German Expressionist architecture. Its fantasy forms were to demonstrate the qualities of reinforced concrete to spectacular effect. However, the cost of formwork, assembled by boat builders, limited the use of the material to the first storey, while the upper floors are plastered brickwork.

The impressive Marble Hall in the Baroque Neues Palais

Chorin

Road map E2. 510. *Kloster Chorin, Amt 11A.* (033366) 703 77. *Apr–Oct: 9am–6pm daily; Nov–Mar: 9am–4pm daily.* *Choriner Musiksommer.*

O N THE EDGE OF the vast **Schorfheide** heathland, which has been listed as a World Biosphere Reserve by UNESCO, stands one of Brandenburg's most beautiful Gothic buildings – the Cistercian **Kloster** (abbey) of Chorin. The Cistercians arrived here in 1258, but work on the present Gothic abbey did not start until 1270. The church is a triple-nave, transeptial basilica, with a magnificent façade. Preserved to this day are two wings of the monastic quarters plus several domestic buildings. Following the dissolution of the monastery in 1542, the entire complex fell into disrepair. Today the church, deprived of its traditional furnishings, is used as a venue for classical concerts. The park established by Peter Joseph Lenné is conducive to pleasant strolls.

ENVIRONS: For visitors to Niederfinow, the giant **Schiffshebewerk** (barge-lift) is a definite must. This wonder of technology was designed for lifting and lowering ships from one canal to another. Commissioned in 1934, it is 60 m (197 ft) tall and capable of lifting barges laden with 1,000 tonnes or more.

Portal of the St Marienkirche in Frankfurt an der Oder

Frankfurt an der Oder

Road map F3. 87,900. *Karl-Marx-Str. 9. (0335-32 52 16).* *Frankfurter Musikfesttage (Mar); Hansefest (Sep); Kleist-Tage (Oct).*

F RANKFURT, on the banks of the river Oder, was granted municipal rights in 1253, prospered in the 13th century and joined the Hanseatic league in 1368. In 1945, the right bank was ceded to Poland and is now known as Słubice.

Viadrin University, founded in 1506, was reopened in 1991 and now educates both German and Polish students. The town's most famous resident was the playwright and writer Heinrich von Kleist who was born here in 1777.

The Gothic **Rathaus** (town hall) in the centre escaped destruction in World War II and now houses an art gallery. The main church, **Marienkirche** (church of St Mary), is a vast, five-nave Gothic hall which has stood in ruins since 1945. Some of the Gothic furnishings were rescued and can now be seen in **St Gertraud** (church of St Gertrude) which dates back to 1368. The main altar from 1489 and the huge, 5m- (16ft)-tall candelabrum from 1376 are particularly valuable. Another Gothic church, originally built for the Franciscans in 1966, has been transformed into the **C.P.E. Bach Konzerthalle** (concert hall), named after Carl Philipp Emmanuel Bach, son of Johann Sebastian.

ENVIRONS: **Neuzelle**, 36 km (23 miles) to the south, has a magnificent former Cistercian Abbey, with an impressive Baroque relief façade and a very striking interior.

Cottbus

Road map F3. 121,000. *Bahnhofstr.* *Karl-Marx-Str. 68. (0355-754 20);* *www.cottbus.de.* *Karnevalsumzug (Feb); Cottbusser Musik-Herbst (Oct).*

T OURISTS RARELY visit Cottbus, despite the many attractions offered by the town. Its enchanting town square is surrounded by impressive Baroque buildings. The house at No. 24 is the quaint Löwen-

The Baroque Schloss Branitz in Cottbus

apotheke (lion's pharmacy), which now houses a small pharmaceutical museum, the **Niederlausitzer Apotheken-museum**, with displays of historical interiors. Nearby, the Gothic **Oberkirche St Niko-lai** features an unusual original late-Gothic mesh vaulting. Another interesting Gothic structure, the **Wendenkirche** (Sorbian church), is a former Franciscan church, from the 14th–15th centuries.

Other attractions of the town include the remains of the medieval city walls with three preserved towers. Perhaps the most attractive building in Cottbus is the **Staats-theater** (state theatre) designed in Jugendstil (Art Nouveau style) by Bernhard Sehring and built in 1908.

The **Wendisches Museum** is devoted to the culture of the Sorbs which is experiencing a revival *(see p171)*.

Schloss Branitz is a late-Baroque palace, originally built in the 18th century, at the southeastern edge of town. It became the residence of Prince Hermann von Pückler-Muskau in 1845, who had its interior redesigned by Gottfried Semper. Today, the palace houses the **Fürst-Pückler-Museum**, which exhibits paintings by Karl Blechen, a local artist from Cottbus. The star attraction of the palace is its **Park**, which was designed by Prince Pückler-Muskau himself. This vast landscaped garden includes a lake with an island on which stands a grass-covered mock-Egyptian earth pyramid containing the tomb of the extravagant and eccentric Prince.

🏛 **Schloss Branitz and Fürst-Pückler-Museum**
Kastanienalle 11. 📞 (0355) 751 50. ⏰ Apr–Oct: 10am–6pm daily, Nov–Mar: 10am–5pm; Tue–Su. ♿

🏛 **Wendisches Museum**
Mühlenstr. 12. 📞 (0355) 79 49 30. ⏰ 8:30am–6pm Tue–Fri, 2–6pm Sat–Sun and bank holidays.

🏛 **Niederlausitzer Apothekenmuseum**
Altmark 24. 📞 (0355) 239 97. ⏰ 10am–5pm Tue–Fri; 2 & 3pm Sat–Sun. ♿

Boats and canoes in the Spreewald, near Lübben

Spreewald ⓫

Road map F3. 🚗 Lübben. ℹ Radduscz, Lindenstr. 1 (035433-722 99), Lübbenau, Ehm-Welk-Str. 15 (03542-36 68). 🚗 🎉 Spreewaldfest in Lübbenau (Jul) and Lübben (Sep).

DESIGNATED AS one of the World Biosphere Reserves, this marshy region, criss-crossed by hundreds of small rivers and canals, attracts large numbers of tourists each year. An all-day trip by **Kahn** (boat) or canoe, which is best started in **Lübben** or **Lübbenau**, can prove to be an unforgettable experience. The splendour of nature, numerous water birds and the endless chain of small restaurants which serve meals straight from the jetty, ensure an exciting day for the visitor. Do not miss the local speciality, pickled gherkins.

Lübben has an original Gothic church and a Baroque palace, rebuilt in the 19th century. Lübbenau features a small Baroque church and the Neo-Classical house of the von Lynar family. In **Lehde** a visit to the small open-air museum and the private collection of the **Bauern-haus- und Gurkenmuseum** – the only gherkin museum in Germany – are to be highly recommended.

ENVIRONS: Luckau, 18 km (11 miles) west of Lübben, has a lovely town square, surrounded by attractive Baroque houses with stucco façades, and the ornamented, 14th-century Gothic Nikolaikirche.

Jüterbog ⓬

Road map E3. 🏘 13,000. 🚆 🚌 ℹ Markt 21 (03372-46 31 13).

JÜTERBOG IS A small, picturesque town featuring many Gothic structures including some well-preserved sections of three city walls with gates and towers, dating back to the 15th century. It also boasts a beautiful town hall with arcades and three churches. **Nikolaikirche** (church of St Nicholas), the largest of them, is a magnificent hall church, with a twin-tower façade, built in several stages. The so-called New Sacristy features a set of medieval wall paintings, while the naves contain many Gothic furnishings.

Statue on Jüterbog town hall

ENVIRONS: Five km (3 miles) to the north of Jüterbog stands **Kloster Zinna**, a former Cistercian Abbey with an early-Gothic stone church. It features 16th-century stained-glass windows depicting the saints Bernhard and Benedikt.

The early-Gothic ex-Cistercian Kloster Zinna, near Jüterbog

SAXONY-ANHALT

THE SCENIC HARZ *mountains, a popular recreation area with fasci-nating rock formations and pleasant walks, are the best known attraction of Saxony-Anhalt. Yet this state also boasts a number of interesting towns, such as Lutherstadt Wittenberg and Magdeburg, steeped in history and blessed with magnificent historic remains, which range from Romanesque churches and abbeys to medieval castles.*

This province consists of the areas of the former Duchy of Anhalt and the Prussian province of Saxony, that part of the Kingdom of Saxony which was incorporated into Prussia after the Congress of Vienna (1815) as punishment for supporting Napoleon.

The landscape in this region is highly varied. Its northern part, the Altmark, is a largely flat area of farmland and heath. The gentle hills of the Harz Mountains in the southwest, although not especially high (their highest peak, the Brocken, rises to only 1142 m/3747 ft), are picturesque and fairly well provided with tourist facilities. The eastern, flat part of the region is more industrialized. It also includes two very important towns: the small town of Wittenberg, where Martin Luther proclaimed his theses in 1517, thus launching the Reformation, and Dessau, the former capital of the Duchy of Anhalt and from 1925 to 1932 the seat of the Bauhaus Art School. The southern part of the province, with its interesting and varied landscape, features one of the land's most impressive historic buildings – the gigantic Naumburg Cathedral.

After World War II Saxony-Anhalt was occupied by the Soviets, and in 1949 it was incorporated into the GDR. It underwent major industrial development, mainly due to lignite mining. The state of Saxony-Anhalt was first created in 1947, only to be abolished five years later. It was finally re-established as a federal state in 1990, with Magdeburg as its capital.

Timber-frame houses in Quedlinburg

◁ **Rousseau Island, in the landscaped gardens of Wörlitz**

Exploring Saxony-Anhalt

Touring Saxony-Anhalt can be an unforgettable experience, especially for admirers of Romanesque art, as this region abounds in churches and abbeys of that period. A visit to Wörlitz provides the opportunity to see one of Germany's most beautiful landscaped gardens. Nature lovers, hill-walkers and, in the winter, cross-country skiers should include a few days in the romantic Harz Mountains in their schedule. An added attraction here is a ride on the narrow-gauge railway drawn by a steam engine which, today as in years gone by, still links some of the most interesting places of the region.

Interior of the Gothic cathedral in Havelberg

Zoo-Park in Dessau

SALZWEDEL

71

ALTMA

188

GARDELEGEN

189

71

E30/2

WOLMIRSTE

MAGDEBURG

MAGDEBURGER
BÖRDE

81

180

❶
HALBERSTADT

❷

6

BERNBU

WERNIGERODE

❹
QUEDLINBURG

6

81

ASCHERSLEBE

6

❸
THE HARZ
MOUNTAIN TRAIL

180

80

LUTHERSTA
EISLEBEN

SANGERHAUSEN ●

QUERFURT ❽

Key

▬	Motorway
▬	Major road
▬	Scenic route
▬	River
☼	Viewpoint

Listening to a summer water concert, in Wörlitz Park

GETTING AROUND

The A2 motorway from Hanover to Berlin runs through Magdeburg to the northern part of the region. Another motorway, the A9 which links Berlin and Munich, provides easy access to Dessau and Halle, which is also served by the A14 motorway from Leipzig to Magdeburg, currently under construction. Other major and minor roads, well signposted, provide access to smaller towns and villages. Larger towns are easily accessed by rail or local bus services. In the Harz Mountains the narrow-gauge train is an alternative form of transport.

SEE ALSO

• **Where to Stay** pp477–8

• **Where to Eat** pp506–7

SIGHTS AT A GLANCE

Interior of the Gothic Cathedral of Halberstadt

Halberstadt ①

Road map D3. 🏃 *42,000.*
🚉 🚌 🛈 *Hinter dem Rathaus 6
(03941-55 18 15).*

HALBERSTADT enjoys a picturesque location in the foothills of the Harz Mountains. Its history goes back to the 9th century, when it became a seat of a mission episcopate. Once an important town, Halberstadt had 80 per cent of its buildings destroyed during World War II. Fortunately, many of its beautiful historic buildings have now been restored to their former glory.

The vast **St Stephans Dom** is the fourth successive church built on the same site. Construction began in the 13th century and the church was consecrated in 1491. The two-tower transeptial basilica ranks as one of the most beautiful pure Gothic forms in Germany. Its oldest part is the 12th-century font. Also notable are the Romanesque Crucifixion group (c.1220), set above the choir screen, and several examples of Gothic sculpture. Stained-glass windows from around 1330 have survived in the Marian Chapel, and 15th-century windows can be found along the cloisters and in the presbytery.

The adjoining chapter buildings contain one of Germany's richest cathedral treasuries – the **Domschatz**, with precious 12th-century tapestries, numerous sculptures and liturgical vessels.

Other interesting churches to have survived in the old town district include the Romanesque 12th-century **Liebfrauenkirche** and the Gothic **Marktkirche St. Martini** with a statue of Roland, symbolizing the freedom of the city. Remaining timber-frame houses can be seen in Gröper- and Taubenstrasse.

Romanesque Crucifixion group in the Dom, Halberstadt

🏛 **Domschatz**
⏰ *10am–5pm Mon–Fri; 10am–4:30pm Sat; 11am–4:30pm Sun.*

ENVIRONS: An original 12th-century Benedictine church stands in Huysburg, 11 km (7 miles) to the northwest.

Wernigerode ②

Road map D3. 🏃 *36,000.* 🚉 🚌
🛈 *Nicolaiplatz 1 (03943-63 30 35).*
🎭 *Rathausfest (Jun); Schlossfestspiele (Jul & Aug).*

WERNIGERODE is attractively situated at a confluence of two rivers. Timber-frame houses lean across its steep, winding streets, and a massive castle rises above the town. The **Harzquerbahn**, a narrow-gauge railway which links the small towns and villages in the Harz Mountains, between Wernigerode and Nordhausen, provides another popular tourist attraction. The Brockenbahn runs between Wernigerode and the Brocken mountain.

Strolling around the Old Town it is well worth stepping into St John's Church, featuring a Romanesque west tower. It contains some late-Gothic features, including the font and the altar. The variety of ornaments adorning the houses in Wernigerode is truly staggering. Particularly interesting are the houses along **Breite Straße**, the town's main shopping street which is closed to traffic.

♜ **Schloss Wernigerode**
Am Schloss 1. 📞 *03943-55 30 30.*
⏰ *May–Oct: 10am–6pm; Nov–Apr: 10am–4pm Mon–Fri; 10am–6pm Sat & Sun.* 🅿️
The fairy-tale castle, spiked with towers, was created during the years 1861–83 on the site of an older fortress. Now a museum, it houses the Stolberg-Wernigerode family art collection. The castle ramparts afford a fantastic view of the town and the nearby Harz mountains.

ENVIRONS: The small town of **Osterwieck**, 22 km (14 miles) to the north, has over 400 timber-frame buildings, dating mainly from the 16th and 17th centuries.

The romantic façade of Schloss Wernigerode, now a museum

The Harz Mountain Trail ❸

THE TOURIST trail across the Harz Mountains leads through charming historic towns and villages, as well as past the other attractions of the region including some fascinating caves and unusual rock formations.

VISITORS' CHECKLIST

Length: 55 km (34 miles)
Stopping places: there are many attractive restaurants all along the trail, in every town.
🎭 Walpurgisnacht, Thale: 30 Apr.

The Rübeland Caves ①
Rübeland's main attractions are the Hermannshöhle and Baumannshöhle, two caves with amazing stalactites and stalagmites.

Blankenburg ②
This charming mountain town is overlooked by an 18th-century castle. The Teufels-mauer, a spectacular 4-km (2-mile) long sandstone cliff, attracts many climbers.

Thale ③
Many mountain walks start in Thale, including one to the Hexentanzplatz, a platform suspended above a cliff, from where witches fly to Sabbath celebrations in the Walpurgis Night.

Wernigerode

Elbingerode

Hasselfelde

BODETA

RAMBERG

STIEGE

Güntersberge

Kurort Stolberg

Quedlinburg

Hoym

Ermsleben

Harzgerode ⑦
The town has charming timber-frame houses in the Old Town, and a 16th-century castle.

Gernrode ④
The star attraction in this town is the 10th-century church of St Cyriacus. Its interior is devoid of ornaments, yet enchantingly pure in form.

Burg Falkenstein ⑥
This huge castle, built in the 12th century and extended many times, is now a museum. From the castle, the visitor can enjoy a splendid view over the surrounding Harz Mountains.

Ballenstedt ⑤
The former home of the von Anhalt-Bemburg family enchants visitors to this day with its imaginative design, including the Baroque castle set in a park.

```
0 km        2
0 miles     2
```

KEY

▬▬ Tour route
══ Other road
▬▬ Scenic route
⚡ Viewpoint

The Renaissance portal of Quedlinburg Schloss

Quedlinburg ❹

Road map D3. 🏂 *26,000*. 🚊 🚌
🛈 *Markt 2 (03946-90 56 24 and 90 56 25).*

THE RISE OF the small town of Quedlinburg was closely connected with its convent, established in 936 by Emperor Otto I and his mother, St Mathilde. On the hill above the town stands the vast Romanesque structure of the **Stiftskirche St Servatius** (Collegiate Church of St Servatius), built between 1017 and 1129. Its old crypt, the Huysburg, which belonged to the previous church, features Romanesque wall paintings and contains tombs of the prioresses and of the Emperor Henry and his wife Mathilde.

An exhibition of treasures is shown in the arms of the transept, including the Romanesque reliquary of St Servatius and the remaining fragments of the 12th-century Knüpfenteppich (tapestry). The **Quedlinburg Schloss**, a Renaissance palace surrounded by gardens, occupies the other side of the hill.

Both Old and New Town of Quedlinburg have valuable examples of timber-frame architecture. The buildings date from various times – the modest house at **Wordgasse 3**, from around 1400, is the oldest surviving timber-frame building in Germany. Also noteworthy are the numerous churches, including the 10th-century **Norbertinenkirche**, the **Wippertikirche** with its early-Romanesque crypt, and the 15th century, late-Gothic **Marktkirche St Benedicti**.

Bernburg ❺

Road map D4. 🏂 *36,000*. 🚊 🚌
🛈 *Rheineplatz 4 (03471-37 20 30).*
🎭 *Rosenfest (Jun).*

ONCE THE CAPITAL of one of Anhalt's Duchies, Bernburg enjoys a picturesque location on the banks of the Saale River. It has a **Bergstadt** (upper town) and a **Talstadt** (lower town), and its attractions include the Gothic

parish churches and the town square with its Baroque buildings. The most important historic building is the **Bernburg Schloss**, a castle built on a rock. It owes its present appearance to refurbishments (1540–70), yet many features of this multi-wing structure are much older, including the 12th-century Romanesque chapels and Gothic towers.

Burg Giebichenstein, in Halle, with the Arts and Crafts College

Halle ❻

Road map D4. 🏂 *232,300*. 🚊 🚌
🛈 *Markt (Roter Turm) (0345-47 23 30).* 🎭 *Händel-Festspiele (Jun); Hallesche Musiktage (Nov).*

HALLE IS AN old town with a rich history in commerce and trade, its wealth founded on the production and sale of salt. Later, the town was turned into a centre for the

The impressive Bernburg Schloss, built on a rock

Renaissance residence in Merseburg

chemical industry. Halle has preserved most of its historic heritage. On the **Marktplatz** (town square) stands an interesting church, **Unser Lieben Frauen** (Our Dear Lady), whose late-Gothic main body (1530–54) was positioned between two pairs of towers that had remained intact from previous Romanesque churches. Nearby is the **Roter Turm** (Red Tower), an 84-m (276 ft) tall belfry, built in 1418–1506. The house at Nikolaistraße 5, the birthplace of Georg Friedrich Händel, now houses a small museum, the **Händel-Haus**. In Domplatz stands the early-Gothic **Dom**, built in 1280–1331 by the Dominicans and restored between 1525 and 1530 in Renaissance style, and elevated to the rank of cathedral. Inside there is an interesting pulpit dating from 1525, and the statues of saints situated by Peter Schroh's pillars.

Halle has some other medieval churches, including the late-Gothic **Moritzkirche** built in the latter part of the 14th century. It is also worth visiting the **Staatliche Galerie**, housed in the refurbished Citadel building known as **Moritzburg** and built during 1484-1503. On the outskirts of town stands **Burg Giebichenstein**, the former castle residence of the Magdeburg bishops. The upper part of the castle remains in ruins, while the lower part houses an Arts & Crafts College.

🏛 **Staatliche Galerie**
Friedemann-Bach-Platz 5. 📞 *(0345) 21 25 90.* ⭕ *11am–8:30pm Tue, 10am–6pm Wed–Sun & public holidays.*

Merseburg 7

Road map D4. 👥 *40,000.* 🚇 🚍
ℹ *Burgstr. 5 (03461-21 41 70).*

THE FIRST sight visitors see as they arrive in Merseburg is the **Domburg** – a vast complex of buildings spiked with towers, consisting of a cathedral and residential premises. The cathedral is not uniform in style; it includes some Romanesque elements (the eastern section and twin towers in the west) erected in the 11th and 12th centuries, and the late-Gothic triple-nave main body, which was built in 1510–17. All that remains of the older, early-Romanesque structure is the crypt, underneath the presbytery. The cathedral contains remarkable Gothic and Renaissance features, as well as numerous sarcophagi of bishops, such as that of Thilo von Troth (1470). The chapter buildings house a library with precious manuscripts, including the **Merseburg Bible** (c. 1200). Adjacent to the cathedral is a three-wing Renaissance-style **Schloss**. Magnificent portals and an attractive oriel in the castle's west wing are noteworthy.

Querfurt 8

Road map D4. 👥 *11,000.* 🚍
ℹ *Markt 14 (034771-237 99).*

THE NARROW streets of Querfurt are crammed with timber-frame houses, and the giant **Schloss** towers over the town square with its Renaissance town hall. The castle's present form is the result of Renaissance refurbishments, but it maintains many Romanesque features, such as the 11th-century donjon (keep), known as **Dicker Heinrich** (Fat Henry) and a 12th-century church. Also worth seeing is the burial chapel, the Baroque **Fürstenhaus** (ducal house) and a small museum, situated in the former armoury and granary.

Naumburg 9

Road map D4. 👥 *30,500.* 🚇 🚍
ℹ *Markt 6 (03445-20 16 14).*
🌐 *www.naumburg.de* 🎭 *Hussiten-Kirsch-Fest (Jun).*

THE TOWN'S star attraction is the **Dom** (cathedral of Saints Peter and Paul *see pp140–41*). There is a late-Gothic **Rathaus** (town hall), restored in Renaissance style, and the main square is surrounded by quaint houses. Further attractions include the **Marientor** gate (1455–6) with the puppet theatre, and the Gothic **Stadtkirche St. Wenzel** (Church of St Wenceslas). The latter has two paintings by Lucas Cranach the Elder as well as the 18th-century organ that Johann Sebastian Bach played on. Friedrich Nietzsche, the philosopher, spent his childhood at No. 18 Weingarten, now a small museum.

Gothic stone retable of the main altar in Naumburg Dom

E A S T E R N   G E R M A N Y

Naumburg Dom

THE IMPRESSIVE Cathedral of Saints Peter and Paul in
Naumburg is one of the finest Gothic structures in
Germany. The present cathedral is the second to be
built on the same site; only a section of the
eastern crypt survived of the earlier Romanesque
church. Construction started before 1213, with
the earliest parts including the late-Romanesque
east choir, the transept and the main body. The
early-Gothic west choir was built in the mid-13th
century, the newer Gothic east choir c.1330.
The northeast towers date from the 15th
century, the southwest towers from 1894.

West choir

**Stained-glass Windows
in the Presbytery**
*The stained-glass windows depict
scenes of the apostles of virtue and
sin. Some sections are original
13th-century work, but two were
completed in the 19th century.*

★ **Founders'
Statues**
*The statues of
Margrave Ekkehard
and his wife, Uta, are
true masterpieces – the
artist succeeded marvellously
in capturing the beauty and
sensitivity of his subjects.*

★ **Portal of
the West
Reading
Room**
*The Gothic twin
portal depicts
the Crucifixion,
a moving and
highly expressive
group sculpture by the
brilliant "Naumburger
Meister" whose identity
remains unknown.*

STAR FEATURES

★ **Founders' Statues**

★ **Portal of the West
Reading Room**

★ **Main Portal**

Pulpit

*The richly orna-
mented pulpit
basket, from 1466,
and the adjoining
stairs have recently
been renovated.*

VISITORS' CHECKLIST

Domplatz. (03445) 20 16 75.
Apr–Sep: 9am–6pm Mon–Sat,
noon–6pm Sun; Mar & Oct:
9am–5pm Mon–Sat, noon–5pm
Sun; Nov–Feb: 9am–4pm Mon–
Sat, noon–4pm Sun.

St Mary's Altar

*This late-Gothic triptych (c.1510) depicts the Virgin
Mary with the Infant, framed by Saints Barbara
and Catherine, with the Apostles in the wings.*

**Sarcophagus
of Bishop
Dietrich II**

**East
choir**

East Choir Altar

*This Gothic altar
features the Virgin Mary
with the Infant Jesus,
surrounded by the
figures of the saints.*

The Main Altar,
built in the mid-
14th-century, is a
stone retable depict-
ing the Crucifixion
with the saints which
was transferred
from another altar.

★ Main Portal

*The late-Romanesque, 13th-century
portal is decorated on the left side
with eagles. The tympanum features
Christ in a mandorla (almond-
shaped area) supported by angels.*

Interior of the Gothic presbytery in the Magdeburg Dom

Magdeburg ⑩

Road map D3. 🏛 *235,000.* 🚊 🚌
ℹ *Julius-Breuer-Str.10 (0391-54 04 903).* 🎭 *Kulturfesttage (Sep/Oct).*

THE LARGE-SCALE development of Magdeburg, today the capital of Saxony-Anhalt and a port on the river Elbe, began in the 10th century when Emperor Otto I established his main residence here. In medieval times the town became a political and cultural centre. Following the abolition of the archbishopric and the destruction wrought by the Thirty Years' War, it lost its political importance. About 80 per cent was destroyed during World War II, making it much less attractive, but it is still worth a visit. Many historic buildings have been reconstructed in the Old Town, in a scenic spot on the banks of the Elbe.

🏯 Dom St Mauritius und St Katharina
Domplatz. ◯ *daily.*
The vast Magdeburg cathedral is one of the most important Gothic churches in Germany. Its construction, which started in 1209 on the site of an earlier Romanesque church, was completed in 1520, although much of it was built by the mid-14th century. The result is a lofty, aisled basilica with transept, cloisters, a ring of chapels surrounding the presbytery and a vast twin-tower façade. The cathedral has several magnificent, original sculptures. Other notable features include the tomb of Emperor Otto I, as well as the 12th-century bronze tomb plaques of archbishops Friedrich von Wettin and Wichmann. The memorial for the dead of World War I is the work of Ernst Barlach, dating from 1929. Visitors to the cathedral may notice several elements that were preserved from ancient structures and have been incorporated into the walls or used as ornaments inside the building.

🏛 Kulturhistorisches Museum
Otto-von-Guericke-Str. 68–73.
📞 *(0391) 54 32 645.* ◯ *10am–5pm Tue–Sun.* 🅿
This museum contains works of art, archaeological finds and historic documents of the town. Its most valuable exhibit is the Magdeburger Reiter (Magdeburg Rider), a sculpture dating from around 1240, depicting an unknown ruler riding on a horse.

🏯 Kloster Unser Lieben Frauen
Regierungsstr. 4–6. **Church**
📞 *(0391) 541 47 22.*
Museum 📞 *(0391) 56 50 20.*
◯ *10am–5pm Tue–Sun.* 🅿
This austere Romanesque church, Magdeburg's oldest building, was built for the Norbertine order during the second half of the 11th and the early 12th centuries. Stripped of all its ornaments, it now serves as a concert hall. The adjacent Romanesque abbey is a museum with medieval and modern sculptures (Barlach, Rodin).

🏯 Halle an der Buttergasse
Alter Markt. Weinkeller Buttergasse.
The basement of a late-Romanesque market hall from c.1200 was rediscovered in 1948, and is used today as a wine cellar.

🏛 Rathaus
Alter Markt.
The present Baroque town hall, built in 1691–8 on the site of an earlier, late-Romanesque town hall, was lovingly restored to its former glory after World War II.

🏯 Pfarrkirche St Johannis
Jacobstr. **Viewing tower** ◯ *10am–6pm Wed–Sun.* 🅿
The ruins of this church, near the market square, are the remains of the Gothic church of St John, which was destroyed during World War II. In 1524 Martin Luther preached here.

Kloster Unser Lieben Frauen in Magdeburg

Stendal ⓫

Road map D3. 🏛 *39,600.*
🚉 🚌 🛈 *Am Markt 1
(03931-65 11 90).*

IN MEDIEVAL times Stendal was one of the richest towns of the Brandenburg margravate, and its most valuable historical remains date from that period. The late-Gothic **St Nikolai** cathedral was built in 1423–67, on the foundations of a Romanesque Augustinian church. Its star attractions are 15th-century stained-glass windows in the presbytery and the transept.

The late-Gothic, 15th-century church **St Marien** (St Mary) has some original Gothic elements, and the oldest parts of the **Rathaus** (town hall) date back to the 14th century. Other attractions include the remains of the town walls, with a beautiful tower, **Uenglinger Torturm**.

Gothic traceries of the cloisters in the Dom, Havelberg

Havelberg ⓬

Road map D3. 🏛 *7,000.* 🚌 🛈
Uferstr. 1. (039387-88 224).

HAVELBERG played an important role in the Christianization of this region, with a mission episcopate established here as early as the mid-10th century. The present cathedral – **Dom St Marien** – was built in 1150–70, and although redesigned in the early 14th century, it nevertheless maintained its Romanesque character. Its most interesting features include

Back of the Gothic Rathaus in the market square in Tangermünde

huge stone candelabra taken from the former reading room, dating back to around 1300, and the present reading room, which is decorated with reliefs carved in the workshop of the Parler Family, in Prague, between 1396 and 1411.

Tangermünde ⓭

Road map D3. 🏛 *10,000.* 🚉 🚌
🛈 *Marktstr. 13 (039322-37 10 and 43 750).*

SITUATED at the confluence of the Tanger and Elbe rivers, this town grew rapidly during medieval times. For centuries it remained the seat of the Brandenburg margraves, and King Charles IV chose it as his second residence. The town joined the Hanseatic League, and grew in status thanks to its trade links.

The present **Rathaus** (town hall) has lovely timber-frame architecture. Today it houses the municipal museum.

The only remains of the old castle are its main tower and the **Kanzlei** (chancellery). In 1377, King Charles IV brought the Augustinian monks to town and had the **St Stephanskirche** (church of St Stephen) built for them. Construction continued until the end of the 15th century. This magnificent, late-Gothic hall church with transept and cloister contains

interesting features: a 1624 organ made in the Hamburg workshop of Hans Scherer the Younger, the 1619 pulpit created by Christopher Dehne and a font dating from 1508, the work of Heinrich Mente.

The east wing of the beautiful Gothic **Rathaus** (town hall) dates back to 1430 and is the work of Heinrich Brunsberg, its richly ornamented spire being typical of his work. The west wing with its arcades was added around 1480, and the external stairs date from the 19th century.

Tangermünde has retained some remains of the city walls, dating from around 1300 and including a magnificent late-Gothic gate, the **Neustädter Tor**, whose tall, cylindrical tower has intricate, lacy ceramic ornaments.

🏛 **Rathaus (Stadtgeschichtliches Museum)**
Markt. 📞 *(039322) 42 153.* 🕙 *15 Feb–Nov 10am–5pm Tue–Sun*

ENVIRONS: A Romanesque **Klosterkirche** (abbey) in Jerichow, 10 km (6 miles) north of Tangermünde, is the earliest brick structure of the region. It was built in the 1150s, for Norbertine monks. The west towers were completed during the 15th century. Its austere, triple-nave vaulted interior is impressive. There are also many remains of the former abbey.

Interior of the former Norbertinenkirche, in Jerichow, north of Tangermünde

Dessau ⓮

Road map E3. 🏘 84,400. 🚆 🚌
🛈 Zerbster Str. 2c (0340-204 14 42).
📅 Mosigkauer Konzertsommer.

D
ESSAU, ONCE A magnificent
city and the capital of the
duchy of Anhalt-Dessau, is
less attractive today, yet it has
some excellent historic sights.
In the town centre are some
interesting Baroque churches
and the **Johannbau**, the
remains of a Renaissance
ducal residence.

Dessau is also known for
the **Bauhaus** complex. Built
in 1925 to a design by Walter
Gropius, it is the home of the
famous art school, which
moved here from Weimar.
The **Bauhausmuseum** is
housed in one of its wings.
Nearby, in Friedrich-Ebert-
Allee, five of the so-called
Meisterhäuser – master
houses for the Art College
professors – have survived
World War II. The houses of
Lyonel Feininger and Paul
Klee are open to the public.
Wassily Kandinsky was also a
former resident. The **Kornhaus**, on Elballee, restored in
1996, contains a restaurant,
café and dance hall.

Many splendid residences
set in landscaped gardens
were built in 18th- and 19th-
century Dessau. In the town
centre stands a Neo-Classical
palace, **Schloss Georgium**,
built in 1780 to a design by
Friedrich Wilhelm von Erdmannsdorff. Today it houses a
collection of old masters,
including works by Rubens,
Hals and Cranach. The palace
is surrounded by a garden.

🏛 Bauhausmuseum
Gropiusallee 38. 📞 (0340) 65 08
250. 🕐 10am–6pm daily. 🖼

⚜ Schloss Georgium
Puschkinallee 100. 📞 (0340) 61 38
74. 🕐 10am–5pm Tue–Sun. 🖼

ENVIRONS: Haldeburg, on
the outskirts of Dessau, has a
Neo-Gothic hunting lodge
built in 1782–3, and Mosigkau
boasts **Schloss Mosigkau**,
Princess Anna Wilhelmina's
Baroque residence, designed
by Christian Friedrich Damm.
It contains some excellent
17th-century paintings.

In **Oranienbaum**, 12 km
(7 miles) east of Dessau, stands
a late-17th-century, early-
Baroque palace built for
Princess Henrietta Katharine
of Orange by the Dutch architect Cornelius Ryckwaert.

⚜ Schloss Mosigkau
Knobelsdorffallee 3. 📞 (0340) 52 11
39. 🕐 Mar: 10am–4pm Sat & Sun;
Apr: 10am–4:30pm Tue–Sun; May–
Sep: 10am–5:30pm Tue–Sun; Oct &
4 Nov: 10am–4.30pm Tue–Sun; 10
Nov–2 Dec 10am–4:30pm Sat & Sun.
⬤ 3 Dec–28 Feb. 🖼 🖼

Lutherstadt Wittenberg ⓯

Road map E3. 🏘 55,000. 🚆 🚌
🛈 Schlossplatz 2 (03491-41 48 48).
📅 Wittenberger Stadtfest & Luthers
Hochzeit (Jun).

T
HIS SMALL town, named
after its most famous resident, **Martin Luther**, enjoys
a scenic position on the
banks of the Elbe River. Its
main development took place
during the 16th century,
under the Great Elector,
Frederick the Wise. Wittenberg became the capital of
the Reformation thanks to the
work of Martin Luther and
Philipp Melanchthon, and as
such it attracts many visitors.
Another famous resident of
that period was the painter
Lucas Cranach the Elder, who
lived here for 43 years.

⚜ Schloss Wittenberg
Schlossplatz. **Museum für
Naturkunde und Völkerkunde**
(Museum of Natural History and
Ethnography) 📞 (2491) 40 26
96. 🕐 9am–5pm Tue–Sun. 🖼
Built for Frederick the Wise
in 1489–1525, the castle was
greatly altered during reconstruction following fire and
wartime damage. A museum
is housed in the west wing.

**The tomb of Frederick the Wise,
in Schlosskirche**

🛐 Schlosskirche
Schlossplatz. 📞 (03941) 40 25 85.
🕐 May–Oct: 2–5pm Mon, 10am–
5pm Tue–Sat, 11:30–5pm Sun;
Nov–Apr: 2–4pm Mon, 10am–4pm
Tue–Sat, 11:30am–4pm Sun.
Built after 1497, this church
was made famous by Martin
Luther, who allegedly posted
his theses on its door in 1517.
The original door no longer
exists, but the church contains many interesting tombs,
including that of Frederick the
Wise, created in 1527 in the
workshop of Hans Vischer, as
well as modest tombs of Martin Luther and Melanchthon.

Schloss Georgium in Dessau

The market square with Baroque fountain, in Lutherstadt Wittenberg

🏛 Cranachhaus

Markt 4. ● *until further notice.*
This beautiful, early 16th-century Renaissance house once belonged to Lucas Cranach the Elder and was the birthplace of his son, Lucas Cranach the Younger. His studio was located at No. 1 Schlossstraße.

🏛 Rathaus

Markt 26. ● *until further notice.*
The Renaissance town hall was built in 1523–35, and later twice extended in the 16th century. In its forecourt are two 19th-century monuments: to Martin Luther by Gottfried Schadow and to Philipp Melanchthon by Friedrich Drake.

⛪ Marienkirche

Kirchplatz. ☎ (3491) 40 32 01.
● *May–Oct: 9am–5pm Mon–Sat, 11am–5pm Sun; Nov–Apr: 10am–4pm Mon–Sat, 11am–4pm Sun.*
The Gothic church of St Mary with its twin-tower façade was built in stages, between the 13th and 15th centuries. Luther was married to Katharina von Bora in this church where he also preached, and six of their children were baptised. Inside there is a magnificent Reformation altar (1547), the work of father and son Cranach, as well as interesting tombs and epitaphs.

🏛 Melanchthonhaus

Collegienstr. 60. ☎ (03491) 40 32 79. ● *Apr–Sep: 9am–6pm Tue–Sun; Oct–Mar: 10am–5pm Tue–Sun.* ✍
This museum is devoted to Luther's closest ally, Philipp Schwarzerd, generally known as Melanchthon.

🏛 Lutherhalle

Collegienstr. 54. ☎ (03491) 42 030. ● *Apr–Nov: Tue–Sun 9am–6pm; Oct–Mar: Tue–Sun 10am–5pm.* ✍
The museum, in the former residence of Martin Luther and his family, also chronicles the work of Lucas Cranach the Elder. It has a large number of documents relating to the Reformation and Luther's translation of the Bible.

LUTHERSTADT WITTENBERG TOWN CENTRE

Cranachhaus ③
Lutherhalle ⑦
Marienkirche ⑤
Melanchthonhaus ⑥
Rathaus ④
Schloss Zamek ①
Schlosskirche ②

KEY

🛈 Tourist information
🅿 Parking
🛐 Church

0 metres 500
0 yards 500

Wörlitz Park ⑯

WÖRLITZ is a charming, English-style landscaped garden, the first of its kind in continental Europe. It was established in stages, commencing in 1764, for Prince Leopold III, Frederick Franz of Anhalt-Dessau. Many famous gardeners worked in Wörlitz, including Johann Friedrich Eyserbeck and Johann Leopold Ludwig Schoch, as well as the architect Friedrich Wilhelm von Erdmannsdorff. In its centre stands a Neo-Classical palace, holding a collection of paintings. Another interesting collection, including stained-glass paintings, can be admired in the Gotisches Haus.

Floratempel
Modelled on an ancient temple with columns, this Neo-Classical temple served as a music pavilion.

★ Gotisches Haus
This pavilion, built in stages, is one of the earliest examples of German Neo-Gothic style. It now houses a collection of stained-glass paintings.

Rousseau-Insel, lined with poplars, was modelled on Ermenonville, the island where the French philosopher was first buried.

SCHOCHS GARTEN

Kleines Walloch

Floratempel

Palmehaus

SCHOCHS GARTEN

Gotisches Haus

Nym

Wörlitzer See

Rosennsel

Rousseau-Insel

Schloss

NAUMARKS-GARTEN

SCHLOSS-GARTEN

Galerie

Kirch

P

Friedericken-brücke

Rosen-Insel
Rose island was created as one of several artificial islands in the part of the garden designed by Johann Christian Neumark.

Gondolas on the Lake
Romantic gondolas wait by the jetties to take tourists across the lake and to the islands.

Boat Concert
*Classical concerts are
held on Wörlitz Lake in
the evening during the
summer season. The
audience, just like the
orchestra, are all afloat
in boats.*

Amalien-Insel
*In keeping with the fashion
of the day, this artificial
island, on Großes Walloch
lake, has a grotto, which
provides a cool
resting place.*

The Pantheon, built in
1795–6, houses a collection of
antique sculptures.

Pantheon

0 metres   500

0 yards   500

WEIDEN-
HEGER

Harderinsel   Großes Walloch   Amalien-Insel

NEUE
ANLAGEN

Wörlitzer See
*The largest of the
four lakes, which
are all joined by
canals, this is
prettiest when
the water lilies
are in bloom.*

Stein, an
artificial volcano
modelled on
Mount Vesuvius
in Italy, emitted
real smoke
and fire.

Stein

★ Synagogue
*Built in 1790 and modelled
on the Vesta Temple in Rome,
the synagogue was gutted
by the National Socialists
in 1938. It has since
been reconstructed.*

STAR FEATURES

★ **Gotisches Haus**

★ **Synagogue**

SAXONY

SAXONY *has a long history and is rich in historic sites. Its capital city, Dresden, ranks among the most beautiful and interesting towns in Germany, despite the devastation it suffered during World War II. The region also boasts the enchanting Erzgebirge Mountains and the glorious scenery of "Saxon Switzerland", where the mighty Elbe river runs amid fantastic rock formations.*

In the 10th century, Emperor Otto I created an eastern border province (margravate) in the area presently known as Saxony. It quickly grew in size as it expanded into neighbouring territories inhabited by the Polabian Slavs. It was divided and part became the Meißen Margravate, ruled by the powerful house of Wettin from 1089. This dynasty's political power increased when it acquired the Saxon Electorate in 1423; subsequently the entire region under their rule became known as "Saxony".

From 1697 until 1763 Saxony was united with Poland, and the Saxon Great Electors, Frederick Augustus the Strong and his son Frederick Augustus II, were also kings of Poland. During this period Saxony flourished, and Dresden became a major centre of the arts and culture until the Seven Years' War (1756–63) put an end to the region's prosperity. In 1806, Saxony declared itself on the side of Napoleon, and the Great Elector acquired the title of King. But Saxony paid a heavy price for supporting Napoleon – following the Congress of Vienna (1815), the kingdom lost the northern half of its territory to Prussia, and in 1871 it was incorporated into the German Empire.

At the end of World War II Saxony was in the Soviet-occupied zone and became part of the GDR in 1949. Since 1990 it has been a state in the Federal Republic of Germany. Saxony is densely populated and in some parts heavily industrialized, but it also has many interesting and unspoiled towns.

The scenic Bastei rocks in Saxon Switzerland

◁ **Kriebstein Castle, overlooking the Zschopau river**

Exploring Saxony

WHEN TRAVELLING in Saxony, a visit to Dresden is a must. Visitors should set aside several days to explore its historic sights and magnificent museums. Dresden is also a convenient base for excursions to the attractive landscapes of the Sächsische Schweiz ("Saxon Switzerland") and further afield – to Bautzen, Görlitz and Zittau, or to the Erzgebirge Mountains, towards Freiberg and Chemnitz. Another town worth visiting, at least for a day, is Leipzig with its historic sights, cultural events, trade fairs and exhibitions.

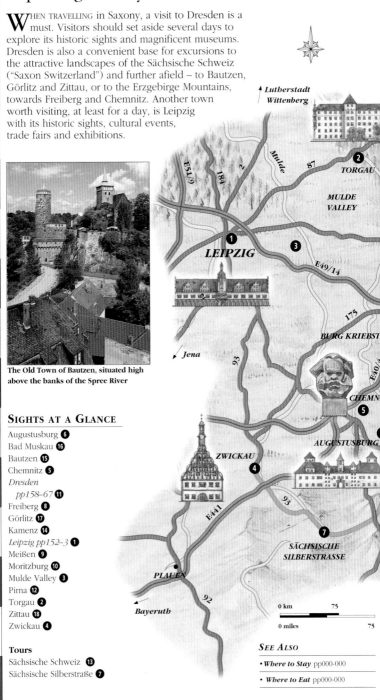

The Old Town of Bautzen, situated high above the banks of the Spree River

SIGHTS AT A GLANCE

Augustusburg ⑥
Bad Muskau ⑯
Bautzen ⑮
Chemnitz ⑤
Dresden
  pp158–67 ⑪
Freiberg ⑧
Görlitz ⑰
Kamenz ⑭
Leipzig pp152–3 ①
Meißen ⑨
Moritzburg ⑩
Mulde Valley ③
Pirna ⑫
Torgau ②
Zittau ⑱
Zwickau ④

Tours

Sächsische Schweiz ⑬
Sächsische Silberstraße ⑦

SEE ALSO

• *Where to Stay* pp000-000

• *Where to Eat* pp000-000

GETTING AROUND

Leipzig and Dresden both have airports, as well
as excellent train and road connections with the
rest of Germany. The A6 motorway runs west
from Görlitz, through Dresden and Chemnitz; the
A13 links Dresden with Berlin, and the A14 with
Leipzig. Other roads, national and regional, are
clearly sign-posted, and all the towns described
in this guide can also be reached by local buses.

**The giant castle and cathedral
complex in Meissen**

16 BAD MUSKAU

Spree

115

Weisser Schöps

Berlin

HOYERSWERDA ●

14 KAMENZ

96

4

GÖRLITZ

E40/4

MORITZBURG

10

17

MEISSEN **9**

15

BAUTZEN

E40

DRESDEN

11

E40/4

96

178

99

101

FREITAL

PIRNA **12**

172

18

ZITTAU

8 FREIBERG

170

KÖNIGSTEIN

SÄCHSISCHE
SCHWEIZ

13

Saddle horses grazing on paddocks near Kamenz

KEY

▰	Motorway
▰	Major road
▱	Scenic route
∿	River
❊	Viewpoint

**Young musicians in the Barock-Garten, in
Gross-Sedlitz, near Dresden**

Leipzig ➊

LEIPZIG, granted town status in 1165, is not only one of Germany's leading commercial towns, but also a centre of culture and learning, with a university founded in 1409. An important centre for the German publishing and book trade, it is the home of the Deutsche Bücherei, the German national library established in 1912. During the Leipziger Messe (autumn and spring trade fairs), it receives a great number of visitors, and it has much to offer in terms of entertainment, including concerts by the renowned Gewandhaus symphony orchestra and the Thomanerchor boys' choir, which boasts Johann Sebastian Bach as a past choirmaster.

Lofty interior of the Neo-Classical Nikolaikirche

Exploring Leipzig

Most of the interesting sights can be found in the old town encircled by the Ring road, which includes Europe's biggest railway station, the **Hauptbahnhof**, built in 1902–15 to a design by William Lossow and Max Kühne. The heart of musical Leipzig beats in the eastern part of the old town, around Augustusplatz. Here stands the **Neues Gewandhaus** (built 1977–81) and the **Opernhaus** (built 1959–60). The University Tower nearby is being redesigned.

In Nikolaikirchhof stands the **Nikolaikirche** (church of St Nicholas). The present church was built during the 16th century, although the lower sections of its north tower date from the 12th century. It has Neo-Classical furnishings. The **Alte Handelsbörse** (old stock exchange) in Naschmarkt is

an early-Baroque building, designed by Johann Georg Starcke. Built in 1678–87 and reconstructed almost from the ground after World War II, it is now a concert hall. In front of the building stands a monument (1903) to Goethe showing him as a student.

In the market square, near the beautiful Renaissance town hall, is the **Alte Waage**, the old municipal weighhouse, a Renaissance work by Hieronymus Lotter. It was built in 1555 and reconstructed in 1964 following damage in World War II.

The area to the south of the town square is taken up by a block of trade fair buildings. The most interesting are the beautifully restored **Specks Hof** (Reichestraße/Nikohinstraße), the oldest arcade in Leipzig with three enclosed courts built between 1908 and 1929, and **Mädlerpassage**, built in 1912–14, a Modernist commercial building with a three-tier passageway connecting Grimmaische Straße and Naschmarkt. Beneath it is the **Auerbachs Keller**, magnificent, 16th-century vaults, immortalized by Goethe in *Faust* and featuring a room bearing his name. The **Commerzbank** (Klostergasse/Grimmaische Straße) and the **Riquet Café**, a fine Viennese-style coffee house, are attractive Art Nouveau buildings.

Lovers of Johann Sebastian Bach's music will wish to visit **Thomaskirche**, the magnificent late-Gothic

church of St Thomas, built in 1482–96, where Bach was the choirmaster from 1723. It now contains the composer's tomb. Worth noting are the beautiful Renaissance galleries built by Hieronymus Lotter, in 1570. The famous Thomanerchor choir still sings at services on Friday evenings and Saturday afternoons, and organ concerts are held in the churches of St Thomas and St Nicholas during the summer months. Bach is also commemorated with a monument in front of the church (1908). Nearby, the **Bosehaus**, a Baroque 17th-century building, is the home of the Bachmuseum, devoted to the composer.

🏛 Grassimuseum

Johannisplatz 5–11. ⬤ until 2004. *Interim Building for* **Museum für Völkerkunde, Museum für Kunsthandwerk** *and* **Musikinstrumentemuseum** Newmarkt 20. ☎ *(0341) 213 37 19.* Ⓦ *www.grassimuseum@liepzig.de* Ⓒ *Library and museum shop with workshops and lectures from April 2001. Exhibitions start in Oct 2001.*

The Grassimuseum complex is being renovated and is currently housed in an Interim Building. Eventually, it will open with three museums: the Museum für Völkerkunde (ethnography) with exhibits from around the world; the Musikinstrumentemuseum (musical instruments) with a magnificent collection, including the world's oldest surviving clavichord, and the Museum für Kunsthandwerk (decorative arts) with its stunning gold and ivory ornaments, as well as the valuable town treasury.

The early-Baroque pavilion of the Alte Handelsbörse, the old stock exchange

The Russische Kirche, a pastiche of the churches in Novgorod

🏛 Deutsches Buch und Schriftmuseum

Deutscher Platz 1. 🕻 (0341) 227 13 24. ◻ 9am–4pm Mon–Sat.
This museum is devoted to the history of German literature. It contains rare manuscripts and old prints as well as a splendid collection of small printed items such as leaflets.

🏛 Museum der Bildenden Künste

Dimitroffplatz 1, until 2003 Grimmaische Str. 1–7. 🕻 (0341) 216 99 14. ◻ 10am–6pm Tue & Thu–Sun, 1–9:30pm Wed.
The Leipzig fine art museum has an excellent collection of

German masters, including Lucas Cranach the Elder, Martin Schongauer and Caspar David Friedrich, as well as magnificent examples of European painting. There are canvases by Jan van Eyck, Rubens, Frans Hals, Tintoretto and sculptures by Balthasar Permoser, Antonio Canova, Auguste Rodin and others. A room is devoted to the work of Max Klinger.

🔒 Russische Kirche

Philipp-Rosenthal-Str.
The Russian Orthodox Church of St Alexius was built in 1912–13 to commemorate the 22,000 Russian soldiers who died in 1813, in the Battle of the Nations. The architect, Vladimir Pokrowski, based his design on the churches of Novgorod in Russia.

🎪 Völkerschlachtdenkmal

Prager Str. 🕻 (0341) 878 04 71. ◻ Apr–Oct: 10am–6pm daily, Nov–Mar: 10am–4pm daily. 📷
This giant, Teutonic-style monument is the work of Bruno Schmitz. Completed for the centenary of the 1813 Battle of the Nations, which pitched the combined Prussian, Austrian and Russian armies against Napoleon, it now houses a museum.

VISITORS' CHECKLIST

Road map E4. 🏘 475,000.
✈ Flughafen Leipzig–Halle.
🚉 Willy-Brandt-Platz. 🕻 (0341) 22 41 155 & 22 40.
🛈 Richard-Wagner-Str. 1 (0341-710 42 60). 🎭 Leipziger Buchmesse (Mar); Leipziger Orgelsommer (Jul–Aug); Internationaler Johann-Sebastian-Bach Wettbewerb (Jul); Leipziger Jazztage (Oct).

🎪 Altes Rathaus

Markt 1. 🕻 (0341) 96 51 30.
Museum für Geschichte der Stadt Leipzig ◻ 2–8pm Tue, 10am–6pm Wed–Sun.
The grand Renaissance town hall, built in 1556 to a design by Hieronymus Lotter, is now the home of the municipal museum. One room is devoted to Felix Mendelssohn-Bartholdy, who conducted the symphony orchestra from 1835 until his death in 1847.

🏛 Bacharchive und Bachmuseum

Thomaskirchhof 16. 🕻 (0341) 96 44 10. ◻ 10am–5pm daily.
This museum houses archives and documents relating to the composer, J. S. Bach, as well as a fine collection of musical instruments from his day.

LEIPZIG CITY CENTRE

Alte Handelsbörse ④
Altes Rathaus ⑥
Alte Waage ⑤
Gewandhaus ②
Mädlerpassage ⑦
Nikolaikirche ③
Opernhaus ①
Thomaskirche ⑧

| 0 m | 200 |
| 0 yards | 200 |

KEY

🛈 Tourist information
⊠ Post office
✝ Church

Doorway of Schloss Hartenfels, with its coat of arms, in Torgau

Torgau ❷

Road map E3. ⚐ 23,000. ▤ ▦
ℹ Schlossstr. 11 (03421-71 25 71).
⚑ Torgauer Auszugsfest (Jun).

THIS SMALL town, with its scenic location on the Elbe, was once the favourite residence of the Saxon Electors. Its main square is surrounded by attractive houses of various styles, in particular Renaissance. The Renaissance **Rathaus** (town hall), built in 1561–77, has a lovely semicircular oriel. Other old town attractions include the **Marienkirche**, a late-Gothic church with an extended Romanesque west section. The interior has many original features, including a painting by Lucas Cranach the Elder, *The Fourteen Helpers*, and the tomb of Luther's wife, Katharina von Bora, who died in Torgau.

The main historic building in Torgau is the Renaissance **Schloss Hartenfels**, built on the site of a 10th-century castle. Its courtyard is surrounded by clusters of residential wings, including the late-Gothic Albrechtspalast built in 1470–85, the Johann-Friedrich-Bau (1533–6) with its beautiful external spiral staircase and the early-Baroque west wing (1616–23). The **Schlosskapelle** (castle chapel), which was consecrated by Martin Luther in 1544, is considered to be one of the oldest churches built for Protestants.

Muldetal ❸

Road map E4.

SEVERAL magnificent old castles nestle in the scenic hills at the confluence of two rivers – the Zwickauer Mulde and the Freiberger Mulde. In the small town of **Colditz**, with its timber-frame houses, lovely Renaissance town hall and Gothic church of St Egidien, stands a huge Gothic castle built in 1578–91 on the site of an 11th-century castle. During World War II it was a famous prisoner-of-war camp known as Oflag IVC.

In **Rochlitz**, 11 km (7 miles) south of Colditz, stands another large castle, built in stages from the 12th to the 16th centuries. Travelling further south you will encounter other castles: the **Wechselburg**, a reconstructed Baroque castle featuring a late-Romanesque collegiate church, as well as the Renaissance castle in **Rochsburg**. In the neighbouring Zschopau valley stands the magnificent, oval **Burg Kriebstein**, built in stages and completed in the late 14th century. This fortress houses a small museum and concert hall, and medieval music concerts are held here during the summer.

Zwickau ❹

Road map E4. ⚐
120,000. ▤ ▦
ℹ Hauptstr. 6 (0375-29 37 13). ⚑ Robert-Schumann-Tage (Jun); TrabiTreffen (Jun).

AN OLD commercial town, Zwickau flourished in the 15th and 16th centuries. Today it is known for the Trabant cars that were produced here during the GDR era. Almost all the town's attractions can be found in the old town, on the banks of the

Zwickauer Mulde river and encircled by the Ring road. The most important historic building in the town is the **Dom St Marien** (cathedral of St Mary), a magnificent late-Gothic hall-church built 1453–1537. Preserved to this day are its original main altar dating from 1479, the work of Michael Wohlgemut, the grand architectural Holy Tomb of Michael Heuffner, dating from 1507, as well as a Renaissance font and a pulpit of 1538, both by Paul Speck.

Also worth visiting in the old town are the **Old Pharmacy**, the **Schumann-Haus**, the composer's birthplace (1810), and the Renaissance **Gewandhaus** (cloth house), once the seat of the Drapers' Guild and now a theatre.

Chemnitz ❺

Road map E4. ⚐ 260,000. ▤
Georgstr. ▦ Bahnhofstr. ℹ
Bahnhofstr. 6 (0371-19 433).

AFTER WORLD WAR II, when 90 per cent of its buildings had been reduced to rubble, the town was rebuilt in the

Gate of the Renaissance pulpit in the Dom St Marien, in Zwickau

Lew Kerbel's monument to Karl Marx at the Stadthalle in Chemnitz

Socialist-Realist style and renamed Karl-Marx-Stadt. Only a handful of historic buildings escaped destruction. The most interesting among these is the **Schlosskirche**, the former Benedictine abbey church St Maria, on the edge of a lake, built at the turn of the 15th and 16th centuries.

Sights in the town centre include the reconstructed **Altes Rathaus** (old town hall), the Gothic **Roter Turm** (red tower) and remains of fortifications. In the main square is the reconstructed Baroque **Siegertsches Haus,** originally built in 1737–41 to a design by Johann Christoph Naumann. The new town centre is dominated by the vast **Stadthalle** (city hall) with Lew Kerbel's 1971 monument to Karl Marx. The **König-Albert-Museumsbau** has a museum of natural history and a fine arts collection, including works by Karl Schmidt-Rottluff.

🏛 **König-Albert-Museumsbau**
Theaterplatz 1. ☐ noon–7pm Tue–Sun. 🖼

Augustusburg ⑥

Road map E4. 🏠 5,000. 🚍
🛈 Marienberger Str. 29b (037291-395 50). **Schloss** ☐ Apr–Oct: 9am–6pm daily, Nov–Mar: 10am–5pm daily.

THE SMALL town is insignificant compared with the vast palace complex bearing

the same name. The best way to get there is by cable car, from Erdmannsdorf. This Renaissance hunting palace was built for the Great Elector, Augustus, in 1567–72, on the site of the former Schloss Schellenberg, which had been destroyed by fire. Constructed under Hieronymus Lotter and Erhard van der Meer, it is a symmetrical, square building with towered pavilions at each corner, joined by galleries, gates and a chapel to the east, with an altar by Lucas Cranach the Younger. Today the palace houses several museums devoted to motorcycles, coaches and hunting.

Sächsische Silberstraße ⑦

See pp156–7.

Freiberg ⑧

Road map E4. 🏠 45,000. 🚉 🚍
🛈 Burgstr. 1 (03731-236 02).
🎉 Bergstadtfest (Jun).

D EVELOPMENT of this mining town was due to the discovery of silver deposits, and Freiberg was granted town status in 1186. It escaped World War II with remarkably little damage.

Today its attractions include the reconstructed old town and many historic buildings, the gem among them being the **Dom St Marien** (cathedral). This late-Gothic hall-church, erected at the end of the 15th century, features a

magnificent main portal, the Goldene Pforte, dating from 1225–30. Inside are many original items, such as a tulip-shaped pulpit (1505), two sets of Baroque organs by Gottfried Silbermann and many sculptures and epitaphs.

When visiting nearby Untermarkt, it is worth going to the **Stadt- und Bergbaumuseum** (municipal and mining museum) which explains the history of mining in the area, as well as the collection of minerals at the **Mineralien- und Lagerstätten-sammlung der Bergakademie**. A stroll along the winding streets will take the visitor to **Obermarkt**, where the 15th-century Gothic town hall and a fountain with the statue of the town's founder as well as attractive houses can be seen.

Otto of Meißen, founder of Freiberg

⛪ **Dom St Marien**
Untermarkt. **Goldene Pforte** 🖼
May–Oct: 10 & 11am, 2, 3 & 4pm daily; Nov–Apr 11am, 2 & 3pm daily.
Organ presentation 11:30am Sun.
🏛 **Stadt- und Bergbau-museum**
Am Dom 1. 📞 (0371) 231 97.
☐ 10am–5pm Tue–Sun. 🖼
⛪ **Mineralien- und Lagerstättensammlung der Bergakademie**
Brennhausgasse 14. 📞 (03731) 39 22 64. ☐ 9am–noon & 1–4pm Wed–Fri, 9am–4pm Sat.

Façade of the Renaissance Schloss Augustusburg

Sächsische Silberstraße ❼

THE SAXON silver route, through the Erzgebirge (mineral ore mountains), takes the visitor to some of the most interesting and scenic places of the region. Silver was mined here from the 12th century, and mining traditions have been preserved to this day. Small towns entice visitors with their interesting parish churches, former mining settlements, museums and disused mines.

Schneeberg ①
A small mining town, which to this day cultivates its art and crafts traditions, Schneeberg is also famous for the St Wolfgangkirche, with an altar masterpiece by Lucas Cranach the Elder.

Oberwiesenthal ②
This important wintersports resort, close to the Czech border and at the foot of the Fichtelberg, offers a ski-jump, downhill ski runs and toboggan runs.

Annaberg-Buchholz ③
Although the town enjoyed only a brief spell of prosperity in the 16th century, its church from that period, St Annen, ranks among the most beautiful examples of late-Gothic architecture in Saxony.

0 km   5
0 miles   5

Marienberg ⑥
This small town, with its wonderful Renaissance town hall, is known mainly for the production of furniture.

KEY

▬▬▬ Suggested route
═══ Other road
▬▬▬ Scenic route
—•— State boundary
🌿 Viewpoint

Greifensteine ⑤
Fantastic, craggy rock formations in the north of the region, shaped like an amphitheatre, attract rock-climbers and hill-walkers.

Frohnau ④
The biggest attraction of this town is its old forge, featuring the Frohnauer Hammer, a huge original hammer that remained in use until 1904.

TIPS FOR DRIVERS

Length of the route: 55 km (34 miles).
Stopping points: inns and restaurants in every town.

Meißen ❾

Road map 4E. 🏙 36,000. 🚉 🚌
🛈 Markt 3 (03521-419 40).
🎭 Stadt- und Weinfest (Sep).

MEISSEN is famous for its porcelain manufacture. Its history began in 929, when Henry I made it the bridgehead for his expansion to the east, into Slav territories. In 966 Meißen became the capital of the newly established Meißen Margravate, and in 968 a bishopric.

This town has retained much of its charm. In the town square is the late-Gothic **Rathaus** (town hall), built in 1472–8, some beautiful Renaissance houses and the **Frauenkirche**, a late-Gothic, 15th-century church boasting the world's oldest porcelain carillon, which was hung here in 1929. It is also worth taking a stroll to St Afra's church, built in the 13th century for the Augustian monks.

⛪ Albrechtsburg

Domplatz 1. 📞 (03521) 47 070.
🕐 Mar–Oct: 10am–6pm daily,
Nov–Feb: 10am–5pm daily.
🔴 10–31 Jan. 🎟
The Albrechtsburg is a vast, fortified hilltop complex with a cathedral and an Elector's palace. The latter was built in 1471–89 for the Wettin brothers, Ernst and Albrecht. Designed by Arnold von Westfalen, its special feature is the magnificent external spiral staircase. From 1710 the palace was used as a porcelain factory. It was restored to its former glory in 1864. Huge wall paintings of this period, showing historical scenes, are the work of Wilhelm Römann. The cathedral church of St John the Evangelist and St Donat, built from the mid-13th century to the early 15th century, has some splendid early-Gothic sculptures, an altar by Lucas Cranach the Elder in the Georgskapelle and ducal tombs in the Fürstenkapelle.

🏭 Staatliche Porzellan-Manufaktur

Talstraße 3. 📞 (03521) 46 87 00 (46 82 08 exhibition). 🕐 May–Oct: 9am–6pm daily; Nov–Apr: 9am–5pm daily.
The first porcelain factory in Europe was set up in 1710 in the castle and moved to its present premises in 1865. Documents relating to the history of the factory and many interesting examples of its products are on display in the exhibition rooms. Guided tours and demonstrations take the visitor through all the stages of the porcelain manufacturing process.

The Baroque hunting lodge in Moritzburg

Moritzburg ❿

Road map 4E. 🚉 🛈 Schlossallee 3b
(035207-85 410). 🎭 Kammermusik-
festival (Aug); Fischzug (Oct).

THE FIRST hunting lodge in this marshy region was built in the mid-16th century, for Moritz of Saxony. The present **Schloss Moritzburg** is the result of extensive alterations ordered by Augustus the Strong, directed by Matthäus Daniel Pöppelmann, and carried out in 1723–26. The result is a square building, with four cylindrical corner towers. Much of the interior has survived, including period furnishings and hunting trophies.

Also open to visitors is the 17th-century castle chapel decorated with splendid stucco ornaments. Augustus the Strong ordered the marshes to be drained, and the newly available land to be transformed into landscaped gardens and lakes. The **Fasanenschlösschen** (little pheasant castle) in the eastern part of the gardens features several interesting Rococo interiors, and also houses a zoological exhibition.

At the end of World War II, the German artist Käthe Kollwitz spent the last years of her life in Moritzburg. The house in which she lived and worked is now the **Käthe-Kollwitz-Gedenkstätte**.

⛪ Schloss Moritzburg

📞 (035207) 8730. 🕐 May–Oct:
10am–6pm daily; Nov–Apr: 10am–
4pm daily. 🎟

⛪ Fasanenschlösschen

⬛ Closed for renovation.

The late-Gothic Rathaus in Meißen

Dresden ⓫

O NE OF Germany's most beautiful cities, Dresden first gained its pre-eminence in the year 1485, when the Albertine Wettins decided to establish their residence here. The town blossomed during the 18th century when, under the rule of the Elector Augustus the Strong, it became a cultural centre and acquired many magnificent buildings. Almost all of these, however, were completely destroyed during the night of 13/14 February 1945, when British and American air forces mounted a vast carpet-bombing raid on the city. Today, meticulous restoration work is in progress to return the historic city centre to its former glory.

Front tower of the Baroque Hofkirche

Statue of the Saxon King Johann, in front of the Sächsische Staatsoper

🏛 Sächsische Staatsoper

Theaterplatz 2. 📞 (0351) 49 110. **Tours** 📞 (0351) 491 14 96.
The imposing, Neo-Renaissance building of the Saxon state opera is one of Dresden's landmarks. It is also known as Semperoper after its creator, the famous architect Gottfried Semper, who designed it twice: the first building, erected in 1838–41, burned down in 1869, the second one was completed in 1878. Reconstruction after World War II dragged on until 1985. The opera house was the venue for many world premieres, including *Tannhäuser* and *The Flying Dutchman* by Richard Wagner, as well as many works by Richard Strauss.

In front of the opera, in Theaterplatz, is a monument to the Saxon King Johann, by Johannes Schilling.

🏛 Schinkelwache

Theaterplatz. **Box office** 📞 (0351) 491 17 05. 🕐 10am–6pm Mon–Fri, 10am–1pm Sat.
This small Neo-Classical building, with its sophisticated lines and its immaculate

proportions, is the work of the famous Berlin architect, Karl Friedrich Schinkel. It was built between 1830 and 1832.

🔒 Hofkirche

Theaterplatz. (Entrance on Schlossplatz). 🕐 daily.
This monumental Baroque royal church, with its open-work tower visible from afar, has served as the Catholic Dom (cathedral church) of the Dresden-Meißen Diocese since 1980. The presence of this Catholic church in staunchly Protestant Saxony was dictated by political necessity: in his struggle for the Polish crown, the Elector, Augustus the Strong, was forced to convert to Catholicism. The church was designed by an Italian architect, Gaetano Chiaveri, and built in 1738–51.

The church's interior has two-tier passageways which run from the main nave to the side naves. Rebuilt after damage in World War II, it features a magnificent Rococo pulpit by Balthasar Permoser, a painting by Anton Raphael Mengus entitled *Assumption*

in the main altar, and the vast organ – the last work of Gottfried Silbermann.

🏛 Residenzschloss

Schlossplatz. **Temporary exhibitions** 🕐 10am–6pm Tue–Sun. **Hausmannsturm** 🕐 Apr–Oct: 10am–6pm Tue–Sun.
This former residence of the Wettin family was built in stages from the late 15th to the 17th centuries. The most recent extensions were added in 1889 and 1901. A vast, irregular, multi-wing complex of buildings, the castle is not yet fully restored. The wings which have been completed are now used for temporary exhibitions. The Hausmannsturm, a tall tower, affords a great view of Dresden.

Façade of a wing of the Residenzschloss, with *sgraffito* decoration

♜ Fürstenzug

Augustusstr.

Langer Gang (long walk) is a long building, erected in 1586–91, which connects the castle with the Johanneum. The elegant façade facing the courtyard is decorated with *sgraffito* and has shady arcades supported by slim columns. It provided an excellent backdrop for tournaments and parades. The wall facing the street features the so-called Fürstenzug (procession of dukes) – a vast, 102 m (111 yd)-long frieze depicting the procession of many Saxon rulers. Originally created by Wilhelm Walther in 1872–6

using the *sgraffito* technique, it was replaced in 1907 by 24,000 Meißen porcelain tiles.

⛫ Verkehrsmuseum (Johanneum)

Augustusstr. 1. **(** (0351) 86 440. ◯ 10am–5pm Tue–Sun.

This late 16th-century Renaissance building, originally designed as royal stables by Paul Buchner, was refurbished in the mid-18th century and housed first a gallery of paintings, later an armoury and a porcelain collection. Since 1956 it has been a museum of transport, with old trams, locomotives and an interesting collection of vintage cars.

Fragment of the Fürstenzug, outside Langer Gang

VISITORS' CHECKLIST

Road map E4 ♙ 480,000. ✈ Dresden-Klotzsche 15 km (9 miles) from centre. 🚉 Hauptbahnhof, Wiener Platz (0351-461 37 10). 🛈 Prager Str. 10–11 (0351-49 19 20). Ⓦ www.dresden.de. 🚢 Sächsische Dampfschifffahrt, Radebeul, Hertha-Lindner-Str. 10. (0351) 86 60 90. 🚢 Flotten-parade der Sächs. Dampfschiff-fahrt (May); Elbhangfest; Stadtfest (Aug); Weihnachtsmarkt.

♟ Frauenkirche

An der Frauenkirche.

This giant church, designed by Georg Bähr and built in 1726–43, used to dominate Dresden's skyline, the bold design of its grand hall, topped by a giant dome, enchanting visitors. Burned out in 1945, its shell seemed to have survived intact, only to collapse two days later. Reconstruction work started in 1993; the crypt has been open since 1996. In front of it is a monument to Martin Luther, built in 1885 by Ernst Rietschel.

DRESDEN CITY CENTRE

Albertinum ⑩
Altstädter Wache ③
Brühlsche Terrasse ⑨
Frauenkirche ⑧
Fürstenzug ⑥
Goldener Reiter ⑮
Hofkirche ④
Japanisches Palais ⑯
Johanneum ⑦
Kreuzkirche ⑫
Museum f. Sächs. Volkskunst ⑭
Neues Rathaus ⑬
Residenzschloss ⑤
Sächsische Staatsoper ②
Stadtmuseum Dresden ⑪
Zwinger ①

0 m   100
0 yards   100

KEY

🛈 Tourist information
⊠ Post office
Ⓟ Parking
🛉 Church

🏛 Brühlsche Terrasse
Brühlsche Terrasse.

Once part of the town's fortifications, this attractive terrace
subsequently lost its military
importance and was trans-
formed into magnificent gardens by Heinrich von Brühl
after whom it is named.
Offering splendid views over
the River Elbe, it is known
as "the balcony of Europe".
There are several great buildings on the terraces – the first
one, seen from Schlossplatz, is
the Neo-Renaissance **Landtag**
(parliament building); next to
it is a small Neo-Baroque building, the **Secundogenitur**
library built for the second
generation of Brühls, now a
popular café; this is followed
by the **Kunstakademie** (art
academy), known as Zitronen-
presse (lemon squeezer)
because of its ribbed glass
dome. Among the statues and
monuments on the terrace are
works by the sculptor Ernst
Rietschel, the architect Gottfried Semper and the painter
Caspar David Friedrich.

🏛 Albertinum
Brühlsche Terrasse. 📞 (0351) 491 45
90. Grünes Gewölbe, Gemäldegalerie
Neue Meister, Skulpturensammlung.
🕐 10am–6pm Fri–Wed.

The Neo-Renaissance Albertinum houses several magnificent collections, the most famous of which is the **Grünes
Gewölbe** (green vaults), a
vast collection of royal jewels,
precious gems, intricately
wrought brooches, large table
decoration sets, hundreds of
vessels made of gold, silver,
amber, mother-of-pearl and
precious stones, and valuable
ivory and ebony figurines.
   Equally interesting are the
collections of the **Gemäldegalerie Neue Meister**, with
paintings from the 19th and

Two Women on Tahiti, Paul Gauguin, 1892, in the Albertinum

20th centuries, including magnificent landscapes by Caspar
David Friedrich, canvases by
the Nazarine group of painters and works by European
masters such as Edgar Degas,
Paul Gauguin, Vincent van
Gogh, Édouard Manet and
Claude Monet. The **Skulpturensammlung** is a small
collection of sculptures,
including remarkable
works by Balthasar
Permoser.

🛐 Kreuzkirche
An der Kreuzkirche.
📞 (0351) 439 39 20.
🕐 Summer: 10am–6pm
Mon–Fri; winter: 10am–4pm
Mon–Fri. **Tower** 10am–5pm
Mon–Sat.

The present
Baroque/Neo-
Classical church
was built in
1764–92 on the site
of a 15th-century
Gothic church, to a design by
Johann Georg Schmidt. To
commemorate the shelling in
World War II, the interior has
not been fully restored. The
Cross of Nails from the ruins
of Coventry Cathedral in
England creates a
powerful symbolic
link between the
two countries.

🏛 Stadtmuseum Dresden (Landhaus)
Wilsdruffer Str. 2.
📞 (0351) 498 660.
🕐 10am–6pm Sat–Thu.

This building was
erected in 1770–76,

*A figurine in the
Grünes Gewölbe*

with a Neo-Classical exterior,
while its interior was
designed and laid out in a
Baroque style. Today it is the
home of the interesting
museum of municipal history,
with exhibits up to the
time of Germany's
reunification.

🏛 Neues Rathaus
Dr.-Külz-Ring.

The giant Neo-Renais-
sance new town hall, in
the southwest of the old
town, was erected in
1905–1910. Its round
tower (70 m/230 ft),
crowned with a gilded
statue of Hercules, offers
the best view of the old
city centre. In the foyer
is a large model of the
city as planned for 2015.

🏛 Museum für Sächsische Volks-kunst (Jägerhof)
Köpckestr. 1. 📞 (0351) 491 46 19.
🕐 10am–6pm Tue–Sun.

This Renaissance hunting
lodge on the north bank of
the Elbe was built between
1568 and 1613. Its west wing
– the only part that escaped
destruction – now houses a
museum of ethnography with
collections of Saxon culture
and traditions, especially from
the Erzgebirge Mountains.

🏛 Goldener Reiter
Neustädter Markt.

The **Neustadt** (new town),
on the right bank of the Elbe,
lost much of its former glory
through destruction in World
War II. Visitors may therefore

Secundogenitur library on Brühlsche Terrasse

be surprised to come across this glistening, gilded equestrian statue of Augustus the Strong in the middle of a square, at the end of the plane tree-lined Hauptstraße. The monument, which is the work of Jean Joseph Vinache, was erected in 1736.

🏛 Japanisches Palais
Palaisplatz. 📞 *(0351) 81 44 50.*
Museum für Völkerkunde
(Museum of Ethnography) ⏰ *10am–6pm Tue–Sun.* **Landesmuseum für Vorgeschichte** (State Museum of Prehistory) ⏰ *10am–8pm daily.*
Originally the Dutch Palais, this three-wing structure was built in 1715. It was extended in 1729–31, by Zacharias Longuelune, for Augustus the Strong's Japanese porcelain collection, at which time the palace changed its name. The porcelain was never actually housed here, however, and for years the palace served as a library. Today it holds two museums. The museum of ethnography is especially good.

🏛 Pfunds Molkerei
Bautzner Str. 79. 📞 *(0351) 808 08 22.* ⏰ *9am–8pm Mon–Fri, 10am–4pm Sat–Sun.*
In the 19th-century part of the Neustadt, with its many bars, galleries, pubs and fringe theatres, stands this old dairy founded by Paul Pfund. Its interior is lined with dazzling, multi-coloured tiles, showing Neo-Renaissance motifs relating to the dairy's products. Today there is a shop which offers hundreds of dairy products, as well as a small bar, where visitors can sample the specialities.

🏛 Kraszewski-Museum
Nordstr. 28. 📞 *(0351) 804 44 50.*
🚫 *Due to renovation.*
This small museum is devoted to the life of the Polish writer

The Baroque Schloss Pillnitz, Augustus the Strong's summer residence

Józef Ignacy Kraszewski who, having escaped arrest in Warsaw, settled in Dresden in 1853. Inspired by the town's history, several of his novels (for example *Hrabina Cosel*, *Brühl*) are set during the time of Augustus the Strong.

🌿 Großer Garten
City centre.
The history of this great garden goes back to the 17th century, although it has been redesigned several times since. At the park's centre stands an early Baroque palace built in 1678–83 to a design by Johann Georg Starcke. A miniature railway takes visitors to Carolasee, a boating lake. It also stops at the botanical gardens in the northwest section of the park, and at the zoo. The Mosaikbrunnen (mosaic fountain) nearby was designed by Hans Poelzig and built in 1926.

🏛 Blaues Wunder
Loschwitz/Blasewitzer Brücke.
The suspension bridge which spans the River Elbe in the eastern part of the town is painted blue and nicknamed "blue wonder". Built in 1891–3, its main span is 141.5 m (464 ft) long. The bridge leads to Loschwitz, a neighbourhood in a picturesque location amidst hills, which has many attractive villas and small palaces built in the 19th century.

🏛 Schloss Pillnitz
📞 *(0351) 261 30.* **Kunstgewerbemuseum Bergpalais** ⏰ *May–Oct: 10am–5:30pm Tue–Sun.* **Wasserpalais** ⏰ *May–Oct: 10am–5:30pm Wed–Mon.*
This charming summer residence, on the banks of the Elbe, was built in 1720–23 by Augustus the Strong and designed by Matthäus Daniel Pöppelmann. There are two parallel palaces: the Bergpalais (mountain palace) and the Wasserpalais (water palace); the latter can be reached by stairs directly from the river jetty. Between 1818 and 1826 the two palaces were joined by a third one, the Neues Palais. Today the Bergpalais houses a fascinating crafts museum. The main attraction, however, is the large park, laid out in English and Chinese styles, with an orangery and pavilions.

🏛 Karl-May-Museum
Radebeul. Karl-May-Str. 5. 📞 *(0351) 837 30 10.* ⏰ *Mar–Oct: 9am–6pm; Nov–Feb: 10am–4pm Tue–Sun.*
Radebeul, 5 km (3 miles) northwest of Dresden, is much visited by the fans of Winnteou, a fictional Indian chief, and his friend Old Shatterhand. A museum is devoted to the life and work of the author, Karl May, who lived and died in Radebeul. It also has a large collection of Native American costumes and items purchased by May.

The suspension bridge across the Elbe River, nicknamed "Blaues Wunder"

The Zwinger

THE MOST FAMOUS building in Dresden is the Zwinger, a beautiful Baroque structure. Its name means 'intermural', and it was built in the space between the former town fortifications. Commissioned by Augustus the Strong, it was constructed in 1709–32 to a design by Matthäus Daniel Pöppelmann, with the help of the sculptor Balthasar Permoser. Its spacious courtyard, once used to stage tournaments, festivals and firework displays, is completely surrounded by galleries into which are set pavilions and gates. Today it houses several museums.

Mathematisch-Physikalischer Salon
A valuable collection of scientific instruments from different ages, this also features clocks, sextants and globes, including a priceless 13th-century Arabic globe of the sky.

Kronentor
This gate owes its name (crown gate) to the crown positioned on top of its dome.

Main entrance

Allegorical figures
crown the balustrades.

★ Porzellansammlung
The porcelain collection holds Japanese and Chinese pieces but its centrepiece is a collection of Meißen porcelain, including parts of the stunning Swan Service made for Heinrich Brühl, to a design by Joachim Kaendler.

Glockenspielpavillon
Once known as Stadtpavilon (town pavilion), the name of this building was changed to carillon pavilion when it acquired a carillon with Meißen porcelain bells, in 1924–36 .

Wallpavillon
A stunning marriage of architecture and sculpture, this Baroque masterpiece is crowned by a statue of Hercules, symbolizing the Elector, Augustus the Strong.

VISITORS' CHECKLIST

Sophienstraße/Ostra-Allee/Theaterplatz. **Porzellansammlung** (0351) 491 46 22. ☐ 10am–6pm Fri–Wed. **Mathematisch-Physikalischer Salon** 491 46 22. ☐ 10am–6pm Fri–Wed. **Rüstkammer** 491 46 22. ☐ 10am–6pm Tue–Sun.

★ **Nymphenbad**
This fountain features tritons and nymphs, sculptures, and grottoes, which were popular in the Baroque era.

Courtyard

Gemäldegalerie Alte Meister
This gallery of old masters occupies the wing which was added by Gottfried Semper (see pp166–7).

★ **Rüstkammer**
Exhibited in the armoury are magnificent arms, with the best examples dating from the 16th century, including a suit of armour made for Erik XIV by Eliseus Libaerts in 1562–4.

STAR FEATURES

★ **Nymphenbad**

★ **Porzellansammlung**

★ **Rüstkammer**

Gemäldegalerie Alte Meister

THE DRESDEN gallery of old masters contains what is considered to be one of Europe's finest art collections. Its core consists of the canvases collected by the Wettin family from the 16th century, but the majority of exhibits were purchased at the order of King Augustus II the Strong and his son Augustus III. It was during that time that the gallery was moved to its own premises – first to the Johanneum and later to its present home in the Zwinger, built by Gottfried Semper in 1847–54.

2nd floor

1st floor

Feast of Love (c.1717)
The so-called fête galante *is one of many splendid paintings by Antoine Watteau, depicting a flirtatious group in a park.*

Madonna and Infant Triptych (1437)
This superb small triptych depicting the Virgin Mary with the Holy Infant, St Catherine and the Archangel St Michael, is one of very few works signed by its creator, Jan van Eyck.

Ground floor

Girl Reading a Letter
(c.1659) *This exquisite painting, of a lone woman by the window reading a letter, is among the finest works by Jan Vermeer van Delft.*

Main entrance

★ **Self-Portrait with Saskia**
(c.1635) *This magnificent painting depicting Rembrandt with his wife, Saskia, is considered by some to be a representation of the Prodigal Son of the Bible.*

GALLERY GUIDE
The ground floor has works by Canaletto; the 1st floor has German paintings and 15th to 18th-century European works, and the 2nd floor has 18th-century and Spanish pastels, paintings and miniatures.

Portrait of a Man (c.1635)
This highly expressive portrait, by Diego Rodríguez de Silva y Velázquez, remained unfinished, yet it still captivates with its powerful imagery.

VISITORS' CHECKLIST

Theaterplatz 1. ☎ *(0351) 491 46 22.* ◻ *10am–6pm Tue–Sun.*

Tribute Money (c.1516)
Titian depicts the theme of this popular New Testament parable in an unusual way, zooming in on the figures of Christ and a Pharisee who shows Him a coin.

Dresden landscapes and portraits

Miniatures

Sleeping Venus (c.1508–10)
This famous nude was probably painted by Giorgione, but recently experts have come to believe that it was the work of his pupil – Titian.

KEY

- ◻ 15th–17th c. Italian painting
- ◻ 15th–16th c. German painting
- ◻ Canaletto and scenes of Dresden
- ◻ 17th-century Dutch and Flemish painting
- ◻ 17th-century French painting
- ◻ Spanish painting
- ◻ 18th-century Italian and French painting
- ◻ German, Czech, Austrian, English and Swiss painting
- ◻ Non-exhibition space

Tapestry room

Underground vaults

★ **Sistine Madonna** (c.1513)
This enchanting picture of the Madonna and Child by Raphael owes its name to St Sixtus's church in Piacenza, for which Pope Julius II had commissioned it.

STAR EXHIBITS

★ **Self-Portrait with Saskia**

★ **Sistine Madonna**

**Market square with Renaissance
Rathaus (town hall) in Pirna**

Pirna ⑫

Road map F4. 🏘 *38,000.* 🚉 🚌
ℹ️ *Am Markt 7 (03501-465 70).*
🌐 *www.touristservice-pirna.de.*
📅 *Stadtfest (Jun).*

IN THE old town, on the banks of the River Elbe, Pirna has preserved an amazingly regular, chequerboard pattern of streets. Time has been kind to the many historic buildings in this town. Its greatest attraction is the **Marienkirche**, a late-Gothic hall-church with fanciful vaulting designed by Peter Ulrich von Pirna and painted by Jobst Dorndorff, in 1545–6. Inside, an original late-Gothic font and a Renaissance main altar can be seen.

Other interesting buildings are the mid-16th century **Rathaus** (town hall) with its Gothic portals, the beautiful houses in the town square and the ex-Dominican, Gothic church of St Heinrich. **Schloss Sonnenstein**, extended during the 17th and 18th centuries, towers above the old town.

ENVIRONS: 10 km (6 miles) southwest of Pirna is the picturesque **Schloss Weesenstein**, much altered from its Gothic origins until the 19th century. It houses a small museum with an interesting collection of wallpapers.

**♟ Museum Schloss
Weesenstein**
Müglitztal, Am Schlossberg 1.
📞 *(035027) 54 26.* 🕐 *Apr–Sep:
9am–6pm; Oct–Mar: 9am–5pm.*

Sächsische Schweiz ⑬

SAXON SWITZERLAND, the wonderfully wild region around the gorge cut into the Lusatian mountains by the River Elbe, features stunningly bizarre rock formations and several formidable castles. The best way to explore the area is on foot as many places are inaccessible to cars. Alternatively you can admire the spectacular scenery from a boat, on the Elbe.

Großsedlitz ①
This vast Baroque park, established after 1719 to a design by Johann Christoph Knöffel, continues to delight visitors to this day with its flower beds and numerous sculptures.

Stolpen ⑦
The 35-year old Countess Cosel, one of Augustus II the Strong's mistresses, was imprisoned in this castle, built on rock.

Bastei ⑥
The "bastion" comprises so-called inselbergs – bizarre, tall rock formations that rise abruptly. Connected by footbridges, they offer splendid views.

Weissig

Hellerau   *Pirna*   *Elbe*

Teplice

6

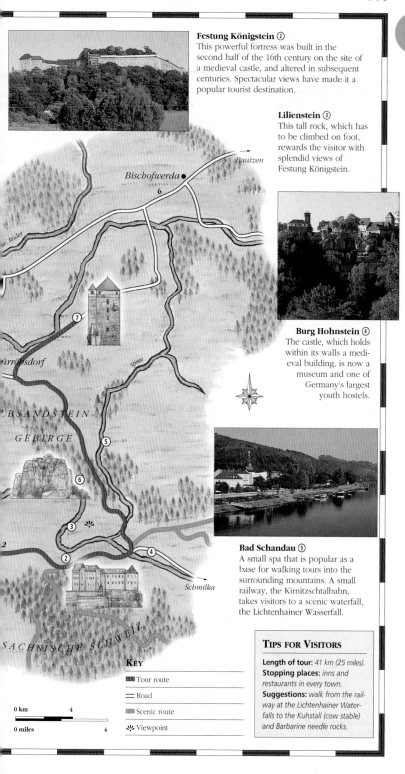

Festung Königstein ②
This powerful fortress was built in the second half of the 16th century on the site of a medieval castle, and altered in subsequent centuries. Spectacular views have made it a popular tourist destination.

Lilienstein ③
This tall rock, which has to be climbed on foot, rewards the visitor with splendid views of Festung Königstein.

Burg Hohnstein ④
The castle, which holds within its walls a medieval building, is now a museum and one of Germany's largest youth hostels.

Bad Schandau ⑤
A small spa that is popular as a base for walking tours into the surrounding mountains. A small railway, the Kirnitzschtalbahn, takes visitors to a scenic waterfall, the Lichtenhainer Wasserfall.

Bautzen

Bischofwerda

or Röder

Spree

irröbsdorf

Spree

BSANDSTEIN-

GEBIRGE

Schmilka

SÄCHSISCHE SCHWEIZ

KEY

▬ Tour route
═ Road
▬ Scenic route
❊ Viewpoint

0 km   4

0 miles   4

TIPS FOR VISITORS

Length of tour: *41 km (25 miles).*
Stopping places: *inns and restaurants in every town.*
Suggestions: *walk from the railway at the Lichtenhainer Waterfalls to the Kuhstall (cow stable) and Barbarine needle rocks.*

Gothic altar from 1513 in St Annen church, in Kamenz

Kamenz ⑭

Road map F4. 🏘 16,800. 🚊 🚌
🛈 *Kirchstr. 1 (03578-30 43 00).*
🎭 *Hutbergfest (May).*

T HE BEST TIME for a visit to
Kamenz is the end of May
or June, when the rhododen-
drons that cover the Hutberg
(294 m/965 ft high) are in
flower. The poet, Gotthold
Ephraim Lessing, was born in
Kamenz in 1729. Although his
house no longer exists, the
Lessingmuseum, founded in
1929, is devoted to his work.

A great fire destroyed much
of the town in 1842, but it
spared the late-Gothic **St
Marien** church, a four-nave
15th century structure with
Gothic altars and other interesting features. Equally noteworthy for their furnishings
are the Gothic ex-Franciscan
St Annen church and
the unusual hall-church
Katechismuskirche.
Originally part of the
town's fortification
system, it has a row of
loopholes on its upper
storey. The old ceme-
tery and the Gothic
funereal church **Begräb-
niskirche St Just** are
also worth a visit. The
latter has a large num-
ber of beautiful 14th-
century wall paintings.

🏛 **Lessingmuseum**
Pulsnitzer Str. 11. 📞 *(03578)
700 01 11.* 🕐 *9am–4pm
Tue–Fri.*

Bautzen ⑮

Road map F4. 🏘 44,000. 🚊 🚌
🛈 *Hauptmarkt 1 (03591-4 20 16).*
🎭 *Vogelhochzeit (Jan;
Internationales Folklorefestival (Jun).*

T HIS TOWN is scenically situated on a high rock over-
hanging the Spree River valley.
Known mainly for its top-secu-
rity jail for political prisoners
during the GDR era, today it
enchants visitors with its
beautifully reconstructed old
town. Many signs are bilingual,
German and Sorbian, reflecting
the fact that Bautzen is the cultural capital of the Sorbs. The
winding streets with their original houses, the city walls, the
curiously crooked **Lauerturm**
tower and the Baroque town
hall in the town square form
a very attractive complex. It
is also worth climbing the

Baroque entrance gate to the Schloss
Ortenburg complex in Bautzen

15th-century **Alte Wasser-
kunst**, a tower that pumped
Spree water up to the town. It
is the symbol of Bautzen and
offers splendid views.

The cathedral **Dom St Peter**
is now used jointly by Catholics (choir) and Protestants
(nave). The late-Gothic
Schloss Ortenburg, built for
the Hungarian king Matthias
Corvinus, houses the **Sorbisches Museum**, devoted to
Sorbian history and culture.

🏛 **Sorbisches Museum**
Ortenburg 3. 📞 *(03591) 42 403.*
🕐 *Apr–Oct: 10–noon, 1–5pm;
Nov–May: 10–12am, 1–4pm.*

Doorway of the Neo-Renaissance
palace in Bad Muskau

Bad Muskau ⑯

Road map F4. 🏘 4,170. 🚌
🛈 *Schlossstr. 3 (035771-504 92).*

B AD MUSKAU, a small town
and spa, boasts one of
Saxony's most beautiful parks,
which has been included in
the UNESCO Cultural Heritage
list. It was created in 1815–45
by the writer Prince Hermann
von Pückler-Muskau. The
Neo-Renaissance palace at its
centre was destroyed in
World War II and is currently
closed for reconstruction, but
the English-style landscaped
park surrounding it, a nature
reserve since 1952, is well
worth visiting. Its main part,
on the northern shores of the
Lusatian Neisse River, is in
Poland. A joint Polish-German
programme, aimed at revita-
lizing the park, has opened
the entire area to visitors from
both sides of the border.

Baroque Neptune fountain in Untermarkt, in Görlitz

Görlitz ⑰

Road map F4. 🏙 66,000. 🚉 🚌
ℹ️ Obermarkt 29 (03581-475 70 & 194 33). 🎭 Oberlausitzer Orgelsommer (May–Oct); Straßentheaterfestival (Jul).

THIS BORDER town, whose eastern part, Zgorzelec, has belonged to Poland since 1945, boasts a long history. Its oldest records date back to 1071. Founded in 1210–20, the town flourished in the 15th and 16th centuries. In 1990 an extensive restoration plan was begun, and now visitors can see its historic buildings in their former glory.

The charming houses in **Obermarkt** (upper market), the Renaissance portals and decorations on houses in Brüderstraße and the fascinating **Untermarkt** (lower market), with its vast town hall complex, enchant everyone. The older wing of the town hall, the work of Wendel Roskopf, has an amazing external staircase with Renaissance ornaments, and winds around the statue of Justice.

One of the most remarkable churches is the imposing five-nave, 15th-century **Hauptstadtpfarrkirche St Peter und St Paul** whose Baroque furnishings are among the finest in Saxony. Also noteworthy is the **Oberkirche**, with an original Gothic main altar and 15th-century wall paintings in the side nave. One of Görlitz's curiosities is the **Heiliges Grab** (Holy tomb), built in 1481–1504, a group of three chapels that are replicas of churches in Jerusalem. Görlitz still has remains of its medieval town fortifications with original towers and gates, including the **Kaisertrutz**, a 15th-century barbican, extended in the 19th century and now home to the town's art collection.

ENVIRONS: The small town of **Ostritz**, 16 km (10 miles) to the south, has a charming original Cistercian abbey, St Marienthal (1230). Its red-and-white buildings are to this day inhabited by nuns, who show visitors around and serve food and home-brewed beer.

Zittau ⑱

Road map F4. 🏙 28,000. 🚉 🚌
ℹ️ Markt 1 (03583-75 21 37). 🎭 Klosterfest (Ascension); Fest am Dreiländereck (Jul).

ZITTAU is an excellent starting point for excursions into the Zittau Mountains, a paradise for rock-climbers, walkers and nature lovers. The town itself has a splendidly preserved old town, with many historic buildings, such as the beautiful, Baroque **Noacksches Haus** (Markt 2). The Neo-Renaissance **Rathaus** (town hall) was built in 1840–45, to a design by Carl Augustus Schramm. The **Johanniskirche**, designed by Karl Friedrich Schinkel, combines elements of Neo-Classical and Neo-Gothic styles and is an excellent example of Historicist architecture.

ENVIRONS: The charming spa town of **Oybrin**, 9 km (6 miles) south of Zittau, can be reached by narrow-gauge railway. Its attractions include the hilltop ruins of a Gothic abbey, immortalized by Caspar David Friedrich. It is worth timing your visit for a Saturday evening in summer, when you can witness the procession of torch-bearing monks or listen to a concert.

Fountain with a statue of Roland, the French knight, in Zittau

THE SORBS

The Sorbs, also known as the Lusatians or Wends, are an indigenous Slav minority who live in the eastern regions of Saxony and Brandenburg. Their ancestors, the Lusatian Slavs, were conquered by Germans in the 10th century. Although condemned to extermination by the National Socialists, today they enjoy complete cultural autonomy. The revival of their language and traditions is apparent in the bilingual signs in towns.

THURINGIA

THURINGIA *is a beautiful state, with much to entice the visitor. The Thuringian Forest, in the south of the state, is a highland area densely covered with spruce, beech and oak forests, inviting visitors to ramble along its enchanted trails, while Thuringia's medieval abbeys, castles and charming small towns are popular destinations with those who are interested in art and history.*

The Kingdom of Thuring, as it was known in the 5th century, was conquered by the Franks in the following century. The demise of the Thuringian landgraves, who had ruled here for hundreds of years, resulted in the outbreak of the Thuringian War of Secession. It ended in 1264, with most of Thuringia falling into the hands of the Wettin dynasty.

Split into several smaller principalities, the region lost its political might, but driven by the ambitions of many of its rulers, magnificent castles, churches and abbeys were built everywhere. Thanks to enlightened royal sponsors many towns became important cultural centres, such as 18th-century Weimar, whose residents at one time included Johann Wolfgang von Goethe, Friedrich Schiller, Johann Gottfried Herder and Christoph Martin Wieland.

After World War II, Thuringia was initially occupied by the US Army, but it soon passed into the Soviet sphere of influence, and in 1949 it became part of the GDR. In 1952 Thuringia lost its status as a federal state, but this was later restored in the reunited Federal Republic of Germany, in 1990.

The majority of tourist attractions can be found in the southern part of the state. The Thuringian Forest has many popular health resorts and wintersport centres, such as Oberhof. This highland area, cut with deep river gullies, is littered with medieval castles built on steep crags. Many of these are now no more than picturesque ruins, but others, such as the Wartburg, have been completely restored to their former glory, and today delight visitors with their magnificent interiors.

Schloss Belvedere, the royal summer residence in Weimar

◁ **The impressive waterfall in Trusetal, in the Thuringian Forest**

Exploring Thuringia

A VISIT TO Thuringia is most enjoyable in late summer, when the magnificent forests of the Thuringian Mountains are set ablaze with all the hues of red and yellow as the leaves turn colour, or in spring when verdant green cloaks the trees. Allow at least one day to explore Erfurt, the state's capital city, with a further two days in Weimar. Eisenach, with its magnificent Wartburg castle, is also a must.

Street vendor selling hand-painted Easter eggs in Erfurt

SIGHTS AT A GLANCE

Petersburg fortress in Erfurt

The fields near Meiningen, in the Thuringian Forest

GETTING AROUND

Erfurt has an airport. The A4 motorway running through Thuringia links Gera with Jena, Weimar, Erfurt, Gotha and Eisenach. Other towns can be reached by local roads, which are clearly signposted. When touring the Thuringian Forest it is well worth following one of the marked tourist routes, such Klassikerstraße (the route of the classics) or Porzellanstraße (porcelain street).

The Renaissance town hall in Gotha

KEY

▬▬	Motorway
▬▬	Major road
▬▬	Scenic route
≈	River
ᯤ	Viewpoint

Eisenach – Wartburg ❶

THE MIGHTY fortress towering above the town is the legendary castle which was probably founded by Ludwig the Jumper, in the late 11th century. Reputedly, it was the setting for the singing contest immortalized by Wagner in his opera *Tannhäuser*. Between 1211 and 1228 the castle was the home of Saint Elizabeth of Thuringia, and from 4 May 1521 until March 1522 Martin Luther found refuge here while he translated the New Testament into German. Major reconstruction in the 19th century gave the castle its old-time romantic character.

Sängersaal
The singing hall in its present form is the result of restoration work. It was allegedly the scene of the famous Minnesänger (minstrels') contest, from Wagner's opera Tannhäuser.

Landgrafenzimmer
In 1854 the landgraves' chambers in the oldest part of the castle, the Palas, were decorated with paintings depicting the castle's history, by Moritz von Schwind.

Landgrafenzimmer

★ Elisabethkemenate
The mosaics adorning the walls of St Elizabeth's rooms illustrate the story of the saint's life. They were designed by August Oetken and placed in 1902–06.

Bergfried
This vast, square tower crowned with a cross is the work of 19th-century restorers.

STAR FEATURES

★ Elisabethkemenate

★ Lutherstube

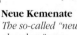

Vogtei
In 1872 this building acquired an original oriel window (c.1475), brought here from the Harsdörffersches House in Nuremberg.

VISITORS' CHECKLIST

Road map C/D4. 👥 *44,000.* 🚉
🚌 ℹ️ *Markt 2 (03691-67 02 60).*
🎭 *Thüringer Bachwochen (Mar–Apr).* **Wartburg** 📞 *(03691) 25 00; www.wartburg-eisenach.de.* ⬜
guided tours Mar–Oct: 8:30am–5pm daily (gate closes 8pm); Nov–Feb: 9am–3:30pm daily (gate closes 5pm). ♿ 🚻 👥 🍴 📷 🛒

★ Lutherstube
The room where Martin Luther lived and worked for ten months is very plainly furnished and has simple wood-panelling on the walls.

Entrance gate

Neue Kemenate
The so-called "new chambers" were added during the mid-19th century. Today they house an art collection with beautiful sculptures from Tilman Riemenschneider's workshop.

Exploring Eisenach

The town, at the foot of the castle hill, was founded in the middle of the 12th century and played an important political role in medieval times. There are interesting remains of fortifications, dating from the late 12th century, which include a Romanesque gate, the Nikolaitor. The Nikolai-kirche nearby, also Roman-esque in style, once belonged to the Benedictine Sisters. In the market square is a 16th-century town hall, and in Lutherplatz stands the house where Martin Luther once lived; it is now a small museum of his work.

🏛 Predigerkirche
Predigerplatz 2. 📞 *(03691) 78 46 78.*
⬜ *9am–5pm Tue–Sun.* 📷
This church, built in honour of Elisabeth von Thüringen shortly after she had been canonized, is part of the Thü-ringer Museum and has been used for changing exhibitions since 1899. It also houses a permanent exhibition, "Medi-eval Art in Thuringia".

🏛 Automobilbaumuseum
Rennbahn 6–8. 📞 *(03691) 78 46 78.*
⬜ *9am–5pm Tue–Sun.*
This car museum celebrates the local car manufacturing industry in Eisenach. Its collection includes old BMWs and Wartburgs.

🏛 Bachhaus
Frauenplan 21. 📞 *(03691) 7 93 40.*
⬜ *Oct–Mar: 1–4:45pm Mon, 9am–4:45pm Tue–Sun; Apr–Sep: noon–5:45pm Mon, 9am–5:45pm Tue–Sun.* 📷
Johann Sebastian Bach, the famous composer, was born in Eisenach in 1685. His birth-place is now demolished, but this small museum nearby is devoted to his life and work.

The Bachhaus and museum, surrounded by a garden

Heiligenstadt ②

Road map C4. 🏛 *17,500.* 🚉 🚌
ℹ *Wilhelmstr. 50 (03606-67 71 41).*

THIS PLEASANT spa and health
resort, well placed for visiting the landscaped gardens
of Eichsfeld, is worth an extended stop. Heiligenstadt is
the birthplace of Tilman Riemenschneider, an outstanding
sculptor of the Gothic era; it
is also the place where the
poet and writer Heinrich
Heine was baptized in 1825,
at the age of 28.

Heiligenstadt has several
churches worth visiting,
including the Gothic **Pfarrkirche St Marien** with its
original wall paintings dating
from around 1500. Not far
from the church stands the
Friedhofskapelle St Annen,
an octagonal Gothic cemetery
chapel. The town's most
interesting church, however,
is the **Stiftskirche St Martin**,
dating back to the 14th–15th
centuries. It has a well-preserved Romanesque crypt and
an amusing Gothic pulpit,
made in the shape of a bookholding chorister.

Mühlhausen ③

Road map D4. 🏛 *38,000.* 🚉 🚌
ℹ *Ratsstr. 20 (03601-45 23 21).*
🎪 *Mühlhauser Stadtkirmes (Aug/Sep).*

MÜHLHAUSEN is one of
Thuringia's older towns,
with its earliest records dating
back to AD 967. In medieval
times it enjoyed the status of
an imperial free town, which
could explain why it became
the centre of political activities during the 1525 Peasants'
War, led by Thomas Müntzer,

**Part of the well-preserved town
walls surrounding Mühlhausen**

a local clergyman. In 1975, on
the 450th anniversary of the
revolt, the town underwent
restoration, and it delights
visitors to this day with its
beautifully preserved old
town surrounded by **city
walls**, including gates and
towers, which have survived
almost intact.

Mühlhausen's winding
streets are lined with charming timber-frame houses. It is
also worth stepping into one
of the six Gothic churches in
this area. The **Pfarrkirche
Divi Blasii**, built for the
Teutonic Knights, has 14th-century stained-glass windows in the presbytery. The
ex-Franciscan **Barfüßerklosterkirche** (on the Kornmarkt) houses a museum
devoted to the Peasants' War.
The huge five-nave 14th-century **Marienkirche**, a hall-church, is one of Thuringia's
largest sacral buildings. It has
a magnificent main portal and
late-Gothic altars. Another
interesting historic structure is
the **Rathaus** (town hall), in a
narrow street between the old
and the new town. This vast
complex was enlarged several
times, from medieval times
until the 18th century.

Sondershausen ④

Road map D4. 🏛 *23,000.* 🚌
ℹ *Markt 9 (03632-78 81 11).*
🎪 *Tag des Bergmanns (Jun).*

SONDERSHAUSEN was the
capital city of the small
principality of Schwarzburg-Sondershausen. The town's
main attraction is the **Schloss**
(ducal palace), a sprawling
building, almost triangular in
shape, built in stages from the
16th to the 19th century. The
palace features some interesting original interiors. Particularly noteworthy are the
Am Wendelstein rooms,
decorated with 17th-century
stucco ornaments, as well as
the Neo-Classical Liebhabertheater (connoisseurs' theatre,
c.1835) and the Baroque
Riesensaal (giants' hall), a
ballroom with 16 enormous
statues of ancient gods. When
strolling around the palace
gardens it is worth looking at
the **Karussell**, an octagonal
building dating from 1700,
now used as a concert hall.

The most interesting Neo-Classical building complex in
town can be found around
Marktplatz (market square).

ENVIRONS: In the **Hainleite**
hills, 4.5 km (3 miles) south
of Sondershausen, stands the
Jagdschloss Zum Possen, once
an 18th-century hunting lodge,
now an inn. The timber-frame
observation tower nearby,
dating from 1781, affords
beautiful views of the district.
Nordhausen, situated 20 km
(12 miles) to the north, is
worth visiting for its attractive
timber-frame houses and its
14th-century cathedral, Dom
zum Heiligen Kreuz, with a
Romanesque crypt.

The extensive façade of the ducal palace in Sondershausen

Monument to Wilhelm I in the Kyffhäuser Mountains

Kyffhäuser Mountains ❺

Road map D4. 🚹 *Bad Franken-hausen, Anger 14 (034671-71 70).*

THIS SMALL mountain range, which runs along the border between Thuringia and Saxony-Anhalt, is not only picturesque but also shrouded in legends and associated with important historic events.

According to one legend, the Emperor Frederick I Barbarossa found his final resting place in one of the caves. Allegedly, he did not drown during the Crusades, as historic records would have us believe, but is waiting here, in the company of six knights. As soon as his beard is long enough to wind three times around the table, it is said, he will return to save Germany from oppression. On the site of the former imperial palace now stands a giant monument with a figure of Barbarossa and an equestrian statue of Emperor Wilhelm I – the work of Bruno Schmitz, erected in 1891–6.

A small health resort, **Bad Frankenhausen**, nestles at the foot of the mountains. It has a number of Gothic churches and a Renaissance palace, now home to a small museum. Nearby, on the **Schlachtberg** (slaughter mountain), the decisive battle in the Peasants' War took place. Today there is a circular pavilion with a vast panoramic picture of the battle, painted in 1971–5.

Gotha ❻

Road map D4. 🏘 *48,000.* 🚉 🚌
🚹 *Hauptmarkt 13 (03621-85 40 36).*
🎭 *Bachwochen (Mar).*

FROM 1640 THE old commercial town of Gotha was the capital of Saxe-Gotha and later of Saxe-Coburg-Gotha Duchy, the dynasty from which Prince Albert, Queen Victoria's husband, descended. The vast ducal palace, **Schloss Friedenstein**, built in 1643–55, towers above the city. This mighty rectangular structure with low square towers in the corners was the first Baroque building in Thuringia. Particularly noteworthy are the ballroom, the palace chapel with the ducal sarcophagi in the crypt and the court theatre, built in 1683. The palace museum houses an art collection including works by famous artists such as Peter Paul Rubens, Anton van Dyck, Frans Hals and Jan van Goyen. The palace gar-

den is also worth a visit. To the south of the palace stands a Neo-Renaissance building, which was purpose-built for the ducal art collection. Now it houses the **Museum der Natur**, a natural history museum. The Renaissance town hall (1567–77) in the old town is surrounded by a number of interesting houses.

Gotha played an important role in the German workers' movement: the Socialist Workers' Party (today's SPD), was founded here in 1875. The conference hall has been reconstructed and now houses the **Gedenkstätte der Deutschen Arbeiterbewegung** (memorial to the German workers' movement).

⚜ **Schloss Friedenstein**
🅲 *03621-82 340.* ⬜ *May–Oct: 10am–5pm Tue–Sun; Nov–Apr: 10am–4pm Tue–Sun.*
🏛 **Gedenkstätte der Deutschen Arbeiterbewegung**
Am Tivoli 3. 🅲 *(03621) 70 41 27.*
⬜ *only by prior arrangement.*

Doorway of the Renaissance town hall on the Hauptmarkt, in Gotha

Thüringer Wald (Thuringian Forest) **⑦**

NARROW, WINDING roads lead through the mountains, which are densely covered with spruce forests. Small towns, charming spas and wintersports resorts nestle in the valleys, while the ruins of once fearsome castles occupy the hilltops. This is prime walking country, and Gotha is the best starting point for a walking holiday. For a longer hike, stop in Ilmenau, and from there follow the upward trail marked G, to a hunters' shelter and a foresters' lodge.

Friedrichroda ①
The Neo-Gothic Reinhardsbrunn castle in Friedrichroda was the place where Queen Victoria met her fiancé, Prince Albert von Sachsen-Coburg-Gotha, in 1840.

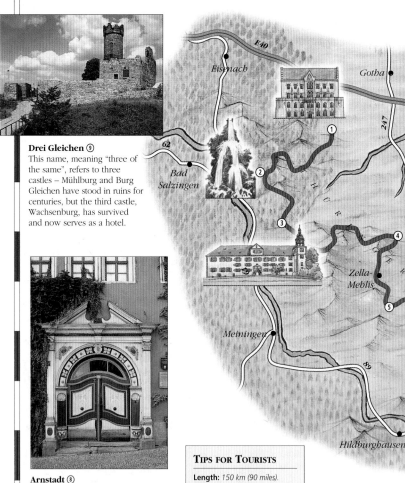

Drei Gleichen ⑨
This name, meaning "three of the same", refers to three castles – Mühlburg and Burg Gleichen have stood in ruins for centuries, but the third castle, Wachsenburg, has survived and now serves as a hotel.

Arnstadt ⑧
This picturesque town, once the home of Johann Sebastian Bach, features a town hall in the Mannerist style, dating from the late 16th century. Other places of interest are an early-Gothic church and a Baroque palace which is now home to a wax museum.

TIPS FOR TOURISTS

Length: 150 km (90 miles).
Stopping places: inns and restaurants in every town.
Suggestions: walk along the Goethe-Wanderweg trail, from Ilmenau. Train journey by Waftbahn, from Gotha via Friedrichroda to Tabarz.

Schmalkalden ③

This charming little town, packed with timber-frame houses, attracts visitors to the Wilhelmsburg, its Renaissance palace, and to Neue Hütte, an interesting old smelting plant dating from 1835.

Trusetal ②

The magnificent waterfall in Trusetal, the work of human hands, was built in the mid-19th century. Another site worth visiting is the Marienglashöhle, an unusual crystal grotto.

0 km   75

0 miles   75

Erfurt   Weimar

E40

8

85

7

6

Rudolstadt

Bad Blankenburg

281

Eisfeld

Oberhof ④

This is a popular winter-sports resort, with excellent ski-jumps. In the summer it is worth visiting the Rennsteiggarten, the town's botanical gardens with a vast collection of alpine plants.

Suhl ⑤

Famous from the 16th century as a centre of arms manufacture, Suhl's history can today be gleaned in the local Waffenmuseum (armaments museum).

Ilmenau ⑥

This small university town, teeming with life, is the starting point of the so-called Goethe-Wanderweg, a walking trail leading to all the places where the famous poet once stayed.

Paulinzelle ⑦

The 12th-century Romanesque abbey, now in ruins, was once a home for Benedictine monks, but it was later abandoned during the Reformation.

KEY

 Suggested route

══ Other road

▬▬ Scenic route

❖ Viewpoint

Erfurt ❽

THE THURINGIAN capital, Erfurt, is also the oldest town in the region – its earliest historic records date from AD729, and in AD742 a bishopric was founded here. As an important trading post between east and west, the town grew quickly. Erfurt University was founded in 1392; it became a stronghold for radical thought, and Martin Luther was one of its distinguished pupils. Until the 17th century, Erfurt was famous for its red dyes extracted from the madder root; in the 18th century the town became a horticultural centre, and to this day it hosts important horticultural exhibitions.

Picturesque half-timbered houses, lining the Krämerbrücke

Exploring Erfurt
The town, on the banks of the river Gera, is dominated by two hills. On the higher one, **Petersberg**, stands a huge fortress surrounding a Romanesque church, while the lower **Domberg** has two churches, the **Dom St Marien** and the **St Severi-kirche**. From the Domplatz, at the foot of the hill, a row of narrow streets leads to Fischmarkt. If you cross the river here, you will get to Erfurt's old commercial district and its market square, the Anger.

🛉 Dom St Marien
Domberg. 🕻 *(0361) 646 12 65.* ⬜ *May–Oct: 2–4pm Sun, 9–11:30am & 12:30–5pm Mon–Fri, 9–11:30am & 12:30–4:30pm Sat; Nov–Mar: 10–11:30am & 12:30–4:30pm Mon–Sat.* **Maria Gloriosa** 🕻 *Apr–Oct: 9am–4pm Mon–Sat, 1–4pm Sun.* 🈹
The wide stairs leading from Domberg to the main entrance of the cathedral provide a good view over the 14th-century Gothic presbytery, which is supported by a massive vaulted substructure, known as the Kavaten. The main body of the cathedral dates from the 15th century,

but its huge towers are the remains of an earlier Romanesque building. **Maria Gloriosa**, a huge bell 2.5 m (8 ft) in diameter, hangs in the centre tower. Cast by Gerhard Wou in 1497, it is one of the largest bells in the world. The church interior has well preserved Gothic decorations and rich furnishings. Particularly valuable are the 14th- and 15th-century stained-glass

Rich furnishings in the Gothic interior of Dom St Marien

windows, the Gothic stalls (c.1370) and Wolfram, a Romanesque bronze candelabra, (c.1160), shaped like a man.

🛉 St Severi-Kirche
Domberg. ⬜ *May–Oct: 9am–12:30pm & 1:30–5pm Mon–Fri; Nov–Apr: 10am–12:30pm & 1:30–4pm Mon–Fri.*
This five-nave Gothic hall-church, next to the cathedral, dates from the late 13th and early 14th century. Inside it has the Gothic sarcophagus of St Severus, from about 1365, a huge font of 1467 and interesting Gothic altars.

✠ Fischmarkt
This small market square, with its Neo-Gothic town hall (1870–74), is surrounded by houses dating from various periods, including the 16th-century Renaissance buildings **Zum Breiten Herd** (No. 13, To the Wide Hearth) and **Zum Roten Ochsen** (No. 7, To the Red Ox). On the streets off the market square are three Gothic churches: Michaeliskirche, opposite the ruins of the late-Gothic university buildings, the twin-nave Allerheiligenkirche (late 13th to early 14th century), and the ex-Dominican Predigerkirche.

✠ Krämerbrücke
The "merchant bridge" which spans the River Gera is one of Erfurt's most interesting structures. The present stone bridge was built around 1325. It is lined by 32 houses with shops, dating mainly from the 17th to 19th centuries, which replaced its 60 original medieval houses. On its eastern viaduct stands Ägidienkirche, a 14th-century Gothic church.

🛉 Augustinerkloster– Augustinerkirche
Augustinerstr. 10. 🕻 *(0361) 576 60 10.* 🕻 *Apr–Oct: 10am–noon & 2–4pm Tue–Sat.* 🈹
This early Gothic church was built for Augustinian monks at the end of the 13th century. Particularly noteworthy are its original Gothic stained-glass windows. In the neighbouring monastery, the reconstructed cell where Martin Luther lived as a monk can be admired.

Fischmarkt, surrounded by houses from various periods

VISITORS' CHECKLIST

Road map D4. 🏘 200,000.
✈ Flughafenstraße 4
(0361-65 60). 🚃 Am
Bahnhofsplatz.
🚌 Bürgermeister-Wagner-
Straße. 🛈 Benediktsplatz
1 (0361-66400);
🆆 www.erfurt.de
🎭 Krämerbrückenfest (June),
Petersbergfest (September).

🏛 Stadtmuseum
Johannesstr. 169. 🕻 (0361) 562 48
88. 🕐 10am–6pm Tue–Sun.
Erfurt's history museum is
housed in a beautiful, late-
Renaissance building called
Zum Stockfisch (To the
Dried Cod), built in 1607.

🏚 Anger
Now pedestrianized, this is a
market square and Erfurt's
main shopping street, lined
with attractive 19th-century
mansions and commercial
premises. There are two
Gothic churches: **Kaufmanns-
kirche** and **Reglerkirche**,
with a huge Gothic altar
dating from around 1470. At
Nos. 37 and 38 there is the
Dacherödensches Haus, a
complex of beautiful Renaissance buildings.

🏛 Angermuseum
Anger 18. 🕻 (0361) 562 33 11. 🕐
10am–6pm Tue–Sun. **Barfüßerkirche**
Barfüßerstr. 20 🕻 (0361) 562 33 11.
🕐 Apr–Oct: 10am–1pm & 2–6pm
Tue–Sun. 🚫
The museum, housed in a
Baroque building, has a
collection of decorative and
sacred arts including paintings
by Lucas Cranach the Elder,
and 19th- and 20th-century
German works. One of its
rooms is decorated with
Expressionist murals (1923–4)
by Erich Heckel. The
medieval section is in the
presbytery of the **Barfüßerkirche**, a former Franciscan
church that was destroyed
during World War II.

🏛 EGA and Gartenbaumuseum
Cyriaksburg, Gothaer Str. 38.
🕻 (0361) 223 22 10. 🕐 9am–6pm
daily. **Museum** 🕻 (0361) 22 39 90.
🕐 10am–6pm Tue–Sun. 🚫
On the hill around Erfurt's
ruined castle (c.1480) are the
grounds of the International
Garden Show (Erfurter
Gartenausstellung International). As well as exhibition
halls, show gardens and palm
houses, there is a museum of
horticulture and apiculture
(breeding and care of bees).

ENVIRONS: Molsdorf, 10 km
(6 miles) to the southeast, has
a lovely 16th-century Baroque
palace set in landscaped
parkland, with a museum.

ERFURT CITY CENTRE

Anger ⑦
Angermuseum ⑧
Augustinerkirche ⑤
Dom St. Marien ①
Fischmarkt ③
Krämerbrücke ④
St Severi-Kirche ②
Stadtmuseum ⑥

0 m   300
0 yards   300

KEY

🛈 Tourist information
🛉 Church
⊠ Post office

Weimar **9**

HAD IT NOT BEEN for the enlightened sponsorship of its rulers, Weimar would have become just another residential town in Thuringia. The town flourished, particularly under Duke Carl Augustus and his wife Anna Amalia, when Goethe, Schiller and Herder lived here. Famous 19th- and 20th-century residents included Franz Liszt, Richard Strauss, Friedrich Nietzsche and many distinguished writers and artists associated with the Bauhaus School, which was founded here in 1919. It also gave its name to the Weimar Republic, the democratic German State, lasting from World War I to 1933.

Exploring Weimar

Weimar is relatively small and most of its tourist attractions are near the town centre, on the left bank of the Ilm River. In the north of the centre are the Neues Museum and the Stadtmuseum (municipal museum). Many interesting buildings can be found around Theaterplatz, from where you proceed towards the Markt to visit the ducal palace. In the south of the centre are the former homes of Goethe and Liszt.

🏛 Neues Museum
Rathenauplatz. **(** *(03643) 54 61 63.*
🕐 *Apr–Oct: 10am–6pm Tue–Sun; Nov–Mar: 10am–4:30pm Tue–Sun.*
This Neo-Renaissance building, once the Landesmuseum (regional museum), was transformed into a gallery in 1999. It displays modern art, with its central collection made up of works by Paul Maenz.

🏛 Stadtmuseum
Karl-Liebknecht-Str. 5–9. **(** *(03643) 90 38 68.* 🕐 *Apr–Oct: 10am–6pm Tue–Sun; Nov–Mar: 10am–5pm Tue–Sun.*
This museum is devoted to the history of Weimar, but it also holds an interesting natural history collection. It is housed in a Neo-Classical house, built in the late 18th century for the publisher Justin Bertuch.

St Peter und St Paul, also known as the Herderkirche

🎭 Deutsches Nationaltheater
Theaterplatz 2. **(** *(03643) 75 53 01.*
The present Neo-Classical building, built in 1906–7 to a design by Heilmann & Littmann, is the third theatre to stand on this site. Famous conductors who worked here include Franz Liszt and Richard Strauss, and it was also the venue for the world premiere of Wagner's *Lohengrin*. In 1919 the National Congress sat in the Nationaltheater and passed the new constitution for the Weimar Republic. In front of the theatre is a monument to Goethe (who founded the theatre) and Schiller, by the sculptor Ernst Rietschel (1857).

🏛 Bauhaus-Museum
Theaterplatz. **(** *(03643) 54 67 30.*
🕐 *Apr–Oct: 10am–6pm Tue–Sun; Nov–Mar: 10am–4:30pm Tue–Sun.*
This museum is devoted to the famous art school, which was founded in Weimar in 1919, moved to Dessau in 1925 *(see p144)* and later, in 1933, to Berlin *(see p84)*.

🏛 Wittumspalais und Wieland-Museum
Theaterplatz. **(** *(03643) 54 51 02.*
🕐 *Mar–Oct: 9am–5pm Tue–Sun; Nov–Feb: 10am–4pm.*
The Dowager Duchess Anna Amalia lived in this Baroque palace, designed by Johann Gottfried Schlegel and built in 1767–9. Visitors can admire fine interiors and mementos of the Enlightenment figure Christoph-Martin Wieland.

🏛 Schillerhaus
Schillerstr. 12. **(** *(03643) 54 51 02.*
🕐 *Apr–Sep: 9am–6pm Wed–Mon; Oct–Mar: 9am–4pm Wed–Mon.*
The museum is in the house where Friedrich Schiller wrote *Wilhelm Tell* (1804) and spent the last years of his life.

🛐 St Peter und St Paul
Herderplatz. **(** *(03643) 85 15 18.*
🕐 *Easter–9 Nov: 10am–noon & 2–4pm Mon–Sat, 11am–noon & 2–3pm Sun; 10 Nov–Easter: 11am–noon & 2–3pm Mon–Sat, 2–3pm Sun.*
This late-Gothic hall-church has Baroque furnishings and an original altar painted by the Cranachs. It is also known as the Herderkirche, after the poet who preached here and was buried inside in 1803.

🏛 Krims-Krackow-Haus
Jakobstr. 10. **(** *(03643) 54 51 02.*
🕐 *as Wittumspalais above.*
This Renaissance house, which was extended in the late 18th century, is now the Herder-Museum and a literary centre.

♣ Schloss
Burgplatz 4. **Schlossmuseum**
(*(03643) 54 61 30.* 🕐 *as Bauhaus-Museum above.*
This vast ducal castle was rebuilt in the Neo-Classical style for Duke Carl Augustus. It has original interiors and fine paintings by the Cranachs and Peter Paul Rubens.

The Schloss in Burgplatz, with its tall Renaissance tower

Picturesque Baroque summer residence known as Schloss Belvedere

♣ Herzogin-Anna-Amalia Bibliothek

Platz der Demokratie 1. 【 (03643)
54 52 00. ◯ Apr–Oct: 11am–12:30pm
Mon–Sat.

This former Mannerist palace,
also known as Grünes Schloss
(green castle), was converted
into the duchess' library, in
1761–6. Its oval Rococo
interior is one of the finest of
its type in Europe.

♣ Schloss Belvedere

【 (03643) 54 61 30. ◯ as
Bauhaus-Museum opposite. 🏷
This ducal summer residence,
built 1724–32 in the attractive
Belvedere Park, has a fine
collection of decorative art
from the Rococo period, and a
collection of vintage vehicles.

🏛 Goethe-Museum

Frauenplan 1. 【 (03643) 54 53 20.
◯ as Wittumspalais opposite. 🏷
This house was presented to
Goethe by the Duke Carl
Augustus. It was here that the
writer studied and wrote his
most famous work, *Faust*.
Today the museum shows
items associated with Goethe
and other Enlightenment
poets from Weimar.

♣ Goethes Gartenhaus

Park an der Ilm. ◯ as Wittumspalais
opposite. 🏷
Goethe's first home in Weimar, and later his summer
house, this small villa stands
in the pleasant park alongside
the River Ilm which Goethe
helped design.

🚇 Liszt-Haus

Marienstr. 17. 【 (03643) 54 51 02.
◯ Apr–Sep: 9am–1pm & 2–6pm
Tue–Sun; Oct–Mar: 10am–1pm &
2–4pm Tue–Sun. 🏷
Franz Liszt lived here in
1869–86, while he composed
the *Hungarian Rhapsody*. His
apartment and the room in
which he worked have been
preserved to this day.

ENVIRONS: Buchenwald,
8 km (5 miles) north of
Weimar, was the site of a
concentration camp set up by
the Nazis. In 1937–45, over
54,000 people were killed
here. It is now a place of
remembrance, a museum and
a documentation centre.

🏛 Buchenwald

【 (03643) 43 02 00. ◯ May–Sep:
9:45am–6pm Tue–Sun; Oct–Apr:
8:45am–5pm Tue–Sun.

WEIMAR CITY CENTRE

Bauhaus-Museum ③
Deutsches
    Nationaltheater ②
Goethe-Museum ⑩
Grünes Schloss ⑨
Krims-Krackow-Haus ⑦
St Peter und St Paul ⑥
Schillerhaus ⑤
Schloss ⑧
Stadtmuseum ①
Wittumspalais und Wieland
    Museum ④

KEY

🚶 Tourist information

✝ Church

⊠ Post office

The modest Gothic town hall on
Marktplatz, in Jena

Jena ⑩

Road map D4. 🏠 100,000. 🚌 🚆
ℹ️ Johannisstr. 23 (03641-80 64 00).
🌐 www.jena.de.

JENA is famous for the world-
renowned Carl-Zeiss-Jena
Optical Works and its university, founded in 1558. One of
the most important schools in
Germany, its former tutors
included Schiller, Fichte and
Hegel. The oldest university
building is the **Collegium
Jenense**. The main building
was built by Theodor Fischer
in 1905–8. The complex
includes a 120-m (394-ft)
cylindrical tower block, completed in 1972 and known as
the "phallus Jenensis".

In the town's main square,
Marktplatz, stands the late-
Gothic **Rathaus** (town hall),
dating from the early 15th
century. Once every hour, a
figure known as the Schnapp-
hans tries to catch a ball, a
symbol of the human soul.
The Gothic church of **St.
Michael** nearby was built in
the 15th and the 16th centuries. The **Stadtmusem Alte
Göhre** has an interesting
collection of regional history.
In Unterer Markt the **Romantikerhaus** is worth a visit;
formerly the home of Johann
Gottlieb Fichte, it now houses
a museum devoted to the
Romantic period.

Also worth visiting are the
fascinating **Optisches Museum** on the history of the
Carl Zeiss Works and the
Zeiss-Planetarium, the
world's oldest of its type. In
the north is the **Goethe-
Gedenkstätte**, a museum
devoted to Goethe's work as
poet, politician and scientist.

🏛 **Stadtmuseum Göhre**
Markt 7. 📞 (3641) 359 80.
🕐 10am–5pm Tue & Thu–Sun,
10am–6pm Wed.
🏛 **Romantikerhaus**
Unterer Markt 12A. 📞 (03641) 44 32
63. 🕐 10am–1pm & 2–5pm Tue–Sun.
🏛 **Optisches Museum**
Carl-Zeiss-Platz 12. 📞 (03641) 44 31
65. 🕐 10am–5pm Tue–Fri, 10am–
4:30pm Sat, 9:30am–1pm Sun.
Historical Zeiss-Workshop 🕐
10am Sun.

ENVIRONS: Dornburg, 12 km
(8 miles) to the northeast, has
three palaces: the Altes
Schloss, a Gothic castle transformed in the Renaissance;
the Renaissanceschloss
(1539–47) and the charming
Rokokoschloss (1736–41).

Rudolstadt ⑪

Road map D4. 🏠 28,000. 🚌 🚆
ℹ️ Marktstr. 57 (03672-42 45 43).
🎭 Tanz-und Folk Fest.

ALTHOUGH Rudolstadt has
the Gothic-Renaissance St
Andreas church, a fascinating
16th-century town hall and
some historic houses in the
old town, tourists come here
mainly to see majestic
Schloss Heidecksburg, a
vast palace perched on a hill.
Its present form is mainly the
result of reconstruction work
carried out in the mid-18th
century by Johann Christoph
Knöffel and Gottfried Heinrich Krohne. Inside are some
beautifully arranged Rococo

**Baroque Schloss Heidecksburg
towering over Rudolstadt**

state rooms. The museum also
holds a splendid porcelain
collection (much of it locally
manufactured), a gallery of
paintings and the so-called
Schiller's Room. From the
castle there are fantastic views
of the Schwarza valley.

♣ **Schloss Heidecksburg**
Schlossbezirk 1. 📞 (03672) 42 90
22. 🕐 10am–5:30pm Tue–Sun.

**Entrance gate to the 11th-century
Schloss Ranis, near Saalfeld**

Saalfeld ⑫

Road map D4. 🏠 34,000. 🚌 🚆
ℹ️ Am Markt 6 (03671-339 50).

SAALFELD flourished in the
14th–16th centuries. From
1680 it was the seat of the
Duchy of Sachsen–Saalfeld,
and the magnificent Baroque
Schloss, built between 1676
and 1720, dates from this
period. The former palace
chapel, now used as a concert hall, is particularly noteworthy. Also worth visiting is
the **Johanniskirche**, a late-
Gothic hall-church with interesting furnishings, a valuable
Gothic Holy Tomb and the
sculpted life-size figure of
John the Baptist, carved by
Hans Gottwalt, a student of
Tilman Riemenschneider.

Another interesting building
in Saalfeld is the early-Renaissance **Rathaus** (town hall),
built in 1529–37. The town
also has remarkably well preserved medieval town fortifications with gates and
towers. In the southern part
of the town stands the **Hoher
Schwarm**, ruins of a Gothic
castle from the 13th century.

In Garnsdorf, on the outskirts of Saalfeld, are the **Feengrotten,** much-visited grottoes created by both natural and human activity. From the mid-16th century until 1846 alum slate was mined in this cave, called "Jeremiasglück" (Jeremiah's good fortune). It was finally closed due to humidity, and the dripping water has since created some astonishingly colourful stalagmites and stalactites.

Picturesque Altenburg Castle complex

♣ Feengrotten
Garnsdorf. ☐ Dec–Feb: 10am–3:30pm daily; Mar–Oct 9am–5pm daily.

ENVIRONS: From Saalfeld it is worth taking a trip to the Hohenwarte-Talsperre, an artificial lake and paradise for watersports enthusiasts. **Schloss Ranis,** a scenic hilltop castle, was probably built in the 11th century for an emperor. Later it became the seat of the Thuringian landgraves, Meißen margraves and the counts of Schwarzburg. Now it houses a museum of the region's natural history.

Gera ⑬

Road map D4. 👥 121,000. 🚉 🚌
ℹ Ernst-Toller-Str. 14 (0365-800 70 30). 🎭 Geraer Höhlerfest (Sep).

THE SECOND largest town in Thuringia, Gera is not very impressive at first sight, although it has many attractions, including a picturesque **Rathaus** (town hall) whose oldest, Renaissance part dates from 1573–6. The Geraer Elleblon, on the righthand side of the entrance, is a unit of measurement equal to 57 cm (22 in). A short distance from the market square, in Nikolaiberg, you will find the **Salvatorkirche.** This Baroque church received its Secessionstyle interior in 1903, after a fire. The theatre (1900–02) was designed in the same style, by

Heinrich Seeling. The Küchengarten (kitchen garden) surrounds the ruins of **Schloss Osterstein** of which only the Baroque orangerie remains. It now houses the **Kunstsammlung,** with paintings by Lucas Cranach the Elder, Max Liebermann and others.

Otto Dix, a leading artist of the *Neue Sachlichkeit,* was born in Gera, and his birthplace has been turned into the **Otto-Dix-Haus.**

♣ Kunstsammlung
Küchengartenallee 4. 🌑 (0365) 832 21 47. ☐ 1–8pm Tue, 10am–5pm Wed–Fri, 10am–6pm Sat & Sun.

🏛 Otto-Dix-Haus
Mohrenplatz 4. 🌑 (0365) 832 49 27. ☐ 10am–5pm Tue–Fri, 10am–6pm Sat & Sun.

The multi-coloured Renaissance doorway of the Rathaus in Gera

Altenburg ⑭

Road map E4. 👥 45,000. 🚉 🚌
ℹ Moritzstr. 21 (03447-59 41 74).
🎭 Skatbrunnenfest (May); Sommerfestspiele (Jul).

I N GERMANY, Altenburg is known as "Skatstadt", the town of skat, a traditional and very popular card game. But there is more to Altenburg than the game; it also has some fascinating historic remains. The **Schloss** (ducal castle), which towers over the old town, has a 10th-century tower, reconstructed mainly in the Baroque style. Today the castle houses the **Spielkartenmuseum** (museum of playing cards). The late-Gothic castle church is also worth seeing. It has rich Baroque furnishings and an organ which was played by the composer Bach. Next to the castle gardens is the **Lindenau-Museum,** with Augustus von Lindenau's collection of 16th–20th century paintings and sculptures, including works by Simone Martini, Fra Angelico, Auguste Rodin, Ernst Barlach and Max Liebermann. The old town, at the foot of the hill, has a beautiful Renaissance town hall with an enormous octagonal tower. In Brühl Platz is a fountain and the figures of skat players, as well as the Baroque **Seckendorffsche Palais** and the Renaissance chancellery.

🏛 Schloss und Spielkartenmuseum
Schloss 2. 🌑 (03447) 31 51 93.
☐ 9:30am–5:30pm Tue–Sun.

🏛 Lindenau-Museum
Schloss. 🌑 (03447) 25 10.
☐ 10am–6pm Tue–Sun.

SOUTHERN GERMANY

Southern Germany at a Glance

THE SOUTHERN REGIONS of Germany, with their wealth of natural beauty, historic sights and folk culture, are particularly attractive to tourists. This part of the country includes two *Länder*: Bavaria, famous for its Alps, beer and the fairytale castle of Ludwig II at Neuschwanstein, and Baden-Württemberg, whose highlights include the Bodensee lake, Heidelberg and taking a trip on the scenic Schwarzwaldbahn railway line between Offenburg and Villingen.

LOCATOR MAP

Würzburg Residenz
Set in a magnificent park on the eastern outskirts of the town, this imposing bishop's palace was built between 1719 and 1773, to a design by Balthasar Neumann. The palace is constructed in a U-shape, with a central pavilion flanked by four two-storey courts.

BADEN-
WÜRTTEMBERG
(see pp274–313)

Heidelberg Castle *is one of Germany's finest examples of a Gothic-Renaissance fortress. Its origins go back to the 13th century, but new buildings sprang up around the inner courtyard during the 16th century as the castle gained importance as a royal residence.*

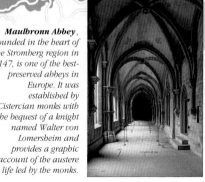

Maulbronn Abbey, *founded in the heart of the Stromberg region in 1147, is one of the best-preserved abbeys in Europe. It was established by Cistercian monks with the bequest of a knight named Walter von Lomersheim and provides a graphic account of the austere life led by the monks.*

Vierzehnheiligen Church, *built in 1743–72 to a design by Balthasar Neumann, is one of the most famous examples of South German Rococo. The monumental "Altar of Mercy" (Gnadenaltar) includes statues of the Fourteen Saints of the Intercession, to whom the church is dedicated.*

| 0 km | 50 |
| 0 miles | 50 |

BAVARIA
(See pp224–73)

Nördlingen Town Hall *was built in the 14th century, but its present form dates from the early 17th century. Prisoners used to be held in a space beneath the external stone stairway. By the wooden entrance is a wall carving of a medieval fool bearing a Latin inscription that translates as "Now there are two of us."*

Neuschwanstein Castle *is one of the three castles built for the Bavarian King Ludwig II (1845–86), involving enormous effort and expenditure. Standing on a high rock, overlooking a stream, the castle was the fulfilment of the King's vision, which was greatly inspired by the operas of Wagner.*

The Frauenkirche *in Munich was completed in 1488 and features two 99-m (325-ft) high towers crowned with copper domes. The church is one of the largest in southern Germany.*

The Baroque in Southern Germany

BECAUSE OF RELIGIOUS CONFLICTS and the Thirty Years' War (1618–48), the Baroque style did not flourish in Germany until the 18th century. Then it did so most lavishly in the southern, Catholic regions of the country. Here, influenced by Italian architecture, the Baroque reached new heights of flamboyance: the impressive spaciousness of religious buildings provided the setting for dynamic compositions in sculpture, fine stuccowork and vividly coloured *trompe l'oeil* paintings. Southern Germany's major artists of the 18th century included Balthasar Neumann, Francois Cuvilliés and the Asam brothers.

The main altar in Rohr, which was created by Egid Quirin Asam in 1723, is in the form of a proscenium (stage) with wings. The sculptural group depicts the Assumption of the Virgin Mary into Heaven.

Ceiling frescos were a basic element of the Baroque interior. This example by Johann Baptist Zimmermann in the Wieskirche in Steingaden, presents a glowing vision of the afterlife.

Galleries with curved balustrades add vitality to the interior.

Light plays a vital role in enlivening the interior decoration.

Figures of saints clad in flowing, dynamic robes and standing in curving, asymmetrical poses, complement the rich iconography and complex composition of the altars.

18th-century monasteries in southern Germany, like this one in Ottobeuren with its imposing stairway, are reminiscent of royal residences.

Late Baroque church façades, such as that of the Theatinerkirche in Munich, have a "rippled" design that creates an unusual effect of light and shadow.

Vaults with fine painting and exquisite stuccowork round off the architectural elements.

BAROQUE RESIDENCES

South German Baroque was not limited solely to religious architecture. As well as the magnificent monasteries and pilgrimage churches, it was also the inspiration for the impressive residences that were built by abbots as well as by bishops. As in the rest of Europe, these were modelled on the French royal palace in Versailles with its imposing grandeur, striking interiors and breathtaking gardens.

The monstrance in Passau is a fine example of the art of 18th-century goldsmiths, who created these receptacles for the consecrated Host.

The Baroque vestibule in the Neues Schloss in Schleissheim (see pp250–51) is decorated with exquisite stuccowork and frescos.

BAROQUE INTERIORS
Although they may seem over-elaborate, the late Baroque interiors of southern German churches are carefully-planned compositions intended to have a powerful effect. Their magnificent combination of architecture, sculpture and painting, and often organ music, resulted in "Gesamtkunstwerk" – a homogenous work that combines all the arts.

The Nymphenburg was a summer residence of the rulers of Bavaria. The plan includes a grand driveway and a park (see pp214–15).

The pulpit and other furnishings are designed to blend harmoniously with the decoration.

Stuccowork fills every interior space that is not decorated with paintings. Sometimes gilded, sometimes white, it may depict complex scenes or, in some cases, be adorned with ornamental designs.

Schloss Favorite is a small palace that forms part of a huge Baroque-style residence in Ludwigsburg (see pp292–3).

The German Alps

PART OF GERMANY extends into a fairly moderate section of the Alps, Europe's highest mountain range. They stretch from the Bodensee (Lake Constance) to Berchtesgaden. A section of the northern calcareous Alps belonging to the Eastern Alps of Allgäu, Bavaria and Salzburg falls within Germany. The mountains are a holidaymaker's paradise all year round. In the summer mountain walks can be enjoyed, with well-marked trails, as well as climbing, hang-gliding and paragliding; in the winter skiing is possible in superbly equipped resorts.

Alpine Chough

Alpine meadows are rich pasture lands, providing premium quality hay. They are also home to a rich variety of wildflowers.

Mountain peaks with their breath-taking jagged rocks.

Mountain streams have, over the years, cut a path through the rocks to create picturesque ravines. One of the most beautiful is this one at Wimbachklamm.

Local architecture blends happily into the landscape.

THE ALPINE LAKES

A melting glacier created many lakes in Bavaria. Their clear, unpolluted waters attract all kinds of watersports enthusiasts, while the picturesque surroundings are equally popular with other recreational users.

The Königssee, with its crystal-clear waters, is located high in the Berchtesgaden National Park.

The Watzmann is Germany's second highest peak.

Schwarzeck

Ski lifts

Reit im Winkl

Schlier

Oberstdorf

The Zugspitze, at 2,963m (9,700 ft), is the highest peak in all of Germany.

ALPINE FLORA AND FAUNA

Alpine vegetation varies according to height above sea level. On the lower slopes are mixed deciduous forests. Higher up are Alpine forests, generally coniferous. Above the tree line, dwarf mountain pine grow and higher still are stretches of high-altitude meadows. Beyond this is bare rock. Wild goats are found above the tree line and chamois in the foothills.

The Alpine ibex lives only in the Italian and Swiss Alps. This wild goat with long, backward-curving horns is a rare sight.

The mouflon is a wild sheep with large horns. It is also found in Corsica and Sardinia

Alpine rock jasmine forms carpets of colour on the mountain slopes.

The Alpine pasqueflower is a white variant of the species that tolerates the harsh soil and climatic conditions of its Alpine habitat.

The peacock butterfly is a common Eurasian species that has adapted successfully to the harsh Alpine environment.

Alpine thrift, with its round heads of pink and purple flowers, is a delightful sight.

Tegernsee

Kochelsee is overlooked by one of the largest hydroelectric power stations in Germany.

Garmisch-Partenkirchen is one of the venues of the annual Four Ski Jumps competition.

Walchensee

Augspitze

The Zugspitze is the highest peak in Germany.

MUNICH

THE CAPITAL OF BAVARIA, *Munich is sometimes called "Germany's secret capital". Lying right at the heart of Europe, the city rapidly overshadowed once powerful neighbours, such as Ingolstadt, Augsburg and Nuremberg, to become southern Germany's main metropolis. With its vibrant cosmopolitan atmosphere, fine buildings, museums and shops, it is one of the country's most popular tourist destinations.*

The citizens of Munich have been known for centuries for their love of the arts. The masterpieces that were created here during the Baroque and Rococo periods were equal to Italian and French works.

In the 19th century, the town's development continued along Neo-Classical lines, gaining for it the name of "Athens on Isar". Just how appropriate the name is can be seen when strolling along Ludwigstrasse or Königsplatz or visiting the Glyptothek, which houses Ludwig I's collection of Greek and Roman sculptures.

In the late 19th century the Munich Academy of Fine Arts was amongst Europe's best art schools. Not many cities have as great a choice of world-class theatres, operas and museums as can be found here in Munich.

But it is not only art that gives Munich its unique charm. The country's biggest folk festival, the Oktoberfest, is held each year in Theresienwiese, where visitors to the town can join in the revelries or just sit and watch, ordering a plate of sauerkraut with sausages and washing it down with some of the excellent Bavarian beer.

When planning a shopping trip to Munich visitors can be sure that its shops are equal to those of Paris and Milan, not only in the breadth of their range but also in terms of their prices.

The town is also one of Germany's main centres of high-tech and media industries. Many TV stations and film studios, as well as over 300 book and newspaper publishers, have their main offices in Munich.

The Neo-Gothic Rathaus in Marienplatz, Munich's central square

◁ **Interior of the Baroque Asamkirche, built between 1733 and 1746 by the Asam brothers**

Exploring Munich

M UNICH, THE CAPITAL OF BAVARIA, is exceptionally rich in interesting museums, churches and historic sights. This urban conurbation of over 1.5 million inhabitants increasingly swallows up the neighbouring areas. Many tourist attractions are located outside the town centre but, thanks to excellent public transport, it is easy to visit them. It is worth taking a trip to Nymphenburg to visit the famous palace and gardens there. Another interesting excursion is a stroll along Leopoldstrasse or Theresienwiese, where the huge, annual Oktoberfest is held.

GETTING THERE
Munich is an important railway junction and has its own international airport. It also has motorway connections with all the major towns and cities in Germany.

The distinctive towers of Munich's skyline

STAR SIGHTS

Churches
Asamkirche **6**
Bürgersaal **1**
Dreifaltigkeitskirche **3**
Frauenkirche **4**
Ludwigskirche **21**
Michaelskirche **2**
Theatinerkirche (St Cajetan) **15**

Buildings
Altes Rathaus **9**
Bayerische Staatsbibliothek **20**
Feldherrnhalle **14**
Neues Rathaus **10**
Propyläen **26**
Residenz (pp206–7) **13**
Schloss Nymphenburg (pp214–15) **28**
Villa Stuck **32**

Museums and Galleries
Alte Pinakothek (pp212–13) **23**
Bayerisches National-
museum **17**

Deutsches Jagd- und
Fischereimuseum **5**
*Deutsches Museum
(pp218–19)* **31**
Glyptothek **24**
Haus der Kunst **16**
Lenbachhaus **27**
Neue Pinakothek **22**
Prähistorische
Staatssammlung **19**
Schack-Galerie **18**
Staatliche Antiken-
sammlungen **25**
Stadtmuseum **7**
Völkerkundemuseum **11**

Other Attractions
Bavaria-Filmstadt **33**
Englischer Garten **30**
Hofbräuhaus **12**
Olympiapark **29**
Theresienwiese **34**
Viktualienmarkt **8**

KEY

▨	Street-by-Street map *pp200–201*
🅿	Parking
🛈	Tourist information
✉	Post office
🚖	Taxi-rank
✝	Church, cathedral, chapel
Ⓢ	S-Bahn
Ⓤ	U-Bahn

SEE ALSO

- *Where to Stay* p481
- *Where to Eat* p510

LOCATOR MAP

MUNICH

ENGLISCHER GARTEN

HOFGARTEN

Television Tower in Olympiapark

GREATER MUNICH

0 metres 400
0 yards 400

Street-by-Street: Around Marienplatz

IN MEDIEVAL TIMES, Marienplatz was Munich's salt- and corn-market. The origins of Munich itself lie with a handful of monks who built their abbey here, giving the place its name (from the word for 'monks') and its heraldic arms. In 1158 Welf Henry the Lion bestowed town status on Munich and 30 years later the town was allocated to the Wittelsbachs, who soon established a residence here. During the Reformation, Munich became a bastion of Catholicism and an important centre of the Counter-Reformation. Its magnificent churches, the Altes Rathaus (old town hall) and the Residenz all bear witness to that era.

Karlstor
Known as the Karl's Gate, the west entrance to the old town was part of the medieval fortifications. It was given its present name in 1791, in honour of Prince Karl Theodore.

★ Bürgersaal
Bürgersaal was built in 1709–10 for a Marian congregation (followers of the Virgin Mary), as a place of meeting and worship. It includes an upper and lower church. Rupert Mayer, an opponent of Nazism, is buried in the crypt. He was beatified in 1987 **1**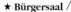

Augustinerbräu
The oldest and most celebrated brewery in Munich was founded by Augustinian monks in 1328. It currently occupies two 19th-century houses with picturesque façades.

0 metres   50
0 yards   50

Michaelskirche
The interior of St Michael's Church is surprisingly large. The massive barrel vaulting over the nave is the second largest after St Peter's Basilica in Rome **2**

STAR SIGHTS

★ Altes Rathaus

★ Bürgersaal

★ Frauenkirche

★ Neues Rathaus

KEY

– – – Suggested route

Deutsches Jagd- und Fischereimuseum
A huge collection of hunting and fishing exhibits is housed in the Augustinerkloster. The deconsecrated church, which has an ornate Rococo interior, once belonged to the Augustinian order ⑤

LOCATOR MAP

★ Frauenkirche
Partially demolished in 1944–45, this imposing church, with its landmark dome-topped towers, has been rebuilt along Gothic lines ④

★ Neues Rathaus
The ornate façade of the new town hall includes figures from Bavarian legend and history. The bronze statue at the top is the "Münchner Kindl" – a character that features in the city's heraldic arms ⑩

St Mary's Column

KAUFINGERSTRASSE

TSTRASSE

RÖSENSTRASSE

MARIEN-PLATZ

RINDERMARKT

Isartor

★ Altes Rathaus
The old town hall was remodelled in its original 15th-century style in the late 19th century. It was rebuilt again after World War II. It now houses a collection of historic toys ⑨

Interior of the Bürgersaal, featuring original 19th-century frescos

Bürgersaal **❶**

Neuhauser Straße 14. **Map** 1 F4.
U or **Ⓢ** Karlsplatz. **🚋** 18, 19, 20, 21, 27. **Lower church hall** 🔲
8am–8pm daily. **Upper church hall**
🔲 11am–1pm daily.

THIS CHURCH belonging to the Marian congregation was designed by Giovanni Antonio Viscardi and built by Johann Georg Ettenhofer in 1709–10. (The Marian congregation, founded in 1563, is a Catholic organization linked to the Jesuit order.)

The church was damaged during World War II, but still features original frescos. In the oratory is a figure of the *Guardian Angel* by Ignaz Günther (1770), a fine example of south-Bavarian Rococo. Rupert Mayer, parish priest during World War II and Munich's leading opponent of Nazism, is buried in the crypt.

Michaelskirche **❷**

ST MICHAEL'S CHURCH

Neuhauser Straße 52. **Map** 2 A4.
U or **Ⓢ** Karlsplatz. **🚋** 18, 19, 20, 21, 27. 🔲 8am–7pm daily.

THE MONUMENTAL St Michael's Church was built by Prince Wilhelm V for the Jesuits who arrived here in 1559. The foundation stone was laid in

1585 and initial building work on the first church, which was smaller than the present one, commenced in 1588. Before work had progressed very far, however, the tower in front of the presbytery collapsed, demolishing a large part of the building. A transept and new presbytery were added to the remaining part of the building and the church – which was the first Jesuit church in northern Europe – was consecrated in 1597. The interior of Michaelskirche is

Statue of St Michael at the entrance to Michaelskirche

awe-inspiring, with its wide, well-proportioned nave, three pairs of shallow chapels on either side, a short transept and an elongated presbytery. It is not certain who was the architect of the project, but it is believed that Wolfgang Müller created the main body of the church and Wendel Dietrich the Mannerist façade. Later extensions are thought to be the work of a Dutch architect, Friedrich Sustris.

In the church crypt, which is open to the public, are the tombs of many members of the Wittelsbach dynasty, including that of the famous castle-builder, King Ludwig II.

Dreifaltigkeits-kirche **❸**

HOLY TRINITY CHURCH

Pacellistraße 6. **Map** 2 A3. **🚋** 19.
🔲 7am–7pm daily.

THE BAROQUE church of the Holy Trinity is one of the few historic buildings in the city to have avoided bomb damage during World War II. The church was built as a votive gift from the city's burghers, aristocracy and clergy in the hope of averting the dangers threatened by the War of the Spanish Succession (1702–14). The foundation stone was laid in 1711 and the church was consecrated seven years later. The royal architect, Giovanni Antonio Viscardi, assisted by Enrico Zucalli and Georg Ettenhofer, created a building that is one of the most beautiful examples of Italian Baroque in Munich. The church's original features include the dome fresco by Cosmas Damian Asam, *The Adoration of the Trinity*.

Frauenkirche ❹

Frauenplatz 1. **Map** 2 B4. **U** or **Ⓢ** *Karlsplatz & Marienplatz.* 🚋 *19.* **Tower** ⏰ *Apr–Oct: 7am–7pm Sat–Wed, 7am–8:30pm Thu, 7am–6pm Fri.* ● *Sun & holidays.*

THE SITE OF THE Frauen-kirche was originally occupied by a Marian chapel, which was built in the 13th century. Some two hundred years later, Prince Sigismund ordered a new, much bigger church to be built on the site. Its architects were Jörg von Halspach and Lukas Rottale. The Frauenkirche was completed in 1488, though the distinctive copper onion-domes were not added to its towers until 1525. The church is one of southern Germany's biggest Gothic structures, which can accommodate a congregation of about 20,000.

A triple-nave hall with no transept features rows of side chapels, a gallery surrounding the choir and a monumental western tower. The whole huge structure measures over 100 m (330 ft) in length and almost 40 m (130 ft) wide.

The church treasures that escaped destruction during World War II include a Marian painting, dating from around 1500, by Jan Polak; the altar of St Andrew in St Sebastian's chapel, with statues by Meister von Rabenden and paintings by Jan Polak, dating from 1510; and the monumental tomb of Emperor Ludwig IV of Bavaria, the work of Hans Krumpper (1619–22).

Carving on main Frauenkirche portal

Deutsches Jagd- und Fischerei- museum ❺

GERMAN MUSEUM OF HUNTING AND FISHING

Neuhauser Straße 2. **Map** 2 A4. 📞 *(089) 22 05 22.* **U** *or* **Ⓢ** *Marienplatz.* 🚋 *18, 19, 20, 21, 27.* ⏰ *9:30am–5pm Tue–Sun, 9:30am–9pm Mon, Thu.* 🎫

IMMEDIATELY ADJACENT to St Michael's Church is the Augustinerkloster, the former Augustinian church, which now houses the Museum of Hunting and Fishing. The original building dates from around 1300 (the first August-inian monks arrived here in 1294). It was rebuilt in the mid-15th century and then remodelled in the Baroque style in 1620–21. The church was decon-secrated in 1803. Since 1966, the building's ornate Rococo interior has housed a very interesting museum, with a collection of weapons dating from the Renais-sance, Baroque and Rococo periods, as well as hunting trophies and related paintings, prints and

dioramas. Artists represented in the museum's collection include several great names such as Rubens, Snyders and Antonio Pisanello.

Asamkirche ❻

ASAMS' CHURCH

Sendlinger Straße 32. **Map** 2 A5. **U** *Sendlinger Tor.* 🚋 *18, 20, 21, 27.* 🚌 *31, 56.* ⏰ *7:30am–6pm Mon–Fri, 8am–7pm Sat, 8am–3pm Sun.* ✝ *5pm Mon–Fri, 6pm Sat, 9am, 10:30am Sun.* 🎫 *noon Sat.*

OFFICIALLY known as St Johann-Nepomuk, this gem of Rococo architecture stands in Sendlingerstrasse and is part of a complex built by the Asam brothers in the mid-18th century. In 1729–30, the sculptor and stuccoist Egid Quirin Asam acquired two properties that he intended to convert into a family home for himself. He subsequently acquired a plot adjacent to these properties, where he wished to build a church devoted to the newly canonized St Nepomuk, a Bohemian monk who had drowned in the Danube. Above the entrance to the church is a statue of the saint.

At the same time, Cosmas Damian, the brother of Egid Quirin Asam, bought a plot on which he built the presbytery. The church building adjoins the residential house of Egid Quirin. The two buildings were joined by a corridor and from one of his bedroom windows the artist could see the main altar.

In this small but unique church, the Asam brothers achieved a rare unity of style. In the church's dimly lit interior, with its rich, dynamically shaped single nave, no surface is left unembellished. The eye is drawn to the altar, which features a sculpted group of the Holy Trinity.

Pulpit in the Rococo-style Asamkirche

A painting by Wilhelm von Kaulbach (1847) from the Stadtmuseum collection

Stadtmuseum ❼

TOWN MUSEUM

St Jakobsplatz 1. **Map** 2 A5.
C (089) 23 32 23 70. **U** or
S Marienplatz. **U** Sendlinger Tor.
🕐 10am–6pm Tue–Sun. 📷 📱

A FEW STEPS away from the Viktualienmarkt, on St Jakobsplatz, stands the Town Museum. Its rich collection has been housed since 1880 in the former arsenal building, which was built in 1491–93 by Lucas Rottaler. It is one of Munich's most fascinating museums, where everyone will find something to their taste, with exhibits illustrating the everyday lives of Munich's citizens of all classes through-out the centuries.

The museum's greatest treasures are the famous set of dancing Moors by Erasmus Grasser (1480). Originally this was a group of eighteen lime-wood carvings of dancing figures in highly expressive postures, surrounding the figure of a woman. Only ten of the figures, which were created originally to decorate the ballroom of the Altes Rathaus, have survived. Also on the ground floor, in the Waffenhalle, is a splendid collection of arms. Other displays include furniture (with pieces in styles ranging from Baroque to Art Deco), photographs, film, brewing equipment and musical instruments. There is also a fascinating doll collection, which is one of the largest in the world. It includes paper dolls from India and China, European mechanical dolls and a variety of original puppets. Also worth seeing is the museum's collection of paintings and prints, particularly the posters. As well as its permanent displays about the history of the city, the museum regularly stages special exhibitions.

The museum also houses a cinema, the *Filmmuseum*, which puts on nightly showings of English-language films.

Viktualienmarkt ❽

Peterplatz-Frauenstraße. **Map** 2 B5.
U or **S** Marienplatz. 🚌 52, 56.

R IGHT AT THE heart of the city is the Viktualienmarkt, a large square that has been the city's main marketplace for the last two hundred years. The locals say that a tourist who fails to visit this "rustic heart" of Munich can never boast that he has seen the Bavarian capital. Apart from stalls selling vegetables and fruit brought in daily from suburban orchards or

Colourfully laden market stalls in Munich's Viktualienmarkt

village gardens, the local beer garden provides a welcome retreat for a beer or snack.

One of the features of the square is a statue of a famous Munich actor and comedian, Karl Valentin (1882–1948).

An impressive view over the market and nearby Marien-platz can be enjoyed from the tower of Peterskirche (St Peter's Church), which stands alongside the square.

Signs of the Zodiac adorning the clock face on the Altes Rathaus

Altes Rathaus ❾

OLD TOWN HALL

Marienplatz 15. **Map** 2 B4. **U** or
S Marienplatz. ⬤ to visitors.
Spielzeugmuseum **C** (089) 29 40
01. 🕐 10am– 5:30pm daily. 📷

M UNICH'S old town hall stands in the eastern part of Marienplatz, immediately next to the new town hall. The original building, which has been remodelled several times over the centuries, was built in 1470–75 by Jörg von Halspach, who also designed the Marian church.

The building's present Neo-Gothic look is the result of remodelling work carried out between 1877 and 1934, when the nearby dual carriageway ring road was being built.

The interior of the building, which was restored following World War II bomb damage, features the Dance Hall with a wooden cradle vault. It is adorned with an old frieze featuring 87 (originally 99) heraldic arms painted by Ulrich Fuetrer in 1478, and a further seven carved by Erasmus Grasser in 1477. The figures standing by the walls are copies of the famous dancing Moors, whose originals by Erasmus Grasser (1480) are kept in the Town Museum (Stadtmuseum).

The lofty tower rising above the old city gate (Talbrucktor) was reconstructed in 1975. The design of the tower was based on pictures dating from 1493. Since 1983, the tower has housed the toy collection of the Spielzeugmuseum.

Neues Rathaus ⑩
NEW TOWN HALL

Marienplatz. **Map** 2 B4. 🆒 (089) 23 30 33 00. Ⓤ or Ⓢ Marienplatz. ⬜ **Town Hall and Tower:** 9am–4pm Mon–Thu, 9am–1pm Fri. 🅷 ⬛ Carillons: May–Oct: 11am, noon, 5pm, 9pm daily.

THE NEO-GOTHIC new town hall standing in Marienplatz was built by Georg Hauberrisser in 1867–1909. Its 100-m (330-ft) high façade features a fascinating set of statues depicting Bavarian dukes, kings and electors, saints, mythical and allegorical figures as well as a variety of gargoyles inspired by medieval bestiaries. The central façade features a huge 80-m (260-ft) high clock tower, known as Glockenspiele. Each day, at 11am and 5pm, the bells ring out a carillon, while the mechanical figures of knights fight a tournament and a crowd dances. The latter is a reenactment of the first coopers' dance, which was held in 1517 to boost the morale of citizens when the town was beset by the plague. Other mechanical figures appear in the windows on the building's seventh floor in the evenings (9:30pm in summer, 7:30pm in winter). These are flanked by figures of the town guardsman carrying a lantern and the Guardian Angel blessing a Munich child, the "Münchner Kindl".

tue on façade of Neues Rathaus

Richly decorated entrance to the Völkerkundemuseum

Völkerkundemuseum ⑪
STATE MUSEUM OF ETHNOGRAPHY

Maximilianstraße 42. **Map** 2 D4. 🆒 (089) 210 13 60. ⬜ 9:30am–4:30pm, Tue–Sun. 🚏 19. ⬛

ON THE OPPOSITE side of the ring road from the Maximilianeum (the Upper Bavaria Government building) is the State Museum of Ethnography. Built in 1858–65, to a design by E. Riedel, its façade is decorated with eight figures personifying the virtues of the Bavarian people: patriotism, diligence, magnanimity, piety, loyalty, justice and courage. Originally intended to house the Bavarian National Museum (now located in Prinzregentenstraße), the building has been home to the State Museum of Ethnography since 1925. It is the second largest (after Berlin) ethnographic museum in Germany.

The origins of the museum's collection go back to 1782, when curios taken from the treasures of various Bavarian rulers were exhibited in a gallery in the gardens of the residence. Attention began to focus on ethnography after expansion of the collection in 1868. The museum currently houses some 300,000 exhibits depicting the art and culture of non-European nations, with a particular emphasis on the Far East (China and Japan), South America and Eastern and Central Africa. The collection is presented in a series of changing exhibitions.

Hofbräuhaus ⑫

Platzl 9. **Map** 2 C4. 🆒 (089) 22 16 76. Ⓤ or Ⓢ Marienplatz. ⬜ 9am–midnight daily.

THE HOFBRÄUHAUS is the most popular beer hall in Munich and a great tourist attraction. Established as a court brewery in 1589 by Wilhelm V, it was originally housed in Alter Hof, but moved to Platzl in 1654. In 1830 permission was granted to build an inn where beer could be sold to the public.

The Neo-Renaissance form of the building dates from 1896. The Schwemme, on the ground floor, is a large hall with painted ceiling and room for about 1,000 guests. The Festall, on the first floor, has a barrel-shaped vault and can accommodate 1,300 guests.

In a courtyard, surrounded by chestnut trees, is the beer garden, which is always very popular during the summer.

Guests enjoying a drink in the beer garden of the Hofbräuhaus

Residenz ⓭

Tʜɪs ꜰᴏʀᴍᴇʀ residence of Bavarian kings has housed a museum since 1920. Over the years, the original Wittelsbachs' castle, which had stood on the site since the 14th century, was gradually extended. Major work in the 17th century included new surroundings for the Brunnenhof and the construction of buildings around the imperial courtyard, Hofkapelle and Reiche Kapelle. Königsbau and Festsaalbau were added in the first half of the 19th century. The Renaissance façade includes two magnificent portals and features a statue of the Holy Virgin as Patroness of Bavaria (Patrona Boiariae).

Necklace dating from 1557

Hofkapelle
This imposing chapel, dating from the early 17th century, was modelled on St Michael's Church. Vault decorations date from 1614.

Reiche Kapelle
This was the private chapel of Maximilian I. Though smaller than the Residenz's other chapel, it is richly furnished.

Entrance

Grottenhof
In the eastern section of this courtyard is this grotto lined with crystal, coloured shells and tufa.

★ Nibelungensäle
Built by Leo von Klenze, Königsbau features five Halls of the Nibelungs. The rooms owe their name to the wall paintings, which depict scenes from the famous German medieval epic Nibelungenlied.

★ **Cuvilliés-Theater**
Built in 1751–53, this masterpiece of theatre architecture was designed by François de Cuvilliés and his son, with stuccos and frescos by Johann Baptiste Zimmermann. The world premiere of Mozart's Idomeneo *was staged in the theatre on 29 January 1781.*

★ **Schatzkammer V**
Room V's collection includes items such as the Bavarian Reichsappel and a sword belonging to Duke Christoph of Bavaria.

Nationaltheater

Schatzkammer III
Besides royal insignia, liturgical vessels and various everyday objects, the treasure house contains some unusual gold and jewellery items. The star attraction of Room III is this small equestrian statue of St George, the work (1586–97) of Friedrich Sustris.

STAR SIGHTS

★ **Cuvilliés-Theater**

★ **Nibelungensäle**

★ **Schatzkammer V**

Feldherrnhalle ⓮

Odeonsplatz. **Map** 2 B3.
U *Odeonsplatz.* 🚋 *19.* 🚌 *53.*
◗ *to the public.*

UNTIL 1816, the site of this monumental building was occupied by a Gothic town gate – Schwabinger Tor. In the early 19th century, however, when Kings Maximilian I Joseph and Ludwig I decided to expand Munich northwards and westwards, their chief architect, Leo von Klenze, ordered the gate to be pulled down, as it stood in the way of the prestigious thoroughfare (Ludwigstrasse) that he intended to build.

Built in 1841–44, the Feldherrnhalle was designed by Friedrich von Gärtner, who modelled it on the Loggia dei Lanzi in Florence. Intended as a monument to the heroes of Bavaria, the interior contains statues of two great military leaders, Johann Tilly and Karl Philipp von Wrede by Ludwig Schwanthaler.

The central carved composition devoted to the heroes of the 1870–71 Franco-Prussian War is much newer, dating from 1882. It was designed by Ferdinand von Miller.

The Feldherrnhalle was the scene of Hitler's unsuccessful "Beer Hall Putsch" in November 1923. As a result, it acquired a certain cult status with the Nazis, and is no longer open to the public.

Theatinerkirche (St Cajetan) ⓯

ST CAJETAN'S CHURCH

Theatinerstraße 22. **Map** 2 B3. **U** or ⑤ *Marienplatz.* 🚋 *19.* ◗ *6am–7:30 pm Mon–Sat, 7am–7:30pm Sun.*

IN ODEONSPLATZ, next to Feldherrnhalle, stands one of the most magnificent churches in Munich, St Cajetan's Church.

When Henrietta Adelaide of Savoy presented the Elector Ferdinand with his long-awaited heir, Maximilian, the happy parents vowed to build an abbey in the town to commemorate the birth. Henrietta wished to give the abbey to the Theatine monks, whose mission was to raise intellectual and moral standards amongst the clergy.

The foundation stone for the church was laid in 1662. The project was entrusted to an Italian architect, Agostino Baralli, who based his design on St Andrea della Valle, in Rome. From 1669 the building works were continued by Enrico Zucalli, who succeeded Baralli as court architect. This single-nave church, with its side chapels, transept and a high stuccoed dome over the nave intersection, shows obvious signs of Roman influence. Added

Venetian touches are visible in the scrolls on the towers' copings, which resemble those on the church of Santa Maria Della Salute in Venice.

Although construction work on the church ended in 1690, the façade – designed by François de Cuvilliés – was not completed until 1765–68. The interior of the church is adorned with stuccos by Giovanni Antonio Viscardi and furnished in rich Baroque style. Its twin towers and copper dome are dominant features on the Munich skyline.

Henri Matisse's *Still Life with Geranium* (1910) from the Haus der Kunst collection

Haus der Kunst ⓰

ARTS HOUSE

Prinzregentenstraße 1. **Map** 3 D2. 📞 *(089) 21 12 70.* 🚌 *53, 55.*
◗ *10am–10pm daily.* 💷 *(free on Sundays and national holidays).*

SINCE THE END of World War II, the Haus der Kunst in Prinzregentenstrasse has housed a fine collection of modern art. Built between 1933 and 1937, the Neo-Classical building is the work of a Nazi architect, Paul Ludwig Trost. It opened its doors in 1937 with a display of propaganda art, which was proclaimed by the Nazis as "truly German". This was followed by a second presentation, "The Exhibition of Degenerate Art", in which several masterpieces of modern art were ridiculed.

Despite its original intended purpose, the building is now a dynamic museum of modern art that is famous far beyond the bounds of Munich for its regular special exhibitions. Its rich collection includes many representative works by major

Pediment on the gable of Theatinerkirche, with copper dome behind

German artists of the 20th century, alongside modern works by major foreign artists including Picasso, Matisse, Mondrian and Magritte. As well as Expressionist and Abstract paintings, examples of modern sculpture are on display in the museum.

Bayerisches Nationalmuseum ⑰

BAVARIAN NATIONAL MUSEUM

Prinzregentenstraße 3. **Map** 3 E3.
📞 (089) 211 24 01. 🚇 20. 🚌 53, 55. ⏰ 9:30am–5pm Tue–Sun.
⬤ Mon.

THE BAVARIAN National Museum was founded in 1855 by King Maximilian II. Between 1894 and 1900 it acquired a new building in Prinzregentenstrasse, which was designed by Gabriel von Seidel; this building alone is worth a closer look. The complex structure consists of wings representing various architectural styles, while the ground floor features halls that are built in styles that are appropriate to their exhibits. Romanesque and Gothic art can thus be seen in Neo-Romanesque and Neo-Gothic rooms, Renaissance art in Neo-Renaissance rooms and Baroque in Neo-Baroque rooms. The individual rooms have been arranged in interesting subject groups, with paintings and sculptures supplemented by superb collections of decorative art and everyday objects. The exhibits include a beautiful sculpture of the Madonna by Tilman Riemenschneider.

The first-floor collections are arranged thematically and include German porcelain, clocks, glass paintings, ivory carvings, textiles and gold items. Particularly interesting

rad Meit's *Judith* **(1515), Bavarian ational Museum**

is a collection of small oil sketches, painted by artists when designing some large-scale compositions, such as an altar or a ceiling painting.

In the basement rooms is a collection of folk art, of which the Christmas cribs are highly popular with visitors. These fascinating multi-figure compositions are the works of Bavarian and Italian artists.

Poster advertising an exhibition at the Schack-Galerie

Schack-Galerie ⑱

Prinzregentenstraße 9. **Map** 3 E3.
📞 (089) 23 80 52 24. ⏰ 10am–5pm Wed–Mon. 🚌 53. 🚇 20.

THE MAGNIFICENT collection of German paintings on display in this gallery come from the private collection of Adolf Friedrich von Schack. They are housed in this elegant building built in 1907 by Max Littmann for use by the Prussian Legation.

As Schack's main interest was in 19th-century painting, the gallery features works that represent the Romantic period, including Leo von Klenze and Carl Spitzweg, as well as witty, fairy-tale works by Moritz von Schwind. Particularly notable are his *Morning*, *In the Woods* and *Rübezahl* – in which the mythical Guardian of the Riesengebirge Mountains wanders through an enchanted

forest. Late 19th-century painters are represented by Franz von Lenbach, Anselm Feuerbach and, above all, by Arnold Bocklin. Bocklin's Romantic works, which are full of symbolism, include *Villa on the Coast* and *Man Scaring a Deer*. The gallery has a large collection of landscapes, including interesting sun-soaked Italian scenes by German masters, as well as a valuable collection of paintings devoted to historic themes.

Prähistorische Staatssammlung ⑲

PREHISTORY MUSEUM

Lerchenfeldstraße 2. **Map** 3 E2.
📞 (089) 211 24 02. 🚇 17. 🚌 53.
⏰ 9am–4:30pm Tue–Sun. 🎟 admission free Sun and national holidays. ♿

IMMEDIATELY adjacent to the Bavarian National Museum is the Prehistory Museum, which was founded in 1885 by King Ludwig II. Since 1976, this spacious building has housed a rich collection of artifacts excavated in various parts of Bavaria. The oldest items in the collection date from the Palaeolithic era while later exhibits illustrate the region's early history. The collection includes Bronze Age, Roman and early Medieval treasures.

A 3rd-century mosaic floor from a Roman villa, on display in the Prehistory Museum

Bayerische Staatsbibliothek ⓴
BAVARIAN NATIONAL LIBRARY

Ludwigstraße 16. **Map** 2 C1, C2.
☎ (089) 28 63 80. Ⓤ Odeon,
Universität. ◯ 9am–7:30pm
Mon–Fri, 9am–4:30pm Sat. ♿
(telephone bookings required).

THE MONUMENTAL Bavarian national library was designed by Friedrich von Gärtner, who took over, in 1827, from Leo von Klenze as the main architect on the prestigious Ludwigstrasse project – commissioned by King Ludwig I. Gärtner was also responsible for the Feldherrnhalle, Siegestor, St Ludwig's Church, and the University building.

This massive structure, in a style reminiscent of the Italian Renaissance, was erected between 1832 and 1843. Its external staircase is adorned with the seated figures of Thucydides, Hippocrates, Homer and Aristotle, by Ludwig von Schwanthaler.

Equally impressive are the stairs leading to the main rooms, which are modelled on the Scala dei Gianti of the Doge Palace in Venice. With its collection of 5 million volumes, the library is on a par with the Berlin Staatsbibliothek (see p64) as the biggest in Germany.

A statue of Hippocrates at the Bavarian National Library

The imposing twin-tower façade of Munich's Ludwigskirche

Ludwigskirche ㉑
ST LUDWIG'S CHURCH

Ludwigstraße 20. **Map** 2 C1.
Ⓤ Universität. ◯ 7am–8pm daily.

INSPIRED BY the Romanesque churches of Lombardy, Friedrich von Gärtner built this monumental triple-nave basilica with transept and twin-tower façade between 1829 and 1844.

The building's vast interior features magnificent original frescos that were designed by the main exponent of the Nazarene style, Peter von Cornelius, and painted by his associates. Von Cornelius himself painted the massive choir fresco, *The Last Judgement*. One of the biggest frescos in the world, it rivals in size Michelangelo's *Last Judgement*, which hangs in the Sistine Chapel, Rome.

Neue Pinakothek ㉒
THE NEW PINAKOTHEK

Barerstrasse 29. **Map** 2 A1. ☎ (089)
23 80 51 95. Ⓤ Theresienstraße.
🚊 18. 🚌 53. ◯ 10am–5pm
Wed–Mon, 10am–10pm Thu. 📷

THE BAVARIAN collection of modern European paintings and sculptures is housed in a building built by Alexander von Brancas between 1975 and 1981. It holds a representative collection of German works, from Neo-Classicism through Romanticism, the "Nazarenes", German and Austrian Biedermeier, Realism, Historicism, Impressionism, Pointillism and Secession paintings.

The collection also includes works by renowned French Realists, Impressionists, Post-Impressionists and Symbolists, purchased in 1909–11, when the gallery's director was the art historian Hugo von Tschudi.

The collection includes Ferdinand Georg Waldmüller's *Young Peasant Woman with Three Children Standing at the Window* (1840), Friedrich Overbeck's *Italia and Germania* (1828), Edouard Manet's *Breakfast in the Studio* (1868), Honoré Daumier's *Don Quijote* (1868), Edgar Degas' *Ironing Woman* (1869), Paul Gauguin's *Birth of Christ* (1869), Walter Crane's *Neptune's Horses* (1892), Gustav Klimt's *Music* (1895) and Lovis Corinth's *Portrait of Count Eduard von Keyserling* (1900). The gallery ends with a small selection of Symbolist and Art Nouveau paintings.

The space between the Old and New Pinakothek has been turned into a sculpture park that features, among others, a work by Henry Moore.

Goya's *Die Marquesa de Caballero* in the Neue Pinakothek

Alte Pinakothek ㉓
THE OLD PINAKOTHEK

See pp212–13.

Façade of the Glyptothek, with its central column portico

Glyptothek ㉔

GLYPTOTHECA

Königsplatz 3. **Map** 1 F2.
C (089) 28 61 00. **U** Königsplatz.
O 10am–5pm Tue, Wed, Fri, Sat,
Sun, 10am–8pm Thu.

THE KÖNIGSPLATZ complex, including Glyptothek and Propylaeum, was the work of Leo von Klenze. It was built in 1816–34 to house Ludwig I's collection of Greek and Roman sculptures and was the first public museum to be devoted to a single art discipline. Klenze designed not only the building but also the arrangement of the exhibits within it.

The most famous pieces in the collection are the ancient statue of a young man, *Apollo of Terentia* (560 BC), the tomb stele of Mnesareta (380 BC) and sculptures from the front of the famous Aphaia temple of Aegina, which depict battle scenes from the Achaean-Trojan wars.

Staatliche Antikensammlungen ㉕

THE NATIONAL COLLECTION OF ANTIQUITIES

Königsplatz 1. **Map** 1 F2.
C (089) 59 83 59. **U** Königsplatz.
O 10am–4:30pm Tue, Thu–Sun,
noon–8:30pm Wed **⬚** Mon–Sat,
free on Sunday.

BUILT IN 1838–48 by Georg Friedrich Ziebland, this building is on the south side of the Königsplatz. Since 1967, it has housed one of the world's finest collections of antique vases from the 5th and 6th centuries BC – a collection so vast that it occupies five rooms. In addition to these, there are many other masterpieces of Greek, Etruscan and Roman ornamental art, jewellery and small statues. The museum's most famous exhibits include a golden Greek necklace, dating from the 4th century BC, and a *kylix* (a shallow, two-handled drinking vessel), with a painted interior that depicts Dionysius in a boat. This is signed by Eksekias, an outstanding exponent of the Attic black figure style and dates from around 530 BC.

Propyläen ㉖

Königsplatz. **Map** 1 F2.
U Königsplatz.

DERIVED FROM the Propylaea to the Athenian Acropolis, this magnificent Neo-Classical structure stands at the end of Brienner Strasse and is visible from as far as Karolinenplatz. Built by Leo von Klenze in 1846–62, its austere form, featuring Doric porticos, provides an excellent final touch to the composition of Königsplatz by linking together the National Collection of Antiquities and the Glyptotheca.

The Propyläen is also a symbolic gateway to the new parts of the city. It was funded by the private foundation of King Ludwig I, although by the time it was built the king had already abdicated.

The carved decorations depict scenes from the Greek War of Liberation against Turkey (1821–29), led by King Otto I, son of Ludwig I. The battle scenes on the frieze and in the tympanum are the work of Ludwig Schwanthaler.

Lenbachhaus ㉗

Luisenstraße 33. **Map** 1 F2. **C** (089) 23 33 20 02. **U** Königsplatz.
O 10am–6pm Tue–Sun. **⬚**

THIS ITALIAN-STYLE villa was built between 1887 and 1891 by Gabriel von Seidl for Franz von Lenbach, a painter who was very popular with the establishment.

Since 1929, the villa has housed the Municipal Art Gallery. Apart from masterpieces such as *Portrait of a Man*, by Jan Polak (c.1500), *Friends from the Young Days* by Carl Spitzweg (1855) and *Self-portrait with a Skeleton* by Lovis Corinth (1896), it also has the world's biggest collection of works by a group known as *Der Blaue Reiter* (The Blue Rider) artists. The Russian painter Wassily Kandinsky was a leading proponent of this movement; he took the first steps towards abstract painting in 1910 when he was living in Murnau, a small town in south Germany.

Fountain in the beautiful front garden of the Lenbachhaus

Alte Pinakothek ㉓

CONSTRUCTION WORK on the Alte Pinakothek, one of the world's most famous art galleries, began in 1826 and was completed 10 years later. Leo von Klenze designed the Italian-Renaissance-style building. The history of its collections goes back to the Renaissance period, when Wilhelm IV the Steadfast (ruled 1508–50) decided to adorn his residence with historic paintings. His successors were equally keen art collectors and, by the 18th century, an outstanding collection of 14th- to 18th-century paintings had been amassed.

St Luke Painting the Madonna (c.1440)
This is one of the most frequently copied masterpieces by the Dutch painter Roger van der Weyden.

★ Four Apostles (1526)
These two panels were painted by Albrecht Dürer, a founding figure of the German school of art. They were purchased in 1627 by Maximilian I from the town of Nuremberg.

Seated Portrait of Charles V (1548)
This portrait was painted by the Venetian artist Titian during the Emperor's visit to the Reich's Parliament in Augsburg.

Main entrance

Homage of the Three Kings (1504)
The depiction of the homage is just one small part of the most important work by Hans Holbein the Elder.

KEY

- ☐ Flemish and Dutch paintings
- ☐ German paintings
- ☐ Italian paintings
- ☐ French paintings
- ☐ Spanish paintings
- ☐ 16th–17th century paintings

STAR EXHIBITS

- ★ **Deposition from the Cross**
- ★ **Four Apostles**
- ★ **Land of Cockaigne**

Abduction of the Daughters of Leukippos (1618)
A highlight of the museum is the Rubens collection, which includes his depiction of the abduction of Hilaeria and Phoibe by Castor and Pollux.

VISITORS' CHECKLIST

Barer Straße 27. **Road map**
2 A1. 🄲 *(098) 23 80 52 15.*
🅄 *Königsplatz.* 🚌 *53.* 🚊 *27.*
🄾 *10am–5pm Wed, Fri–Sun,
10am–9pm Tue.* 🄰 *(Admission
free to children up to age 14.)*
🚻 ♿ 🄾 ↕

GALLERY GUIDE
The ground-floor rooms of the gallery are devoted to the works of German old masters dating from the 16th and 17th centuries. On the first floor are works by Dutch, Flemish, French, German, Italian and Spanish artists.

First floor

★ **Deposition from the Cross** (1634)
Rembrandt's dramatic vision of the Saviour's sacrifice was originally intended to be part of a triptych.

Disrobing of Christ (c.1590)
The gallery's small but interesting collection of Spanish paintings includes this work by El Greco, one of his three most important compositions.

Ground floor

★ **Land of Cockaigne** (1567)
In this vividly detailed painting by Pieter Brueghel the Elder, the Flemish artist depicts the mythical land of plenty. The work is an ironic condemnation of gluttony and laziness, themes that are depicted in its many humorous scenes.

Schloss Nymphenburg ㉘

ONE OF EUROPE'S most beautiful palaces, Schloss Nymphenburg grew up around an Italianate villa built in 1663–64 for the Electress Henrietta-Adelaide to a design by Agostino Barelli. The palace was dedicated to the pastoral pleasures of the goddess Flora and her nymphs, hence the name. Several additions were made over the years, including four pavilions. These were designed by Joseph Effner who directed works from 1715. Built to the side of the original villa, these were connected by arcaded passageways.

Porcelain parrot in front of the factory

Gallery of Beauties
Portraits of royal favourites include this one of Helene Sedlmayr, a 17-year-old girl from Munich.

Entrance to Schloss Nymphenburg
Seen in this view are the original Italianate villa and two of the side pavilions that were added later.

Marstallmuseum
The former stables house a collection of carriages that once belonged to Bavarian rulers. They include the magnificent carriages of Ludwig II.

Porcelain Factory
Established in 1747 by Franz Anton Bustelli and transferred to Nymphenburg in 1761, this is one of the oldest porcelain factories in Europe.

KEY

– – –   Suggested route

STAR SIGHTS

★ **Amalienburg**

★ **Festsaal**

★ **Lackkabinett**

★ Amalienburg
The interior of this hunting lodge in the Schlosspark is a superb example of Rococo style by François de Cuvilliés.

Magdalenenklause
After a lifetime of revels, Maximilian Emmanuel commissioned a hermitage where he could pray and meditate. By the time of its completion in 1725, however, the king was dead.

Badenburg

Pagodenburg

Museum Mensch und Natur
This museum is devoted to geology and human biology.

★ Lackkabinett
This small 17th-century cabinet owes its name to its panels of black and red Chinese lacquer. It is on display in the Pagodenburg.

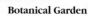

Botanical Garden
A collection of botanical specimens, including many rare plants, is featured in this fascinating garden.

★ Festsaal
Featuring decorations devoted to the goddess Flora, this vast Rococo ballroom is the work of father and son – Johann Baptiste and Franz Zimmermann.

View from the platform of the television tower in Olympiapark

Olympiapark 🄯

📞 (089) 30 67 24 14. 🅄 Olympia-
zentrum. 🚋 20, 25, 27. **Pavilion**
🕐 9am–midnight daily. 📷

BUILT FOR the 1972 Olympic
Games, this vast sports
stadium can be spotted from
almost anywhere in Munich,
as it is the site of a 290-m
(950-ft) high television tower,
the Olympiaturm. The entire
complex was designed by
Germany's leading architects,
Benisch and Partners.

The stadium has three main
facilities: the Olympic Stadium,
which seats 62,000 spectators,
the Olympic Hall and the
Swimming Hall. In what is
one of the most original
constructions of 20th-century
German architecture, all three
are covered by a vast transparent canopy, stretched
between a series of tall masts
to form an irregular tent.

The stadium includes many
other facilities, such as an
indoor skating rink, a cycle
racing track and tennis courts.

The sports complex is located
beside the park's artificial
lake. Opposite it is a hill that
was constructed from rubble
removed from the city after
war destruction.

Apart from sporting events,
the Olympiapark hosts many
popular events, including fireworks displays and regular
open-air rock and pop concerts
in the summer months.

Englischer Garten 🄰

🅄 Giselastraße. 🚌 54.

THE IDEA OF creating this
garden, which would be
open to all the inhabitants of
Munich and not only to its
aristocracy, came from Count
von Rumford, an American-
born chemist and physicist
who lived in Bavaria from
1784. As the region's Minister
of War, he was responsible
for reorganizing the Bavarian
army. His idea of creating a
garden of this size – the
garden covers an area
of 5 sq km (1,235
acres) – right in the
centre of a large city,
was quite unique in
Germany. In 1789,
taking advantage of
his influential position,
he persuaded Karl
Theodor to put his
plans into action.

The project leader
was Friedrich Ludwig
von Schell. He was
brought to Munich
from Schwetzingen by
the Elector to create
the garden on an area
of former marshland.

Chinese Tower in the Englischer Garten

Opened in 1808, the Karl-
Theodor-Park is today known
simply as the Englischer
Garten (English Garden). It
is a popular place for long
walks, jogging or just lying on
the grass in the cool shade of
a spreading old tree.

There are some interesting
old buildings in the park,
such as the Monopteros, a
Neo-Classical temple by Leo
von Klenze (1837), and the
Chinese Tower (1789–90),
which is similar to the pagoda
in London's Kew Gardens.
The Tower stands in one of
the park's beer gardens.

It is also worth dropping
in to the Japanese Teahouse,
where the gentle art of tea
brewing is demonstrated.

Deutsches Museum 🄱

See pp218–19.

**Franz von Stuck's *Die Sünde*, on
display in the Villa Stuck**

Villa Stuck 🄲

Prinzregentenstraße 60. 📞 (089) 45
55 51 25. 🚋 18. 🚌 51, 55.
🕐 10am–6pm Tue–Sun. 📷

THIS VILLA was the home of
the famous painter Franz
von Stuck, the co-founder of
the Munich Secession school
of painting. As well as
numerous portraits, nudes
and sculptures, Von Stuck
was the creator of many
mythological and allegorical
scenes, all painted in dark

Submarine used in the film *Das Boot*, displayed in Bavaria-Filmstadt

colours and full of eroticism. These include eight variations (1893) on the theme of sin. His *Amazon* (1897) stands in front of the villa.

Franz von Stuck built the villa in 1897–98, to his own design, decorating it with his own paintings and sculptures. Since 1968, it has housed a museum. A permanent exhibition of Stuck's work is displayed in the magnificent music room on the ground floor, while the second-floor rooms are used for temporary exhibitions devoted mainly to early 20th-century art.

Bavaria-Filmstadt 33

Bavariafilmplatz 7. *(089) 64 99 23 04.* 25. 10am–3pm daily.

COMMONLY known as Hollywood on Isar, this vast site in the southern suburb of Geiselgasteig covers an area of over 3.5 sq km (865 acres).

Since 1919 the world's greatest cinema stars have worked here, including Orson Welles and Billy Wilder. The British film director Alfred Hitchcock made his first films here (*The Pleasure Garden*, 1925 and *The Mountain Eagle*, 1926). Elizabeth Taylor, Gina Lollobrigida and Romy Schneider have all stood in front of the cameras here.

Strolling visitors to the site will often come across some well-known characters who have appeared in films such as *E.T.* or *The Neverending Story*, which were filmed here. The sets of other films made here, including *Enemy Mine* and *Cabaret*, can also be seen. You can also peep into the submarine that was

reconstructed for Wolfgang Petersen's classic film *Das Boot* (1981) – the film follows the voyage of one such boat during World War II.

VIP tours of the Filmstadt include stuntmen shows and fascinating demonstrations of many technical film-making tricks and techniques. A special attraction is the cinema called Showscan, whose seats move according to the story on the screen, giving visitors the sensation of a trip through the universe or of flying through the tunnels of an old silver mine.

While taking a look behind film sets you may even catch a glimpse of a movie star or a celebrity, as the studio is also used for recording TV shows, in which visitors can take part as the studio audience.

Theresienwiese 34

Theresienhöhe. *Theresienwiese.* Oktoberfest (Sep–Oct).

FOR MOST OF THE YEAR this is simply a vast oval meadow encircled by the Bavariaring. Theresienwiese comes into its own once a year, however, during the Oktoberfest. Then it turns into a gigantic, boisterous beer-drinking venue, with stalls, marquees, funfair and loud music.

Towering above the meadow is a monumental 18-m (59-ft) high statue, symbol of the state of Bavaria. Made in 1844–50, the statue is the work of Ludwig Schwanthaler. It incorporates an internal staircase leading to the figure's head, where there is a viewing platform.

Just behind the statue is the Ruhmesalle, a Neo-Classical building surrounded by a colonnade. Designed by Leo von Klenze and built in 1843–53, the building contains numerous busts of eminent Bavarians.

Bavaria statue in Theresienwiese

OKTOBERFEST

Munich's Oktoberfest is one of the biggest folk fairs in Europe. In 1810 the site on which it is held was the venue for a horse race, held to celebrate the marriage of Ludwig (later King of Bavaria) and Thérèse von Saxe-Hildburghausen. A few years later it became the venue for an autumn fair that has grown into an enormous event over the years. Chief amongst the attractions is beer, drunk in vast quantities, in marquees erected by the breweries. The festival starts in late

Revellers at the annual Oktoberfest in Theresienwiese

September with a huge procession through the town and the ceremonial opening of the first barrel of beer. It finishes, 16 days later, on the first Sunday of October.

Deutsches Museum ③

THIS IS REPUTED TO BE the largest museum of science and technology in the world. It is also, according to statistics, the most popular museum in Germany, averaging 1.3 million visitors per year. Inspired by the vision of Oskar von Miller, the foundation stone for the first group of buildings was laid in 1904. The project, located on an island east of the city centre, was directed by Gabriel von Seidl and, after his death, completed by his brother, Emanuel. The vast exhibition area, spread over four floors, features an ever-growing collection of over 16,000 exhibits.

Decorative Arts
Exquisite glass, porcelain and decorative textiles illustrate the artistic and technical development of these crafts.

MUSEUM GUIDE

The collections are housed on four floors, divided into 45 sections. In the basement and on the ground floor, large models and original heavy vehicles, such as trains and motor cars, are displayed. The first floor is devoted to exhibits relating to chemistry, physics and scientific instruments. The space between the ground floor and the first floor is given over to aeronautics, while the second floor houses exhibits relating to decorative arts and crafts, such as ceramics, glass, paper, textiles and photography. The exhibition on the museum's fourth floor represents the most advanced technologies, and includes astronomy, computers and micro-electronics.

Physics
As well as featuring many modern technological exhibits, this section includes a huge and fascinating collection of scientific instruments and equipment from the past.

★ **Aeronautics**
In a room devoted to the history and development of air travel, many rare exhibits are on display, including the 1896 Lilienthal's biplane, an aeroplane belonging to the Wright brothers and a 1936 Messerschmitt ME 109.

Ground floor

Sailing
In a room charting the history of sailing, a 14th-century cog is displayed alongside a submarine and a luxury ferry ship.

Third floor

Second floor

First floor

★ **Astronomy**
In this section the exhibits illustrate the structure of the cosmos and the instruments used for its exploration.

Measurements
The mechanisms used to measure time, weight and distance were often very beautiful and complex, as illustrated by the exhibits here.

Music
Beautiful musical instruments are presented here as technical appliances that are used for producing sound.

★ **Automobiles**
Built by Carl Benz in 1885, the first petrol-driven car is displayed here. It could reach a top speed of 12 km/h (7 mph).

Land Transport
In this vast hall, models of bridges, viaducts and tunnels are featured along with coaches, railway engines and bicycles.

KEY

☐ Design and technology

☐ Land transport

☐ Water transport

☐ Physics and chemistry

☐ Music

☐ Aeronautics and astronomy

☐ Decorative art

☐ Telecommunications

☐ Agriculture

☐ Astronomy

☐ Measurements

STAR EXHIBITS

★ **Aeronautics**

★ **Astronomy**

★ **Automobiles**

MUNICH STREET FINDER

MAP REFERENCES given in this chapter for sights (and in the Munich hotel and restaurant listings at the back of the book) refer to the maps here. The key map below shows the area of Munich covered by the *Street Finder*. The maps include the major sightseeing areas, historic attractions, railway stations, bus stations, U-Bahn and S-Bahn stations and train stations. The word Straße (Str.) indicates a street, Platz a square, Brücke a bridge and Bahnhof a railway station.

| 0 metres | 750 |
| 0 yards | 750 |

KEY TO THE MUNICH STREET FINDER

Major sight	Tourist information	One-way street
Place of interest	Parking	Pedestrianized street
Other building	Hospital with casualty unit	
S S-Bahn station	Police station	
U U-Bahn station	Church	
Railway station	Post office	**SCALE OF MAPS 1–3**
Taxi stand	Railway line	0 metres 200
		0 yards 200

1

TIVOLISTRASSE

OETINGERSTRASSE

KÖNIGINSTRASSE

ENGLISCHER

GARTEN

DIANASTRASSE

LERCHENFELDSTRASSE

EMIL-RIEDEL-STRASSE

OETINGENSTRASSE

PARADIESSTRASSE PARADIESSTRASSE

KÖNIGINSTRASSE

ROSENBUSCHSTRASSE

2

IFFLANDSTRASSE

LERCHENFELDSTRASSE

SEEAUSSTRASSE

Präbhistorische
Staatssamm-
lung

Haus der Kunst

PRINZREGENTENSTRASSE

RETMORSTRASSE

AM GRIES

Schackgalerie

SEITZSTRASSE

BRUDERSTRASSE

WAGMÜLLERSTRASSE

UNSÖLDSTRASSE

Bayerisches
Nationalmuseum

OETTINGENSTRASSE

ALEXANDRASTRASSE

3

Luitpold-
brücke

LIEBIGSTRASSE

LIEBIGSTRASSE

RETMORSTRASSE

Friedensengel

EUROPA-
PLATZ

ST.-ANNA-STRASSE

ST.-ANNA-
PLATZ

TRIFTSTRASSE

TATTENBACH-
STRASSE

SEITZSTRASSE

Anna
Klosterkirche

Anna Kirche

Lehel U

R.-KOCH-STRASSE

STERNSTRASSE

RETMORSTRASSE

Isar

BÜRKLEINSTRASSE

GEWÜRZMÜHL-
STRASSE

WIDENMAYERSTRASSE

MARIA-THERESIA-STRASSE

Regierung von
Oberbayern

PFARRSTRASSE

4

WIMMER-RING

Völkerkunde-
museum

THIERSCH-
STRASSE

KNÖBELSTRASSE

Maximilianbrücke

Praterwehr-
brücke

Maximilianeum

M.-PLANCK-

STRASSE

Max-Weber-Platz

U

KNÖBELSTRASSE

ADELGUNDENSTRASSE

THIERSCHSTRASSE

MARIANNEN-
PLATZ

Mariannen-
brücke

Alpines
Museum

PRATERINSEL

SCKELLSTRASSE

GRÜTZNER-
STRASSE

MAX-WEBER-
-PLATZ

MANNHARDT-
STRASSE

STEINSDORFSTRASSE

5

LAND-
STRASSE

WÖRTHSTRASSE

KABELSTEG

MÜLLERWEG

INNERE WIENER STRASSE

METZGERSTRASSE

JOHANNIS-
PLATZ

BAVARIA

*B*AVARIA *is the biggest federal state in the Federal Republic of Germany. It is made up of regions that, in the past, were either independent secular territories or bishoprics. It includes former free towns of the Holy Roman Empire, such as Nördlingen, Rothenburg ob der Tauber, Dinkelsbühl, Nuremberg and Augsburg, which lost their independence to Bavaria only in the early 19th century.*

The area that is now known as Bavaria was inhabited in early times by Celts and Romans. The German Baiovarii, which gave the territory its name, arrived here during the 5th and 6th centuries. In the second half of the 6th century, the area was conquered by the Franks then, from 1180 until 1918, Bavaria was ruled by the Wittelsbach dynasty. During Medieval times, this split into the Upper Bavarian line (Straubing, Ingolstadt and Munich) and the Lower Bavarian line (Landshut). In 1505, separate provinces were once again combined into a single country. During the 16th and 17th centuries the duchy of Bavaria was the bulwark of Roman Catholicism within the Holy Roman Empire and during the reign of Maximilian I, Bavaria fought against the Protestant Union in the Thirty Years' War. For his loyalty to Rome, Maximilian I was rewarded in 1623 with the title of Elector, which meant that he could vote in elections for the Emperor. Following the fall of the Holy Roman Empire, Bavaria became a kingdom and remained as such until 1918.

Bavaria's turbulent history has left behind a rich architectural and cultural heritage. In addition to Roman antiquities, Baroque fortresses and fairy-tale castles, the region also has more than its share of glorious Alpine scenery, beer halls and colourful festivals, all of which make this one of the most popular parts of Germany for tourists. The capital, Munich, is a lively cosmopolitan city of wide boulevards and leafy squares with a wide choice of shops, restaurants, cinemas and theatres.

Girls dressed in national costume celebrating St Leonard's Festival

◁ **Interior of the Abbey library, in Metten**

Exploring Bavaria

BAVARIA IS A PARADISE for tourists. Its beautiful lakes attract lovers of water sports, while the mountainous regions of the Bavarian Forest offer the unspoiled charms of nature. The Alps, with their charming mountain hostels and numerous ski-lifts, provide endless possibilities for enjoyment. Towns and villages feature magnificent historic sights and the capital, Munich, combines the advantages of a lively metropolis with a peaceful atmosphere that is not often found in large cities.

Frankfurt

ASCHAFFENBURG ①
MILTENBERG
Men
WÜRZBURG ⑥
POMMERSFE
BAMBER
ROTHENBURG ⑰
Heilbronn
ANSBACH ⑬
DINKELSBÜH ⑪
⑫
NÖRDLINGEN

The façade and central rotunda of Bayreuth's Eremitage

SIGHTS AT A GLANCE

AUGSBUR
LANDSB
AM LEC
OTTOBEUREN ㊺
KEMPTEN ㊶
LINDAU
LINDENBERG
LINDERHOF
Bodensee
FÜSSEN
NEUSCHWANSTEIN
㊳
Feldkirch
OBERSTDORF

0 km   30

0 miles   30

Halle

Chemnitz

HOF

BURG

85

VIERZEHN-
HEILIGEN

93

22 **8** BAYREUTH

22

F R Ä N K I S C H E
S C H W E I Z

15

5

The beautiful town of Passau, on the river Danube

KEY

▨ Motorway

▨ Major road

▨ Scenic route

═ River

☆ Viewpoint

10 AMBERG

O B E R -
P F Ä L Z E R
W A L D

22

20

B A Y E R I S C H E R
W A L D

NBERG

E45/9

9

RCHING

28 **15** DONAUSTAUF

85

31

REGENSBURG

27

E56/3

KELHEIM

STRAUBING

15

12

4

STÄTT

23 INGOLSTADT

DEGGENDORF

PASSAU

BURG

93

E53/92

Dunaj

32

E45/9

Izara

26 DINGOLFING

E52/8

25

LANDSHUT

Linz

CHAU

22 FREISING

Salzach

12

21 SCHLESSHEIM

15

ALTÖTTING

99

29

Inn

MÜNCHEN

304

30

BURGHAUSEN

18 ANDECHS

304

20

2

*Starnberger
See*

ROSENHEIM

34 *Chiemsee*

472

E52/8

RAMMERGAU

B E R C H T E S G A D E N E R
L A N D

TTAL

33

GARMISCH-
PARTENKIRCHEN

NSCHWANGAU

SEE ALSO

• Where to Stay pp470–497

• Where to Eat pp498–527

Nuremberg's imposing Kaiserburg,
overlooking the city

GETTING AROUND

Munich, Nuremberg and Augsburg are all served by
international airports, while fast train services operate
throughout the region. The main motorways are the A93
linking Saxony with Ratisbon, the A9 between Thuringia
and Munich, the A5 between Frankfurt and Passau and the
A8, which runs between Stuttgart and Salzburg.

Red sandstone exterior of Schloss Johannisburg, Aschaffenburg

Aschaffenburg ❶

Road map C5. 🚹 67 000. 🚆
🏛 *Schlossplatz (06021-39 58 00).*

Situated in Lower Franconia, Aschaffenburg enjoys a scenic position on the hilly right bank of the river Main. The town became the second seat of the Mainz bishops in the 13th century, the first being Mainz.

The northwest part of the old town features a majestic, red sandstone riverside castle, **Schloss Johannisburg**, which was once occupied by the Mainz bishops-electors.

The castle gallery holds a fine collection of European paintings, dating from the 15th to the 18th century. It includes canvases by Lucas Cranach and Hans Baldung Grien. In the castle library are valuable medieval codices, such as the 10th-century *Book of Gospel Readings* (*Evangelarium*) from Fulda. Elegant interiors in the west wing are also noteworthy.

Occupying a scenic position above a vineyard a short distance to the northwest of the castle is Pompejanum. The Bavarian king Ludwig I was so fascinated with the discovery of Pompeii that he ordered a replica of the Castor and Pollux villa (*Casa di Castore e Polluce*) to be built. This he filled with his rich collection of antiquities.

After undergoing restoration work to repair war damage, the museum opened its doors to the public again in 1994.

⚓ Schloss Johannisburg
Schlossplatz 4. 📞 *(06021) 38 65 70.*
🕐 *Apr–Sep: 9am–5:30pm Tue–Sun;*
Oct-Mar: 10am–3:30pm Tue–Sun. 🖼

Pommersfelden ❷

Road map D5. 🏛 *Hauptstraße 11 (09548-922 00).*

On the edge of the Steiger-wald – a popular hiking area – is the small village of Pommersfelden, which is dominated by its magnificent Baroque palace, **Schloss Weissenstein**. The palace was commissioned by the Mainz Archbishop and Elector and the Prince-Bishop of Bamberg, Lothar Franz von Schönborn. It was built, in only five years (1711–16), to a design by the famous architect, Johann Dientzenhofer.

This masterpiece of secular Baroque architecture is worth visiting for several reasons. Particularly interesting is the three-storey-high ornamental ceiling by Johann Rudolf Byss. The most spectacular room is the Marble Hall, which features paintings by Michael Rottmayer. The well-preserved interior of the palace houses a gallery, a library, and a valuable collection of furniture. After visiting the palace, you can take a stroll around its gardens, which were

created by Maximilian von Welsch in 1715, in what was the then fashionable, geometric French style. It is now laid out in English-garden style.

⚓ Schloss Weissenstein
📞 *(09548) 203.* 🕐 *Apr–Oct: 10am–5pm daily.* 🕐 *every hour. (Short tour: 11:30am and 4:30pm.)* 🖼

Coburg ❸

Road map D5. 🚹 *44,000.* 🚆
🏛 *Herrngasse 4 (09561-741 80).*

Former residence of the Wettin family, Coburg is situated on the bank of the river Itz. It is dominated by a massive fortress, the **Veste Coburg**, which is one of the largest in Germany. Coburg's origins go back to the 11th century, but its present-day appearance is mainly the result of remodelling that was carried out in the 16th and the 17th centuries.

The fortress consists of a number of buildings clustered around several courtyards and surrounded by a triple line of walls. The complex is now a museum, housing various collections, including prints and drawings, arms and armour.

In 1530, the fortress provided refuge to Martin Luther who, as an outlaw, hid here from April until October. The room in which he hid is

Ornate entrance to Coburg's Stadthaus

furnished with antique furniture and features a portrait of Luther, painted by Lucas Cranach the Younger.

Among the most important buildings in the old town are the late-Gothic church of St Maurice and a beautiful Renaissance college building that was founded by Prince Johann Casimir in 1605. On the opposite side of the market square is the town hall, originally built in 1577–79 and remodelled in the 18th century.

Further along is the town castle, **Schloss Ehrenburg**, which was built in the 16th century on the site of a dissolved Franciscan monastery. The castle burned down in 1693 and was subsequently rebuilt. The façade facing the square was remodelled by Karl Friedrich Schinkel in Neo-Gothic style.

The castle has some fine interiors, including the Baroque Reisensaal and Weisser Saal and a chapel with rich stucco decorations.

♣ **Veste Coburg**
(09561) 87 90. Apr–Oct: 10am–5pm Tue–Sun; Nov–Mar: 1–4pm Tue–Sun.

♣ **Schloss Ehrenburg**
Schlossplatz 1. (09561) 808 80. Apr–Sep: 9am–5pm Tue–Sun; Oct–Mar: 10am–3pm Tue–Sun. every hour.

Vierzehnheiligen ❹

Staffelstein. **Road map** D5.
(09571) 950 80. Apr–Oct: 7am–6pm; Nov–Mar: 8am–5pm.

HIGH ABOVE the river Main is Banz Abbey, a Benedictine monastery built in 1695 by Johann Leonhard and Leonhard Dientzenhofer. Directly opposite stands the pilgrimage church of the Fourteen Saints of Intercession. The first chapel, erected on this site in the 16th century, proved to be too small to accommodate the growing numbers of pilgrims so, in 1741, the foundation stone

Interior of the monumental, Baroque Vierzehnheiligen church

was laid for the monumental new church, designed by Balthasar Neumann. Built in 1741–72, this is one of the most famous masterpieces of South German Baroque, with magnificent Rococo furnishings. The building is a cross-shaped basilica, with a monumental twin-tower façade.

The interior has an exceptionally dynamic style, achieved by combining longitudinal and central planes: the three ovals laid along the main axis join with the two circles of the transept. The centrepiece of the nave is the "Altar of Mercy", which stands at the spot where, according to a 1519 legend, a shepherd had visions of Christ with the fourteen Saints of Intercession. The altar features statues of the fourteen saints, the work of J.J.M. Kühel (1763). The rich stucco decorations and wall paintings are the work of J.M. and F.X. Feuchtmayr, J.G. Übelherr and Giuseppe Appiani.

Madonna from Marienkapelle in Ebermannstadt

Fränkische Schweiz ❺

Road map D5.

THE AREA POPULARLY known as Franconian Switzerland (*Fränkische Schweiz*) covers the area between Nuremberg, Bamberg and Bayreuth. One of Germany's most beautiful tourist regions, it offers its visitors picturesque green meadows, magnificent highlands covered with cornfields, imposing castles perched on top of high rocks, fabulous dolomite rocks and deep caves with stalactites. Its towns and villages, with their charming inns and timber-frame houses, look like a setting for *Snow White and Seven Dwarfs*. The main routes across the area run alongside its rivers – the Wiesent, Leinleiter, Püttlach and Trubach. The Wiesent, which is ideal for canoeing, cuts across the region from east to west, joining the river Regnitz near the town of Forchheim. The town features many timber-frame houses, including the old town hall dating from the 14th to the 16th century. Near Forchheim, in **Ebermannstadt**, is a Marian church with a fine Madonna.

The federal route B470 leads to the picturesque village of Tüchersfeld, which is built into the rocks. A good base for exploring this area is the village of Pottenstein. St Elizabeth of Thuringia is said to have stayed here in 1227. To the east of the castle is a cave with impressive stalactites.

Schloss Greifenstein in Heiligenstadt, in Fränkische Schweiz

Würzburg **6**

THE BOMBING RAID on Würzburg on 16 March 1945 lasted for about 20 minutes and destroyed over 80 percent of the town's buildings. It seemed that Würzburg, which occupies a picturesque position on the banks of the river Main, had been erased from the face of the earth. Like Dresden, however, the town rose from the ashes and once again it enchants visitors with its rich heritage of historic sights. As well as being a popular tourist destination, Würzburg is also an important commercial and cultural centre for Lower Franconia and home of the excellent Franconian wine.

View over Würzburg, with Dom St Kilian in the foreground

♛ Residenz
See pp231–2.

♙ Dom St Kilian
Domplatz. ☏ (0931) 321 18 30.
🕓 Easter–1 Nov: 10am–5pm Mon–Sat, 1–6pm Sun and holidays; 2 Nov–Easter: 10am–noon, 2–5pm Mon–Sat, 12:30–1pm, 2–6pm Sun and holidays.

Next to the cathedral churches of Mainz, Speyer and Worms, this is Germany's fourth largest Romanesque church. It was built in 1045–1188, its patron saint an Irish monk who came to Würzburg in AD 686 and died a martyr's death.

The church is a three-nave basilica with a transept and a twin-tower façade. Inside, the Romanesque main nave with its flat roof contrasts sharply with the Baroque stucco embellishments of the choir.

In the north nave is an interesting group of bishops' tombs, including two that are the work of Tilman Riemenschneider. At the end of the north transept is a chapel, which was built by Balthasar Neumann for the bishops of the House of Schönborn.

♙ Neumünster-Kirche
St-Kilians-Platz.

Just north of the cathedral, the Neumünster-Kirche was built in the 11th century at the burial site of St Kilian and his fellow Irish martyrs, St Kolonat and St Totnan.

The church's imposing Baroque dome and its red sandstone façade date from the 18th century. Featured in

The beautiful red sandstone façade of Neumünster-Kirche

the interior are numerous works of art, including a late 15th-century Madonna and the *Man of Sorrow* by the 15th-century German sculptor Tilman Riemenschneider. The north door leads to a lovely small courtyard; the remains of the cloister date from the Hohenstauf period. Under a lime tree is the resting place of a famous medieval minstrel Walther von der Vogelweide.

A procession is held each year on St Kilian's day (8 July) when theological students carry the skulls of the martyrs, contained in a transparent box, from the west crypt to the cathedral where they are put on public display.

✚ Bürgerspital
Theaterstraße.

The Bürgerspital was founded in 1319 by Johann von Sternen. Hospitals like this originally provided charitable care for the old as well as the infirm, and today this institution provides care for over one hundred elderly residents of Würzburg. It operates as a self-financing foundation, its main source of income being from vine-growing. Residents are given a quarter of a litre (½ pint) of an excellent home-produced wine each day, with double the ration on Sundays. Visitors can also sample various vintages.

✚ Juliusspital
Juliuspromenade.

Just a short distance away from Bürgerspital is another hospital. Founded in 1576 by Julius Echter, Juliusspital was remodelled in the 17th and the 18th centuries. The Rococo pharmacy (1760–65) in the hospital arcades has survived intact and is well worth a visit.

♛ Rathaus
Rueckermainstraße.

Würzburg's picturesque town hall was built in several stages. Begun in the 13th century, it was subsequently extended in the 15th and 16th centuries. Particularly noteworthy are the beautiful 16th-century paintings on the façade and the late-Renaissance tower, Roter Turm, which dates from around 1660.

An old crane near Alte Main-brücke over the river Main

🚇 Alte Mainbrücke

Crossing the river Main between the old town and Festung Marienberg is this beautiful bridge. Built in 1473–1543, it is the oldest bridge over the Main.

⛰ Festung Marienberg
Fürstenbau-Museum

📞 (0931) 438 38. ⏰ Apr–Oct: 9am–6pm Tue–Sun; Nov–Mar: 10am–4pm Tue–Sun. 🏷

Mainfränkisches Museum

📞 (0931) 430 16. ⏰ 10am–5pm Tue–Sun. 🏷

Burgführungen 📅 Apr–Oct: 11am, 2pm, 3pm Tue–Fri; 10am, 11am, 1pm, 2pm, 3pm, 4pm Sat–Sun.

Built on the site of an old Celtic stronghold, the Marienberg Fortress towers above the town. In AD 707 a church was built here and, in 1201, work commenced on a fortress that served as the residence of the prince-bishops until 1719. Within its fortifications stands the first original donjon church dating from the 13th century, and the Renaissance-Baroque palace. The museum exhibits illustrate the 1,200-year history of the town. The former arsenal now houses the Franconian Museum with its valuable collection of sculptures by Tilman Riemenschneider.

VISITORS' CHECKLIST

Road map C5. 🏘 128,000. ✈ 7 km (4½ miles) west. 🚉 Haupt-bahnhof. 🛈 Am Congress Centrum (0931-37 23 35). 🎭 Afrika-festival (May), Würzburger Wein-dorf (May/Jun), Mozartfest (Jun), Kilianifest (Jul), Bachtage (Nov–Dec).

🔒 Käppele
Mergentheimer Strasse.
Standing at the top of a hill at the southwestern end of the city, this twin-towered Baroque chapel is the work of Balthasar Neumann (1747–50). Its interior is lavishly decorated with beautiful wall paintings by Matthias Günther.

Festung Marienberg, built on a hill overlooking the river Main

WÜRZBURG CITY CENTRE

Alte Mainbrücke ❼
Bürgerspital ❹
Dom St Kilian ❷
Festung Marienberg ❽
Juliusspital ❺
Neumünster–Kirche ❸
Rathaus ❻
Residenz ❶

0 metres   300
0 yards   300

KEY

🛈 Tourist information
P Parking
🏛 Church

Residenz in Würzburg

Sculpture from Residenz garden

THIS VAST COMPLEX on the eastern edge of the town was commissioned by two prince-bishops, the brothers Johann Philipp Franz and Friedrich Karl von Schönborn. Its construction between 1720 and 1744 was supervised by several architects, including Johann Lukas von Hildebrandt and Maximilian von Welsch. However, the Residenz is mainly associated with the name of Balthasar Neumann, the creator of its famous Baroque staircase.

Napoleon's bedroom

Main entrance

★ Treppenhaus
The work of the Venetian artist Giovanni Battista Tiepolo, the largest fresco in the world adorns the vault of the staircase.

Martin-von-Wagner-Museum entrance

Ehrenhof
A fountain, designed by Gabriel von Seidel, was constructed in the parade square in front of the Residenz in 1896. It was funded by donations from the inhabitants of Würzburg.

The Arms of the Patron
The richly decorated façade by Johann Wolfgang von der Auwery bears the personal arms of Friedrich Karl von Schönborn, Prince-Bishop of Bamberg and Würzburg.

★ Kaisersaal
The centrepiece of the palace, the sumptuous emperor's chamber, testifies to the close relationship between Würzburg and the Holy Roman Empiure.

VISITORS' CHECKLIST

Residenzplatz 2. (0931) 35 51 70. Apr–Oct: 9am–6pm daily; Nov–Mar: 10am–4pm daily.

Garden Chamber
This vast, low hall has rococo stucco works by Antonio Bossi, dating from 1749. There is also a painting on the vaulting by Johan Zick dating from 1750, depicting The Feast of the Gods *and* Diana Resting.

Venetian Room
This room is named after a tapestry depicting the Venetian carnival. Further ornaments include decorative panels with paintings by Rudolph Byss and his pupils.

★ Hofkirche
The church interior is richly decorated with paintings, sculptures and stucco ornaments. The side altars were designed by Johann Lukas von Hildebrandt and feature paintings by Giovanni Battista Tiepolo.

STAR SIGHTS

★ **Hofkirche**

★ **Kaisersaal**

★ **Treppenhaus**

Bamberg ❼

SITUATED ON SEVEN HILLS like ancient Rome, Bamberg features a splendidly preserved old town, encircled by the branches of the river Regnitz. The town is famous not only for its exceptional artistic heritage but also for its excellent beer, produced by one of the nine breweries that operate here. Its long history goes back to AD 902, when the Babenberg family established their residence here. The town grew and prospered in the wake of the Thirty Years' War, in which the townsfolk declared themselves on the Catholic side.

Beautiful rose garden at the rear of the Neue Residenz

Exploring Bamberg

A good place to start sight-seeing is the Domplatz, one of Germany's loveliest squares, with its magnificent cathedral church and the old bishop's palace. After visiting the Neue Residenz you can go down to the river, where you will find the water palace, Concordia. The old town is reached by crossing one of two bridges – Untere or Obere Brücke.

⛪ Dom
See pp236–7.

⛪ Alte Hofhaltung
Historisches Museum
Domplatz 7. ☎ (0951) 87 11 42.
🕐 9am–5pm Tue–Sun. 📷
On the west side of Domplatz stands a magnificent portal, featuring statues of the imperial couple Heinrich II and Kunigunde. This is the gate to the former bishop's residence, built at the turn of the 15th and 16th centuries in place of an old fortress of Heinrich II. Within the wings of the building is a pleasant courtyard. The museum that is housed here focuses on the history of the region.

🏛 Neue Residenz und Staatsgalerie
Domplatz 8. ☎ (0951) 563 51.
🕐 Apr–Sep: 9am–noon, 1:30–5pm daily; Oct–Mar: 9am–noon, 1:30–4pm daily. 📷
The Neue Residenz, with its richly decorated apartments and the Emperor's Room, was buit in 1695–1704 and is the work of Johann Leonhard Dietzenhofer. Its walls are adorned with magnificent frescos painted by the Tyrolean artist Melchior Steidl. The walls and pillars feature the Habsburg family tree, while 16 statues represent Emperors of the Holy Roman Empire. The Neue Residenz houses a collection of old German masters, including *The Flood* by Hans Baldung Grien and three canvases by Lucas Cranach the Elder.

⛪ Bishop's Palace
Behind the cathedral, along the quiet, picturesque Dom-strasse, are a number of ecclesiastical buildings, the oldest of which date from the 16th century. Domstrasse leads to the Baroque Bishop's Palace, built in 1763 by Johann Michael von Küchel.

⛪ Karmelitenkloster
Kreuzgang 🕐 8:30–11.30 am, 2:30–5:30pm daily.
The hospital-abbey complex of St Theodore was founded in the late 12th century by Bishop Eberhard. Since 1589 the church and abbey have belonged to the Carmelite order. The south tower and Romanesque portal are the remains of the massive 12th-century basilica. The interior of the church was redesigned in the late 17th and early 18th centuries so the altar is now situated at its western end, while the entrance is on the site of the previous presbytery. The layout of the cloisters on the south side of the church is typical of Cistercian designs.

♣ Wasserschloss Concordia
Concordiastrasse. ⬤ *to the public.*
This magnificent Baroque palace, which enjoys a scenic position on the water's edge,

Façade of the Baroque Bishop's Palace, flanked by two towers

Picturesque fishermen's cottages in Klein-Venedig

was built for Counsellor
Böttinger between 1716 and
1722, to a design by Johann
Dientzenhofer. The building
now houses a science institute.

🏛 Altes Rathaus

The Baroque lower bridge,
Untere Brücke, provides a
magnificent view over the
upper bridge, Obere Brücke,
with its fabulous town hall.
This originally Gothic seat of
the municipal authorities was
remodelled in 1744–56 by
Jakob Michael Küchel. The
half-timbered structure of the
Rottmeisterhaus, which seems
to be gliding over the waves
of the river Regnitz, was
added in 1688.

🏛 Klein-Venedig

Kranenstrasse.
"Little Venice" is a district
of fishermen's cottages, their
picturesque façades adorned
with pots of geraniums.
Visitors come here for a glass
of Rauchbier – a local beer
with a smoky flavour.

🏛 Grünermarkt

With its historic houses and
adjacent Maximilianplatz,
Grünermarkt lies at the heart
of the old town. Here you
will find the magnificent
Baroque St Martin's Church,
built in 1686–91 by the
Dientzenhofer brothers. Also
notable are the late-Baroque
buildings of the St Catherine
Hospital and Seminary, built
by Balthasar Neumann, which
now serves as the town hall.

⛪ Kirche St Michael

Michaelsberg.
Fränkisches Brauereimuseum
🕐 Apr–Oct: 1–5pm Wed–Sun. 📷
The Benedictine abbey that
stood on this site was founded
in 1015. The surviving church

was built after 1121 and later
remodelled in the 16th and
17th centuries. On the ceiling
of the church, nicknamed
the "Botanical Gardens", are
paintings depicting almost
600 species of medicinal
plants. The abbey's Baroque
buildings date from the 17th
and 18th centuries and are
the work of Johann Dientzenhofer and Balthasar Neumann.
The domestic quarters include
the abbey's brewery, which
now houses a museum.

**The Baroque palace Concordia on
the bank of the river Regnitz**

**BAMBERG CITY
CENTRE**

Alte Hofhaltung ❷
Altes Rathaus ❼
Bishop's Palace ❹
Dom ❶
Karmeliterkloster ❺
Klein-Venedig ❽
Neue Residenz
   und Staatsgalerie ❸
Wasserschloss
   Concordia ❻

KEY

ℹ Tourist information
🅿 Parking
⛪ Church

Bamberg Cathedral

BAMBERG'S SKYLINE is dominated by the cathedral of St Peter and St George, which combines the late Romanesque and early French-Gothic styles. Its construction started about 1211 and the church was consecrated in 1237. This is a triple-nave basilica with two choirs, whose apses are flanked by two pairs of towers. The cloisters were built between 1399 and 1457, while the monumental sculptures adorning the portals date from the 13th century. The western choir of the cathedral holds the only papal grave in Germany, that of Pope Clement II, who had been the local bishop.

Sculpted figure of Ecclesia

★ **Bamberger Reiter**
By the northwestern pillar of the eastern choir stands the famous equestrian statue of the "Bamberg Rider", dating from 1225–30. Many scholars have puzzled over the identity of the rider, but the riddle remains unsolved.

Interior
The illuminated main nave features a graceful, early Gothic, cross-ribbed vault.

St George's Choir

★ **Tomb of Heinrich II and Kunigunde**
This beautiful sarcophagus of the imperial couple is the work of Tilman Riemenschneider, completed in 1513.

Main entrance

VISITORS' CHECKLIST

Domplatz 5. *(0951) 50 23 30.* 10am–6pm daily.
Diözesanmuseum *(0951) 50 23 25.* 10am–5pm Tue–Sun. Good Friday, 25, 31 Dec.

St Peter's Choir

Emperor's Cloak
The Diocesan Museum houses an exhibition of sacral art. It also features a collection of imperial vestments, including Heinrich II's blue cloak of stars.

Hochaltar des Peterschores
The main altar of the west choir is adorned with sculptures depicting the Crucifixion (1648–49) by Justus Glesker.

★ Marian Altar by Veit Stoss
Veit Stoss was commissioned to create this altar by his son, Andrew Stoss, who was a Carmelite prior in Nürnberg. After the victory of the Reformation in Nürnberg, however, he moved to Bamberg. The altar was later moved to Bamberg in 1543.

Fürstenportal

Gnadenpforte
This magnificent stonework adorns the main entrance. The tympanum features reliefs depicting scenes from the Last Judgement.

STAR SIGHTS

- ★ Bamberger Reiter
- ★ Marian Altar by Veit Stoss
- ★ Tomb of Heinrich II and Kunigunde

Bayreuth **❽**

LOVERS OF GERMAN music associate this town with the composer Richard Wagner (1813–83), who took up residence here in 1872. Established in 1231, Bayreuth originally belonged to the family of Count von Andechs-Meran; in 1248 it passed to the Margraves of Nuremberg (von Zollern) and, since 1806, Franconian Bayreuth has belonged to Bavaria. The town flourished during the 17th and 18th centuries when it was the residence of the Margraves, particularly during the time of Margravine Wilhelmine, sister of the Prussian King Frederick the Great and wife of Margrave Frederick.

Extraordinary Baroque interior of the Markgräfliches Opernhaus

🖼 Markgräfliches Opernhaus

Opernstraße 14. █ (0921) 759 69 22. ○ Apr–Sep: 9am–6pm Fri–Wed, 9am–8pm Thu; Oct–Mar: 10am–4pm daily. 🈺

One of the finest theatres in Europe, the Markgräfliches Opera House was built in the 1740s by Joseph Saint-Pierre. Its interior was designed by Giuseppe Galli Bibiena and his son Carlo, who came from a famous Bolognese family of theatre architects.

♣ Neues Schloss

Ludwigstraße 21. █ (0921) 759 69 21. ○ Apr–Sep: 9am–6pm Fri–Wed, 9am–8pm Thu; Oct–Mar: 10am–4pm daily. 🈺

The Neues Schloss (New Castle) was commissioned by Margravine Wilhelmine and built by Joseph Saint-Pierre. Built in a horseshoe shape, the elongated, three-storey structure combines classical lines with a rustic ground floor. The Italian wing was added in 1759. Nearly all the rooms have retained their original Baroque and Rococo decor. The park is arranged in a typically English style.

🖼 Villa Wahnfried

Richard-Wagner-Museum. Richard-Wagner-Straße 48. █ (0921) 75 28 16. ○ 10am–5pm Mon, Wed, Fri– Sun; Nov–Mar: 10am– 5pm daily. 🈺 ● Easter Sunday.

On the northeast side of the castle garden is Villa Wahnfried. Built for Wagner by Carl Wölfel, the villa was destroyed during World War II but was restored in the 1970s. In the garden is Wagner's tomb and that of his wife Cosima, the daughter of Franz Liszt.

🏛 Franz-Liszt-Museum

Wahnfriedstraße 9. █ (0921) 757 28 18. ○ Sep–Jun: 10am–noon, 2–5pm daily; Jul-Aug: 10am–5pm daily. 🈺

A short distance from Villa Wahnfried, at the junction of Wahnfriedstrasse and Liszt-strasse, stands the house in which Hungarian composer Franz Liszt died in 1886. It now houses a museum dedicated to the composer.

🖼 Eremitage

4 km (2.5 miles) northeast of town █ (0921) 759 69 37. ○ Apr–Sep: 9am–6pm Fri–Wed, 9am–8pm Thu. ● Oct–Mar.

In 1715–18, following the example of the French king Louis XIV and the fashion among the nobility for playing at ascetism, Margrave Georg Wilhelm ordered the building of the Eremitage complex as a retreat. When the hermitage (or Altes Schloss) was given to Margravine Wilhelmine as a birthday present, however, she transformed it into a glamorous, self-indulgent, pleasure palace.

Tomb of Wagner and his wife in the garden of Villa Wahnfried

RICHARD WAGNER (1813–1883)

The German composer is inseparably linked with Bayreuth, where he enjoyed his greatest artistic triumphs. His career, which did not run smoothly in early days, began in Magdeburg, Königsberg and Riga. From there he had to flee, via London to Paris, from his pursuing creditors. His reputation was firmly established by successful performances of his romantic operas *The Flying Dutchman* (1843) and *Tannhäuser* (1845) in Dresden. Wagner's long-time sponsor was the eccentric Bavarian king, Ludwig II. From 1872 Wagner lived in Bayreuth, where Festspielhaus was built specifically for the operas.

Bust of Wagner by Arno Breker (1939)

Festspielhaus, specially designed venue for the annual Wagner Festival

Festspielhaus

Festspielhügel. ((0921) 787 80. 10am, 10:45am, 2:15pm, 3pm, Tue–Sun (mornings only during the Festival). Nov.

Each July and August, Wagner festivals are held in this theatre, which was built in 1872–75 to a design by Gottfried Semper. The world premiere of *The Ring of the Nibelung* was performed here in 1876.

ENVIRONS: Approximately 20 km (12 miles) to the northeast of Bayreuth is the town of **Kulmbach**. Famous for its countless breweries, the town hosts a big beer festival each year, in July and August.

Its town hall has a beautiful, Rococo façade dating from 1752. From here you can walk to the castle hill to visit the Plassenburg Fortress, which has belonged to the Hohenzollern family since 1340. Until 1604, this was the seat of the von Brandenburg-Kulmbach Margraves. This vast structure was built in 1560-70. The gem in its crown is the Renaissance courtyard with arcades (Schöner Hof). The castle houses a vast collection of tin figurines, with some 30,000 items.

In **Ködnitz**, just to the south-east of Kulmbach, can be seen the Upper Franconian Village School Museum. Based on the original school furnishings and various old photographs, the exhibition illustrates the teaching methods that were used in this region more than a hundred years ago.

Some 25 km (16 miles) from Bayreuth, in Sanspareil Park near Hollfeld, is the **Felsentheater** – an unusual 80-seat theatre set in a natural grotto.

Felsentheater, in a natural grotto in Sanspareil Park near Bayreuth

BAYREUTH CITY CENTRE

Franz-Liszt-Museum ❹
Markgräfliches
Opernhaus ❶
Neues Schloss ❷
Villa Wahnfried ❸

0 metres   200
0 yards   200

KEY

🛈 Tourist information
P Parking
✝ Church

Berching

Map D6. 🏛 *7,500.* ⓘ *Petten-koferplatz 12 (08462-20 50).*

THIS CHARMING little town, situated in the valley of the river Sulz, boasts a history that stretches back to the 9th century. To this day it retains the complete enclosure of its medieval city walls, including towers and gates with old oak doors. The most beautiful of the towers is the *Chinesische Turm* (the Chinese Tower).

The regional museum is well worth visiting, as are some of the local churches. These include an early Gothic church, Mariae Himmelfahrt, remodelled after 1756 by M Seybold and featuring some beautiful Rococo stucco ornaments. The Baroque St Lorenz, with its 13th century tower and original late-Gothic altar, is also noteworthy.

Amberg ⑩

Map D5. 🏛 *43,000.* ⓘ *Zeug-hausstraße 1A (09621-102 39).*

SITUATED AT THE EDGE of the Franconian Jura, on the banks of the river Vils, Amberg owes its development to local iron ore deposits and the steel industry. The well-preserved, oval-shaped old town is still encircled by medieval walls. At the centre is an enchanting market square with the vast 15th-century late-Gothic hall-church, Pfarrkirche St Martin, and Gothic town hall (1356), both still with their original interiors.

Amberg was once the residential town of the Rhine palatines, whose Renaissance palace and chancellery have survived to the present day.

The symbol of Amberg is the Stadtbrille, the bridge spanning the river Vils, whose arches reflected in the river resemble a pair of spectacles – hence its nickname "the town's spectacles".

The late-Gothic main altar in St George's Church, Dinkelsbühl

Dinkelsbühl ⑪

Map D6. 🏛 *11,000.* 🚊 ⓘ *Segringerstraße 2 (09851-902 40).* 🎭 *Kinderzeche (mid-Jul).*

THIS OLD Franconian town is one of the best-preserved medieval urban complexes in Germany. The walls surrounding the city include four towers – Wörnitzer, Nördlinger, Seringer and Rothenburger Tor – which are all almost intact. The residential district of the town consists

mainly of timber-framed houses. The finest example of these is the Deutsches Haus, which stands opposite St George's Church. Dating from the late 15th to the early 16th century, the house once belonged to the Drechsel-Deufstetten family and is now a hotel-restaurant.

The late-Gothic Church of St George is a triple-nave hall-church with no transept. Together with the presbytery, it forms one large interior crowned with magnificent network vaults. The most valuable items of the interior furnishings include the pulpit, the font – which dates from around 1500 – and the Crucifixion in the main altar, which is attributed to Michael Wolgemut. A fine view of the town can be obtained from the church tower.

In Turmgasse stands the Baroque palace of the Teutonic Order, built in 1760–64 by Mathias Binder.

Nördlingen ⑫

Map D6. 🏛 *20,000.* 🚊 ⓘ *Marktplatz 2 (09081-43 80 or 841 16.* 🎭 *Stabenfest (May), Nördlinger Pfingstmesse Schar-lachrennen (Jun–Jul), Sommer-festspiele (Jul), Historisches Stabt Mauernfest (every third year in Sep).*

THE TOWN IS situated in the Ries Basin, which is an immense and well-preserved crater formed millions of years ago by a meteor.

During the Middle Ages Nördlingen was a free town of the Holy Roman Empire and an important trade centre. The fortification walls which surround the city, including fifteen towers (dating from the 14th to the 15th centuries) have survived almost intact to this day.

The late-Gothic church of St George was built by Nikolaus Eseler, who also built the St George Church in Dinkelsbühl. The church is a triple-nave hall-church with round pillars and network vaults. Its imposing west tower, known as the Daniel Tower, offers a magnificent panoramic view of the town

The symbol of Amberg is the bridge named "the town spectacles"

and its environs.

The St Salvator's Church features original Gothic altars and a portal that has the scene of the *Last Judgement* in the tympanum.

The former hospital of the Holy Spirit is now home to an interesting **Municipal Museum**. The 14th century town hall features a striking external stone stairway (1618).

🏛 **Municipal Museum**

Vordere Gerbergasse 1. 📞 (09081-273 82 30). 🕐 Mar–Nov: 1:30–4:30pm Tue–Sun. 🎫 Dec–Feb: open only to guided tours (reserve a place in advance by telephone). 🈂

Ansbach ⓭

Map D6. 🏛 40,000. 🚉 🛈 Johann-Sebastian-Bach-Platz 1 (0981- 512 34 or 194 33. 🎭 Ansbacher Frülingsfest (May), Bach-Woche (Jul), Ansbacher Rokokospiele (Jul), Heimatfest (Jul).

THE TOWN, situated west of Nuremberg, began its history in 748 AD with the foundation of a Benedictine Abbey by a man named Gumbert. A settlement called Onoldsbach, which sprang up nearby, is now called Ansbach. From 1460 until 1791 Ansbach was the home of the von Brandenburg-Ansbach margraves and in 1791 the town was incorporated into the Kingdom of Prussia; after 1806 it passed into Bavaria. The Hohen-zollern residence is situated

in the north-eastern part of the Old Town. Remodelled several times it is now a Baroque neo-Classical structure. Its 27 original state apartments include the Mirror Room, Mirror Gallery, Dining Room and Audience Room. It now houses the Museum of Faience and Porcelain. The nearby Hofgarten has a 102-metre (335-ft) long Orangery. It also houses a Kaspar Hauser Collection. Hauser was killed in the town in 1833.

🏛 **Markgrafenmuseum**
Kaspar-Hauser-Platz 1.
📞 (0981) 977 50 56.
🕐 10am–noon, 2–5pm Tue–Sun. 🈂
🏛 **Markgräfliche Residenz "Ansbacher Fayence und Porzellan"**
Promenade 27. 📞 (0981) 953 83 90.
🕐 Apr–Sep: 9am–5pm Tue–Sun; Oct–Mar: 10am–4pm Tue–Sun.
🎫 hourly. ♿

Eichstätt ⓮

Map D6. 🏛 15,000. 🚉

WILLIBALD, a close com-panion and compatriot of the Anglo-Saxon missionary Boniface, established a missionary-abbey (Eihstat) here. Soon afterwards Eichstätt became an episcopal town. In 1634 a devastating fire ripped through the town, destroying four-fifths of its houses and four churches; after this the town was rebuilt in Baroque style.

Eichstätt is home to the country's only Catholic uni-versity, established in 1980. On the outskirts of town, on

Majestic Walhalla near Donaustauf

a hill overlooking the River Altmühl, stands the pictur-esque Willibald Castle, which until the 18th century was the residence of prince-bishops. Now it houses an interesting museum of artifacts from the Jurassic era, where visitors can see a very well preserved skeleton of *archaeopteryx*.

A new bishop's residence was built nearby from 1702 until 1768. Its west wing features a magnificent staircase and the Mirror Room, in which the works of Mauritio Pedetti, Johann Jakob Berg and Michael Franz are displayed.

Donaustauf ⓯

Walhalla. 📞 (09403) 96 16 80. 🕐 Apr–Sep: 9am–5:45pm; Oct: 9am–4:45pm; Nov–Mar: 10am–noon & 1–3:45pm. 🈂

IN 1830-1841 Leo von Klenze built the Walhalla *(see above).* This monument to the national glory occupies a scenic location on the River Danube. The building stands on a raised terrace and has the form of a neo-Classical columned temple (similar to the Parthenon in Athens). It is adorned with 121 marble busts of artists and scientists.

Orangery of the Hohenzollern residence, in Ansbach

Nürnberg (Nuremberg) ⑯

SITUATED ON THE RIVER PEGNITZ, Nuremberg is not only
a paradise for lovers of its famous gingerbread and
sausages but is also the symbol of Germany's history.
The earliest records of the town, the second largest in
Bavaria, date from 1050 when it was a trading settlement. From 1219 Nuremberg, a free town of the Holy
Roman Empire, was an important centre of craft and
commerce. Its most rapid development took place in
the 15th and 16th centuries, when many prominent
artists, craftsmen and intellectuals worked here, making
Nuremberg one of the cultural centres of Europe.

Picturesque alley near Frauentor

Exploring Lorenzer Seite

The southern part of the old
town, known as Lorenzer
Seite, is separated from the
northern part by the river
Pegnitz and encircled to the
south by the city walls. Many
of the area's historic treasures
were carefully reconstructed
following severe bomb
damage during World War II.

🏰 Frauentor
Frauentorgraben.
Frauentor is one of the most
attractive gates into the old
town. It is installed in the
massive city walls that were
constructed during the
15th and 16th centuries.
The vast tower, Dicker
Turm, was erected
nearby in the 15th
century. Königstor, a
magnificent gate that
once stood to the right
of Dicker Turm, was
dismantled in the 19th
century. Beyond Frauen-
tor are a number of
alleys with half-timbered
houses, shops and
cafés, built after the war.

🏛 Marthakirche
Königstraße 74–78.
Dating from the 14th century,
the small hospital church of St
Martha is tucked between the
surrounding houses. Though
its interior is virtually devoid
of furnishing, it features some
magnificent Gothic stained-
glass windows, which date
from around 1390.

🏛 Mauthalle
Hallplatz 2.
The massive structure that
dominates Königstrasse is a
Gothic granary built in 1498–
1502 by Hans Beheim the
Elder. It originally housed the
town's municipal scales and
the customs office. In the 19th
century, the building was
converted into a department
store and continues in that
role today, following post-
war reconstruction.

🏛 Germanisches Nationalmuseum
See pp246–7.

🏛 St Lorenz-Kirche
Lorenzer Platz.
The most important building
in Nuremberg is the Gothic
church of St Lorenz, whose
basilica-style main body
was built around
1270–1350. The vast
hall presbytery was
added much later,
in 1439–77. On
entering the
church it is worth
taking a look at
the magnificent
main portal,
which is
adorned
with

SIGHTS AT A GLANCE

Panoramic view over the rooftops of Nuremberg

One of four imposing gateways in the encircling city walls

sculptures. In the main nave of the church, suspended from the ceiling above the altar, is a superb group sculpture, *Annunciation*, the work of Veit Stoss (1519). He was also the creator of the crucifix within the main altar and the magnificent statue of the Archangel Michael standing by the second pillar of the main nave. There are

also several Gothic altars and some magnificent 15th-century stained-glass windows (1493–95) by Adam Kraft. The pillars of the nave are adorned with a number of fascinating statues of the Apostles, dating from the late 14th century.

🜲 Lorenzer Platz

Overlooked by the church of St Lorenz, Lorenzer Platz is a popular meeting place for the citizens of Nuremberg and visitors alike. Outside the church is the Fountain of the Virtues, *Tugendbrunnen* (1589), with water cascading from the breasts of its seven Virtues. Nearby is a statue of St Lorenz, which is a copy of the 1350 Gothic original. Diagonally across the square

KEY

🛈 Tourist information

🅿 Parking

🜲 Church

0 metres 300
0 yards 300

VISITORS' CHECKLIST

Road map D6. 🜲 *490,000.*
🛬 *on the northeast outskirts of town.* 🚍 🛈 *Frauentorgraben (0911-233 60).* 🎵 *Internationale Nürnberger Orgelwoche (June–July); Christkindlesmarkt (late Nov-23 Dec).*

is the Nassauer Haus, a Gothic mansion whose lower storeys were built in the 14th century. The upper floors were added in the 15th century.

A short distance from the square, in Karolinenstrasse, is a fine sculpture by Henry Moore, which stands in the middle of this shopping street.

🜲 Heilig-Geist-Spital

In the centre of town, on the banks of the river Pegnitz, stands the Hospital of the Holy Spirit. Founded in 1332, this is one of the largest hospitals built in the Middle Ages and features a lovely inner courtyard with wooden galleries. The wing that spans the river was built during extension works in 1488–1527. Lepers were kept at some distance from the other patients, in a separate half-timbered building that was specially erected for the purpose. From 1424 until 1796, the insignia of the Holy Roman Empire were kept here rather than in the castle.

The Heilig-Geist-Spital now houses an old-folks' home and a restaurant. The entrance to the building is on the northern side of the river.

Heilig-Geist-Spital reflected in the waters of the river Pegnitz

Exploring Nürnberg (Nuremberg)

NUREMBERG WAS ONCE an important publishing centre. Schedtl's *Liber Cronivarum* was published here in 1493 and, in 1543 – following the town's official adoption of the Reformation in 1525 – *The Revolutions of the Celestial Spheres* by Copernicus was published. The Thirty Years' War ended the town's development but, during the 19th century, it became the focus for the Pan-German movement. In 1945–49 the town was the scene of the trials for war crimes of Nazi leaders.

Detail of *Schöner Brunnen*, in Hauptmarkt

♛ Hauptmarkt

Each year the Hauptmarkt provides a picturesque setting for the town's famous Christkindlesmarkt, which goes on throughout Advent. At this famous market you can buy gingerbread, enjoy the taste of German sausages, warm yourself with a glass of red wine spiced with cloves and buy locally made souvenirs.

Nuremberg's star attraction is the Gothic *Schöner Brunnen* (Beautiful Fountain), which was probably erected around 1385 but replaced in the early 20th century with a replica. It consists of a 19-metre (62-ft) high, finely carved spire

standing at the centre of an octagonal pool. The pool is surrounded by a Renaissance grille that includes the famous golden ring: the local tradition is that if you turn the ring three times, your wishes will come true. The pool is adorned with the statues of philosophers, evangelists and church fathers, while the spire is decorated with the statues of Electors and of Jewish and Christian heroes. Features and details of the original fountain are kept in the **Germanisches National-museum** (*see pp246–7*).

♟ Frauenkirche

Hauptmarkt. ○ *9am–6pm Mon–Sat, 9am–12:30pm Sun.*
Commissioned by Emperor Charles IV, this Gothic hall-church dates from 1352–58. Over its richly decorated vestibule is the oriel of the west choir. Its gable contains a clock from Männleinlaufen, installed in 1509. Each day at noon the clock displays a procession of Electors paying homage to the Emperor. Also noteworthy is the Gothic altar (*Tucher Altar*), which dates from 1445.

♛ Rathaus

Rathausplatz.
The present town hall consists of several sections. Facing the Hauptmarkt is the oldest, Gothic part, built in 1332–40 and remodelled in the early 15th century. Behind, facing Rathausplatz, is the Renaissance part, built in 1616–22 by Jakob Wolff. Its magnificent portals are decorated with heraldic motifs. The courtyard features a fountain dating from 1557.

⛬ Spielzeugmuseum

Karlstraße 13. 【 *(0911) 231 31 64.*
○ *10am–5pm Tue–Sun, 10am–9pm Wed.* ● *Good Friday, 24, 25, 26, 31 Dec.* 🗓
This enchanting toy museum, established in 1971, houses a magnificent collection of tin soldiers and a huge collection of dolls and puppets. Its greatest attraction, however, is a collection of antique dolls' houses, filled with miniature furniture and equipment.

♟ Kirche St Sebaldus

Winklerstraße 26. ○ *Jan–Feb: 9:30am–4pm Mon–Sat, 9:30am–12:30pm Sun; Mar–Whitsun & Oct–Dec: 9:30am–6pm Mon–Sat, 9:30am–12:30pm Sun; Whitsun–Sep: 9:30am–8pm Mon–Sat, 9:30am–12:30pm Sun.*
The oldest of Nuremberg's churches, Kirche St Sebaldus was built in 1230–73 as a Romanesque, two-choir basilica. During remodelling in the 14th century, it was given two side naves and a soaring western hall-choir. The Gothic towers were completed in the late 15th century. At the centre of the presbytery is the magnificent tomb of St Sebald. This cast bronze structure was made by Peter Vischer the Elder. It houses a silver coffin (1397) containing relics of the saint. The church features some splendid carvings by Veit Stoss, including a statue of St Andrew (1505), standing in the ambulatory around the presbytery, the Volckamersche Passion (1499) and the Crucifixion scene in the main altar (1520). Also noteworthy is the magnificent Gothic font and the Tucher family epitaph by Hans von Kulmbach (1513).

Heraldic arms adorning the tympanum of the town hall portal

The timber-frame building of the Dürerhaus

⛪ Egidienkirche
Egidienplatz.
Egidienkirche is the only surviving Baroque church in Nuremberg. Its façade, built after the fire of 1696, hides a building containing elements of the previous Romanesque-Gothic Benedictine church. The older chapels, including the Euchariuskapelle, Tetzel-kapellethe and Wolfgang-kapelle, survive to this day.

♟ Kaiserburg
Kaiserburg-Museum. Innerer Burghof. ☎ (0911) 200 95 40.
◻ Apr–Sep: 9am–6pm Fri–Wed, 9am–8pm Thu; Oct–Mar: 10am–4pm daily. ◙
The three castles that tower over Nuremberg include the central burgraves' castle, with the Free Reich's buildings to the east, and the Imperial castle (whose origins go back to the 12th century) to the west. When climbing up the Burgstrasse you will first reach the Fünfeckturm (Pentagonal Tower), which dates from 1040. The oldest building in town, it is a relic of the von Zollern burgraves' castle. At its foot are the Kaiserstallung (Emperor's stables), which now houses a youth hostel. A continued climb will bring you, on the left, to the courtyard of the imperial palace, which features a round tower (*Sinwellturm*) dating from the 12th century, and a deep well – the *Tiefe Brunnen*. Passing through the inner gate of the castle you will finally reach its heart, the residential building.

🏛 Albrecht-Dürer-Haus
Albrecht-Dürer-Straße 39.
☎ (0911) 231 25 68. ◻ 10am–5pm Tue, Wed, Fri–Sun, 10am–8pm Thu. ◙ ◙
Born in 1471 in a house on the corner of Burgerstrasse and Obere Schmiedgasse, the renowned artist and engraver Albrecht Dürer lived in this house from 1509 until his death in 1528. On the three-hundredth anniversary of his death, the building was bought by the town and many rooms have since been reconstructed. The ground-floor room now contains a printing press dating from Dürer's time. Copies of his pictures provide a useful insight into the work of this famous Nuremberg citizen.

One of the most outstanding painters of the Renaissance era, Dürer was born in Nuremberg. He began his career as a goldsmith in his father's workshop, and learned painting at Michael Wolgemut's studio. He achieved fame not only as a painter, but also as a brilliant engraver and respected theoretician. He was a shrewd observer of the surrounding world and a sensitive artist, whose works are highly valued.

Dürer's self-portrait

⚰ St-Johannis-Friedhof
Am Johannisfriedhof.
The St John's Cemetery is one of the best preserved and most important in Europe. Since it was established in 1518, it has provided a resting place for many famous people, including Albrecht Dürer (No. 649), the sculptor Veit Stoss (No. 268), the goldsmith Wenzel Jamnitzer (No. 664) and the painter Anselm Feuerbach (No. 715).

The cemetery also contains a rich array of beautiful tombs dating from the 16th, 17th and 18th centuries.

🏛 Ehemaliges Reichsparteitagsgelände
Zeppelintribüne. ☎ (0911) 231 56 66. ◻ 10am–6pm Tue–Sun.
The vast, unfinished building complex in the southern part of town dates from the Nazi era. Its construction began in 1933 and it was intended to be a venue for National Party gatherings. The building now houses a historical exhibition and archive.

The buildings of the Kaiserburg, towering over the town

Nuremberg: Germanisches Nationalmuseum

THIS MUSEUM, WHICH WAS officially opened in 1852, was founded by a Franconian aristocrat named Hans von Aufsess. It houses a unique collection of antiquities from the German-speaking world. In 1945, towards the end of World War II, the buildings that had originally housed the museum were bombed. The modern architecture of the new building, which was completed in 1993, cleverly incorporates the remaining fragments of a former Carthusian abbey. Among the most valuable items in the museum's collection are works by Tilman Riemenschneider, Konrad Witz, Lucas Cranach the Elder, Adolf Altdorfer, Albrecht Dürer and Hans Baldung Grien.

Madonna with Child Crowned by Angels
This picture was painted by Hans Holbein the Elder (c.1465–1524) who created many festive altarpieces using warm colours.

Archangel (1516)
This enchanting wood-carving of the archangel Raphaël is one of many works produced by Veit Stoss after his return from Cracow.

Library

★ Cover of the Codex Aureus
The richly ornamented cover of the Codex Aureus, also known as the Golden Gospel Book of Echternach, was produced in Trier in the 11th century.

Former Carthusian church

Brooch from Domagnano
This Ostrogothic buckle from the 5th century AD, shaped like an eagle, was discovered in the late 19th century in Domagnano, in San Marino. It probably belonged to a rich Ostrogothic aristocrat.

Kupferstich-kabinett

GALLERY GUIDE
The exhibits have been arranged in sections, ranging from prehistory to the early Middle Ages. They include a painting and sculpture gallery, decorative arts, a collection of toys, folk art, drawings and stamps.

VISITORS' CHECKLIST
Kornmarkt. (0911) 133 10.
10am–5pm Tue, Thu–Sun,
10am–9pm Wed. 1 Jan, Good
Fri, 1 May, 24, 25, 31 Dec.

First floor

Ground floor

★ Torquetum
Johannes Praetorius from Nuremberg produced this engraved copper device in 1568, designed to measure the positions of the stars.

KEY

- Prehistory
- Medieval art
- 15th–16th-century German art
- 19th-century German paintings
- 20th-century art
- Musical instruments
- Arms and armour
- Crafts
- Folk art
- Nuremberg carpets
- Temporary exhibitions

★ Schlüsselfeld Vessel
This beautiful silver-gold sailing ship, supported by a two-tailed mermaid, is an ornamental table vessel made in 1503 by an unidentified Nuremberg goldsmith.

★ Portrait of Michael Wolgemut (1516)
Albrecht Dürer painted this portrait of his predecessor and master, Wolgemut, 30 years after commencing studies at his studio.

STAR SIGHTS

- ★ **Cover of Codex Aureus**
- ★ **Portrait of Michael Wolgemut**
- ★ **Schlüsselfeld Vessel**
- ★ **Torquetum**

Street-by-Street: Rothenburg ob der Tauber ⑰

IF YOU WANT TO sample the atmosphere of the Middle Ages, visit Rothenburg on the river Tauber, whose origins go back to the 12th century. Rothenburg was granted the status of a free town within the Holy Roman Empire in 1274 but its major growth took place in the 15th century. During the Thirty Years' War (1618–48) the town, which fought on the Protestant side, was captured by the Emperor's army. Little has changed since that time and the city walls still surround Gothic cathedrals and an array of gabled houses.

Eagle crest from the town hall

Reichstadtmuseum
The former Dominican abbey now houses a museum devoted to the town's history. The abbey kitchen – the oldest surviving kitchen in Germany – is also open to visitors.

Franziskanerkirche
In this Gothic church is a retable depicting The Stigmatization of St Francis, *believed to be an early work by Tilman Riemenschneider.*

★ St Jakobs Kirche
In the Gothic church of St Jakob, which was built between 1373 and 1464, is this magnificent high altar by Friedrich Herlin.

★ Mittelalterliches Museum
Many blood-curdling exhibits are on display at this museum, which houses an extensive collection of instruments of torture and punishment.

View from Burggarten
The castle garden (Burggarten) is reached through Burgtor, the tallest of the town's gates. The garden, which during the Middle Ages was the site of the Hohenstaufen family castle, provides a magnificent view over the town and the river valley.

Galgentor
Galgentor, an old execution place, is also known as Würzburger Tor, since it is the gate leading to Würzburg.

Spitaltor
The best preserved segments of the old city walls are around Spitaltor. From here you can walk through Rödertor to Klingentor.

KEY

– – – Suggested route

★ Rathaus
The town hall consists of the surviving Gothic section with a tower, and the later Renaissance structure with Baroque arcades.

STAR SIGHTS

★ **Mittelalterliches Museum**

★ **Rathaus**

★ **St Jakobs Kirche**

Andechs

Road map D7. 🅸 *Am Kirchplatz
(08151-906 00).*

THE VILLAGE OF Andechs, at the summit of the 700-m (2,300-ft) high Holy Mountain of the same name, is not only the destination of pilgrimages to the local church, but also of many less spiritual trips to the *Braüstüberl*, where visitors can refresh themselves with a glass or two of the excellent beer brewed by local monks.

The present triple-nave Gothic hall-church was built in 1420–25. Its Rococo interior dates from 1755. The lower tier of the main altar contains the famous *Miraculous Statue of the Mother of God* (1468), while the upper tier features the *Immaculata* by Hans Degler (1609). On selected feast days, holy relics are displayed on the altar gallery.

Lake at the foot of the Holy Mountain of Andechs

Landsberg am Lech ⑲

Road map D7. 🅰 *24,000.* 🚆
🅸 *Hauptplatz 1 (08191-12 82 46).*

THE HISTORY of Landsberg goes back to 1160 when Henry the Lion built his castle here, on the right bank of the river Lech. During the 13th century, the surrounding settlement grew into a town, which soon became a major trading centre. Religious conflicts, culminating in the Thirty Years' War, put an end to the town's development but, in the late 17th century, the town once again became an important commercial and cultural centre. Adolf Hitler wrote *Mein Kampf* here, while serving a prison term for his unsuccessful coup attempt in Munich.

At the heart of Landsberg is the Hauptplatz with its Baroque town hall and the intricately carved 14th-century tower, Schmalztor.

In Ludwigstrasse is the late-Gothic parish church, Stadtpfarrkirche Mariä Himmelfahrt, whose Baroque-style interior features a statue of the *Madonna and Child* by Hans Multscher. Bayertor, the original town gate, is in the west part of the old town.

The town's **Neues Stadtmuseum** is a useful source of information on local history.

🏛 **Neues Stadtmuseum**
Von-Helfenstein-Gasse 426. 🅲 *(08191) 94 23 26.* ☐ *Apr–Jan: 2–5pm Tue–Sun.* 🈚

Dachau ⑳

Road map D6. 🅰 *35,000.* 🚆
🅸 *Konrad-Adenauer-Straße 1 (08131-845 66).*

FOR MOST PEOPLE the name Dachau is inextricably linked with the concentration camp that was built here by the Nazis in 1933. Since 1965, the whole site has been designated as a memorial to the 32,000 prisoners who died there, with a permanent exhibition in the former domestic quarters of the camp.

Dachau is a beautiful town with many historic buildings. On the southwestern edge of the old town stands **Schloss Dachau**, summer residence of the Wittelsbachs. In earlier times this was the site of a fortified castle, replaced in the 16th century by a fortress. The palace that stands here today was created in the 18th century from the western wing of the earlier castle, the work of Joseph Effner.

Relief from the church façade in Landsberg

In the early 19th century the castle housed a colony of artists who had tired of city life. They were known as *Gruppe Neu Dachau*. Even earlier, however, the beauty of the surrounding countryside had been discovered by the impressionist painter Max Liebermann (1847–1935). Many works of art inspired by local scenery, including one by Liebermann, can be seen in the **Dachauer Gemäldegalerie**.

🏛 **Dachauer Gemäldegalerie**
Konrad-Adenauer-Straße 3.
🅲 *(08131) 56 75 16.* ☐ *11am–5pm Tue–Fri, 1–5pm Sat–Sun.* 🈚
🏰 **Schloss Dachau**
Schlossstraße 7. 🅲 *(08131) 879 23.*
☐ *Oct–Mar: 10am–4pm Tue–Sun; Apr–Sep: 9am–6pm Tue–Sun.* 🈚

Schleissheim ㉑

Road map D6. Oberschleissheim.

SCHLEISSHEIM IS SITUATED barely 14 km (9 miles) from Munich, making it within easy reach for an afternoon visit to its Baroque palace and park.

Surrounded by canals and now somewhat neglected, the park was established in the 17th and 18th centuries and includes three palaces. The

Baroque façade of the Wittelsbach palace, Schloss Dachau

modest **Altes Schloss** was
built in 1623 for Prince
Wilhelm V. Now it houses an
exhibition of religious folk art.

Schloss Lustheim is a
small, Baroque, hermitage-
type palace, built in 1684-87
by Enrico Zucalli for the
Elector Max Emanuel. As well
as its beautiful interiors and
stunning frescoes, it boasts a
magnificent collection of
Meissen porcelain, which is
displayed in the **Museum
Meissener Porzellan**.

The imposing bulk of the Neues Schloss in Ingolstadt

The newest building is the
Neues Schloss, designed by
Enrico Zucalli. Work began in
1701 but was not com-
pleted until the second
half of the 18th
century. Despite
wartime damage,
it retains many
original features.
It now houses
exhibits belonging
to the Bavarian
State Museum.

Detail from Neues
Schloss in Schleissheim

brothers, in 1724–25. The
four-nave Romanesque crypt
features a famous column,
which is decorated with
carvings of fantastic
animals *(Bestien-
säule)*. Nearby is
the **Diözesan-
museum**, whose
vast ecclesiastical
collection includes
two paintings by
Rubens.

At the south-
western end of
the old town
stands a former monastery,
Weihenstephan, which is
home to the world's longest-
established brewery.

Middle Ages and the Renaissance and Baroque periods.
Among the most outstanding
is the Church of the Virgin
Mary, a triple-nave hall
structure with circular pillars,
chapels and choir with an
ambulatory. Inside is the
original Gothic-Renaissance
main altar dating from 1572.

Another notable building is
the Neues Schloss, built
between the 15th and 18th
centuries, with its stately
rooms and Gothic chapel. It
now houses the **Bayerisches
Armeemuseum**.

A true gem of Bavarian
architecture is the **Church of
St Maria Victoria**, the work
of Cosmas Damian Asam.

The **Deutsches Medizin-
historisches Museum** has a
comprehensive collection of
medical instruments.

♣ **Altes Schloss**
◯ 10am–5pm Tue–Sun. 📷

♣ **Neues Schloss**
📞 (089) 315 87 20. ◯ Apr–Sep:
9am–6pm Tue–Sun; Oct–Mar: 10am–
4pm Tue–Sun. ◯ Mon.

♣ **Schloss Lustheim**
◯ Apr–Sep: 9am–6pm Tue–Sun;
Oct–Mar: 10am–4pm Tue–Sun. 📷

Museum Meissener Porzellan
📞 (089) 315 87 20. ◯ Apr–Sep:
9am–6pm Tue–Sun; Oct–Mar: 10am–
4pm Tue–Sun. ◯ Mon.

Freising ㉒

Road map D6. 🏠 40,000. 🚆
🛈 Marienplatz 7 (08161-541 22).

SITUATED ON THE banks of the
river Isar is the old town of
Freising. Its history is closely
connected with St Korbinian,
who founded the bishopric
here in the early 8th century.
Korbinian died around AD
725 and his remains still lie in
the crypt of the Dom – the
Cathedral Church of the Birth
of the Virgin Mary and St
Korbinian (1159–1205). This
is a five-nave basilica, without
transept, with an elongated
choir and a massive twin-
tower western façade. Its
interior was remodelled in
Baroque style by the Asam

🏛 **Diözesanmuseum**
Domberg 21. 📞 (08161) 487 90.
◯ 10am–5pm Tue–Sun. 📷

Ingolstadt ㉓

Road map D6. 🏠 115, 000. 🚆
🛈 Rathausplatz 2 (0841-305 10 98).

LYING ON THE river Danube,
this former seat of the
Wittelsbach family features
many important historic
buildings dating from the

🏛 **Bayerisches
Armeemuseum**
Neues Schloss, Paradeplatz 4.
📞 (0841) 937 70. ◯ 8:45am–
4:30pm Tue–Sun. 📷

🏛 **Deutsches Medizin-
historisches Museum**
Anatomiestraße 18–20.
📞 (0841) 305 18 60. ◯ 10am–
noon, 2–5pm Tue–Sun. 📷

Striking Baroque interior of the Church of St Maria Victoria, Ingolstadt

Arcaded courtyard of Neuburg Castle

Neuburg an der Donau ㉔

Road map D6. 🏛 *25,000.* 🚉
ℹ️ *Residenzstraße 166 (08431-552 40).*

PERCHED ON A promontory overlooking the river Danube, Neuburg is one of Bavaria's loveliest towns. During the Middle Ages, it changed hands frequently but was eventually ruled by Otto Heinrich the Magnanimous, under whom the town grew and prospered on an unprecedented scale. He was the founder of the castle, built between 1534 and 1665, whose massive round towers still dominate the town. Its earliest part is the east wing. The courtyard, which is surrounded by arcades, features beautiful frescos by Hans Schroer. In the tower is a staircase adorned with paintings. The castle chapel, completed in 1543, is one of the oldest, purpose-built Protestant churches in Germany.

In Amalienstrasse, leading down towards the town, stands the former Jesuits' College and the Court Church (Hofkirche). Work on the church began in the late 16th century and was completed in 1627. It was intended to be a Protestant church, but the ruling family converted back to Catholicism during its construction and it was taken over by the Jesuits who turned it into a counter-reformation

Marian church. The triple-nave hall-structure has an exquisite interior decorated in gold, white and grey.

Among many old buildings that survive in the town centre are the Graf-Veri-Haus and the Baron-von-Hartman-Haus in Herrenstrasse. To the east of town stands the Grünau Castle (Jagdschloss), built for Otto Heinrich in 1530–55.

ENVIRONS: 18 km (11 miles) to the south, Schrobenhausen is the birthplace of the painter Franz von Lenbach, who was born in 1836. A museum in Ulrich-Peisser-Gasse is devoted to his life and work. While there, it is worth visiting St Jacob's Church, to see the fine 15th-century wall painting there.

Heraldic crest on Neuberg Castle

🏛 **Schlossmuseum Neuburg**
Residenzstraße 2.
📞 *(08431) 88 97.* ⬜
May–Oct: 10am–6pm Tue–Sun; Nov–Apr: 10am–4pm Tue–Sun. 📷

Landshut ㉕

Road map E6. 🏛 *57,000.* 🚉
ℹ️ *Altstadt 315 (0871-92 20 50).*
🎉 *Fürstenhochzeit (every 5 years), Hofmusiktage (every 2 years), Frühjahrsdult (Apr–May), Bartlmädult (end Aug), Haferlmarkt (Sep).*

THE EARLIEST records of Landshut date from 1150. One hundred years later this was already a town and the main centre of power of the Dukes of Lower Bavaria. In

1475 the town was the scene of a lavish medieval wedding, when Duke Georg of the House of Wittelsbach married the Polish Princess Jadwiga, daughter of Casimir Jagiellon. Since 1903 the town has held regular re-enactments of the wedding feast (Landshuter Fürstenhochzeit).

Landshut has preserved its medieval urban layout, with two wide parallel streets, Altstadt and Neustadt, with clusters of historic 15th–16th century buildings. Opposite the town hall in Alstadt is the **Stadtresidenz**, a town house modelled on the Palazzo del Tè in Mantua. Sometimes known as the "Italian House", this was the first Renaissance palace to be built in Germany.

The vast brick church of St Martin (1385–1500) is a triple-nave, narrow hall-church featuring a presbytery, network vaults (1459) and the tallest church tower in Bavaria.

Landshut is dominated by the fortified 13th–16th century **Burg Trausnitz**, which features a medieval tower and a Renaissance palace dating from 1568–78. The palace features arcades around the courtyard and a series of frescos by Alessandro Scalzi, which date from 1578.

ENVIRONS: From Landshut, it is worth taking a trip to Moosburg, situated 14 km (9 miles) to the west. Its early

Stained-glass window in Landshut depicting Duke Georg and Jadwiga

13th-century Church of St Castulus features a 14-m (46-ft) high Marian altar by Hans Leinberger (1514). Leinberger was probably also the creator of the epitaph of Theoderich Mair and of the crucifix on the west wall.

⚜ Burg Trausnitz
🕿 (0871) 92 41 10. ⏱ Apr–Sep: 9am–6pm; Oct–Mar: 10am–4pm. ✍

⚜ Stadtresidenz
Altstadt 79. 🕿 (0871) 92 41 10. ⏱ Apr–Sep: 9am–6pm; Oct–Mar: 10am–4pm. ✍ ⬤ Mon.

Interior of St George's Chapel in Landshut

Dingolfing ㉖

Road map E6. 🚶 15,400.
🛈 Dr-Josef-Hastreiter-Straße 2 (08731-50 10).

THE MAIN TOURIST attraction in this small town on the banks of the river Isar is its Gothic castle. Built in the 15th century by the Bavarian dukes, this vast edifice now houses the Regional Museum. It is also worth taking a stroll to see Pfarrkirche St Johannes, a late-Gothic brick building dating from the late 15th century. Although what remains of its furnishings are merely the poor remnants of its former glory, nevertheless the church is still considered one of the most beautiful Gothic buildings in Bavaria.

ENVIRONS: In Landau an der Isar, situated 13 km (8 miles) to the east of Dingolfing, stands the picturesque Baroque church of Mariä Himmelfahrt, dating from the first half of the 18th century. There is also an interesting small church, the Steinfelskirche (c.1700) inside a natural rock cave. In Arnstorf, 30 km (19 miles) to the east, is one of the few remaining Bavarian castles on water. Known as the Oberes Schloß, the castle was probably built in the 15th century and remodelled during the 17th and 18th centuries.

Straubing ㉗

Road map E6. 🚶 44,500. 🚉
🛈 Theresienplatz 20 (09421-94 43 07). 🎭 Gäubodenvolksfest Agnes-Bernauer-Festspiel (July, every four years).

THIS MARKET TOWN enjoys a picturesque setting on the river Danube. The 60-m (200-ft) long Strassenmarkt, which consists of two squares, Theresienplatz and Ludwig-platz, is a part of the former trade route that led to Prague. The area is lined with historic buildings in Baroque, Neo-Classical and Secession styles.

At the centre of Strassen-markt stands the 14th-century municipal tower, which offers a splendid view over the towns of the Bavarian Forest. At Ludwigplatz 11 is the "Lion's Pharmacy", where the famous Biedermeier painter, Karl Spitzweg, worked as an apprentice in 1828–30.

Turning from Theresienplatz into Seminargasse or Jakobs-gasse, you will reach the monumental brick structure of the parish church of St Jakob (1400–1590). This triple-nave hall-church, crowned with a network vault, retains many original features, including stained-glass windows in the chapels of Maria-Hilf-Kapelle (1420) and St Bartholomew. The so-called Moses' Window in the Chapel of St Joseph was made in 1490 in Nuremberg, based on a sketch provided by Wilhelm Playdenwurff. In the Cobbler's Chapel (Schusterkapelle) hangs a painting of *Madonna and Child*, by Hans Holbein (c.1500). Overlooking the Danube is a 14th–15th century castle, part of which is now used as a museum, **Museum im Herzogschloss**. The **Gäubodenmuseum** has a magnificent collection of Roman artifacts.

ENVIRONS: In the tiny village of Aufhausen, 21 km (12 miles) to the west, is the beautiful late-Baroque pilgrimage church of Maria Schnee. Built by Johann Michael Fischer in 1736–51, it includes magnifi-cent wall paintings by the Asam brothers and a statue of the Madonna. Commissioned by Duke Wilhelm V of Bavaria, the Gnadenmadonna is believed to pardon sins.

In Oberaltech, some 10 km (6 miles) to the east, is the beautiful church of St Peter and St Paul built in the early 17th century for the Benedictine order. Inside, an unusual hanging staircase leads to the galleries, while the vestibule is decorated with stucco ornaments, depicting bird motifs.

In Windberg, 22 km (14 miles) east of Oberaltech, is a Romanesque Marian church whose main portal (c.1220) features an image of the Madonna in the tympanum.

🏛 Gäubodenmuseum
Frauenhoferstraße. ⏱ 10am–4pm Tue–Sun. ✍

🏛 Museum im Herzogschloss
🕿 (09421) 211 14. ⏱ 10am–4pm Tue–Sun. ✍

Main altar in Ursulinenkirche, Straubing

Regensburg (Ratisbon) ㉘

THE AREA OF Regensburg was once a Celtic settlement and later a campsite of the Roman legions. The outline of the Roman camp is still visible around St Peter's Cathedral. In the early 6th century, Regensburg was the seat of the Agilolfa ruling family and, in AD 739, a monk named Boniface established a bishopric here. From AD 843, Regensburg was the seat of the Eastern Frankish ruler, Ludwig II the German. From 1245 it was a free town of the Holy Roman Empire and throughout the Middle Ages remained South Germany's fastest growing commercial and cultural centre.

Picturesque Steinere Brücke leading to the old town of Regensburg

🜋 Steinere Brücke
An outstanding example of medieval engineering, this 310-m (1,000-ft) long bridge over the Danube was built in 1135–46. It provides the best panoramic view of Regensburg. Near the bridge gate, Brückentor, stands an enormous salt warehouse topped with a vast five-storey roof.

🜋 Wurstküche (Wurstkuchel)
Thundorferstraße.
🕐 *8am–4pm daily.*
Immediately behind the salt warehouse is the famous *Wurstküche* (sausage kitchen), which has probably occupied this site since as early as the 12th century and may have served as a canteen for the builders of the bridge. Its Rothenburger sausages are regarded by local residents as the best in the world.

🜋 Altes Rathaus
Rathausplatz.
Reichstagsmuseum. 【 (0941) 507 44 11. 🖼 3:15pm Mon–Sat (except public holidays). Large groups by appointment. 📷
In Rathausplatz stands an old 15th-century town hall with a 13th-century tower. It contains a splendid, richly decorated

room – *Beratungszimmer der Reichsstände* –where the Perpetual Imperial Diet (the first parliament of the Holy Roman Empire) sat between 1663 and 1806. Benches in the chamber were coloured to indicate who could sit where: for example, red benches for Electors. The adjoining new town hall dates from the late 17th–early 18th century.

Late-Gothic oriel on the side elevation of the Altes Rathaus

🔒 Dom St Peter
Domschatzmuseum
Krautermarkt 3.
【 (0941) 595 32 25 30.
🕐 *Apr– Nov: 10am–5pm Tue–Sat, noon–5pm Sun; Dec–Mar: 10am–4pm Fri-Sat, noon–4pm Sun (except 25 Dec–6 Jan: 10am–4pm Tue–Sat, 10am–4pm Sun).* 📷
Towering above the city, on the site of the former Roman military camp, is the massive brick structure of St Peter's Cathedral. Built between 1250 and 1525, its western towers were added only in 1859–69. The master architect, Ludwig, modelled his design on French examples (the

SIGHTS AT A GLANCE

19th-century towers on the Gothic St Peter's Cathedral

Rayonnant style). The stained-glass windows of the choir date from the early 14th century. The **Domschatz-museum** has a collection of ecclesiastical vestments.

☩ Alte Kapelle
Alter Kornmarkt.

The Old Chapel is really a Marian collegiate church. It stands on the foundations of an older, early Romanesque chapel dating from the Carolingian period. The building has been remodelled several times and contains some beautiful Rococo stuccoes by Anton Landes.

♣ Schloss Thurn und Taxis
Emmeramsplatz 5. ☎ (0941) 504 81 33. ◯ daily. ☑ Apr–Oct: 11am, 2pm, 3pm, 4pm (also 10am Sat–Sun); Nov–Mar: 10am, 11am, 2pm, 3pm Sat–Sun. ⬚

In the south end of the town you will find the buildings and churches of the former St Emmeram Abbey, which have been tastefully

Enchanting Rococo interior of Alte Kapelle

the burial chapel. In 1998, the Bavarian State Museum opened a branch here, which includes valuable collections of decorative art.

☩ Baumburgerturm
Watmarkt

Regensburg has many unique ancestral palaces dating from the 14th–15th centuries, with high towers modelled on Northern Italian architecture. Some 20 of the original 60 towers have survived. One of the most beautiful is the residential tower, Baumburger Turm. Nearby, at Watmarkt 5, stands the equally beautiful Goliathhaus, where Oskar Schindler lived for a time in 1945. A commemorative plaque has been placed at the rear of the building.

Gothic portals of St Emmeram Abbey in Schloss Thurn und Taxis

0 metres 300

0 yards 300

KEY

🛈 Tourist information

P Parking

✝ Church

incorporated into the palace complex of the ducal family von Thurn und Taxis. These include a Gothic cloister dating from the 12th–14th centuries, a library with magnificent frescos by Cosmas Damian Asam and

Winter view of Gnadenkapelle complex, from Altötting

Altötting ㉙

Road map E6. 👥 *11,000.* ℹ️
Kapellplatz 2a (08671-80 68). 🚉
🎭 *pilgrimages to Altötting (Whitsun).*

A LTÖTTING IS RENOWNED as the earliest destination of pilgrimages to the "Miraculous Statue" of the Virgin Mary (1330). The statue stands in the Wallfahrtskapelle St Maria, which consists of two parts. The central, octagonal chapel, **Gnadenkapelle** (c.AD 750) was once the baptistery. The external chapel was built in 1494 and the ambulatory in 1517. As well as the Miraculous Statue, it houses the so-called "Silver Prince", representing the miraculously cured son of the Prince-Elector, Karl Albrecht. Many Bavarian kings and princes wished to be buried here, including King Ludwig II, who requested that his heart be placed here after his death.

Nearby is the interesting Romanesque-Gothic church of St Philip and St Jacob (1228–30 and 1499–1520). Its Neo-Classical interior contains many tombstones, while a separate chapel, Tillykapelle, is the burial place of Johann Tserclaes von Tilly, a hero of the Thirty Years' War and the Emperor's general.

The **Schatzkammer** (Treasury) is housed in the former sacristy. Its collection includes an exquisite example of French enamel and gold artwork, the *Goldenes Rössl* (Golden Steed), which dates from around 1400. Despite its name, the theme of this work, by a celebrated Parisian goldsmith, is the Adoration of the Magi. It was commissioned by Isobel of Bavaria as a New Year gift for her husband, Charles VI of France.

Schatzkammer
Kapellplatz 21. 📞 *(08671) 67 97.*
🕐 *Apr–Oct:10am–noon, 2–4pm Tue–Sun.* 🖼️

Walkway around Gnadenkapelle, in Altötting, filled with offerings

Burghausen ㉚

Road map E6. 👥 *17,000.* ℹ️ *Stadt-platz 112 (08677-967 69 31).* 🚉

T HE VERY PICTURESQUE town of Burghausen is situated on the river Salzach. Towering over the town, the river and the lake is Wöhrsee Castle, a large castle complex built on a high ridge stretching for 1,100 m (1,200 yds). Work on the castle started in 1253, but most of the buildings were erected during the reign of King George the Rich and therefore have magnificent, late-Gothic forms. The king's wife, Jadwiga Jagiellon, whom he married in grand style in Landshut *(see p252)*, was later rejected by him and she spent her final days in the fortress of Burghausen.

The **Burg** consists of two main parts: the main castle, with tower, the residential quarters, the courtyard and domestic buildings; and the castle approach (Vorburg). The residential building has some fine 15th- and 16th-century paintings. A special door links the Prince's quarters with the "internal" Chapel of St Elizabeth. Next to the chapel is the mid-13th-century Dürnitz, which served originally served as a ballroom and banqueting hall .

The castle approach consists of five courtyards (Vorhof). In the fourth courtyard is the "external" Chapel of St Jadwiga (Aussere Burgkapelle St Hedwig) – the work of Wolfgang Wiesinger, a native of Salzburg (1489). This has numerous original buildings, including the town hall, which was created by combining three burgher houses dating from the 14th–15th centuries The parish church of St Jakob (1353-1513) in Burghausen is a three-nave basilica.

Burg
📞 *(08677) 967 69 20.*
Staatliche Sammlung 🕐 *Apr–Sep: 9am–5pm daily; Oct–Mar: 9am–noon, 1–4pm Tue–Sun.*

Panoramic view of Burghausen, with its vast castle complex on the hill

Bayerischer Wald ③

THE BAVARIAN FOREST stretches north to the river Danube, between Regensburg and Passau. It is part of Central Europe's largest woodland and provides idyllic grounds for a variety of outdoor pursuits. The local rocks contain large quantities of quartz, which contributed to the early development of the glass industry here. To this day, the region produces some fine, blown-glass artifacts. The region also hosts a number of popular festivals throughout the year.

Spiegelau ③
Spiegelau is one of the most popular starting points for tourists planning hiking trips into the mountains.

Zwiesel ①
In the old glassworks, which survive to this day, you can watch workers using blow irons to produce vases, jugs and other objects made of glass.

Grafenau ④
The main attractions of this small town are its tobacco and furniture museums and the Baroque church.

Frauenau ②
Along with Zwiesel, this is the oldest centre of glass production in the area. The local museum illustrates the town's history.

Freyung ⑤
The main attraction of the town is the Wolfenstein Castle, which now houses a museum of hunting and fishing.

Finsterau ⑥
Situated close to a vast artificial lake, Finsterau has an interesting open-air museum that displays examples of the local building trade.

KEY

▮▮▮	Suggested route
══	Other road
▮▮	Scenic route
�належ	Viewpoint

0 km   8
0 miles   8

TIPS FOR WALKERS

Starting point: *Zwiesel.*
Distance: *82 km (51 miles)*
Getting there: *Train to Frauenau, on the Zwiesel-Granau line; or Bodenmais, terminus of another branch line from Zwiesel.*

Street-by-Street: Passau ℘

PASSAU, WHOSE LONG HISTORY goes back to Roman times, lies on a peninsula between the rivers Danube and Inn, near the Austrian border. During the second half of the 5th century, St Severinus established a monastery in Passau as well as several more nearby. In 739, an Irish monk called Boniface, known as "Germany's Apostle", founded a bishopric here and for many years this was the largest diocese of the Holy Roman Empire. Large parts of the town were destroyed by fires in 1662 and 1680. Reconstruction was carried out by Italian artists, who gave the town its Baroque, Rococo and Neo-Classical façades. However Passau retains a medieval feel in its narrow alleys and archways.

Passauer Glasmuseum
Opposite the old town hall is the beautiful patrician Hotel Wilder Mann, which now houses the Glasmuseum. The museum's vast collection includes valuable examples of Bohemian, Austrian and Bavarian glasswork.

★ **Dom St Stephan**
St Stephan's Cathedral is a true masterpiece of Italian Baroque, built by Italian architect Carlo Lurago to replace the original Gothic structure, which was largely destroyed by fire in the 17th century.

Deggendorf

ANGER STR

DOMPLATZ

MESSERGASSE

Passau-Hauptbahnhof

University

INNPROMENAD

★ **Altes Rathaus**
Dating from the 14th–15th century, the old town hall was created by combining eight patrician houses. The structure features a Neo-Gothic tower.

MARIEN-BRÜCKE

Neue Bischofsresidenz
Built by Domenico d'Angeli and Antonio Beduzzi in 1713–30, the Neue Residenz has a pilaster façade with protruding balconies and roof balustrade.

VISITORS' CHECKLIST

🏠 50,000. 🚉 ⓘ *Rathaus-platz 3, 94032 Passau (0851 95 59 80).* 🎭 *Festival Europäische Wochen (Jun-Jul) music and theatre events, plus exhibitions by artists from many European countries (mainly Austria, Hungary, the Czech Republic, Slovakia and Poland).*

★ Veste Oberhaus
This former castle of the prince-bishops now houses the Kultur-historischesmuseum, with displays on local and regional history and the work of local artists.

PRINZREGENT LUITPOLD BRÜCKE

Schaiblingsturm
On the bank of the river Inn are the remains of Passau's Gothic town walls. They include this tower, built in 1481.

★ Wallfahrtskirche Mariahilf
High above the banks of the river Inn stands this early-Baroque abbey complex dating from 1627–30. It includes a pretty twin-towered pilgrimage church.

STAR SIGHTS

★ **Altes Rathaus**

★ **Dom St Stephan**

★ **Veste Oberhaus**

★ **Wallfahrtskirche Mariahilf**

KEY

0 metres   100
0 yards   100

– – – Suggested route

Berchtesgadener Land ⓷

BERCHTESGADENER LAND is one of the most beautiful regions, not just in Germany, but in the whole of Europe. It occupies the area of the Berchtesgadener Alps whose boundaries are defined by the river Saalach to the west, the river Salzach to the east, the "Stony Sea" *(Steinernes Meer)* to the south to and, to the north, Untersberg, which is 1,972 m (7,500 ft) above sea level. To the south of Berchtesgaden village lies the National Park (Nationalpark Berchtesgaden).

★ Ramsau an der Ache
Set in an enchanting location in the Ramsau Valley, this town is a popular base for visitors to the area. Spectacular views of the mountains can be enjoyed from the small parish church.

Hintersee
This scenic lake has given its name to a picturesque hamlet nearby. A walk around the lake takes about one hour.

KEHLSTEINHAUS

Standing on the summit of Kehlstein, this stone building resembling a mountain shelter is known as the Adlerhorst (Eagle's Nest). It was given to Hitler as a birthday present in 1939 by one of his closest allies, Martin Bormann, and it became the Führer's favourite residence. The approach to the building is a true engineering masterpiece: the initial section, the Kehlsteinstrasse, is a scenic mountain road, which passes through five tunnels and offers some breathtaking views. The final ascent is via a lift. The whole project took 13 months to complete. After the war, the Eagle's Nest fell into the hands of the Americans, then, in 1960, it passed into private hands. The building now houses a restaurant that is very popular with tourists, not only because of its history but also for the spectacular views that it provides over part of the Alps.

LATTE
GEBIR

REITER
ALPE

HINTERSEE   Ramsau

Wimbachkl

NATIONAL-

PARK

BERCHTESGADE

Nationalpark Berchtesgaden
This magnificent national park, which is home to many rare species of plants and animals, can be visited by joining organized tours between May and October.

Berchtesgaden
The capital of the region features many historic buildings. The Schloss, originally an Augustinian priory, now houses the art treasures collected by Crown Prince Ruprecht. The local salt mine has been a source of wealth since the 16th century.

VISITORS' CHECKLIST

Road map E7. 🏘 8,500. 🚉
Berchtesgaden. 🛈 Kurdirektion,
Königsseerstrasse 2, Berchtesgaden (08652-96 70).

Wallfahrtskirche Maria Gern
One of the loveliest Baroque buildings in the region, the pilgrimage church of Maria Gern was built in 1709 in this idyllic location.

UNTERS-BERG

kl

Maria Gern

Bischof-wiesen

Halten

Berchtes-gaden

Mitterbach

önau nigssee

Königssee

KÖNIGSSEE

OBERSEE

KEY

■ Major road
= Minor road
≈ River
☼ Viewpoint

STAR SIGHTS

★ Königssee

★ Ramsau an der Ache

★ Königssee
Germany's highest lake, Königssee is the focal point of Berchtesgadener Land. Lying 600 m (2,000 ft) above sea level, it covers an area of 5.5 sq km (1,360 acres) and reaches a depth of 188 m (616 ft).

0 km 5
0 miles 5

Touring Chiemsee 🔞

B AVARIA'S LARGEST LAKE, Chiemsee is a real
paradise for watersports enthusiasts, with
sailors, water-skiers, swimmers and divers all
enjoying the opportunities it offers. The lake is
set amidst magnificent Alpine scenery in the
region known as the Chiemgau, which
stretches eastwards from Rosenheim to the
border with Austria along the river Salzach.
Chiemsee is surrounded by numerous small
towns and villages and dotted with islands,
some of which feature fascinating historic
buildings. Excellent land, water and rail
transport facilities ensure trouble-free travel
to all destinations in the area.

Fraueninsel
*Like its neighbour Herreninsel, this
island is rich in art treasures. Its
abbey (Klosterkirche) was
founded in 766 and taken
over by Benedictine
nuns in the mid-
9th century.*

Stock
*The harbour town of Stock is
connected by narrow-gauge steam
railway to the Chiemsee's main resort
of Prien. The railway, the Chiemsee-
bahn, is over one hundred years old.*

(map labels) Obi, Hinzing, Halfing, HARTSEE, Eggstäd, Bad Endorf, LANGBURGNER SEE, SIMSSEE, Stock, Prien, Harras, Urschalling, Bernau

Urschalling
*The 12th-century church of
St James features magnificent
wall paintings dating from the
13th and 14th centuries.*

KEY

▬	Motorway
═	Major road
═	River
✵	Viewpoint

Herrenchiemsee Palace
*In 1873, King Ludwig II
bought Herreninsel, with
the intention of building
a replica of the Palace of
Versailles here. Funds ran
out and the project was
not completed, but
the magnificent central
section and park are well
worth visiting.*

Seeon Abbey

This post-Benedictine abbey, surrounded by the waters of Klostersee, was built in stages during the 11th and 12th centuries. It was remodelled in 1438–43 by Konrad Pürkel, a master-builder from Burghausen.

Castle in the Rock

One of the most interesting curiosities of this region is the "Hohlenburg" – a castle carved into a rock on the bank of the river Fraun, some 30 m (98 ft) above water level. Visits are allowed only with a guide.

Chieming

Chieming lies on the eastern shore of the lake. Its 6-km (4-mile) long beach is an ideal place for sunbathing and swimming in the waters of the lake.

Chiemsee

Lying at an altitude of 518 m (1,700 ft), the lake covers an area of 80 sq km (20,000 acres) with a depth of 70 m (230 ft). Its size makes it popular with sailing enthusiasts.

Colourful Alpine inn, dating from 1612, in Oberammergau

Garmisch-Partenkirchen ③⑤

Road map D7. 👥 *27,000.* 🚉
ℹ️ *Richard-Strauss-Platz 2 (08821-18 07 00).* 🎿 *Hornschlitten-Rennen (6 Jan).*

LYING IN THE valley of the river Loisach, Garmisch-Partenkirchen is the best-known resort in the Bavarian Alps. To say that it offers ideal skiing conditions would be to state the obvious. In 1936, it hosted the Winter Olympic Games and, in 1978, the World Skiing Champion-ships. From Garmisch-Partenkirchen, Germany's highest peak, Zugspitze (2964 m/9,720 ft), can be reached by taking the narrow-gauge railway to Zugspitzblatt and from there a cable car, which reaches the summit in a few minutes. Garmisch-Partenkirchen's parish church of St Martin (Alte Pfarrkirche St Martin) is worth a visit. It was built in the 13th century and extended in the 15th century and features some well-preserved Gothic wall paintings and net vaulting. The **Werdenfelser Museum** shows how people in this region lived in the past, with a fine collection of wooden furniture and clothing, as well as room reconstructions.

Oriel window in Garmisch-Partenkirchen

🏛️ **Werdenfelser Museum**
Ludwigstraße 47. 📞 *(08821) 21 34.* ⭕ *Dec–Oct: 10am–1pm, 3–6pm, Tue–Fri, 10am–1pm Sat–Sun.* 🎫

Oberammergau ③⑥

Road map D7. 👥 *4,700.* ℹ️ *Eugen-Papst-Straße 9A (08822-923 10).* 🎭 *Oberammergauer Passionsspiele May–Oct, every ten years: next 2010); König-Ludwig-Lauf (Feb); König-Ludwig-Feiern (24 Aug).*

SITUATED SOME 20 km (12 miles) north of Garmisch-Partenkirchen, and standing on the site of a 9th-century Welfs' fort, Villa Ambrigow, Oberam-mergau is world famous for its folk art and passion plays. The Thirty Years' War (1618–48) and the plague of 1632 came close to wiping out the entire popu-lation of the village. Its surviving inhabi-tants pledged that if they were saved from extinction they would stage for ever more a play about Christ's Passion. No further deaths occurred and, to this day, the villagers have kept their pledge. Every ten years, some 2,000 people take part in the six-hour-long spectacle, in which they transform themselves from Bavarians into Jews and Romans from the time of Christ. About one hundred performances are staged between mid-May and mid-October. The venue for these magnificent plays is the huge Passionsspielhaus.

Buildings worth seeing in Oberammergau include the Rococo church of Saint Peter and Saint Paul (1735–40) and the famous *Pilatushaus*, with its illusionist painting of Christ before Pilate on the façade. The **Heimatmuseum** has a notable collection of carved wooden cribs.

🏛️ **Heimatmuseum**
Dorfstraße 8. 📞 *(08822) 941 36.* ⭕ *15 May–15 Oct: 2–6pm Tue–Sun, Oct-May: 2–6pm Sat.* 🎫

Ettal ③⑦

Road map D7. 👥 *974.*

ABOUT 4 km (2.5 miles) from Oberammergau is the tiny resort of Ettal, which is best known for its Benedictine abbey, founded by Emperor Ludwig IV of Bavaria. The abbey's foundation stone was laid in 1330, while the Church of the Virgin Mary and the convent were consecrated in 1370. The church building is a Gothic structure but, in 1710–52, Josef Enrico Zuccalli and Franz Schmuzer carried out major remodelling work in the Baroque style. The church interior is decorated with rich Rococo stuccowork by Johann Baptist and Johann Georg Ubelhör, and wall paintings by Martin Knoller.

The monastery produces some fine fruit liqueurs, flavoured brandies and beer.

The Baroque Benedictine abbey in Ettal

Linderhof ❸

İN THE EARLY 1850s, Linderhof was bought by the Bavarian King Maximilian II. This remote mountain district had great appeal to the young heir to the throne and later to the eccentric King Ludwig II. In 1874, work started on remodelling the existing *Königshäuschen* (royal cottage) in the neo-Rococo style. The palace is surrounded by a delightful garden, which is dotted with romantic little buildings, including *Schwanenweiher* (Swan Lake), *Venusgrotte* (Venus grotto) and the *Marokkanisches Haus* (Moroccan house).

VISITORS' CHECKLIST

Road map D7. **Schloss Linderhof**. 🄲 (08822) 920 30. ◯ Apr-Sep: 9am–5:30pm Fri–Wed, 9am–7:30pm Thu; Oct–Mar: 10am–4pm daily. 🅿

Tapestry Room
The walls of this room are painted in a style that is reminiscent of tapestry work, with depictions of pastoral scenes.

Reception Room
Although the palace was intended as a private residence, King Ludwig II insisted on the provision of a suitably ornate and regal reception room.

Dining Room
Designed by Christian Jank, the dining room was completed in 1872. It features gilded panelling by Phillip Perron and stuccowork by Theobald Behler.

Mirror Hall
The design of Linderhof's Mirror Hall was based on the Mirror Room of the royal residence in Munich *(pp206–7)*.

Terraces
Terraces in front of the palace are adorned with sculptures and include a pool with a fountain.

Schloss Neuschwanstein ③

Sᴇᴛ ᴀᴍɪᴅsᴛ ᴍᴀɢɴɪꜰɪᴄᴇɴᴛ mountain scenery on the shores of the Schwansee (Swan Lake), this fairy-tale castle was built in 1869–86 for the eccentric Bavarian King Ludwig II, to a design by the theatre designer Christian Jank. When deciding to build this imposing residence, the king was undoubtedly inspired by the sight of Wartburg Castle in Thuringia *(see pp176–7)*, which he visited in 1867. The pale grey granite castle, which draws on a variety of historical styles, is a steep 20-minute walk from the nearby village of Hohenschwangau and offers spectacular views of the surrounding scenery.

★ Singing Room
The Sängersaal was modelled on the singing room of the Wartburg castle in Eisenach.

Study

Vestibule
The walls of the vestibule and of other rooms in the castle are lavishly covered with paintings depicting scenes from old German myths and legends.

★ Throne Room
The gilded interior of the throne room reminds one of Byzantine temples and the palace church of All Saints in the Residenz (see pp206–7) in Munich.

Dining Room
Like other rooms in the palace, the dining room includes fabulous pictures, intricately carved panels and beautifully decorated furniture, all bearing witness to the skill and artistry of the 19th-century craftsmen.

★ Castle Building
Schloss Neuschwanstein is the archetypal fairy-tale castle and has provided the inspiration for countless toy models, book illustrations and film sets.

VISITORS' CHECKLIST

Road map D7. Neuschwanstein-str. 20. ☎ (08362) 8 10 35. ◷ Oct–Mar: 10am–4pm daily; Apr–Sep: 9am–6pm Fri–Wed, 9am–8pm Thu. ♨ ✔ ♿ (limited access). ⓘ ▢ ◻ ⓘ

Courtyard
The heart of the castle was supposed to have been a mighty 90-m (295-ft) high tower with a Gothic castle church. It was never built, but in 1988 its planned position was marked in white stone.

Two-storey arcades surround the castle courtyard.

Main entrance

Gatehouse
During construction, temporary accommodation was built for the king on the second floor of the gatehouse, completed in 1872.

STAR FEATURES

★ **Castle Building**

★ **Singing Room**

★ **Throne Room**

Hohen-schwangau ⑳

Road map D7. 🏔 *Schwangau 3,818.* ⓘ *Kurverwaltung Schwangau, Münchener Straße 2 (08362-8 19 80).*

THE SKYLINE OF Schwangau is dominated by two castles, Schloss Neuschwanstein (left) and the majestic **Schloss Hohenschwangau.** The fortified castle that occupied this site in the Middle Ages was remodelled in 1538–47 and, in 1567, it passed into the hands of the Wittelsbach family. The property was destroyed during the course of the Tyrolean War but in 1832 the heir to the throne (later Maximilian II) ordered the ruins to be rebuilt in Neo-Gothic style. The plans were prepared by the painter Domenico Quaglio; after his death, work on the castle was continued by the architects Georg Friedrich Ziebland and Joseph Daniel Ohlmüller.

This four-storey building, standing on medieval foundations, is flanked by angular towers. The wall paintings that decorate the rooms of the castle date from 1835–36. Their iconographic content, which is based on old Germanic sagas, is the work of Moritz von Schwind. A walk around the castle provides an excellent opportunity to study the Wittelsbach family history and to see the mid-19th century furnishings. Magnificent views of the surroundings are offered from the lovely terraced gardens of the castle.

♜ **Schloss Hohenschwangau**
☎ (08362) 811 27. ◷ Apr–Sep: 9am–6pm Mon–Wed & Fri–Sun, 9am–8pm Thu; Oct–Mar: 10am–4pm. ● 24 Dec. ♨

Neo-Gothic castle of Maximilian II in Hohenschwangau

The Rococo Throne Room in the Kempten Residenz.

Kempten 🄐

Road map C7. 👥 62,000. 🚊
🅸 Rathausplatz 24 (0831-252 52 37 or 194 33).

Kempten lies at the centre of one of Germany's most attractive tourist regions, the Allgäu, which stretches from Bodensee lake to the west and the river Lech to the east. The town, which boasts a history of over 2,000 years, was first mentioned by the Greek geographer and historian Strabon as a Celtic settlement, Kambodounon. Later, the Romans established Cambodunum on the right bank of the river Iller. Along with Augusta Vindelicorum (Augsburg) and Castra Regina (Regensburg), this was one of the most important towns in the Roman province of Raetia.

Medieval Kempten grew around a Benedictine Abbey, founded in 752. In the northwestern part of town, near the former abbots' residence,

is the church of St Lorenz. A triple-nave, galleried basilica with an octagonal cupola and a twin-tower façade, this is the work of Michael Beer and Johann Serro. The town's parish church of St Mang dates from the 15th century. In the Rathausplatz is an attractive town hall dating from 1474 and other historic buildings, including the Londoner Hof with its Rococo façade (1764). The **Römisches Museum** has a collection illustrating the town's Roman history and, on the right bank of the river Iller, is the **Archäologischer Park**, with impressive excavated remains of Roman Cambodunum.

🏛 Römisches Museum
Residenzplatz 31. 📞 (0831) 123 67.
🕙 10am–4pm Tue–Sun. 🎫
🏛 Archäologischer Park Cambodunum
Cambodunumweg 3. 📞 (0831) 57 42 50. 🕙 May–Oct: 10am–5pm Tue–Sun; Nov–Apr:10am–4:30pm Tue–Sun.

Epitaph of the family of Andreas Bertsch, in the Stadtmuseum Lindau

Lindau 🄑

Road map C7. 👥 24,000. 🚊 🅸
Ludwigstraße 68 (08382-26 00 30 or 19 433).

In roman times Lindau was a fishing settlement, which used to lie over three islands. The first historic records of the town date from 882. On the south side of the old-town island lies the harbour with its 13th-century lighthouse (Mangturm). The new lighthouse (Neuer Leuchtturm), built in 1856, stands on the neighbouring pier and offers a splendid view over the lake and the Alps. The marble Lion of Bavaria opposite is the symbol of Lindau.

The old town features many historic buildings, such as the Gothic-Renaissance town hall in Reichsplatz, which was built in 1422–36 and later remodelled in 1578. The picturesque Maximilianstrasse is lined with the houses of rich patricians; their shady arcades (*Brodlauben*) are typical of Lindau architecture.

In Schrannenplatz, in the northwest area of the town, stands the church of St Peter. Since 1928 this has been the war memorial chapel for World War I victims. Its eastern section dates from the mid-12th century while the bigger, western section was built between 1425 and 1480. The interior contains many wall paintings, including some by Hans Holbein the Elder dating from 1485–90. Nearby stands the *Diebsturm* (Thief's Tower) of 1380. The **Stadtmuseum** (town museum) is housed in Haus zum Cavazzen (1729) in Marktplatz, which also features a lovely Neptune fountain.

On the south side of the Market Square stands the Protestant Church of St Stephen, which dates from the 12th century and was remodelled in Baroque style in 1782. The Catholic Church of St Mary, built in 1748–52, has a lovely Rococo interior.

🏛 Stadtmuseum Lindau
Marktplatz 6. 📞 (08382) 94 40 73.
🕙 Apr–Oct: 10am–noon, 2–5pm Tue–Sun. ● Nov–Mar.

Oberstdorf 43

Road map C7. 🏔 *11,000.* 🚌 🛈
*Verkehrsamt, Marktplatz 7 (08322-
70 00).*

OBERSTDORF LIES in the valley of the River Iller.
The ideal skiing conditions and the mild all-year-round climate make this one of the most popular health resorts and winter sports centres in Germany. Nearby is the skiing stadium (Schattenberg-Skistadion) with its famous ski-jump, where the annual "four ski-jump" tournament starts each year.

Although the fire of 1865 destroyed large sections of the settlement here, some of the most important historic buildings escaped. These include Seelenkapelle, whose façade is decorated with a 16th-century wall painting typical of the region, and two chapels, Loreto-kapelle and Josephskapelle, which were joined together in 1707. Just to the east of Oberstdorf is the 2,224-m (7,300-ft) Mount Nebelhorn, whose summit can be reached in a few minutes by cable car. This offers a spectacular view over the majestic Allgäuer Alps as well as providing an excellent starting point for mountain hiking.

Füssen 44

Road map D7. 🏔 *16,000.* 🚌 🛈
*Kurverwaltung, Kaiser-Maximilian-
Platz 1 (08362-938 50).*

SITUATED CONVENIENTLY on an important trade route,
Füssen experienced its most rapid growth in the late Middle Ages, as witnessed by many of the buildings in Reichensstrasse and the remains of the town fortifications, which include Sebastiantor and sections of the walls with five turrets. Perched on a rock, high above the town, stands the palace of the Augsburg prince-bishops. Started in 1291 by the Bavarian Prince Ludwig II the Severe, construction was continued in 1490-1503 by the Augsburg bishops. The residential buildings of the palace range around a courtyard whose walls are

**Madonna in the
Church of St Mang,
in Füssen**

decorated with trompe l'oeil door and window frames.

At the foot of the castle stands the former Benedictine Abbey (Kloster St Mang), which was erected in the 9th century at the burial site of St Magnus, the "Apostle of the Allgäu". The only surviving part of the abbey is the late 10th-century crypt with the remains of wall paintings.

**Late-Baroque interior of the Abbey
Library, in Ottobeuren**

Ottobeuren 45

Road map D7. 🏔 *7,500.* 🛈
Marktplatz 14 (08332-92 19 50).

SITUATED 8 km (5 miles) from Memmingen, the small
health resort of Ottobeuren is the site of one of Germany's most famous Benedictine abbeys. Founded in 764, the abbey is still a place of prayer and work for the monks who live here, having withstood even the radical secularization of 1803. In the 18th century the abbey was remodelled by the Abbot Rupert II. The foundation stone for the building complex was laid in 1717 and work began under the direction of Simpert Kramer. The new buildings were completed in 1731. The richly decorated interiors, with stuccoes by Andrea Maini, still survive. A new abbey church was built between 1737 and 1766 with construction supervised initially by Simpert Kramer. In 1748, this was taken over by Johann Michael Fischer, who was responsible for its final appearance.

The interior of the church has a magnificent unity of style: Rococo stuccoes by Johann Michael Feuchtmayr are in perfect harmony with the vault frescos by Jakob Zeiller as well as the splendid altars and stalls by Martin Hörmann and Joseph Christian. The abbey's three organs, which are considered to be among the most beautiful in the world, can be heard at regularly held recitals.

Ski-jump complex in Oberstdorf

Augsburg 46

SITUATED ON THE river Lech, Augsburg is the third largest town in Bavaria and one of the oldest in Germany. As early as 15 BC this was the site of a Roman camp, which later became a town known as Augusta Vindelicorum. Until the end of the 13th century, the town was ruled by powerful bishops. From 1316, as a Free Imperial City of the Holy Roman Empire, Augsburg grew and developed, becoming one of the richest and most powerful cities in Germany. The Thirty Years' War (1618–48), however, put an end to the town's prosperity.

Augustusbrunnen
Incorporating a statue of the Emperor Augustus, the fountain was created in the workshop of Dutchman Hubert Gerhard in 1588.

Dom

RATHAUS PLATZ

PHIL.-WEISER-STRASSE

Church of St Anna
The star attraction of this unassuming ex-Carmelite church is the Renaissance memorial chapel endowed by the brothers Ulrich and Jacob Fugger in 1509.

St Moritz Kirche

ANNASTRASSE

BGM.-FISCHER-STRASS

Maximilian-museum
Set in a Renaissance patrician mansion, the museum has a splendid collection of work by local gold- and silversmiths.

KÖNIGS-PLATZ

ZEUGGASSE

Zeughaus
A bronze group by Hans Reichle, St Michael Overcoming Satan (1607), adorns the façade of the former arsenal building.

VISITORS' CHECKLIST

Road map D6. 🏠 *265,000.*
✈ *5 km (3 miles) to the
north.* 🚃 🛈 *Bahnhofstraße 7
(0821-50 20 70).* 🎭 *Plärrer,
Frühjahrsplärrer (week following
Easter), Herbstplärrer (Aug/Sep),
Friedenfest (8 Aug),
Mozartsommer (Aug).*

★ Rathaus
*The magnificent town hall,
built by Elias Holl in 1615–16,
is generally regarded as
Germany's finest example
of Mannerist architecture.*

★ Maximilianstraße
*Augsburg's main thoroughfare is the most
beautiful street in southern Germany, with
notable fountains by Adrian de Vries.*

★ Fuggerhäuser
*Commissioned by Jacob II
Fugger (1495–1525) for
himself and his family,
this Italian-style
building, with
two arcaded
courtyards,
was built in
1512–15.*

St Ulrich-
und-Afra

KEY

– – – Suggested route

STAR SIGHTS

★ Fuggerhäuser

★ Maximilianstraße

★ Rathaus

View of the monumental Gothic
Dom of the Holy Virgin

🔒 **Dom of the Holy Virgin
(Maria Heimsuchung)**
Frauenstraße 1. ⬜ *9am–5:30pm.*
Originally a Romanesque
twin-choir, pillared basilica
with crypt, western transept
and two towers, dating from
994–1065, the structure was
remodelled between 1331 and
1431 along Gothic lines. The
church was given two further
side aisles, a choir with an
ambulatory and a French-style
ring of chapels. Original
features include the richly
carved portals and the famous
Romanesque bronze door
with 35 panels depicting
allegorical figures. There are
some unique stained-glass
windows, dating from 1140.

🏛 **Fuggerei**
Fuggerei-Museum, Mittlere Gasse 13.
📞 *(0821) 319 88 10.* ⬜ *1 Mar–23
Dec: 9am–6pm daily.* ⬛ *24 Dec–28
Feb.* 🎫
The Fuggerei, in Augsburg's
Jakobervorstadt (Jacob's
Suburb), is Europe's oldest
social housing estate. It was
founded in 1516 by Jacob
Fugger, a member of what
was then the richest family in
Europe. The intention was to
provide homes for the town's
poorest citizens, particularly
families with children. Today,
however, it has evolved into a
home for retired citizens.

The 52 houses in Fuggerei
were built in 1516–25 and line
six streets. They are surrounded by gardens. One of the
buildings houses the **Fuggerei-
Museum**, which is devoted to
the history of the estate. Entry
to the Fuggerei is via one of
its four guarded gates.

BADEN-WURTTEMBERG

THIS GERMAN STATE, *which includes territories of the former Grand Duchy of Baden, is one of the country's most popular tourist destinations. Its charming old university towns, such as Tübingen and Heidelberg, historic castles, luxurious resorts and the magnificent recreation areas of the Schwarzwald (Black Forest) and Bodensee (Lake Constance) guarantee enjoyable and memorable holidays.*

This region's turbulent history, which has been ruled over the years by Palatinate electors, counts and finally kings of Wurttemberg, as well as by margraves and Grand Dukes of Baden, has given the province its cultural and religious diversity.

This southwestern area of Germany was the cradle of two great dynasties that played a significant part in German and European history and culture. The Hohenstauf family – which originated from Swabia – produced kings and emperors who ruled during the most magnificent period of the German Middle Ages (1138–1254). These included Frederick I Barbarossa and Frederick II. The Hohenzollern family, also from Swabia, produced Brandenburg dukes, Prussian kings including Frederick the Great and German emperors from 1871–1918.

In Heidelberg the enlightened elector Ruprecht I founded the first university in Germany in 1386 and shortly after this epoch-making event, further universities were established in Tübingen and Freiburg im Breisgau. Many towns and villages in the region can boast a history going back to Roman times. The Romans used to grow vines in the area of Baden-Wurttemberg and now wines from the region are renowned worldwide for their high quality.

Baden-Wurttemberg, however, does not only represent an illustrious past, but also an impressive present. Unemployment figures for the region are the lowest in Germany, and many companies that are known and respected throughout the world – such as Bosch, DaimlerChrysler, Porsche and the software company SAP – have their production plants here.

Magnificent French-style garden in front of the palace in Ludwigsburg

◁ Bodensee (Lake Constance), in the foothills of the Alps

Baden-Wurttemberg

BADEN-WURTTEMBERG is one of Germany's most popular tourist destinations. Its magnificent castles, luxurious resorts and the beautiful recreation areas of the Black Forest guarantee memorable holidays, while the region's long and turbulent history has given it a rich cultural and religious diversity. The southwest region of Germany was the cradle of two dynasties that played important roles in German and European history and culture – the Hohenstaufen and Hohenzollern families. The great number of urban centres in the state is due to the influence of these two families. Baden-Wurttemberg also has more universities than any other state in Germany, the oldest being located at Heidelberg, Tübingen and Freiburg im Breisgau.

The picturesque castle in Sigmaringen, in the region of Schwäbische Alb

KEY

🟥 Motorway

🟥 Main road

🟥 Scenic route

— River

☀ Viewpoint

The Gothic town hall in Ulm

SEE ALSO

• *Where to Stay* pp470–97

• *Where to Eat* pp498–527

GETTING AROUND

The main communication centres of the area are Stuttgart, which has an international airport, and Mannheim. Main motorways include the A5 from Frankfurt to Basle, via Heidelberg, Karlsruhe, Baden-Baden and Freiburg; the A81 from Würzburg to Constance, via Tauberbischofsheim, Heilbronn, Stuttgart and Schwäbische Alb; the A6 from Mannheim to Ansbach, via Heilbronn and Crailsheim; and the A8 from Karlsruhe to Ulm, via Stuttgart.

SIGHTS AT A GLANCE

Palace façade in Bruchsal

0 km   20

0 miles   20

Wertheim ❶

Road map C5. 🏘 *24,500*. 🚆
🛈 *Wenzelplatz (09342-30 11 60)*. 🚗
Altstadtfest (Jul), Burgweinfest (Aug).

S TANDING AT THE point where
the rivers Tauber and Main
meet is the town of Wertheim,
whose earliest historic records
date from 1183. A gunpowder
explosion in 1619 plus the
destruction caused by the
Thirty Years' War turned the
Wertheimer Burg, the von
Wertheim family castle, into a
romantic ruin. Its tall watchtower offers panoramic views.

Wertheim's market square
is lined with half-timbered
houses, while the Baroque
Protestant church nearby,
dating from the 15th–18th
centuries, contains ten tombs
of members of the von Wertheim family. The most spectacular of these is the tomb of
Count Ludwig I von Löwen-
stein-Wertheim and his wife,
Anna von Stolberg. This is the
work of Michael Kern (1618).
Also worth visiting are the
Glasmuseum and the **Grafschaftsmuseum Wertheim**,
with collections of Frankish
costumes, paintings and coins
and displays on wine-making.

🏛 **Glasmuseum**
Mühlenstraße 24. 📞 *(09342) 68 66*.
⬜ *Apr–Oct: 10am–noon & 2–5pm
Tue–Sun*. **Glassmaking demon-
strations** *Sat & national holidays
10am–12noon*. 🚗
🏛 **Grafschaftsmuseum
Wertheim**
Rathausgasse 10. 📞 *(09342) 30 14
10*. ⬜ *9:30am–noon & 2–4:30pm
Tue–Fri, 2:30–5pm Sat & Sun*. 🚗

**Half-timbered houses and tower
by Schloss Tauberbischofsheim**

Tauberbischofs-
heim ❷

Road map C5. 🏘 *13,000*. 🚆
🛈 *Marktplatz 8 (09341-803 13)*.

B ONIFACE, the Anglo-Saxon
missionary to the German
tribes, established Germany's
first nunnery in AD 735. Its
first prioress, Lioba, who
was related to
Boniface, gave
her name to the
Baroque church
that stands in
Tauberbischofs-
heim's market
square.

The town, which
enjoys a picturesque
location in the
valley of the river
Tauber, still has a group of
original half-timbered houses.
On the market square is the
Baroque Rehhof (1702) and
the old "Star Pharmacy" in a

house once occupied by
Georg Michael Franck, grand-
father of the Romantic poets
Clemens and Bettina Brentano.

In the eastern section of
Hauptstraße stands Haus
Mackert – a Baroque mansion
built in 1744 for a wealthy
wine merchant. In Schlossplatz is the Kurmainzisches
Schloss, an imposing edifice
built in the 15th–16th centuries, that now houses the
Landschaftsmusum.

🏛 **Landschaftsmuseum
Kurmainzisches Schloss**
📞 *(09341) 37 60*. ⬜ *Easter–Oct:
2:30–4:30pm Tue–Fri, 10am–noon &
2–4:30pm Sat & Sun*. 🚗

Bad Mergentheim ❸

Road map C5. 🏘 *25,000*. 🚆
🛈 *Marktplatz 3 (07931-5 71 35)*. 🚗
*Markelsheimer Weinfest (after
Whitsun)*.

L YING IN A CHARMING spot
on the river Tauber, Bad
Mergentheim was, from
1525 until 1809, the
seat of the Grand
Masters of the
religious order
of the "House of
the Hospitallers
of Saint Mary of
the Teutons in
Jerusalem", more
commonly known
as the Teutonic
Knights. When
three Hohenlohe brothers
entered the Order in 1220,
they contributed to it their
share of their father's estate.
This laid the foundations for
one of the most powerful
Teutonic commands at the
heart of the Holy Roman
Empire. From 1244 until 1250
Heinrich von Hohenlohe held
the office of Grand Master.

The former Hohenlohe's
castle, built in the 12th–13th
centuries, was remodelled in
Renaissance style in 1565–74
by Michael Bronner and
Blasius Berwart. They gave
the castle its winding stairs
and the opulent ornamental
decor of the staircase. The
Baroque-Rococo Schlosskirche
dominates the complex. Its
interior was designed by
François Cuvilliés, while the

**Heraldic crest from the
castle in Bad
Mergentheim**

Scenic castle ruins in Wertheim

ceiling fresco *(The Victorious Cross)* is the work of Nicolaus Stuber. The castle is now the home of a very interesting museum of the Order, the **Deutschordensmuseum**.

Many of the town's historic buildings survive to this day, including the 13th-century Church of the Knights of St John of Jerusalem and the Dominican church containing the epitaph of the Grand Master Walther von Cronberg. The **Pfarrkirche** (Parish church) in the Stuppach district contains a masterpiece by Grünewald (1519), known as the *Madonna of Stuppach*.

🔒 Pfarrkirche in Stuppach

Kapellenpflege. 📞 *(7931) 26 05.*
🕐 *Mar–Apr: 10am–5pm daily;*
May–Oct: 9am–6pm daily; Nov–Feb:
11am–4pm daily. 📷

🏛 Deutschordensmuseum

Schloss. 📞 *(07931) 522 12.*
🕐 *10am–5pm Tue–Sun.* 📷

Weikersheim ❹

Road map C5. 🏘 *8,000.* ℹ *Am Marktplatz 12 (07934-99 25 75).*

ELEVEN KILOMETRES (7 miles) east of Bad Mergentheim is the picturesque little town of Weikersheim. A Rococo fountain from 1768 stands at the centre of its market square while, on the north side, stands the late-Gothic parish church. The latter is a triple-nave hall-church with a single-tower western façade and two towers by the choir. Inside are many tombs of the von Hohenlohe family. Also on the market square stands the **Tauberländer Dorfmuseum**, which charts the history of rural life in Franconia. In the western part of town stands the very well preserved **Schloss Weikersheim**, the palace complex of the Counts von Hohenlohe, which dates

ure of drummer
Weikersheim's Hofgarten

from the 16th–18th centuries. Its highlight is undoubtedly the vast Rittersaal, a sumptuous banqueting hall that measures 35 m (115 ft) long × 12 m (39 ft) wide × 9 m (29 ft) high. The counts and their aristocratic guests used to enter this room on horseback. Its very rare, original furnishings include paintings and reliefs depicting hunting scenes.

A true rarity is the original Baroque Hofgarten (palace garden), designed by Daniel Matthieu and built in 1709.

♣ Schloss Weikersheim

🕐 *Apr–Oct: 9am–6pm daily; Nov–Mar: 10am–noon & 1:30–4:30pm daily.* 📷

🏛 Tauberländer Dorfmuseum

Marktplatz. 📞 *(07934) 12 09.* 🕐 *Easter–Nov: 2–5pm Tue–Fri, 10am–noon & 2–5pm Sat, Sun, holidays.* 📷

Creglingen ❺

Road map C5. 🏘 *5,000.* 🚉
ℹ *Rathaus (07933-6 31).*

UPSTREAM FROM Weikersheim, on the Bavarian border, is the small town of Creglingen. Here, sometime in the distant past, a ploughman found a luminous holy wafer in a clod of earth while working in a field. The news of this miraculous find spread quickly and, within a few years, the **Herrgottskirche** was built,

Altar by Tilman Riemenschneider, in Creglingen's Herrgottskirche

where the host was put on display for visiting pilgrims. In 1500, Tilman Riemenschneider was commissioned to make an altar for the church, which he carved from limewood between 1502 and 1506. The main theme of the polyptych is the *Assumption of the Virgin Mary*, considered to be the artist's masterpiece. The altar survived the turbulent times of the Reformation, when many precious religious images were destroyed.

🔒 Herrgottskirche

Kohlersmühle. 📞 *(07933) 631.*
🕐 *Apr–Oct: 9:15am–5:30pm daily;*
Nov–Mar: 10am–noon & 2–4pm Tue–Sun. ⬤ *24, 25, 31 Dec.*

TEUTONIC ORDER

The Order of the Hospital of St Mary of the German House in Jerusalem was officially founded in Acre (Akko) in 1190. Its aim was to care for sick pilgrims or Crusaders wounded in fights with the Saracens. In 1231–83, the Teutonic Knights took over all of Prussia and, in 1308–09 all Eastern Pomerania around Danzig, and they moved their headquarters from Venice to Marienburg on the river Nogat. In 1525 the Grand Master, Albrecht von Hohenzollern-Ansbach, converted to Lutheranism and secularized Teutonic Prussia. However, the Order remained in existence in the Holy Roman Empire: its German Master, Walter von Cronberg, who had his residence in Mergentheim, became *de facto* Grand Master. Napoleon abolished the Order in 1809, but it still exists today, with its headquarters based in Vienna since 1809.

The Wasserturm (Water Tower) in Friedrichsplatz, Mannheim

Mannheim ⑥

Road map B5. 🏠 326,000. 🚉 🚌
Willy-Brandt-Platz 3 (0190-77 00 20).
🎭 *Mannheim-Heidelberger Filmfestival (mid-October).*

Mannheim existed as a small fishing hamlet as far back as 766. In 1606, Elector Frederick IV the Righteous ordered a fortress to be built on the site, at the junction of the rivers Rhine and Neckar. A trading settlement sprang up nearby, which was soon granted town status. Having been repeatedly destroyed through the years, the town was finally rebuilt in Baroque style during the reign of the Elector Johann Wilhelm.

The town-centre layout follows the regular Baroque pattern of the early 18th century, when the town was divided into 136 regular squares. In 1720, when Elector Charles III Philip decided to move his residence from Heidelberg to Mannheim, the foundation stone for a Baroque palace was laid in the grounds of a former citadel.

With over 400 rooms, this became one of the largest and most opulent of all German palaces. Like many other residences built by European rulers at that time, the palace was modelled on Versailles. The main palace is built to a horseshoe layout, and its symmetry is emphasized by a central projecting entrance. Building work was carried out by Johann Clemens Froimont, Alessandro Galli da Bibiena, Guillaume d'Hauberst and Nicolas de Pigage.

The second largest town of the region, Mannheim boasts many other historic buildings, including the post-Jesuit Church of St Ignatius and St Francis Xavier, designed by Alessandro Galli da Bibiena and built in 1733–60. Original wall-paintings by Egid Quirin Asam no longer exist, but the altars have survived to this day. These include J I Saler's *Silver Madonna in Radiant Glory* (1747). Also worth visiting are the Baroque Altes Rathaus (1701–23) and Secessionist buildings in Friedrichsplatz such as the Kunsthalle and Wasserturm – the symbol of Mannheim.

The town has several interesting museums: the **Städtische Kunsthalle** has a large collection of 19th- and 20th-century art, including Francis Bacon's *Study After Velasquez's Portrait of Pope Innocent X*. The museum is renowned for its major temporary exhibitions. The **Reiss-Museum** has a fine collection of 18th-century Dutch paintings and sections devoted to early history and ethnography. Another big attraction is the **Landesmuseum für Technik und Arbeit** (Museum of Technology and Labour). Opened in 1990, this houses a collection of historic machinery. Mannheim saw the first official

Statue of Elector Karl Theodor in Mannheim's Jesuitenkirche

demonstration of many inventions that have now become part of everyday life. In 1817, Baron Karl Friedrich von Sauerbronn demonstrated his first bicycle here and, in 1886, Carl Friedrich Benz unveiled his first automobile, produced at the nearby factory.

🏛 **Städtische Kunsthalle**
Moltkestraße 9. 🔔 *(0621) 293 64 13.* 🕐 *10am–5pm Tue–Wed, Fri–Sun, noon–5pm Thu.* ● *during Carnival, 1 May, 24, 31 Dec.* 🖼

🏛 **Landesmuseum für Technik und Arbeit**
Museumsstraße 1. 🔔 *(0621) 429 89.* 🕐 *9am–5pm Tue, Thu & Fri, 9am–8pm Wed, 10am–5pm Sat, Sun.* ● *Good Friday, 24, 25, 31 Dec.* 🖼

🏛 **Reiss-Museum** Quadrat D5 and C5. 🖥 *www.mannheim.de/ reiss_museum.de* 🔔 *(0621) 293 31 50.* 🕐 *10am–5pm Tue, Thu & Fri, 10am–9pm Wed, 1–5pm Sat, 10am–6pm Sun.* 🖼

Paul Cézanne's *Pipe Smoker* (c.1890), in the Städtische Kunsthalle, Mannheim

Schwetzingen ⑦

Road map B5. 🏠 21,500. 🚌
Dreikönigstr. 3 (06202-94 58 75).
🎭 *Schwetzinger Festspiele (May), Mozartkonzerte (Sept).*

Schwetzingen's Baroque-Renaissance palace was built during the reign of the Electors Johann Wilhelm, Charles II Philip and Karl Theodor as their summer residence. Erected on the site of a medieval castle that was later converted into a hunting lodge, it is one of the best known palace complexes of

Baroque Schwetzingen Palace, set amid beautiful gardens

18th-century Europe. The conversion of the 16th-century hunting lodge was carried out by J A Breuning and the side wings were built by Alessandro Galli da Bibiena. The magnificent Rococo theatre, designed by Nicolas de Pigage, was built in 1752, while the palace garden is the work of Johann Ludwig Petri, who designed it in the French-style, following the fashion prevalent in continental Europe at that time. The garden features several interesting pavilions, including a mosque with two minarets and a bathhouse. In 1776 Friedrich Ludwig von Sckell converted it into an English-style garden.

Heraldic insignia from Bruchsal Palace

Philippsburg to Bruchsal. He not only initiated the town's development but, most importantly, ordered a palace to be built for himself and his court. The foundation stone of **Schloss Bruchsal** was laid in 1720 and the building works were carried out by Maximilian von Welsch, who was responsible for the right wing, and Michael Rohrer, who built the left wing between 1723 and 1728. The main body, preceded by a ceremonial courtyard, was designed by Baron Anselm von Grünstein. The central part of the palace is

occupied by a magnificent staircase built by the great Balthasar Neumann, with stuccowork by Johann Michael Feuchtmayer and paintings by Johann and Januarius Zick. The palace suffered severe bomb damage in 1945, but its major part was reconstructed between 1952 and 1977.

St Peter's church was built in 1740–49 by Michael Rohrer to Balthasar Neumann's 1736 design. The church features magnificent Baroque tombs of Schönborn and his successor Cardinal Franz Christoph von Hutten. The palace garden was designed in the French style by Johann Scheer.

This former residence of prince-bishops now houses a section of the Karlsruhe Museum, which features the largest collection of Flemish and French tapestries in Germany. It is also home to the **Museum Mechanische Musikinstrumente**, which includes 200 mechanical musical instruments. Short demonstrations are given on these throughout the day.

♠ **Schloss Bruchsal**
☎ (07251) 74 26 61. ◯ 9:30am–5pm Tue–Sun. ● 25, 31 Dec. ◢
Museum Mechanische Musik-instrumente ◯ 10am–5pm Tue, 9:30am–5pm Wed–Sun. ◢ 10am, 11am, 1pm, 2pm, 3pm, 4pm. ● Shrove Tuesday, 24, 25, 31 Dec. ◢

♠ **Schloss Schwetzingen**
☎ (06202) 814 81. ◯ Apr–Sept: 8am–8pm Tue–Sun; Oct & Mar: 9am–6pm Tue–Sun; Nov–Feb: 9am–5pm Tue–Sun. ◢

Bruchsal ❽

Road map B6. 🏠 40,000. 🚉 🛈 Am Alten Schloss 2 (07251-727 71).

BRUCHSAL BELONGED to the Bishops of Speyer from 1056 until 1806, since when it has been part of Baden. The town rose to prominence in the 17th century, when the Prince-Bishop of Speyer, Damian Hugo von Schönborn moved his residence from

Central façade of the Baroque Schloss Bruchsal

Street-by-Street: Heidelberg 🄾

SITUATED ON THE BANKS of the river Neckar, Heidelberg is one of Germany's most beautiful towns. For centuries it was a centre of political power, with a lively and influential cultural life. In 1386, Germany's first university was established here by the Elector Ruprecht I. Building of the palace began during his reign, continuing until the mid-17th century. However, in the late-17th century, French incursions totally destroyed medieval Heidelberg, including the castle. The town was subsequently rebuilt in the early 18th-century in Baroque style.

Marktplatz
Now adorned with the Neptune Fountain, the market square was, in the past, the site of executions and the burning of witches and heretics.

★ Heiliggeistkirche
Built in 1400–41 on the site of a late-Romanesque basilica, the Church of the Holy Spirit is the town's oldest sanctuary.

HAUPTSTRASSE

HEILIGGEISTSTRASSE

FISCHM

OBERE NECKARSTRASSE

STEINGASSE

NECKARSTADEN

0 metres 60
0 yards 60

Philosophenweg
Built in 1817 on the slopes of Heiligenberg, at an altitude of 200 m (650 ft), the "Philosophers' Walk" offers magnificent views of Heidelberg and its castle.

★ Alte Brücke
This imposing, nine-span bridge over the river Neckar was built in 1786–88 by Mathias Maier. It was rebuilt after its destruction during World War II.

★ **Haus zum Ritter**
Built in 1592 for the family of a rich cloth merchant, the Haus zum Ritter is a fine example of German Mannerist style. It now houses a luxury hotel and restaurant.

VISITORS' CHECKLIST

Road map C6. 🚶 *139,000.*
🚉 🚌 *Hauptbahnhof (06221-194 33).* 🎭 *Mannheim-Heidelberger Filmfestival (mid-Oct), Schlossfestspiele (Jul & Aug), Weindorf (Sep), Heidelberg Herbst (Sep).*

Hexenturm
The tower was once part of the 13th-century Medieval town fortifications.

MERIANSTRASSE

UNIVERSITÄTS-PLATZ

HEUGASSE

HAUPTSTRASSE

Universitätsbibliothek

UNTERE STRASSE

Alte Universität
The old university building, designed by local architect Johann Adam Breuning, was built in 1712—35.

BUSSEMERGASSE

LAUERSTRASSE

Jesuitenkirche
This church was built in 1712–51 for the Jesuits, who arrived in Heidelberg in 1698. The ornaments on the monumental façade were carved by Paul Egell.

STAR SIGHTS

★ **Alte Brücke**

★ **Haus zum Ritter**

★ **Heiliggeistkirche**

KEY

– – – Suggested route

Heidelberg Castle

Detail from Ruprechtsbau

Towering over the town, the majestic castle is really a vast residential complex that was built and repeatedly extended between the 13th and 17th centuries. Originally a supremely well-fortified Gothic castle, but now mostly in ruins, this was the seat of the House of Wittelsbach palatines. After remodelling in the 16th century, the castle became one of Germany's most beautiful Renaissance residences. However, its splendour was extinguished by the Thirty Years' War and the 1689 war with France, during which most of the structure was destroyed.

★ Ottheinrichsbau
The Deutsches Apotheken-museum is housed within the shell of this Renaissance building. It features Baroque and Rococo workshops and a travelling pharmacy.

The bell tower, which was erected in the early 15th century, was remod-elled frequently in subsequent years.

★ Friedrichsbau
One of the latest parts of the castle is Friedrich's Palace, which dates from 1601–07. Inside are statues of members of the Wittelsbach dynasty, including Charles the Great.

Castle moat

Englischer Bau
These imposing ruins in the castle complex are the remains of a 17th-century building that Friedrich V built for his wife Elizabeth Stuart.

STAR SIGHTS

★ Friedrichsbau

★ Ottheinrichsbau

★ Ruprechtsbau

VISITORS' CHECKLIST

Schlossberg. ▐ (06221) 53 84
31. ◻ Apr–Oct: 9am–5pm;
Nov–Mar: 9am–6pm. **Grosses
Fass** ◻ 9am–6pm daily. ▨
**Deutsches Apotheken-
museum** ▐ (06221) 258 80.
◻ 10am–5:30pm. ● 31 Dec,
1 Jan. ▨

Pulverturm
*Built during the reign of the
Elector Ruprecht, this 14th-
century tower once formed
part of the castle defences.*

Brunnenhalle
This Gothic loggia features early-
Romanesque columns taken from the
palace of Charles the Great in Ingelheim.

Torturm

**Main
entrance**

★ Ruprechtsbau
*Built around 1400 by a
master builder from
Frankfurt, this is the oldest
surviving part of the castle.*

🏛 Alte Universität
Grabengasse 1. ▐ (06221) 54 21 52.
Universitätsmuseum ◻ 10am–
4pm Mon–Sat. ▨

Designed by Mainz architect
Johann Adam Breuning, the
university was built in 1712–35
on the site of the 16th-century
structure. On the north wall
and ceiling are allegorical
paintings by Ferdinand Keller.
In front of the building is a
fountain crowned by a
sculpture in the form of the
heraldic Palatinate lion.

🏛 Universitätsbibliothek
Plöck 107–109. ▐ (06221) 54 23 80.
◻ 9am–5pm Mon–Wed, 9am–6pm
Thu, 9am–3:30pm Fri.

The monumental building of
the university library, designed
by Joseph Durm of Karlsruhe,
was erected in 1901–05 near
the church of St Peter. The
Heidelberg library, with over
2 million volumes, is one of
the largest in Germany. The
exhibition rooms hold many
precious manuscripts and old
prints, including the famous
Codex Manesse, illustrated
with 137 beautiful miniatures.

🏛 Kurpfälzisches Museum
Hauptstraße 97. ▐ (06221) 58 34
02. ◻ 10am–5pm Tue, Thu–Sun,
10am–9pm Wed. ▨

The French Count Charles de
Graimberg spent the bulk of
his considerable fortune on
building up an extensive
collection of fine drawings,
paintings, arms and various
curios associated with the
history of the Palatinate and
the castle of Heidelberg. In
1879, his collection became
the property of the town and
forms the core of this very
interesting museum, which
also includes a fascinating
archaeology section.

🏛 Heiliggeistkirche
Hauptstraße.

This collegiate church, whose
Baroque dome is one of the
city's landmarks, was built in
1400–41. The canons of the
college were also university
scholars and therefore the
church aisle features special
galleries for the extensive
collections of library books –
Bibliotheca Palatina. The
choir features a tombstone of
Ruprecht III and his wife,
Elisabeth von Hohenzollern.

Karlsruhe ⑩

Road map B6. 🏛 269,000. 🚉
🛈 *Bahnhofsplatz 6 (0721-355 30 & 194 33; www.karlsruhe.de).*
🎭 *Internationales Trachten-und-Folklorefest (Jun).*

KARLSRUHE, which is one of the "youngest" towns in Germany, flourished during the 19th century as a centre for science and art. In 1945, it lost its status as a regional capital, but is now the seat of the Bundesverfassungsgericht – the highest courts of the Federal Republic.

The town originated in 1715 when the margrave of Baden, Karl Wilhelm von Baden-Durlach, ordered a lodge to be built in the middle of his favourite hunting grounds. Karl liked the area and the lodge so much that he decided to move his residence here and live the remainder of his days in peace – hence the town's name, meaning "Karl's rest". The original Baroque-style design was expanded during the reign of his successor, Karl Friedrich.

The palace, which forms the hub of 32 streets, was designed by Leopoldo Retti, Mauritio Pedetti, Balthasar Neumann, Philippe de la Gaupière and others, and built in 1749–81. The town is based on a fan-like plan, spreading from a base formed by the open-sided wings of the palace. The rest of the circle, whose centre is marked by the octagonal palace tower (1715), is filled with green areas, including the palace garden.

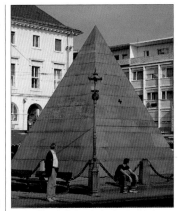

A pyramid containing the tomb of Karl Wilhelm von Baden-Durlach in Karlsruhe

In the early 19th century, the town was remodelled along Neo-Classical lines. The main architect of this large-scale project was Friedrich Weinbrenner, who created this masterpiece of urban design. The equilateral market square is positioned along the palace axis. It is filled with similar but not identical buildings and features a central pyramid containing Karl Wilhelm's tomb. South of Marktplatz is the circular Rondellplatz. Weinbrenner's other works include the monumental town hall (1811–25), the Protestant town church and the Catholic parish church of St Stephen.

Karlsruhe has some very interesting museums. The Badisches Landesmuseum in the castle features a large collection of antiquities, decorative arts, sculpture, porcelain and furniture, from the Middle Ages to the present day. In a Neo-Renaissance building (1843–46) is the **Staatliche Kunsthalle**, with its large collection of mainly German and Dutch paintings from the 16th–19th centuries. These include the famous *Crucifixion* by Grünewald (1523).

Entirely different in character are the collections of the Zentrum für Kunst und Medientechnologie (ZKM) – an establishment that has combined the role of art college and museum since 1997. It occupies a former ammunitions factory in the western part of the town. Its core is the **Museum für Neue Kunst**, featuring installations, computer art and videos and other work by contemporary artists. The **Stadtmuseum im Prinz-Max-Palais**, based in a mansion named after the last chancellor of the Second Reich, contains the local history museum.

🏛 **Staatliche Kunsthalle**
Hans-Thoma-Straße 2–6. 📞 *(0721) 9 26 33 55.* ⏰ *10am–5pm Tue–Fri, 10am–6pm Sat–Sun.* 🖼
🏛 **Museum für Neue Kunst**
Lorenzstraße 9. 📞 *(0721) 81 00 13 00.* ⏰ *10am–6pm Thu–Sat, 10am–10pm Wed.* 🖼
🏛 **Stadtmuseum im Prinz-Max-Palais**
Karlstraße 10. 📞 *(0721) 1 33 42 30.* ⏰ *10am–6pm Tue, Wed, Fri & Sun, 10am–8pm Thu, 2–6pm Sat.*

The Baroque residence of the Dukes of Baden in Karlsruhe

Baden-Baden ⓫

Road map B6. 🏘 50,000. ✈ Baden Airport (5 km/3 miles northwest of town). 🚉 ℹ Solmsstraße 1 (07221-27 52 00).

K NOWN AS THE "summer capital of Europe", this elegant spa resort is one of the oldest towns in Germany and was once the favourite destination of European aristocracy from Russia to Portugal. Even before the Romans built their camp here around AD 80, the site was occupied by a Celtic settlement of the Latenian period.

In the early years of the modern era, *Civitas Aurelia Aquensis* – known simply as Aquae – was already known in Italy for the therapeutic properties of its waters. In the 3rd century AD, Aquae was conquered by the Germanic tribe of Alamains and in the 6th century AD by the Francs, who built a fortress in the town. The Margrave Hermann II, known as "Marchio de Baduon", was the first important ruler of Baden.

During the horrific Black Death, the qualities of the local waters were once again recognized as being beneficial to health. During the Palatinate War of Succession, Baden-Baden was almost totally destroyed but, by the end of the 18th century, it had became one of Europe's most fashionable resorts.

The old town of Baden-Baden lies at the foot of the Schlossberg (castle hill). The oldest surviving building in the town is the Gothic collegiate church, built during the 13th–15th centuries and then remodelled in the 18th century. It contains several valuable epitaphs. To the south of the church is the bathing hall – Friedrichsbad – which was built in neo-Renaissance style in 1877. Nearby stands the magnificent New Palace, which was the residence of margraves from the 15th century

Baden-Baden's casino, set in the elegant Kurhaus

onwards. It was remodelled along German Renaissance lines in the 16th century by Kaspar Weinhart. The interiors are decorated with paintings by Tobias Stimer.

Most of the spa buildings are the work of Friedrich Weinbrenner. His elegant Kurhaus in Werderstraße has been used as a casino since 1838. The most famous gamester at the casino was Fyodor Dostoevsky, who was not always lucky at roulette. His novel *The Gambler* (1866) is supposedly set in Baden-Baden. Nearby is the Trinkhalle (pump room), with its mineral water fountains. Built in 1839–42, it is decorated with wall paintings illustrating Black Forest legends.

Rising behind the spa area is the last project completed by Leo von Klenze before his death – the Orthodox burial chapel of a Romanian aristocratic family, the Stourdza

Mausoleum. In Schillerstraße you will find a villa built in 1867 for the famous Russian writer, Ivan Turgenev, who lived here until 1872.

🎵 Brahmshaus
Maximilianstraße 85. ☎ (07221) 50 49 10. ◯ 3–5pm Mon, Wed, Fri, 10am–1pm Sun. 🈴
The exhibition displayed in this house is devoted to the life and works of the German composer Johannes Brahms who lived here from 1865 until 1874.

🔒 Kloster Lichtental
Hauptstraße 40. ☎ (07221) 7 23 32. 🏃 Group tours (minimum 7 persons), advance telephone booking required. 🈴
This Cistercian nuns' abbey, situated on the outskirts of town, has a church dating from the 14th–15th centuries. Its ducal chapel contains many epitaphs of the Baden margraves. The abbey also has an interesting museum.

🏛 Stadtgeschichtliche Sammlungen
Schlossstraße 2. ☎ (07221) 2 21 80. ◯ Apr–Oct: 10am–12:30pm & 2–5pm Tue–Sun. 🈴
This exhibition includes many Roman archaeological finds from the Baden-Baden region, including cooking utensils, an interesting collection of toys, dolls, medals and spectacles.

🏛 Stadtmuseum
Küferstraße 3. ☎ (07221) 93 22 71/2. ◯ 10am–12:30pm & 2–5pm Tue–Sun. 🈴
The Stadtmuseum includes sections devoted to glass, porcelain and paintings, as well as some fascinating old gambling equipment.

The Neo-Renaissance Trinkhalle (pump room) in Baden-Baden

Maulbronn ⑫

MAULBRONN, in the heart of the Stromberg region, grew up around a Cistercian Kloster (monastery). One of the best-preserved examples of medieval architecture in Europe, the monastery was founded in 1147 in the valley of the river Salzach by monks who came here from Alsace. The Klosterkirche, built in 1147–78, is an elongated, triple-nave basilica with a transept and a choir. The Gothic atrium on the western side was added in 1210–15. Outside the enclosure are domestic buildings, an inn and the guest chapel, which date from the 15th–17th centuries. Defence walls with turrets and a gate tower encircle the entire complex.

★ Chapter House
The monks assembled in this Gothic hall to discuss their private and public affairs. The hall has two naves, supported by three pillars.

★ Brunnenkapelle
Built opposite the entrance to the refectory, the Well Chapel, with its intricate Gothic forms, is where the monks used to wash their hands before meals.

Inner Courtyard
Once a garden, the monastery's inner courtyard is surrounded by cloisters. It is a place that inspires contemplation.

Cloisters

STAR FEATURES
★ Brunnenkapelle
★ Chapter House
★ Mourning
★ Stalls

The Porch
The porch, also known as "Paradise", was built onto the church façade in the early 13th century.

Cloisters
In the 13th century, monks meditated as they walked around the cloisters, which gave them protection from the vagaries of the weather. Talking was strictly forbidden.

Church Interior
Originally the church had a wooden roof. In 1424 it was replaced with a network vault, which stands in stark contrast to the plain walls.

★ **Mourning**
This Gothic relief, made in around 1390 in the Parler family workshop, was part of an altar, which no longer exists. Today, it can be seen on the altar in the monastery's choir.

★ **Stalls**
Richly decorated with carved ornaments, the late-Gothic stalls date from around 1450.

Heilbronn ⑬

Road map C6. 🚶 *119,000.* 🚉
ℹ️ *Marktplatz (07131-56 22 70).*
🎭 *Pferdemarkt (Feb), Neckarfest (Jun), Stadtfest (Jun), Heilbronner Herbst (Sep).*

H EILBRONN'S earliest records date from the 8th century, when the town was known as "Heilicbrunno". By the late 19th century, Heilbronn had become Wurttemberg's main industrial centre, with a large port on the river Neckar.

Having suffered major destruction during World War II, the town's surviving buildings include the church of St Kilian, a Gothic basilica from the second half of the 13th century, with a triple-nave hall-choir flanked by two towers. The western tower was built in 1508–29. The magnificent altarpiece is an original late-Gothic polyptych, the work of Hans Seyffer (1498).

Near the 15th–16th-century Rathaus (town hall) is a house reputed to have been the home of Käthchen, a character in Heinrich von Kleist's play *Das Käthchen von Heilbronn*. Near the rebuilt church of St Peter and St Paul (originally the church of the Teutonic Order) stands the former Teutonic convent – the Deutschhof.

Isaak Habrecht's astronomical clock on Heilbronn town hall

Half-timbered houses on the bank of the river Kocher, in Schwäbisch Hall

Schwäbisch Hall ⑭

Road map C6. 🚶 *35,000.* 🚉
ℹ️ *Am Markt 9 (0791-75 12 46).*
🎭 *Kuchen- und Brunnenfest der Haller Salzsieder (Whitsun).*

A RCHAEOLOGICAL excavations in 1939 proved the existence of a Celtic settlement on this site as early as 500 BC. The town features a great number of historic buildings from various periods, including many half-timbered 15th–16th-century houses, Baroque town houses, and a Rococo town hall and town palace (Keckenburg). The most interesting building is the hall-church of St Michael, whose Gothic main body was built in 1427–56. The Romanesque tower on the western façade, however, dates from the 12th century. The late-Gothic hall-choir (1495–1527) is famous for its decorative network vaults. Original furnishings include the main altar, the stalls and the Holy Sepulchre.

Schwäbisch Gmünd ⑮

Road map C6. 🚶 *63,400.* 🚉 ℹ️
Kornhausstraße 14 (07171-60 34 55).
🎭 *Internationales Schattentheater Festival (Jun), European Church Music.*

T HIS TOWN – the birthplace of the architect Peter Parler and painters Hans Baldung Grien and Jerg

Madonna with Child, in Marktplatz, Schwäbisch Gmünd

Ratgeb – was once renowned throughout Europe for the magnificent goods produced by its goldsmiths. It has many great historic buildings, mainly churches, such as the late-Romanesque church of St John, which dates from around 1220, but was subsequently remodelled. The church of St Cross is famous not only for being the first Gothic hall-church in southern Germany, but also the first major work of the famous family of architects – the Parlers. This triple-nave hall with a hall-choir, featuring an ambulatory and a ring of side chapels, was built in several stages, between 1320 and 1521. Its western façade has a high triangular top with blind windows.

Inside the church are many valuable historic relics, such as the Holy Sepulchre (1400), the stalls, which date from around 1550, and the organ gallery (1688).

Other interesting structures in the town include large fragments of the town fortifications, including towers, and several half-timbered houses.

Bad Wimpfen ⑯

Road map C6. 🚶 *6,676.* 🚉 ℹ️
Carl-Ulrich-Straße 1 (07063-9 72 00).
🎭 *Talmarkt (Jun/Jul), Zunftmarkt (Aug), Weihnachtsmarkt (Dec).*

T HE TOWN of Bad Wimpfen was created out of two settlements, Bad Wimpfen am Berg and Bad Wimpfen im Tal, which remain distinct to this day. The settlement on top of the hill grew around the Hohenstauf family palace, whose chapel and well-preserved arcade windows, resting on pairs of decorated columns, can still be seen.

Built at the order of Frederick I Barbarossa in 1165–75, this was the main and the biggest imperial palace (Kaiserpfalz) of the Holy Roman Empire. One of the surviving towers offers a spectacular view over the Neckar valley.

Set in a picturesque location, Bad Wimpfen features many half-timbered houses dating from the 16th–18th centuries.

Bad Wimpfen im Tal is built around the former collegiate church of St Peter and St Paul. This is a triple-nave basilica with transept, two eastern towers and cloister, dating from the 13th–15th centuries. The south façade of the transept and the portal are richly decorated with carvings, which are probably the work of Erwin von Steinbach, one of the builders of Strasbourg Cathedral. The church interior features many original carved statues and stalls.

Marbach ⑰

Road map C6. 🏰 1,450. 🚉
🛈 Marktstraße 23 (07144-10 20).

THIS SMALL TOWN would probably never merit an entry in any guidebook were it not for the fact that the great writer Friedrich Schiller was born here in 1759. The modest, half-timbered house, in which the famous poet spent his childhood, has survived to this day and is now a small museum – the **Schiller-Geburtshaus**. The town also possesses a vast museum of literature (**Schiller-Nationalmuseum**), which is housed in a Neo-Baroque palace. Its collection is not limited to the life and work of Schiller, but also includes many documents relating to German literature.

Other attractions in Marbach include some of the original half-timbered houses and the remains of the town walls and town gates in the old town. The late-Gothic Alexanderkirche is also worth a visit. Built in the second half of the 12th century by Albert Jörg, it features interesting network vaulting covered with ornamental paintings.

Friedrich Schiller statue in Marbach

🏚 **Schiller-Geburtshaus**
Nicklastorstraße 31. 📞 (07144) 175 67. 🕐 9am–5pm daily. ⬤ 24–31 Dec. 🖼

🏛 **Schiller-Nationalmuseum**
Schillerhöhe 8–10. 📞 (07144) 84 86 01. 🕐 9am–5pm daily. ⬤ 24–31 Dec. 🖼

Esslingen ⑱

Road map C6. 🏰 92,000.
🛈 Marktplatz 16 (0711-3 96 93 90).

SET AMONG vineyards on the banks of the river Neckar, the beautiful town of Esslingen is famous for its sparkling wines. The town's historic buildings were fortunate in surviving intact the ravages of World War II. A walk through the winding streets and narrow alleys of the old centre will yield many interesting sights, while a climb to the top of the hill affords a splendid view of the town and the Neckar valley, as well as the amazing **Innere Brücke**, a 14th-century bridge. From there visitors can descend towards the market square, stopping on the way to visit Frauenkirche, a Gothic hall-church dating from the 14th century. Its front tower, the work of Ulrich and Matthäus Ensingers, was added later. In the market square is the Stadtkirche St Dionysius, the oldest church in town, built in the 13th century on the site of an earlier, 8th-century building. Inside are magnificent early-Gothic stained-glass windows and late-15th-century Gothic furnishings, including the choir partition, the sacrarium and the font. The nearby church of St Paul, built in the mid-13th century for the Dominicans, is the oldest surviving Dominican church in Germany. In neighbouring Rathausplatz stands the half-timbered old town hall, Altes Rathaus, with its beautiful Renaissance façade, and the Baroque new town hall. Designed as a palace for Gottlieb von Palm by Gottlieb David Kandlers, the Neues Rathaus was built between 1748 and 1751.

The picturesque houses and chapel of Esslingen's 14th-century Innere Brücke

Ludwigsburg ⑲

Palace crest

S ITUATED NEAR Stuttgart and known as the "Versailles of Swabia", Ludwigsburg was founded in 1704 on the initiative of Eberhard Ludwig, Prince of Wurttemberg. At the heart of the town is the vast palace complex, which the Prince ordered to be built for his mistress, Countess Wilhelmina von Graevenitz. The construction of the palace, which was carried out between 1704 and 1733, involved many outstanding architects and interior decorators, including Philipp Jenisch, Johann Nette, Donato Frisoni and Diego Carlone.

Northern Garden
This magnificent Baroque park is the venue for a flower show ("Blooming Baroque") that is held here during the summer.

★ **Western Gallery**
The gallery features opulent stucco ornaments by Ricardo Rotti and Diego Carlone (1712–15).

★ **Marble Hall**
This vast hall in the new wing of the palace was remodelled in 1816, but still retains some of its Baroque interior decor.

★ **Queen's Library**
The library is housed in the east wing of the palace, in the apartments arranged for Queen Charlotte Mathilde.

The new wing of the palace houses a museum devoted to court art of the Baroque period.

★ **Schloss Favorite**
The "Favorite" hunting lodge was built between 1718 and 1723, but its interior has been remodelled in Neo-Classical style.

VISITORS' CHECKLIST

Road map C6. 👥 *80,000.*
🚏 ℹ️ *Wilhelmstr. 10 (07141-910 22 52).*
Residenzschloss Ludwigsburg
Schlossstraße 30. ☎️ *(07141) 18 64 40.* ⏰ *summer: 9am–noon, 1–5pm; winter: 10am–noon, 1–4pm.* **Museum** ⏰ *Tue–Sun 10am–6pm.* 📷

The old wing
contains the palace's oldest apartments.

Märchengarten
The landscaped section of the park includes the "Fairy-tale Garden", which contains figures and models from German fairy-tales.

The upper fruit garden attracts visitors with its picturesque paths, which are lined with apple trees and grapevines.

Restaurant and café

STAR SIGHTS

★ **Marble Hall**

★ **Queen's Library**

★ **Schloss Favorite**

★ **Western Gallery**

Emichsburg
This romantic castle, built in 1798–1802, was named after the founder of the Wurttemberg dynasty.

Stuttgart ⑳

THE CAPITAL of Baden-Wurttemberg, Stuttgart is one of the largest and most important towns of the Federal Republic. It grew from a 10th-century stud farm, known as Stutengarten, to become the ducal (1321) and later the royal (1806) capital of Wurttemberg. Beautifully situated among picturesque hills, the town is a major industrial centre with many important manufacturing plants. It is also a well-known publishing and cultural centre, with a world-famous ballet company, chamber orchestra and splendid art collections.

Exploring Stuttgart

Start your tour of Stuttgart at Schlossplatz, continuing along Königstrasse towards the Palace Gardens, with their many interesting buildings, and stopping to pay a visit to the Staatsgalerie, whose extension was designed by the British architect James Stirling. From there you can return via Konrad-Adenauer-Strasse, heading towards Karlsplatz, then to Schillerplatz and Marktplatz with its magnificent town hall, finally ending the walk at Hegelhaus museum.

⛲ Schlossplatz

At the centre of the square stands the **Jubiläumssäule** – a column erected in 1842–46 to celebrate the 25-year reign of Wilhelm I. The square also features sculptures by many famous artists, including Alexander Calder and Alfred Hrdlicka. The east side of the square features a huge palace complex, **Neues Schloss**, built in 1746–1807, while on the opposite side stands **Königsbau**, a Neo-Classical structure erected in 1856–60.

Neo-classical façade of Stuttgart's Staatstheater

🏛 Kunstgebäude

Schlossplatz 2. **Galerie der Stadt Stuttgart** 【 (0711) 216 21 88. **Württembergischer Kunstverein** 【 (0711) 22 33 70. ◯ 11am–6pm Tue, Thu, Sun, 11am–8pm Wed. 📷

Erected between 1912 and 1913, this building houses the municipal art gallery and the regional association of the arts. The gallery features 19th- and 20th-century art, with an emphasis on the work of artists from southern Germany, including Adolf Hölzel, Joseph Kosuth and Otto Dix.

♣ Schlossgarten

The magnificent gardens stretching north of the Neues Schloss were established in the early 19th century. They have maintained, to this day, much of their original charm, with neat avenues and interesting sculptures. The attractions include the **Carl-Zeiss-Planetarium**, which runs an excellent science programme, using equipment made by the famous optics company.

On the edge of the park stands a vast Neo-Classical theatre building, the **Württembergisches Staatstheater**, built in 1907–12 by Max Littmann. In 1982–3 it was given a new, dome-covered wing, the Theaterpavilion, designed by Gottfried Böhm.

🏛 Staatsgalerie

See pp298–9.

♠ Altes Schloss

Württembergisches Landesmuseum Schillerplatz 6. 【 (0711) 279 34 00. ◯ 10am–1pm Tue, 10am–5pm Wed–Sun. 📷

When Wurttemberg castle burned down in 1311, it was decided to move the family seat to Stuttgart. In 1325, the existing small castle was extended, creating Dütnitzbau. This wing has survived and can be seen from Karlsplatz. A large-scale Renaissance remodelling project, designed by Aberlin Tresch and carried out in 1553–78, gave the castle its square layout, with three-storey arcaded cloisters encircling the inner courtyard. The southwestern wing contains the Schlosskapelle (chapel), the first sacral building in Stuttgart built especially for the Protestants. The castle now houses the **Württembergisches Landesmuseum**,

The façade of Stuttgart's Neues Schloss, combining Baroque and Neo-Classical elements

Cloistered courtyard of the Renaissance Altes Schloss

which includes vast collections of decorative art, including those displaying the ducal and royal insignia of Wurttemberg. The prehistory section includes jewellery from the Frankish period and the preserved tomb of a Celtic nobleman from Hochdorf.

🏛 Schillerplatz

This is undoubtedly one of Stuttgart's most beautiful areas. It is here that the stud farm that gave Stuttgart its name is said to have stood. Today, a pensive statue of Friedrich Schiller, the work of the Danish sculptor Bertel Thorwaldsen (1839), occupies the centre of the square.

Schillerplatz is surrounded by historic buildings: the **Old Chancellery**, built in 1542–44 and extended upwards in 1566,

now houses a restaurant, the Prinzenbau (1605–78) and the Stiftsfruchtkasten, an attractive gabled granary (1578), now home to a museum of musical instruments.

🏛 Stiftskirche (Hl. Kreuz)

Stiftstraße 12.
From the south side of Schillerplatz there is a view of the presbytery of the collegiate church of the Holy Cross. This Gothic church, the work of Hänslin and Aberlin Jörg, was built in the 15th century and incorporated the walls of the previous, early-Gothic church. Despite World War II damage, the church still has the original stone gallery of the dukes of Wurttemberg, built in 1576–84 by Simon Schlör to a design by Johann Steiner. The church also has many Gothic furnishings.

VISITORS' CHECKLIST

Road map C6. 🏙 586,000.
🛫 south of town. 🚉
ℹ *Königstraße 1A (0711-222 82 40).* 🎭 *Stuttgarter Weindorf (Aug/Sep), Cannstatter Volksfest (Sep/Oct), Stuttgarter Weindorf (Oct/Nov), Fellbacher Herbst (Oct), Weihnachtsmarkt (Dec).*

🏛 Hegelhaus

Eberhardstraße 53. 📞 *(0711) 216 67 33.* 🕐 *10am–5:30pm Tue & Fri, 10am–6:30pm Thu.* 🚫
Georg Wilhelm Friedrich Hegel – the creator of one of the most important modern philosophical systems – was born in this house on 27 August 1770. The house is now a museum, which houses an exhibition devoted to the life and work of the famous philosopher.

Figures of saints adorning the façade of the Stiftskirche

STUTTGART CITY CENTRE

Altes Schloss ❺
Hegelhaus ❽
Kunstgebäude ❷
Schillerplatz ❻
Schlossgarten ❸
Schlossplatz ❶
Staatsgalerie ❹
Stiftskirche
  Hl. Kreuz ❼

KEY

ℹ Tourist information

🅿 Parking

✝ Church

0 metres   300
0 yards   300

🏛 Linden-Museum/ Staatl. Museum für Völkerkunde

Hegelplatz 1. 🕿 *(0711) 2 02 24 08.*
🕐 *10am–5pm Tue, Thu, Sat–Sun, 10am–8pm Wed, 10am–1pm Fri.* ♿

The Linden Museum is one of Germany's finest ethnology museums. It was founded by Count Karl von Linden, who was also its director from 1889 until 1910. The museum contains many fascinating exhibits from all over the world, including figures from the Indonesian theatre of shadows, a Tibetan sand mandala, a 6th–8th-century mask from Peru in South America and a full-size reproduction of an Islamic bazaar.

Peruvian mask in the Linden-Museum

🏟 Weißenhofsiedlung

Weißenhof 10. **Exhibition rooms**
🕿 *(0711) 2 57 91 87.* 🕐 *10am–2pm Tue–Sat.* 📷 *from Am Weißenhof 15, 11am Sat.* **Architektur-Galerie**
🕿 *(0711) 257 14 34.* 🕐 *2–6pm Tue–Sat, 11am–4pm Sun.*

A building exhibition held in 1927 in Stuttgart had housing as its main theme. It left behind a complete housing estate that still exists today, although it was badly bombed during World War II. Most of the houses represent functionalism, which was being promoted at the time by the Bauhaus. The estate, which was to serve as an example to other towns and estates, has some interesting houses,

including works by Mies van der Rohe (Am Weißenhof 14–29), Le Corbusier (Rathenaustraße 1–3), Peter Behrens (Hölzelweg 3–5) and Hans Scharoun (Hölzelweg 1).

🎵 Liederhalle

Berliner Platz 1.

A must for all lovers of modern architecture, Liederhalle, in the centre of Stuttgart, is a successful synthesis of tradition and modernism. Built in 1955–56 by Adolf Abel and Rolf Gutbrod, this fine cultural and congress centre, with three concert halls clustered around an irregular hall, is still impressive today.

🏛 Mercedes-Benz-Museum

Mercedesstraße 137. 🕿 *(0711) 172 25 78.* 🕐 *9am–5pm Tue–Sun.* ⬤ *public holidays.*

To the east of the town centre, in the Obertürkheim district, is the famous Mercedes-Benz-Museum. Its splendid collection illustrates the development of motorcar production, from the earliest models to today's state-of-the-art, computerized products. Set up to celebrate the centenary of their inventions, the museum features over 70 historic vehicles, all in immaculate condition. The collection includes the world's two oldest automobiles, Gottlieb Daimler's horseless carriage and Carl Benz's three-

Some of the models on display in the Mercedes-Benz-Museum

wheeled automobile from 1886. Also on display is a hand-made limousine that was built in the 1930s for the Emperor of Japan and the first "Popemobile", which was built for Pope Paul VI.

Another interesting exhibit is the famous 1950s racing car, *Silberpfeil* (Silver Arrow), as well as models that were built for attempts on world speed records. Also on display are scores of the latest models that have been produced by the company.

The visitor can also learn the history of Daimler-Benz AG, which was created by the merger in 1926 of Daimler-Motoren-Gesellschaft and Benz & Cie., Rhein. The company's subsequent 1999 merger with Chrysler created one of the world's largest car manufacturing concerns, DaimlerChrysler.

🗼 Fernsehturm

Built between 1954 and 1956 this television tower was the world's first television transmitter built entirely from ferro-concrete. It is 217 m (712 ft) high and stands on top of a wooded hill, Hoher Bopser. Its observation platform provides splendid views over Schwäbische Alb, Schwarzwald and, on a clear day, even the Alps.

🏛 Porsche-Museum

Porschestraße 42. 🕿 *(0711) 9 11 56 85.* 🕐 *9am–4pm Mon–Fri, 9am–5pm Sat, Sun, public holidays.*

Stuttgart's other famous car manufacturer also has its own museum, which includes

House designed by Le Corbusier in Weißenhofsiedlung

around 50 examples of these fast and expensive vehicles, some of which are built to order. The history of the company is documented in a film shown in the museum's cinema. Free guided tours of the factory production lines are available. These are very popular and it is advisable to book well in advance.

🜆 Markthalle
Dorotheenstraße 4. ☐ *7am–6pm Mon–Fri, 7am–4pm Sat.*
Stuttgart's market hall, built in 1912–14 in Art Nouveau style on the site of an earlier veg-etable market, is one of the finest in Europe. Built as a food exchange, it has magni-ficent frescos. Today it still sells fresh fruit and vegetables to the general public, and it now also houses a small restaurant and café.

♣ Schloss Solitude
Solitudestraße. 🄴 *(0711) 69 66 99.* ☐ *Apr–Oct: 9am–noon, 1:30–5pm; Nov–Mar: 10am–noon, 1:30–4pm.*
This exquisite small palace, standing on the slopes of a hill, was built for Prince Karl Eugene between 1763 and 1767. The Prince not only commissioned the project, but also took an active part in the design of the residence, which is the work of Pierre Louis Philippe de la Gupière, who was responsible for intro-ducing the Louis XVI-style to Germany. Many consider this palace to be his masterpiece.

Following its full restoration in 1990, and the provision of 45 residential studio apart-ments, the palace now serves art students from all over the world, who come here on scholarships. A 15-km (9-mile) long, straight road connects Schloss Solitude with Ludwigsburg.

JOHANNES KEPLER (1571–1630)

This outstanding astronomer and mathematician was born in Weil der Stadt. He studied theology in Tübingen, where he encountered the work of Nicolaus Copernicus, becoming a fervent advocate of his theory. Forced to flee in 1600, Kepler went to Prague where he worked with Tycho Brahe. Many years of research led him to formulate three laws of planetary motion. Kepler is also the inventor of the twin-lens telescope.

🜆 Bad Cannstatt
Once an independent health resort, Bad Cannstatt is now a district of Stuttgart. Set in a beautiful park, it has a late-Gothic parish hall-church, a Neo-Classical town hall and a Kursaal (spa-house), built in 1825–42. One of its attractions is the Neo-Classical Schloss Rosenstein, built in 1824–29 at the request of King Wilhelm I, based on amended designs by John Papworth. The King was also the initiator of the beautiful "Wilhelm's complex". This includes a Moorish-style villa located in a symmetrical-ly laid-out park, with many Oriental-style pavilions and other decorative elements. Completed in the 1840s, its main designer was Karl Ludwig Wilhelm von Zanth. The park has now been transformed into a botanical-zoological garden.

ENVIRONS: Stuttgart provides a convenient base for explor-ing the surroundings. In **Sin-delfingen**, 15 km (9 miles) southwest, it is worth visiting the Romanesque Church of St Martin Canons, which was founded in 1083. While you are there, take a stroll along Lange Straße to the old town hall, which dates from 1478 and is joined with the Salt House (1592). The two buildings, both half-timbered in their upper sections, now house the town museum.

A little further to the west, **Weil der Stadt** is the birth-place of the astronomer Johannes Kepler and the reformer Johannes Brenz. The town's late-Gothic church of St Peter and St Paul was com-pleted in 1492 by Aberlin Jörg. Inside is a beautiful Renaissance sacrarium, dating from 1611. The Marktplatz, with a statue of Kepler at its centre, has a Renaissance town hall (1582). Nearby, at Keplergasse 2, stands the house in which the famous astronomer was born and which now houses a small museum, the Kepler-Museum.

Another place worthy of a visit is **Waiblingen**, 10 km (6 miles) to the northeast of Stuttgart. It features a Roman-esque church, the vaults of which are decorated with some splendid wall paintings dating from 1515.

The façade of the Schloss Solitude, in the hills to the west of Stuttgart's centre

Staatsgalerie

THE STAATSGALERIE grew from the museum of fine arts founded in 1843 by King Wilhelm I and containing the King's private collection. Now it ranks among the finest of German galleries. As well as its own magnificent collection of old masters and modern artists, the gallery has an extensive collection of graphics. In 1984 the art gallery acquired an extension designed by James Stirling.

★ The Mourning of Christ
This subtle depiction of Christ is the work of the Venetian artist Giovanni Bellini.

Bathsheba at her Toilet (c.1485)
In this painting, which is a fragment of a lost triptych illustrating Justice, Hans Memling uses the Old Testament story of Bathsheba to exemplify the abuse of power, intervention by God and the reformation of a sinner.

★ St Paul in Prison (1627)
In this, one of his earliest works, Rembrandt depicted the Apostle Paul awaiting death in a humble cell.

Entrance to Alte Staatsgalerie

Entrance to Neue Staatsgalerie

Crossing of the Rhine near Rhenen (1642)
The Dutch painter Jan von Goyen became famous for his evocative landscapes, which were often executed in uniform tones of lead-grey or brown-green.

STAR EXHIBITS

★ **Iphigenie**

★ **St Paul in Prison**

★ **The Mourning of Christ**

KEY

- Italian painting
- German painting
- Dutch painting
- 19th-century painting
- 20th-century painting
- Private rooms
- Collection of graphic arts
- Non-exhibition rooms

★ **Iphigenie** (1871)
Anselm Feuerbach's painting was inspired by a play by Goethe, Iphigenie on Tauris.

VISITORS' CHECKLIST

Konrad-Adenauer-Straße 30–32.
((0711) 2 12 40 50 or 2 12 40 28; www.staatsgalerie.de. ☐ 10am–6pm Tue, Wed, Fri–Sun, 10am–9pm Thu. ⚑ (Wed free).

GALLERY GUIDE

Permanent exhibitions are on the first floor. In the old building are works by old masters, while 19th-century work is in the right wing. 20th-century works are displayed in the new building. In the left wing of the ground floor are temporary displays of items from the graphics collection.

Spring Fields (1887)
One of the leading members of the French Impressionist movement, Claude Monet was unsurpassed in his rendition of iridescent light.

Mother and Child (1905)
This painting by Pablo Picasso represents his "pink period", which preceded the famous Cubist experiments of this great Spanish artist.

First floor

Ground floor

Female Nude Reclining on a White Pillow (1917)
Amedeo Modigliani became famous for his idiosyncratic portraits and female nudes.

Schwäbische Alb ㉑

THE MOUNTAIN RANGE of Schwäbische Alb (the Swabian Jura) extends like an arc, 220 km (137 miles) long and 40 km (25 miles) wide, from the Upper Rhine around Schaffhausen, in Switzerland, to Ries, at the border between the federal counties of Baden-Wurttemberg and Bavaria. The highest peak in the range is Lemberg (1,015 m/3,330 ft). Beech woods and scented juniper shrubs dominate the mellow landscape, whose whole system of inter-connected stalagmitic caves was carved from the underlying sedimentary limestone rocks.

Hechingen
On the outskirts of Hechingen, the remains of a 1st–3rd-century AD Roman villa are open to the public.

Haigerloch
In the vaults of this castle is a vast bunker that was used as an atomic research laboratory towards the end of World War II.

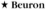

★ **Burg Hohenzollern**
The ancestral seat of the Hohenzollern family was remodelled in 1850-67. Only the 15th-century St Michaelkapelle survives from the original fortress.

★ **Beuron**
Beuron's magnificent Benedictine Abbey was founded in the 11th century. Its subsequent remodelling resulted in a Baroque structure, which survives to this day.

STAR SIGHTS
★ **Burg Hohenzollern**
★ **Sigmaringen**
★ **Beuron**

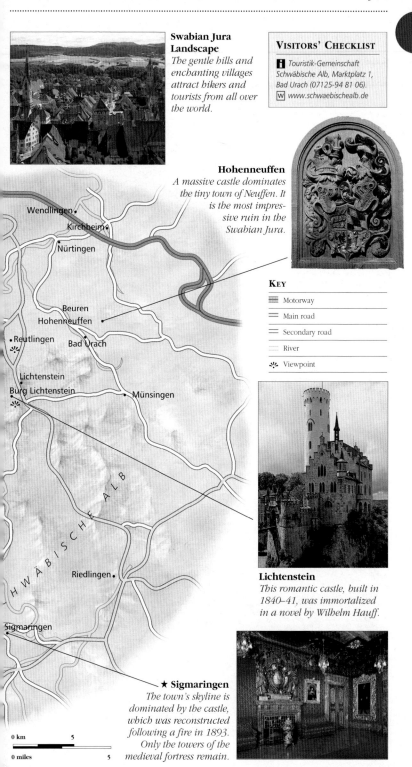

Swabian Jura Landscape
The gentle hills and enchanting villages attract hikers and tourists from all over the world.

VISITORS' CHECKLIST

i *Touristik-Gemeinschaft Schwäbische Alb, Marktplatz 1, Bad Urach (07125-94 81 06).*
w *www.schwaebischealb.de*

Hohenneuffen
A massive castle dominates the tiny town of Neuffen. It is the most impressive ruin in the Swabian Jura.

KEY

▦	Motorway
▬	Main road
═	Secondary road
⋯	River
�	Viewpoint

Map locations: Wendlingen, Kirchheim, Nürtingen, Beuren, Hohenneuffen, Reutlingen, Bad Urach, Lichtenstein, Burg Lichtenstein, Münsingen, Riedlingen, Sigmaringen, SCHWÄBISCHE ALB

Lichtenstein
This romantic castle, built in 1840–41, was immortalized in a novel by Wilhelm Hauff.

★ Sigmaringen
The town's skyline is dominated by the castle, which was reconstructed following a fire in 1893. Only the towers of the medieval fortress remain.

0 km	5
0 miles	5

Tübingen ②

Road map C6. 🏠 85,000. 🔲 🚹
An der Neckarbrücke 1 (07071-913 60). 🔵 *Mon, Wed, Fri.*

ALONG WITH Heidelberg and Freiburg im Breisgau, Tübingen is the home of one of southern Germany's three most famous universities. It was founded in 1477 by Count Eberhard the Bearded.

The first records of the fortress that later gave rise to a settlement on this site date from 1078. By around 1231, the settlement had become a town. In 1342, Tübingen passed into the hands of the counts of Wurttemberg, having previously belonged to the counts Palatinate.

Schloss Hohentübingen, which towers over the town, has a magnificent gateway (Äusseres Tor). Built in 1606, it is richly adorned with the coat of arms of the House of Wurttemberg. The walled castle complex, with its central courtyard and long approach, was built in stages during 1507–15, 1534–42 and 1606.

A walk along the Burgsteige will bring you to the pictur-esque old town. Here, at the centre of Marktplatz, is the Neptune Fountain, the work of Heinrich Schickardt, dating from 1617. In the western corner of the square is a lovely Renaissance town hall, built in 1435 and extended in the

Tübingen's Gothic-Renaissance town hall

16th century. It features an astronomical clock, which dates from 1511. *Sgraffiti* on the western façade dates from 1876; those on the elevations facing Haaggasse date from the 16th century.

The collegiate church of St George (**Stiftskirche St Georg**), built in 1440–1529, is a triple-nave hall with rows of side chapels, galleries and a single tower. Of particular note are the ducal tombs, the late-Gothic reading-room and the stained-glass windows of the choir, dating from 1475. Magnificent stalls, adorned with carved figures of the Prophets, date from the late 15th century.

The bookstore in Holzmarkt (*Buchhandlung Heckenhauer*) is where Hermann Hesse

once served as an apprentice bookseller. On the banks of the Neckar stands the **Hölderlinturm**, in which the German poet Hölderlin lived from 1807 until his death. Not far from here stands the large building of the Alte Bursa, which was built in 1478–80 and later remodelled in 1803-1805. The building was once used to accommodate students and as a lecture hall. Martin Luther's close associate, Philipp Melanchthon, lectured here between 1514 and 1518.

The Protestant seminary in Neckarhalde was founded by Prince Ulrich in 1536. Its graduates include the poets Hölderlin, Möricke and Schiller and the philosophers Hegel and Schelling.

The **Kunsthalle** is famous throughout Germany not only for its temporary exhibitions, but also for its fine collection of modern art. Other popular attractions in Tübingen include the **Stadtmuseum**, which is devoted to the town's history, and the **Auto- und Spielzeugmuseum**.

🏛 **Museum Schloss Hohentübingen**
Burgsteige 11. 【 (07071) 297 73 84. ⭕ May–Sep: 10am–6pm Wed–Sun, Oct–Apr: 10am–5pm Wed–Sun. 🈸

⛪ **Stiftskirche St Georg**
【 (07071) 525 83. ⭕ Apr–Sep: 9am–5pm daily, Oct–Mar: 9am–4pm daily. 🈸

🏚 **Hölderlinturm**
Bursagasse 6. 【 (07071) 220 40. ⭕ 10am–noon, 3–5pm Tue–Fri, 2–5pm Sat, Sun, public holidays. 🈸

🏛 **Kunsthalle**
Philosophenweg 76. 【 (07071) 969 10. ⭕ variable – phone for details.

🏛 **Stadtmuseum**
Kornhausstraße 10. 【 (07071) 204 17 11 or 94 54 60. ⭕ 3–6pm Tue–Sat, 11am–1pm, 3–6pm Sun. 🈸

🏛 **Auto- und Spielzeug-museum**
Brunnenstraße 18. 【 (07071) 55 11 22. ⭕ Apr–Oct: 10am–noon, 2–5pm Wed–Sun; Nov–Mar: 10am–noon, 2–5pm Sun and public holidays only. 🈸

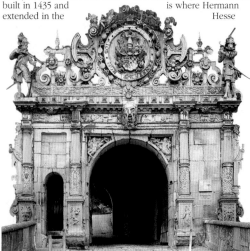

Ausseres Tor leading to Schloss Hohentübingen

Rottweil ❷

Road map C7. 🏛 24,000. 🚉 🛈
Hauptstraße 2 (0741-49 42 80).
🎭 *Fasnet (last Mon of Carnival),
Jazzfest (May), Klassikfestival (Jun),
Ferienzauber (Aug).*

SITUATED ON THE banks of the river Neckar, Rottweil is one of the oldest towns in Baden-Wurttemberg. It grew from a Roman settlement that was established on a hilltop here in AD 73. In 1234 Rottweil was granted town status and, by 1401, it had become a free town of the Holy Roman Empire. Between 1463 and 1802 it belonged to the Swiss Confederation, which was founded in 1291 by the cantons of Uri, Schwyz and Unterwalden. In 1802, the town passed into the rule of the dukes of Wurttemberg.

Rottweil has many historic remains, including sections of the fortified city walls, with several well-preserved turrets.

The parish church of St Cross (Heilig-Kreuz-Münster), built in 1230–1534, has a triple-nave basilica with stellar and network vaults. Late-Gothic altars, including St Bartholomew's, by Michael Wolgemut and a crucifix attributed to Veit Stoss, are among its features.

To the south of the church stands the late-Gothic town hall (1521). On the opposite side of the street, at Haupt-straße 20, the **Stadtmuseum** has an outstanding collection

Crucifixion attributed to Veit Stoss in Heilig-Kreuz-Münster, Rottweil

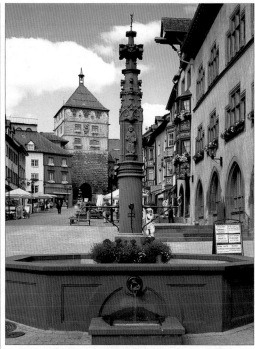
Fountain and "Black Tower" in Rottweil's main street, Hauptstraße

of prehistoric remains. The **Dominikanermuseum** has an interesting exhibition of Roman relics. These include the famous Orpheus mosaic, dating from the 2nd century AD, and an outstanding collection of late-Gothic sculpture, including the statue of St Barbara by Multscher (c.1450).

The Hauptstraße is lined with burghers' houses, displaying characteristic oriel windows. One of the most beautiful historic buildings in Rottweil is the Kapellenkirche, built in 1330–1478. Its 70-metre (230-ft) tower and three portals are adorned with carved ornaments reminis-cent of the French Gothic style. The Baroque interior features frescos by Josef Fiertmayer, who was a pupil of renowned painter and architect Cosmas Damian Asam. The Gothic Dominican church, built in 1266–82 and remodelled in the 18th

Kapellenturm, Rottweil

century, has some frescos by Joseph Wannenmaher (1755). Roman baths dating from the 2nd century AD have been excavated at the corner of what is now the cemetery.

Rottweil is famous for its carnival processions *(Fasnet)*, a tradition that goes back to the Middle Ages. A collection of carnival costumes can be seen in the Stadtmuseum.

The **Puppen- und Spielzeugmuseum** has a fine collection of historic dolls and toys.

🏛 **Stadtmuseum**
Hauptstraße 20. 📞 *(0741) 942 96 34.* ◻ *10am–noon, 2–5pm Tue–Sun.* ⬤ *Mon & Sun afternoons.* 🖼

🏛 **Dominikaner-museum**
Am Kriegsdamm.
📞 *(0741) 78 62.*
◻ *10am–1pm, 2–5pm Tue–Sun.* ⬤ *public holidays.* 🖼

🏛 **Puppen- und Spielzeugmuseum**
Hochbrücktorstraße 9.
📞 *(0741) 942 21 77.* ◻ *2–5pm Wed–Sat, 11am–5pm Sun.* 🖼

Ulm ②

Road map B6. 🏙 115,000. 🚉
ℹ️ Münsterplatz 5 (0731-161 28 30.
📅 Fischerstechen (every fourth year in
Jul: 2001, 2005 etc.), Schwörmontag
(3rd Mon in Jul), Stadtfest (Jun).

LYING ON the river Danube,
Ulm dates back to 854. It
became a town in 1165 then,
in 1274, a free town of the
Holy Roman Empire. During
the 15th century Ulm was one
of the richest towns in Europe
but the Thirty Years' War put
an end to its rapid development. In 1810 Ulm came
under the rule of the Wurttemberg kings. The town is
renowned as the
birthplace of Albert
Einstein. During
World War II, most
of the old town was
destroyed during
bombing raids.

The Münster is a
true masterpiece of
European Gothic
architecture. A vast,
five-nave basilica, its
161-m (530-ft) high
west tower is the
highest church
tower in the
world. The
cathedral's

**Gothic font in Ulm
Cathedral**

construction, from
1377 until 1545,
was overseen by the greatest
builders of the German
Gothic – Heinrich and
Michael Parler, Urlich
Ensinger, Hans Kun and
Matthäus Böblinger. The
unfinished cathedral was
extended in 1844–90, based
on the original medieval
design. The interior contains
many outstanding features,

including the altar by
Hans Multscher (1443),
the famous stalls with
figures of philosophers,
poets, prophets and
apostles carved by
Jörg Syrlin the Elder,
15th-century stained-
glass windows, and
the font, by Jörg Syrlin
the Younger.

The town has many
fine historic buildings,
including the Gothic-
Renaissance town
hall, which is decorated with
brightly coloured frescos and
features an astronomical
clock. Other features of
Marktplatz include the Gothic
fountain *Fisch-
kasten brunnen*
(Fish Crate), dating
from 1482, and the
Reichenauer Hof,
which dates from
1370–1535.

The **Ulmer
Museum**, which is
housed in a number
of historic 16th- and
17th-century build-
ings, has a collection
of art spanning a
period from the
Middle Ages to
the present day.
The collection
includes the work
of local artists,
such as Hans Multscher. The
Deutsches Brotmuseum
specializes in artifacts related
to bread, including items
depicting bread in art and
graphic designs.

🏛 **Ulmer Museum**
Marktplatz 9. 📞 (0731) 161 43 30.
🕐 10am–5pm Thu-Tue, 10am–
8:30pm Wed. 🖼

🏛 **Deutsches Brotmuseum**
Salzstadelgasse 10. 📞 (0731) 699
55. 🕐 10am-5pm Tue, Thu–Mon,
10am–8:30pm Wed. 🖼

Ravensburg ②

Road map C7. 🏙 45,000. 🚉
ℹ️ Kirchstraße 16 (0751-823 24).
📅 Fasnet (Jul), Rutenfest (Jul).

THE FIRST HISTORIC records of
the "Ravespurc" fortress
date from 1098, when it was
one of the seats of the Welf
family. It is believed to be the

**Main altar by Hans Multscher in
Ravensburg's Liebfrauenkirche**

birthplace of Henry the Lion,
the powerful Duke of Saxony
and Bavaria, born in 1129.
The settlement that sprang up
at the foot of the castle was
granted town status in 1251.
From 1395, paper was
produced here and, during
the 15th century, the town
became one of the richest in
Germany from its involve-
ment in the linen trade.

Standing in Kirchstraße is
the 14th-century parish church
of Liebfrauenkirche, which
retains original 15th-century
features, including the main
altar and some fine stained-
glass windows.

In Marienplatz stands the
late-Gothic town hall (14th–
15th century), with its lovely
Renaissance bay window.
Also in Marienplatz is the
Waaghaus (1498), which
housed the weigh-house and
mint on the ground floor,
with a trading hall upstairs,
when Ravensburg was
engaged in coin production.
The watchtower (*Blaserturm*)
is crowned by a Renaissance
octagon that has become the
symbol of the town. Another
attractive building here is the
Laderhaus, which dates from
1513–14. Near the town hall is
the old 14th–15th century
granary (*Kornhaus*).

Marktstraße features many
old burgher houses. No. 59,
the oldest house in town, dates
from 1179. The neighbouring
house was built in 1446. The
tall white cylindrical tower
that can be seen from here is
known as the "sack of flour"
(*Mehlsack*). It was erected in
the 16th century. A mgnificent
view of the town can
be obtained from Veitsburg,
which occupies the site of
the original Welf castle.

**Astronomical clock on Ulm's
Gothic-Renaissance town hall**

Former Cistercian abbey complex in Salem, now a secular building

Weingarten 26

Road map C7. 👥 22,500. 🚉
ℹ️ Münsterplatz 1 (0751-40 51 25).
🎉 Heilig-Blut-Fest.

COUNT HENRY of the House of Welf founded a Benedictine abbey in Weingarten in 1056. During the Romanesque period, around 1190, the monks of the abbey produced a chronicle of the House of Welfs, known as the *Welffenchronik*.

Ambitious plans, drawn up in the 18th century at the initiative of Abbot Sebastian Hyller, provided for an extension of the abbey and the construction of another vast complex of buildings. Two side courtyards and four external courtyards, encircled with curved galleries with smaller pavilions, were planned to be grouped around the church. These were designed by Casper Moosbrugger, Franz Beer, Giuseppe Frisoni and others, and built in 1715–24.

The church is reminiscent of the Basilica of St Peter's in Rome. Although it is half the size of the latter, it is nevertheless an immense structure. Inside are some magnificent ceiling frescos by Cosmas Damian Asam, while the carved and inlaid choir stalls are the work of Joseph Anton Feuchtmayer. Also of note is the organ by Josef Gabler. In an ingenious design, the organ pipes are concealed within a series of towers to avoid obscuring the windows of the façade.

The **Alamannenmuseum** has a fascinating exhibition of relicts that have been found in graves dating from the Merovingian period.

🏛 **Alamannenmuseum**
Karlstr. 28. ☎ (0751) 493 43. ◯ 3–5pm Tue–Sun, 3–6pm Thu. 🔲

Salem 27

Road map C7. 👥 8,500.

THE FIRST CISTERCIAN monks arrived in Salmansweiler (now known as Salem) in 1134. Between 1299 and 1414 they built a church according to the rules of their order, which espoused poverty and banned any decoration of the monastic buildings.

The abbey is a triple-nave basilica with transept and straight-end choir. Its austere façade is relieved by blind windows, some of which have attractive traceries. In later years the restraints of poverty were relaxed to the extent that the abbey now has an interesting tabernacle (1500), stalls (1594) and early-Renaissance altars (dating from the 18th century).

The new abbey buildings were built between 1700 and 1710 and constitute **Schloss Salem**. The buildings include some richly decorated abbot's apartments and the extremely impressive Emperor's room (*Kaisersaal*), which was built between 1708 and 1710.

Since its secularization in 1802, the abbey has been the private property of the Baden margraves who keep some of their art collection here. The west wing houses a private boarding school founded by Kurt Hahn, who also founded Gordonstoun in Scotland.

⚜ **Schloss Salem**
☎ (07553) 814 37. ◯ Apr–Oct: 9:30am–6pm Tue–Sat, 10:30am–6pm Sun. 🔲

Ceiling fresco in Weingarten's abbey

The Bodensee

SOMETIMES KNOWN as Lake Constance, the Bodensee lies on the border of Germany, Switzerland and Austria. The area surrounding the lake is one of the most attractive in Germany, in terms of both natural beauty and cultural heritage. Towns and villages around the shores feature countless reminders of past times and cultures. The best time for a visit is summer, when local fishermen stage colourful fairs and water sports are possible.

The Bodensee
The lake is 15 km (9 miles) across at its widest point and 74 km (46 miles) long. It lies at an altitude of 395 m (1,295 ft) and reaches 252 m (826 ft) in depth.

Reichenau
The greatest attraction of this island is the Benedictine abbey, which was famed during the era of Otto the Great (10th century) for its illuminated manuscripts. It has a beautiful Romanesque-Gothic church and an intoxicating herb garden.

★ **Mainau**
Mainau is known as the "Island of Flowers". The most beautiful displays are in the park surrounding the Baroque palace, which was built in 1739–46. It is currently owned by the Lennart Bernadotte family.

STAR SIGHTS
★ **Konstanz**
★ **Mainau**
★ **Wasserburg**

★ **Konstanz (Constance)**
The largest town in the region, its main attraction is the magnificent 11th-century Romanesque cathedral. The vaults over the central aisle were built between 1679 and 1683.

Map labels: Stockach, Ludwigshafen, ÜBERLINGER SEE, Überlingen, Singen, Radolfzell, ZELLERSEE, Gottmadingen, Reichenau, Mainau, Konstanz, UNTERSEE, Kreuzlingen

Meersburg

The exquisite Baroque town of Meersburg has two residences – the Baroque Neues Schloss and the Altes Schloss. The latter is a 16th-century structure built on top of a hill. It contains within its walls an old Carolingian palace.

VISITORS' CHECKLIST

Map 7 C. 🛈 *Bahnhofsplatz 13, Konstanz (07531-13 30 30).*
🎆 *Seenachtfest (mid-August); Büllefest (1st Sunday in October).*
Bodensee-Naturmuseum
Hafenstr. 9, Konstanz (07531-12 87 39 00). ◯ *10am–6pm.*
🏛 **Heimatmuseum**
Reichenau Ergat 1. 📞 *(07534) 920 70.* ◯ *May–Oct: 3–5pm Tue–Sun.* 🏛

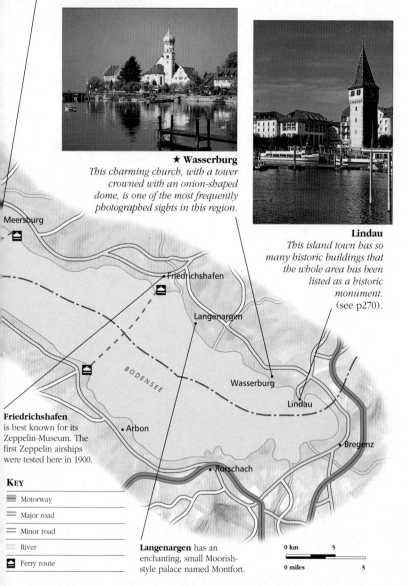

★ Wasserburg
This charming church, with a tower crowned with an onion-shaped dome, is one of the most frequently photographed sights in this region.

Lindau
This island town has so many historic buildings that the whole area has been listed as a historic monument. (see p270).

Meersburg ⚓

Friedrichshafen ⚓

Langenargen

BODENSEE

Wasserburg

Lindau

Friedrichshafen
is best known for its Zeppelin-Museum. The first Zeppelin airships were tested here in 1900.

Arbon

Bregenz

Rorschach

KEY

🟫	Motorway
═	Major road
═	Minor road
	River
⚓	Ferry route

Langenargen has an enchanting, small Moorish-style palace named Montfort.

0 km   5

0 miles   5

Freiburg im Breisgau ㉙

THE COUNTS von Zähringen first established Freiburg in 1120. The town, which later belonged to the counts von Urach, became so rich over the years that, in 1368, it bought its freedom and voluntarily placed itself under the protection of the Habsburgs. Marshal Vauban fortified the town in the 17th century, when Freiburg briefly belonged to France. Since 1805 it has been part of Baden. Situated between Kaiserstuhl and Feldberg, it is a natural gateway to the southern Black Forest.

Freiburg University
Freiburg University occupies a Baroque post-Jesuit complex. In the main entrance stands this statue of the pensive Aristotle.

This former Jesuit church belongs to the university complex.

Tourist information

RATHAUS PLATZ

RATHAUSGASSE

Railway station

BERTOLDSTRASSE

Fischerau
Fischerau and, parallel to it, Gerberau are picturesque streets in the old town, running along the Gewerbebach stream.

Bertoldsbrunnen
(Bertold's fountain) stands at the intersection of Bertoldstraße and Kaiser-Joseph-Straße, known as "Kajo".

| 0 metres | 50 |
| 0 yards | 50 |

Martinstor
St Martin's Gate was part of the 13th-century town fortifications. Its present appearance is the result of work carried out in 1900.

KEY

--- Suggested route

STAR SIGHTS

★ **Bächle**

★ **Münster – the Main Altar**

★ **Kaufhaus**

◁ **Picturesque scene with fruit trees in blossom in the Schwarzwald (Black Forest)**

Haus zum Walfisch

The façade of the Whale House in Franziskanergasse, with its lovely bay window, is a magnificent example of late-Gothic style.

VISITORS' CHECKLIST

Road map B7. 🏰 197,000.
🚉 ℹ *Rotteckring 14 (0761-388 18 80).* 🎭 Fasnet (end of carnival), Frühlingsmesse (May), Internationales Zeltmusikfest (Jun), Weintage (Jun), Weinkost (Jun), Herbstmesse (Oct), Umwelt-Film-Festival (Oct).

Münsterplatz

The picturesque square at the foot of the cathedral, lined by houses of various periods, from Gothic to Rococo, is still used for markets.

★ Bächle

From the Middle Ages, fast-flowing canals have been running along the streets, draining excess surface waters, and providing the water needed to extinguish the frequent fires.

★ Münster – the Main Altar

The cathedral, which started in c.1200 as a Romanesque basilica, was completed by 1260 in the French Gothic style. Inside is the original main altar by Hans Baldung Grien.

★ Kaufhaus

Completed in 1520, with ground-floor arcades and richly adorned gables, the Kaufhaus (literally buying house) was used by local merchants for meetings, conferences and lively festivities.

Schwarzwald (Black Forest) 🌐

COVERED WITH TALL FIR TREES and spruces, the Schwarz-
wald is one of Germany's most picturesque regions.
The area is famous not just for its cuckoo clocks,
Kirschwasser (schnapps) and *Schwarzwälder Kirschtorte*
(Black Forest Gâteau); in the past, Celts and later the
Romans came to appreciate the therapeutic qualities
of the local spring waters. (The sources of the rivers
Donau and Necker are here.) The area is also
a paradise for skiers, climbers, ramblers,
hang-glider pilots and sailors.

★ Staufen
im Breisgau
*The town is also
known as Faust-
stadt: Dr Faustus,
who had resided
here, died in 1539
– he is variously
reputed to have
blown himself up,
to have been stran-
gled or to have had
his neck broken.*

Todtnau
*Todtnau is not only a sports centre and a
base for hikers: it is also a major centre of
toothbrush production and the birthplace
of Karl Ludwig Nessler (1872–1951), who
invented the process of hair-perming.*

Todtmoos
*The heart of this resort is the Baroque
pilgrimage church, which dates from the
17th–18th centuries. Popular dog-sleigh
races are held annually in the town.*

Fraisenheim
Lahr
Herbholzheim
Tenningen
Emmend
Denzlinge
Freibur
im Breis
Bad Krozingen
Staufen im Breisgau
Müllheim
To
SCHWARZWALD
Todtn
Kandern
Wiese
Wei
Lörrach
Rheinfelden

Gutach

In the open-air museum near the small town of Gutach visitors can see the Schwarzwald's oldest house – the Vogtsbauernhof – which dates from the 16th century.

★ Furtwangen

The main attraction of Furtwangen is its clock museum (Uhrenmuseum), which houses a collection of more than 4,000 varied chronometers.

0 km	10
0 miles	10

Hangloch-Wasserfall

This magnificent mountain waterfall near Todtnau is one of the most beautiful in the Black Forest.

KEY

▦	Motorway
▬	Main road
═	Secondary road
	River
✻	Viewpoint

★ St Blasien

In the beautiful health resort of St Blasien is a Benedictine Abbey, founded in the 9th century. Crowned with a vast dome, its church (1783) is an excellent example of early Neo-Classical style.

STAR SIGHTS

★ **Furtwangen**

★ **St Blasien**

★ **Staufen im Breisgau**

WESTERN
GERMANY

Western Germany at a Glance

WESTERN Germany is the country's wealthiest and most heavily industrialized region. The Ruhr district still harbours enormous industrial potential, while Frankfurt am Main is Germany's largest financial centre. The region is also rich in tourist attractions – visitors are drawn to the romantic castles which line the Rhein and Mosel valleys, to Cologne with its majestic cathedral, the spa town of Aachen, the museums of Frankfurt and Kassel and the imposing Romanesque cathedrals of Speyer, Worms and Mainz. Western Germany is also famed for its excellent wines and the festivities of Cologne's carnival.

NORTH RHINE-WESTPHALIA
See pp368–401

Cologne Cathedral (see pp388–9), *which was not completed until the 19th century, is generally considered one of the most outstanding Gothic buildings in Germany.*

```
0 kilometres        100

0 miles             100
```

Maria Laach *(see pp344–5) is a charming, beautifully preserved Romanesque abbey in a tranquil, isolated setting on the shores of the Laacher See.*

RHINELAND-PALATINATE & SAARLAND
See pp322–45

Detmold is best known for its magnificent castle (see p401) – one of the most beautiful examples of the "Weser Renaissance" style of architecture.

Fulda Cathedral (see p354) is one of the finest Baroque churches in Hesse. It was built on the site of the previous Romanesque church and follows the original layout.

HESSE
See pp346–67

The Museum Fridericianum in Kassel (see pp350–51), *originally built to house Friederich II's art collection, has hosted the* documenta *since 1955, a four-yearly exhibition of contemporary art that has achieved international acclaim.*

The old town in Frankfurt am Main (see p361) *is centred around the Römerberg – a square surrounded by attractive half-timbered houses, with the Fountain of Justice as a focal point.*

Wine in Western Germany

O F THE GREAT EUROPEAN vineyards, Germany's are the
farthest north. There are 13 wine-growing regions in
Franconia, Baden-Wurttemberg and Saxony, but the most
famous German vineyards are those in the western part of
the country, especially the Rheingau, Pfalz, Rheinhessen
and Mosel-Saar-Ruhr regions. The most widely drunk alcoholic beverage in Germany is beer – unlike in France, Italy
or Spain – and therefore the wines produced here are
mainly high-quality wines of named vineyards, with a
relatively low production of table wine.

The Mosel-Saar-Ruhr
region produces superb white
wines from the Riesling
grape. The highest quality
wines are those marked with
the letters QmP.

Vineyards in Edenkoben, in the
southern part of the Weinstraße
(see p333), in the Palatinate

IMPORTANT FACTS ABOUT GERMAN WINE

Region and climate
Gentle, rocky hills stretching along the river
bends – perfect for Rieslings – are typical of the
Mosel-Saar-Ruhr and Rheingau regions. Clay and
limestone soil, appropriate for the Müller-Thurgau variety, are
found in Hesse on the Rhine. The German climate is considerably more severe than that of southern countries, which gives
the wines a slightly sharp, refreshing taste.

Typical grape varieties
The red grape is not cultivated in great quantities.
The most popular red variety is the Spätburgunder,
known in France as Pinot Noir, which produces a
heavy wine with a strong flavour. White grapes are
much more popular, especially the famous Rieslings, from
which the best white wines are produced, the Müller-Thurgau,
which gives a light wine with a fruity bouquet, the Grauburgun-
der (Pinot Grigio) and the Weißburgunder (Pinot Blanc). Less
well-known are: Silvaner, Gewürztraminer, Grüner Veltliner and
Gutedel. Rosé wines are produced from the Portugieser variety,
cultivated in the Rhineland–Palatinate (Pfalz) and Rheinhessen.

Famous wine producers
Mosel-Saar-Ruhr: Fritz Haag, Heymann-Löwenstein,
Karthäuserhof, Dr. Loosen, Egon Müller, J.J. Prüm,
C. von Schubert, Willi Schaefer; **Rheingau:** Georg
Breuer, Robert Weil; **Rheinhessen:** Gunderloch,
Keller; **Pfalz:** Müller-Catoir, Georg Mosbacher, Dr.
Bürklin-Wolf Hessische-Bergstraße.

The Nahe is famous for
its white wines, produced
from Silvaner as well as
Riesling and Müller-
Thurgau grapes.

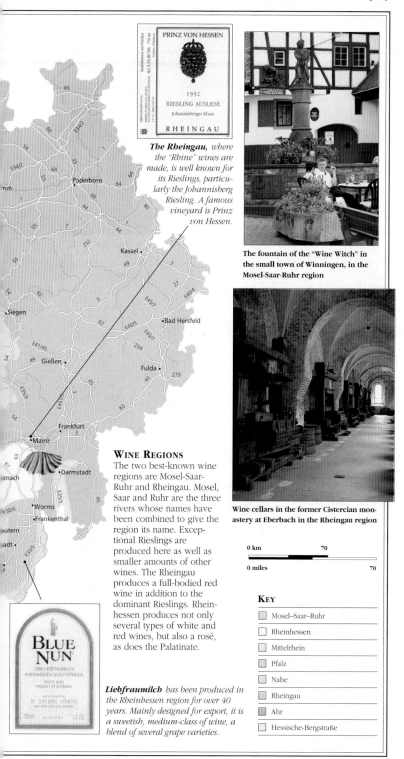

PRINZ VON HESSEN

1992

RIESLING AUSLESE

Johannisberger Klaus

RHEINGAU

The Rheingau, where the "Rhine" wines are made, is well known for its Rieslings, particularly the Johannisberg Riesling. A famous vineyard is Prinz von Hessen.

The fountain of the "Wine Witch" in the small town of Winningen, in the Mosel-Saar-Ruhr region

Wine cellars in the former Cistercian monastery at Eberbach in the Rheingau region

WINE REGIONS

The two best-known wine regions are Mosel-Saar-Ruhr and Rheingau. Mosel, Saar and Ruhr are the three rivers whose names have been combined to give the region its name. Exceptional Rieslings are produced here as well as smaller amounts of other wines. The Rheingau produces a full-bodied red wine in addition to the dominant Rieslings. Rheinhessen produces not only several types of white and red wines, but also a rosé, as does the Palatinate.

BLUE NUN

1988 LIEBFRAUMILCH
RHEINHESSEN-QUALITÄTSWEIN

WHITE WINE
PRODUCT OF GERMANY

H. SICHEL SÖHNE

750 ml

Liebfraumilch has been produced in the Rheinhessen region for over 40 years. Mainly designed for export, it is a sweetish, medium-class of wine, a blend of several grape varieties.

| 0 km | 70 |
| 0 miles | 70 |

KEY

	Mosel–Saar–Ruhr
	Rheinhessen
	Mittelrhein
	Pfalz
	Nahe
	Rheingau
	Ahr
	Hessische-Bergstraße

Romanesque Architecture

WESTERN GERMANY boasts some of the most interesting examples of Romanesque architecture in the whole of Europe. Charlemagne's famous chapel in Aachen was erected as early as the Carolingian period. The cathedral in Trier and the church of St Maria im Kapitol in Cologne are among the most outstanding creations of early-Romanesque architecture of the Frankish dynasty. In the 12th century, the most important German centres of art were Cologne and the towns of the central Rhineland, with three magnificent cathedrals in Speyer, Mainz and Worms, and the monastery in Maria Laach, preserved to this day.

The choir of St Martin in the Dom in Mainz is an example of the spaciousness that is typical of the late-Romanesque style.

The front elevation of the St Gotthard-Kapelle in Mainz has upper galleries with arcades decorated with friezes – a common feature of Romanesque architecture.

Twin western towers

Gallery above the vestibule

Lavishly decorated main portal

The northern portal of the Dom in Worms is framed by an offset architrave and flanked by pairs of columns, as are the portals of many other Romanesque cathedrals.

The monastery in Maria Laach has many capitals with intricate decorations, such as these carvings with human faces.

Cross-vaulting (or cross-ribbed vaulting)

Tower at the intersection of the nave and transept

The portal of the Dom in Trier *has a magnificent tympanum, depicting Christ with the Virgin Mary and St Peter.*

ROMANESQUE CATHEDRALS

Cathedrals of the type shown here were built with a basilica-type internal arrangement, including a transept and presbytery, and a double choir usually ending in a semicircular apse. The Dom in Speyer has a massive twin-towered west front, as shown here. The other pair of towers rises above the presbytery, and the intersection of the nave and transept has a lower, broad fifth tower.

The system of vaults also acts as support.

Twin eastern towers

ROMANESQUE CAPITALS

Romanesque churches in the Rhine Valley feature exquisite stone sculptures. The capitals, with their extraordinary variety of form, ranging from simple blocks to fine figurative or animal-decorated compositions, are of particular interest.

Water-leaf capital of a bonded column

Simplified Corinthian capital

Cushion (or block or cube) capital

Zoömorphic (animal-decorated) capital

The St Gotthard-Kapelle in Mainz, *next to the Dom, was the archbishop's personal chapel for private prayer. It is comparable to similar private buildings in secular palaces.*

RHINELAND–PALATINATE AND SAARLAND

THE RHINELAND-PALATINATE *is one of Germany's most romantic regions, attracting visitors with its vineyards, gentle hills and fairy-tale castles along the Rhine and Mosel valleys. Several towns, such as Trier, have kept reminders of their Roman heritage.*

These two states, which border France in the west, did not emerge in their present form until after World War II. The Rhineland-Palatinate was created from the previously independent Bavarian Palatinate and the southern part of the Central Rhineland, making it a true jigsaw-puzzle of territories without a coherent history. The Saarland was under French rule until 1956. Today, it forms a bridge between France and Germany, the two driving forces of European unity.

The turbulent history of the region has left many traces. The picturesque Mosel Valley is lined with grand Medieval fortresses, such as Burg Eltz, while Worms on the Rhine is the setting for most of the Nibelungen legend as well as the residence of the mythical king of Burgundy, Gunther.

The Nibelung treasure is still said to lie at the bottom of the Rhine. The impressive cathedral in Worms, along with the Romanesque cathedrals of Speyer and Mainz, is a fascinating example of Medieval sacral architecture.

The "Deutsches Eck" in Koblenz is the strategic spot where the Mosel flows into the Rhine, and Koblenz also marks the beginning of the romantic Rhine Valley. A boat trip upriver, justifiably popular with visitors, will pass some spectacular rocky scenery, including the famous Lorelei Rock and countless castles set among vineyards on either side of the gorge.

The famous ironworks complex in Völklingen is a reminder of a bygone era, when most of the Saarland's inhabitants were active in mining, steelworks and other heavy industries.

Panorama of Saarbrücken, with the Saar river in the foreground

◁ **The snow-covered Medieval fortress of Burg Eltz, in the Mosel Valley**

Exploring Rhineland-Palatinate and Saarland

WHITE WINE enthusiasts come here, attracted by the beautiful, picturesque valleys of the Rhine and Mosel rivers, with their Medieval castles and small towns. Travelling along the Deutsche Weinstraße (German wine route), Germany's oldest tourist route, visitors can see fascinating historic buildings and taste the different types of wine made by the numerous small vineyards scattered throughout the entire region. Speyer and Mainz have monumental Romanesque cathedrals, while Trier boasts many interesting Roman relics. The huge ironworks in Völklingen is a surprising sight, transporting visitors back to a time when heavy industry ruled much of the region.

SEE ALSO

- *Where to Stay* pp487–8
- *Where to Eat* pp516–17

The imposing red-sandstone building of the Dom in Mainz

The proud complex of Schloss Stolzenfels near Koblenz, designed by Karl Friedrich Schinkel

Bonn

Cologne (Köln)

BAD NEUENAHR- AHRWEILER

MARIA LAAC

HOHE EIFEL

SCHNEE-EIFEL

PRÜM

Kyll

257

Our

BITBURG

50

E42/60

MOSELTAL ❸

TRIER ❶

Luxembourg

257

268

327

E422/1

50

Mosel

Saar

268

ST. WELDEN

E422/1

41

SAARLAND ❷   **NEUKIRCHEN**

SAARBRÜCKEN

E29

Metz

E50/6

0 km   20

0 miles   20

The interior of the Dom in Trier

SIGHTS AT A GLANCE

GETTING AROUND

The A65 motorway links Karlsruhe with Ludwigshafen, and
continues from there towards
Luxembourg or Lorraine, via
Homburg and Saarbrücken.
The A32, and later the A4,
leads from Saarbrücken to
Metz or Strasbourg. The A1
runs northwards from
Friedrichsthal to Trier and
the Mosel Valley. Inter-City
trains offer a frequent and
convenient service; Frankfurt
am Main and Köln/Bonn
(Konrad-Adenauer-Flughafen)
have international airports.

KEY

▥▥	Motorway
▥▥	Main road
▬▬	Scenic route
—	River
☼	Viewpoint

Trier ❶

ONE OF Germany's oldest towns, Trier was founded in 16 BC as *Augusta Treverorum*, supposedly by the Emperor Augustus himself. In the 3rd and 4th centuries it was an imperial seat and the capital of the *Belgica prima* province. In the 5th century the town, which now numbered 70,000 inhabitants, was conquered and destroyed by Germanic tribes. Trier never returned to its former importance – in the 17th century it had a mere 3,600 inhabitants, and 100 years later they still numbered fewer than 4,000. The town, which is also the birthplace of Karl Marx, has a rich architectural heritage.

🏛 Porta Nigra
📞 *(0651) 97 80 80.*
🕐 *Apr–Sep: 9am–6pm daily;*
Jan–Mar & Oct–Nov: 9am–5pm daily;
Dec: 10am–4pm daily. 📷

This town gate, named *Porta Nigra* (black gate) in the Middle Ages because of its weathered stone, was erected in the 3rd century. The oldest German defensive structure, it still impresses with its colossal size: 36 m (118 ft) long, 21.5 m (70.5 ft) wide and 30 m (27 ft) high. Two gateways lead onto a small inner courtyard, and there are two tiers of defence galleries with large open windows. It is flanked by two towers – the four-storey western tower and the three-storey unfinished eastern tower. The entire structure was made of huge blocks of sandstone, connected by iron rods, without mortar.

In the 12th century, the building was transformed into the two-storey church of St Simeon and served as such until the early 19th century.

The magnificent *Porta Nigra*, gigantic Roman gateway into Trier

Petrusbrunnen (fountain of St Peter) in Hauptmarkt

🏛 Hauptmarkt
Trier's main market square, undoubtedly one of the most attractive in Germany, dates back to the 10th century. The Marktkreuz (market cross) erected around the same time symbolized the town's right to hold markets. Today there is a copy of the original cross mounted on a granite Roman column, with a relief of the Lamb of God. On the south-eastern side of the square is the Petrusbrunnen (St Peter's fountain), from 1595, with sculptures of St Peter and the Four Virtues. On the south-western side stands the 15th-century Steipe, with a steep gabled roof. Originally it was used by the town councillors as guesthouse and banqueting hall. The Baroque Rotes Haus (red house) next door dates from 1683. Löwenapotheke, in a 17th-century building on the southeastern side of the square, is Germany's oldest pharmacy, its records dating back to the 13th century.

🏛 Bischöfliches Dom- und Diözesanmuseum
Windstraße 6–8. 📞 *(0651) 710 52 55.* 🕐 *9am–5pm Mon–Sat, 1–5pm Sun.* ⬤ *1 Jan, 24 & 25 Dec.* 📷
A 19th-century building near the cathedral, once a Prussian prison, now houses the art collection of the Diocese, including early Christian works of art. Its pride of possession is a 3rd-century ceiling painting from the imperial palace which once stood on the site of the cathedral. The fresco was rediscovered in 1945, and some 70,000 pieces were painstakingly reassembled over the following decades. Another important historic exhibit is the reconstructed crypt of the Benedictine church of St Maximin, which has important 9th-century Carolingian wall paintings.

🏛 Dom St Peter
📞 *(065) 75 801.* 🕐 *Apr–Oct: 9am–6pm; Nov–Mar: 9am–5pm.* 📷
The present cathedral incorporates the remains of an older 4th-century church. The oldest cathedral in Germany, it was constructed in stages – in the early 11th century, late 12th century, mid-13th century and 14th century. It is a triple-nave, two-choir basilica with transept and six towers, and its furnishings include several outstanding objects, such as the tomb of the papl envoy Ivo (1144) and the tomb altar of Archbishop Richard von Greifenclau (1531).

🏛 Liebfrauenkirche
An der Meerkatz 4. 📞 *(0651) 425 54.* 🕐 *8am–6pm daily.* 📷
Adjoining the cathedral is the Liebfrauenkirche (Church of Our Dear Lady), built in 1235–60. Along with the

The Liebfrauenkirche – one of the country's earliest Gothic churches

cathedral in Magdeburg, this is one of the earliest examples of German Gothic architecture. Its ground plan is based on the Greek cross, and the tower above the dome accentuates the intersection of the naves. Its western portal is richly decorated with carved ornaments and iconographic symbols. The interior features many outstanding relics, including 15th-century wall paintings on twelve columns, which symbolize the 12 apostles. There are also some impotant tombs, including that of a local nobleman, Karl von

Metternich (1636), which is found in the northeast chapel.

🏛 Aula Palatina

Konstantinplatz. **☎** (0651) 42 570.
🕐 Apr–Oct: 9am–6pm Tue–Fri, noon–6pm Sat & Sun; Nov–Mar: 11am–noon & 3–4pm Tue–Fri, noon–1pm Sat & Sun.

The *Aula Palatina* (Palatinate hall) dates from AD 310. An elongated, rectangular brick building 67 m (220 ft) long, 27.5 m (90 ft) wide and 30 m (98 ft) high with a vast semi-circular apse, it served as the throne hall of the Roman emperor or his representative. Following the town's sacking by Germanic tribes, the building was reduced to rubble. In the 12th century the apse was converted into a tower, to

VISITORS' CHECKLIST

Road map A5. 👥 99,000.
🚉 Theodor-Heuss-Allee.
ℹ Simeonstraße 60 (0651-97 80 80).

accommodate the archbishop. In the 17th century, the *Aula Palatina* was integrated into the newly-built palace and its eastern wall partly demolished. During Napoleonic and Prussian times, the hall served as army barracks. The Prussian king Friedrich Wilhelm IV eventually ordered its reconstruction. From 1856 it has served as the Protestant church of St Saviour. Restored after bombing in 1944, its giant size still seems remarkable.

The monumental, austere exterior of the Aula Palatina

TRIER CITY CENTRE

Aula Palatina ⑥
Basilika & Kurfürstliches Schloss ⑦
Bischöfliches Dom- und
   Diözesanmuseum ③
Dom St Peter ④
Hauptmarkt ②
Kaiserthermen ⑩
Liebfrauenkirche ⑤
Porta Nigra ①
Rheinisches
   Landesmuseum ⑧
Stadtbibliothek ⑨

0 m   400
0 yards   400

KEY

ℹ Tourist information
🅿 Parking
✝ Church

Portal of the Kurfürstliches Schloss

♣ Basilika und Kurfürstliches Schloss

Konstantinplatz. **Basilica** 🎯 *(0651) 425 70.* ⏲ *Apr–Oct: 9am–6pm Mon–Sat, noon–6pm Sun; Nov–Mar: noon–1pm & 3–4pm Tue–Sat, 11am–noon Sun.*

Built around AD 305, Emperor Constantine's basilica witnessed a turbulent history. From the 12th century it served as residence of the Archbishop-Electors; in the 16th century part of the site was incorporated into a Renaissance castle. This was followed by an early Baroque palace and finally a late Baroque electoral palace, which has survived to this day and includes the remains of the earlier buildings.

The present palace was designed by Johannes Seiz and built in 1756–62 for Johann Philipp von Walderdorff. The central tympanum shows Pomona, Venus, Apollo and a group of angels. The stairs, which lead from the garden to the inner staircase, were designed in the 18th century, but not built until 1981. They have beautiful handrails with typical Rococo motifs.

🏛 Rheinisches Landesmuseum

Weimarer Allee 1. 🎯 *(065) 977 40.* ⏲ *9:30am–5pm Tue–Fri, 10:30am–5pm Sat & Sun.* ⬤ *1 Jan, 24, 25 & 26 Dec.* 🎫 *(free 1st Mon of the month).*

Only a few steps separate the electoral palace from the

Rhine regional museum founded in 1877. Its collections are grouped into four sections: pre-historic, Roman, Franconian-Merovingian, and medieval to contemporary. The largest space is devoted to Roman relics. Star exhibits include a magnificent mosaic depicting Bacchus, from the dining room of a Roman villa, and the lovely statuette of a nymph, undoubtedly the work of a major artist. Equally impressive is a stone carving showing a ship loaded with four giant barrels, sailing on the Mosel River. Dating from AD 220, it decorated the tomb of a local wine-merchant. Also noteworthy is the tombstone of a cloth-merchant from the town of Igel. The original tombstone has surprisingly colourful paint-work, restored in 1993, but the museum displays a copy.

🏧 Stadtbibliothek

Weberbach 25.

The municipal library contains a number of important collections that were assembled here in the early 19th century, when many monastic libraries closed down. Apart from countless documents dating from various periods, the library holds 74 full-page miniatures of the famous Trier Apocalypse (c.800), as well as one of the few surviving copies of the first Bible printed by Gutenberg.

Nymph in Rheinisches Landesmuseum

⋔ Kaiserthermen

Weimarer Allee/Kaiserstr. 🎯 *(0651) 442 62.* ⏲ *Apr–Sep: 9am–6pm daily; Jan–Mar & Oct–Nov: 9am–5pm daily; Dec: 10am–4pm daily.* 🎫

Not far from the Rheinisches Landesmuseum are the remains of the vast imperial baths. Built in the early 4th century, during the reign of Constantine, they were the third largest bathing complex in the Roman world. The remaining sections of the walls and foundations indicate the former layout. Best preserved are the walls of the *caldarium*, the room with the hot water pool. Next to it is the round *tepidarium*, the warm baths. The spacious *frigidarium* was used for cold baths. Considerable room was given to the *palaestra*, an outdoor exercise area. Another surviving feature is the underground heating system (*hypocaustum*), where the air was heated by stoves and conducted under the floors.

⋔ Jesuitenkolleg

Brotstraße. ⏲ *8:30am–5:30pm daily.*

The Gothic Church of the Holy Trinity was built for Franciscan monks, who settled in Trier before 1238. The surviving church, from the late 13th century, went to the Jesuits in 1570. The college (1610–14) was transferred to the university following the dissolution of the Jesuit Order. It now houses a theological seminary. Inside the church it is worth viewing the epitaph of Elisabeth Görlitz (c.1470).

Vast complex of the Kaiserthermen (imperial baths)

⋔ Amphitheater

Petrisberg. 📞 *(0651) 97 80 80.*
🕐 *Apr–Sep: 9am–6pm; Oct–Mar:
9am–5pm.*

Near the imperial baths are
the ruins of the Roman amphitheatre, dating from the 1st
century AD. This was the
scene of gladiatorial fights
and animal contests. The
entire structure, consisting
of an elliptical arena and a
stepped auditorium, was
surrounded by a high wall,
divided into individual storeys
by colonnaded arcades. The
complex was designed to seat
up to 25,000 people. In the
5th century the inhabitants of
Trier used the amphitheatre
as a place of refuge from the
increasingly frequent raids by
Germanic tribes.

⌂ Heiligkreuzkapelle

Arnulfstraße/Rotbachstraße.

The Chapel of the Holy Cross,
in a secluded spot, is one of
Trier's more interesting
historic buildings. Built in
the Romanesque style in the
second half of the 11th century, at the initiative of the
parson of Arnulfa Cathedral,
it is a small building with a
ground plan in the shape of
the Greek cross and an octagonal tower set within the
cross. Although it suffered
serious damage during World
War II, it was meticulously
restored to its original state in
the years 1957–8.

⌂ Pfarrkirche St Matthias

Matthiasstraße. 85. 📞 *(0651) 310
79.* 🕐 *6:30am–8pm daily.*

This church's history dates
back to the 5th century, when
it became the burial place of
St Eucharius, the first bishop
of Trier. From the 8th century,
the church was run by Benedictine monks. In the 10th–
11th centuries a new church
was erected as burial site of
the relics of the apostle, St
Matthew. It was twice remodelled at the turn of the 15th to
16th centuries, when it
acquired its rich Gothic
vaults. The present abbey
dates from the 16th century.
The shrine holding the
apostle's relics ensured that
the church became one of the
most important destinations
for pilgrims in the region.

The ruins of Barbaratherme, ancient Roman baths

⋔ Barbaratherme

Südallee. 📞 *(0651) 97 80 80.*
🕐 *Apr–Sep: 9am–6pm; Oct–Mar:
9am–5pm.*

Not far from the Roman
bridge across the Mosel River
are the ruins of the Barbara
baths, dating from the 2nd
century AD. Although above
ground not much has been
preserved, the extensive
system of underground heating channels, the *hypocaustum*, clearly demonstrates the
original size of this public
bath complex. In the Middle
Ages, Patrician and
aristocratic families transformed the baths into their
residences. In the 17th century Jesuit monks dismantled
the remaining structures, and
used the recovered building
materials to construct their
own college.

⋔ Kirche St Maximin

Maximinstraße. 📞 *(0651) 710 52 55.*

In the Middle Ages there were
as many as four abbeys in
Trier. St. Maximin Abbey was
founded on the burial site of
its patron saint, who died in
AD 325. The surviving church
was built in the 13th century,
on the foundations of the
previous buildings. Its
Romanesque–Gothic forms
were partly obscured by the
remodelling work carried out
in 1580–1698. The church's
most valuable historic remains
were the Carolingian wall
paintings, which originally
adorned the crypt. Following
meticulous restoration work
these can now be seen in the
Rheinisches Landesmuseum.

⌂ Kirche St Paulinus

Thebäerstraße. 📞 *(0651) 27 08 50.*
🕐 *10am–6pm Mon, 9am–4:30pm
Tue, Fri, Sat, 9am–6pm Wed, Thu,
1–5:30pm Sun.*

This church was built in the
12th century, on the foundations of an older Christian
chapel. In 1674 it was blown
up by the French army. St
Paulin, its patron saint and
bishop in Trier, was one of the
few to voice his opposition to
the Aryan credo of Emperor
Constantine II, in which he
rejected the divinity of Christ
and proclaimed himself alone
to be made in God's image.
Paulin did not meet with a
martyr's death, but was exiled
to Phrygia (now Turkey),
where he died in 358. The
present church, a true gem of
Rococo architecture, was
designed by Balthasar Neumann, who also created the
main altar. The wall paintings
are by Thomas Scheffler.

Baroque ceiling paintings in the
Rococo Kirche St Paulinus

Saarland ❷

THIS GERMAN state, bordered by Luxembourg and France, was long disputed between France and Germany, but has now been firmly integrated into the Federal Republic. Almost forgotten are its coal and steel industries, which declined in the 1960s and 70s. The region has seen a turbulent history – it was ruled in turn by Celts, Romans and Franks. In the 17th century, on the order of Louis XIV, Vauban built the town-fortress of Saarlouis. Saarbrücken, an 18th-century town, is famous for its Baroque architecture, mostly created by Friedrich Joachim Stengel.

Von Nassau-Saarbrücken family tombs in Saarbrücken

Saarbrücken

Road map B6. 🏠 190,000. 🚉
🛈 Hauptbahnhof (0681-184 33).
🎭 Max Ophüls-Preis (Jan),
Perspectives du Théâtre (May).

The capital of Saarland, Saarbrücken was first built as the Franconian fortress of *Sarabrucca*. The town, situated on the banks of the Saar River, flourished in the 17th and particularly in the 18th century, under the rule of Duke Wilhelm Heinrich von Nassau-Saarbrücken.

The churches and other prestigious buildings are largely the work of Friedrich Joachim Stengel, court architect to the von Nassau-Saarbrücken family. He designed the Catholic **Basilika St Johann** (1754–8) in the market square, as well as the monumental **Schloss**, the palace on the opposite bank of the Saar (1739–48). Its original, modern façade, created in 1989 after damage in World War II, is the work of the architect Gottfried Böhm.

Opposite the Schloss stands the **Altes Rathaus** (old town hall), dating from 1748–50, which today houses an interesting museum of ethnography. The Protestant **Ludwigskirche** (1762–75) is one of the last works completed by Stengel. A true architectural gem, it is laid out in the shape of a Greek cross. The **Stiftskirche St Arnual**, in the southwestern part of the town, contains the splendid Gothic and Renaissance tombs of the von Nassau-Saarbrücken family. Since 1960 it has also featured a "German–French Garden". One of the garden's entrances leads to Gulliver-Miniwelt (miniature world of Gulliver), where small versions of the world's most famous buildings are exhibited.

Völklinger Hütte, the historic steelworks in Völklingen

Völklingen

Road map B6. 🏠 43,500.
🛈 Rathausstr. 57 (06898-211 00).
About 10 km (6 miles) west of Saarbrücken lies the small industrial town of Völklingen, which was granted town status in 1937. In 1881, Carl Röchling, a native of Saarbrücken, bought a small steel mill, the **Völklinger Hütte**, which he soon developed as the heart of his family's industrial empire. The steel mill still exists, and in 1994 it became a UNESCO World Heritage Site, listed as a historical object of international importance. Another attraction is an original, early 20th-century housing estate.

Homburg

Road map B6. 🏠 42,000. 🛈 Rathaus, Am Forum 5 (06 841-20 66).
This town grew up around the Hohenburg castle, which now is just a picturesque ruin. In the Schlossberg nearby were unearthed the remains of a fortress, which was built in 1680–92 by Sébastien Le Preste Vauban on the orders of the French King Louis XIV. The greatest attraction of Homburg, however, is its Schlossberg caves, the largest man-made caves in Europe, cut into the red sandstone.

Ottweiler

Road map B5. 🏠 16,000.
🛈 Schlosshof 5 (06 824-35 11).
The small picturesque town of Ottweiler has a beautifully preserved old town. The Alter Turm (old tower), which in the 15th century formed part of the town's fortifications, now serves as a belfry to the parish church, whose origins go back to the 15th century. Its present Baroque form was the work of Friedrich Joachim Stengel from 1756–7.

Rathausplatz is a beautifully proportioned complex of historic houses, mostly the homes of wealthy citizens, dating from the 17th and 18th centuries. Many have half-timbered upper halves. The Altes Rathaus (old town hall, 1714) combines two different building methods – the base is stone, the top half-timbered. In Schlossplatz is the Renaissance Hesse Haus (c.1590).

Moseltal ❸

THE MOSEL river, 545 km (338 miles) long, is one of the longest tributaries of the Rhine. The Mosel valley between Trier and Koblenz, where the Mosel flows into the Rhine, is one of the most beautiful parts of Germany. On both sides of the river, romantic castles tower over endless vineyards, where excellent white grapes are grown – both are typical features of the charming landscape.

Burg Thurant ②
Near the town of Alken stands Thurant castle, which was built in the 13th century. It is the only twin-towered castle along the Mosel.

Kobern-Gondorf ①
An ancient cemetery, dating from Roman and Franconian times, was discovered here in 1874. It yielded many interesting artifacts, including necklaces, rings and weapons.

Burg Pyrmont ⑤
Pyrmont's grim 13th-century medieval castle was remodelled and extended several times during the Baroque era.

Cochem ⑥
The castle in Cochem, originally built in the 11th century, was completely destroyed by French soldiers in 1869. The present castle was rebuilt in the 19th century.

Ehrenburg ③
The first fortress, rising to 235 m (771 ft) above sea level, was built in 1120. It was frequently remodelled in later years.

Burg Eltz ④
The von Eltz family castle, whose history goes back to the 16th century, remains in private hands to this day, but it is open to visitors.

416

49

Mosel

Baybach

Dünnbach

Bremm

Burg Arras ⑦
This fortress was built in 938 as part of the fortifications against frequent pillaging raids by Magyars.

KEY

▮▮▮	Suggested route
▬	Scenic route
═	Other road
┄	River, lake
☀	Viewpoint

0 km   5
0 miles   5

TIPS FOR DRIVERS

Length of the route: *about 75 km (46 miles).*
Stopping-off points: *There are numerous restaurants and cafes in Cochem; small pubs can be found along the entire route.*
Additional attractions: *A boat trip on the Mosel River, from Koblenz to Cochem or Trier.*

Altar in the Dreifaltigkeitskirche, in Speyer

Speyer ❹

Road map B6. 🏛 46,000. 🚇 🛈
Maximilianstraße 13 (06232-14 23 92).
🎪 *Brezelfest (Jul), Kaisertafel (Aug).*

IN THE 7th century, Speyer was the seat of a diocese. As a free city of the Holy Roman Empire from 1294 until 1779, 50 sessions of the imperial parliament took place here. The most famous session was in 1529, when the Protestant states of the Holy Roman Empire lodged a protest (hence the term "Protestant") against the decisions of the Catholic majority.

The most important historic building in Speyer is the Romanesque **Dom St Maria und St Stephan**, a World Heritage Site. For a time, before being superseded by the gigantic abbey of Cluny in Burgundy, this was the largest monumental Romanesque building in Europe. The Dom, built in 1025–61 on the initiative of Conrad II, is a triple-nave, cross-vaulted basilica with transept, vestibule, choir, apse and several towers. Its magnificent triple-nave crypt, the burial place of Salian emperors, has stunning stone carvings, some worked by Lombard stonemasons. **St Afra's**, dating from around 1100, has some interesting sculptures, including *Christ Bearing His Cross* and *Annunciation* (c.1470). The Domnapf, a vast stone bowl seen at the forecourt of the cathedral, dates from 1490. It was used during enthroning

ceremonies, when the newly anointed bishop would order it to be filled with wine right to the brim in order to win the hearts of his flock.

Another 11th-century interesting building is the **Mikwe** in Judenbadgasse, a ritual Jewish bath for women, and the remains of a synagogue nearby. To the west of the Dom stand the remains of the medieval fortifications including the **Altpörtel**, a 14th- to 16th-century town gate. The late-Baroque **Dreifaltigkeitskirche** (church of the Holy Trinity), built in 1701–17, is an architectural masterpiece with marvellous interiors.

Worms ❺

Road map B5. 🏛 82,000. 🚇
🛈 *Neumarkt 14 (06241-250 45).*

WORMS is one of the oldest towns in Germany. In the Middle Ages it was the home of the Reich's Parliament, hosting more than 100 sessions. The **Dom St Peter** is one of the largest late-Romanesque cathedrals in Germany, along with the cathedrals in Mainz and Speyer. It was built in 1171–1230 as a two-choir basilica, with eastern transept, four towers and two domes. Its northern nave includes five beautiful sandstone reliefs from a Gothic cloister, which no longer exists. The interior furnishings date mainly from modern times. Particularly noteworthy is the high altar designed in the 18th century by Balthasar Neumann, and the stalls dating from 1760.

A relief from 1488, in the Dom in Worms

Tombstones in the Heiliger Sand Jewish cemetery in Worms

A short distance from the cathedral is the Marktplatz (market square), with the interesting **Dreifaltigkeitskirche** church of the Holy Trinity (1709–25). Northeast of the square stands the **Stiftskirche St Paul** (church of St Paul), built in the 11th–12th centuries and completed in the 18th century, with original 13th century wall paintings. Nearby is the only surviving Renaissance residential building in Worms, the **Rotes Haus** (red house).

In the western part of the old town is the **Heiliger Sand** (holy sands), the oldest Jewish cemetery in Europe, where the earliest tombstones date from the 11th and 12th centuries. Also worth a visit is the 14th-century **Liebfrauenkirche** (Church of Our Dear Lady). The most noteworthy feature of the **Magnuskirche** (11th–12th centuries) is its crypt, from around AD 800, while the **Stiftskirche St Martin** (late 11th century) has some interesting portals.

The vast Romanesque Dom St. Peter in Worms

Deutsche Weinstraße ⑥

THE "German Wine Route" starts in Bockenheim and ends in Schweigen, near the Alsatian town of Weißenburg. The tour suggested here includes the most interesting sections of this route. This is one of the most beautiful parts of Germany, where visitors will encounter aspects of German and European historical and cultural heritage at every step, set among the picturesque scenery of the endless vineyards covering the sun-drenched slopes of the Pfälzer Wald.

Bad Dürkheim ⑧
This famous resort is best known for its annual Wurstmarkt, held in September. Despite its name, it celebrates the wine harvest, and sausages take second place.

St Martin ⑥
Not much remains of the Romanesque church of St Martin, but the 16–18th-century buildings surviving in the town continue to enchant visitors.

Hambacher Schloss ⑦
Only a romantic ruin remains of this vast hilltop fortress, whose fame is based on the Hambacher Fest when, on 27 May 1832, students protested against the fragmentation of Germany.

NATURPARK
PFÄLZER
WALD

Landau ⑤
This little town has the remains of the fortress built by Vauban, and an extraordinarily beautiful post-Augustinian church.

Trifels ④
This grim, ruined castle once served as a prison for many important people, including the King of England, Richard the Lionheart.

0 km   5
0 miles   5

Leinsweiler ③
Hilltop Hof Neukastel was once the home of the German impressionist artist Max Slevogt, and to this day, wall paintings by the artist can be seen here.

Klingbach

Bad Bergzabern ②
This town has some interesting Renaissance remains, including the Gasthaus zum Engel (Angel's Inn) and a royal castle.

Dörrenbach ①
The star attractions in this small town are the half-timbered town hall and the Gothic church surrounded by fortifications.

KEY

 Suggested route

Scenic route

Other road

River, lake

Viewpoint

TIPS FOR DRIVERS

Length: 83 km (51 miles).
Stopping-off points: Landau has many cafés and restaurants. The spa town of Bad Dürkheim, with its cafés and wine bars, is also a good place to stop.
Signs: Look for signposts showing a bunch of grapes or a wine jug.

Mainz ❼

THE TOWN, which grew out of the Roman military camp *Moguntiacum* established in 39 BC, is today the capital of the Rhineland-Palatinate. Mainz is the home of two important German television stations (ZDF and SAT 1). It is also the main centre of trade for the popular Rhine wines. Its late-Romanesque cathedral symbolizes the power of the Kurfürsten, the prince-electors, who used to crown German kings. Indisputably the town's most famous son is Johannes Gutenberg – the inventor of printing.

⊞ Kurfürstliches Schloss

Dieter-von-Isenburg-Straße.
Römisch-Germanisches Museum 🄲 *(0631) 912 40.* ◻ *10am–6pm Tue–Sun.*

Construction of the Baroque electoral palace, which began in 1627 during the rule of Archbishop Georg von Greifenclau, was completed more than a century later, in 1775–6, under Johann Friedrich Carl Joseph von Erthal. Today the palace houses the fascinating museum of Roman and Germanic history.

🏛 Gutenberg-Museum

Liebfrauenplatz 5. 🄲 *(0631) 12 26 40.* ◻ *9am–5pm Tue–Sat, 11am–3pm Sun.* ● *Public holidays.* 🎫

Johannes Gensfleisch zum Gutenberg became famous as the inventor of the printing process using movable metal type. The letters were cast in a special apparatus and set in

Statue of Gutenberg in Gutenbergplatz

columns. Gutenberg himself prepared the Bible for printing and publication in 1454–5. From the original 200 copies, only 46 have survived to this day.

The museum, which opened in 1900, shows a reconstruction of the master's workshop from 1450. The collection comprises priceless early books, including the Gutenberg Bible and the Psalter published in 1457 by Fust & Schöffer, Gutenberg's erstwhile partners and latterday creditors. The Psalter was the first work to be printed using three different colours of inks.

⊞ Kaiserdom

See pp336–7.

⊞ Gutenbergplatz

A short distance from the Protestant parish church of St John is Gutenbergplatz, a pleasant square with a statue of the inventor. Set in its

paving stones is a line marking the 50th parallel. The Staatstheater (state theatre) in the square is an interesting late Neo-Classical building from 1829–33.

Historic half-timbered houses in Kirschgarten

⊞ Kirschgarten

Near the Baroque hospital of St Roch, built in 1721 and now an old people's home, runs a street called Kirschgarten (cherry orchard). This is one of the loveliest parts of old Mainz, which suffered serious damage in World War II. The well-preserved complex of historic half-timbered houses, dating from the 16th–18th centuries, makes this district worth visiting and a pleasant place for a stroll.

⛪ Kirche St Stephan

Kleine Weißgasse 12. 🄲 *(06131) 23 16 40.* ◻ *10am–noon & 2–5pm daily.*

A short distance from Kirschgarten stands the Gothic parish church of St Stephen. It was built in stages, on the site of an older building dating from the 10th century. Construction began in the mid-13th century and continued until the end of the 15th century. The resulting church is a triple-nave hall with eastern transept and a single-nave choir. The adjacent late-15th century cloisters are a true gem of late-Gothic design. The original stained-glass windows in the presbytery, destroyed during World War II, were replaced by six new ones in 1978–81, designed and partly made by Marc Chagall. Set against a

The Baroque Kurfürstliches Schloss and museum

Landing stage for boats on the Rhine

VISITORS' CHECKLIST

Road map B5. *190,000.*
 *Im Brückenturm am
Rathaus (06131-28 62 10).*
 *Mainzer Fastnacht (Jan/Feb),
Johannisnacht (22–25 Jun),
OpenOhr Festival (Jun), Mainzer
Zeltfestival (end of Jun/early Jul)
Weinforum Rheinhessen (last
weekend in Oct).*

beautiful blue background, they depict biblical scenes, including Abraham with the three travellers, the Patriarch pleading to God to spare the righteous in Sodom and Gomorrah, Jacob's dream, and Moses with the Tablets of the Ten Commandments.

The church interior contains many other interesting original features. The four large brass candelabra were cast in Mainz in 1509. The small polyptych depicting the Crucifixion dates from around 1400, while its movable wings were made some 100 years later. The niche below the tower contains the Holy Tomb (c.1450).

⋔ Römersteine

Southeast of the University campus are the impressive remains of the Roman aqueduct, dating from the 1st century AD. The Zahlbach valley was a vantage point for the southwestern flank of the Roman camp, *Castrum Moguntiacum*, but it presented a major technical problem of supplying the camp with drinking water. The aqueduct was built by Roman engineers. Although some of its pillars were 23 m (75 ft) high, the present remains only reach up to 10 m (32 ft).

ENVIRONS: It is also worth making an excursion to **Oppenheim**, a centre of the wine trade 20 km (12 miles) to the south. The pride of this town is its Gothic Katharinenkirche, a church built of red sandstone in the 13th–14th centuries. The neighbouring hill and the ruins of Landskron castle provide the most spectacular view over the Rhine valley. The Weinbaumuseum, museum of viticulture, is also worth visiting.

MAINZ CITY CENTRE

Gutenberg-Museum ②
Gutenbergplatz ④
Kaiserdom ③
Kirche St Stephan ⑥
Kirschgarten ⑤
Kurfürstliches Schloss ①

0 metres 250
0 yards 250

KEY

 Tourist information
P Parking
 Church

Mainzer Dom

Crucifix in the St Gotthard-Kapelle

T HE GREATEST attraction of Mainz is its superb cathedral, gleaming red in the sunshine. Together with those of Speyer and Worms it is one of the only three Romanesque imperial cathedrals to have survived almost intact to this day. Its basic framework was laid out in 1081–1137 and 1183–1239, but its oldest parts date from the early 11th century, with the rows of Gothic side chapels added during the 13th and 14th centuries. Although neither the Gothic altars nor the magnificent choir screen have survived to this day, it is still possible to see the large group of bishops' monuments from the 13th to the 19th century.

Portal of the "Memorie" Burial Chapel
The late-Gothic portal, leading to the Romanesque burial chapel of the cathedral canons, was made by Madern Gerthener, after 1425.

Pulpit
This Neo-Gothic pulpit was made in 1834 by Joseph Scholl.

Two large and two small towers are symmetrically positioned on the ends of the cathedral.

St Stephen's Choir
The Romanesque eastern choir, one of the first parts to be built, is simpler in style than other parts of the cathedral.

Round staircase towers are from the previous building, built in the early 11th century.

★ **Monument of Heinrich Ferdinand von der Leyen**
This Baroque monument of the Dom rector, the work of Johann Mauritz Gröninger, was erected during his lifetime, in 1706.

St Martin's Choir
The late-Romanesque western choir with its trefoil closing is an early 13th-century addition.

★ **Stalls**
These superb Rococo oak stalls encircle almost the entire presbytery. They were created by Franz Anton Hermann, who completed them in 1767.

Main entrance

Tomb of Jakob von Liebenstein
The late-Gothic tomb of the archbishop von Liebenstein, who died in 1508, is the work of Hans Backoffen. It depicts the deceased in draped robes, lying under an ornate canopy.

STAR FEATURES

★ **Monument of Heinrich Ferdinand von der Leyen**

★ **Stalls**

Rhine Valley (Rheintal) ➑

T HE CELTS called it *Renos*, the Romans *Rhenus*,
while to Germanic tribes it was the Rhein, or
Vater Rhein ("Father Rhine"), as it is known
today. The source of this mighty, 1320-km
(825-mile) long river is in Switzerland, from
where it flows through Liechtenstein,
Germany, Luxembourg and Holland, yet
the Germans regard it as "their" river.
The Rhine is steeped in many legends
– it was into this river that Hagen von
Tronje, faithful follower of King
Gunther and slayer of Siegfried, threw
the treasure of the Nibelungs, and
Lohengrin's swan is said to appear
near the town of Kleve *(see p374)*
to this day.

Stolzenfels ①
The existing castle com-
plex has little in common
with the original 13th-cen-
tury fortress, which burned
down in 1688. In the early
19th century, the ruins
were bought by the future
king Friedrich Wilhelm IV.
The castle, designed by the
famous Prussian architect
Karl Friedrich Schinkel,
was built in 1833–45.

| 0 kilometres | 5 |
| 0 miles | 5 |

Boppard ②
Boppard's most famous sights are
the remains of the Roman military
camp of Bodobric, the church of
St Severus (12th–13th centuries),
famous for its wall paintings, and
the Medieval market square, built
on the site of Roman hot baths.
Michael Thonet, the creator of
famous chairs made from bent
wood, was born here in 1796.

TIPS FOR DRIVERS

Length of the route: *About
125 km (78 miles).*
Stopping-off points: *The best
places to stop are Boppard or
Bacharach, offering the widest
choice of bars and restaurants.*
Further attractions: *A boat trip
on the Rhine river, from Koblenz
to Mainz.*

St Goar ③
The town takes its
name from Goar, an
Aquitanian hermit who
settled here in the
mid-6th century. His
burial place is in the
magnificent 11th-
century crypt of the
Stiftskirche (the parish
church, which today is
a Protestant church).

Marksburg ⑧

From 1117 this castle, which towers over the Rhine and the small town of Braubach, has been owned at different times by the von Braubachs and the powerful Epstein family. The Marksburg is the only castle along this stretch of the Rhine which has never been damaged.

Lorelei ⑦

The Lorelei Rock, onto which many boats have been smashed by the strong currents, has been a source of inspiration for many poets. A 19th-century legend tells of a beautiful blonde combing her hair and luring unlucky sailors to their deaths with her song.

Pfalzgrafenstein ④

In the middle of the Rhine River stands the proud and mighty fortress of Pfalzgrafenstein – one of the most beautifully situated castles in the Rhineland. Its origins date back to 1326, but its present shape is the result of Baroque refurbishments in the 17th–18th centuries.

Bacharach ⑤

The town has a unique complex of historic buildings, with fortified town walls, the church of St Peter, the ruins of the Gothic chapel of St Werner, and Burg Stahleck – the castle towering over the town which today houses a youth hostel.

Burg Sooneck ⑥

In the 13th century, Sooneck castle was the home of various robber knights. The fortress fell into ruin in the late 17th century, due to frequent raids by the French. In the 19th century it was bought by the Hohenzollerns, who rebuilt the castle in its original form.

Limburg

rüesel   *Kaub*

Lorch

Rüdesheim

Bingen

Kaiserslautern   *Mannheim*

KEY

▦	Motorway
▰	Main road
▬	Scenic route
═	River
☆	Viewpoint

Koblenz ❾

THE NAME which the Romans gave to their camp in 9 BC – *castrum ad confluentas*, meaning the "camp at the confluence" – reflects the town's strategic importance, for it is here that the Mosel flows into the Rhine. From the Middle Ages until the 19th century, Koblenz was the seat of the powerful archbishop–electors of Trier. It was also the birthplace of Prince von Metternich, the 19th-century Austrian statesman. Today it is a modern metropolis which attracts many visitors, and is the main centre of the region's cultural life.

Romanesque twin-tower façade of the Basilika St Castor

🏛 Deutsches Eck

Ludwig-Museum im Deutschherrenhaus. ☎ (0261) 30 40 40. ◷ 10:30am–5pm Tue–Sat, 11am–6pm Sun & public holidays.
The "German corner" is the place where the Mosel flows into the Rhine. Here stands the enormous equestrian statue of Emperor Wilhelm I. Designed by Bruno Schmitz, it was erected in 1897, destroyed in World War II and replaced with a copy in 1993. The name refers to the complex of buildings known as Deutschherrenhaus belonging to the Order of Teutonic Knights. Only part of the three-wing residence of the Order's Commander, built in the early 14th century, has survived to this day. Following its refurbishment in 1992 the building now houses the Ludwig-Museum, with a collection of modern art (mainly German and French post-1945 artists) donated by Peter and Irene Ludwig.

⛪ Basilika St Castor

Kastorstraße 7.
The collegial church of St Castor was built in 817–36 on the initiative of the archbishop of Trier, on a site previously occupied by an early Christian church. The treaty of Verdun, which divided the Carolingian Empire between the three sons of Ludwig I the Pious, was signed here in 843. The present appearance of the church is the result of extensions from the 11th–13th centuries. Inside are beautiful wall epitaphs of the Trier archbishops Kuno von Falkenstein (1388) and Werner von Königstein (1418). Also noteworthy is the pulpit dating from 1625.

🏛 Florinsmarkt

Mittelrheinisches Museum
Florinsmarkt 15. ☎ (0261) 129 25 02. ◷ 10:30am–5pm Tue–Sat, 11am–6pm Sun.
This square takes its name from the Romanesque-Gothic church of St Florin, dating from the 12th and 14th centuries. The Mittelrheinisches Museum with its collection of archaeology and medieval art of the Central Rhine region occupies three historic buildings. The Kaufhaus, in the centre, dates from 1419–25 and 1724. The image of a horse-rider shows the robber baron Johann von Kobem, beheaded in 1536, who now sticks his tongue out at passers-by every half hour. To its right stands the late-Gothic Schöffenhaus, and to its left is the Baroque Bürresheimer Hof, from 1659–60.

The Renaissance Alte Burg, now housing archives and a library

♠ Alte Burg

Burgstraße 1.
In the Middle Ages, the powerful von Arken family had a fortified residence built for themselves in the north-western section of the Roman fortifications. In 1277 it was taken over by Heinrich von Finstingen, the archbishop of Trier, who ordered its extension. The fortress was to protect him from the citizens of Koblenz who were striving for independence. Successive archbishops continued with the conversion of the building, which acquired its final shape in the 17th century. The eastern Renaissance façade of the complex is particularly attractive. Today it houses the municipal archives and parts of the library.

The spur between the Mosel and the Rhine, called Deutsches Eck

Liebfrauenkirche

Florinspfaffengasse 14.

(0261) 315 50.

At the highest point in the old town stands the Romanesque church of Our Dear Lady. Its history dates back to early Christian times, but its present form is the result of remodelling work carried out in 1182–1250. A triple-nave basilica with galleries, it has a twin-tower western façade. The beautiful, elongated Gothic choir was added in 1404–30. Inside are some historic remains from the 17th and 18th centuries.

Statue of the Madonna in Liebfrauenkirche

Kurfürstliches Schloss

Clemensplatz.

Not far from the bridge across the Rhine stands the electoral palace, an example of the Rhineland's early Neo-Classical architecture. It was built, and for a short time occupied, by Clemens Wenzeslaus von Sachsen, the last of Trier's electors. Construction of the castle began in 1777, to a design prepared by Michael d'Ixnard, and continued until 1786, overseen by Antoine François Peyère the Younger.

Festung Ehrenbreitstein

Landesmuseum Koblenz

(0261) 970 30.

15 Mar–15 Nov: 9am–12:30pm & 1–5pm daily.

On the opposite side of the Rhine stands the mighty fortress of Ehrenbreitstein, one of the largest in the world. A smaller fortress was erected on this site in 1000, and extended in subsequent years by the archbishops and electors of Trier, who lived in this indomitable fortress from 1648 to 1786. Trier's holiest relic, the Rock Christi (vestments of Christ) was kept here. The appearance of the fortress has not changed much since Prussian days. It offers splendid views over Koblenz, the Rhine and the Mosel. Today, it is home to the **Landesmuseum Koblenz** (regional museum) with an interesting collection on the development of technology, and to the **Rhein-Museum** with hydrological collections. At Wambachstraße 204, in the same district, is the house of Beethoven's mother.

The Classical façade of the Kurfürstliches Schloss

KOBLENZ CITY CENTRE

Alte Burg ④
Basilika St Castor ②
Deutsches Eck ①
Festung Ehrenbreitstein ⑦
Florinsmarkt ③
Kurfürstliches Schloss ⑥
Liebfrauenkirche ⑤

0 metres 250
0 yards 250

KEY

🕆 Church

🅿 Parking

ℹ Tourist information

Maria Laach ⑩

Capital of a
vestibule column

A TRUE MASTERPIECE of German and European Romanesque architecture, the Maria Laach Abbey stands next to the Laacher See, a lake formed in the crater of an extinct volcano. Its construction started in 1093 at the behest of Heinrich II, who also lies buried here. Building continued from 1093 until 1220. Until secularization in 1802, the Abbey was the home of the Benedictines. Since 1892 the church has once again been resounding with Gregorian chants, which are sung here several times a day.

View from the West
The monumental western façade of the abbey consists of the semicircular apse, a massive, square 43-m (141-ft) tall central tower, and two slim 35-m (115-ft) tall flanking towers.

★ Tomb of Heinrich II
The tomb of the Palatine Heinrich II, who died in 1095, dates from about 1280. His effigy has been reproduced in a magnificent walnut wood block, which to this day has kept its original colours.

Löwenbrunnen
The lion fountain, which adorns the atrium, was made in 1928. It was modelled on the famous Alhambra fountain in Granada, Spain.

Main entrance

Detail from a Column Capital
The western door is surrounded by columns with interesting capitals. Carved figures can be seen, including that of a devil recording the sins of each entrant and others which are pulling each other's hair out.

The "Paradise", the courtyard, is meant to symbolize the Garden of Eden.

Church entrance

Mosaics
The interior is decorated with paintings and mosaics created over centuries by artists of the Beuron School. In the eastern apse is a mosaic of Christ the Ruler dating from 1911.

VISITORS' CHECKLIST

Road map B5. 6032 from Niedermendig or Mayen, 6031 from Andernach.
(0265) 590.
5:30am–8pm daily.
Crypt – information by video show.

The church towers have arcaded galleries, typical of Romanesque style.

Stained-glass Windows
Three vast stained-glass windows in the eastern apse were made by a contemporary artist, W. Rupprecht, in 1956.

★ High Altar
Among the most precious works preserved in the church is the late-Romanesque canopy of 1220–50, rising above the high altar.

★ Crypt
The vaults of the exquisite early-Romanesque crypt are supported by austere square capitals. This is also the resting-place of Gilbert, the first abbot at Maria Laach.

STAR SIGHTS

★ Tomb of Heinrich II

★ High Altar

★ Crypt

HESSE

HESSE LIES IN *the very heart of present-day Germany. Scattered over the region are reminders of its former glory: Roman camps, Carolingian buildings, Romanesque churches and Gothic cathedrals with lofty spires. Territorial partitions, so typical of the former German Reich, brought about the blossoming of art and architecture during the Renaissance and the Baroque eras.*

A post-World War II creation, the borders of this federal state roughly approximate those of its 13th-century forerunner. For most of its history, Hesse was divided between Hesse-Darmstadt and Hesse-Kassel.

Today, when admiring the distinctive panorama of Frankfurt am Main – its towering banks and skyscrapers more reminiscent of New York's Manhattan than of a European metropolis – it is hard to believe that this was the birthplace of Goethe. The importance of this city extends far beyond Hesse: it is the financial centre of the European Union, and its annual Book Fair is the largest event of its kind in the world.

Darmstadt became famous as a centre for Jugendstil (Art Nouveau) early in the 20th century. Wiesbaden is the seat of Hesse's state government, and Marburg is one of the best-known university towns. In the 16th century, at the times of fierce religious feuds, the first Protestant university was built here. The Church of St Elizabeth is one of the earliest examples of Gothic architecture in the region. Lovers of modern art will know of Kassel – every five years it hosts the *documenta*, an exciting exhibition of artistic developments.

Hesse has much more to offer. The Waldecker Land, near Kassel, boasts the Eder lake and attractive health resorts. Eberbach in the picturesque Rheingau, the wine-growing area around Eltville, has a well-preserved former Cistercian abbey, which was used as a film setting.

Park and Baroque Orangery of the palace complex in Fulda

◁ Frankfurt's skyscraper district, nicknamed "Mainhattan"

Exploring Hesse

Eltville, situated in the Rheingau, one of Germany's most important wine-producing regions, is famous for its Riesling wine. Frankfurt am Main, known around the world as a great financial and commercial centre, also has fantastic museums, drawing visitors with their outstanding art collections, while the International Book Fair is a true paradise for readers and bookworms. In the 19th century, wealthy socialites chose Bad Homburg as their favourite spa, while the romantic town of Marburg still has the lively atmosphere of a university town.

Ruins of the abbey in Limburg

The giant Niederwalddenkmal near Rüdesheim

Sights at a Glance

KASSEL ①

② FRITZLAR

WALDECKER
LAND
③

BAD HERSFELD

⑤
ALSFELD

UTERBACH

254 ④ FULDA

RHÖN

279

GELS-
BERG   40

SCHLÜCHTERN

Göttingen

Kassel

Schweinfurt

Würzburg

| 0 km | 20 |
| 0 miles | 20 |

**The Messeturm in the Frankfurt
fairgrounds, designed by Helmut Jahn**

SEE ALSO

- *Where to Stay* pp488–90.

- *Where to Eat* pp517–19.

GETTING AROUND

The A7 motorway, cutting across Hesse
in a north–south direction, provides a
fast transport link. Starting from Hannover, it runs through Göttingen, Kassel
and Fulda to Würzburg in Bavaria. The
A4 runs from Dresden, via Weimar, to
Bad Hersfeld. From there visitors can
take the A7 or the A5, towards Gießen,
Bad Homburg, Frankfurt am Main and
onwards to Darmstadt and Heidelberg.
The fast ICE railway connects Kassel
and Frankfurt am Main with Basel (in
Switzerland), Stuttgart, Berlin and
Munich. Frankfurt am Main has one
of Europe's largest airports.

KEY

▨	Motorway
▨	Main road
▨	Scenic route
═	River
☆	Viewpoint

Statue of the Brothers Grimm in Hanau

Kassel ❶

K ASSEL, the cultural, scientific and commercial centre of northern Hesse, suffered severe damage during World War II due to the armaments industries based here, and much of the town has been rebuilt in functional 1950s style. Today, Kassel has become synonymous with one of the most important shows of contemporary art – *documenta* – held here every five years (the 11th documenta is scheduled for 2002). The town is equally famous for its outstanding collection of European art, housed in the splendid Schloss Wilhelms-höhe, as well as for its parks and gardens, especially the large forest-park adjoining the castle.

17th century cameo-decorated tureen in the Landesmuseum

🏛 Hessisches Landesmuseum

Brüder-Grimm-Platz 5. [(0561) 784 60.] 10am–5pm Tue–Sun. ● 1 May, 24, 25, 31 Dec. 📷 (free Sat.)

Outstanding items in the Neo-Baroque Hesse Regional Museum, built in 1910–13, are the astronomical instruments, originally installed in 1560 in a landgrave's castle, which no longer exists. The ethnographic section has displays of Hessian folk costumes and regional craft items.

The Landesmuseum also houses one of Europe's most unusual museums: the fascinating Tapetenmuseum (wallpaper museum). Established in 1923, the museum presents the history of wallpaper and the methods of its production around the world. The collection includes examples of leather wall coverings (cordovans) and wallpapers representing Secession and Art-Deco styles as well as the "world's literature on wallpaper". *Vues de Suisse* (views of Switzerland), dating from 1802, is one of the earliest examples of scenic wallpaper. It was printed using 95 different inks and 1,024 wooden blocks. The splendid panoramic *Rénaud et Armide,* from the workshop of Joseph Dufours, printed in 1828 using 2,386 wooden blocks.

🏛 Neue Galerie

Schöne Aussicht 1. [(0561) 70 96 30.] 10am–5pm Tue–Sun. ● 1 May, 24, 25 & 26 Dec. 📷

The New Gallery, founded in 1976 and devoted to 19th- and 20th-century art, occupies a Neo-Classicist building from 1871–4. The main emphasis of the gallery's collection is on Romantic and Impressionist paintings. It includes canvases by artists such as Carl Schuch, Max Slevogt and Lovis Corinth.

The splendid collection of 20th-century paintings focuses on German Expressionism. An entire room is also devoted to the installations of the controversial sculptor and performance artist Joseph Beuys.

Wallpaper (1670–80), in the Tapetenmuseum

🏛 Brüder-Grimm-Museum

Schöne Aussicht 2. [(0561) 787 20 33.] 10am–5pm daily. ● 1 Jan, Good Friday, 24, 25, 31 Dec.

Next to the New Gallery is the small Schloss Bellevue, built in 1714 by Paul du Ry. Although brothers Jacob and Wilhelm Grimm were born in Hanau, they lived in Kassel from 1798 until 1830, and in 1960 a museum devoted to the lives and work of the famous fairy-tale tellers and philologers was opened, containing the first editions of their most important works.

An illustration for Cinderella, one of the Grimm fairy-tales

🎭 Kunsthalle Fridericianum

Friedrichsplatz 18. [(0561) 707 27 20.] 10am–6pm Wed & Fri–Sun, 10am–8pm Thu. 📷 (free Wed.)

Königsplatz and Friedrichsplatz were designed by the court architect, Simon Louis du Ry. The northwestern side of the latter is occupied by the Neo-Classical Fridericianum, built by du Ry in 1769–76. Its founder, Landgrave Friedrich II, had always intended it to be a museum, and it became the second public museum (after the British Museum in London) to be built in Europe, and the first one on the European mainland. Since 1955, the Fridricianum has been the main venue for Kassel's multimedia contemporary art show – the *documenta*, which every five years takes over the entire city. An additional exhibition hall, the Documentahalle, was opened in 1992, in the nearby Staatstheater.

The Ottoneum, home of the first permanent theatre in Germany

🔲 Ottoneum

Steinweg 2. **Naturkundemuseum**
📞 (0561) 787 40 14. ⭕ 10am–5pm Tue–Sun. 🖼

The Ottoneum (1604–5), built for Landgrave Maurice the Learned, was Germany's first permanent theatre. Designed by Wilhelm Vernukken and remodelled in the late 17th century by Paul du Ry, it was converted into a natural history museum in 1885.

🍃 Karlsaue

An der Karlsaue 20c. 📞 (0561) 715 43. **Museum für Astronomie und Technikgeschichte** ⭕ 10am–5pm Tue–Sun. **Zeiss-Planetarium** 🎞 2pm Tue, Sat, 2 & 8pm Thu, 3pm Wed, Fri, Sun. 🖼 (free Fri.)

The southern part of Kassel is home to Karlsaue, a vast palace and garden complex named after its founder, Landgrave Karl. The site was earlier occupied by a small Renaissance Schloss (1568), surrounded by a garden. In 1702–10 Pierre-Etienne Monnot built the large Orangery, which now houses a museum of astronomy and technology. Monnot is also the creator of Marmorbad, a bath pavilion from 1722, while the kitchen pavilion was designed by Simon Louis du Ry in 1765.

🏛 Wilhelmshöhe

Gemäldegalerie Alter Meister.
Schloss Wilhelmshöhe. 📞 (0561) 937 77. ⭕ 10am–5pm Tue–Sun. ⬤ 1 May, 24, 25, 31 Dec. 🖼

At the top of Wilhelmshöher Allee, designed in 1781, stands Wilhelmshöhe, a magnificent palace and park. The palace is situated along the axis of the avenue that runs up the hill, through a long forest glade. The original intention was to fill it with a series of cascades, but only a few of these were ever built. At the top of the hill is the Octogon, crowned with the statue of Hercules, the symbol of the town. The palace was designed by Simon Louis du Ry and Heinrich Christoph

Jussow and built in 1793–1801 for the Elector Wilhelm. Now it houses the Gemäldegalerie Alte Meister with its outstanding collection of European masters including paintings by Rubens, Titian, Rembrandt, Dürer and Poussin. The large and attractive park has many pavilions and sculptures.

Cascades, with Octogon and Hercules statue, in Wilhelmshöhe

KASSEL CITY CENTRE

Brüder-Grimm-Museum ③
Fridericianum ④
Hessisches Landesmuseum and Deutsches Tapetenmuseum ①
Karlsaue ⑥
Neue Galerie ②
Ottoneum ⑤

0 metres 300
0 yards 300

WILHELMSHOHE ←

KEY

🛈 Tourist information
🅿 Parking
✝ Church

Fritzlar ❷

Road map C4. 🏯 15,000. 🚇 🚌
Kasseler Straße. 🛈 Rathaus,
Zwischen den Krämen 5 (05622-98
86 43). 🎭 Pferdemarkt (Jul),
Stadtfest (Aug).

THE BEAUTIFUL town of Fritzlar has preserved its original, nearly complete ring of
medieval walls with watch-
towers, bastions and over 450
half-timbered houses from
various periods. In the early
8th century, St Boniface, the
apostle of Germany, had the
holy oak of the Germanic god
Donar, which grew here, cut
down to build a Christian
chapel. In 724 he founded the
Benedictine **Dom** (abbey of
St Peter). In 1118 the original
church was replaced by a cruci-
form, vaulted basilica with a
triple-nave crypt, and this was
remodelled in the 13th and
14th centuries. Adjacent to the
church is a lovely 14th-cen-
tury ambulatory. The church
interior is rich in historic
treasures. The east wall of the
transept is decorated with
wall paintings from c.1320,
and the south nave includes a
Pietà (1300). The 14th-century
parish church of the Franciscan Order nearby has a lovely
painting of the Madonna, on
the northern wall of the choir.
   In Fritzlar's picturesque old
town stands the **Rathaus**
(town hall), whose lower
floors date from the 12th
century, while the upper ones
were added in the 15th century. The exquisite **Hochzeitshaus** (wedding house),
in the street of the same
name, is a Renaissance half-
timbered house, built in
1580–90, which now houses a
museum. Another interesting
sight is the **Alte Brücke**, a
13th-century stone bridge
spanning the Eder River.

**Relief of St Martin, on the walls of
the Rathaus in Fritzlar**

Waldecker Land ❸

THE WALDECKER LAND, situated west of Kassel, was
once an independent county and later, until
1929, a free state within the German Reich. Today
this region, with its Eder-Stausee (reservoir), is
one of the most attractive tourist regions in
Germany. The wooded hills provide a perfect
setting for long rambles, the roads and tracks
are ideally suited for cycling tours and the
rivers and lakes permit visitors to practise
a wide variety of watersports.

Korbach ②
Korbach is a beautiful
old town with many
half-timbered houses.
Worth seeing are the
Gothic church of St
Kilian with its inter-
esting 14th-century
pulpit, and the
church of St Nicho-
las, with the
Baroque tomb of
Georg Friedrich
von Waldeck
(1692).

Frankenberg ⑤
This small town is brimming
with half-timbered houses.
The town hall (1509), also
half-timbered, has humorous
polychrome wood-carvings.
The Gothic Marienkirche with
its 15th-century wall paintings
is also worth visiting.

Pac

| 0 km | | 10 |
| 0 miles | | 10 |

KEY

▦▦▦	Motorway
▮▮▮▮	Suggested route
▦▦▦	Scenic road
═══	Other road
───	River, lake
☀	Viewpoint

Bad Arolsen ①
Both the sculptor Christian Daniel Rach and the painter Wilhelm von Kaulbach were born in this spa town, and they are commemorated in two museums. The star attraction, however, is the Baroque castle (1713–28) of the von Waldeck family, designed by Julius Ludwig Rothweil.

Höxter

Warburg

Twiste

Diemelstadt

Watter

Warme Bach

Wolfhagen

Eder-Stausee

Eder

Fritzlar

Bad Hersfeld

Wohra

Marburg

Waldeck ③
The old fortress of Waldeck is now a hotel. It offers superb views over the Eder-Stausee reservoir and the small town of Waldeck with its 18th-century half-timbered houses. The Gothic town church has a high altar (c.1500), devoted to the Virgin Mary.

TIPS FOR VISITORS

Length of route: *110 km (68 miles).*

Stopping-off points: *There are many good cafés and restaurants in every town along the route.*

Further attractions: *Cruises and ferries run on the Edersee. A viewing platform on top of the Peterskopf hill, near Hemfurth, can be reached by electric train.*

Bad Wildungen ④
This popular spa town has many charming half-timbered houses. The church has a priceless altar painted with scenes of the Passion by Konrad von Soest (1403).

Projecting gate of the Baroque Stadtschloss in Fulda

Fulda ❹

Road map C5. 🏠 *60,000.* 🚉
ℹ️ *Schlossstr. 1 (0661-10 23 26).*

FULDA'S HISTORY began in March 744, when Sturmius, a pupil of St Boniface, laid the foundation stone for the Benedictine abbey. Ten years later the body of St Boniface, who had been murdered by Frisian pagans, was laid to rest here. The town, which grew around the abbey, experienced its heyday during the Baroque period, and a new Baroque building, designed by Johann Dietzenhofer, was built in 1704–12 on the foundations of the old abbey. The **Dom St Salvator und Bonifatius** is a triple-nave basilica with a dome above the nave intersection, a monumental eastern façade and a shrine with the saint's relics under the high altar, in the western section.

Opposite the cathedral stands the **Stadtschloss** (former episcopal palace), a shoe-shaped edifice, built by Johann Dietzenhofer and Andreas Gallasini, with richly decorated Baroque and Rococo interiors. Particularly noteworthy are the Kaisersaal (imperial hall) on the ground floor, the magnificent Mond-saal (moon chamber, formerly the ballroom) and the charming Rococo-style Spiegelsaal (chamber of mirrors) on the first floor. Today, some of the palace chambers hold an impressive collection of porcelain. The palace complex includes a large landscaped garden and an orangery, which houses a café.

THE BROTHERS GRIMM

The two brothers are known around the world as collectors of German folk-tales, which were first published in 1812 and sub-sequently translated into most languages. Fairy-tales such as *Hänsel and Gretel*, *Cinderella* and *Little Red Riding Hood* have been favourites for generations of children. Above all, however, the brothers were scholars. In his *German Grammar*, published in 1819, Jacob Grimm proved that all German dialects sprang from a common origin, and thus laid the foundations of German philology. The Grimm Brothers also initiated the publication of the *Dictionary of the German Language*.

To the north of the Dom stands the round **Michaels-kirche**, a Carolingian chapel dating from 822, one of the oldest church buildings in Germany. Inside the church has a ring of eight columns and a crypt supported by a single column. The circular gallery, the long side nave and the western tower are 11th-century additions.

Other interesting sights in Fulda are the Baroque **Heilig-Geist-Kirche** (church of the Holy Spirit), built in 1729–33 by Andreas Gallasini, and the late-18th century parish church of St Blasius. In the 8th century, five abbeys were established on the four hills surrounding the town. On Petersberg stands the former Benedictine **Peterskirche**, from the 9th–15th centuries, with a Carolingian crypt.

Inside the church is one of Germany's oldest wall paintings, dating from 836–47.

Alsfeld ❺

Road map C4. 🏠 *18,000.* 🚉 ℹ️
Obergasse 6 (06631-18 21 65). 🌐
Pfingstfest (Whitsun), Stadt- und Heimat-fest (Aug), Historischer Markt (Sep).

THE FIRST historic records of Alsfeld date from the late 9th century. Today the town attracts visitors with its pretty old town with numerous 16th–17th century half-tim-bered houses. On the eastern side of the town square stands a grand late-Gothic **Rathaus** (town hall), built in 1512–16, and one of the finest examples of half-timbered structures anywhere in Germany. It has an attractive council chamber.

Half-timbered houses in Alsfeld

Other interesting features in the market square are the stone **Weinhaus**, with its distinctive stepped gable (1538), and the Renaissance **Hochzeitshaus** (wedding house), dating from 1565. Oposite the town hall stands the **Stumpfhaus** (1609), its façade beautifully decorated with wood carvings and paintings. From the town hall runs the picturesque Fulder Gasse, with the Gothic parish church **Walpurgiskirche** (13th–15th centuries), which has 15th-century wall paintings. In Rossmarkt stands the former Augustian **Dreifaltigkeits-kirche** (church of the Holy Trinity), from the 13th–15th centuries. It was from here that in 1522 the monk Tilemann Schnabel began to spread the Reformation in Alsfeld. The 18th-century **castle** in Altenburg, 2km (1 mile) from Alsfeld, enjoys a hilltop position.

Detail on the Rathaus, in Marburg

Marburg ❻

Road map C4. 🏯 *80,000.* 🚉
🛈 *Pilgrimstein 26 (06421-991 20).*
📅 *Marktfrühschoppen (Jul), 3-Tage Marburg (Jul), Elisabethmarkt (Oct).*

WHEN IN 1248 the county of Hesse broke away from Thuringia, Marburg became one of the most important seats of the landgraves. The first landgrave, Heinrich II, lived in the castle that towers over the town. The town's history is insepar-ably linked with the 13th-century figure of Elisabeth of Thuringia, wife of Ludwig IV, who devoted her life to the poor and died here. In 1527, Philipp the Magnanimous founded the first Protestant university in the Reich at Marburg. He also instigated the first Marburg Colloquy in 1529, to unify the Protestant faith. The "articles" presented by Martin Luther to Melanch-thon and Zwingli later formed the basis for the Augsburg Creed. Today, Marburg is a picturesque university town.

A tour of the town should start from the **Elisabethkir-che**, at the bottom of the hill. Built in 1235–83, it is (after Trier) Germany's second purely Gothic church. The interior is blessed with many valuable items. There is a large set of Gothic altars from the early 16th century, includ-ing the altars of St Elisabeth (1513) and of the Holy Family (1511). Next to the north choir entrance stands the statue of St Elisa-beth with a model of the church (1480). The choir contains the tomb of the Saint, positioned under the baldachin (c.1280). The vestry houses the greatest treasure, the reliquary of St Elisa-beth (1235–49). In the south choir is an interesting group of monuments to the Hessian landgraves, from the 13th–16th centuries.

The **Universitätsmuseum für Bildende Kunst** holds a collection of paintings prod-uced after 1500, with a pre-dominance of 19th- and 20th-century German artists. Around the market square stands a group of historic, half-tim-bered houses from the 14th–17th centuries. Particularly pretty are the Sonne (sun, No. 14), the Stiefel (boot, No. 17) and the house at No. 19. The Steinhaus (stone house, No. 18), built in 1318, is the oldest in Marburg, along with that at No. 13 Hirschgasse. At No. 16 Markt is the Renaissance Künstlerhaus (artists' house).

The Gothic portal of the Elisabeth-kirche in Marburg

High above the town (287 m/ 942 ft above the sea) towers the **Landgrafenschloss**, the landgraves' castle dating from the 10th–16th centuries. The two-storey Fürstenbau (dukes' building) has a large ducal chamber, dating from 1330. The Wilhelmsbau was built in 1492–8. It houses a museum of sacral art with mementos of the debate between Luther, Zwingli and Melanchthon.

🛐 **Elisabethkirche**
Elisabethstraße. 📞 *(06421) 655 73.*
🕐 *Apr–Sep: 9am–6pm; Oct: 9am–5pm; Nov–Mar: 10am–4pm Mon–Sat, 11:15am–4pm Sun.*

🏛 **Universitätsmuseum für Bildende Kunst**
Biegenstraße 11. 📞 *(06421) 282 23 55.* 🕐 *11am–1pm & 2–5pm Tue–Sun.*

🏰 **Landgrafenschloss und Universitätsmuseum für Kulturgeschichte im Wilhelmsbau**
Schloss 1. 📞 *(06421) 282 58 71.* 🕐 *Apr–Oct: 10am–6pm Tue–Sun; Nov–Mar: 11am–5pm Tue–Sun.*

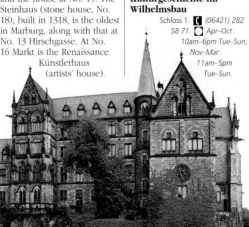

The vast Landgrafenschloss, high above Marburg

Gießen ❼

Road map C4. 👥 72,000. 🚉 ℹ️
Berliner Platz 2 (0641-30 624 89).

GIESSEN was granted town status in 1248, and in 1607 it acquired its university. In Brandplatz stands the partially reconstructed **Altes Schloss** (old palace), dating from the 14th–15th centuries. Now the home of the Oberhessisches Museum, it holds a large collection of art dating from the Gothic period to today.

The **Botanischer Garten** is one of Germany's oldest botanical gardens, established in 1609 for the purposes of scientific research. To the north of it stands the **Neues Schloss** (new palace), built in 1533–9 for Landgrave Philipp the Magnanimous. It miraculously escaped damage when the town was bombed in 1944. The Wallenfelssches Haus nearby houses interesting ethnological collections. The only remaining part of the Gothic **Pfarrkirche St Pankratius**, which was almost completely destroyed in 1944, is its tower, dating from 1500.

At No. 2 Georg-Schlosser-Straße is the **Burgmannenhaus**, an attractive half-timbered mansion dating from the 14th century.

Portal of the Altes Schloss in Gießen

Along with the old stable block in Dammstraße, it is the only half-timbered building that has survived to this day.

Wetzlar ❽

Road map C5. 👥 54,000. 🚉
ℹ️ *Domplatz 8 (06441-993 38).*

OCCUPYING A picturesque spot on the banks of the Lahn river, Wetzlar is overlooked by the ruins of the 12th-century **Kalsmunt** fortress. It was built for the Emperor Friedrich I Barbarossa (1122–90). Only parts of the tower remain intact. The **Dom** (Collegiate Church of St Mary) was begun in 897 but by the late 15th century had only been partly completed. The splendid western double portal has remained unusable for the last 500 years – although the iconography of the tympanum was finished, the stairs leading to the entrance were never built. If they had been built, they would have led not to the church's nave, but to a courtyard. Wetzlar's Dom is a rare, perhaps even unique surviving example of the typical appearance of most European churches in the mid-15th century. Inside the church are several interesting historic artifacts, including the statue of the *Madonna on the Moon Crescent* (mid-15th century) and a late-Renaissance *Crucifixion.*

In 1772, the young Johann Wolfgang von Goethe spent three months in Wetzlar working as an apprentice at the court of appeal. During this time he fell in love with Charlotte Buff, called Lotte, who was engaged to one of Goethe's friends. The **Lottehaus**, her former home, has a collection of items relating to Goethe and Lotte. It was the suicide of a friend, Karl Wilhelm Jerusalem, who lived in the 18th-century **Jerusalemhaus** at No. 5 Schillerplatz, that inspired Goethe to write his tragic novel, *The Sorrows of Young Werther* (1774). Jerusalem had suffered unrequited love, just like Goethe. The novel, which was published two years later, made Goethe famous around Europe, but it also unwittingly led many young men to commit suicide.

The Gothic south tower of the Dom in Wetzlar

Weilburg ❾

Road map B5. 👥 13,500. 🚉
ℹ️ *Mauerstraße 6 (06471-76 71).*

WEILBURG enjoys a particularly scenic location in a bend of the Lahn River. The town is dominated by the majestic Renaissance–Baroque **Schloss** of the Nassau-Weilburg family. The monumental castle complex was created in stages. Its main section dates from the Renaissance era; the east wing was built in 1533–9; the south and west wings in 1540–48 and the west tower in 1567. The northern part of the palace was completed in 1570–73. In the late-17th century, various Baroque additions were made, mainly to the interior of the castle. The 16th-century furnishings show the rich ornamentation typical of the German Renaissance. The **Obere Orangerie** (upper orangery), built in 1703–5 and today used for temporary exhibitions, and the **Hofkirche** (castle church), dating from 1707–13, are the work of Ludwig Rothwell. Terraces lead from the castle to the Lahn river, which is crossed by an 18th-century stone bridge. In Frankfurt-straße stands the **Heiliggrabkapelle** (Chapel of the Holy Sepulchre), dating from 1505.

Limburg

Road map B5. 🚶 *31,000.* 🚉
ℹ️ *Hospitalstraße 2 (06431-61 66).*

L IMBURG'S history dates back to the 8th century. In 1821, the town became the see of a newly created diocese.

The **Dom** (collegiate cathedral church of St George) towers high above the Lahn river. This monumental building, whose style combines late-Romanesque and early French-Gothic, was erected in 1190–1250. Its well-proportioned interior contains a rich variety of historic artifacts, including some 13th-century wall paintings in the presbytery and the transept, a font dating from the same period and the tombstone of Konrad Kurzbold, who founded the first church on this site.

To the south of the Dom stands the **Burg** (castle), an irregular structure built in the 13th–16th centuries. It houses the interesting **Diözesanmuseum** (Diocese museum).

Limburg has many original examples of beautiful half-timbered buildings. The houses at No. 6 Römer, No. 6 Kolpingstraße, No. 4 Kleine Rütsche and No. 11 Korn-

Romanesque–Gothic wall paintings in the Dom in Limburg

markt date from the last decade of the 13th century. Near the 14th-century **Alte Lahnbrücke** (old Lahn bridge), with its defensive towers, stands a mansion belonging to the Cistercians of Eberbach. The post-Franciscan Sebastiankirche (church of St Sebastian) dates from the 14th and 18th centuries.

Bad Homburg ⓫

Road map C5. 🚶 *52,000.* 🚉
ℹ️ *Kurhaus, Louisenstraße 58 (06172-17 81 10).* 🎭 *Fugato (Sep).*

B AD HOMBURG grew up around a fortress whose earliest records date back to 1180. Friedrich II von Hessen-Homburg initiated the conversion of the medieval castle into the **Schloss**, a Baroque

palace built in 1678–86. It features a magnificent Festsaal (ballroom) and Spiegelkabinett (hall of mirrors). The only part of the former complex remaining today is the 14th-century Weißer Turm (white tower). Following the annexation of Hesse-Homburg by Prussia in 1866, the palace became the favourite summer residence of the royal (and, from 1871, of the imperial) family.

Along with Baden-Baden and Wiesbaden, Homburg was one of Germany's most fashionable spas, and today the town reflects its former splendour. The **Kurpark**, a landscaped park established in 1854–67, was designed by Peter Joseph Lenné.

The **Spielbank** (1838), in Brunnenallee claims to be the oldest casino in the world. Built in 1887–90, the **Kaiser-Wilhelm-Bad** is still used as the main bath complex for therapeutic treatments. An Orthodox chapel, designed by Leontyi Mikholayevich Benois specifically for the Russian Orthodox nobility, was completed in 1899.

ENVIRONS: Saalburg, 7 km (4 miles) to the northwest, has a Roman fortress, which was completely reconstructed in 1898–1901. The fortress formed part of the *limes*, the fortified border that separated the Roman Empire from its Germanic neighbours from the 1st to 3rd century AD.

The grand edifice of the Kaiser-Wilhelm-Bad in the Kurpark, Bad Homburg

Eltville

Road map B5. 🏛 *17,000.* 🚌 🛈
Schmittstr. 2 (06123-90 98 20). ⚑
Biedermeier- und Sektfest (Jul).

In the 2nd century, the area that is now the old town was a Roman *latifundium,* a large agricultural estate. In 1332, Eltville was granted town status. Part of the Mainz diocese, it is today known for its excellent sparkling wine.

In 1337–45 the **Burg** (castle) was extended at the request of Archbishop Heinrich von Virneburg. The east wing of the castle was added in 1682–3 by Giovanni Angelo Barell. The only part of it remaining today is the fivestorey residential tower; the rest of the building is a picturesque ruin. In the tower are original 14th-century wall paintings and friezes.

The twin-naved **Pfarrkirche St Peter und St Paul** (parish church) was built in 1350–1430. The vestibule has wellpreserved wall paintings (1405) showing scenes from the Last Judgement. The town boasts several attractive mansions, including Hof Langwerth von Simmern (1773), Stockheimer Hof (1550) and Gräflich-Eltzscher Hof (16th–17th century).

Crest of the Hessische Staatsweingüter-Vinothek, in Eltville

Wiesbaden

Road map C5. 🏛 *270,000.* 🚌
🛈 *Markstr. 6 (0611-172 97 80).*
⚑ *Internationale Maifestspiele (May),
Theatrium (Jun).*

Wiesbaden is the modern capital of Hesse. Highly valued as a spa by the Romans, who exploited the healing properties of its waters, the town grew from a small settlement known as *aquae mattiacorum* after the Germanic tribe of the Mattiacs. In 1774 the Nassau-Usingen family chose Wiesbaden as their residence. This, as well as the subsequent rapid

The Baroque Biebrich Palace, south of Wiesbaden

growth of the town as a spa resort in the 19th century, laid the foundations for its lasting prosperity. Today, the town is still dominated by large-scale developments carried out in the spirit and style of Classicism and Historicism.

The **Stadtschloss** (municipal castle), today the seat of the state parliament, was built in 1835–41. In Schlossplatz the Neo-Renaissance **Marktkirche,** built in 1853–62, soars above the town's other buildings. In front of the church stands a statue of Wilhelm I the Great von Nassau-Oranien. The oldest building in the town is the **Altes Rathaus** (old town hall), dating from 1610. In Wilhelmstraße is the imposing Neo-Renaissance and Neo-Baroque **Hessisches Staatstheater** (state theatre). It was built in 1892–4 for Kaiser Wilhelm II to the designs of the theatre

architects Felder and Heller. Adjacent to the Marktkirche is the attractive Kurhauskolonnade (spa house colonnade). It was erected in 1825 and is the longest colonnade in Europe. The early 20th-century **Kurhaus** (spa house) itself, with its grand façade and portico, is the work of Friedrich Thiersch. Inside is the original **Spielbank** (casino), where Fyodor Dostoyevsky and Richard Wagner tried their luck at the tables.

To the south of the town centre stands **Schloss Biebrich**, where the counts von Nassau-Usingen resided until the early 19th century, when they moved to the newly built palace in the town centre. The Schloss was built in stages during the 18th century. The north pavilion was built first, in 1700, followed nine years later by the south pavilion. The wings, which join the two pavilions, and the central rotunda were added during the first two decades of the 18th century. Finally, the two external wings were added in 1734–44, creating an overall horseshoe layout. The interior is richly furnished, predominantly in Baroque-Rococo style.

On the northern outskirts of the town is a large hill, the Neroberg, whose summit can be reached by funicular railway. At the top is the socalled **Griechische Kapelle** (Greek chapel). Built in 1847–55 by Philipp Hoffmann, it served as a mausoleum for Princess Elisabeth von Nassau, the niece of Alexander I Tsar of Russia, who died young.

The attractive façade of Hessisches Staatstheater in Wiesbaden

The ornate Gothic portal of Pfarrkirche St Valentin, in Kiedrich

Kiedrich ⓮

Road map B5. 👥 3,400. 🚉
🛈 Markstr. 27 (06123-90 50 11).

THE EARLIEST recorded mention of Kiedrich was in the mid-10th century, in a document produced by the Archbishop Friedrich of Mainz. One of the town's main attractions is the **Pfarrkirche St Valentin**, a gem of Gothic architecture. The church was built in stages, beginning with the main hall (1380–90). The west tower was added in the early 15th century and the light, lofty choir in 1451–81. Some time later the central nave was raised to the level of the choir, creating a row of galleries above the aisles, and at the same time the magnificent star vaults were created. The whole project was financed from donations made by countless pilgrims who came to pray to the relics of St Valentine, kept here since 1454. A statue of the saint adorns the western portal. The early 15th-century tympanum depicts the *Annunciation* (on the left) and the *Coronation of the Virgin Mary* (on the right);

above is an image of *God the Father giving His Blessing*, with two archangels playing musical instruments. Inside, the church harbours an incredible wealth of ancient art treasures. The high altar and St Catherine's altar in the south aisle date from the late-Renaissance period. The magnificent Gothic stalls were created in 1510, while the church organ is one of the oldest in Germany, with pipes made in 1310. Next to the parish church stands a late-Gothic, two-storey funeral chapel built in 1445.

Kiedrich has several interesting old mansion houses, such as the Schwalbacher Hof (1732). The **Rathaus** (town hall), with its steep roof, is evocative of the late-Gothic style, although it was built much later (1585–6).

ENVIRONS: Five km (3 miles) west of Kiedrich, in Östrich, is **Kloster Eberbach**, a former Cistercian abbey. This vast complex, built between the 12th and 14th centuries, was once home to nearly 300 monks and is one of the best-preserved medieval monasteries in Germany. The church interior provided the setting for some of the scenes in the film *The Name of the Rose*, based on the novel by Umberto Eco. The Cistercians used to have their own vineyards here, and today the

abbey buildings are used by the Hessian Wine Co-operative to press, ferment, store and sell Ebenberger Steinberg, a famous white Rheingau wine.

A short way to the west, in **Winkel**, stands the Baroque castle of Reichardshausen, which in the early 19th century was the home of Princess Luise von Nassau.

🏠 **Kloster Eberbach** ☎ (06723) 99 32 99. 🕐 11:30am–10pm daily. 📷

Rüdesheim ⓯

Road map B5. 👥 10,000. 🚉
🛈 Geisenheimerstr. 22 (06722-194 33). 🎆 Fireworks (Jul), Weinfest (Aug).

RÜDESHEIM, enjoying a picturesque location on the banks of the Rhine, has a long history going back to Roman times. The town is famous for its main street, the **Drosselgasse**, which is lined with countless wine bars and shops. There are also the remains of three castles: the **Boosenburg**, the **Vorderburg** and the 12th-century **Brömserburg**. The Brömserburg's keep today houses a wine museum.

Rüdesheim also has several historic mansions, including the half-timbered Brömserhof (1559) with a collection of musical instruments, and the early 16th-century Klunkhardshof. Above the town towers the **Niederwalddenkmal**, a statue of Germania, 10.5 m (34 ft) high, built to commemorate victory in the Franco-Prussian War of 1870–71, which resulted in German unification. The monument affords excellent views of Bingen and the Rhine valley.

Gabled and half-timbered houses in Drosselgasse, in Rüdesheim

Frankfurt am Main ⑯

FRANKFURT, nicknamed "Mainhattan" and "Chicago am Main" because of its skyscrapers, is one of the main economic and cultural centres of both Germany and Europe. The headquarters of many major banks and newspaper publishers are based here, including those of the *Frankfurter Allgemeine Zeitung*, one of Europe's most influential newspapers. The city's International Book Fair is the world's largest event of its kind. Goethe was born in Frankfurt, and the Johann-Wolfgang-Goethe-Universität is one of Germany's most famous universities. The city also boasts magnificent art collections.

The Neo-Renaissance façade of the Alte Oper

🔲 Alte Oper
Opernplatz 8. 📞 *(069) 34 04 00.*
The monumental old opera house stands near the Stock Exchange. Built in 1872–80, it was completely burned down during World War II. Subsequently rebuilt, it is today used as a conference centre. Its façade and decorations are a fine imitation of the Italian Renaissance style.

🚌 Eschenheimer Turm
Große Eschenheimer Straße
The Eschenheimer Turm, at the corner of Hochstraße, presents a silhouette typical of old Frankfurt. A relic of the medieval town's fortifications, it was designed by Klaus Mengoz; construction began in 1400 and was completed in 1428 by Madern Gerthener. The façade of the tower features

Putti with model ship, at the front of the Börse

many attractive bay windows; it also has two reliefs depicting eagles, the symbol of the German empire and the city of Frankfurt.

🚌 Börse
Börsenplatz.
According to historical records, local merchants founded the town's first Stock Exchange in 1558. The new building, designed by Heinrich Burnitz and Oskar Sommer, was erected in 1864–79. It has been used again by stockbrokers since 1957, and is open to the public. Like the old opera house, the stock exchange is designed in Neo-Renaissance style.

🚌 Hauptwache
An der Hauptwache.
Built in 1671, the Hauptwache was originally a guardhouse. In 1730 it was turned into a prison. Dismantled stone by stone during the construction of the town's underground system, it was reassembled in its original form following the completion of the project. Since 1904 the Hauptwache has been a chic café and a popular meeting place.

🚌 Goethehaus
Großer Hirschgraben 23. 📞 *(069) 13 88 00.* ⏰ *9am–4pm Mon–Fri, 10am–4pm Sat & Sun.* 🈯
Southwest of the Hauptwache is Johann Wolfgang Goethe's family home. The great German poet, novelist and dramatist was born here on 28 August 1749. The house, along with many other buildings in Frankfurt, was totally destroyed in World War II, but later lovingly restored. Its interior was reconstructed to represent the style typical of the mid- to late- 18th century. Goethe lived in this house until 1775, when he moved to Weimar. The desk at which he wrote his early works, including the first version of *Götz von Berlichingen* (1771), *The Sorrows of Young Werther* (1774) and the first version of *Egmont* (1774), has been preserved.

The adjacent building now houses the Goethemuseum. Opened in 1997, the museum recreates the atmosphere of the 1750–1830 period, and holds a collection of items related to the writer. There is an excellent library, which contains some of his writings.

The distinctive Neo-Classical rotunda of the Paulskirche

Portal of the Goethehaus, with the ancestral family crest

Paulskirche

Paulsplatz. *(069) 21 23 85 89.*
10am–5pm daily.

The distinctive Neo-Classical rotunda of the church was begun in 1786 but not completed until 1833, due to continuous hostilities with France. Today, however, this building is no longer thought of, or indeed used as, a church. After the first, albeit ill-fated, German National Assembly met here following the revolutionary upheavals of 1848–9, the church became a symbol of republican and liberal Germany. The Paulskirche now serves as a venue for many important events. Each year the awards ceremony for the prestigious German Publishers' Peace Prize takes place here.

Römerberg

Located in the centre of Frankfurt's old town, this square contains the Gerechtigkeitsbrunnen (fountain of justice). Its highlight, however, is the **Römer** (literally the Roman). So-called after the remains of ancient settlements, it is a complex of 15th- to 18th-century houses, including the Altes Rathaus (old town hall), which were rebuilt after World War II. Opposite is a group of half-timbered houses, commonly referred to as Ostzeile. The Steinernes Haus (stone house) was originally built in 1464 for a Cologne silk merchant. Recently reconstructed, it is now the home of the Frankfurter Kunstverein (artists' league).

VISITORS' CHECKLIST

Road map C5. 660,000.
Hauptbahnhof (069-21 23 88 49); Kaiserstr. 56 (069-21 23 88 00). Dippemesse (spring, autumn), Wäldchestag (Whitsun), Kunsthandwerk Heute (May/Jun), Mainfest (Aug), Book Fair (Oct), Christkindlmarkt (Dec).

The Ostzeile on the Römerberg, one of the symbols of Frankfurt

FRANKFURT CITY CENTRE

KEY

Post Office
Church
Parking

0 metres   75
0 yards   75

🏛 Jüdisches Museum

Untermainkai 14–15. ☎ *(069) 21 23 50 00.* ⏰ *10am–5pm Tue & Thu–Sun, 10am–8pm Wed.* ♿

The Jewish community of Frankfurt was the second largest in Germany, after that of Berlin. This museum, in the former Rothschild Palace, documents the rich cultural heritage of Frankfurt's Jews.

⛪ St Leonhardkirche

Alte Mainzer Gasse.

Close to the banks of the Rhine stands the church of St Leonhard, a fine example of Gothic and Romanesque architecture. A five-naved hall-church with an elongated choir, it was built in stages in the 13th and 15th centuries. Inside are many treasures, including at the front of the main nave a copy of Leonardo da Vinci's *Last Supper* by Hans Holbein the Elder, from 1501. Next to it is St Mary's altar, created by master craftsmen from Antwerp in 1515–20. On the north wall of the choir visitors can see a fresco depicting the *Tree of Life and the Apostles* (1536) by Hans Dietz.

🏛 Historisches Museum

Saalgasse 19. ☎ *(069) 21 23 55 99.* ⏰ *10am–5pm Tue, Thu–Sun, 10am–8pm Wed.* ♿

The new building housing the history museum was finished in 1972. The museum has an interesting display of items relating to Frankfurt's history, including a fascinating model of the medieval town, a collection of local prehistoric finds and several decorative

The early-Gothic Nikolaikirche, in Frankfurt's Römerberg

architectural fragments from buildings that were destroyed during World War II.

The adjacent building is the Saalhof, which dates back to the time of the Emperor Friedrich I Barbarossa (1122–90). In 1333, the building passed into private hands and from then on it frequently changed its appearance.

⛪ Nikolaikirche

Römerberg.

The twin-naved church of St Nicholas, also known as Alte Nikolaikirche, was consecrated in 1290. Used as a court church until the late 15th century, it now serves a Lutheran congregation. Popular attractions are its many statues of St Nicholas (Santa Claus) and the 40-bell carillon, which twice a day plays German folk songs.

🏛 Kunsthalle Schirn

Römerberg. ☎ *(069) 299 88 20.* ⏰ *11am–7pm Tue & Sun, 11am–10pm Wed–Sat.* ♿

One of Europe's most prestigious exhibition buildings, the Kunsthalle opened in 1986. It hosts temporary art exhibitions featuring archaeological themes and the work of old masters and contemporary artists.

⛪ Kaiserdom

Domplatz 14. ☎ *(069) 297 03 20.* ⏰ *Mar–Oct: 9am–6pm Mon–Sat, 3–6pm Sun; Nov–Feb: 9am–5pm Mon–Sat, 3–5pm Sun.* 🕒 *3pm daily.* **Dommuseum** ☎ *(069) 29 92 29.* ⏰ *9am–5pm Tue–Fri, 11am–5pm Sat & Sun.*

Near the archaeological park, where the ruins of a Carolingian fortress have been unearthed, stands the imperial cathedral, used for the coronation of German kings from 1356, and of Holy Roman Emperors from 1562. The cathedral, dedicated to St Bartholomew and Charlemagne, was built during the 13th, 14th and 15th centuries, on the site of a Carolingian chapel. It has several priceless masterpieces of Gothic art, including the magnificent 15th-century Maria-Schlaf-Altar and a high altar dating from the second half of the 15th century. The choir has original 14th-century stalls; above these, a fresco painted in 1427 depicts scenes from the life of the cathedral's patron saint, Bartholomew.

The Dom's huge tower affords magnificent views of the town. In the cloisters is the Dommuseum with an interesting collection of liturgical objects, sacred art and precious artifacts.

🏛 Museum für Moderne Kunst

Domstraße 10. ☎ *(069) 21 23 04 47.* ⏰ *10am–5pm Tue & Thu–Sun, 10am–8pm Wed.* ♿

The modern art museum occupies a building that looks like a slice of cake. It was designed by Hans Hollein in 1989–92. The museum's collection represents all the major artistic trends from the 1960s until the present day, and includes works by Roy Lichtenstein, Andy Warhol

The magnificent late-Gothic high altar in the Kaiserdom

Hollein's modern design, housing the Museum für Moderne Kunst

and Claes Oldenburg. Temporary exhibitions held here focus on multi-media shows, incorporating photography and video art.

⚏ Ikonen-Museum

Brückenstraße 3–7. ▐ (069) 21 23 62 61. ⏰ 10am–5pm Tue & Thu–Sun, 10am–8pm Wed.

The museum of icons holds an extensive collection of Russian-Orthodox icons from the 16th–19th centuries. It is housed in the Deutschordenshaus, originally built in 1709–15 by Maximilian von Welsch for the Order of the Teutonic Knights. The present building is a faithful copy of the earlier Baroque three-wing structure, which was destroyed in World War II. Hidden inside is the 14th-century Teutonic Church of St Mary, which has attractive original altars and 14th- to 17th-century wall paintings.

The Deutsches Architekturmuseum, in Schaumainkai

⛫ Museum für Angewandte Kunst

Schaumainkai 17. ▐ (069) 21 23 40 37. ⏰ 10am–5pm Tue & Thu–Sun, 10am–8pm Wed.

The museum of applied arts was opened in 1983, in a building designed by Richard Meier. He used a Biedermeier house, the Villa Metzler, and added a modern wing. The museum has a striking collection of around 30,000 objects of applied art from Europe and Asia.

Nearby, in a villa with a large garden in Schaumainkai, is the small but fascinating Museum für Völkerkunde (ethnography museum).

⛫ Deutsches Architekturmuseum

Schaumainkai 43. ▐ (069) 21 23 84 71. ⏰ 10am–5pm Tue & Thu–Sun, 10am–8pm Wed.

One of the most interesting museums in the Schaumainkai complex is undoubtedly the museum of architecture, opened in 1984 in an avant-garde building designed by Oswald Mathias Ungers. The museum has a permanent collection as well as temporary exhibitions concentrating mainly on developments in 20th-century architecture.

Nearby, at No 41 Schaumainkai, is the Deutsches Filmmuseum, which holds documents and objects relating to the art of film-making and the development of film technology. The museum has its own cinema, which shows old and often long-forgotten films.

⛪ Liebieghaus

Schaumainkai 71. ▐ (069) 21 23 07 01. ⏰ 10am–5pm Tue & Thu–Sun, 10am–8pm Wed.

The Liebieghaus was built in 1896 for the Czech industrialist Baron Heinrich Liebieg. Today it houses a museum of sculpture, with works ranging from antiquity through to Mannerism, Baroque and Rococo. The museum also has superb examples of ancient Egyptian and Far Eastern art, as well as works from the Middle Ages and the Renaissance. Its highlights are the works of Neo-Classical masters such as Antonio Canova, Bertel Thorwaldsen and Johann Heinrich Dannecker.

The Liebieghaus, home of the museum of sculpture

⛫ Naturmuseum Senckenberg

Senckenberganlage 25. ▐ (069) 754 20. ⏰ 9am–5pm Mon, Tue, Thu & Fri, 9am–8pm Wed, 9am–6pm Sat & Sun.

This museum, near the university, is one of the best natural history museums in Germany. Besides a vast collection of plants and animals, including dinosaur skeletons, it contains human and animal mummies from Egypt.

ENVIRONS: Hanau, 30 km (19 miles) east of Frankfurt, is the birthplace of the brothers Wilhelm and Jakob Grimm. An exhibition devoted to their lives and work is held at the local history museum, in Philippsruhe, a Baroque palace.

Frankfurt – Städelsches Kunstinstitut

THE FOUNDER of this excellent museum, the banker Johann Friedrich Städel, bequeathed his art collection to the town in 1815. He also founded an art college for the training of new artists and the upkeep of the collection. Since then, the museum has grown through acquisitions and donations. It moved to a Neo-Renaissance building in 1878, on the picturesque "museum embankment" by the Main. In the 1920s it acquired the Hohenzollern collection from Sigmaringen. The building gained a new wing in 1990 (designer Gustav Peichl), and was renovated in 1995–9.

Portrait of a Woman (c.1480)
Simonetta Vespucci, mistress of Giuliano Medici, is the subject of this painting by Sandro Botticelli. Her pendant belonged at the time to the Medici collection.

Ecce Homo
Members of the family who commissioned this painting from Hieronymus Bosch also originally figured in it, but they were later painted over and now only a few figures are partially visible.

First floor

★ **Lucca Madonna**
This small painting by Jan van Eyck, which evokes an intimate and intensely private atmosphere, takes its name from its former owner, Charles Ludwig de Bourbon, Duke of Lucca.

KEY

- 19th-century paintings
- 20th-century paintings
- German, Dutch and Flemish 17th- and 18th-century paintings
- Italian, French and Spanish 17th- and 18th-century paintings
- German and Dutch 14th–16th-century paintings
- Italian 14th–16th-century paintings

Around 100,000 prints and drawings, dating from the 14th century to the present day and making up one of Germany's most valuable collections, are exhibited in this exhibition hall.

Main entrance

Library

★ The Geographer (1669)
Although the signature on the painting is not genuine, there is no doubt that this picture, depicting a scholar at work, is the work of Jan Vermeer van Delft.

VISITORS' CHECKLIST

Schaumainkai 63.
(069) 605 09 80.
www.staedelmuseum.de
10am–5pm Tue & Thu–Sun,
10am–8pm Wed. (free Wed.)

Second floor

★ Blinding of Samson (1636)
Rembrandt's dramatic painting depicts the violent blinding of Samson by the Philistines after Delilah cut off his hair.

GALLERY GUIDE
The ground floor of the building houses the collection of Dutch and German prints and drawings, the hall where these are exhibited, a bookstore and a museum shop. The first floor is devoted to 19th- and 20th-century art and the second floor to the Old Masters.

Isle of Cythera (c.1710)
Jean-Antoine Watteau painted three pictures on this theme, inspired by Dancourt's play The Three Sisters. *The museum holds the earliest of the three, which shows a Flemish influence.*

Ground floor

Orchestra Players (1870–74)
Edgar Degas, not completely satisfied with his painting, retrieved it from its owner. In 1874, he cropped it on three sides, added a bit at the top and repainted the entire painting.

STAR EXHIBITS

★ Lucca Madonna

★ Blinding of Samson

★ The Geographer

Darmstadt ⑰

Road map C5. 🚗 138,000. 🚉
🛈 Hauptbahnhof (06151-13 27 82);
Luisenplatz 5 (06151-13 27 81).
🎭 Frühlingsfest (Mar/Apr), Heinerfest
(early Jul), Herbsfest (Oct).

THE EARLIEST historical
records of Darmstadt,
which was probably named
after Darimund, a Frankonian
settler, date from the 12th
century. Until 1479, the castle
and the town belonged to the
Counts von Katzenelnbogen,
and later to Hessian landgraves. In 1567, the Landgraves von Hessen-Darmstadt
chose Darmstadt as their residence, and they continued to
live here until 1918.

To the north of the old
town stands the **Residenzschloss**, initially a ducal
palace, and from 1806 residence of the Landgraves von
Hessen-Darmstadt. The Re-
naissance-Baroque complex is
centred around three courtyards. The earlier medieval
castle, which stood on the
same site, burned down in
1546. The present palace was
created in stages, with its
earliest parts, the Renaissance
wings, dating from 1567–97.
The Glockenbau has a 35-bell
carillon which can be heard
every half hour; it was completed after the Thirty Years'
War, in 1663. Further modifications, planned in 1715–30,
were never completed. Two
Baroque wings, the so-called

Neubau or Neuschloss (new
castle), surround older buildings to the south and west.
The Schloss was bombed in
World War II and subsequently rebuilt. Today it houses the
provincial and university
library, while the Glockenbau
is home to the fascinating
Schlossmuseum (castle
museum). As well as a
splendid collection of
coaches and furniture,
it contains the famous
Darmstadt Madonna
(1526), by the painter
Hans Holbein.

Also worth seeing,
the late-Renaissance
Rathaus (town hall),
built in 1588–90, sur-
vived World War II.
The 15th-century choir
of the **Stadtkirche** has
an enormous monu-
ment (1587) to Magda-
lena zur Lippe, first
wife of Landgrave
Georg I the Pious. To
the southwest of the
Stadtkirche stands the
Pädagog, built in
1629 as an educa-
tional establishment.

To the north of the Schloss
is the **Hessisches Landesmuseum** (regional museum
of Hesse), erected in 1892–
1905. Its collection includes
artifacts dating from the Roman era to the 20th century.
The museum also has an
excellent natural history section, whose exhibits include
the impressive skeleton of a

mammoth as well as birds of
every species native to
southern Hesse. Set in the
park behind the museum is
the Baroque Prinz-Georg-
Palais (1710), which houses
the **Großherzogliche Porzellansammlung**, an extensive porcelain collection.

The last Grand Duke of
Hesse, Ernst Ludwig, was
an important patron of the
Jugendstil, the German
Art Nouveau move-
ment. He initiated the
building of an exhib-
ition and residential
complex, the
Mathildenhöhe,
which was established
in 1901 in the grounds
of the former ducal
park, to serve the
existing artists' colony
led by Joseph Maria
Olbrich. Olbrich
designed the Ernst-
Ludwig-Haus, which
now houses the
**Museum Künst-
lerkolonie**, an ex-

**Statue on the door
of the Behrens-
Haus in Darmstadt**

hibition space for
the colony's artists.
He also created sev-
eral villas in Prinz-Christian-
Weg and the famous **Hochzeitsturm** (wedding tower),
erected in 1907–8 to celebrate
the Grand Duke's wedding.
The **Behrens-Haus**, designed
by the Hamburg architect
Peter Behrens, is sober in contrast. The Orthodox church of
St Mary Magdalene was built
in 1897–9 by the Russian architect Leontin Mikolayevich
Benois, in honour of Alice,
wife of the last tsar of Russia
and sister of Ernst Ludwig.

🏛 **Schlossmuseum**
Residenzschloss. 📞 (06151) 240 35.
⏰ 10am–1pm & 2–5pm Mon–Thu,
10am–1pm Sat & Sun.
🏛 **Hessisches
Landesmuseum**
Friedensplatz 1. 📞 (06151) 16 57
03. ⏰ 10am–5pm Tue & Thu–Sat,
10am–9pm Wed, 11am–5pm Sun. 🔲
🏛 **Museum
Künstlerkolonie**
Olbrichweg/Bauhausweg. 📞 (06151)
13 20 23. ⏰ 10am–5pm Tue–Sun. 🔲
🏛 **Großherzogliche
Porzellansammlung**
Schlossgartenstr. 10. 📞 (06151) 71
32 33. ⏰ 10am–1pm & 2–5pm
Mon–Thu, 10am–1pm Sat & Sun.

Hochzeitsturm and Orthodox Church in Mathildenhöhe, Darmstadt

The Carolingian Torhalle (gate-house) of the Kloster (abbey) in Lorsch

Lorsch 🔞

Road map B5. 🏛 *10,700.* ℹ *Rathaus, Marktplatz 1 (06251-596 74 00).*

THIS SMALL town is mainly known for the **Kloster**, a Benedictine abbey first founded in 764 by Chrodegang of Metz and one of the most important cultural and intellectual centres in Europe in the Carolingian era. It reached the peak of its power in the 8th–13th centuries, before being sold to the Archbishop of Mainz in 1228. The Benedictines were forced to leave, and in their place the Cistercians arrived. The monastery was dissolved during the Reformation, and in 1621 the Spanish Army destroyed and plundered the greater part of the complex.

Fragments of the 13th-century nave, the towers and the gate-house, dating from c.790, are all that has survived. The original 8th-century church, a basilica without transept, burned down in 1090 and was rebuilt in the 12th century. The original crypt is the burial place of Ludwig II the German, the first ruler of the Eastern Franks. The **Torhalle** (gate-house) is one of the most important architectural remains of the Carolingian period, and it was listed as a UNESCO World Heritage Site in 1992. Its lower section is made up of three arcades, equal in height and width, modelled on Roman triumphal arches. The first-floor

quarters above were probably used as a guest room or courtroom, and from the 14th century they served as a chapel. Remains of the original wall paintings are still visible here. The façade is decorated with red and white stone mosaics, which were inspired by Franco-Merovingian art. The vertical divides, created by pilasters and entablature, are copies of ancient designs – an architectural feature typical of the Carolingian Renaissance. The chapel's high roof and vaults date from the 14th century.

Michelstadt 🔞

Road map B5. 🏛 *16,000.* ℹ *Marktplatz 1 (06061-194 33).* 🎪 *Bienenmarkt (May).*

MICHELSTADT, set among the hills of the Odenwald, is first mentioned in historical records in 741. From the 13th century the town belonged to the von Erbach family (the future Counts von Erbach).

The town has preserved many historic half-timbered houses and presents a typical image of medieval Germany. The 16th-century **Kellerei** is built around the remains of an earlier castle dating from 970. It now houses a regional museum. The sight most popular with photographers is the half-timbered **Rathaus** (town hall), dating from 1484, with its three towers and an

open ground-floor gallery. Nearby stands the late-Gothic, 15th-century **Pfarrkirche St Michael** (parish church of St Michael). Inside are some interesting epitaphs including the double tombstone of Philipp I and Georg I, dating from the late 15th century. A true rarity is the 18th-century **synagogue**, which escaped being burned by the National Socialists in 1938.

In the Steinbach district of Michelstadt stands the **Einhardsbasilika**, a church dating from around 821. The first church built on this site, at the initiative of Einhard, a courtier of Charlemagne, was a small, pillared and vaulted basilica with a short choir ending with a rounded apse. Under the eastern section is a crypt. The parts which remain to this day include the main nave, the north aisle with an apse and the crypt which holds precious religious relics.

ENVIRONS: In **Fürstenau**, situated about 1 km (0.6 mile) northwest of Michelstadt, is a beautiful complex including the Altschloss (old palace), remodelled from a medieval castle, the Neuschloss (new palace), dating from 1810, the park and its garden pavilions.

Erbach, 5 km (3miles) south of Michelstadt, became famous as a centre for the art of ivory carving. In No. 1 Otto-Glenz-Straße is the Deutsches Elfenbeinmuseum (German ivory museum), which is devoted to this craft. Other attractions in this town include the overbearing Baroque Schloss (castle) and its interesting art collection.

The Carolingian Einhardsbasilika in Michelstadt-Steinbach

NORTH RHINE-WESTPHALIA

ORIGINALLY *consisting of two distinct provinces with somewhat diverging histories, the region of North Rhine-Westphalia today has its own strong identity. It encompasses the vast valley of the Ruhr river, rich in mineral deposits, where over the past 200 years huge conurbations have developed, comprising dozens of industrial cities that are gradually merging into one another.*

As a province, the North Rhineland, situated along the lower Rhine valley, goes back to Roman times. In the Middle Ages most of this area was ruled by the Bishops of Köln. The North Rhineland cities grew and prospered thanks to their trade links, and in the 19th century they became major centres of mining and heavy industry.

Westphalia forms the eastern part of the land. Once a Saxon territory, its history was often intertwined with that of the Rhineland. Only its western end has been heavily industrialized.

North Rhine-Westphalia is not the largest of the German regions, but with a population of nearly 18 million it is the most heavily populated one. It is often thought that the region, and in particular the heavily industrialized Ruhr valley, has little to offer to its visitors, but this is a mistaken belief. Its splendid past has left many priceless historic monuments and more recently, thanks to great investment, its industrial cities have transformed themselves into attractive cultural centres.

The history of towns such as Bonn, Aachen, Cologne (Köln) and Xanten goes back to Roman times, and they have preserved much of their ancient heritage to this day. Evidence of Romanesque art, which flourished in the Rhineland, is today apparent in numerous impressive abbeys dotted throughout the region and in the churches of Cologne, which also boasts the colossal Gothic Dom.

Much of North Rhine-Westphalia is rural, and the region offers thousands of kilometres of tracks for walking in the Teutoburg Forest and in the Northern Eifel mountains, as well as splendid conditions for watersports and fishing in the Sauerland. It also has surprisingly good ski slopes, such as in the Rothaar Mountains.

A typical lowland landscape near Xanten, in the Rhineland

◁ The imposing Gothic Dom St. Peter in Cologne (Köln), lit up at night

Exploring North Rhine-Westphalia

DESPITE BEING heavily industrialized, the land of North Rhine-Westphalia has many attractions for visitors. At least two days should be set aside to admire the historic treasures in Cologne, while those who prefer museums – or shopping – might allocate more time for Düsseldorf. The towns of Bonn, Aachen and Münster should also feature on every visitor's schedule. The best areas for rest and relaxation are the mountain ranges of the Eifel and the Teutoburg Forest, ideally suited for walking and cycling holidays.

SEE ALSO

• *Where to Stay* pp490–92
• *Where to Eat* pp519–23

Burg Altena in the Sauerland

SIGHTS AT A GLANCE

GETTING AROUND

There are international airports at Düsseldorf, Köln–Bonn (Konrad-Adenauer-Flughafen) and at Münster–Osnabrück. North Rhine-Westphalia has the highest density of motorways anywhere in Germany, making it easy to travel between cities, and providing links with other German regions, Belgium and the Netherlands.

Delmenhorst

215

MINDEN
29

Hannover

65

E30/30

E30/30

51   68

HERFORD

Osnabrück

BIELEFELD 28

26 LEMGO

27 TEUTOBURGER
WALD

DETMOND

1 MÜNSTER

54

43

MÜNSTERLAND

E37/1

E34/2

33

1

HÖXTER

25

64

55   PADERBORN
24   64

HAMM

LIPPSTADT

68

E34/2

SOEST 23

1

44

5 DORTMUND

E331/44

55

7

GEN
21

7

ARNSBERG

Kassel

22

SAUERLAND

PLETTENBERG

E41/45

55

E40

54

E41/45

20 SIEGEN

Gießen

The Gothic Münster St Maria in
Essen, in the Ruhr valley

Koblenz

| 0 km | 20 |
| o miles | 20 |

KEY

▬ Motorway

▬ Main road

— River

✲ Viewpoint

Roman amphitheatre in the Archäologischer Park in Xanten

Münster **0**

MÜNSTER and its surroundings were already inhabited in Roman times, but its history proper started in the 9th century, with the establishment of a bishopric. Town status was granted in 1137, and in the 13th century Münster joined the Hanseatic League. In 1648 the Westphalian Peace Treaty was signed here, ending the Thirty Years' War. Münster's Westfälische Wilhelms-Universität (1773) is one of Germany's largest universities. World War II saw 90 percent of Münster laid to ruins, but most of the town has now been rebuilt.

⊞ Erbdrostenhof
Salzstraße 38. ● *Closed to the public.*
This beautiful mansion was skilfully positioned diagonally across a corner site. Designed by Johann Conrad Schlaun, it was built in 1753–7, and despite destruction in World War II it still enchants with its "wavy", late-Baroque façade.

⊞ Rathaus
Prinzipalmarkt. **Friedensaal**
▐ (0251) 492 27 24. ◯ 9am–5pm Mon–Fri, 9am–4pm Sat, 10am–1pm Sun. ● 25 Dec. ▨
The imposing Gothic town hall, the pride of Münster, was almost completely destroyed during World War II. After its splendid reconstruction, it is again a major draw for visitors. The only parts that had escaped destruction were the furnishings of the main council chamber, which have been returned to their rightful place after the rebuilding work. It

The beautifully restored façade of the late-Gothic Rathaus

Houses on Prinzipalmarkt, reconstructed in the medieval style

was here that on 16 May 1648 part of the Westphalian Treaty was signed, ending the Thirty Years' War.

🔒 Lambertikirche
Prinzipalmarkt.
St Lamberti is an excellent example of the hall-churches characteristic of Westphalia. It was built in 1375–1450, but the openwork finial of the tower dates from 1887. The cages hanging on the tower held the bodies of the Anabaptists, following the crushing of their commune in 1536. It is also worth taking a look at the relief depicting the *Tree of Jesse*, above the north entrance, and the figures of the apostles (c.1600) by Johann Koess.

⊞ Dom St Paul
Domplatz. **Domkammer**
◯ 11am–4pm Tue–Sun. ▨
The most precious historic relic in Münster is undeniably

its massive St Paul's cathedral, built in 1225–65 and representing a transitional style between late-Romanesque and early-Gothic. The vast basilica has two transepts, two choirs and a couple of massive towers at the western end. The northern cloister was added in the 14th century, and in the 16th–17th centuries the passage that runs around the presbytery acquired a ring of chapels. In the vestibule stands a group of 13th-century sculptures. Especially worth seeing are the two altars by Gerhard Gröninger (1st half of the 17th century), the early 16th-century stained-glass windows brought here from Marienfeld, the Gothic candelabra and monuments of many bishops. The cathedral's best-known treasure is the astronomical clock (1540), with paintings by Ludger tom Ring the Elder and sculptures by Johann Brabender. At noon, moving figures show the Magi paying tribute to the infant Jesus to the sounds of the carillon.

🏛 Westfälisches Landesmuseum für Kunst und Kulturgeschichte
Domplatz 10. ▐ (0251) 590 72 01. ◯ 10am–6pm Tue–Sun. ▨ (free Fri.)
The Westphalian regional museum specializes mainly in Gothic art, with a large collection of sculptures and altars rescued in World War II. Its most noteworthy exhibits include the works by Heinrich and Johann Brabender. The upstairs galleries show works by Conrad von Soest and the tom Ring family. Contemporary art is represented by, among others, August Macke's work.

Figure of a saint in Dom St Paul

🔒 Überwasserkirche
Überwasserkirchplatz.
The Liebfrauenkirche (Church of Our Lady) is popularly named Überwasserkirche (church above the water), after the district on the banks

The Baroque-Classical Schloss, residence of Münster's prince-bishops

of the tiny Aa river. This
Gothic edifice was built in
c.1340–46, on the site of a
Romanesque Benedictine
church. Inside are 16th-cen-
tury votive paintings by Ludger and Hermann tom Ring.

♣ Residenzschloss
Schlossplatz 2.
This beautiful Baroque residence was built in 1767–87,
by Prince-Bishop Maximilian
Friedrich. It was designed by
Johann Conrad Schlaun, a
local master of Baroque architecture. Maximilian Friedrich
started the redevelopment of
Münster in the northern
Baroque style. On his initiative the town acquired a large
park, part of which was transformed into a botanical garden in 1803. After World War
II, the castle was rebuilt and
became the headquarters of
Münster university.

🏛 Museum für Lackkunst
Windthorststraße 26. 【 (0251) 41 85
10. ◯ noon–8pm Tue, noon–6pm
Wed–Sun & public holidays. 🌐
This unique museum, devoted
to lacquer ware, has a good
collection with items from
around the world and from
different periods, making a
visit to the museum a treat for
those interested in this craft.

Watermill in the open-air museum
in Mühlenhof

⛪ Mühlenhof
Theo-Breider-Weg 1. 【 (0251) 98 12
00. ◯ 16 Mar–Oct: 10am–6pm
daily; Nov–15 Mar: 1–4:30pm
Tue–Sat, 11am–4pm Sun. 🌐
This small but interesting
open-air museum is situated
on the banks of the picturesque Aasee, Münster's lake
and main recreation area.
Displayed are a number of
rural dwellings with authentic
furnishings and two mills
(17th and 18th centuries).

♣ Drostenhof
Wolbeck, Am Steintor 5.
Southeast of the town, in Wolbeck (now part of the city),
is an original Renaissance
mansion from the mid-16th
century. Its exquisite gate-
house leads into the courtyard
of the mansion, which has
original fireplaces, doors and
ceiling paintings.

MÜNSTER CITY CENTRE

Dom St Paul ④
Erbdrostenhof ①
Lambertikirche ③
Museum für Lackkunst ⑦
Rathaus ②
Überwasserkirche ⑥
Westfälisches Landesmuseum
  für Kunst und Kultur-
  geschichte ⑤

0 metres   100

0 yards   100

KEY

🛈 Tourist information

🅿 Parking

🕆 Church

Münsterland ②

THE REGION stretching in a narrow strip to the north of Münster is the land of horses and Wasserburgen (moated castles). The castles were surrounded by moats or built on islands to give their owners protection in the surrounding lowlands. Almost 50 Wasserburgen have survived, some converted into residences. Not all are open to visitors as most remain to this day in the hands of the family of the original owners. The best way to tour the flat Münsterland region is by car or bicycle.

Vischering ②
The magnificent Burg Vischering is one of the oldest and best-preserved castles in Westphalia. Founded in 1270, it was extended in the 16th and 17th centuries.

Schloss Raesfeld ⑤
The beautiful 17th-century castle has some original 14th-century elements. Particularly worth seeing is the castle chapel with its Baroque altar.

Havixbeck ①
Two interesting castles are near this small town: the Renaissance Haus Havixbeck and the Renaissance-Baroque Burg Hülshoff, birthplace of and museum to the 19th-century writer Annette von Droste-Hülshoff.

Schloss Nordkirchen ③
This vast moated castle, nicknamed the "Westphalian Versailles", was designed by Gottfried Laurenz Pictorius and built in 1703–34 for the Plettenberg family.

Schloss Lembeck ④
In its present shape, the Lembeck castle complex is the result of Baroque remodelling, under the direction of Johann Conrad Schlaum. Nearby is a nature reserve.

0 km _____ 16

0 miles _____ 16

KEY

▦ Suggested route

▦ Scenic route

═ Other road

═ River, lake

☀ Viewpoint

TIPS FOR DRIVERS

Length of route: 97 km (58 miles).
Stopping-off points: Every town has inns, and there is a hotel in Schloss Lembeck.
Suggestions: All castles are open to visitors Tuesday to Sunday, with the exception of Nordkirchen, which opens only at weekends.

Map labels: Enschede, Coesfeld, Nottuln, Osnabrück, Münster, Borken, Haltern, Lüdinghausen, Hamm, Dorsten, Marl, Hamm

Kleve (Cleves) ❸

Road map A3. 🏔 *50,000.* 🚊 🚌 ⓘ
Kavariner Str. 20–22 (02821-844 22).

THE TOWN OF Kleve is
named after the high cliff,
on which a castle was built in
the 10th century. Around it a
settlement developed, which
became a town in 1242. It
was ruled by the dukes of
Kleve, whose ambitions were
far greater than the size of
their dominions and reached
their peak in 1539, when
Anne of Cleves married the
English King Henry VIII.

During World War II Kleve
lost most of its historic buildings. One that has survived to
this day is the imposing Gothic
church of the Assumption of
the Virgin Mary, **St Mariä
Himmelfahrt** (1341–1426). It
has remains of the high altar,
dating from 1510–13, with
reliefs by Henrik Douvermann
and Jakob Dericks, as well as
beautiful monuments and epitaphs to the von Kleve dukes.
Equally worth seeing is the
former Franciscan **St Mariä
Empfängnis**, a Gothic twin-
nave hall-church from the first
half of the 15th century. Its
noteworthy features include
the Gothic stalls (1474) and a
magnificent Baroque pulpit
(1698). The well-preserved
ducal castle of **Schwanenburg** was remodelled twice:
in Gothic style in the late 15th
century, and in Baroque style
in 1636–66. Testifying to
former splendour are the
parks established in the mid-
17th century by Johann Moritz
von Nassau. The most beautiful of these is the **Tiergarten**
(animal garden). **Haus Koekkoek**, located nearby, once
belonged to the Romantic
painter, Barend Cornalis
Koekkoek, after whom it was
named.

⚜ **Schwanenburg**
Am Schlossberg. 📞 *(02821) 475 33.*
🕐 *11am–5pm daily.* 📷

ENVIRONS: The suspension
bridge across the Rhine – at
1,228 m (4,028 ft) the longest
such structure in Germany –
connects Kleve with **Emmer-
ich**. Here it is worth visiting
the Martinskirche, which has
the exquisite, late-10th-century
shrine of St Willibrod.

Twelve km (7 miles) to the
southeast of Kleve lies the
charming town of **Kalkar**
which, in around 1500, was
home to the famous Kalkar
School specializing in wood-
carving. The church of St
Nicolai has superb furnishings
dating from the same period,
including three outstanding
works by Henrik Douvermann.

Six km (4 miles) southeast
stands **Moyland**, a moated
castle. It houses a modern art
collection, which belongs to
the brothers von der Grinten
and includes over 4,000 works
by the artist Joseph Beuys.

Xanten ❹

Road map B4. 🏔 *19,500.* 🚊 🚌
ⓘ *Kurfürstenstr. 9 (02801-983 00).*

THE HISTORY of Xanten goes
back to the Romans, who
founded the settlement of
Colonia Ulpia Traiana near
the local garrison. The
present town,
however, did
not rise out of
the ruins of the
Roman town.
It was estab-
lished nearby,
around the
memorial
church built
on top of
the grave

The Hafentor in the Archäologischer Park in Xanten

of the martyr St Viktor. It was
named *ad sanctos* (by the
saints), soon to be shortened
to Xanten. A powerful town
in the Middle Ages, Xanten
also features in the Nibelung
myth, and was said to be the
birthplace of Siegfried.

Undoubtedly the most im-
portant historic building in
the town is the **Dom St
Viktor**, built on the graves of
St Viktor and members of the
Thebian Legion. The surviving Gothic cathedral dates
from 1263–1517. It is worth
taking a look at the Gothic
sculptures standing by the
pillars of the main nave, the
shrine of St Victor (1129), the
early-Gothic stalls (c.1240)
and, above all, the exquisite
Marienaltar by Henrik Douvermann. Equally fascinating
are the collegial buildings and
the cloister holding the tombs
and epitaphs of the canons.

Xanten also has many pretty
old houses, mainly clustered
around the central market
square. Another sight worth
visiting is the **Klever Tor**, a
magnificent double town-
gate, dating from the late 14th
century, in the northwest of
the town. The **Archäologischer Park**, established in
1974 on the site of the
Roman town, displays
many reconstructed Roman
public buildings and
town walls, including
the impressive Hafentor
(harbour gate).

🌼 **Archäologischer
Park**
Wardter Str. 📞 *(02801)
29 99.* 🕐 *Mar–Nov:
9am–6pm daily; Dec–Feb:
10am–4pm.* 📷

The Gothic Dom St Victor in Xanten

The Young Horses by Emil Nolde, in the Museum am Ostwall

Dortmund ❺

Road map B4. 🏙 *600,000.* 🚉 🚌
ℹ️ *Königswall 18A (0231-502 56 66).*
🎭 *Dortmunder Bücherfest (Aug), Dortmund à la carte (Jun), Hansetage (Nov).*

THE LARGE city of Dortmund
is famous not only for its
excellent beer and highly
developed industry, but also
for its more than 1,000
years of history. In the
Middle Ages, the town
grew rich through
trade and joined
the Hanseatic
League; after a
period of decline
it flourished again
in the 19th century.
  A walk through the
small old town will take
visitors to the **Museum
für Kunst-und
Kulturgeschichte**
(museum for art and
cultural history)
with displays of
interiors from
various periods,
including Secessionist designs
by Joseph Maria Olbrich. A
short distance from here is
the **Petrikirche**, a Gothic
14th-century hall-church,
whose greatest attraction is its
high altar (1521), the work of
Gilles, a master from Antwerp.
Also noteworthy is the former
Dominican **Propsteikirche**,
with its exquisite late-Gothic
main altar. A shortcut across
the market square and along
Ostenhellweg takes the visitor
to two more churches: the
Reinoldikirche and the
Marienkirche. The former,

**Statue on Alter Markt,
in Dortmund**

dedicated to St Reinold, the
patron saint of Dortmund, has
an early-Gothic 13th-century
main body and a late-Gothic,
15th-century presbytery. It
includes many Gothic sculptures and furnishings. The
second one, the church of St
Mary, is a 12th-century Romanesque structure. It has a magnificent main altar, by Conrad von Soest (1415–
20) and a statue of the
Madonna (c.1230). The
Museum am Ostwall
has an excellent
modern art collection.

🏛 **Museum für Kunst-
und Kulturgeschichte**
Hansastr. 3. 📞 *(0231) 502 55
22.* ⏰ *10am–8pm Tue–Sun.* 🅰️
🏛 **Museum am Ostwall**
Ostwall 7. 📞 *(0231) 502 32 47.*
⏰ *10am–6pm Tue, Wed, Fri,
Sun, 10am–8pm Thu,
noon–6pm Sat.* 🅰️

ENVIRONS: 10 km
(6 miles) northwest, in
Waltrop, on the Dort-
mund-Ems Canal, is the Schiffshebewerk Henrichenburg, a
hoist built in 1899 to lift ships.

Essen ❻

Road map B4. 🏙 *600,000.* 🚉 🚌
ℹ️ *Im Handelshof (0201-887 20 42).*
🎭 *Essen Original (Aug).*

IT IS HARD to believe that this
vast industrial metropolis
has grown from a monastery,
established in 852. The town
owes its growth and prominence to the Krupp family,

who, over several generations
from the mid-19th century,
created the powerful German
steel and arms industry.
  The most important historic
building in the town is the
Münster, the former collegiate church of the canonesses.
This unusual edifice consists
of the 15th-century Gothic
church of St John, an 11th-
century atrium and the main
church, which in turn has a
Romanesque 11th-century
frontage and a Gothic 14th–
century main body. Without
doubt the most precious
object held by the church is
the *Goldene Madonna*, a
statue of the Virgin Mary with
the Infant, made from sheet
gold, probably c.980. The
treasury has an outstanding
collection of gold items from
the Ottonian period.
  Another important sight in
Essen is the **Synagogue** built
by Edmund Körner in 1911–13.
The largest synagogue in Germany, it managed to outlast
the Third Reich and is now a
place of commemoration.
  Visitors who are interested
in 20th-century architecture
should see the church of
St Engelbert in Fischerstraße,
designed by Dominikus Metzendorf (1934–6), the town-
garden in **Margarethenhöhe**
built from 1909 to a design by
Georg Metzendorf, and the
opera house designed by the
Finnish architect, Alvar Aalto.
  Essen has much to offer to
modern art enthusiasts. The
Museum Folkwang boasts
an excellent collection of
20th-century paintings, mainly
German Expressionists. It also
has a division devoted to the
graphic arts and posters.
  The **Grugapark** is a large
green area with botanical
gardens, zoo and the Gruga-
halle, where major concerts
are held. To the south of the
centre, on the banks of the
Baldeneysee, stands **Villa
Hügel**, which belonged to the
Krupp family until 1945.
Today interesting art exhibitions are frequently hosted
here. Further south, in **Wer-
den**, is the former Benedictine church of St Ludger,
consisting of a 13th–century
body preceded by a 10th-
century imperial frontage. The

The grand Villa Hügel, former home of the Krupp family in Essen

treasury holds many precious objects including a bronze crucifix from around 1060.

🏛 Museum Folkwang
Goethestr. 41. 📞 (0201) 884 53 14. 🕐 10am–6pm Tue–Thu, Sat & Sun, 10am–midnight Fri. ⬤ 1 Jan, Easter, 1 May, 24 & 31 Dec. 🈺

ENVIRONS: Visitors interested in technology should visit **Bochum**, which is also the seat of the excellent Ruhr-Universität. There are two excellent museums: the **Deutsches Bergbau-Museum** devoted to mining, and the **Eisenbahnmuseum** (railway museum) in Dahlhausen. Both have world-class exhibits.

Duisburg ❼

Road map B4. 🏙 540,000. 🚉 🚏 ℹ Königstr. 53 (0203-305 25 61).

DUISBURG, on the edge of the Ruhr region, underwent a period of rapid development in the 19th and 20th centuries. Once a small town, it became the world's largest inland harbour thanks to its location at the spot where the Ruhr flows into the Rhine.

The small old town was almost totally destroyed in World War II, but the 15th–century Gothic **Salvatorkirche** (church of St Saviour) has been rebuilt. Some of the town's greatest attractions are its museums. The **Wilhelm-Lehmbruck-Museum** focuses on the work of the sculptor Lehmbruck, who was born in Duisburg. The museum has an interesting collection of 20th–century sculptures, including works

by famous artists such as Salvador Dali, Henry Moore, Max Ernst, Emil Nolde and Joseph Beuys. Also worth visiting is the **Museum der Deutschen Binnenschifffahrt** with its collection of barges and inland waterway vessels. In the 16th century, Duisburg was the home of the famous geographer and cartographer Gerhard Mercator, whose huge collection of globes, maps and charts can now be seen in the **Niederrheinisches Museum**.

🏛 Wilhelm-Lehmbruck-Museum
Düsseldorfer Str. 51. 📞 (0203) 283 26 30. 🕐 11am–5pm Tue–Sat, 10am–6pm Sun. 🈺

ENVIRONS: CentrO in **Oberhausen**, 14 km (9 miles) north of Duisburg, is the largest shopping and leisure complex in Europe.

Krefeld, 6 km (4 miles) southwest of Duisburg, has been a centre of silk fabric production from the 17th century, and the Deutsches Textilmuseum has over 20,000 exhibits, ranging from antiquity to the present day.

Wuppertal ❽

Road map B4. 🏙 380,000. 🚉 ℹ Elberfeld, Informationszentrum am Döppersberg (0202-194 33); Rathaus (0202-563 66 88).

WUPPERTAL, capital of the Bergisches Land area, was created in 1929 by combining six towns strung along a 20-km (12-mile) stretch of the Wupper river. The towns are joined by the **Schwebebahn**, a monorail constructed in 1900. Carriages are suspended from a single rail, which rests on tall pillars.

The most interesting of the former towns is Elberfeld, with a museum of clocks, and the **Von-der-Heydt–Museum** of 19th- and 20th-century German art. The museum in the Friedrich-Engels-Haus in Barmen (Engelsstr. 10) is worth seeing, and Neviges has a Baroque pilgrimage church, with a much-visited miraculous picture of the Virgin Mary.

🏛 Von-der-Heydt-Museum
Elberfeld, Turmhof 8. 📞 (0202) 563 62 31. 🕐 11am–6pm Tue, Wed, Fri–Sun, 11am–8pm Thu. 🈺 🚻 🈺

The unusual monorail, linking Wuppertal's six constituent towns

Düsseldorf ❾

Düsseldorf, the administrative capital of North Rhine-Westphalia, received its municipal rights in 1288. From the late 14th century it was the capital of the Duchy of Berg, and from 1614 that of the Palatine. The town owes much to Duke Johann Wilhelm (called Jan Wellem), who lived here in 1690–1716. One of the most important industrial and cultural centres in the Rhine Valley, this European metropolis has a renowned university, superb museums and theatres and, as the German capital of fashion, many excellent shops.

🏛 Museum Kunst Palast

Ehrenhof 5. **(** *(0211) 89 92 42 42.*
🕐 *noon–8pm Tue–Sun.* 🖼 🚻 🛗
🛗

This art museum is one of the most interesting in Germany, with a collection of paintings dating from the 16th to the 20th centuries, including works by Rubens, Cranach and Dutch masters of the 17th century. It also holds a large collection of paintings by the Düsseldorf Academy, active in the first half of the 19th century, whose best known artists were Peter von Cornelius and Friedrich Wilhelm Schadow.

🏯 Altstadt

The small old town area suffered severe damage during World War II. Among the surviving monuments it is worth seeing some of the beautiful town houses and the late-Gothic **Rathaus** (town hall), built in the years 1570–73. In front of it stands a famous equestrian statue of the Elector Jan Wellem, built in 1703–11 by Gabriel Grupello. The Düsseldorf castle, burned down in 1872, only has the **Schlossturm** (castle tower) remaining, which now houses a museum of navigation. Another building worth visiting is the Baroque, post-Jesuit **Pfarrkirche St Andreas** (parish church of St Andrew), from the years 1622–9. It has a central ducal mausoleum complex situated behind the presbytery, where the remains of Jan Wellem and others are kept. The **Lambertuskirche**, the former collegiate church of St Lambertus, is a Gothic hall-church with a tall front tower, built in 1288–1394. Some valuable furnishings have survived, including the Gothic sacramentarium and important Gothic ducal tombs, such as that of Duke Wilhelm V, from 1595–9.

Interior of the Pfarrkirche St Andreas

Detail from the façade of the Lambertuskirche

🏛 Kunstsammlung Nordrhein-Westfalen

Grabbeplatz 5. **(** *(0211) 838 10.* 🕐 *10am–6pm Tue–Thu & Sat–Sun, 10am–8pm Fri.* ● *24,25 & 31 Dec.* 🖼 🚻 🛗 🛗

The art collection of the state of North Rhine-Westphalia is enormous, featuring mainly the work of 20th-century artists. Particularly valuable are 88 paintings by Paul Klee, which were acquired in 1960. There are also fascinating works by Wassily Kandinsky, Marcel Duchamp, Piet Mondrian, Pablo Picasso and more recent artists such as Frank Stella, Roy Lichtenstein and Robert Rauschenberg. Temporary exhibitions are held in a building near the Kunsthalle, at No. 4 Grabbeplatz.

🏛 Hetjens-Museum

Schulstraße 4. **(** *(0211) 899 42 10.* 🕐 *11am–5pm Tue & Thu–Sun, 11am–9pm Wed.* 🖼

This museum, in the Nesselrode Palace, is the oldest German museum devoted entirely to ceramics. Here the visitor can find out about the techniques for producing faïence and porcelain, and admire exhibits from prehistory to the present day, from around the world.

🎠 Königsallee

The "kings' avenue", often just referred to as Kö, was laid out at the beginning of the 19th century, along the edge of the old city moat. One of the most elegant shopping streets in Europe, the Kö is lined with expensive shops. Luxurious galleries, exclusive boutiques, department stores, fashion houses and modern shopping malls are interspersed with numerous bars and restaurants. Particularly noteworthy is the Art Nouveau Warenhaus Tietz (now housing the Kaufhof-Galleria department store), which was built in the years 1907–9, to a design by Joseph Maria Olbrich.

🍀 Hofgarten

Jägerhofstr. **Goethemuseum:** Jacobistraße 2. **(** *(0211) 899 62 62.* 🕐 *11am–5pm Tue–Fri & Sun, 1–5pm Sat.* 🖼

This charming park, originally laid out in 1769 for Elector Karl Theodor, was recreated in the English style at the beginning of the 19th century. The park is a marvellous setting for Schloss Jägerhof, a Baroque hunting lodge dating from the years 1752–63 and built according to a design by

The late-Baroque Schloss Benrath

Johann Josef Couven and Nicolas de Pigage. The castle was rebuilt after World War II. It now houses the Goethe-Museum, holding memorabilia and documents related to the writer's life, and a collection of 18th-century art, funded by Ernst Schneider.

🏛 Heinrich-Heine-Institut

Bilker Str. 12–14. ((0211) 899 55 71.) 11am–5pm Tue–Fri & Sun, 1–5pm Sat. 🖼

The celebrated German poet Heinrich Heine was born in Düsseldorf in 1797. This institute was established to preserve his legacy, to conduct research into his work and to organize exhibitions. Düsseldorf's university and a number of streets have also been named after Heine.

♠ Schloss Benrath

Benrather Schlossallee. ((0211) 899 72 71.) Apr–Oct: 10am–4pm Tue–Sun; Nov–Mar: 11am–4pm Tue–Sun. 🖼 🎫

Benrath, part of Düsseldorf since 1929, is home to this beautiful Neo-Classical hunting palace, built for the electors of the Palatine in 1755–73 by Nicolas de Pigage. Decor, beautiful furnishings and an extensive park have survived.

The former city moat which runs alongside Königsallee

Kaiserswerth

Today a part of Düsseldorf, this area prides itself on a history dating back to the 8th century. Its Pfarrkirche St Suitbertus, a Romanesque basilica from the 12th century, has the magnificent 13th-century golden relic of its patron saint. There are also the ruins of a palace, built in the 12th century for Friedrich I Barbarossa.

ENVIRONS: The "Neanderthal" part of the Düssel valley was originally named after the poet Joachim Neander. It became famous in 1856, when the remains of ape-like creatures were uncovered in a cave. A museum dedicated to these "Neanderthal Men" is located in Mettman, 17 km (11 miles) east of Düsseldorf.

DÜSSELDORF CITY CENTRE

Altstadt ②
Hetjens-Museum ④
Hofgarten ⑥
Königsallee ⑤
Kunstsammlung Nordrhein-
    Westfalen ③
Museum Kunst Palast ①

0 metres   500

0 yards   500

KEY

🛈 Tourist information

🅿 Parking

✝ Church

Neuss

Road map B4. 150,000.
Oberstr. 7 (02131-90 83 00).

THE HISTORY of Neuss goes back to Roman days. The town developed around a Bernhardine monastery, which became a girls' boarding school in the 12th century. The most famous building is the magnificent 13th-century Romanesque **Stiftskirche St Quirinus**. After a fire in 1741, a Baroque dome with a statue of St Quirin, the patron saint, was added to the eastern tower of the church. Also worth seeing is the Obertor (upper gate), built in 1200, one of the mightiest fortified gates in the Rhineland.

Dormagen ⑪

Road map B4. 62,000.
Zons, Schlossstraße 2–4 (02133-53 787 51). Freilichtspiele in Zons (Jun–Sep).

THIS MEDIUM-SIZED town, which principally relies on its chemical industry, would not be found in a guide book were it not for two remarkable historic monuments within the city limits. On the banks of the Rhine lies the fortified customs town of **Zons**, established around 1373–1400 at the instigation of archbishop Friedrich von Saarwerden. This small regular, four-sided fortress has survived in excellent condition. The buildings in the settlement are mainly from a later time, but the walls and gates, as well as the ruined castle **Schloss Friedestrom** are among the most fascinating examples of Medieval fortifications in the Rhine Valley.

Equally interesting is an excursion to **Knechtsteden,** west of Dormagen, where an amazing monastery was built for the Norbertines in the 12th century. Set amid woods and orchards, the vast twin-choired basilica has mighty towers in the eastern section. There are impressive murals, including a 12th-century mural of Christ in the western apsis, as well as attractive cloisters.

The Gothic post-Cistercian Bergischer Dom in Altenberg

Solingen ⑫

Road map B4. 165,000.
Cronenberger Str. 59–61 (0212-290 23 33). Frühjahrskirmes (Mar).

SOLINGEN is almost synonymous with its famous factory, where quality scissors and knives are produced. The main attraction in town is the **Klingenmuseum**, which shows cutting tools from the Stone Age to the present day.

ENVIRONS: Remscheid, 7 km (4 miles) east of Solingen has the Röntgenmuseum, dedicated to the German Nobel Prize winner Alfred Röntgen, who was born here and discovered the X-ray. One of the

Baroque façade of the local Heimatmuseum in Remscheid

most beautiful buildings is the Heimatmuseum with displays of typical regional interiors and local artists' work.

Schloss Burg, on the Wupper river, is the 12th-century fortress of the von Berg family. Many times rebuilt, it now houses a museum.

Altenberg ⑬

Road map B4. 5,745.
Platz des Bergmanns 2 (035056-333 41).

ALTENBERG near Odenthal has preserved its **Bergischer Dom**, a former Cistercian cathedral and one of the most important destinations for pilgrims. Built in 1259–1379, it is also one of the most beautiful Gothic buildings in Germany. In accordance with their rules, the Cistercians built the church without a tower. The interior is furnished with Gothic works of art and has stunningly beautiful stained-glass windows, the altar of the *Coronation of the Blessed Virgin Mary* from the late 15th century, a beautiful 14th-century *Annunciation* and a sacrarium (1490). After the dissolution of the Order in 1803, the cathedral suffered a turbulent history. It now serves as a church for both Catholics and Protestants.

Children also enjoy a visit to Altenberg because of its **Märchenwald** (fairy-tale wood), an enchanted forest, with interactive scenes and statues representing all the most popular fairy tales.

Köln (Cologne) ⑭

See pp384–91.

Aachen ⑮

Road map A4. 🏠 254,000. 🚗 🚆
🅸 Elisenbrunnen (0241-194 33).
🎭 Frühjahrsbend (Apr), horse-riding competitions CHIO (Jul), Europamarkt des Kunsthandwerks (Sep).

AACHEN owes its fame to its hot springs, whose healing powers were already highly valued by the Romans when they established baths here in the 1st–2nd centuries AD. The name of the town, *aquae granni* or Aquisgrani, also relates to the source.

The settlement grew mainly in the 8th century, when Charlemagne chose it as his principal residence in 768. He built a huge palace complex with chapel, cloistered courtyard and hall for himself.

When Charlemagne was crowned emperor in 800, Aachen became the capital of the Holy Roman Empire. Although the town soon lost this title, it remained an important destination for pilgrims because of the valuable relics brought here by Charlemagne. From the 10th to the 14th centuries, all German kings were crowned in the palace chapel.

Subsequently, in the 18th and 19th centuries, Aachen gained great importance as a spa. Many magnificent buildings dating from this splendid era have long since vanished. A further wave of destruction was inflicted by World War II, yet some particularly magnificent historic

monuments have survived. The most important of these, in the centre of the old town, is the **Pfalz**, a complex of buildings belonging to Charlemagne's former palace. They include the **Münster**, a cathedral with a palace chapel and a hall which was rebuilt as the **Rathaus** *(see pp382–3).*

In the old town, not far from the cathedral complex, it is worth visiting the church of St Folian, where a Gothic Madonna dating from 1411 has survived. A short distance south from here stands the Elisenbrunnen (fountain of St Elizabeth), an exceptionally beautiful building where mineral water can be taken. It was built in 1822–7 according to designs by Johann Peter Cremers and Karl Friedrich Schinkel.

Statue of David Hansemann

After admiring the attractive houses around the central market square visitors can enjoy the **Couven-Museum**. Based in an historic middle-class town house, it has an interesting collection dedicated to the life of the bourgeoisie in the 18th and 19th centuries. There is also a collection of ceramic tiles from the 17th–19th centuries.

The house where Israel Berr Josaphat Reuter established the first-ever news agency in 1850 (transferred to London

a year later) now houses the **Internationales Zeitungsmuseum**, devoted to the history of the press, with over 100,000 newspapers from the 17th century to today.

It is also worth visiting the **Suermondt-Ludwig-Museum**, a short distance beyond the compact town centre, which has a great collection of art from the Middle Ages until the present day, including some beautiful sculptures and paintings from the 17th century.

To the northeast of the old town extends the spa district of Aachen. Here, visitors can stroll through the spa park at their leisure or spend an evening at the casino.

Aachen also has much to offer lovers of modern art: the Ludwig-Forum für Internationale Kunst hosts interesting exhibitions, performances and concerts.

🏛 **Internationales Zeitungsmuseum**
Pontstr. 13. 📞 (0241) 432 45 08.
🕐 9:30am–1pm & 2:30–5pm Tue–Fri, 9:30am–1pm Sat; May–Sep: additionally 2:30–5pm Sun & Mon.

🏛 **Suermondt-Ludwig-Museum**
Wilhelmstr. 18. 📞 (0241) 47 98 00.
🕐 11am–7pm Tue & Thu–Fri, 11am–9pm Wed, 11am–5pm Sat & Sun. 🈂

🏛 **Couven-Museum**
Hühnermarkt 17. 📞 (0241) 432 44 21. 🕐 10am–5pm Tue–Fri, 10am–7pm Sat & Sun. ⚫ public holidays. 🈂

ENVIRONS: Kornelimünster, 6 km (4 miles) southeast of the centre, is a beautiful place with a well-preserved old town and churches. The most important of these is the Pfarrkirche St Kornelius, a former Benedictine monastery from the early 9th century. The surviving building is a 14th-century Gothic basilica, extended by the early 16th century to an imposing five-nave structure. In the 18th century the octagonal chapel of St Kornelius was added at the axis of the presbytery.

The Neo-Classical building which houses the casino in Aachen's spa park

The Pfalz in Aachen

Charlemagne, effigy on his shrine

THE ORIGINAL palace of Charlemagne in Aachen did not survive; of his vast construction only the Pfalzkapelle (palatine chapel) remains. Modelled on the church of San Vitale in Ravenna, Italy, it was built by Odo von Metz in 786–800. In the mid-14th century a front tower was added, and in the years 1355–1414 a new presbytery was built. Side chapels were added later, and in the 17th century the central section was covered by a dome.

Antique Columns
The arcaded ambulatory is divided by beautiful columns, made from red marble and porphyry which had been brought from Ravenna and Rome.

Hubertus- and Karls-kapelle

Main entrance

Ungarn-kapelle

Charlemagne's Throne
This modest throne, fashioned from marbled tiles, served as the coronation throne for successive German leaders.

Candelabra
This copper candelabra, a masterpiece of Romanesque craftsmanship, was a gift from Emperor Friedrich I Barbarossa.

STAR SIGHTS

* ★ **The Shrine of Charlemagne**
* ★ **Lotharkreuz**
* ★ **Pala d'Oro**

Bronze doors
The doors, dating from the time of Charlemagne, are the oldest historic monument of their kind in Germany.

★ Lotharkreuz
This magnificent cross (c.1000), decorated with a cameo showing a portrait of Emperor Augustus, is one of the most valuable exhibits in the Schatzkammer.

The Gothic presbytery was modelled on Sainte-Chapelle in Paris.

★ The Shrine of Charlemagne
The Emperor Charlemagne was canonized as a saint in 1165 and shortly after, probably at the beginning of the 13th century, a golden shrine was made to keep his bones in. It is now on display in the presbytery.

★ Pala d'Oro
The front of the main altar is adorned with valuable gold sheets from c.1020, which were funded by Heinrich II.

Matthiaskapelle

Annakapelle

Proserpina's Sarcophagus
This sarcophagus, in the Schatzkammer (treasury), is an exceptionally beautiful example of Roman sculpture. It is thought that the body of Charlemagne rested in this coffin until he was canonized.

Ambo
The ambo, a pulpit fashioned from gold-plated copper and inlaid with precious stones and ivories, was donated by Heinrich II in 1014.

Köln (Cologne) ⓮

ORIGINALLY FOUNDED by the Romans as *Colonia Claudia Ara Agrippinensum,* Köln is one of the oldest towns in Germany. The Franks ruled the town from the end of the 5th century, and Charlemagne raised its status to that of an archbishopric. Köln remained a powerful ecclesiastical centre – it boasts 12 Romanesque churches as well as the famous Gothic cathedral. The city also played a significant role in the Hanseatic League, and from 1388 it had a university.

Detail on the Rathaus

🏠 St Andreas

Komödienstraße 4–8.
This late-Romanesque basilica was founded c.1200, with a presbytery added in 1414–20. The saint Albertus Magnus lies buried in the crypt. Particularly noteworthy are the beautiful capitals, which link the pillars between the naves, and the stalls (c.1420–30).

🏠 Pfarrkirche St Mariä Himmelfahrt

Marzellenstraße 32–40.
The parish church of the Assumption of Mary is one of the few Baroque buildings in Köln. It was built for the Jesuit Order in 1618–89, under the direction of Christoph Wamser. It is easy to discover numerous Romanesque and Gothic elements, although these are not surviving parts of an earlier building, but the result of a consciously created link with earlier styles.

Picturesque houses on Fischmarkt

🏠 Dom St Peter und Santa Maria

See pp388–9.

🏛 Römisch-Germanisches Museum

Roncalliplatz 4. ☎ (0221) 22 12 44 38. ◯ 10am–5pm Tue–Sun.
This modern, glazed building houses archaeological finds dating from the Roman and pre-Roman eras that have been uncovered in Köln and the Rhine Valley. On display are weapons, many items of everyday use, ornamental and artistic objects as well as the superb Dionysus mosaic and the monument to Poblicius.

🏛 Museum Ludwig

Bischofsgartenstraße 1. ☎ (0221) 22 12 23 70. ◯ 10am–8pm Tue, 10am–6pm Wed–Fri; 11am–6pm Sat & Sun. 📷
This museum, combining the private collection of the Ludwig family with the 20th-century works originally held by the Wallraf-Richartz-Museum, has one of Europe's best collections of modern art. There are paintings by Picasso, German Expressionists, Surrealists, American Pop Artists and the Russian Avantgarde as well as many sculptures.

🏠 Groß St Martin

An Groß St Martin 9. ☎ (0221) 16 42 56 50. ◯ 10am–6pm Mon–Fri, 10am–12:30pm & 1:30–6pm Sat, 2–4pm Sun.
This church, with its attractive triangular presbytery and vast tower dominating Fischmarkt, was founded for the Benedictine Order in the late 12th century. The Romans built a sports arena on this site with a swimming pool, remains of which have been uncovered under the crypt. The houses in the surrounding Martinsviertel are post-World War II, however they were built to historic designs and with a medieval street lay-out, making this an intimate and romantic area to explore.

Panorama with the Rathaus, Groß St Martin and the Dom, with the Rhine in the foreground

A detail of the Gothic section of the Rathaus façade

🏛 **Wallraf-Richartz-Museum**
See pp390–91.

🏛 **Rathaus**
Alter Markt. ● due to renovation, information (0221) 22 10. **Jewish Baths:** ◯ 8am–4pm Mon–Thu, 8am–noon Fri, 11am–3pm Sat & Sun. **Praetorium:** Kleine Budengasse. ◯ 10am–4pm Tue–Fri, 11am–4pm Sat & Sun.
The town hall is an irregular shape created by successive modifications. In the first phase, around 1330, a wing with a Hanseatic Hall was

built, decorated with Gothic sculptures of heroes and prophets. In 1407–14 a vast Gothic tower was added, and in the 16th century the arcaded Renaissance Lions Courtyard and a magnificent front lodge were built. In front of the town hall, under a glass pyramid, are the remains of 12th-century ritual Jewish baths, that were destroyed after the expulsion of the Jews in 1424. From Kleine Budengasse an entrance leads to the *Praetorium*, the remains of a Roman town hall.

🏛 **Gürzenich**
Gürzenichstraße
This Gothic building has a huge celebration hall (1437–44), which occupies the entire first floor. Next to it are the ruins of the Romanesque church Alt St Alban. It has a copy of the sculpture *Parents* by Käthe Kollwitz.

🏠 **Minoritenkirche Mariä Empfängnis**
Minoritenstraße
This modest Gothic Franciscan church was established in the 13th–14th centuries. It is an

elegant three-naved basilica without a tower, modelled on the Elisabethkirche in Marburg. There are historic furnishings and a 14th-century shrine with the remains of Johannes Duns Scotus, a Scottish Minorite.

Place of remembrance, in Alt St Alban, near the Gürzenich

KÖLN CITY CENTRE

KEY
🛈 Tourist information
P Parking
🕂 Church

Exploring Köln (Cologne)

PRESENT-DAY Köln is a metropolis, known primarily for its trade fairs. It is also an important centre of art and culture, its reputation forged by several excellent museums, numerous historic buildings and superb art galleries. Book and newspaper publishers have their head offices here, as do radio and television stations. The highest number of visitors, however, come to Köln for the five days preceding Ash Wednesday, to join in the fun and watch the grand carnival processions.

🏛 Schnütgen-Museum

Cäcilienstraße 29. **[** (0221) 22 12 36 20. ○ 10am–5pm Tue & Thu–Fri, 10am–8pm Wed, 11am–5pm Sat & Sun. ▨

The Romanesque church of St Cecilia, built in 1130–60 as a nunnery, was taken over in 1479 by the Augustinian Sisters; today it houses the Schnütgen-Museum. Destroyed during World War II and subsequently rebuilt, this museum specializes in religious art, mainly from the Middle Ages. Its collection includes magnificent sculptures, gold and ivory items and sacral objects.

The Romanesque church of St Gereon, with its vast dome

🔒 St Peter

Leonhard-Tietz-Straße 6.

The late-Gothic church of St Peter is a galleried basilica, built in 1515–39. Following its destruction in World War II, the former vaulting was replaced by a ceiling. The church's greatest attractions include its Renaissance stained-glass windows (1528–30) and the magnificent *Crucifixion of St Peter*, painted after 1637 by Peter Paul Rubens, who spent his childhood here and whose father lies buried in the church.

Detail from Stadtmuseum

🔒 St Maria im Kapitol

Marienplatz 19.

Originally built in the early part of the 11th century, as a convent, the church's extension and remodelling took until the early 13th century. Noteworthy among the furnishings are its extensive crypt and the mid-11th-century wooden door in the west closure, richly carved with reliefs depicting scenes from the life of Christ. It also has a superb Renaissance rood screen, and is the only church in Köln with cloisters.

🏠 Overstolzenhaus

Rheingasse 8.

World War II deprived Köln of many of its historic residential buildings, but this one has been lovingly restored. Built for a prosperous patrician family in the second quarter of the 13th century, it is regarded as one of the town's finest Gothic houses.

🔒 St Maria Lyskirchen

An Lyskirchen 12.

This, the smallest Romanesque church in Köln, was built around 1220 and slightly remodelled in the 17th century. Its greatest attractions are magnificent frescos depicting scenes from the Bible and the lives of the saints, which adorn the vaults (c.1250), as well as the *Schöne Madonna*, a huge statue of the Virgin with the Infant Christ (c.1420).

🏛 Imhoff-Stollwerck-Museum

Rheinauhafen 1a. **[** (0221) 931 88 80. ○ 10am–6pm Tue–Fri, 11am–7pm Sat & Sun. ▨

This fantastic museum of chocolate explains the history of cocoa bean cultivation as well as the cultural significance, use and marketing of chocolate. It also shows the production process, and lets visitors sample the product.

🔒 St Georg

Georgsplatz 17.

This church was built around the middle of the 11th century, originally as a transept basilica with two choirs. In

---

ROMANESQUE CHURCHES

Köln has 12 surviving Romanesque churches, bearing testimony to the importance of the Church in the town's development. Built on the graves of martyrs and early bishops of Köln, the forms of the churches influenced the development of Romanesque architecture well beyond the Rhineland. Almost all the churches were damaged in World War II. Some, such as the church of St Kolumba, have not been restored, but most were returned to their former glory.

Towerless westwork

Tower at the junction of the naves

St Andreas

Front tower

Trefoil eastern closure

St Aposteln

The attractive Romanesque church of St Kunibert, seen from the Rhine

the mid-12th century the west choir was replaced by a massive frontage (westwork), but the towers were never added.

St Pantaleon
Am Pantaleonsberg 2.

A little way from the centre is this exquisite church, a former Benedictine monastery founded c.950 by Archbishop Bruno, brother of Emperor Otto I. The archbishop and the Empress Theophanu, who completed the building, are both buried here. The church has a superb late-Gothic choir screen with richly carved ornamentation. From the crypt, the remains of a Roman villa are accessible.

Severinsviertel

The Severin Quarter, a district on the southern edge of the old town, owes its name to the 13th-century Romanesque church of St Severinus. The church, largely remodelled in the Gothic style in the 15th and 16th centuries, features rich original furnishings and has a mid-10th-century crypt.

St Aposteln
Neumarkt 30.

This enormous 12th-century church of the Apostles, which towers over Neumarkt, a central square in Köln, is one of the most interesting Romanesque churches in the Rhineland. The original basilica has a trefoil eastern closure, a low tower at the junction of the naves and a tall front tower. It was given two further slim turrets flanking the apse of the presbytery.

From Neumarkt, Hahnenstrasse leads to Rudolfplatz and the Hahnentor, perhaps the most beautiful of all surviving medieval gates.

St Gereon
Gereonsdriesch 2–4.

This church must be the most unusual edifice not only in the Rhineland, but in all of Germany. Its oldest part, an oval building surrounded by small conchas, was built in the late 4th century on the graves of martyrs and – according to legend – founded by St Helen. The Romanesque

presbytery is an 11th-century addition and, in 1219–27, the oval was encircled with a ten-sided, four-storey structure in early-Gothic style. This is topped with a massive dome, 48 m (157 ft) in diameter, with ribbed vault.

St Ursula
Ursulaplatz 24.

This church was built in the 12th century, on the site of an earlier church probably dating from c.400. In the late 13th century the presbytery was rebuilt in Gothic style. The Baroque golden chamber at the southern end, added in the 17th century, is lined with many shrines. According to legend, these hold the remains of St Ursula and 11,000 virgins, all of whom were reputedly killed at the hands of the Huns. The town insignia of Köln also testify to the veneration of the virgins.

St Kunibert
Kunibertskloster 2.

Bishop Kunibert was buried in a church on this site in 663. The present Romanesque church (1215–47) has precious Romanesque stained-glass windows (c.1220–30).

The medieval Hahnentor, exit from Köln towards Aachen

Tower at the junction of the naves

Trefoil eastern closure

Groß St Martin

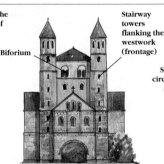

Biforium

Stairway towers flanking the westwork (frontage)

St Pantaleon

Pair of front towers

Semi-circular apse

St Kunibert

Cologne Cathedral (Kölner Dom)

10th-century Gero Cross

T HE MOST FAMOUS Gothic structure in Germany, the Kölner Dom is also unusually complex, whether in terms of its splendour, its size or even simply the date of its construction. The foundation stone was laid on 15th August 1248, the presbytery consecrated in 1322. The cathedral was built gradually until c.1520. It then remained unfinished until the 19th century, when Romanticists revived interest in it. The building was finally completed in 1842–80, according to the rediscovered, original Gothic designs.

Pinnacles
Elaborately decorated pinnacles top the supporting pillars.

Cathedral Interior
The presbytery, the ambulatory and the chapels retain a large number of Gothic, mainly early-14th-century, stained-glass windows.

Engelbert Reliquary (c.1630)
The cathedral treasury is famous for its large collection of golden objects, vestments and the fine ornamentation of its liturgical books.

Main entrance

Petrusportal, or the portal of St Peter, the only one built in the second half of the 14th century, has five Gothic figures.

STAR SIGHTS

★ **Gothic Stalls**

★ **Shrine of the Three Kings**

★ **Altar of the Magi**

★ Gothic Stalls
The massive oak stalls, built in 1308–11, were the largest that have ever been made in Germany.

VISITORS' CHECKLIST

Cathedral ◯ *6am–7:30pm daily.* Treasury *Domkloster 4.*
◻ *(0221) 27 28 01 65.*
◯ *10am–5pm daily.* ☒ ☒
Viewing platform ◯ *summer: 9am–5pm; winter: 10am–4pm.* ☒
Organ recitals *Jun–Aug:* 8pm Tue. Exhibition of Rubens tapestries *Whit Sunday until Ascension Day.*

Semicircular arches transfer the thrust of the vaults onto the buttresses.

Buttresses support the entire bulk of the cathedral.

High Altar
The Gothic altar slab, which dates back to the consecration of the presbytery, depicts the Coronation of the Virgin Mary, flanked by the twelve apostles.

★ Shrine of the Three Kings
This huge Romanesque reliquary was made by Nikolaus von Verdun in 1181–1220, to hold the relics of the Three Kings. These relics were brought to Köln in 1164 for Emperor Friedrich I Barbarossa.

Mailänder Madonna
This fine early-Gothic carving of the Milan Madonna and Child dates from around 1290. It is currently displayed in the Marienkapelle.

★ Altar of the Magi
This splendid altar (c.1445), the work of Stephan Lochner, is dedicated to the Three Kings, the patrons of Köln.

Wallraf-Richartz-Museum in Köln

THIS MUSEUM was named after Ferdinand Franz Wallraf, who bequeathed his art collection to the city in 1824, and Johann Heinrich Richartz, who funded the first building. In 1977, all 20th-century works of art were combined with the private collection of the Ludwig family and exhibited in the Museum Ludwig, initially located on the upper floors of the museum. In 1986, the Museum Ludwig moved to its own premises. The Wallraf-Richartz-Museum itself moved to a brand-new building in 2001.

Bleaching the Linen (1882)
Max Liebermann created this painting in the early stages of his career, when his work was largely concerned with Realism.

★ Stigmatization of St Francis (c.1616)
This dark and mysterious painting, originally created by Peter Paul Rubens for the Capuchin church in Köln, is untypical of the artist's work.

Third floor

Reclining Girl (1751)
This young nude, arranged on her bed in a provocative pose, is an example of the light-hearted works of so-called "boudoir art" that François Boucher specialized in.

Ground floor

★ Fifer and Drummer (1502–4)
This subtle painting, the wing of an altarpiece, is the work of Albrecht Dürer, who included himself in the scene – the drummer is a self-portrait of Dürer himself.

Main entrance

Girls on a Bridge
(1905)
*Edvard Munch covered
the same subject several
times (see p423). The version
held in Köln is one of the
earliest, and features an
urbanized landscape.*

Fifth floor

VISITORS' CHECKLIST

Wallraf-Richartz-Museum
Martinstraße 39.
(0221) 22 12 11 19.
10am–8pm Tue, 10am–6pm
Wed–Fri, 11am–6pm Sat & Sun.

GALLERY GUIDE
*Each floor in the museum
displays paintings belonging to one era. On the first
floor, the exhibition begins
with the collection of 14th-
century art; the third floor
holds 16th–17th century
art, and on the fifth floor
works of art from the 19th
century are displayed,
organized by the schools of
art they represent.*

**Jacob accuses
Laban of giving him
Lei instead of
Rachel as a wife**
(1628)
*This biblical scene
was painted by one of
the most outstanding
Dutch masters,
Hendrick ter
Brugghen.*

**First
floor**

**Old Woman
and Boy**
(c.1650–60)
*This scene was
painted by Bartolome
Esteban Murillo. The
artist excelled not
only as the master of
charmingly senti-
mental depictions of
the Madonna, but
was also an excellent
observer of everyday
life in 17th-century
Spain.*

Madonna and Child
(1325–30)
*This central panel of a trip-
tych by Simone Martini is
thought to have originated
from the San Agostino
church in San Giminiano.*

KEY

- Medieval paintings
- 17th- and 18th-century paintings
- 19th-century paintings
- Non-exhibition space

STAR EXHIBITS

★ **Fifer and Drummer**

★ **Stigmatization of
St Francis**

One of the artificial reservoirs in the northern Eifel

Northern Eifel 16

Road map A4. ℹ️ *Bad Münstereifel, Marktstraße 15 (02253) 922 20.* 🎭 *Bad Münstereifel: Burg in Flammen (Jul).*

BARELY 20 percent of the Eifel mountain range is in North Rhine-Westphalia. Low, forested mountains line the valley of the Rur river, which has been dammed in several places. The resulting artificial lakes provide a perfect opportunity for relaxation and sporting activities. There are also many attractive towns and fascinating monuments.

Blankenheim is famed for its picturesque half-timbered houses, the late-Gothic church and the frequently modified 12th-century castle of the counts von Manderscheid-Blankenheim, which today is a youth hostel. The source of the Ahr river can also be seen here – a house was built over the top of it in 1726.

In **Schleiden**, the castle, built in the 12th century and frequently rebuilt up until the 18th century, is worth visiting. There is also a late-Gothic church with valuable stained-glass windows and an impressive organ dating from 1770.

Probably the most beautiful town in this region is **Monschau**, which until 1919 was called Montjoie. It is known also for the Montjoier Düttchen (croissants) and an excellent mustard. The ruin of a 13th-century castle towers on a hill. At its foot, the Rur river runs through a narrow valley, with attractive small towns, narrow, steep streets and timber-frame houses from various eras. In Hasenfeld

visitors can see a dam dating from 1904, and an amazing hydro-electric building, decorated in a way that reflects its purpose. One of the most interesting monuments of this region is the Steinfeld monastery, with a history dating from the 10th century. In 1121 the Augustinians settled here, and in 1126 they accepted the rule of St Norbert of Xanten, and this became the first monastery on German territory. A beautiful Romanesque basilica was built in the second half of the 12th century. It has retained wall paintings from the 12th and 14th centuries, and vaulted ceilings from the 16th century. The **Rheinisches Freilichtmuseum Kommern** is an open-air museum with examples of the building styles typical of the Northern Eifel. It is also worth visiting the town of **Euskirchen**, which has an attractive Gothic church with superb furnishings, and the moated castle of Veynau (14–15th centuries).

Picturesque half-timbered houses in Monschau

The spa town of **Bad Münstereifel** dates back to 830, when a Benedictine monastery was established here. The present church is a 12th-century Romanesque basilica with impressive 11th-century frontage. Also worth seeing are the Gothic town hall and a Romanesque house, now housing a museum.

🏛 **Rheinisches Freilichtmuseum Kommern**
Auf dem Kahlenbusch. Mechernich-Kommern. 📞 *(02443) 998 00.* ⏰ *Apr–Oct: 9am–6pm; Nov–Mar: 10am–4pm.* 🎫

Brühl 17

Road map B4. 🚶 *42,000.* 🚉 🚌 ℹ️ *Uhlstr. 1 (02232-79 34 50).* 🎭 *Hubertusmarkt (Oct).*

THE SMALL town of Brühl has one of the most beautiful residential complexes, since 1984 a UNESCO World Heritage Site. As early as the 13th century, a palace was established here for the archbishops of nearby Köln, but this was destroyed in the 14th century. A Baroque palace, **Augustusburg**, was built on its foundations in 1725–8, according to a design by Johann Conrad Aschlaun. It was named after the instigator of the building, Elector Klemens August.

Merry-go-round at the Phantasialand in Brühl

The building was almost immediately refurbished, with a new façade and furnishings, the work of François Cuvilliés, and in the 1940s a new staircase was completed to a design by Balthasar Neumann. After devastation in World War II, the palace was carefully restored, and the magnificently furnished late-Baroque and Rococo interior, especially a stunning dining room designed by Cuvilliés, can now be seen again. A path leads from the orangery to a Gothic church built for the Franciscans in the 15th century. The *Annunciation* on the high altar is the work of Johann Wolfgang van der Auwer, while the magnificent

Phantasialand, the largest theme park in Germany, near Brühl

canopy above was designed by Balthasar Neumann. The castle is surrounded by a Baroque park, designed by Dominique Girard.

About 2 km (1 mile) east of the main residence is another castle, **Falkenlust**, built in 1729–40, to a design by Cuvilliés. Its captivating interior includes a lacquered and a mirror cabinet. Nearby stands an octagonal chapel, its interior decoration modelled on a secluded grotto.

It is also worth visiting the small villa near Augustusburg where the great Surrealist artist Max Ernst was born. It now houses a small display commemorating his work.

Another attraction, which draws a large number of visitors is **Phantasialand**, Germany's largest theme park. Visitors will need several days to see all the attractions of this vast fairground with its roller-coaster, water-rides and numerous merry-go-rounds.

♠ **Augustusburg**
(02232) 440 00. ○ Feb–Nov: 9am–noon & 1:30–5pm Tue–Fri, 10am–6pm Sat & Sun.

○ **Falkenlust**
(02232) 121 11. ○ Feb–Nov: 9am–12:30pm & 1:30–5pm Tue–Fri, 10am–6pm Sat & Sun.

○ **Phantasialand**
Berggeiststr. 31–41. (02232) 362 00. ○ Apr–Oct: 9am–6pm daily, later in summer. ⓳

ENVIRONS: Two moated houses await the visitor at **Kerpen**, 27 km (17 miles) to the north: the small 16th-century castle of Lörsfeld, and the Baroque palace of Türnich, built in 1756–66.

In **Pulheim-Brauweiler**, 30 km (19 miles) to the north, is an extremely beautiful Benedictine monastery, founded in 1024. Building began in 1048, funded by Rycheza, the wife of the Polish King Boleslav Chrobry.

From here it is worth travelling another 23 km (14 miles)

west to **Bedburg**, where the moated castle is worth seeing. This is a vast brick structure with four wings, which was established in stages over 300 years, starting in around 1300.

Bonn ⓲

See p394.

Königswinter ⓳

Road map B4. 🏘 35,000. 🚉 🚌
ℹ Drachenfelsstr. 11 (02223-91 77 11).

KÖNIGSWINTER lies in the centre of the Siebenge-birge, an attractive range of small, wooded mountains (the "seven mountains"), excellently suited for walking. The most popular mountain is the Drachenfels (dragon's rock). The oldest mountain railway in Germany, built in 1883, takes visitors to the top (321 m/1,053 ft). During the ascent visitors can see the Neo-Gothic Drachenburg, a palace dating from 1879–84, and on the top are the ruins of the Gothic Drachenburg, dating from the 12th century. The "dragon" in the name relates to the myth of the Nibelungs – the dragon slain by Siegfried was supposed to have lived here.

The little town of Königswinter, at the foot of the mountains, has picturesque 17th-century half-timbered houses, town houses and late 19th-century hotels.

ENVIRONS: Bad Honnef, 6 km (4 miles) to the south, is a charming spa town known as "Nice on the Rhine", where the former chancellor Konrad Adenauer lived until his death. A museum commemorates this great politician.

Situated 15 km (9 miles) to the north is **Siegburg**, where a Benedictine monastery (1064) is worth visiting. The walls of the crypt are from the 11th century, but the present church is a 17th-century building, rebuilt after World War II. The Anno-Schrein is a magnificent Romanesque reliquary box dating from 1183.

The Baroque Schloss Augustusburg in Brühl

Bonn ⑱

BONN was founded by the Romans in 11 BC, and flourished thanks to the archbishops of Cologne. It gained fame because of Ludwig van Beethoven, who was born here in 1770, and Robert Schumann, who spent the final years of his life here. The world heard of Bonn when, on 10 May 1949, it was elevated to the status of capital of the Federal Republic of Germany. When parliament decided in 1991 to make Berlin the capital of the newly unified country, Bonn was deprived of its role, although seven ministries stayed on.

The Baroque portal of the Beethovenhaus in Bonn

⛪ Beethovenhaus
Bonngasse 20. ☎ *(0228) 981 75 25.*
⏱ *Apr–Sep: 10am–6pm Mon–Sat, 11am–4pm Sun; Oct–Mar: 10am–5pm Mon–Sat, 11am–4pm Sun.* 🅿
The museum is housed in the Baroque 18th-century house where the composer Ludwig van Beethoven was born and lived until the age of 22. He never returned to his home town, but there is a large and impressive collection of memorabilia from his entire life.

⛪ Markt
The central market square in Bonn, shaped like a triangle, owes its present appearance to a mixture of modern and Baroque architecture. Its most outstanding feature is the late-Baroque **Rathaus** (town hall), built in 1737–8, to a design by Michel Leveilly. The centre of the market square is decorated with the Marktbrunnen, a fountain in the shape of an obelisk, erected in 1777 in honour of the Elector Maximilian Friedrich.

Not far from the Markt are some churches worth seeing. The first is the Gothic **Remigius-kirche**, built for the Franciscans in the years 1274–1317, and the second is the Baroque **Namen-Jesu-Kirche** built for the Jesuits according to a design by Jacob de Candreal in the years 1686–1717.

⛪ Rheinufer
The Rhine embankment, which changes its name several times along its course, runs along the western bank of the Rhine. Many of Bonn's attractions are grouped along this street. To the north of Kennedybrücke (Kennedy bridge) lies the Beethovenhalle, a vast concert and congress hall, and to the south of the bridge is the Bonn opera house.

Next to the opera is the Alter Zoll, the former customs house, based in one of the bastions that was part of the 17th-century city defences.

⛪ Universität
Am Hofgarten.
Founded in 1818, Bonn University is based in what is probably the most beautiful home for an educational institution anywhere in Germany. The stunningly attractive Baroque castle was built for the Elector Joseph Klemens in 1607–1705, to a design by Enrico Zuccalle, and extended after 1715 by Robert de Cotte.

⛪ Münster St Martin
Münsterplatz.
Bonn's cathedral is a magnificent example of Romanesque architecture in the Rhine Valley. The church was built in around 1150–1230, on the site of an earlier 11th-century cathedral, of which a three-naved crypt has survived. South of it, the romantic 12th-century Romanesque cloister is also worth seeing.

🏛 Rheinisches Landesmuseum
Colmantstraße 14–16.
☎ *(0228) 988 10.*
⏱ *Reopening after renovation end 2002; until then the collection is displayed at "Alte Rotation", Justus-von-Liebig-Str. 115.* ⏱ *11am–5pm Tue-Sun, 11am–8pm Wed.*

Gold clasps in the Rheinisches Landesmuseum

This interesting regional museum has a vast collection of excavated items dating back to Roman times, as well as medieval and modern art. The skull of a Neanderthal Man is also exhibited here.

The Baroque Elector's palace, housing Bonn University

🏛 Regierungsviertel

Until recently this was the central authority of one of the most powerful countries in Europe, and teeming with life. Now it creates a somewhat desolate impression. Some ministries and offices have remained in Bonn, and the transfer to Berlin is taking time, but the town is definitely changing.

The former Bundestag building, in the Regierungsviertel

🏛 Haus der Geschichte der BR Deutschland

Willy-Brandt-Allee 14. **(** *(0228) 916 50.* ○ *9am–7pm Tue–Sun.* 🖭
This excellent new history museum details the history of Germany after World War II, with fascinating multi-media displays and vast amounts of illustrative material.

🏛 Kunstmuseum Bonn

Friedrich-Ebert-Allee 2. **(** *(0228) 77 62 60.* ○ *10am–6pm Tue & Thu– Sun, 10am–9pm Wed.* ● *24, 25 & 31 Dec; Sat, Sun & Mon in carnival.*
This superb museum of 20th-century art, in an interesting building designed by Axel Schultes, has a great collection of Expressionist paintings, including many works by August Macke. Next to the museum is the Kunst- und

Ausstellungshalle, which opened in 1992 as a venue for temporary exhibitions.

🎭 Bad Godesberg

The small spa town of Bad Godesberg was incorporated into Bonn as recently as 1969. An elegant neighbourhood, its villas line the spa park. On top of the hill is the Godesburg, a castle dating from the 13th century, which has been a ruin since the 16th century.

⚓ Poppelsdorf

In this leafy southwestern suburb, the Baroque Schloss Clemensruhe (1715–18) is well worth visiting. Both the castle and its extensive park with an attractive botanical garden belong to the university. It is also worth making a detour to the Baroque pilgrimage church on the Kreuzberg, a low hill. The church houses the chapel of the Holy Steps, attributed to Balthasar Neumann.

The Baroque Schloss Clemensruhe, in Poppelsdorf

BONN CITY CENTRE

Beethovenhaus ①
Markt ②
Münster St Martin ⑤
Rheinufer ③
Universität ④

0 metres 300
0 yards 300

KEY

🛈 Tourist information
🅿 Parking
✝ Church

The medieval Oberes Schloss in Siegen

Siegen ⑳

Road map B4. 🚶 100,000. 🚗 🚌 ℹ️ Markt 2 (0271-404 13 16). 🎭 Kultur Pur (May/Jun), Rubensfest (Jun/Jul), Weihnachtsmarkt (Dec).

Beautifully located amidst the hills on the high banks of the Sieg river, Siegen is the largest town in the Siegerland region. For centuries the city was the residence of the dukes of Nassau. Religious divisions in the family resulted in two castles being built in Siegen. The **Oberes Schloss** (upper castle) is a medieval building, frequently refurbished in the 16th, 17th and 18th centuries. The museum, which has been opened inside the castle, has some paintings by Peter Paul Rubens, who was born in Siegen. The lower **Unteres Schloss** is a Baroque palace, which replaced an earlier building. In the centre of Siegen it is also worth visiting the **Nicolaikirche**, a 13th-century hexagonal church with a presbytery and tower, which served as the ducal family mausoleum.

Environs: In **Freudenberg**, 10 km (6 miles) northwest of Siegen, is the small settlement of Alter Flecken, which is reproduced in virtually all German guidebooks. Founded in 1666 at the instigation of Duke Johann Moritz von Nassau, the village consists of identical half-timbered houses.

Hagen ㉑

Road map B4. 🚶 210,950. 🚗 🚌 ℹ️ Pavilion im Volkspark (02331-207 58 88). 🎭 Marktschreiertage (Jan).

Hagen would probably not feature in the guidebooks, were it not for Karl Ernst Osthaus, who created an artists' colony here at the beginning of the 20th century, inviting Art Nouveau designers such as Peter Behrens and Henry van de Velde. The magnificent **Hohenhof**, Osthaus' home, was created by van der Velde. It houses the **Karl-Ernst-Osthaus-Museum**, with a collection of modern art. Behrens designed the crematorium in the suburb of Delstern and the beautiful villas **Haus Como** (Hafleyer Str. 35) and **Haus Goedeke** (Amselgasse). In the south of the town is the Westfälisches Freilichtmuseum, a popular open-air museum, which displays many historic workshops and factories with reconstructed equipment.

Sauerland ㉒

Road map B4. ℹ️ Sauerland-Touristik, Brilon, Heinrich-Jansen-Weg 14 (02961-94 32 29).

The Sauerland is the region to the south and east of the Ruhr coalfields, making an obvious holiday destination for the inhabitants of this large, industrialized conurbation. Embracing the northern part of the Rhenish slate massif, its densely wooded mountains are not high – the highest peak is Hegekopf at 843 m (2,766 ft). Crossed by rivers teeming with fish and full of artificial lakes, the area is perfect for walking, cycling and fishing.

Enjoyable days can be had on an excursion to one of the caves such as **Attahöhle**, **Dechenhöhle** and **Heinrichshöhle** near Iserlohn. There are charming towns, too, and in **Breckerfeld**, the Gothic parish church has preserved a superb altar, from around 1520. The main attraction in **Altena** is the superb, gigantic Burg (castle), built in the 12th century and restored in the early 20th century. In 1910 the world's first youth hostel for tourists

One of the charming villages, nestling in the hilly landscape of the Sauerland

Timber-frame house, typical of the Sauerland landscape

was created here. The 14th-century Schloss Wocklum in **Balve** was rebuilt in the 18th century. One of the greatest tourist draws in the Sauerland is the **Möhnesee**, a lake with a huge dam, built in 1908–12 and bombed by Allied "dambusters" in 1943 with catastrophic consequences. **Arnsberg** has a regional museum and the lovely Neo-Gothic moated castle Herdringen with assorted furnishings from other castles.

In the south extend the Rothaargebirge (red-haired mountains). Their most beautiful town is the spa resort of Bad Berleburg, while the Kahler Asten mountain and the town of Winterberg are popular winter sports areas.

Soest ㉓

Road map B4. 🏘 *50,000.* 🚉 🚌 🛈 *Am Seel 5 (02921-103 14 14).* 🎪 *Bördetag (May), Gauklertag (Sep), Jahrmarkt Allerheiligenkirmes (Nov).*

THE WESTPHALIAN town of Soest made its mark in history when, in about 1100, the town's civic rights were formulated and subsequently adopted by 65 other towns. Today the town captivates visitors with its well-preserved old town, its historic churches, and the almost completely intact walls which surround the town. The focus of the old town is the Romanesque **Propsteikirche St Patrokli**, founded in 965 by Bruno, archbishop of Cologne, and built in stages until the 13th century. Further historic buildings are grouped around the church: the 18th-century, Baroque **Rathaus** (town hall),

the 12th-century Romanesque **Petrikirche** with its Gothic presbytery, and the 12th-century **Nicolaikapelle**, a chapel with 13th-century wall paintings and an altar painted by Konrad von Soest.

In the northern part of the old town, two churches are worth seeing: the **Hohnekirche** with beautiful Gothic and early Baroque furnishings, and the **Wiesenkirche** with equally valuable furnishings and a magnificent group of stained-glass windows from the 14th and 15th centuries. The window above the northern portal shows the so-called Westphalian Last Supper, depicting a table laden with plentiful Westphalian smoked ham and local pumpernickel bread.

ENVIRONS: In **Lippstadt**, 23 km (14 miles) east of Soest, it is worth visiting the Gothic Marienkirche. In the suburb of Bökenförde is the 18th-century Baroque moated palace Schwarzenraben, and there is an early-Baroque castle in Overhagen.

Paderborn ㉔

Road map C3. 🏘 *140,000.* 🚉 🚌 🛈 *Marienplatz 2 (05251-88 29 80).* 🎪 *Puppenfestspiele (Jan), Schützenfest (Jul), Liborifest (Jul–Aug), Liborikirmes (Oct).*

PADERBORN has featured on the historical map for over 1,000 years. In the 8th century Charlemagne built a palace here, and in about AD 800, a bishopric was established. The town's most important monument is the beautiful **Dom St Maria, St Kilian und St Liborius**, a Romanesque-Gothic cathedral. This enormous hall-church with two transepts and tall front tower suffered greatly during World War II, but it continues to captivate visitors with its magnificent decor on the richly carved portal, the great

An ornate window in the Dom in Paderborn

Romanesque crypt, interesting plaques and richly decorated bishops' tombs and epitaphs. The diocesan museum holds the Imad-Madonna, funded by Bishop Imad, an outstanding figure of the Madonna and Child dating from 1051–8. On the northern side of the cathedral a section of the foundations of the emperor's palace can be seen, together with the **Bartholomäuskapelle** (chapel of St Bartholomew), the oldest hall-church in Germany, completed in 1017. To the south of the cathedral complex, on Rathausplatz, is the exceptionally beautiful **Rathaus** (town hall) dating from 1613–20. An example of the Weser-Renaissance style, it is crowned with richly ornamented gables. The **Heinz-Nixdorf-Museumsforum** provides a pleasant break from the past – this museum is dedicated to the history of computers.

ENVIRONS: Near **Stukenbrock**, 15 km (9 miles) north of Paderborn, is the theme park Hollywood-Park and the fascinating Safariland, where more than 500 African animals roam freely.

Tower of the Romanesque-Gothic Dom in Paderborn

Front of the early-Romanesque Abtei Corvey in Höxter

the centre of Höxter is a Gothic church built for the Franciscans in 1248–1320.

The city's greatest attraction, however, is the magnificent **Abtei Corvey**, a monastery founded in 822. It was originally built as the church of St Stephen and St Vitus, but only the grandiose two-storey frontage completed in 885 survived. It became the model for several other churches built in Westphalia, while the main body of the church was rebuilt in the 17th century.

Höxter **㉕**

Road map C3. 🏚 35,000. 🚊 🚌
ℹ️ Weserstraße 11 (05271-96 34 31).
🎭 Corveyer Musikwochen (May–Jun), Huxorimarkt (Sep), Kirchenmusiktage (Nov–Dec).

IN A PICTURESQUE situation on the Weser river, Höxter can pride itself on its beautiful old town with many timber-frame houses, fragments of the city walls, a Renaissance **Rathaus** (town hall) from 1610, and important churches. The history of **Kilianikirche**, in the centre of the old town, goes back to the late 8th century, although in its present form it is a Romanesque building from the 11th–12th centuries. Also in

Lemgo **㉖**

Road map C3. 🏚 42,000. 🚊 🚌
ℹ️ Papenstr. 7 (05261-98 87 10).

THIS EXCEPTIONALLY pretty town was founded in 1190 by Bernhard II von Lippe. Lemgo was a member of the Hanseatic League, and had its heyday during the witch hunts of the 17th century. Today, Lemgo has numerous Renaissance monuments – the charming old town was spared during World War II, and the Gothic Nicolaikirche and Marienkirche, with Gothic wall paintings and a Renaissance organ by Georg Slegel, have survived. The pearl of the city is the beautiful **Rathaus** (town hall), built in the 15th–17th centuries. It contains an original pharmacy that is still in use. Many timber-frame houses have also survived, the best ones in Papen-, Mittel- and Echternstraße.

The picturesque Renaissance Rathaus in Höxter

Façade of a Renaissance pharmacy inside the Rathaus in Lemgo

The most beautiful house in Lemgo is the **Hexenbürger-meisterhaus**. This "witches' mayor's house" (1571), an excellent example of Weser Renaissance, belonged to the mayor, Hermann Cothmann, who started the witch hunt. It now houses a town museum. Also worth visiting are the **Junkerhaus** (1891), the architect's home, and **Schloss Brake** (13th-16th centuries), a castle which now houses the **Weserrenaissance-Museum**.

🏛 **Weserrenaissance-Museum**
Schloss Brake. 📞 (05261) 94 50 25. ⏰ 10am–6pm Tue–Sun.

Teutoburger Wald (Teutoburg Forest) **㉗**

Road map C3. ℹ️ Detmold, Rathaus Am Markt 5 (05231-97 73 28).
🎭 Andreas-Messe in Detmold (Nov).

A RANGE OF LOW mountains extending from Osnabrück through Bielefeld right up to Paderborn, the Teutoburg Forest is one of the most attractive tourist regions in Westphalia. The best base for walking and cycling holidays is **Detmold**, which has a very attractive old town with well-preserved timber-frame buildings from various periods, and the elegant Residenz-schloss, the castle of the zur Lippe family. Originally medieval, the palace was rebuilt in the 16th century in the Weser-

Renaissance style. The interior is composed of 17th and 19th century furnishings. The star feature is a set of eight gobelins crafted in a Brussels workshop around 1670, showing scenes of Alexander the Great's triumphs. Furnishings from the 19th century include designs by Charles Le Brun.

Three km (2 miles) south of Detmold is the spot where in the year AD 9 Cherusko Arminius, known as Hermann, leader of the Germanic tribes, triumphed against the Roman army led by Varus. At the top of the mountain, the **Hermannsdenkmal**, a huge monument designed by Ernst von Bandel, was erected in 1838–75. It was supposed to symbolize the German struggle for unification.

Two fascinating attractions near Detmold are the **Adlerwarte Berlebeck**, an ornithological research station, where eagles and many other birds of prey can be observed, and the **Vogelpark Heiligenkirchen**, a bird park with over 2,000 varieties of birds in all shapes and sizes from around the world.

Hermannsdenkmal, near Detmold

Bielefeld ㉘

Road map C3. ㊊ 325,000. 🚉 🚌
🛈 Niederwall 23 (0521-51 69 98).
🎭 Hermannslauf (Apr), Leinenweber-Markt (May), Bielefelder Kultur-Sommer (May–Sep), Sparrenburgfest (Jul), Weinmarkt (Sep), Weihnachtsmarkt (Dec).

ON THE EDGE of the Teutoburg Forest, Bielefeld owes its evolution to the production of and trading in linen. The old town is dominated by the **Sparrenburg** castle, built in the 13th century for the von Ravensburg family. In the 16th century the castle was surrounded by new fortifications including new bastions, and in the 19th century the residential part of the city was greatly extended.

The central feature of the old town is Alter Markt (old market), on which stands the

Nicolaikirche. This Gothic church suffered heavily in World War II, although the marvellous Antwerp altar (c.1520) was preserved. Nearby, on Obernstraße, stands the **Crüwell-Haus**, an interesting late-Gothic town house from the early 16th century. The street leads to St Jodokus-Kirche, a late-Gothic church, whose greatest treasure is the amazing figure of the Black Madonna (c.1220). Further south is the **Kunsthalle**, a modern building with a significant collection of 20th-century art. It is also worth visiting the **Marienkirche** in the new town. Built in 1280–1330, this Gothic church holds the tomb of one of the von Ravensburg dukes (c.1320) and a high altar (c.1400) with a central Gothic section.

ENVIRONS: Picturesque **Herford**, 17 km (11 miles) north of Bielefeld, has a lovely old town with timber-frame houses and beautiful Gothic churches.

In **Enger**, 21 km (13 miles) to the north, in the former church of the canons, a tomb dating from 1100 has been preserved, which holds the remains of the Saxon Duke Widukind, buried in 807.

The spa town of **Bad Salzuflen** with its pretty old town and spa park is the ideal place for those seeking relaxation.

An observation tower in the Sparrenburg complex in Bielefeld

The Wasserstraßenkreuzung (waterway junction) in Minden

Minden ㉙

Road map C3. ㊊ 85,000. 🚉 🚌
🛈 Domstraße (0571-829 06 59).
🎭 Klassik-Open-Air (Aug).

CHARLEMAGNE created a bishopric here as early as 798. The town evolved thanks to its strategic location on the Weser river. The city's most important monument is the cathedral, **Dompfarrkirche St Petrus und St Gorgonius**. It has a Romanesque presbytery, transept and monumental frontage built in the 11th–12th centuries, although the body of the church is an example of early-Gothic style from the 13th century. It is worth visiting the church treasury with its 11th-century crucifix.

The **Rathaus** (town hall), with 13th-century lower sections, is worth seeing, as are Minden's many charming houses around the market square. A great attraction is the **Wasserstraßenkreuzung** (waterway junction), where a 375-m (1,230-ft) long bridge takes the Mittellandkanal across the Weser river.

ENVIRONS: On top of a hill in **Porta Westfalica**, 6 km (4 miles) south of Minden, is a giant monument to Kaiser Wilhelm (1892–6), designed by Bruno Schmitz.

The **Westfälische Mühlenstraße**, (Westphalian mill route), signposted around Minden, takes visitors past 42 different mills and windmills.

NORTHERN GERMANY

Northern Germany at a Glance

NORTHERN GERMANY has very varied landscapes, ranging from the sandy beaches on the Baltic and North Sea coasts to the moraine hills of Schleswig-Holstein and the moorlands of the Lüneburger Heide. Nature-lovers are enchanted by the countless lakes in Mecklenburg and the Harz mountains, while those interested in history or architecture enjoy the Renaissance castles along the Weser River and the Gothic brick architecture in former Hanseatic towns. Historic buildings in Goslar and Hildesheim testify to the importance of these two towns.

Helgoland is a popular tourist destination. Red cliffs as high as skyscrapers, a picturesque town and the sea aquarium are the star attractions of this island.

SCHLESWIG-HOLSTEIN
(see pp440–51)

LOWER SAXONY, HAMBURG AND BREMEN
(see pp410–39)

Oldenburg, symbolized by its heraldic shield, is famous for its large collection of paintings and interiors in its Kunstmuseum (art museum).

Bremen, a historic harbour town, draws visitors with its many historic buildings and monuments, including a Renaissance-Gothic town hall.

Fehmarn, the second largest German island, is linked with the German mainland by a railway bridge constructed in 1963.

Rügen enchants visitors with its chalky white cliffs, which contrast starkly with the deep blues and greens of the surrounding Baltic Sea.

MECKLENBURG
LOWER POMERANIA
(see pp152–67)

Lübeck suffered massive damage in World War II, but its Gothic town hall survived the attacks and the city's beautiful old town has been rebuilt.

0 km   50

0 miles   50

Hamburg not only has attractive museums and valuable monuments, but also such lively and bustling places as the Fischmarkt, a huge market held every Sunday morning where it is possible to purchase virtually anything.

Gothic Brick Architecture

BRICK WAS used as a building material in many parts of medieval Europe, but in Northern Germany it gave rise to the distinctive style of *Backsteingotik* (brick Gothic). Brick technology was introduced in the mid-12th century by Norbertine monks arriving from Lombardy. The style is characterized by a rich variety of vaults, the use of buttresses instead of supporting arches, and colourful designs achieved by using glazed bricks. Through trade and the activities of religious orders these forms spread throughout the Baltic region.

Terracotta decoration

The storeys are divided by friezes.

MARIENKIRCHE IN LÜBECK
Considered the crowning achievement of *Backsteingotik*, this church, built from around 1260, became the model for countless others, including the cathedral in Schwerin. It is a triple-naved basilica, with a twin-towered façade, braced with buttresses.

The eastern façade of many churches, such as the Marienkirche in Prenzlau (above) was often crowned by an elaborate, ornamental gable.

A pointed arched portal, decorated with ceramic borders, was a typical feature of many village churches.

Main portal

Gables with tiled decorations and intricate openwork, such as this gable of the south chapel of the Nikolaikirche in Wismar, are a feature of many Lower Pomeranian churches.

The vast twin-towered façade symbolizes the power of its founders – wealthy Lübeck patricians.

Terracotta tiles with raised decorative motifs were used in brick architecture in place of stone bas-reliefs.

Turret for smallest church bell

The arcades between the naves are tall and narrow, culminating in acutely pointed arches.

Complex star vaulting with intricate ribbing replaced the earlier cross-ribbed vaulting.

Flying buttresses are rare in brick-built churches.

Stepped walls were used to dress the façades of the church. They were an important element in the construction.

Beam openings indicate that a robust type of scaffolding was used in the course of construction. The ends of the beams are incorporated in the walls.

Friezes on the arcades, such as this interlaced motif made from brick, are frequently used as a decorative element, even in village churches.

SECULAR BRICK ARCHITECTURE

Backsteingotik was not confined to churches – this style was used in magnificent town halls, weigh-houses, gateways and houses, mostly on narrow plots, with elaborate gables decorated with glazed bricks and white plasterwork.

Gothic house on the market square in Greifswald

The German Coastline

THE WATERS of two seas – the North Sea and the
Baltic Sea – lap on northern Germany's
shores, linked by the Kiel Canal, which cuts
across the base of the Jutland peninsula. The
cool climate on the coast makes for short
summers yet, on a sunny day, the beaches are
packed with holidaymakers, and a holiday here
can have a lot to offer. Heiligendamm was the
first seaside resort to be established in Germany,
in 1783 by a duke of Mecklenburg. By the end of
the 19th century, spas with elegant villas, prome-
nades and piers were springing up everywhere.
A popular attraction are the *Strandkörbe*
– huge wickerwork beach chairs.

*The sand dunes form
part of a nature reserve
in the northern part of
Sylt, the largest of the
North Frisian islands.*

*The Cliffs of Helgoland have
a characteristic reddish hue
indicating the red sandstone
from which they are composed.*

NORDFRIESISCHE INSELN

Sylt

NORDFRIESLAND

11

42

41

199

199   201

Flensburg

5

201

Schleswig

201

76   Kiel

Rendsburg

203

Helgoland

205

23

77

Neumünster

5

Itzehoe

206

E45/7

E234/27

73

Elmshorn

495

73

Pinneberg

Hambu

Reinbek

E22/1

NORDSEE (NORTH SEA)

OSTFRIESLAND

72

Wilhelmshaven

210   72   436

437

Bremerhaven

71

Emden

31

E22/28

29

74

71

E22/A7

70

72

Oldenburg

*The Kiel Canal,
known in Ger-
many as the Nord-
Ostsee-Kanal, was
constructed in
1887–95. Around
40,000 vessels pass
through the canal
every year.*

Borkum, *one of the East Frisian
islands, was once inhabited by
whalers. Garden fences were
often constructed from whale
bones, and some have survived
to the present day.*

Bremerhaven *is a vast port at the
mouth of the Weser river. It was constructed from 1837 to support the
port of Bremen, which is located
farther inland, away from the sea.*

Stralsund, a Hanseatic harbour town with a medieval lay-out, has a large number of well-preserved historic monuments.

On the small, flat island of *Hiddensee* all car traffic is banned. The island was much loved by the writer Gerhart Hauptmann, who lies buried here in the local cemetery.

THE COASTLINE

The hinterland of the Baltic region is generally flat and sandy, but in some areas it is steep and rocky. For visitors the greatest draw are the islands: Rügen with its steep chalky cliffs, Usedom with its wide, sandy beaches and Hiddensee. Off the lowlands and the marshy coastal region in the hinterland of the North Sea coast extends the chain of Frisian islands.

The beach at Ablbeck and the pier with its restaurant are the greatest attractions on the island of Usedom, at the mouth of the Oder river.

OSTSEE (BALTIC SEA)

207

LÜBECKER BUCHT

105

Wismar

20

103

Rostock

Ribnitz- Damgarten

Güstrow

104

Schwerin

Stralsund

96

E251/96

Greifswald

Anklam

Bergen
RÜGEN

ODERBUCHT

109

Ueckermünde

Rügen, famous for its unusual chalky cliff formations, was immortalized by Caspar David Friedrich and continues to inspire artists.

0 km ————— 60
0 miles ————— 60

CROSS-SECTION OF WATT

The Watt is a flat, boggy stretch of coastline, up to several kilometres wide, which is covered by the sea as the tide comes in, and laid bare as it goes out again. The Watt land-scape is fairly monoton-ous, but it is fascinating to observe the rich flora and fauna, which has adapted to cope with life both underwater and exposed to the air.

Winkles and other small snails live in the coastal zone by the sea.

Starfish

Lugworm and sand cast

Sand gaper (mussel)

LOWER SAXONY, HAMBURG AND BREMEN

*T*HREE *federal states – Lower Saxony and the independent city states of Hamburg and Bremen – cover an enormous terrain, embracing the whole of northwestern Germany. For the visitor they provide a series of memorable snapshots: the mighty cosmopolitan port of Hamburg, enchanting towns and villages with half-timbered houses and the blooming heather of the Lüneburger Heide.*

Lower Saxony was formed in the 19th century through the merging of the kingdom of Hannover with the duchy of Brunswick, Oldenburg and Schaumburg-Lippe and other parts of northern Germany. The second-largest German state after Bavaria, it only ranks fourth in terms of the number of its inhabitants, being less densely populated than other states.

Lower Saxony is characterized by lowlands that become hillier in the south, culminating in the Harz Mountains. The only large cities are Hannover, a modern centre renowned for its trade fairs and for hosting Expo 2000, and Braunschweig, a venerable town that cherishes its link with the Saxon king Heinrich der Löwe, its first important ruler. The Romanesque splendour of Hildesheim is a magnet for visitors, as are the Renaissance centres along the Weser River including Hameln, the charming towns of Celle, Lüneburg and Einbeck, and Wolfenbüttel, Stadthagen and Bückeburg which contain some remarkable Mannerist works of art.

Nature lovers will enjoy excursions to the Lüneburger Heide or paddling in the endless expanses of mud-flats in the North Sea. Tourists are also attracted by the sandy beaches of the East Frisian islands, as well as the solitary rock of the island of Helgoland.

The "free and Hanseatic" towns of Hamburg and Bremen rejoice in a different atmosphere, urban and urbane, tolerant and multicultural, based on centuries of trade with the world.

The glorious moorlands of the Lüneburger Heide, with tall juniper bushes and flowering heathers

◁ The charming Gänselieselbrunnen (goose girl fountain) in the market square in Göttingen

Exploring Lower Saxony, Hamburg and Bremen

Hamburg and Bremen, the region's largest cities, are also the most convenient bases for tourists, offering accommodation in every price category. The most attractive area in this region is the southeastern section, extending to the foothills of the Harz Mountains with picturesque towns, such as the university town of Göttingen, Romanesque Hildesheim or the stunningly beautiful merchant town of Goslar. A visit to the seaside and an excursion to the islands are also enjoyable.

SEE ALSO

• **Where to Stay** pp492–5

• **Where to Eat** pp523–5

OSTFRIESISCHE INSELN ❶

OSTFRIESLAND ❷

WILHELMSHAVEN

EMDEN

OLDENBURG ❹ E22/28 BREM[EN] ❼

CLEMENSWERTH ❸   E233/213   CLOPPENBURG ❺

NORDHORN

OSNABRÜCK ❻

WIEHENGEBIRGE

BÜCKEB[URG]

436   29   437   E234/27   31   72   E37/29   31   70   Obe   69   51   51   E37/1   65   51

The crowning feature of the bay window of the Dempterhaus in Hameln

The massive edifice of the Neues Rathaus in Hannover

0 km		40
0 miles		40

KEY

▦	Motorway
▦	Main road
	Scenic route
	River
✷	Viewpoint

GETTING AROUND

There are international airports in Hamburg, Bremen and Hannover. A network of motorways links Lower Saxony with Scandinavia (via Schleswig-Holstein), and with the rest of western Europe (via the Netherlands or southern Germany). There are good ferry connections between Hamburg and Harwich (England). An extensive rail network makes the entire state accessible, although bus connections are limited.

The Grosse Wallanlagen Park in Hamburg, laid out along the city's former fortifications

SIGHTS AT A GLANCE

Altes Land **9**
Braunschweig (Brunswick) **18**
Bremen pp416–19 **7**
Bückeburg **17**
Celle **14**
Clemenswerth **3**
Cloppenburg **5**
Duderstadt **25**
Einbeck **23**
Goslar pp436–7 **22**
Göttingen **24**
Hamburg pp420–25 **8**
Hannover (Hanover) pp430–31 **20**
Hildesheim pp434–5 **21**
Lüneburg **11**
Lüneburger Heide **12**
Oldenburg **4**
Osnabrück **6**
Ostfriesische Inseln (East Frisian Islands) **1**
Ostfriesland (Eastern Frisia) **2**
Soltau **13**
Stade **10**
Stadthagen **16**
Wolfenbüttel **19**
Wolfsburg **15**

Tours
The Weser Renaissance Trail **26**

Ostfriesische Inseln (East Frisian Islands) ❶

Road map B2. ⛴ *Emden-Borkum, Norden-Norddeich to Juist and Norderney, Nessmersiel-Baltrum, Bensersiel-Langeoog, Neuharlingersiel-Spiekeroog, Harlesiel-Wangerooge.*
🏠 *(01805) 20 20 96.*
ⓦ *www.die-nordsee.de*

Moormuseum in Elisabethfehn, Ostfriesland

A LONG THE North Sea Coast extends the belt of East Frisian Islands consisting of, from west to east: Borkum, Juist, Norderney, Baltrum, Langeoog, Spiekeroog and Wangerooge. All around them is the **Nationalpark Niedersächsisches Wattenmeer**, a large national park established to protect the unique ecosystem of the shallow seas. At low tide it turns into vast mud-flats, extending to the horizon. This is the time to tour the Watt, as it is known locally, either by horse-drawn carriage or barefoot – always making sure to return before the tide comes in!

The islands themselves, with their beautiful sandy beaches, sand dunes and healthy climate, are among the most popular holiday destinations in Germany.

The car-free island Juist, a 17-km (11-mile) strip of land less than 500 m (1,640 ft) wide, and Norderney with its main town of the same name are the most interesting islands. Neo-Classical villas recall the days when such figures as Heinrich Heine and Otto von Bismarck spent their holidays here. It is also worth

visiting Wangerooge, another island where cars are banned. Three lighthouses – Westturm, Alter Leuchtturm and Neuer Leuchtturm – indicate the island's role in the navigation of the Weser River estuary.

Ostfriesland (East Frisia) ❷

Road map B2. 🚉 *Emden, Leer, Norden.* 🏠 *(01805) 20 20 96.*
ⓦ *www.die-nordsee.de* 🏛 *Kiewittmarkt (end Mar); Altstadtfest (Aug).*

E AST FRISIA is a peninsula near the border with the Netherlands and the Jadebusen bay, at Wilhelmshaven. This is a land of flat meadows, grazing cows and windmills.

It is worth visiting **Emden**, the region's capital, with its attractive town hall resembling that in Antwerp, and a town centre crossed by many canals. The **Nannen-Kunsthalle Emden**, founded in the early 1990s by Henri Nannen, publisher of the weekly news magazine *Stern*, holds a remarkable collection of 19th-century paintings, including the works of many German Expressionists such as Emil Nolde, Max Beckmann and Oskar Kokoschka.

Another attraction is the **Moor- und Fehnmuseum** (moor and fen museum) in Elisabethfehn, which is dedicated to the extraction of peat. Its exhibits include the world's largest plough, as well as the story of Jever, the local beer. Also worth visiting are the Renaissance palace whose reception hall has a ceiling with sunken panels, and next

to the parish church the wood and stone tomb of the Frisian leader Edo Wiemken, made in 1561– 4 by master craftsmen from Antwerp.

🏛 Nannen-Kunsthalle Emden
Hinter dem Rahmen 13. 📞 *(04921) 974 00.* ⏰ *10am–8pm Tue, 10am–5pm Wed–Fri, 11am–5pm Sat & Sun.* ⬛ *1 May, 25 & 31 Dec.* 📷

🏛 Moor- und Fehnmuseum
Elisabethfehn. 📞 *(04499) 22 22.*
⏰ *end Mar–end Oct: 10am–6pm Tue–Sun & bank holidays.*

Clemenswerth ❸

Road map B3. 🚉 *Sögel or Lathen.* 🏠 *Papenburg, Hauptkanal rechts 68/69 (04961-194 33).*

E MSLAND, to the south of East Frisia, extends along the Dutch border, a poor area since time immemorial, with moors and boglands. Only the discovery of oil in the 20th century engineered its progress. Sögel, 33 km (21 miles) south of Greater Papenburg, has the region's greatest attraction, the palatial hunting lodge Clemenswerth, built from 1737– 49. In search of solitude, the elector and archbishop of Cologne Clemens August commissioned the lodge from Johan Conrad Schlaun. The design was modelled on the pavilion-pagoda of Nymphenburg in Munich. Altogether it comprises seven pavilions with mansard roofs and a chapel. All the brick buildings were laid out on a green lawn, creating a star shape around the palace. The landscaped park adds to the romantic atmosphere. The Baroque interior accommodates a museum of the region.

Nationalpark Niedersächsisches Wattenmeer in the Greefsiel area

Oldenburg ❹

Road map B2. 🏚 155,000. 🚉
🛈 Wallstr. 14 (0441-157 44).
🎪 Hafenfest (7 days after Whitsun); Altstadtfest (end Aug); Kramermarkt (Sep/Oct).

A THOUSAND YEARS old, and once part of Denmark, this town remained the seat of a duchy until 1918.

The **Lambertikirche**, in the central market square, is a late-Gothic hall-church with a Neo-Classical rotunda added in 1797. The **Schloss**, the ducal residence, displays a similar marriage of styles, particularly Baroque and Neo-Classical. The **Landesmuseum für Kunst und Kulturgeschichte** (state museum of art and culture), based in the castle, is known mainly for its collection of paintings assembled by Wilhelm Tischbein, who lived here for 25 years. The affiliated **Augusteum**, a Neo-Renaissance building in a picturesque spot, holds the museum's modern collection.

🏛 **Landesmuseum für Kunst und Kulturgeschichte**
Elisabethstr. 1. 📞 (0441) 220 73 00.
🕐 9am–5pm Tue, Wed & Fri, 9am–8pm Thu, 10am–5pm Sat & Sun.
⬤ 1 Jan, Good Friday, Easter, 1 May, 24, 25 & 31 Dec. 🖼

ENVIRONS: The small spa town of **Bad Zwischenahn** is worth a visit. Its star attraction is the Gothic St Johanniskirche with frescoes from 1512.

A windmill in the open-air museum in Cloppenburg

Cloppenburg ❺

Road map B2. 🏚 29,000.
🛈 Eschstr. 9 (04471-152 56).
🎪 Mariä Geburtsmarkt (Sep).

T HE SMALL market town of Cloppenburg boasts the **Museumsdorf**, the oldest open-air museum in Germany, established in 1934. On a vast site, 50 architectural monuments from all over Lower Saxony have been assembled. There are houses, including charming examples of the half-timbered style of Wehlburg, windmills and a small 17th-century church from Klein-Escherde near Hildesheim.

To the east of Cloppenburg lies Visbek. Here the visitor is taken back to the Stone Age, with megalithic graves from 3,500 to 1,800 BC, including the 80-m (262-ft) long grave known as "Visbeker Bräutigam" (bridegroom) and the even larger, 100-m (321-ft) long "Visbeker Braut" (bride).

🏛 **Museumsdorf Cloppenburg**
Bether Straße 6. 📞 (04471) 948 40.
🕐 Mar–Oct: 9am–6pm daily, Nov–Feb: 9am–4pm daily. 🖼

Osnabrück ❻

Road map B3. 🏚 157,000. 🚉
🛈 Kranstr. 58 (0541-32 32 202).

T HIS WESTPHALIAN town has been a bishop's see since the time of Charlemagne. In 1648, negotiations took place here between representatives of Sweden and the Protestant duchies of the Reich. The signing of the Peace of Westphalia in 1648, which ended the Thirty Years' War, was announced from the town hall steps. It was also the birthplace of the writer Erich Maria Remarque in 1899.

Despite damage in World War II, the **Dom St Peter**, Osnabrück's 13th-century cathedral, is worth visiting. It has a bronze baptismal font and enormous triumphal cross, and the late-Gothic Snetlage-Altar of the Crucifixion. From here a short walk takes the visitor to the market square, Marienkirche and the Gothic **Rathaus** (town hall), with a sculpture of Charlemagne.

Epitaph for Albert von Bevessen in the Dom in Osnabrück

ENVIRONS: South of Osnabrück is the western part of the Teutoburger Wald (Teutoburg Forest). The spa town of **Bad Iburg**, 12 km (8 miles) to the south of Osnabrück, has a monumental Benedictine monastery and bishop's palace. The Rittersaal (knights' hall) is worth seeing, with its giant ceiling fresco depicting an architectural fantasy of foreshortened perspectives.

The Schloss in Oldenburg, featuring Baroque and Neo-Classical styles

Bremen ●

BREMEN, together with its deep-water port Bremerhaven, constitutes a separate town state. Not so much a bustling modern metropolis as a peaceful country town, it is conscious of its historical origins dating back to Charlemagne. The townscape is not dominated by the port as in Hamburg, but by the old town with its magnificent cathedral and town hall. Bremen enjoyed prosperity from 1358 when it joined the Hanseatic League, its wealth based on the coffee and wool trade. Today, Bremen still benefits from its port, which ships around 700,000 cars a year.

Statue of the Bremen Town Musicians, by Gerhard Marcks

Gabled houses and the statue of Roland in the Marktplatz

Exploring Bremen

Most of Bremen's tourist attractions are in the old town, on the east bank of the Weser River. The area is easy to pick out on a map as it is surrounded by a green belt, established when the town's fortifications were demolished. The Übersee-museum (ethnography museum) is close to the old town, and trams run to Schwachhausen, where the Focke-Museum is based.

🏛 Marktplatz

On the main square of Medie-val Bremen stand the town hall and the cathedral, and, on the west side, several gabled houses. This lovely view is slightly marred by the unattractive 1960s Haus der Bürgerschaft, the state parliament building.

In front of the town hall stands a 10-m (32-ft) statue of Roland, dating from 1404. It is the largest of many similar statues in German towns, and the prototype for others. A nephew of Charlemagne, Roland symbolizes a town's

independence. His gaze is directed toward the cathedral, the residence of the bishop, who frequently sought to restrict Bremen's autonomy. Roland's sword of justice symbolizes the judiciary's independence, and the engraved motto confirms the emperor's edict, conferring town rights onto Bremen.

The second, more recent (1953) monument in the square is dedicated to the Bremen Town Musicians – a donkey, dog, cat and cockerel,

who according to the Grimm fairy tale trekked to Bremen.

🏛 Rathaus

Marktplatz. **☎** (0421) 32 12 29. ◻ 11am, noon, 3pm, 4pm daily.

The original Gothic building dating from the years 1405–10 was clad with a magnificent Renaissance façade, one of the finest examples of Weser Renaissance architecture in northern Germany, designed by Lüder von Bentheim. He masterfully incorporated the Gothic figures of Charle-magne and seven Electors, as well as four prophets and four wise men. In the 40-m (131-ft) Große Halle (great hall) new laws were passed, as symbolized by the fresco (1932) of Solomon's court. Among its many other treasures, the meticulously crafted Renaissance spiral staircase is worth mentioning. On the western side of the town hall is the entrance to the "Ratskeller" where you can sample 600 different wines, and delight in the murals from 1927, by the Impressionist Max Slevogt.

The late-Renaissance façade of Bremen's Rathaus

⚜ Schütting
Marktplatz.

On the southwestern side of Marktplatz stands this mansion used by the Merchants' Guild for their conventions. It was built in 1537–9 by the Antwerp architect Johann der Buschener in Dutch Mannerist style. The eastern gable, more classically Renaissance in style, is the work of the local builder Carsten Husmann.

The Mannerist Schütting, a meeting place for merchants

⛪ Dom
Tower and "Bleikeller":

🕐 *Easter–1 Nov: 10am–5pm Mon–Fri, 10am–2pm Sat, 2–5pm Sun.*

This magnificent Romanesque cathedral with its vast twin-towered façade dates from the 11th century. Over the years it was extensively refurbished. At the end of the 19th century, while the southern tower was rebuilt, the façade was also reconstructed and a tower was added at the junction of the naves. Inside, it is worth looking at the sandstone bas-reliefs which divide the western choir stalls as well as fragments of Gothic stalls that were destroyed in the 19th century, with scenes of the Passion and the battle

Bas-reliefs on the western choir stalls in the Dom

of Judas Machabeus. There is also a Baroque pulpit paid for by Christina the Queen of Sweden in 1638, and numerous multi-coloured memorials, including one to Segebad Clüver by the entrance to the north tower (1457). The larger eastern crypt has interesting Romanesque capitals, while in the second eastern crypt visitors can admire the oldest Bremen sculpture of Christ the Omnipotent (1050) as well as the baptismal font. The latter has 38 bas-reliefs, and a bowl supported by four lions with riders. In the so-called "Bleikeller" (lead cellar) underneath the former church cloisters, eight perfectly preserved mummies are on show.

VISITORS' CHECKLIST

Road map C2. 🏠 556,000. 🚉
ℹ️ *Am Bahnhofplatz (0421-30 80 00).* 🚢 *Tours of the port (1.5 hours) (0421-32 12 29).*
Cruises: *Apr–Oct: 11:45am, 1:30 & 3:15pm daily.* 🚌
📅 *Sat & Sun.* 🎭 *6 Tage Rennen (Jan); Oserwiese (Apr); Vegesack Harbour Festival (Jun); Bremer Freimarkt (second half Oct/early Nov).*

BREMEN TOWN CENTRE

Böttcherstrasse ⑤
Dom ③
Kunsthalle ⑦
Marktplatz ①
Rathaus ②
Schnoorviertel ⑥
Schütting ④
Übersemuseum ⑧

0 metres	500
0 yards	500

KEY

ℹ️ Tourist information

✉️ Parking

⛪ Church

♟ Böttcherstraße
Paula-Modersohn-Becker-Museum and **Roseliushaus**

Böttcherstr. 6–10. ☎ *(0421) 336 50 77.* ◯ *11am–6pm Tue–Sun.*

This once insignificant lane where coopers lived was transformed into Art Deco style in 1926–30 by Ludwig Roselius, a wealthy coffee merchant. The National Socialists preserved the street as an example of degenerate art. At the entrance to the street is a bas-relief by Bernhard Hoetger from 1920, of the Archangel Michael fighting a dragon.

The **Paula-Modersohn-Becker-Museum**, built in the Expressionist style, contains an art museum, while in the neighbouring 16th-century **Roseliushaus** the original period interiors can be admired. The street's other attraction is a carillon which chimes tuneful melodies every day at 12:15 and 6pm.

♟ Schnoorviertel
Spielzeugmuseum im Schnoor

Schnoor 24. ☎ *(0421) 32 03 82.* ◯ *11am–6:30pm Mon–Fri, 11am–6pm Sat; 1 Apr–31 Dec: 11am–4pm Sun.*

The Schnoorviertel is a historic district of small houses dating from the 15th–18th centuries. One of Bremen's poorest areas before World War II, it miraculously escaped destruction. It has been restored gradually since

Archangel Michael fighting a dragon, on a bas-relief in Böttcherstrasse

1958 and now teems with restaurants, cafés, souvenir shops and tourists. In the centre of the district is the Gothic **Johanniskirche**, which once belonged to the Franciscans. In accordance with the order's rules it has no tower, although this is compensated for by a decorative gable on the western façade, and three levels of arched alcoves and herringbone brickwork. The **Spielzeugmuseum** (toy museum) nearby is also worth visiting.

🏛 Kunsthalle
Am Wall 207. ☎ *(0421) 32 90 80.* ◯ *10am–9pm Tue, 10am–5pm Wed–Sun.* 🖼

On the edge of the old town is this art gallery, which actually lost most of its collection to Russia during World War II. The pieces that remained, as well as works subsequently acquired, make the collection of great importance. There

are works by Dürer, Altdorfer, Rubens, Jan Breughel, van Dyck and Rembrandt. There is also an excellent French section, with works by Delacroix, Denis, Monet and Manet, as well as 19th- and 20th-century German painters such as Beckmann and Kirchner. At the heart of the collection are about 40 paintings by Paula Modersohn-Becker.

🏛 Übersee-Museum
Bahnhofplatz 13. ☎ *(0421) 36 19 176.* ◯ *10am–6pm Tue–Sun.* 🖼

This museum of overseas countries transports the visitor to faraway destinations. Founded in 1891, it was originally a museum of German colonialism and is now dedicated to the culture of non-European nations. Of special interest are exhibits on Pacific cultures, with life-sized models of houses and boats from the Solomon Islands.

🏛 Focke-Museum
Schwachhauser-Heerstr. 240. ☎ *(0421) 361 35 75.* ◯ *10am–6pm Tue–Sun.* 🖼

The excellent collections of this museum compensate for its distant location. Founded in 1918, when the history museum was amalgamated with the decorative arts museum, it presents Bremen's art and culture from the Middle Ages to the present day. Exhibits from patrician houses and original sculptures from the façade of the town hall testify to the wealth of the Hanseatic town. Other sections are devoted to the archaeology of the region as well as to whaling and emigration to the US in the 19th and 20th centuries.

The nearby Rhododendronpark offers a pleasant respite from the museums. It includes 1,600 varieties of rhododendron which turn the park into a sea of flowers from late April to June.

ENVIRONS: Three places in the Bremen area are particularly worth a detour. About 50 km (31 miles) to the north lies Bremen's deep-sea harbour **Bremerhaven,** with the **Deutsches Schifffahrtsmuseum**. This wonderful,

Camille Pissarro, *Girl lying on a grassy slope*, Kunsthalle

PAULA MODERSOHN-BECKER (1876–1907)

A pupil of Fritz Mackensen and wife of Otto Modersohn, Paula Modersohn-Becker was the most significant artistic figure in Worpswede. She learned about the Impressionist use of colour during visits to Paris, and her own unique

sensibility made her a precursor of Expressionism. She became famous for her naturalistic paintings of poor, starving and even dying country folk. She died in childbirth, aged only 31, and this is how she was comme-morated on her tombstone, in the peaceful village cemetery in Worpswede, by the sculptor Bernhard Hoetger.

Girl playing a flute in birch woods (1905)

Exhibits in the Große Kunstschau in Worpswede near Bremen

marine museum, designed by the renowned architect Hans Scharoun, displays both ori-ginals and models of a wide range of ships, dating from the Roman Empire to the present day. A special hall displays the *Hanse Kogge,* a merchant ship dredged from the bottom of the Weser River in 1962. This type of ship was capable of holding 120 tons of cargo, and handled the entire merchandise of north-ern Europe during the late Middle Ages. Displayed out-side, in the open-air part of the museum, are the last great German sailing boat *Seute Deem,* the polar ship *Grön-land* and *Wilhelm Bauer,* a U-boat from World War II.

The small village of **Worps-wede**, northeast of Bremen, takes the visitor into the world of art. From 1889 until the end of World War II it was a famous artists' colony, situated in the middle of peat bogs. Apart from poets, such as Rainer Maria Rilke, and such architects as Bernhard Hoetger, the fame of this vil-lage rested principally on the painters: Fritz Mackensen, Otto Modersohn, Hans am Ende, Fritz Overbeck and Heinrich Vogeler. Unques-tionably the greatest artist in Worpswede was Paula Moder-sohn-Becker, whose sad fairy-tale world of rustic subjects cannot be defined within one style. Work by the founding members is on display in the **Große Kunstschau** and the **Worpsweder Kunsthalle**.

Verden an der Aller, the picturesque bishops' residence and once a free town of the Reich, is known to sports enthusiasts thanks to its horse-racing tracks, training centres and stadiums, and the **Deutsches Pferde-museum** (horse museum), with a large collec-tion of equestrian artifacts. Seven horse auctions are held in the town each year, and the most important are in April and October.

Apart from horses, Verden an der Aller has a picturesque town centre with small houses, the Andreaskirche, a church with the famous brass tomb of bishop Yso, as well as the Johanniskirche with a rain-bow-arched wall dating from the 18th century, depicting the Last Judgement.

Above the town rises the Dom with a large, steep roof. The hall of this cathedral, a modification of earlier basil-icas, is architecturally inter-esting, with a multi-sided presbytery, a passageway dating from 1268–1311 and Romanesque cloisters and a tower. To the north of the cathedral is the Domherren-haus housing the Historisches Museum, with exhibits on regional history as well as interesting archaeological and ethnographic departments.

🏛 **Deutsches Schifffahrtsmuseum**
Bremerhaven, Hans-Scharoun-Platz 1.
📞 *(0471) 482 07 22.* ⬤ *10am– 6pm Tue–Sun.* ⬤ *24, 25 & 31 Dec.* 📷
Wilhelm Bauer ⬤ *Apr–Oct.* 📷
🏛 **Große Kunstschau**
Worpswede. Lindenallee 3 & 5. 📞
(04792) 13 02. ⬤ *10am–6pm daily.* 📷
🏛 **Worpsweder Kunsthalle**
Bergstr. 17. 📞 *(04792) 12 77.*
⬤ *10am–6pm daily.* 📷
🏛 **Deutsches Pferdemuseum**
Andreasstr. 7. 📞 *(04231) 80 71 40.*
⬤ *10am–5pm Tue–Sun.*

The Dom in Verden an der Aller, with its unusually large roof

Hamburg

Crest on the town hall

GERMANY'S second largest city, Hamburg has an openness to the world and a variety of architectural styles in its districts, making it a fascinating place to visit. For many years, Hamburg was a leading member of the Hanseatic League and an independent trading town, and in 1945 it became a city-state of the Federal Republic. Visitors are attracted by Hamburg's enormous port, situated right in the centre of the city, colourful entertainments in the red-light district St Pauli, many attractive parks and lakes as well as the warm welcome extended by the locals who, on first encounter, may seem a little cool.

A fountain in the Neo-Renaissance Rathausmarkt

Exploring Hamburg
The best way to get around Hamburg is by metro (U-Bahn and S-Bahn), using an all-day ticket (Tageskarte) since parking space is scarce. The city centre can be explored on foot, including the area between the main railway station and the lake, along with the rest of the old town, the port and Hamburg's two largest museums.

�
 Rathausmarkt
The symbol of Hamburg is the enormous Neo-Renaissance town hall, the fifth in the city's history. Previous town halls were destroyed by wars as well as a catastrophic fire in 1842. Little remains of the old town. The city's current appearance is characterized by 19th-century style as well as Modernism. The town hall itself, with its ornamental halls representing the pride of Hamburg's middle class, is worth visiting.

The town hall square is enclosed on one side by Alsterfleet. Originally a small river, it is today one of numerous canals which have given Hamburg the name "Venice of the North". A monument in memory of the victims of World War I is the work of the artist Ernst Barlach. Between Rathausmarkt and Gänsemarkt runs a network of elegantly roofed shopping arcades. These were built in the 19th century, and have since been continually extended.

🚏 Alster
Elegant arcades lead from the Rathausmarkt to Binnenalster, a large lake in the middle of the city. Like the much larger Außenalster lake further north, it was created by damming the Alster River. On a sunny day, the Jungfernstieg, an elegant boulevard running the length of the Alster, is a pleasant place for a walk.

Great views of the city can be had from the café in the Alsterpavilion. There is a small quay from which boats depart for the "Alsterrundfahrt", an excursion which takes the visitor all the way to the Außenalster and to smaller canals with views of the villas in the north of Hamburg and the cityscape of the centre with its five main towers.

Door knocker on St Petrikirche

🔒 St Petrikirche
Mönckebergstr. 🇨 (040) 325 74 00. ◯ 8am–6pm Sun–Fri, 9am–5pm Sat.
The church of St Petri, originally Gothic, was extensively rebuilt in the Neo-Gothic style after the Great Fire of 1842. The Grabower Altar that once belonged to the church has been transferred to the Kunsthalle (see pp422–3). Tourists can still admire the Gothic sculpture of the Madonna, dating from 1470.

🚏 Jakobikirche
Jakobikirchhof 22. 🇨 (040) 32 77 44. ◯ 10am–4pm Mon–Fri, 10am–1pm Sat.
The church of St Jacobi, from 1340, was bombed during World War II, and subsequently rebuilt in its original style. Its captivating interior includes the largest Baroque

The main altar in Jakobikirche

organ in northern Germany, the work of Arp Schnitger. The triptych of St Luke in the presbytery of the southern nave, a magnificent example of late-Gothic art, was originally created in 1499 for Hamburg's cathedral, which was pulled down in 1804.

🏛 Kontorhausviertel

Deichtorhallen Deichtorstr. 1–2 📞 (040) 32 10 30. ⬜ during exhibitions.

After World War I a district of commercial offices known as Kontorhausviertel was built between Steinstraße and Messberg. The **Chilehaus**, built by Fritz Höger in 1922–4, was an experiment in creating a traditional brick building with a Modernist design. This ten-storey building, with its pointed eastern façade resembling a ship's bow, became internationally famous as a symbol of Expressionist architecture.

Nearby are the enormous **Deichtorhallen**, market halls of the port built in 1911–12. Transformed into dramatic exhibition halls in 1997, they are now a splendid setting for major art exhibitions.

The Expressionist Chilehaus in Kontorhausviertel

🏛 Speicherstadt

Deutsches Zollmuseum

Alter Wandrahm 16a. 📞 (040) 33 97 63 86. ⬜ 10am–5pm Tue–Sun.

The atmosphere of the giant warehouse district by the port will seem depressing to some, charming to others. Located within the toll-free area of the port, this district is reached after crossing the customs post. It is the largest complex of warehouses in the world. The Neo-Gothic buildings, dating from the end of the 19th century, are separated by canals. They still serve as

storerooms for coffee, tea and carpets, waiting here in customs-free limbo until the owners are ready to sell them. Recently listed as one of the city's historic monuments, Speicherstadt is waiting for a new owner and a new purpose. The **Deutsches Zollmuseum** (German customs museum), temporarily located here by Kornhausbrücke, (corn house bridge), tells the story of customs and excise over the past hundred years.

HAMBURG CITY CENTRE

Alster ②
Altstadt (Old Town) ⑧
Jakobikirche ④
Kontorhausviertel ⑤
Kunsthalle ⑦
Rathausmarkt ①
St Petrikirche ③
Speicherstadt ⑥

0 m   250
0 yards   250

KEY

ℹ Tourist information

🏛 Church

🅿 Parking

Kunsthalle

THE MOST interesting art gallery in northern Germany, the Kunsthalle in Hamburg has a tradition dating back to 1817, when the Kunstverein (friends of the fine arts), proud of its middle-class, non-aristocratic background, was established. The museum opened to the public in 1869. The collection has a standard chronological review of European art movements, with an emphasis on 19th-century German Romantics, including works by Caspar David Friedrich and Philipp Otto Runge. An annexe, the Galerie der Gegenwart (contemporary gallery), was built in 1996 to a design by the architect Matthias Ungers. Shaped like a stark cube, it accommodates the museum's modern art collection.

The Polar Sea (1823–4)
Caspar David Friedrich's dramatic seascape, with a sinking ship in the background behind the rising flow, is pregnant with symbolism.

★ Offering in the Temple (c.1627)
Thanks to his mastery of a sense of drama, Rembrandt succeeded in depicting the psychological make-up of his elderly subjects, who have recognized the Saviour in an unspoken message conveyed to the temple by Mary and Joseph.

First floor

Main entrance

Ground floor

High Altar of St Peter in Hamburg (1383)
This panelled painting, displaying a stunning wealth of detail, was produced by Master Bertram of Minden, the first artist in Germany to be identified by his name. He worked in Hamburg for most of his life.

STAR EXHIBITS

- ★ **Girls on the Pier**
- ★ **Morning**
- ★ **Offering in the Temple**

Self-Portrait with Model (1910 and 1926) *Sixteen years after first painting this picture, Ernst Ludwig Kirchner repainted some sections, in order to emphasize the distance between model and artist.*

VISITORS' CHECKLIST

Glockengießerwall. (040) 4 28 54 26 12. 10am–6pm Tue–Sun, 10am–9pm Thu.
Library 10am–5pm Tue–Sat.
Café Liebermann 10am–5pm Tue–Sun, 10am–8pm Thu.

GALLERY GUIDE
On the ground floor, Rooms 2–10 and 16–19 contain works of art from the first half of the 19th century. On the first floor, Rooms 101–116 display the works of old masters. In Rooms 117–137 paintings from the 19th century are exhibited, and works from the first half of the 20th century are shown in Rooms 138-148.

★ **Girls on the Pier**
(c. 1900) This painting is one of six variations on the same theme painted by Edvard Munch. The painter omitted the landscape, concentrating on the relationship and tensions between the girls.

Nana (1877)
In 1877 Édouard Manet painted Nana, the heroine of a Zola novel. Manet was not allowed to exhibit the painting in the Paris Salon because Nana was known as a Parisian courtesan.

Café Liebermann and entrance to the Modern Times gallery

★ **Morning** (1808)
This painting by Phillip Otto Runge was intended to be part of a series called "Times of the Day", but this was never completed due to the artist's untimely death.

KEY

- Gallery of old masters
- 19th-century paintings
- 20th-century paintings (first half)
- Gallery of drawings
- Non-exhibition space

⛪ Altstadt (Old Town)

Hamburg's old town extends to the south of the Rathaus (town hall) but, following the Great Fire of 1842 and bombing during World War II, only a few original buildings remain. **Katharinenkirche** (St Catherine's), with its characteristic tower, was begun in the 13th century and completed in the 17th century. It has been restored after damage in World War II. Of the neighbouring Neo-Gothic **Nikolaikirche** only a single tower remained after 1945, the Nikolaiturm, which is the third tallest in Germany. It serves as a monument to the tragic consequences of war.

Deichstrasse is one of a few surviving streets in the old town, with the original façades visible from both the road and the canal (the best view is from Hohe Brücke, a bridge). One of the many famous restaurants is at No. 25, "Zum Brandanfang", where The Great Fire of 1842 was said to have broken out, which eventually destroyed most of the city.

Ornate Baroque pulpit in Hamburg's Michaeliskirche

🛕 Michaeliskirche

Observation tower ☎ *(040) 37 67 81 00.* ◷ *Apr–Sep: 9am–6pm Mon–Sat, 11:30am–6pm Sun; Oct–Mar: 10am–5pm Mon–Sat, 11:30am–5:30pm Sun.*
The massive Baroque church of St Michaelis, visible from afar with its 132-m (433-ft) tower (the "Michel"), is the main symbol of Hamburg. The interior is preserved in a white, grey and gold colour

The neon-lit Reeperbahn in St Pauli

scheme, and some of the fittings are made from tropical wood. The observation platform affords splendid views of the city and its harbour.

⛪ Krameramtswohnungen

Krayenkamp 10. ☎ *(040) 31 10 26 24.* ◷ *10am–5pm Tue–Sun.*
Near the Michaeliskirche a section of the old town, the Krameramtswohnungen, has miraculously survived. These half-timbered houses, linked by a courtyard, were funded by the merchants' guild and built to house the widows of shopkeepers. Today they are occupied by tourist shops, cafés and restaurants.

⚓ The Port

Cap San Diego ☎ *(040) 36 42 09.* ◷ *10am–6pm daily.* **Rickmer Rickmers** ☎ *(040) 319 59 59.* ◷ *10am–6pm daily.*
Situated 104 km (62 miles) inland along the Elbe River, Hamburg is Europe's second largest port after Rotterdam,

and the port dominates the panorama. Every year 12,000 ships dock here from 90 countries. From the U3 Baumwall metro station it is best to walk to **Landungsbrücken**, past the museum ships moored here: the freighter *Cap San Diego* and the sailing boat *Rickmer Rickmers* (1896). Landungsbrücken is a 200-m (656-ft) long building from where the passenger ferries depart. A tour of the harbour is highly recommended. Near Landungsbrücken, in a copper-domed building, is the entrance to Alter Elbtunnel (the old tunnel under the Elbe) where people and cars are lowered in a giant lift.

⛪ St Pauli

Infamous around the world, this area is also known as **Reeperbahn**, after the main street. It is a world of nightclubs and bars, pubs and theatres, sex clubs and brothels. It is here, in Hamburg's red-light district, that some teenage seasonal workers from Liverpool, the Beatles, started their careers. On Herbertstrasse, scantily clad women offer their services behind a metal barrier – women and those under 18 are forbidden entrance. St

---

FISCHMARKT – A MARKET FOR EVERYTHING

This is an attraction for early risers or for those who never get to bed at all. From 5am (7am in winter) the Auktionshalle (auction hall) and the nearby waterside turn into a colourful market place. Fishermen returning from the sea with their freshly caught fish compete with noisy greengrocers offering their wares and bric-à-brac merchants setting out stalls. Thousands of tourists mingle with sailors and ladies of the night relaxing with a cup of steaming mulled wine after a hard night's work in St Pauli. Here and there you can hear Plattdeutsch being spoken, the northern patois. Morning mass at 10am used to mark the end of this colourful spectacle, but today's public lingers on and then hurries off to bed instead of church.

Bric-à-brac on sale at a market stall in Fischmarkt

Pauli even has an Erotic-Museum, where next to the exhibits are reproductions of works by artists from Rembrandt to Picasso, which are said to "prove" that everything revolves around the female posterior.

ENVIRONS: The magnificent palace in **Ahrensburg** (1595), 23 km (14 miles) to the northeast, has Baroque and Rococo interiors open to visitors.

Façade of Schloss Ahrensburg, flanked by towers

Altes Land ❾

Road map C2.

ON THE FLOOD plains stretching for more than 30 km (19 miles) between Hamburg and Stade, along the Lower Elbe River, is the Altes Land (old land). This area is fertile and has the largest number of orchards in Germany. Many visitors come here in May, when cherry and apple tree blossom turns everything into a sea of white and pink. In this riot of colour stand sturdy red-brick houses with white half-timbered panels, thatched roofs and carved gates. The most beautiful villages are **Neuenfelde**, **Jork**, **Borstel**, **Steinkirchen** and **Hollern**, with their richly furnished Baroque churches.

Stade ❿

Road map C2. 🏯 47,000.
🚆 U3 to Neugraben, then by train or catamaran from Landungsbrücken.
ℹ️ Schiffertorstr. 6. (04141-40 91 70 & 40 91 75).

THIS MEDIEVAL Hanseatic town has retained most of its half-timbered buildings, with the most attractive in the **Alter Hafen** (old harbour). There is a also a quaint crane and the **Schwedenspeicher** (Swedish granary) dating from the Swedish occupation during the Thirty Years' War (1692–1705). It is now home to the **Schwedenspeicher-Museum**, Stade's regional museum with exhibits on the town's history and defence system, including wheels from 700 BC, which were part of a Bronze-Age cart. Nearby, an interesting building at Am Wasser West 7 houses the **Kaufmann Collection**, with works by Worpswede artists. The entire old

The Baroque portal of the Dutch-influenced Rathaus in Stade

town is surrounded by preserved modern fortifications. Other attractions are the **Bürgermeister-Hintze-Haus** at Am Wasser West 23, a house built for the mayor, Hintze, in 1617–46, and the exquisite Baroque **Rathaus** (town hall) from 1667, its design revealing Dutch influence.

It is also worth visiting two Gothic churches: **St Wilhadi** from the 14th century which boasts an interesting Gothic hall and a leaning tower, and **St Cosmas and Damiani**, founded after the Great Fire of 1659, with marvellous Baroque furnishings.

🏛 **Schwedenspeicher-Museum**
Am Wasser West 39. 📞 (04141) 32 22. 🕙 10am–5pm Tue–Fri, 10am–6pm Sat & Sun. ⬜

The half-timbered houses along the waterside of Alter Hafen in Stade

Lüneburg ⓫

Road map D2. 🏰 *70,000.*
🚉 🛈 *Rathaus, Am Markt (04131-30 95 03).*

IT IS HARD to believe that this small, former Hanseatic town was once one of the wealthiest in Germany. Its prosperity was founded on salt mines. Opened in 956, they provided work for more than 2,000 people by the late Middle Ages and were the largest industry in Europe.

Lüneburg's most important monument is the **Rathaus** (town hall). The interior is even more intriguing than the frequently re-built façade, in particular the **Großer Ratssaal** (the main hall) with its Gothic stained-glass windows and 16th-century frescoes of the Last Judgement, as well as the **Große Ratsstube** (council chamber) with Renaissance woodwork by Albert von Soest. The **Museum im Rathaus** (town hall museum) holds a remarkable collection of municipal silverware.

Johnniskirche, one of Lüneburg's three Gothic churches, stands on Am Sande. It has a 108-m (354-ft) west tower, which leans more than 2 m (6 ft) from the perpendicular. In one of its five naves there is a panelled painting dating from 1482–5, the masterful work of the German painter Hinrik Funhof. Also interesting is the soaring basilica of **Michaeliskirche**, consecrated in 1409.

Not far from here is the old port on the Ilmenau River. On Lüner Straße stands the **Altes Kaufhaus**, a former herring warehouse with a Baroque façade. The 14th-century wooden crane was rebuilt in the 18th century. It was used to load salt onto ships. The decorative wavy brick lines (*Taustäbe*) on many of the old buildings are characteristic of the town.

🏛 Museum im Rathaus
Am Markt. 📞 *(04131) 30 92 30.* 🕐 *10am–5pm Tue–Sun.* 🔴 *1 Jan, 24–26 & 31 Dec.* 🎫

A typical farmstead in Lüneburger Heide

Lüneburger Heide ⓬

Road map D2. 🛈 *Lüneburg, Barghausenstr. 35 (04131-737 30).*

SOUTH OF Hamburg, between the rivers Elbe and Aller, is an area of around 100 sq km (39 sq miles) of heathland, grazed by heifers and sheep and buzzing with bees in the heathers and pine forests. Until the Middle Ages, this area was covered by dense mixed forests, but these were felled in order to satisfy demand for wood in the saltworks of Lüneburg. The half-stepped terrain provides grazing land for Heidschnucken, the local breed of sheep. The heather moors are best seen at the **Naturschutzpark Lüneburger Heide**, a large area of nature reserve founded in 1921. From the village of Undeloh it is best to continue by foot, bike or carriage to the traditional village of Wilsede. From Wilsede it is not far to Wilseder Berg, the highest peak of this moraine region. The view of the surrounding countryside is particularly beautiful at the end of August, when the purple heather is blooming.

Soltau ⓭

Road map C3. 🏰 *23,000.* 🛈 *Bornemannstr. 7 (05191-82 82 82).*

THE MAIN attraction of the town of Soltau is **Heidepark Soltau**, a vast funfair with trains, water rides and a genuine Mississippi steamboat. For nature lovers, the **Vogelpark Walsrode**, 20 km (12 miles) southwest of Soltau, may be a more attractive alternative. It holds about 1,000 species of birds from every continent, from penguins to birds of paradise. Aviaries, some 12-m (40-ft) tall, seek to simulate an impression of the birds' natural environment.

🍀 Heidepark Soltau
🕐 *Apr–Oct: 9am–6pm daily (admission till 4pm).*
🍀 Vogelpark Walsrode
🕐 *Mar–Oct: 9am–7pm daily; Nov–Feb: 10am–4pm.*

ENVIRONS: In grim contrast to both parks stands **Bergen-Belsen**, a concentration camp built by the National Socialists in the moorland of Osterheide, about 30 km (19 miles) south of Soltau. A monument and small museum commemorate the place where 50,000 people were murdered, among them Anne Frank.

🏛 Gedenkstelle Bergen-Belsen
Lohheide. 📞 *(05051) 60 11.*
🕐 *9am–6pm daily.*

Eighteenth-century wooden crane in Lüneburg

Vogelpark Walsrode – a paradise with 1,000 different bird species

Celle ⓮

Road map C3. 🚶 74,000.
🚉 Bahnhofplatz. 🛈 Markt 14–16
(05141-12 12). ◐ May–Oct:
9am–7pm Mon–Fri, 10am–4pm Sat,
11am–4pm Sun; Nov–Apr: 9am–5pm
Mon–Fri, 9am–1pm Sat.

BETWEEN THE years 1378 and 1705, Celle was the seat of distant relations of the Welf family, the reigning dynasty in the Duchy of Brunswick-Lüneburg. The **Schloss** (castle), rebuilt in Renaissance style after 1533, has a preserved eastern façade with octagonal towers at the corners, gables and bay windows. It is one of the most important early-Renaissance buildings in Germany. The Gothic chapel is worth visiting. It was rebuilt in a Mannerist style to a design by Martin de Vos, who painted 76 of its paintings, including the famous *Crucifixion* (end of the 16th century).

Celle prides itself on 500 half-timbered houses, with the most interesting ones in picturesque Kalandgasse and Zöllnerstrasse.

Hoppner Haus, at Poststrasse 8, is richly decorated with reliefs of mythological beasts. Equally interesting is the painted decoration of the **Rathaus** (town hall), a great example of Weser Renaissance *(see p439)* from 1579. From the **Stadtkirche** church tower great views unfold. The Baroque **Synagoge**, beyond the old town, is the only one surviving in northern Germany.

⛪ Schloss
[(05141) 12 373. ◐ Apr–Oct: 10 & 11am, noon, 1, 2, 3 & 4pm Tue–Sun; Nov–Mar: 11am & 3pm Tue–Sun. 🎧

🏛 Stadtkirche
[(05141) 7735. ◐ 10am–6pm Tue–Sat. **Tower:** Apr–Oct: 10am–noon, 1–6pm Tue–Sat.

✡ Synagoge
Im Kreise 24. ◐ 3–5pm Tue–Thu, 9–11am Fri, 11am–1pm Sun.

ENVIRONS: The town of **Wietze**, 11 km (7 miles) west of Celle, has been a centre of petroleum since 1858. The **Deutsches Erdölmuseum Wietze** provides a very interesting overview on the history of oil extraction.

The neighbouring village of **Wienhausen** has a Cistercian **Kloster** (monastery) with a beautiful 13th–14th century church. Worth seeing are its Gothic frescoes, the presbytery vaults and the 14th- and 15th-century tapestries.

🏛 Deutsches Erdölmuseum
Schwarzer Weg 7–9. [(05146) 92 340. ◐ Mar–Nov: 10am–5pm Sun; Jun–Aug: 10am–6pm Tue–Sun. 🎧

🏛 Wienhausen Kloster
[(05149) 357. 🗓 Apr–Oct: 10 & 11am, 2–5pm Tue–Sat, noon–5pm Sun. 🎧

Wolfsburg ⓯

Road map D3. 🚶 123,000. 🚉
🛈 Porschestr. 47a (05361-21 832).

DURING THE 1930s, this small village began to develop into a sizeable town, based around the Volkswagen car works. Production of the "people's car" was conceived by Hitler – every German was to be able to afford this inexpensive car, designed by Ferdinand Porsche. The model reached its peak during the post-war economic boom years. The **Volkswagenwerk** factory is open to visitors.

Wolfsburg also has some outstanding examples of modern architecture: a cultural centre designed by Alvara Aalto, a city theatre designed by Hans Scharoun and a planetarium.

🚗 Volkswagenwerk Autostadt
Stadtbrücke. [(0800) 28 86 78 23. ◐ 9:30am–4:15pm Mon–Thu 🎧 guided tours every 15 mins.

The façade of the Schloss with octagonal towers at the corners, in Celle

The Renaissance Schloss in Stadthagen

Stadthagen **⑯**

Road map C3. 🏠 *23,800.* 🚉
🛈 *Rathauspassage 1 (05721-78 20).*

THE COUNTS OF Schaumburg-Lippe used the Renaissance **Schloss** (castle) as their private residence. Apart from this and the town hall, the main attraction is the church of **St Martini** which has an early Baroque mausoleum of Ernst zu Holstein-Schaumburg built onto its eastern wall. Adrian de Vries, court artist to Rudolf II in Prague, created a masterful monument of bronze figures.

🔒 St Martini
Schulstr.18. ◷ *3–5pm Wed & Fri.*

ENVIRONS: A gem of Romanesque architecture can be found at **Idensen** near Wunsdorf, 22 km (14 miles) from Stadthagen. The church interior (1120) is entirely painted with scenes from the Old and New Testaments, and there is a vast, Byzantine-style image of Christ's Enthronement (*maiestas domini*) on the vaulted ceiling of the apsis.

Bückeburg **⑰**

Road map C3. 🏠 *21,000.* 🚉
🛈 *Lange Str. 45 (05722-20 61 81).*

IN THE 16TH century this town became the capital of the principality of Schaumburg-Lippe. The philosopher Johann Gottfried von Herder was the preacher here. The **Stadtkirche** (town church), one of the first Protestant churches in Germany, is a pinnacle of Mannerism with its fantasy façade. Another attraction is the **Schloss** with its enchanting chapel. The Goldener Saal (golden hall), from 1605, has a Götterpforte (portal of the divinities) and a beautiful panelled ceiling.

🔒 Stadtkirche
Lange Str. 📞 *(05722) 957 70.* ◷ *15 Apr–15 Oct: 10:30am–noon, 3–5pm Mon–Sat; 3–5pm Sun; 16 Oct–14 Apr 2:30–4:30pm daily.*

⛪ Schloss
📞 *(05722) 50 39.* ◷ *Apr–Sep: 9:30am–6pm; Oct–Mar: 9:30am–5pm.*

The opulent Goldener Saal in Schloss Bückeburg

Braunschweig (Brunswick) **⑱**

Road map E3. 🏠 *240,000.* 🚉
🛈 *Vor der Burg 1 (0531-27 35 50).* 🎭 *Festival of Chamber Music (May); Medieval Fair (May/Jun).*

AN IMPORTANT commercial and political centre from the early Middle Ages, Braunschweig was chosen as town of residence by Heinrich der Löwe (Henry the Lion), ruler of Saxony and Bavaria. A member of the Welf family, he eventually lost in his struggle against the German emperor.

Very different in character but equally famous was Till Eulenspiegel, an ordinary man who poked fun at dim-witted citizens, the aristocracy and the clergy. His exploits were fictionalized in the 16th century, and he was immortalized with a fountain on Bäckerklint Square.

Braunschweig's continued decline culminated in the almost total destruction of the town in 1944. During reconstruction, the concept of the "Traditionsinsel" was developed: small islands of reconstructed historic monuments adrift in a sea of modernism.

A tour of the town is best started from Burgplatz (castle square). Here is the **Burg-löwe**, the monument of a lion funded by Heinrich in 1166 (the original is in a museum). Symbolizing Heinrich's rule, it was the first such sculpture to be erected since Roman days. The **Dom** (cathedral), Romanesque in style but modified, is well worth seeing. In the north nave, an extension, are unusual turned pillars, and in the transept and presbytery are 13th-century frescoes. Its marvellous treasures include a gigantic seven-armed bronze candlestick, the tomb of Heinrich and his wife Mathilde, the Crucifix of Imerward and a wooden cross with the figure of Christ modelled on the sculpture of *Voltosanto* in Lucca. Visitors can also see the column of the Passion with the figure of Christ, the work of Hans Witten, a well-known sculptor.

To the west of the cathedral lies the **Altstadtmarkt** (old town market). Here are the L-shaped **Rathaus** (town hall), with a two-storey open

The Burglöwe, Heinrich der Löwe's monument in Braunschweig

cloister, and the Gothic church of **St Martini**. The beautiful **Gewandhaus** (cloth hall), rebuilt in the Renaissance, is also worth seeing.

East of the cathedral is the **Herzog-Anton-Ulrich-Museum**, the oldest in Germany. It was opened to the public as a gallery by Duke Anton Ulrich and holds such gems as Rembrandt's *Family Portrait*, a Giorgioni self-portrait and Vermeer van Delft's *Girl with a Glass of Wine*.

🛈 Dom
Burgplatz. ◻ 10am–5pm daily.

🛈 St Martini
Altstadtmarkt. ◻ 10am–1pm, 3–5pm Tue–Fri, 10am–1pm Sat, after Mass at noon Sun.

🏛 Herzog-Anton-Ulrich-Museum
Museumsstr. 1. 📞 (0531) 484 24 00. ◻ 10am–5pm Tue & Thu–Sun, 10am–8pm Wed. 🖼

The richly decorated portal of the Gewandhaus in Braunschweig

ENVIRONS: In **Königslutter**, 35 km (22 miles) east of Braunschweig, Emperor Lothar initiated the building of the Benedictine **Abteikirche**, a monastery church and later his burial place. The portal with figures of lions, a frieze with figures of fishermen on the exterior of the apse and the cloisters reflect the taste of the times and the northern Italian origin of architects and sculptors; only the frescoes are late 19th-century additions.

Helmstedt, 45 km (28 miles) to the east, is unjustifiably only associated with the former border crossing between East and West Germany. In 1576,

The Marienbrunnen fountain on Altstadtmarkt in Braunschweig

Duke Julius of Brunswick founded the Julius Academy, one of Germany's most popular Protestant universities, where the Italian philosopher Giordano Bruno taught. Juleum (1592–7), the main building, has a central tower and two decorative gables. Repainted in the original bold red, it is now home to the **Kreisheimatmuseum**, a regional museum and library.

🛈 Abteikirche
Königslutter. ◻ 9am–6pm daily, in winter until 5pm.

🏛 Kreisheimatmuseum
Helmstedt. ◻ 9–11am, 3–5pm Mon–Fri, 3–5pm Sat, 11am–12:30pm Sun. **Library** ◻ 3–5pm Tue, Thu.

Wolfenbüttel ⑲

Road map E3. 🏠 53,000. 🚉
🛈 Stadtmarkt 9 (05331-86 280). 🖼 *Theaterfest (Jun/Jul); Altstadtfest (Aug).*

THIS SMALL town has had a remarkably turbulent past. From 1432 until 1753 the Welf dukes moved their seat here from Braunschweig, because of their conflicts with the local council. In the 16th century, innovative town design introduced wide avenues and spacious squares. Largely unscathed by World War II attacks, the town has 500 historic half-timbered houses, and a magnificent library. The **Herzog-August-Bibliothek** contains

130,000 volumes, including the most valuable book in the world, Heinrich der Löwe's Gospel book. Associated with the town are the philosopher Gottfried Wilhelm Leibniz and writer Gotthold Ephraim Lessing. The **Lessinghaus** houses a literature museum.

The centre of the town is dominated by the **Schloss**, the largest castle in Lower Saxony, refurbished in the Baroque style in 1714–16. It houses the **Heimatmuseum** with regional items such as furniture and tapestries. The Venussaal (hall of Venus) has beautiful Baroque ceiling frescoes. Opposite the castle is the **Zeughaus** (armoury), with its interesting Mannerist façade, built in 1613–19 to a design by Paul Francke.

Continuing eastwards the visitor will get to the **Hauptkirche**, the 16th-century church dedicated to *Beatae Mariae Virginis*, the ducal pantheon and the leading example of Protestant Mannerist architecture. Begun in 1608, the church's façade has delicate reliefs, while the interior reveals an unusual combination of styles, including the very late-Gothic.

♣ Schloss and Heimatmuseum
Schlossplatz. 📞 (05331) 924 60.
Herzog-August-Bibliothek, Lessinghaus & Zeughaus
📞 (05331) 80 80. ◻ 10am–5pm Tue–Sun. ● 24 & 31 Dec. 🖼
🛈 Hauptkirche
Michael-Praetorius-Platz 9.
📞 (05331) 28 92.

Baroque façade of Schloss Wolfenbüttel

Hannover (Hanover) ⑳

THE CAPITAL OF Lower Saxony, Hannover does not at first glance seem particularly exciting, but appearances can be deceptive: the town boasts interesting architecture in the historic centre, magnificent Baroque gardens and one of Europe's most important museums of modern art. Hannover's past was marked by its dynastic links with England, sharing the same ruler during the years 1714–1837. Annual industrial trade fairs have earned the town an international reputation, and in 2000 Hannover hosted the international exhibition Expo 2000 which attracted 18 million visitors.

Exploring Hannover

After the near-total destruction of the old town in 1944, many historic monuments have been rebuilt, and large green spaces encourage the visitor to explore the town on foot. It is best to follow an extensive circuit, starting from and returning to the railway station. The Baroque gardens at Herrenhausen in the northwest of the town are reached by metro (U-Bahn 4, 5).

🎭 Opernhaus

Opernplatz 1. **(** (0511) 99 99 11 11.
The opera house was built in 1845–57 by George Ludwig Friedrich Laves, Hannover's most important architect, to a fine Neo-Classical design. Particularly charming is the façade with portico columns.

🏛 Niedersächsisches Landesmuseum

Willy-Brandt-Allee 5. **(** (0511) 980 77 25. ○ 10am–5pm Tue–Wed, Fri–Sun, 10am–7pm Thu. 🖼
The most interesting part of the state museum of Lower Saxony is the picture gallery, which holds excellent German medieval and Renaissance paintings (Dürer, Spranger, Cranach), a good section with Dutch and Flemish paintings (Rubens, Rembrandt, van Dyck) as well as German paintings of the 19th and 20th centuries, with fine examples of Romanticism and Impressionism (Friedrich, Corinth, Liebermann).

🏛 Sprengel-Museum

Kurt-Schwitters-Platz. **(** (0511) 16 84 38 75. ○ 10am–10pm Tue, 10am–6pm Wed–Sun. 🖼
One of Europe's finest museums of modern art, the Sprengel-Museum reflects the city's role as an artists' mecca in the 1920s, before the National Socialists destroyed works of art that they designated as "degenerate". Hannover's controversial artist Kurt Schwitters worked here, as did El Lissitzky, whose *Kabinett der Abstrakten* (school of abstraction, 1928, reconstructed) is worth seeing. Funded by Bernhard Sprengel, a chocolate magnate, the museum was built in 1979, and holds works by Munch, Chagall and Picasso, as well as many more recent artists, including Christo.

The museum is located by Maschsee, a large artifical lake created in the centre of the city in 1936. During the summer it teems with motor and sailing boats, while Hanoverians stroll around its banks.

Müller's *The Lovers* (1920), in the Sprengel-Museum

🏛 Neues Rathaus

Trammplatz 2. **(** (0511) 168 49.
Dome ○ Apr–Oct: 9:30am–noon & 2–5pm.
The gigantic town hall symbolizes the lofty ambitions of the wealthier citizens at the beginning of the 20th century. It was built from 1901–13, on more than 6,000 beech pillars, modelled on a Baroque palace with a central dome, and decorated with Neo-Gothic and Secessionist detail. The Swiss artist Ferdinand Hodler created a vast painting entitled *Einigkeit* (unity) for the Debating Hall, which depicts the arrival of Protestantism in the town in 1533. A unique oblique lift takes you up to the dome from where there are wonderful views.

⚜ Leineschloß

Hinrich-Wilhelm-Kopf-Platz.
In the historic city centre by the Leine River stands the Leineschloß, a 17th-century palace completely rebuilt by the local architect Laves between 1817 and 1842. It had to be rebuilt again after destruction in World War II, and now serves as headquarters for the Niedersächsischer

Façade of the vast Neues Rathaus, with its central dome

Interior of the church of St Georg und St Jacobus, in Marktplatz

Landtag (Lower Saxony state parliament). The porticos on the façade were modelled on ancient Greek temples.

🏛 Marktplatz
Although the houses on this square had to be almost completely rebuilt after World War II, this is one of the best examples of 15th-century red-brick architecture, with amazing gables with projections as well as figurative friezes of glazed terracotta. Nearby, the Marktkirche St Georg und St

Jacobus (church of St George and St Jacob) features a 14th-century nave with a characteristic four-pinnacled tower. The most valuable object among its furnishings is the Gothic altar, with scenes of the Passion and copper engravings by the renowned artist Martin Schongauer.

♣ Herrenhäuser Gärten
Despite having been razed to the ground during World War II, the gardens in Hannover's Herrenhausen district are among the most beautiful Baroque gardens in Germany. They were established by Duchess Sophie von der Pfalz, daughter of Elizabeth Stuart and mother of England's

VISITORS' CHECKLIST

Road map C3. 🚆 522,000.
🚇 Ernst-August-Platz.
ℹ Ernst-August-Platz 2 (0511-16 84 97 00). 🛍 Sat.
🎪 Schützenfest (Jun/Jul).

George I. The Großer Garten, the most important of the four gardens, has a formal layout modelled on 17th- and 18th-century Dutch parks. It is a botanical garden with fountains, including the Große Fontäne, the tallest in Europe with a 82-m (269-ft) water spout. There are grottoes, mazes, sculptures and decorative urns, and the hedges are some 21 km (13 miles) long.

The stunningly beautiful Baroque gardens in Herrenhausen

HANNOVER CITY CENTRE
Leineschloss ⑤
Marktplatz ⑥
Neues Rathaus ④
Niedersächsisches Landesmuseum ②
Opernhaus ①
Sprengel-Museum ③

0 m   300
0 yards   300

KEY
ℹ Tourist information
🅿 Parking
✝ Church

Hildesheim ⑳

T HE UNDISPUTED capital of Romanesque culture, the old town of Hildesheim was transformed into a heap of rubble by heavy bombing on 22 March 1945. The most important monuments have now been re-created, with mixed results, surrounded by modern developments. Two churches, the Michaeliskirche and the Dom St. Mariä, are UNESCO World Heritage sites, and the Roemer-Pelizaeusmuseum of Egyptian Culture also makes a visit to Hildesheim worthwhile.

Wedekindhaus, a beautiful half-timbered house on Marktplatz

Exploring Hildesheim

Contrary to received wisdom, the city is best visited on foot. Visitors can park in the centre, for example near the church of St Michael, and then explore the main sights from here. A round tour, including the museums, should not take longer than around 4–5 hours. It is also possible to follow the Rosenroute (rose trail) around town which is marked on the pavements by white roses.

♙ Marktplatz

Since gaining civic rights in the 11th century, the heart of the bishopric town has been its market square. Every detail has now been faithfully reconstructed, and it is easy to forget that the square looked totally different only a few years ago. In 1987, the Knochenhaueramtshaus (butchers' guild hall) was rebuilt, the largest and most famous half-timbered house in Germany, dating from 1529. Opposite are the Gothic town hall and the Tempel-haus, an original 15th-century building with round turrets and a half-timbered annexe, added in 1591. Reliefs depict the story of the Prodigal Son.

🛉 Andreaskirche

Andreasplatz. ◻ *Apr–Sep: 9am–6pm Mon–Sat, 11:30am–6pm Sun; Oct–Mar: 10am–4pm Mon–Sat, 11:30–4pm Sun.*

The reconstructed Gothic church of St Andrew transports the visitor to a different world, characterized by the brightness and the quality of the light that passes through its vast windows, as well as its soaring proportions. The 115-m (377-ft) tower was added in the 19th century.

🛉 Michaeliskirche

Michaelisplatz. ◻ *Apr–Sep: 9am–6pm Mon–Fri, 1–6pm Sun; Oct–Mar: 9am–4pm Mon–Sat, 1–4pm Sun.*

Built on the instructions of Bishop Bernward, the church is a textbook example of what became known as the Ottonian style, the early Romanesque culture of the Otto dynasty. Its characteristic feature is the streamlined simplicity of interior and exterior, with square pillars intersecting with the naves. The sarcophagus of the founder, St Bernward, is in the crypt in the western part of the church.

Luckily, a rare painted 12th-century ceiling was removed during World War II and thus largely survived. It depicts the story of Redemption, from Adam and Eve with the Tree of Life, through to Mary and the Saviour.

🏛 Roemer-Pelizaeus-museum

Bas-relief on the façade of Andreaskirche

Am Steine 1. ☎ *(0521) 93 690.* ◻ *9am–6pm Mon–Fri, 10am–6pm Sat, Sun.*

The pride of this museum is the Ancient Egyptian collection, one of the best in Europe, which includes the burial figures of Hem Om and the writer Heti from the Old Kingdom (c.2600 BC). It also has fine collections of Chinese porcelain and Inca artefacts, and it is famed for its temporary exhibitions on ancient cultures, from Tutankhamun to the Mayans.

🛉 Dom St Mariä

Domhof. ☎ *(0521) 179 17 60.* ◻ *Apr–Sep: 9:30am–5pm Mon–Sat, noon–5pm Sun; Oct–Mar: 10am–4pm Mon–Fri, 9:30am–3pm Sat, noon–5pm Sun.*

During a hunting expedition in 815, Ludwig der Fromme (the devout), son of Charlemagne, allegedly hung relics of the Virgin Mary on a tree. When he tried to remove them they would not budge – which he took to be a heavenly sign that a church should be founded on this site and a town alongside it. The Tausendjähriger Rosen-

Presbytery of Michaeliskirche

The Bernwardsäule in the Dom St. Mariä – a huge bronze column

stock (1,000-year-old rose) of this legend grows to this day in the cathedral's cloisters, and even survived bombing. The cathedral was reconstructed after World War II, using a model of the church's 11th-century appearance.

Original works of art bear witness to the cathedral's foundry which flourished under bishop Bernward. Bronze double doors depict the Old Testament version of the Creation on one side, and the life of Christ according to

the New Testament on the other. The Bernwardsäule, a huge bronze column from 1022, was once topped by a crucifix. The column, with scenes from the life of Christ arranged as a spiralling picture story, recalls the column of Emperor Trajan in Rome. Two further important works of art are a chandelier from 1060, with a diameter of 3 m (10 ft), and a baptismal font (c.1225) based on the personifications of the four rivers of the Garden of Eden.

🔒 Godehardkirche
Godehardsplatz. ☐ 9am–6pm Mon–Fri, 9am–2:30pm Sat, 11:30am–4:30pm Sun.
This church is dedicated to Bernward's successor, bishop Godehard, who like him has been included in the canon of saints. Built in 1133–72, it is typical of local architecture, and also recalls the earlier church of St Michaelis. It has interesting carved capitals as well as a northern doorway with the Blessed Jesus Christ accompanied by St Godehard and St Epiphany.

🔒 Mauritiuskirche
Moritzberg.
Another Romanesque church worth visiting in Hildesheim

is the church of St Maurice, west of the centre. Founded by bishop Hezilo and built in the years 1058–68, the church has enchanting cloisters, dating from the 12th century, and the sarcophagus of the founder of the church.

Presbytery of the massive Godehardkirche, flanked by towers

HILDESHEIM CITY CENTRE
Andreaskirche ②
Dom St. Mariä ⑤
Godehardkirche ⑥
Marktplatz ①
Michaeliskirche ③
Roemer-Pelizaeusmuseum ④

0 m   300
0 yards   300

KEY
ⓘ Tourist information
⊠ Post office
✝ Church

Street-by-Street: Goslar ②

GOSLAR, at the foot of the Harz mountains, is a captivating town with 1,800 charming, half-timbered houses, the largest number in Germany. For 300 years the Holy Roman Emperors of Germany resided in Goslar, a member of the Hanseatic League also known as "the treasure chest of the North". Goslar's main source of wealth was the nearby mine in Rammelsberg, where zinc, copper and especially silver were mined. The townscape has remained largely unchanged, making it a great tourist attraction as well as a UNESCO world heritage site.

Guildhouse (Hotel Kaiserworth)

Jakobikirche

KORNSTRASSE

MARKT

HOHER WEG

KAISERBLEEK

DOM PLATZ

★ Rathaus
On the western side of the market square stands the 15th-century town hall. Its beautiful Huldigungssaal (hall of homage) has a ceiling and walls with Gothic frescos.

Siemens-haus

★ Pfarrkirche
The Gothic Church of Saints Cosmas and Damian has Romanesque stained-glass windows and a bronze Renaissance baptismal font.

Statue of the Emperor Barbarossa

KEY

– – – Suggested route

The Kaiserpfalz
The Emperors' palace is a stone building (1005–15), largely rebuilt in the 19th century. The chapel and the Emperors' hall with its superb paintings are worth seeing.

★ **Historic Half-
Timbered Houses**
*Many charming
half-timbered
buildings from
various periods
have survived in
Goslar, creating
compact rows of
houses in the streets
of the city centre.*

0 meters	50
0 yards	50

St Annen-
Stift

STAR SIGHTS

★ **Rathaus**

★ **Pfarrkirche**

★ **Historic Half-
Timbered Houses**

🏛 Siemenshaus
Schreiberstraße 12. 📞 (05321) 238
37. ☐ 9am–noon Tue & Thu.
This half-timbered house, one
of the most attractive, was
once owned by the Siemens
family who have their roots in
Goslar. The former brewery
on this site is open to visitors.

🏠 St Peter and St Paul
Frankenberger Platz.
Located in the Frankenberg
neighbourhood, this was one
of 47 churches which once
stood in the town. It was built
in the 12th century, and the
tympanum of the south portal
dates from this period. Extensively refurbished, the church
prides itself on its magnificent
Baroque furnishings.

🏠 St Jakobi
Jakobi-Kirchhof. 📞 (05321) 235 33.
☐ Apr–Sep: 8:30am–5pm daily.
The present appearance of
this church, the only Catholic
one in Goslar, is the result of
Gothic additions, although the
structure of the walls remains
Romanesque. The famous
work of art in the church is
the *Pietà* by Hans von Witten,
but it is also worth looking at
the wall paintings, the organ
and the baptismal font.

🏠 Neuwerkkirche
Rosentorstraße. 📞 (05321) 228 39.
☐ Apr–Oct: 10am–noon & 2:30–
4:30pm Mon–Fri, 10am–noon Sat.
This impressive late-Romanesque church was built in the
12th–13th centuries for the
Cistercian Order, although the
surviving monastic buildings
date from the early 18th century. Inside, the wall paintings
and the choir partition are
of interest. The church is surrounded by a peaceful garden.

**The train in the Bergbaumuseum
in Rammelsberg**

🏛 Breites Tor
Breite Straße.
Some parts of the defensive
system, dating mainly from
c.1500, are well preserved.
This "wide gate", which can
be seen on the eastern
approach of the town, is the
most imposing part.

🏛 St Annen-Stift
Glockengießerstraße 65. 📞 (05321)
247 62. ☐ 10am–1pm & 2–4pm
Mon–Thu, 11am–1pm Fri & Sat.
The hospice of St Anna for
orphans, the elderly and infirm still fulfills the same function. Behind its picturesque
façade is a beautiful small
chapel with superb paintings
on a wooden ceiling.

🏛 Bergbaumuseum Rammelsberg
Bergtal 19. 📞 (05321) 75 00.
☐ 9am–6pm daily
Goslar's mining museum is
based in the 10th-century
silver mine. One of the oldest
surviving industrial structures
in the world, it was entered in
UNESCO's list of world heritage sites. On display are the
mining tools and utensils that
were used in various periods.
Visitors can take a train ride
through the mine and learn
about the history of mining.

The above-ground buildings of the silver mine in Rammelsberg

Einbeck ㉓

Road map C3. 🏘 29,400. 🚉
🛈 *Rathaus, Marktplatz 6 (05561-91 61 21).*

IN THE MIDDLE AGES, this town had 600 breweries – more than houses – and today it is still known for its beers; Bockbier, the famous German strong beer, was invented here. Burned down in 1540 and 1549, the town was subsequently rebuilt in a uniformly Renaissance style. The historic town centre is enclosed by the city walls. More than 100 half-timbered houses have survived to this day. **Eickesches Haus** (Marktstraße 13) is particularly eye-catching, with a sculpted façade based on biblical and Classical stories. Other picturesque houses can be found in Tiedexer Straße and in **Marktplatz**. The latter boasts the **Rathaus** (town hall), Einbeck's main attraction, as well as the **Ratswaage** (municipal weigh house) and **Ratsapotheke** (chemist). The tower of the neighbouring **Pfarrkirche St Jakobi** (parish church) leans 1.5 m (5 ft) from the perpendicular. In 1741, a Baroque façade was added to hide this.

ENVIRONS: 15 km (9 miles) from Einbeck is the spa town of **Bad Gandersheim**. It grew up around a Benedictine monastery established here in 852, which in the 10th century was the home of Roswitha von Gandersheim, the first known German poet.

Göttingen ㉔

Road map C4. 🏘 129,000. 🚉
🛈 *Altes Rathaus, Markt 9 (0551-540 00).* 🎭 *Händel-fest (Jun); Literaturherbst (Oct), Jazzfestival (Nov); student festivals, such as Stiftungsfest.*

ALONG WITH Tübingen, Marburg and Heidelberg, Göttingen is one of the most renowned German university towns. Established in 1737 by the English King George II, who was also the ruler of Hannover, the university taught the sons of wealthy German, English and Russian aristocrats. Important cultural figures worked here, including the writer Heinrich Heine, the brothers Grimm and the explorer Alexander von Humboldt. Göttingen's reputation as an educational centre continues today, partly due to the establishment of the Max Planck Institute, named after the scientist who was born in the city and developed the quantum theory.

Göttingen is a lively town thanks to its student population, with dozens of cafés, cosmopolitan restaurants and bars. University buildings are scattered all over town, and the **Aula**, a Neo-Classical Assembly Hall, is worth a visit.

On the Marktplatz in the town centre stands the **Rathaus** (town hall) with a Gothic stone façade. The **Gänselieselbrunnen**, the goose girl fountain, in front dates from 1901. It is kissed by students who have passed their exams, and much loved by tourists.

From the southeastern end of the market square, Göttingen's four main churches can be seen: St Michael to the south, St Johannis to the west, St Albani to the east and St Jakobi to the north. The latter two boast late-Gothic altars worth visiting. Together, they testify to Göttingen's early importance in the Middle Ages.

Stone crest on Göttingen's Rathaus

The twin-towered Gothic façade of St Cyriakus in Duderstadt

Duderstadt ㉕

Road map C4. 🏘 24,500. 🚉
🛈 *Marktstr. 66 (05527-84 12 00).*

TO THE SOUTH of the Harz mountains, not far from the former border with East Germany, lies this often overlooked gem. A walk around the medieval town is best started on **Obermarkt** (upper market). Here stands the half-timbered **Rathaus** (town hall), with an interesting façade and spiky towers. Inside it has exhibition halls and a cultural centre. East of the town hall rises the Catholic **Probsteikirche St Cyriakus** with its rich interior of altars and 15 Baroque statues. **St Servatius**, its Protestant counterpart, combines Gothic architecture with a Secessionist interior. Nearby is the **Westertorturm**, the only surviving town gate. Its strangely spiralling finial is not a decorative feature, but the consequence of a weakness in its design.

The Gothic Rathaus on Marktplatz in Göttingen

The Weser Renaissance Trail 26

THE WESER Renaissance is an architectural and decorative style of northern Germany, dating from the mid-16th to the mid-17th century. Its tall roofs and gables were inspired by Dutch architecture, although it has many original features: the *Zwerchhäuser* (bay windows, one or more storeys high), the *Utlucht* (protruding sections of the façade), lavish decorations and multi-wing castles, some with spiral staircases in their towers.

WESERGEBIRGE

Emmer   Weser

SOLLING

Bevern ③
Another gem of the Weser Renaissance style, the castle in Bevern, near Holzminden, was built from Prussian stone in the years 1602–12. It has four wings as well as two towers in the corners of its courtyard.

Hameln ①
Rattenfängerhaus (rat catcher's house), Hochzeitshaus (wedding house) and Demptersches Haus (Dempsters' house) are good examples of the Weser Renaissance style. The Romanesque-Gothic Münster (collegiate church) is also worth seeing.

Hämelschenburg ②
The castle, built in 1588–1612, is a three-winged building, surrounded by a moat. It has an impressive exterior with towers and decorative gables; its original interiors are also preserved.

Münden ④
The principal buildings that exemplify the Weser Renaissance style are the town hall and the castle, now a regional museum with a collection of ceramics. Fragments of a Renaissance fresco of Duke Eryk II of Calenberg can also be admired here.

0 km   20

0 miles   20

TIPS FOR DRIVERS

Starting point: *Hameln.*
Length: *112 km (70 miles).*
Stopping-off places: *good restaurants and bistros can be found in all the towns and villages along the route.*

SCHLESWIG-HOLSTEIN

S CHLESWIG-HOLSTEIN *is the northernmost German state, situated between the Baltic and the North Sea and bordered by the Elbe River and Denmark. Weather-beaten by the unstable marine climate, the Gothic brick buildings of Lübeck, queen of the Baltic coast, testify equally to the turbulent history of this region. Today, tourists visit Schleswig-Holstein for its wide sandy beaches and impressive lakes.*

Originally, this state comprised two territories: Schleswig in the north, which was inhabited by Germanic tribes (Angles, Saxons, Vikings and Danes) in the Middle Ages, and Holstein in the south, mainly populated by Slavs, who converted to Christianity as late as the 12th century. Its more recent history was characterized by struggles between the Hanseatic towns and the rulers of Denmark. In the 18th century, the entire region, from Altona in the south (now part of Hamburg) to Kolding in the north, belonged to Denmark, but in 1866 it was annexed to Bismarck's Prussia. In 1920, the political borders that exist today were established when Denmark regained the northern part of Schleswig after a plebiscite, leaving a significant Danish minority on the German side.

Schleswig-Holstein is principally an agricultural region, and less densely populated than any other state in Germany. Art lovers are mainly drawn to Lübeck, the most powerful Hanseatic town in the Baltic during the Middle Ages. Lübeck's old town, an architectural gem, has now been listed as a world heritage site by UNESCO. Other places offer surprises aplenty – the visitor will be captivated by the Romanesque churches around Flensburg, while the magnificent countryside more than compensates for the lack of major cultural monuments. A walk through the national park of Schleswig-Holsteinisches Wattenmeer, the moving sand dunes of the elegant island of Sylt, or a romantic sunset on the lake shores in Plön will leave lasting impressions.

The moated Renaissance Wasserschloss in Glücksburg

◁ **Idyllic landscape with a lighthouse on Sylt island**

Exploring Schleswig-Holstein

UNDOUBTEDLY the greatest attraction in this two-part state is Lübeck, and at least one day should be set aside to visit this town. Kiel is a popular destination during the annual Kieler Woche, the world's largest sailing festival. The sun-kissed island of Sylt invites the visitor to linger for a few days, while the stunning scenery of Helgoland is best explored in a one-day trip from Cuxhaven or Husum. Hotels in the larger towns, such as Schleswig, Kiel or Flensburg, and many provincial boarding houses, provide a good base for excursions.

0 km   25
0 miles   25

↘ *Esbjerg (Denmark)*

❹
SYLT

N O R D F R I E S L A

199

N O R D F R I E S I S C H E

5

H A L L I G E N

I N S E L N

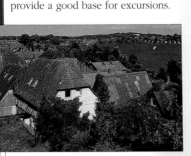

Buildings in Plön, in the Holstein Switzerland Nature Reserve

Nordsee

E I D E R S T E D T

5

(North

203

Sea)

❶
HELGOLAND

HUSUM

GETTING AROUND
The nearest international airport is Hamburg. Two motorways bisect Schleswig-Holstein: leaving Hamburg and the long queues for the Elbe Tunnel behind, the E47 (No 7) takes the visitor to Kiel and via Flensburg on to the Danish peninsula of Jutland, while the E22 (turning off the E47) leads via Lübeck to the Danish capital, Copenhagen.

❸
MELDORF

D I T H M A R S C H E

CUXHAVEN

73

49

The lake at Westensee Nature Reserve, where visitors can experience the captivating nature and wildlife close up

SIGHTS AT A GLANCE

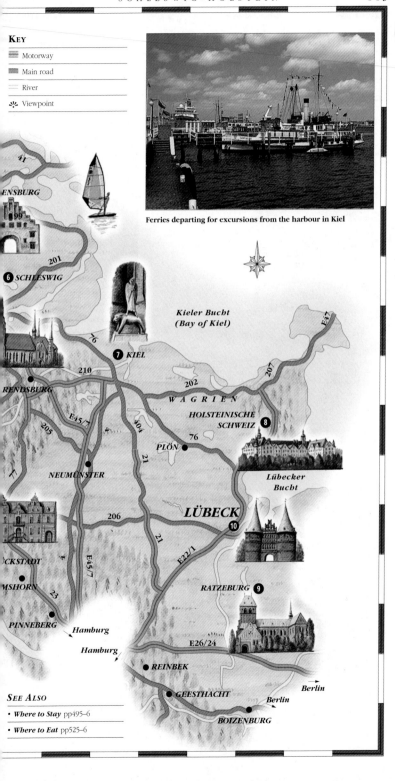

KEY

- ▬ Motorway
- ▬ Main road
- ═ River
- ☆ Viewpoint

Ferries departing for excursions from the harbour in Kiel

41

FLENSBURG
99

201

6 SCHLESWIG

*Kieler Bucht
(Bay of Kiel)*

E47

76

7 KIEL

210

202

RENDSBURG

E45/7

205

404

4

W A G R I E N

**HOLSTEINISCHE
SCHWEIZ** 8

77

21

PLÖN 76

NEUMÜNSTER

*Lübecker
Bucht*

207

206

LÜBECK

21

10

ÜCKSTADT

E45/7

4

MSHORN

23

E22/1

RATZEBURG 9

PINNEBERG *Hamburg*

Hamburg

E26/24

REINBEK

Berlin

GEESTHACHT

Berlin

BOIZENBURG

SEE ALSO

- **Where to Stay** pp495–6
- **Where to Eat** pp525–6

Helgoland ●

FOR LOVERS OF SPICES in Germany, it may have seemed a bad deal when in 1890 Germany received Helgoland from Britain in return for Zanzibar, but the island is nevertheless worth a visit. Farthest out in the open sea (50 km/31 miles from the mainland), the island always had great strategic importance, and after 1945, Britain used it as a bombing target before it was returned to Germany in 1952. Today its fresh air and spectacular red cliffs attract thousands of tourists.

VISITORS' CHECKLIST

Road map B1. 🏃 *1,900.*
🚢 *Bremerhaven, Cuxhaven and Wilhelmshaven.* 🏠 *Lung Wai 28 (04725-81 37 11 & 14).*

Port ①
On the flat part of the island is Unterland, a small post-war town with 1,900 inhabitants and a port. Fishermen store their nets in the colourful little houses, referred to as Hummerbuden (lobster huts).

Lange Anna ③
Tall Anna, measuring about 40 m (131ft) high, is the best known red sandstone cliff. Nearby is the so-called Lummenfelsen, the idiots' rock, which is also the smallest nature reserve in Germany.

0 metres   100

0 yards   100

Oberland ②
In the upper part of the island stands the Nikolai-kirche, dating from 1959. Close by, and worth a visit, are 16th-century tombs.

KEY

– – – Suggested route

TIPS FOR TOURISTS

Starting point: *the port of Helgoland*
Length: *1.7 km (1.1 miles).*
Stopping places: *there are numerous restaurants, bars and cafés all over the island .*

Glückstadt ❷

Road map C2. 🏠 *12,000.* 🚌 🛈
Grosse Nübelstraße 31 (04124-93 75 85).

THE DANISH king, Christian IV, founded this little town in 1617 and although less impressive than Hamburg, the town is worth a visit for its layout – roads radiate out from the hexagonal market square, once surrounded by fortifications. On the square stands the reconstructed 17th-century town hall as well as the Baroque Stadtkirche (town church). In 1648, parts of the duchy of Holstein were transferred to Glückstadt. Most of the palaces built to house the Dukes survived, for example the Palais Werner with its amazing ballroom. The regional **museum** is now in Brockdorf-Palais, another palace from 1632.

🏛 **Detlefsen-Museum**
Am Fleth 43. 📞 *(04124) 93 67 30.*
🕑 *2–5pm Tue; 2–6pm Fri; 10am–noon, 2–5pm Sun.*

Meldorf ❸

Road map C1. 🏠 *7,500.* 🚌
🛈 *Nordermarkt 10 (04832-70 45).*

MELDORF has preserved the **Dithmarscher Dom**, its cathedral, a 13th-century basilica with an exterior extensively rebuilt in the 19th century. The vaulting in the transept, resembling a cupola, is decorated with Gothic frescos, depicting the legends of saints Catherine, Christopher and Nicholas. There is a richly decorated dividing wall (1603) and a grand triptych of the Crucifixion (c.1520).

The port and waterfront of Flensburg

Sylt ❹

Road map B1. 🏠 *50,000.* 🚌 *in Westerland.* 🛈 *Westerland, Am Bundesbahnhof (04651-99 88).*

THE ISLAND of Sylt, the largest of the North Frisian islands, has long attracted wealthy German visitors. The 50-km (31-mile) long island offers a rich variety of landscapes: white, sandy beaches, shifting sand dunes near List, towering up to 25 m (82ft) high, steep shorelines, the Rotes Kliff (red cliff) near Kampen and the Watt, the endless expanse of mudflats in the national park, Schleswig-Holsteinisches Wattenmeer. **Westerland** is Sylt's main town, and its promenade, Friedrichstrasse, is "the" place to be seen. There is also an interesting casino in a former Secessionist spa building.

Flensburg ❺

Road map C1. 🏠 *84,500.* 🚌
🛈 *Speicherlinie 40 (0461-230 90).* 🎪 *Rum-Regatta in Flensburger Förde (Jun).*

THE MOST northerly town in Germany, Flensburg was an important trading centre in the 16th century with 200 ships, although at times it belonged to Denmark. The **Nordertor** (northern gate), dating from 1595, is an emblem of the city. The shipping museum is fascinating while the Marienkirche has a Renaissance altar, sculptures and the painting *The Last Supper* (1598). Nearby is the **Heilig-Geist-Kirche** (church of the Holy Ghost), which has belonged to the town's Danish community since 1588. Other interesting churches are **Nikolaikirche** which boasts a magnificent Renaissance organ, and Johanniskirche with a vaulted ceiling dating from around 1500. Its painted scenes show people disguised as animals, which was a covert way of criticizing the church and the system of indulgences.

ENVIRONS: Schloss Glücksburg, 9 km (6 miles) northeast of Flensburg, a square castle with massive corner towers on a granite base, was built from 1582–7. Visit its captivating castle chapel, the Roter Saal (red hall) with its low vaulting, and the valuable collection of 18th-century tapestries from Brussels. The artist Emil Nolde lived and worked in **Seebüll**, west of Flensburg, from the age of 20 until his death in 1956.

The sandy beaches of the North Frisian island of Sylt, extending far to the horizon

The inner courtyard of Schloss Gottorf in Schleswig

Schleswig ❻

Road map C1. 👥 *27,000*. 🚆
ℹ️ *Plessenstr. 7 (04621-98 16 16).*
🎭 *Schleswig-Holstein Musik Festival throughout the region (Jul/Aug); Wikinger-Tage (Aug every other year).*

THE MAIN seat of the Vikings, Schleswig became a bishop's see as early as 947, and from 1544 to 1713 it was the residence of the dukes of Schleswig-Holstein-Gottorf, once related to the rulers of Denmark and Russia. They resided in **Schloss Gottorf**, a castle with four wings which now houses the **Schleswig-Holsteinisches Landesmuseum** (regional museum) as well as northern Germany's most famous archaeological museum, the **Archäologisches Landesmuseum**,

exhibiting the *Moorleichen*, prehistoric corpses preserved in peat. It is also worth seeing the two-storey chapel (1590).

The **Dom** (cathedral) was built in stages between the 12th and 15th centuries. Its largest treasure is the Bordesholmer Altar, a triptych altar carved by Hans Brüggemann in 1514–21. A masterpiece of Gothic carving, it is 12 m (39 ft) high and comprises 392 figures; the only one to look straight at the visitor is the sculptor himself, bearded and hat askew (in the house of Abraham and Melchisede).

Visitors can also walk around the historic fishermen's district of **Holm**, and visit the **Wikinger-Museum Haithabu**, about 4 km (2 miles) from the town centre. The fortifications have survived in the grounds

of this historic Viking settlement. The museum is housed in a modern building, which looks like an upturned boat. Exhibits include the depiction of Viking life, models of boats, jewellery and everyday items.

🏛️ **Schloss Gottorf/ Schleswig-Holsteinisches Landesmuseum/Archäologisches Landesmuseum**
📞 *(04621) 81 32 22.* 🕐 *Mar–Oct: 9am–5pm daily; Nov–Feb: 10am–4pm Tue–Sun.*
🏛️ **Wikinger-Museum Haithabu**
📞 *(04621) 81 32 22.* 🕐 *Mar–Oct: 9am–5pm daily; Nov–Feb: 10am–4pm Tue–Sun.*

Kiel ❼

Road map C1. 👥 *245,000*. 🚆
ℹ️ *Andreas-Gayk-Straße 31 (0431-67 91 00).* **Town hall** 🕐 *May–Sep: 12:20 Wed & Sun.* 🎭 *Kieler Woche (end Jun).*

LOCATED at the end of the Kieler Förde inlet, Kiel marks the beginning of the Nord-Ostsee-Kanal (Kiel Canal), in service since 1895, with two giant locks. Ferries depart from Kiel for Scandinavia, and in the summer the "Kieler Woche" turns the town into a mecca for yachtsmen from around the world.

A walk along the Schweden-Kai (embankment) and surroundings will take visitors to the vast **Rathaus** (town hall), dating from the beginning of the 20th century, and the **Nikolaikirche** (church of St Nicholas) which was rebuilt after the devastation of World War II, with its baptismal font and Gothic altar. Ernst Barlach created *Geistkämpfer*, the sculpture outside the church, which symbolizes the triumph

ROMANESQUE BAPTISMAL FONTS

There are few places in the world where visitors can see as many Romanesque baptismal fonts as in Angeln. Generally fashioned from granite, they have been preserved in enchanting 12th-century churches, which can be visited by following a 63-km (39-mile) route along the roads linking Flensburg and Schleswig, Munkbrarup, Sörup, Norderbrarup, Süderbrarup and finally Ulsnis.

Font in the church in Borbry

Font in the church in Munkbrarup

Font in the church in Sörup

A house in Kiel's Schleswig-Holsteinisches Freilichtmuseum

of mind over matter. Pieces of the sculpture, which had been cut up by the National Socialists, were found and reassembled after the war.

The most interesting of Kiel's many museums is the **Schleswig-Holsteinisches Freilichtmuseum**, an open-air museum in Molfsee, 6 km (4 miles) from the centre of Kiel, where German rural architecture from the 16th–19th centuries is on show. Pottery, basket-making and baking are demonstrated, and the products are sold here.

🏛 **Schleswig-Holsteinisches Freilichtmuseum**
Hamburger Landstraße 97. 📞 (0431) 65 96 60. 🕐 Apr–Oct: 9am–6pm daily; Nov–Mar: 11am–4pm Sun & public holidays. 📷

Holsteinische Schweiz (Holstein's Switzerland) ➑

Road map D1. 🚇 🚍 Bad Malente, Kurverwaltung, Bahnhofstraße 4a (04523-20 01 00). 🎷 Jazz-Festival in Plön; open-air opera during Sommerspiele in Eutin.

THE MORAIN hills, which reach a height of 164 m (538 ft), and 140 lakes are the reasons why this area is known as Holstein's Switzerland. The best means of transport here is the bicycle, allowing visitors to appreciate the beauty of nature and the wealth of the fauna – ornithologists have counted 200 species of birds. The main centre of this holiday area is **Plön** on the

Großer Plöner See (large Plön lake). Nearby is **Preetz**, an old shoemakers' town, which has a towerless Gothic church that belonged to a former Benedictine monastery. Older still is the Romanesque church in **Bosau**, a small town in a picturesque location on the Großer Plöner See. It was the first bishopric in this area, and home to Vizelin – the apostle of the Slavs.

It is also worth visiting **Eutin**, a small town full of picturesque buildings, which is sometimes referred to as the "Weimar of the north". The original Schloss, a brick structure with four wings, was built in the Middle Ages as the residence of the Lübeck bishops, but it was substantially altered in the years 1716–27. Worth seeing inside are the palace chapel, the Blauer Salon (blue salon) with Rococo stucco work, as well as paintings by Johann Heinrich Wilhelm Tischbein, which were inspired by the *Iliad* and the *Odyssey*, epic poems written by Homer.

The Dom in Ratzeburg

Ratzeburg ➒

Road map D2. 🚶 12,500. 🚇
🛈 Schlosswiese 7 (04541-85 85 65).

RATZEBURG, situated on an island in the Großer Ratzeburger See, is linked with the mainland by three causeways. The town was named after Ratibor, the duke of the Elbe River area. Henry the Lion established a missionary bishopric here in 1154, and later it became the residence of the Lauenburg dukes.

The **Dom** (cathedral) is one of the earliest examples of brick architecture, a style that was imported from Lombardy. The southern vestibule of the Romanesque basilica is particularly impressive – with herringbone-pattern brickwork and lines of black tiles as interior decoration. The Romanesque stalls, a 13th-century crucifix in a rainbow arch, the ducal gallery above the nave and the Baroque altar in the southern transept are just some of the impressive treasures in this church.

The 17th-century Schloss in Plön, in Holstein's Switzerland

Street-by-Street: Lübeck ❿

THIS "SPECIFIC NEST", as Lübeck was described by its most famous resident, Thomas Mann, is well worth a visit. The most important town in the Baltic basin by the end of the Middle Ages, it is now a magnet for fans of Backsteingotik, Gothic brick architecture which has been elevated to a national style. In Lübeck it is easy to see why: church interiors, the façades of buildings, the city gates, the unique town hall and even the Medieval hospital resemble pictures from an illustrated history of architecture brought to life. Despite a few blunders, the city has been beautifully rebuilt after World War II and enjoys a positive revival.

Rathaus
Germany's most famous brick town hall, dating from 1226, has unusual walls and turrets.

Mengstraße
This street is full of picturesque Gothic buildings fronted by typical brick façades and crowned by stepped gables.

Heilig-Geist-Hospital

SCHÜSSELBUDEN

HOLSTENSTRASSE

★ Marienkirche
St Mary's Church, larger than the cathedral and situated behind the town hall, holds great art treasures.

Holstentor
This gate, once the only entrance into Lübeck, was built by Hinrich Helmstede in the years 1466–78, based on Flemish designs. It has become the emblem of the town.

Petrikirche
The church of St Peter, from the first half of the 14th century, is Lübeck's only five-naved church.

KEY

– – – Suggested route

View of the Town
Lübeck and its seven towers can be seen from afar. Virtually all the tourist attractions are in the old town, which is enclosed by the river Trave and its channels.

VISITORS' CHECKLIST

Road map D2. 🔼 275,000.
🚉 Am Bahnhof.
ℹ️ Breitenstr. 62 (0451-122 54 20). 🎭 Markt Anno Dazumal (May); Volksfest (Jul); Kunsthandwerker-Weihnachtsmarkt (Dec).

0 metres	150
0 yards	150

St Annen-Museum
This museum, housed inside an Augustinian convent, portrays life and culture in 13th–18th-century Lübeck.

Freilicht-bühne

Theatre Museum
The puppet theatre museum holds one of the world's largest collections of puppets.

ST. ANNEN–STRASSE

MÜHLENSTRASSE

BREITE STRASSE

MARLESGRUBE

DANKWARTSGRUBE

PARADE

STAR SIGHTS

★ **Marienkirche**

★ **Dom**

★ **Dom**
The cathedral, begun in 1173 at the time of Henry the Lion and completed in 1230, is 130 m (426 ft) long.

MARZIPAN FROM LÜBECK

A favourite present from Lübeck is marzipan, which has been popular throughout Europe since the 19th century. The sweets are made from two-thirds sweet almonds imported from Venice and one-third sugar and aromatic oils. The Persians referred to it as *marsaban*, and in 1530 its name was recorded for the first time in Lübeck as *Martzapaen*. From 1806, the Niederegger patisserie perfected the recipe; they established a patisserie on Breite Strasse which operates to this day.

Exploring Lübeck

All the most important monuments, with the exception of the Holstentor, are situated within the old town, which is best explored on foot.

🔒 Marienkirche

🕐 *9am–5pm daily, in winter to 3pm.*

St Mary's church was constructed by the Lübeckers as a monument to themselves. The twin-towered basilica with transept and a passageway around the polygon-shaped presbytery is the brick modification of a Neo-Classical French cathedral.

Its vast interior boasts the highest vaulted brick ceiling in the world (40 m/131 ft) which dominates the other interior features. These include a 10 m (32 ft) bronze Holy Sacrament (1476–9); a baptismal font in the main nave dating from 1337; the altar dedicated to the Virgin Mary in the Sängerkapelle (singers' chapel) made in Antwerp in 1518; and the main, late-Gothic Swarte-Altar with the Madonna. The Brief-kapelle, the south-western side chapel built around 1310, is one of the earliest examples of star vaulting in Europe.

In one of the towers, the shattered fragments of the church bells have been left embedded in the floor where they fell during the bombing in 1942; the present bells are from St Catherine's in Gdansk.

🏛 Buddenbrook-Haus

Heinrich- und Thomas-Mann-Zentrum, Mengstr. 4. 🕐 *mid Apr–Oct 10am–6pm; Nov–mid Apr: 10am–5pm.* ⬤ *24, 25, 31 Dec.* 📷

Literature lovers will wish to visit the Buddenbrook house. Behind its Rococo façade from 1758 is a museum devoted to the Mann family, the great writers who lived here in 1841–91. It is here that Thomas Mann wrote the family saga of the Buddenbrooks, after whom the house is named, and for which he was awarded the Nobel Prize in 1929. The centre exhibits documents relating to this famous family, in particular to Thomas and Heinrich Mann, concentrating on their time in Lübeck and their emigration and exile after 1933.

🏛 Schabbelhaus

Mengstraße 48 & 50.

Originally the western, wealthier half of Lübeck had many patrician houses, facing the streets with their ornate brick gables. Many of these were damaged in the bombing raids of March 1942, but after World War II they were carefully restored. The most interesting buildings survived in Mengstrasse, in particular the famous Schabbelhaus at No. 48. Built in 1558, this house gained a magnificent Baroque hall in the 18th century. Today it is an attraction in its own right as well as a restaurant.

Stepped gables of the Haus der Schiffergesellschaft

🏛 Haus der Schiffergesellschaft

Breite Straße 2.

The house of the Marine Guild, which dates from 1535, has a splendid interior and now houses one of the city's most elegant restaurants. The façade has stepped gables and terraces/forecourts, typical of Lübeck.

🏛 Füchtingshof

Glockengießerstr. 23.

The eastern part of the town is of an entirely different character: narrow streets link charming Höfe (courtyards) and small, modest houses. The most interesting Höfe can be

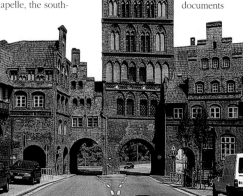

The multi-storey Burgtor, crowned by a Baroque cupola

The façade of the Gothic Heiliger-Geist-Hospital, with its spiky towers

found at numbers 23 and 39. The Baroque portal of the Füchtingshof, at No. 23, leads to houses which, from 1639, were built for the widows of merchants and captains.

Burgtor
On the northern limits of the old town stands the castle gate, a second surviving gate of the historic fortifications. A Baroque finial was added to the gate in 1685. The five storeys of the tower are decorated with uniform rows of windows and windbreaks.

Heiliger-Geist-Hospital
Große Burgstr. ☐ *Apr–Sep: 10am–5pm Tue–Sun; Oct–Mar: 10am–4pm Tue–Sun.*
The Holy Ghost hospital is the best preserved Medieval building of its type in central Europe. Built in the shape of the letter T, it has a shorter western section with a twin-aisled hall-church (c. 1286), containing frescos of *Christ and the Madonna on Solomon's Throne* and *Majestas Domini*. The second section contains the actual hospice. In 1820, small cubicles were created for the elderly, who lived here until 1970.

Jakobikirche
This 15th-century church, which suffered only insignificant damage during World War II, has preserved its original, mainly Baroque features. Of particular note are the main altar as well as the side altar in the south chapel. The latter was established around 1500 by the mayor, Heinrich Brömbse,

and depicts a scene of the Crucifixion carved in sandstone. Both the small and the large organ originate from the 15th century.

Katharinenkirche
Königstraße. **Museumskirche St. Katharinen** ☐ *Apr–Sep: 10am–1pm, 2–5pm Tue–Sun.*
St Catherine's, the only surviving monastic church, was built by the Franciscans, as is apparent from the absence of a tower and its monastic gallery in the presbytery of the main nave. The western façade, with its glazed brickwork, is of a high artistic quality. In the 20th century, sculptures carved by Ernst Barlach were added *(Woman in the Wind, Beggar on Crutches* and *The Singing Novitiate)*. On the western side hangs the painting of *The*

The bright interior of the Gothic Dom

Resurrection of Lazarus by Jacopo Tintoretto, bought by a wealthy patrician; the sculpture of St George and the dragon is a copy of the famous original by the Lübeck artist Bernt Notke, which is now in Stockholm.

St-Annen-Museum
☐ (0451) 122 41 37.
☐ *Apr–Sep: 10am–5pm Tue–Sun; Oct–Mar: 10am–4pm Tue–Sun.*
● *Easter, 24, 25, 31 Dec.*
The Augustinian convent houses unusual Lübeck art treasures. There is an impressive number of wooden Gothic altars, commissioned by wealthy families for their private chapels in one of the five churches. The altars were supposed to bring them eternal salvation after death, and to symbolize the wealth and prestige of the family during their lifetime. Gems of the collection are the Hans Memling altar with Christ's Passion, and the external side wings of the Schonenfahrer Altar by Bernt Notke.

Dom
☐ *Apr–Sep: 10am–5pm daily; Oct–Mar: 10am–3pm daily.*
The cathedral, completed in 1341, takes the form of a Gothic hall-church. Its most precious possession is the Triumphal Cross sculpted from a 17-m (55-ft) oak tree by Bernt Notke, a celebrated local artist. The giant figures, resplendent with emotion, include Adam and Eve, as well as the founder, bishop Albert Krummedick. Among numerous memorials, that dedicated to bishop Heinrich Bocholt, made from bronze, stands out. Additionally, two valuable sculptures can be seen; *Holy Mary Mother of God* with a crown composed of stars, as well as the *Beautiful Madonna* in the southern nave (1509). Note the bronze baptismal font by Lorenz Grove from 1455, with three kneeling angels supporting the bowl.

MECKLENBURG-LOWER POMERANIA

T HE MEDIEVAL *towns of Schwerin, Wismar, Rostock and Stralsund, as well as several magnificent architectural monuments, provide reason enough to visit this part of Germany, yet it also offers a largely untouched landscape of forests and lakes. Along the Baltic coastline, tourists delight in the beautiful sandy beaches of Darß or Usedom, but above all they head for the island of Rügen, with its famous white cliffs.*

Mecklenburg-Vorpommern (Lower Pomerania), a mosaic of regions, can look back on an eventful history. In the 12th century, indigenous Slav tribes were colonized and converted to Christianity. The region became part of the Holy Roman Empire and German colonialism resulted in the Slavs' rapid assimilation. In the Middle Ages, several towns became rich trading centres and joined the Hanseatic League. From the 18th century, the Swedish Empire was the most powerful political force in this part of Europe. It ruled Wismar, Rügen and Stralsund until 1803 and 1815 respectively, when the territories became part of Prussia, and later the German Reich. During World War II the Baltic towns suffered terrible destruction and then from neglect under the German Democratic Republic: in 1953 all the hotels were nationalized and the unique buildings in the Hanseatic towns were left to decay or were destroyed.

After reunification, although still one of the poorest states in Germany, Mecklenburg-Lower Pomerania today has become an idyllic holiday destination. Improvements in the infrastructure, new hotels and restaurants have brought positive change, and it has much to offer. Nature lovers, walkers and cyclists, for example, can enjoy the Mecklenburg lake district and the island of Rügen. Fans of architecture will find a wealth of interest in the palace in Ludwigslust and the castle of Güstrow, as well as the Gothic brick architecture in town halls, churches and smaller buildings.

The beautiful white chalk cliffs on the island of Rügen sweep down to the blue Baltic Sea

◁ The superb Schloss of Schwerin, on an island in the middle of Schwerin lake

Exploring Mecklenburg-Lower Pomerania

THIS IS A large region with only minor roads so visitors are well advised to allow extra time to explore it. The area can be divided into three: the west, stopping off in pretty Wismar or charming Schwerin with its fairy-tale castle; the centre, with the major port of Rostock as a base, and the east, which can be explored from Stralsund or Greifswald. In the central Mecklenburger Seenplatte is Müritz National Park, a vast area of lakes and forests that is ideal for camping, walking and sailing. It is also a good plan to set aside a few days for relaxation on the sandy beaches of Darß, Zingst, Usedom or Rügen.

Mecklenburg's glorious beaches

SIGHTS AT A GLANCE

Mecklenburg Bay

⑤ BAD DOBERAN

Lübeck Bay E22/105 ROSTOCK ⑨

Lübeck WISMAR ④

GADEBUSCH ③ Schweriner See GÜSTROW ⑥

104 ①

Schaalsee SCHWERIN

E26/24 241

E26/24

BOIZENBURG 5

② LUDWIGSLUST

Perleberg

Neuer Markt, surrounded by charming gabled buildings, Rostock

KEY

— Motorway
— Main road
— Scenic route
— River
☆ Viewpoint

Baltic Sea

Sassnitz

E22/E251

BERGEN

Rügen, lit by dawn sunlight

R Ü G E N

E22/105

STRALSUND

RIBNITZ-DAMGARTEN

96

Lecknitz

Trebel

GREIFSWALD

PEENEMÜNDE

WOLGAST

109

ANKLAM

USEDOM

Kummerower See

M E C K L E N B U R G I S C H E
S E E N P L A T T E

104

103

UECKERMÜNDE

NEUBRANDENBURG

Kolpinsee

104

109

Welse

Müritz

U C K E R M A R K

E55/19

E28/11

198

NEUSTRELITZ

PRENZLAU

E251/96

Berlin

Wittstock

Berlin

0 km   30

0 miles   30

GETTING AROUND

International flights land at Hamburg
and Berlin, domestic flights at Rostock and Heringsdorf on Usedom.
Ferries go from Denmark, Sweden
and Lithuania to Saßnitz and Rostock,
and the E55 motorway runs from the
south to Schwerin and Rostock.

The attractive cloisters of Schloss Güstrow

Schwerin

DESPITE protests from Rostock, the smaller town of Schwerin was chosen as the capital of the newly united state of Mecklenburg-Lower Pomerania. This was an inspired choice as the town is picturesquely situated amid several lakes, with a fairy-tale castle on an island, and an enchanting old town with many Neo-Classical and historic buildings that survived World War II largely unscathed. Apart from a brief spell, the Mecklenburg dukes resided in Schwerin from 1318–1918. Intellectual life flourished here in the 16th century and so the city is known as "Florence of the North".

The Neo-Renaissance Schloss on an island in Schweriner See

Exploring Schwerin

The old town of Schwerin is situated between Pfaffenteich railway station and Schweriner See, a vast 65-sq km (25-sq mile) lake. All the town's most important tourist attractions can easily be visited on foot. Close by to the north is Schelf, which was once a separate town.

♨ Schloss

Schlossinsel. 📞 *(0385) 56 57 38.*
⭘ *15 Apr–15 Oct: 10am–6pm Tue–Sun; 16 Oct–14 Apr: 10am–5pm Tue–Sun.*
Situated on Burg Island, this castle is often referred to as the "Neuschwanstein of Mecklenburg", after the famous Bavarian castle. The Schweriner Schloss was in fact largely built in 1843–57 to an eclectic design by Georg Adolph Demmler and Friedrich August Stüler, who were inspired by the turrets of Château Chambord in France. Major refurbishment tried to recreate some of the castle's original Renaissance features,

of which only the ceramic decorations have remained. Inside, the castle chapel built by Johan Batista Parra in 1560–63 has survived. The elegant rooms in the castle – Thronsaal (throne chamber), Ahnengalerie (ancestral gallery), Rote Audienz (red auditorium), Speisesaal (dining chamber) – are decorated with gilded stucco work. Despite the proliferation of their styles these rooms delight visitors, transporting them back to the 19th century.

♣ Burg- und Schlossgarten

The remaining part of the island is occupied by the Burggarten (fortress garden), which has an orangery and an artificial grotto, built from granite around 1850. A bridge leads to the larger Schlossgarten (castle garden) which is a favourite place for the town's inhabitants to relax. The Kreuzkanal, a canal built in 1748–56, one of the garden's axes, is lined with copies of Baroque statues

including the *Four Seasons*, created by the renowned sculptor of the Dresden Zwinger, Balthasar Permoser.

🏛 Staatliches Museum

Werderstr. 📞 *(0385) 595 80.*
⭘ *10am–8pm Tue, 10am–5pm Wed–Sun.* ● *24 & 31 Dec.* 🖼
The state museum stands in Alter Garten, one of the most attractive squares in Germany, where the waters beautifully reflect the castle and the Neo-Renaissance theatre. The museum, which features lions on its façade and a portico with Ionic columns, houses an art collection based on that of Duke Christian Ludwig II, a lasting testimony to his taste and erudition. Apart from works by German artists such as Cranach, Liebermann and Corinth, and the Dutch painters Hals and Fabritius, it holds works by many French artists. This includes 34 paintings by Jean-Baptiste Oudry, who was court painter to Ludwig XIV, as well as a good selection of paintings by the much more recent Dadaist artist Marcel Duchamp.

🏛 Rathausplatz

The town hall square is surrounded by the homes of wealthy citizens, often with 19th-century façades concealing older walls. This is true of the Gothic town hall, which is hidden under an English mock-Tudor-style façade. Demmler was the architect who is responsible for numerous Neo-Renaissance

***Venus and Amor* (1527) by Lucas Cranach in the Staatliches Museum**

The Dom and houses in Schwerin

and Neo-Gothic buildings, the showpieces of Schwerin. One of the outstanding buildings in the market square is Neues Gebäude on the north side. This "new building" is a covered market from 1783–5, with a showpiece façade comprising 12 Doric columns.

🏠 Dom St Maria und St Johannes
Markt. 📞 *(0385) 592 52 12.*
Tower ⏰ *telephone for opening times.* 🎫
This cathedral is regarded as the most important work of Gothic brick architecture in the Baltic region, in spite of its Neo-Gothic tower, which affords a marvellous view of the entire town. The basilica, dating from 1240–1416, with its wide transept and passage-way around the presbytery

and its wreath of chapels, is reminiscent of the design of French cathedrals. A small number of outstanding original features remain in the cathedral, which compare well with the finest works from Antwerp during this time. They include the wooden late-Gothic multi-panelled Crucifixion worked in sandstone, the 14th-century baptismal font, a memorial to Duchess Helen of Mecklenburg created by the Vischer workshop in Nuremberg, as well as the tombstones of Duke Christopher and his wife (1595).

🏛 Freilichtmuseum Schwerin-Mueß
Alte Crivitzer Landstraße 13.
📞 *(0385) 201 30 11.* ⏰ *15 Apr–15 Oct: 10am–6pm Tue–Sun.* 🎫
The museum contains a collection of Mecklenburg folk architecture, including 17 houses of the 17th–19th centuries, which strive to recreate the look of an original village. Combine a visit to this open-air museum with a leisurely day on the beach in nearby Zippendorf.

Houses of an earlier era in open-air Freilichtmuseum in Schwerin-Mueß

SCHWERIN CITY CENTRE

Burg- und Schlossgarten ②
Dom St Maria und
  St Johannes ⑤
Rathausplatz ④
Schloss ①
Staatliches Museum ③

0 metres   300
0 yards   300

KEY

P Parking

ℹ️ Tourist information

🏠 Church

One of 24 waterfalls in Ludwigslust Park

Ludwigslust ❷

Road map D2. 🚶 *12,600.*
🚇 *north of centre, 15 min. walk.*
ℹ️ *Schlossfreiheit 8 (03874-52 62 51).*

AT THE BEGINNING of the 18th century, the small village of Klenow was founded here, which from 1765 grew into a town. The town was laid out around the **Schloss**, residence of the dukes of Mecklenburg-Schwerin until 1837. The "Versailles of Mecklenburg" is in fact quite different from its French namesake. The Baroque palace was built entirely in brick, concealed beneath sandstone from the Ruda hills. The ornate interior, particularly the elegant Goldener Saal (gold hall), was decorated in Ludwigsluster Carton, a type of papier-mâché, in order to cut costs.

In the mid-19th century, the vast **Schlosspark** was redesigned by Peter Joseph Lenné as an English-style landscaped garden. On a scenic walk round the garden, the visitor can discover some 24 waterfalls, a canal, artificial ruins, a stone bridge and the mausoleum of Helena Pavlovna, daughter of Tsar Peter I,

who died tragically young. In the town you will find the Protestant **Stadtkirche**, built in 1765–70 to look like an antique temple. In the presbytery is a giant mural, *The Adoration of the Shepherds.*

⛪ **Schloss**
🎫 *(03874) 281 14.*
🕐 *15 Apr–15 Oct: 10am–6pm Tue–Sun; 16 Oct–14 Apr: 10am–5pm Tue–Sun.* ● *24, 31 Dec.* ♿
🔓 **Stadtkirche**
🎫 *(03874) 284 57.* ● *Until further notice.*

Gadebusch ❸

Road map D2. 🚶 *6,600.* 🚇
ℹ️ *Lübsche Str. 8 (03886-29 76).*

THIS SMALL TOWN, situated right next to the former East–West border, has two interesting historic monuments. The **Stadtkirche**, which dates from 1220, is the oldest brick church in Mecklenburg. Its cross vaulting, chunky pillars and goblet-shaped capitals are Romanesque in style. One of its most precious pieces is the bronze baptismal font (1450). Angels hold the bowl, on which 22 scenes of the Passion were sculpted by an unknown artist.

In the 16th and 17th centuries, the **Schloss** was the

Baptismal font in the Stadtkirche in Gadebusch

residence of distant relations of the dukes of Mecklenburg. Resembling the castle in Wismar, it is decorated with glazed reliefs and pilasters. It is not open to visitors.

Wismar ❹

Road map D2. 🚶 *55,000.* 🚇
ℹ️ *Am Markt 11 (03841-194 33).*

WISMAR is undoubtedly one of the most attractive towns in Mecklenburg. During the Middle Ages, it was an important Hanseatic centre, as evidenced by the monumental brick church, which is completely out of proportion with the provincial town of today. After the Thirty Years' War, in 1648, the Swedes were established in the town, and rebuilt it as the strongest fortress in Europe. In 1803 they leased Wismar to Mecklenburg, but never claimed it back.

The town centre has a grand market square measuring 100 x 100 m (328 x 328 ft), with **Wasserspiele** (water feature), a Dutch-Renaissance pavilion from 1602 in the centre. Water was piped here from a source 4 km (2 miles) away, until 1897, to supply 220 private and 16 public buildings. The most beautiful house on the square is the **Alter Schwede** (old Swede), built about 1380, with a protruding Gothic

The Baroque residence of the dukes of Mecklenburg-Schwerin in Ludwigslust

Alter Schwede and Wasserspiele in the market square in Wismar

brick gable. To the west of the market there are two churches, which act as sad examples of the GDR's neglect of its historical legacy. The reconstruction of the **Georgenkirche**, badly damaged in World War II, was begun in 1989, and it will soon be returned to its former glory. The **Marienkirche** has only one surviving tower – the ruined nave was blown up in 1960. Nearby lies the **Fürstenhof**, residence of the dukes of Wismar. The north wing is the most interesting – its Mannerist style was inspired by the Italian town of Ferrari and northern European ceramic traditions (such as Lübeck workshop). The magnificent sandstone portal is flanked by pairs of intertwined fauns. **Nikolaikirche** is a gem of Wismar architecture. Spared in World War II, the façade of this late-Gothic basilica from the 14th and 15th centuries is decorated with glazed friezes of mythological creatures, saints and, at the peak of the transept, a huge rose window. The proportions of the interior and the height of the vaulted main

A pair of fauns from the portal of Fürstenhof in Wismar

nave measuring 37 m (121 ft) are captivating. Some of the interior fixtures and fittings came from other churches in the city, which were either ruined or no longer exist, including the so-called Krämeraltar with a sculpture of the *Beautiful Madonna and Child* (c.1420). The room by the tower has the most complete cycle of frescos in the region (c.1450).

Bad Doberan **⑤**

Road map D1. 🚶 *11,900.* 🚉
ℹ *Alexandrinenplatz 2 (038203-621 54).*

W HEN Duke Henry Borwin was hunting deer, a passing swan reportedly shouted *"Dobr Dobr"* (a good location) as the deer fell. Borwin duly founded the most important Cistercian monastery of the Baltic region here. The **Münster** was built in 1295–1368, with a severe interior and a small bell, in accordance with the order's rules which stipulate that no tower should be built. The interior is fascinating, its walls surfaced in red, with white plasterwork and colourful ribbing. Most of the original fixtures and fittings have survived almost intact. Among the treasures are a vast, gilded panelled painting, produced in Lübeck in 1310, a 12-m (39-ft) Holy Sacrament made from oak, a small cupboard holding the chalice and relics

from an earlier Romanesque building, as well as a statue of the Virgin Mary. Beautiful tombs mark the resting places of the rulers of Mecklenburg, of the Danish Queen Margaret, and Albrecht, King of Sweden, who died in 1412. Visitors can walk around the outside of the church which has a pleasant lawn. Beyond you can find a small octagonal building, beautifully decorated with glazed brickwork – this lovely piece of 13th-century architecture is the morgue.

A stroll around the health spa is also recommended. Right in its centre it has two early 19th-century pavilions with Chinese features – an ideal place for a coffee break.

ENVIRONS: Another adventure the visitor could try is a trip on the "Molli", a narrow-gauge railway that links Bad Doberan with Heiligendamm and Kühlungsborn, where there is a 4-km (2-mile) long beach. On the way, a little gem of 13th-century country architecture, the church in **Stefenshagen,** calls for a visit. On its south portal, see the terracotta figures of the Apostles. Across the presbytery runs a brickwork relief with mythological creatures and entwined vines.

🏛 **Doberaner Münster**
📞 *(038203) 627 16.* ⏰ *May–Sep: 9am–6pm Mon–Sat, noon–6pm Sun; Mar, Apr, Oct: 9am–5pm Mon–Sat, noon–5pm Sun; Nov–Feb: 10am–4pm Tue–Sat; noon–4pm Sun.* 🗝 *daily.*

The monumental Cistercian Münster in Bad Doberan

The imposing Schloss, dominating the skyline of Güstrow

Güstrow **6**

Road map D2. 👥 *32,500.* 🚉
ℹ️ *Domstr. 9 (03843-68 10 23).*

Güstrow is one of the most harmonious towns of the former German Democratic Republic, with an attractive old town, unmarred by pre-fabricated tower blocks. All the most important monuments are within easy reach. The town is dominated by the **Schloss**, built from 1558 by Franz Parr, a member of a renowned family of sculptors and architects from northern Italy. German, Italian and Dutch elements come together here, including fantastical chimneys and two-storey arcades in the courtyards. The architect's brother decorated the Festsaal (ballroom) with a hunting frieze – the stucco heads of the deer have real antlers.

In the nearby **Dom**, a brick cathedral of the 13th and 14th centuries, there is a fascinating tomb of the Apostles on the pillars of the nave and the 16th century tomb of Duke Ulrich and his two wives, with a large genealogical family tree of all three of them. In the north nave hangs the burly *Schwebende* (Hovering Angel), a remarkable work by Ernst Barlach, who lived here from 1910 until his death in 1938. He described his works to Bertolt Brecht as: "beautiful without beautifying, sizeable without enlarging, harmonious without smoothness, and full of vitality without brutality". Barlach's work bore the brunt of National Socialist condemnation – the original *Schwebende* was melted down and made into cannons but the copy that replaced it was made from the original plaster cast. Other works by Barlach can be seen in the museum dedicated to him.

It is worth concluding a visit to this town in the market, near which rises the **Pfarrkirche St Marien.** This church has a magnificent high altar, a panelled work of art with painted wings, which is the work of Belgian artists (c. 1522).

Environs: The open-air museum in **Groß-Raden**, near Sternberg, is popular with tourists as well as archaeology students. A village has been recreated with houses, workshops and a system of fortifications.

🏛 **Archäologisches Freilichtmuseum**
Groß-Raden. 📞 *(03847) 22 52.*
🕐 *Apr–Oct: 10am–5:30pm daily. Nov– Mar: 10am–4:30pm Tue–Sun.*

Neubrandenburg **7**

Road map E2. 👥 *75 000.* 🚉
ℹ️ *Marktplatz 1 (0395-194 33).*

Founded in 1248 as a sister town to Brandenburg on the Havel, the town was laid out in the form of a regular oval. It prospered as a trading centre until the Thirty Years' War, after which it fell into disrepair. As a result it now has what is probably the only example of post-World War II concrete tower blocks surrounded by medieval town walls, which have survived virtually intact. The walls extend for 2.3 km (2515 yds), originally with a keep open to the interior, and subsequently interspersed with half-timbered houses, known as **Wiekhäuser** (there were once 58, of which 24 survive). Of the four city gates the most interesting are **Friedländer Tor** (begun in 1300), with inner and outer gateways and a tower, as well as Neues and Stargarder Tor, decorated on the town side with mysterious terracotta figures of women with raised hands (c.1350).

In the town centre stands the Medieval **Marienkirche**, which was damaged during World War II and is now restored as a concert hall.

Environs: The castle in **Stargard**, some 10 km (6 miles) to the south, is the oldest secular building in Mecklenburg. Its 4 m (13 ft) walls were begun in 1200; the residence in 1236. Today it houses a youth hostel.

A typical half-timbered Wiekhaus in the town wall in Neubrandenburg

Nationalpark Müritz ❽

THERE ARE ABOUT a thousand lakes between Schwerin and Neubrandenburg; the largest of these is Müritzsee, to the east of which a national park was established in 1990. A particularly attractive part of the lake district is the so-called Mecklenburgische Schweiz (Swiss Mecklenburg), with its hilly moraines, such as Ostberg, 115 m (377 ft) above sea level. Tourists are attracted by the breathtaking scenery, perfect conditions for water sports and fascinating castles and palaces.

VISITORS' CHECKLIST

Road map E2. 🛈 Waren, Neuer Markt 19. (03991-66 61 83); Neustrelitz, Markt 1. (03981-25 31 19).

Schlitz ②
This palace is the most important Neo-Classical monument in Mecklenburg (1800–1823). In its beautiful landscaped park stands the Nymphenbrunnen, the famous fountain of nymphs. Cast in 1903 in Secessionist style for the Berlin department store Wertheim, it was transferred to this site in 1930.

Basedow ①
For 600 years Basedow was in the hands of the von Hahn family, who built this irregular three-winged palace.

Müritzsee ④
Müritzsee (meaning "small sea") is, at 115 sq km (44 sq miles), the second largest lake in Germany after Lake Constance.

KEY

▨ Tour route

▨ Scenic route

= Minor road

= River, lake

🕊 Viewpoint

Neustrelitz ⑤
The palace (1712) was the seat of distant relations of the Mecklenburg-Strelitz dukes who established the town and its church, and after 1733 resided here.

0 km   15

0 miles   15

Waren ③
Waren, an ideal base for tourists, is close to Binnen-müritz with its beaches and shops with watersports equipment for sale or hire.

Rostock ⑨

T HE HISTORY OF THE most important German port in the Baltic has been turbulent. This prosperous Hanseatic town had established trade links with distant ports such as Bergen (Norway), Riga (Latvia) and Bruges (Belgium) as early as the 15th century. In 1419 the first university in northern Europe was founded here, and it flourished again in the 19th century. After it suffered heavy damage in the Allied air raids of 1942, Rostock was rebuilt on a grand scale as the GDR's showpiece, since Szczecin had been lost to Poland.

VISITORS' CHECKLIST

Road map D1. 🚶 200,000.
🚉 🛈 *Schnickmannstraße.*
13–14 (0381-194 33).
🌐 *www.rostock.de*
📅 *Warnemünder Woche (Jul),
Weihnachtsmarkt (Nov–Dec).*

**Kröpelinerstraße – a promenade
with 17th century houses**

Exploring Rostock
A visit to the town is best started from the Neuer Markt (new market), from where the most important monuments can easily be reached on foot.

🏛 Rathaus
The town hall, on Neuer Markt, has a Baroque façade (added in 1727–9), from which seven Gothic towers of the original building emerge. At the rear of the building, in Große Wasserstraße, it is worth seeking out Kerhof-haus, the best preserved Gothic house in Rostock with a splendidly ornate façade featuring glazed brickwork, dating from 1470.

🏛 Steintor
A few minutes south of Neuer Markt is the Steintor, the best known of the gates in the old city wall. One of only three surviving gates of the original fortifications (at one time with 22 gates), it received its characteristic crowning feature during the Renaissance.

🔒 Marienkirche
Am Ziegenmarkt. ⏰ *10am–4pm Mon–Sat, 11:15am–noon Sun.* 📷
This church, meant to exceed the height of its Lübeck counterpart, was completed in the mid-15th century, after almost 250 years of construc-tion. The nave, built after the original roof had collapsed, has an untypical, short body, while the mas-sive western tower is as wide as three naves. Intercon-nected swathes of glazing decorate the exterior of the church, while much of the whitewashed interior features star vaulting. The main attraction is the astrono-mical clock, constructed in 1472 by maestro Düringer of

**Baptismal font in
the Marienkirche**

**The richly decorated pulpit
in the Marienkirche**

Nuremberg. Its mechanism will show the correct time and date until 2047. Every afternoon its clockwork apostles parade before the tourists.

🏛 Kröpelinerstraße
The most popular street in the city is lined by houses from the 17th to the 19th centuries. In summer students congregate around the "Brunnen der Lebensfreude" (fountain of happiness) on the Universitätsplatz (university square). The main university building was built in the years 1867–70 in Neo-Renaissance style. The southern part of the square was occupied by a pal-ace with a beautiful Baroque hall where concerts are performed. A Neo-Classical annexe with a Doric colonnade (1823) stands nearby. A statue on the square commemorates the town's most famous resident, Field Marshal Blücher, who helped defeat Napoleon at Waterloo.

ENVIRONS: Between Rostock and Stralsund lies a delightful coastal area. The peninsula, with the three former islands of **Fischland**, **Darß** and **Zingst**, attracts visitors to its quiet, beautiful beaches and splendid natural scenery. Particularly attractive are the villages of **Ahrenshoop**, which was originally an artists' colony, **Prerow**, which has traditional fishermen's houses and churches, and **Wieck**, with its charming thatched houses. A national park has been established here, and includes Darß and its magnificent forest, Zingst, the west coast of Rügen and the island of Hidensee.

Stralsund ⓾

AFTER LÜBECK, STRALSUND IS the most interesting Hanseatic town in northern Germany. During its history, it has had to defend its independence against Lübeck, Denmark, Holland and Sweden. In the Thirty Years' War, General Wallenstein vowed that he would take the town even if it was chained to heaven – but he failed. Subsequently, Lower Pomerania stayed under Swedish rule for 200 years until 1815, when it became Prussian. Despite its turbulent history, 811 protected buildings survived in the old town, among them some truly remarkable examples of architecture.

The Rathaus with its small turrets

Exploring Stralsund

The town centre of Stralsund is surrounded by water on all sides – in the north by the Strelasund bay, and on the other sides by lakes formed in the moats of the former bastions, Knieperteich and Frankenteich. All the most interesting historic monuments are easily accessible on foot from here.

🏛 Alter Markt

The old market square affords the best view of the filigree façade of the town hall, beyond which stands the vast edifice of St Michael's church. It is surrounded by houses from various eras, of which the two most important are the Gothic Wulflamhaus, and the Commandantenhaus, Baroque headquarters of the town's former Swedish commandant. The Rathaus dates from the 13th century with a 14th-century façade and ground-floor arcades, and resembles the one in Lübeck. In 1370 the Hanseatic League

Portal of the Nikolaikirche

and the defeated Danish king signed a peace treaty here.

The Nikolaikirche, built from 1270–1360, was inspired by French Gothic cathedrals as well as the Marienkirche in Lübeck. It has rare free-standing flying buttresses in brick, which are much more unusual than in stone. Inside there are several intriguing furnishings, for example, the statue of St Anna (c. 1290), an astronomical clock (1394), as well as fragments of the Novgorod stall with various fascinating scenes including one of hunting for sables. The Baroque main altar was designed in 1798 by renowned Berlin architect and sculptor Andreas Schlüter.

🏛 Kulturhistorisches Museum

Mönchstr. 25/27
☎ *(03831) 287 90.*
🕐 *10am–5pm Tue–Sun.*
♿

The Katharinenkloster, a former 15th-century Dominican abbey, now houses two museums. Its abbey rooms provide an appropriate setting for historic exhibitions – the refectory has vaults supported by stylish columns – including copies of the famous Viking treasure from Hiddensee and a collection of 18th- and 19th-century toys and dolls' houses. A branch of the Museum, in Böttcherstraße, has a collection devoted to village life, folklore and costumes of the Baltic region.

🏛 Deutsches Museum für Meereskunde und Fischerei

🕐 *10am–5pm daily; Jul, Aug: 9am–6pm; 25, 26 Dec: 10am–5pm; 1 Jan: noon–5pm.* ⚫ *24, 31 Dec.* ♿

Highlights of this museum of the sea and fishing, based in a former convent, include colourful aquariums and a 16-m (52-ft) long skeleton of a whale. It is also a scientific establishment researching the life of sea organisms.

⛪ Marienkirche

Tower 🕐 *May–Oct: 9am–6pm Mon–Sat, 11:30am–5pm Sun; Nov–Mar: 10am–noon, 2–4pm Mon–Fri, 10am–noon Sat, 2:30–4pm Sun; Apr: 10am–4pm Mon–Sat, 2:30–4pm Sun.* **Organ concerts:** *summer: 11am Mon–Wed, Fri–Sun.* ♿

Dominating the Neuer Mark is the town's largest church, St Mary's, built in 1383–1473, with an octagonal tower (with good views of Stralsund). Star vaulting lightens the impact of the monumental 99-m (325-ft) high interior. Main attractions are Gothic frescos, carved wooden figures of saints and a late-Gothic baptismal font. The huge Baroque organ is used for concerts in summer.

Marienkirche with its dominant, octagonal tower

Rügen ⑪

THE LARGEST of Germany's islands at 926 sq km (357 sq miles), Rügen is also the most beautiful and diverse, boasting steep cliffs next to sandy beaches and a hilly hinterland with forests and peat bogs. The island is only 50 km (31 miles) across, yet its rugged coastline extends for hundreds of miles. The Huns once ruled here, and their tombs can still be seen. It was fortified by the Slavs, then ruled by Danes and Swedes. In 1815 Rügen came under Prussian rule, and in 1936 it was linked to the mainland by the 1 km- (0.6 mile-) long Rügendamm.

Kap Arkona
An attractive walk around the rugged cape, 46 m (150 ft) high, passes the ruins of the Jaromar ancestral home and a temple to the Slav god Svantevit.

Hiddensee
This small island is accessible from Stralsund or Schaprode on Rügen. Horse-drawn carts and bikes replace cars in this oasis of tranquillity.

KEY

▬ Motorway

= Main road

☀ Viewpoint

★ Waase
At this typical fishing village on the island of Ummanz, an unusual work of art has survived: an altarpiece from Antwerp, from around 1520.

STAR SIGHTS

★ Nationalpark Jasmund

★ Putbus

★ Waase

*Map labels:*

Ar
Nobbi
Altenkirchen
Dranske
Wiek
Breege
WITTOW
Lebbi
Bodo
Grieben
BUG
Hiddensee
Schaprode
Trent
HIDDENSEE
UMMANZ
Gingst
Kubitzer Bodden
Samtens
Stralsund
Poseritz
Brandshagen
Reinberg

Jasmund Peninsula

The northeast of the peninsula is occupied by the Stubnitz forest of oak and beech trees, which continues down to the sea, interrupted by dazzling white chalk cliffs. The symbol of Rügen, they inspired artists like Caspar David Friedrich.

VISITORS' CHECKLIST

Road map E1. 🚉 🚌 *Bergen, Markt 23 (03838-25 60 95). Binz, Heinrich-Heine-Str. 7 (038393-306 75); Hiddensee, Norderende 162, Vitte (038300-642 26); Putbus, Alleestr. 4 (038301-4 31).*
🎭 *In Ralswiek (near Bergen) performances take place under the title of "Ballade von Klaus Störtebeker" (Jun–Sep).*

★ Nationalpark Jasmund

An attractive walk starts at the viewpoint of Königsstuhl (king's seat; 119 m/390 ft), continues along the Hochuferweg (cliff-top walk), past Victoriasicht and Wissower Klinken viewpoints, to end at Sassnitz.

Osterseebad Binz

Rügen's largest and most popular seaside resort, Binz has a beautiful white beach, grand early 20th-century villas and a pier.

(map)

romper Wiek

Glowe

Lohme

NATIONAL PARK JASMUND

Sagard • Sassnitz

Kleiner Jasmunder Bodden

Prorer Wiek

Ostseebad Binz

Ostseebad Seillin

Ostseebad Baabe

Ostseebad Göhren

Putbus

Rügischer Bodden

Greifswalder Bodden

0 km 5
0 miles 5

★ Putbus

This elegant late Neo-Classical town was planned after 1807 on the model of Bad Doberan. Its centrepiece is the theatre, which was built in 1819 to a design by Wilhelm Steinbach.

Greifswald ⑫

Road map E1. 🚶 *54,000.* 🚉
ℹ️ *Am Markt (03834-52 13 80).*
🎵 *Musical concerts "Greifswalder Bachwochen" (Jun); Jazz Evenings in Eldena (Jul).*

This former Hanseatic town is situated 5 km (3 miles) from the Bay of Greifswald. From afar the picturesque silhouette of the town with its three church towers, nicknamed Fat Mary, Little Jakob and Long Michael, appears like a painting by Caspar David Friedrich – the town's most famous resident – come to life. Charm pervades the old town, its architectural mix resulting from 40 years of East German rule. Greifswald, an important academic centre and market town, has geared up more for tourism since 1989. It is certainly worth a visit – a short walk from east to west will enable the visitor to see all the most important monuments in town.

The 14th-century **Marien-kirche** has a vast square tower, giving it a rather squat appearance and its nickname, Fat Mary. Inside, the church contains the remains of frescos and an amazing Renaissance pulpit depicting the Reformation figures of Luther, Bugenhagen and Melanchthon. The city museum has a

collection of paintings by Caspar David Friedrich, including his famous landscapes of the ruined monastery of Eldena, *Ruined Eldena in the Riesengebirge*, which he transposed to the mountains of present-day Poland and Slovakia.

The market square with its Baroque town hall is surrounded by patrician houses, with exemplary rich brickwork façades (particularly numbers 11 and 13). Nearby rises the vast **Dom St Nikolai.** The cathedral's octagonal tower, topped with a Baroque helm, affords extensive views of the town. The Rubenow-Bild (1460), one of the paintings inside, depicts the founding professor of Greifswald's university in front of Mary, Mother of God.

ENVIRONS: Wieck, an attractive working fishing village, is now incorporated into Greifswald. It has a drawbridge dating from 1887, reminiscent of typical Dutch bridges. The Cistercian monastery of **Eldena**, just 1 km (0.6 mile) south of Wieck district, was made famous by the Romantic paintings of Caspar David Friedrich. The monastery was founded in 1199 and plundered by the Swedes in 1637. Its ruined red walls amid the green grass and trees look wildly romantic.

Alter Speicher – the half-timbered granary in Wolgast

Wolgast ⑬

Road map E1. 🚶 *15,000.* 🚉
ℹ️ *Rathausplatz 6 (03836-60 01 18).*

From 1295 the seat of the Pomeranian-Wolgast dukes, Wolgast castle was destroyed in 1713, when Peter the Great ordered the town to be burned down. An interesting building still remaining is the 12-sided cemetery chapel with star vaulting, which is supported by a single column. The most valuable work of art can now be seen in **Pfarrkirche St Petri**, a 14th-century parish church.

Renovated houses around the Fischmarkt in Greifswald

Dating from the turn of the 17th to the 18th century, the *Totentanz* frieze is an imitation of the famous *Dance of Death* by Hans Holbein in Basle. Another notable artifact is the epitaph of Duke Philip I, crafted in 1560 by the Saxon artist Wolf Hilinger.

Other attractions in the town are the **Alter Speicher**, an 80 m- (262 ft-) long half-timbered granary (Burgstraße, 1836), and the family home of Philipp Otto Runge, famous romantic painter and adopted son of Hamburg.

🜲 Philipp-Otto-Runge-Gedenkstätte
Kronwieckstraße 45. ◯ *Jun–Aug: 10am–6pm Tue–Fri, 10am–4pm Sat, Sun; Sep–May: 10am–5pm Tue–Fri, 10am–2pm Sat.*

One of the models in the Otto Lilienthal-Museum in Anklam

Anklam ⓮

Road map E2. 🜲 16,400. 🜲
🛈 *Markt 3, Rathaus (03971-21 05 41).*

A FORMER Hanseatic town, Anklam's erstwhile importance is revealed by its vast defensive walls, in which is set the city gate, **Steintor**, dating from the mid-15th century. It is worth visiting the Gothic **Marienkirche**. Inside, the church's octagonal pillars and the arches of its arcades are painted with graceful figures, which reveal a Lübeck influence.

A museum recalls the life and inventions of Otto Lilienthal who was born here in 1848. After observing storks, he constructed a flying machine and completed his first flight in 1891. In total he created some 2000 machines,

Fishing boat on the beach at Usedom

none of which flew further than 350 m (1148 ft). His last flight ended in his death.

🏛 Otto-Lilienthal-Museum
Ellbogenstraße 1. ◯ *May–Sep: 10am–5pm Tue–Fri, 2–5pm Sat, Sun; Oct–Apr: 10am–4pm Tue–Fri, 2–5pm Sun.*

Usedom ⓰

Road map E1. 🜲 🛈 *Heringsdorf, Kurverwaltung, Kulmstr. 33 (038378-24 51); Ahlbeck, Kurverwaltung, Dünenstr. 45 (038378-244 14).*

T HE ISLAND, named after the village of Usedom and separated from the mainland by the Peenestrom, is the second largest in Germany at 445 sq km (172 sq miles). A small corner in the east was incorporated into Poland after 1945. Usedom is almost as attractive as Rügen, possessing white beaches, forests, peat bogs and bays overgrown with rushes in the south. It is linked with the mainland by two drawbridges (near Anklam and Wolgast). The resorts follow one another like pearls on a string: Bansin, Heringsdorf and Bad Ahlbeck, known as the "three sisters", are connected by a wide beach. At the beginning of the 20th century they evolved into elegant holiday resorts, with white villas, hotels and boarding houses, as typical of seaside resorts. Worth a visit is the industrialist

Oechler's house in Heringsdorf (Delbrückstr. 5), which has an antique appearance with mosaics on its façade. During the past few years, the early 20th-century piers in all three spas have been rebuilt and restored. The longest, in Heringsdorf, is also the second largest in Europe, after one in Poland. The Marienkirche, one of the island's main attractions, was erected in the 19th century.

Peenemünde ⓯

Road map E1. 🜲 650.

H ISTORICALLY the most interesting spot on the island of Usedom is the **museum** at Peenemünde, based on military territory. It demonstrates the evolution of space travel, pioneered at this research station since 1936.

During World War II, long-distance rockets, powered by liquid fuel and known as V-2 (*Vergeltungswaffe;* retaliatory weapon), were produced here, which inflicted heavy damage on London and Antwerp in 1944. After the war, the chief engineer, Wernher von Braun, worked for NASA and became one of the pioneers of the Apollo rockets – eventually taking mankind to the moon.

V-2 rocket in Peenemünde

🏛 Historisch-technisches Informationszentrum
Bahnhofstraße. 28.
📞 *(03871-21 32 10).*
◯ *10am–noon, 2–4pm Tue–Fri; 2–4 pm Sun.*

TRAVELLERS' NEEDS

WHERE TO STAY

I T IS RELATIVELY EASY to find a room in a hotel or pension in Germany, even in small towns or large villages. The range of prices for a night's accommodation is wide, depending on the standard of services offered and the location of the establishment. In smaller towns located in attractive tourist areas, you can also find rooms to rent at a reasonable rate in private homes. In large towns and cities it is harder to find inexpensive accommodation.

If cost is a consideration, it may be necessary to take a room in a hotel that is some distance from the city centre. Within the list of hotels provided on pages 474–497 there is a choice of around 250 hotels and pensions, which represent various price categories and a high standard of services. Tourist offices supply lists of accommodation and may be able to find a room for you. Information about other accommodation options can be found on pages 472–3.

The atmospheric lobby of the Kempinski Hotel, Berlin *(see p475)*

THE RANGE OF HOTELS

THE LIST OF recommended hotels on pp474–97 can be navigated by following the star rankings that accompany each entry. This is the same system as is used in other countries, with the number of stars awarded depending on the facilities offered by the hotel rather than the standard of service. This means that it may be possible to enjoy a more pleasant stay in a small hotel that has only a single star than in a three-star hotel that offers lifts, a swimming pool, restaurant and business centre, but where refurbishment is long overdue.

If the name of the hotel includes the appellation "*Garni*", this indicates that there is not a restaurant on the premises, but only a dining room where breakfast is served. "*Hotel Apart*" means that the establishment is comprised of suites that include equipped kitchens or a kitchen annexe. The price

of suites is such that it is not worth booking them for just one night, although a booking of several days for a family or group of friends can turn out to be very economical.

Standards vary enormously between hotels. In large cities there will be no difficulty in finding a deluxe (and, of course, expensive) hotel – typically part of an international chain. The choice of less expensive accommodation usually entails accepting a lower standard of service or a less convenient location.

Away from cities, high prices generally apply to rooms in comfortable hotels in particularly peaceful locations, or to those provided within historic palaces or villas. Smaller hotels in such areas usually offer good accommodation at very affordable prices, where visitors can enjoy their stay in small, but cosy and comfortable rooms.

HOW TO BOOK

A S IN OTHER countries, hotel accommodation can be booked directly by telephone, letter or fax, as well as by e-mail or through the Internet. Reservations can be made directly with the hotel or through a local tourist office. They may request written confirmation of the booking, and will almost certainly ask for a credit card number. Tell the owners what time you will be turning up, and let them know if you are delayed, in order not to lose the room.

For those who have not pre-booked, the local tourist office can usually find a hotel room or provide information about rooms in private homes. They are also a good source of advice about the availability of other accommodation options in the area.

Entrance of Opera Hotel, Munich

◁ **The Hotel Alte Post in Oberammergau**

The deluxe Hotel Vier Jahreszeiten in Hamburg *(see p494)*

INTERNATIONAL AND GERMAN CHAIN HOTELS

THROUGHOUT GERMANY there are hotels belonging to virtually all the well-known international chains, as well as to German national chains. Many places in Germany have an IBIS, which can be relied on to provide inexpensive, usually two-star accommodation. In season, they offer a double room for little more than DM 100 (€51).

Somewhat more expensive, and of a higher standard, are hotels belonging to the Best Western chain. Their excellent standard of service, combined with an affordable price, ensures their popularity with tourists. Hotels belonging to the Sorat group are also recommended. Their standard is similar to that of Best Western establishments and can be two-, three- or even four-star, but their premises always have interesting interiors, designed by renowned architects. Many hotels belonging to chains are, in fact, four- or deluxe five-star. Among the finest are the Kempinski and Vier Jahreszeiten hotels. In addition to these, there is no shortage of hotels belonging to chains such as Hilton, Holiday Inn, Inter-Continental, Mercure, Ramada and Hyatt Regency.

HOTELS IN HISTORIC BUILDINGS

IN GERMANY, as in other countries, there are many palaces, castles and other historic buildings that have been converted into hotels. Often the name *Schlosshotel* is used to indicate that an establishment is a hotel within a palace. Many of these hotels are members of international organizations, such as **European Castle Hotels and Restaurants** or **Romantik Hotels und Restaurants**, who can provide further information.

Sign for the four-star Parkhotel in Dortmund

HOTEL PRICES

IN GERMANY, a complicated hotel categorization system operates, with a diverse range of prices depending on the season, as well as on various events that are taking place. In summer resort areas, it is obviously most expensive during the summer, while in large cities visited frequently by businessmen the most expensive seasons are spring and autumn. In cities where commercial fairs are held, prices may double during the most popular fairs – for example, in Berlin during the tourist fair ITB, in Hanover during the information-computer fair CEBIT and in Frankfurt during the car and publishing fairs. It is the same, of course, in Munich during the October beer festival.

Many hotels offer significant reductions at weekends, and often there is the opportunity of a discount for those who turn up without a reservation. Prices can also sometimes be negotiated for longer bookings, especially during periods when business is slack.

ADDITIONAL COSTS

IN GERMANY, tax is included in the price of a hotel room, but tips should be given for additional services such as having your baggage taken to your room or having theatre tickets reserved for you. Additional costs can come as a surprise when you settle your bill. In the most expensive hotels, for example, breakfast is not included in the cost of the room. Most hotels have their own parking facilities, but the cost may be unacceptably high. Check in advance the cost of making direct-dialled telephone calls from the hotel room, as well as the commission charged by the hotel for cashing traveller's cheques and the rate offered when exchanging currency. Using the mini-bar and pay-to-view TV channels in your room can also prove to be expensive.

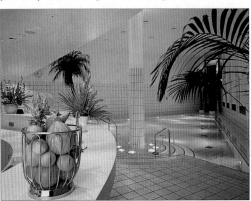

Swimming pool in the Grand Hotel Esplanade in Berlin

The picturesque Alte Wirt Hotel in Bernau

PENSIONS AND GASTHÖFE

A GASTHOF IS A traditional inn with a restaurant on the ground floor and rooms to rent on the upper floor. A wide range of establishments is covered by this simple description, however, from small, inexpensive, family-run hotels, with modestly equipped rooms, to the most luxurious and elegant accommodation in an exquisitely restored country inn.

Pensions are less formal establishments than hotels and are typically run by a family. They usually provide modest accommodation, breakfast and a pleasant family atmosphere. They are always comfortable and very clean, at affordable prices.

INEXPENSIVE ACCOMMODATION

G ERMANY has a very widely developed chain of youth hostels (*Jugendherberge*) and these provide the cheapest option for an overnight stay. A youth hostel can be found in every large town, as well as in small holiday centres. The most attractive are those that are located in old castles, beautiful villas or other historic buildings. Most hostels are of a high standard. Accommodation may be provided in double and triple rooms, as well as in dormitories. In order to be eligible to use youth hostels, you must carry a valid membership card of the Youth Hostels

Association. Membership is available from the YHA of your own country. The fee for overnight accommodation with breakfast is around DM 20–25 (€10–13). Unless you are carrying a sheet sleeping bag with you, you must hire one at the hostel, for which an additional charge will be made. The hostels are usually closed during the day, so you must ensure that all arrangements connected with your stay are arranged before 9am or after 4–4:30pm. In large cities during the high season, when demand for beds is particularly heavy, your stay may be limited to 2–3 days. Apart from in Bavaria, overnight accommodation is open to everyone who is in possession of a valid membership card. In Bavaria, only members aged 26 and under may use the hostels. Older members may stay, however, when they are in charge of a group of youngsters.

The Alpenrose Pension in Neuschwanstein

Private accommodation offers another inexpensive option. In attractive tourist areas, it is common for owners of larger villas and private houses to rent rooms to tourists, often offering breakfast as well. Houses with rooms available to rent are indicated by the sign *Fremdenzimmer* or *Zimmer frei*. Details of such accommodation can be obtained and booked in tourist information offices.

During the summer months, students may also benefit from accommodation in student hotels that otherwise house university students during term times in German university towns. Again, information about such accommodation may be obtained from tourist offices.

Mountain hut at Feldberg, Black Forest

AGROTOURISM

A GROTOURISM is very popular in Germany, and has become an attractive and low-cost alternative holiday, particularly for families with children. The rooms that are available are of a perfectly acceptable standard and meals can often also be provided by the farmers.

For younger children, and especially those from towns and cities, it is a great thrill to observe the daily work on a farm and to have contact with farm animals. Often, farmers who take holidaymakers keep a number of different animals on the farm. They may also offer the possibility of horse-riding, or hiring bicycles, a boat or fishing tackle, so that a full programme of outdoor activities can be enjoyed. Agrotourist holidays can be booked through **Zentrale für den Landurlaub Landschriften** and by **Agratour GmbH**.

Mountain Hostels

Mountainous regions of Germany are generally well prepared to accommodate walkers. Shelters, hostels and mountain hotels can be found not only along Alpine trails, but also in the Thuringian Forest, the Black Forest and the Harz Mountains. Details about such accommodation can be obtained from local tourist information bureaus.

Camping

Travelling with a camping trailer, camper van or just a tent continues to be very popular in Germany, with a highly developed network of more than 2,000 camping sites throughout the country. Of a generally high standard, sites are equipped with washrooms and kitchens. There is usually a shop and café and some have swimming pools.

Disabled Travellers

Virtually all hotels of a higher standard are equipped to accommodate disabled guests. At least one entrance will have ramp access, and a few rooms will have bathrooms adapted to the needs of those who are confined to a wheelchair. Facilities for the disabled are worse in lower-category hotels, where specially adapted fixtures and fittings are rarer. In such hotels, you may have to negotiate steep stairs, as many rooms are located on the upper floors of buildings.

In order to receive additional help during a journey, a disabled person can contact the **Bundesarbeitsgemeinschaft Hilfe für Behinderte e.V.**, or the **Bundesverband Selbsthilfe Körperbehinderter e.V**.

A mountain shelter in Oybin, Saxony

Travelling with Children

Travelling with children through Germany should not present any problems. In most hotels, facilities such as cots and high chairs can be obtained and there is often no additional accommodation charge for a young child. In better hotels, a few hours of babysitting for the children can usually be booked. Few hotels, however, provide children's playrooms. The standard equipment in every restaurant includes a high chair for toddlers, while menus always include the option of children's portions.

DIRECTORY

INFORMATION ON ACCOMMODATION & RESERVATIONS

Hotel Reservation Service (HRS)
Drususgasse 7–11,
50 667 Cologne.
☎ (0221) 207 76 00.
🌐 www.hrs.com

YOUTH HOSTELS

Deutsches Jugendherbergswerk DJH Service GmbH
Bismarckstr. 8,
32 760 Detlmold.
☎ (05231) 740 10.

Youth Hostels Association (YHA)
Trevelyan House,
8 St Stephen's Hill,
St Albans,
Hertfordshire AL1 2DY.
☎ (01727) 85 52 15.

AGROTOURISM

Agratour GmbH (DLG)
Eschborner Landstr. 122,
60 489 Frankfurt
am Main.
☎ (069) 24 78 80.

Zentrale für den Landurlaub Landschriften––Verlag GmbH
Heerstraße 73,
53 111 Bonn.
☎ (0228) 96 30 20.

MOUNTAIN SHELTERS

Dav Summit Club
Am Perlacher Forst 186,
81 545 Munich.
☎ (089) 64 24 00.

Verband Deutscher Gebirgs- und Wandervereine e.V.
Wilhelmshöher
Allee 157–159,
34 121 Kassel.
☎ (0561) 93 87 30.
🖷 (0561) 938 73 10.

CAMPING & CARAVANNING

Caravan Club Bonn e.V.
Postfach 30 03 42,
53183 Bonn.
☎ (0228) 67 91 91.

Deutscher Camping-Club e.V.
Mandlstr. 28,
80 802 Munich.
☎ (089) 380 14 20.

DISABLED TRAVELLERS

Bundesarbeitsgemeinschaft Hilfe für Behinderte e.V.
Kirchfeldstr. 149,
40 215 Düsseldorf.
☎ (0211) 31 00 60.
🖷 (0211) 30 06 48.

Bundesverband Selbshilfe Körperbehinderter e.V. (BSK)
74 238 Krautheim/Jagst.
☎ (06 294) 681 10.
🖷 (06 294) 953 83.

Touristik Union International (TUI)
3000 Hanover 61.
☎ (0511) 56 70.

Choosing a Hotel

THE HOTELS IN THIS GUIDE have been chosen on the basis of good value, attractive location and range of amenities offered. Entries are listed by price category within each town or region, with colour-coded thumb tabs in the margins to indicate the areas covered on each page. A map of Berlin can be found on pages 104–109; a road map is featured inside the back cover.

	Number of Rooms	Restaurant	Garden or Terrace	Swimming Pool	Air Conditioning
BERLIN					
BERLIN – EASTERN CENTRE: *DeragHotel Grosser Kurfürst* (DM)(DM)(DM) Neue Rosstr. 11–12, 10 179. **Map 5 E3.** (030) 24 60 00. FAX (030) 24 60 03 00. www.deraghotels.de A good medium-class hotel, furnished in a modern style and located near a U-Bahn station. It belongs to the DeragHotel chain of hotels that specialize in providing additional services. Here, for example, hire of a bicycle is included in the room price, while a card issued to guests by the hotel acts as a ticket on the city transport system.	144	●			
BERLIN – EASTERN CENTRE: *Hackescher Markt* (DM)(DM) Grosse Präsidentenstr. 8, 10 178. **Map 5 D1.** (030) 28 00 30. FAX (030) 28 00 31 11. www.hackescher-markt.com Charming small hotel opposite Hackeschen Höfen, with excellent restaurant, terrace and elegantly furnished rooms.	31		■		
BERLIN – EASTERN CENTRE: *Berlin Hilton* (DM)(DM)(DM)(DM) Mohrenstr. 30, 10 117. **Map 5 C3.** (030) 202 30. FAX (030) 20 23 42 69. www.hilton.com Excellent location with views from front rooms of Deutscher Dom and Französischer Dom. Rooms are comfortably furnished and spacious. Three excellent restaurants.	500	●	■	●	■
BERLIN – EASTERN CENTRE: *Maritim proArte Hotel Berlin* (DM)(DM)(DM)(DM) Friedrichstr. 151, 10 117. **Map 1 C4, 5 C2.** (030) 203 35. FAX (030) 20 33 42 09. www.maritim.de One of the city's most attractive hotels, furnished with modern furniture and contemporary works of art. Some luxury rooms have bathrooms finished with marble and granite.	401	●		●	■
BERLIN – EASTERN CENTRE: *Four Seasons Hotel* (DM)(DM)(DM)(DM)(DM) Charlottenstr. 49, 10 117. **Map 5 C2.** (030) 203 38. FAX (030) 20 33 61 66. www.fourseasons.com Located near the Gendarmenmarkt, this is regarded as one of Berlin's top-three hotels. The façade of the modern building is inlaid with travertine and marble, while the interiors are furnished in a lavish Neo-Baroque style.	204	●			■
BERLIN – EASTERN CENTRE: *Hotel Adlon* (DM)(DM)(DM)(DM) Unter den Linden 77, 10 117. **Map 1 B4, 4 B2.** (030) 22 61 11 11. FAX (030) 22 61 11 16. www.hotel-adlon.com Deluxe hotel near the Brandenburg Gate. Its acclaimed designers used the most expensive materials, including marble, leather and cherry and myrtle wood. Special rooms cater for those with allergies.	337	●		●	■
BERLIN – WESTERN CENTRE: *Hotel Brandenburger Hof* (DM)(DM)(DM)(DM) Eislebener Str. 14, 10 789. **Map 2 B5.** (030) 21 40 50. FAX (030) 21 40 51 00. www.brandenburger-hof.com An elegant atmosphere, perfect service, tranquil location and luxury rooms ensure this hotel's reputation as one of the best in Berlin. Dating from the Wilhelm era, the captivating building has been restored, furnished with furniture in the Bauhaus style and decorated with works of art.	82	●			
BERLIN – WESTERN CENTRE: *Hotel Palace Berlin* (DM)(DM)(DM)(DM) Budapester Str. 45, 10 787. **Map 2 C4.** (030) 250 20. FAX (030) 25 02 11 61. www.palace.de Luxury hotel located in the Europa-Center. Elegant interiors are concealed within a rather uninteresting exterior. Guests, including major politicians and film stars, value its intimate atmosphere, excellent service and renowned gourmet restaurant, First Floor (*see p504*).	282	●			■

Price categories for a twin room with bathroom or shower, and including breakfast, service and tax (in Deutsch Marks and Euros):
- (DM) up to DM150 (up to €77)
- (DM)(DM) DM150–250 (€77–128)
- (DM)(DM)(DM) DM250–350 (€128–179)
- (DM)(DM)(DM)(DM) DM350–450 (€179–230)
- (DM)(DM)(DM)(DM)(DM) above DM450 (above €230).

RESTAURANT
The hotel has a restaurant that is open to non-residents as well as to hotel guests.

GARDEN OR TERRACE
The hotel is set in a garden or has an outside terrace or courtyard, often with tables for eating outside.

SWIMMING POOL
The hotel has a swimming pool.

AIR CONDITIONING
All rooms are air-conditioned.

	NUMBER OF ROOMS	RESTAURANT	GARDEN OR TERRACE	SWIMMING POOL	AIR CONDITIONING
BERLIN – WESTERN CENTRE: *Savoy Hotel* (DM)(DM)(DM) Fasanenstr. 9–10, 10 623. Map 2 A4. ((030) 31 10 30. FAX (030) 31 10 33 33. W www.hotel-savoy.com Perfectly located, with well-furnished rooms and a charming atmosphere. In addition to excellent restaurants and bars, its Casa del Habano is Berlin's first cigar lounge. 1 ▭ ⚡ ▯ ⬚ ⬚ P ⬚	125	●			■
BERLIN – WESTERN CENTRE: *Grand Hyatt Berlin* (DM)(DM)(DM)(DM) Marlene Dietrich Platz 2, 10 785. Map 4 A3. ((030) 25 53 12 34. FAX (030) 25 53 12 35. Reservations ((0180) 523 12 34. W www.hyatt.com This is one of the most luxurious hotels in Berlin, with a good restaurant (Vox), a sushi bar, bistro and the discreet Café Tizian. Nearby is a vast commercial centre, with music theatre, casino and giant multi-screen cinema in which the Berlin Film Festival is held. 1 ▭ ▯ ⬚ ⬚ P ⬚	342	●		●	■
BERLIN – WESTERN CENTRE: *Kempinski Hotel Bristol Berlin* (DM)(DM)(DM)(DM)(DM) Kurfürstendamm 27, 10 719. Map 2 B4. ((030) 88 43 40. FAX (030) 883 60 75. W www.kempinskiberlin.de One of the most famous hotels in Berlin, the Kempinski occupies a distinctive semi-circular building. It has a classic interior with luxurious rooms, an excellent restaurant and bistro-café. 1 ▭ ⚡ ▯ ⬚ ⬚ P ⬚	301	●		●	■
FURTHER AFIELD: *Artemisia* (DM)(DM) Brandenburgische Str. 18, 10 707 Berlin-Wilmersdorf. ((030) 873 89 05. FAX (030) 861 86 53. The Artemisia is the only women-only hotel in Berlin. The rooms, on the fourth and fifth floors of an old building, are comfortable though some have only washbasins, with a bathroom on the landing. 1 ▭	8		■		
FURTHER AFIELD: *Märkischer Hof* (DM)(DM) Linienstr. 133, 10 115. Map 1 C2. ((030) 282 71 55. FAX (030) 282 43 31. Housed within a historic 19th-century building, not far from Oranienburger Strasse, this small hotel has a family atmosphere. The standard is astonishingly high in relation to the prices. 1 ▭ P ⬚	20				
FURTHER AFIELD: *Best Western Hotel City-Consul, Berlin* (DM)(DM) Rathausstr. 2–3, 10363. ((030) 55 75 70. FAX (030) 55 75 72 72. W www.consul-hotels.com This modern hotel is just a 10-minute walk from Alexanderplatz. It is furnished to a high standard, and equipped with video, fax and modem facilities for guests' use. An excellent breakfast buffet is served. 1 ▭ ⚡ ▯ ⬚ ⬚ P ⬚	99	●			■
FURTHER AFIELD: *Villa Kastania* (DM)(DM)(DM) Kastanienallee 20, 14 052 Berlin-Charlottenburg. ((030) 300 00 20. FAX (030) 30 00 02 10. W www.berlin-info.de/villa-Kastania Situated in a tranquil street, with good connections by U-Bahn to the city centre, this intimate hotel maintains high standards. Standard rooms are fitted with small kitchens. 1 ▭ ⚡ ▯ ⬚ ⬚ P ⬚	43	●		●	■
FURTHER AFIELD: *Blue Band Hotel Berlin* (DM)(DM)(DM)(DM) Lützowplatz 17, 10 785. Map 2 D4. ((030) 260 27 00. FAX (030) 26 05 27 15. W www.blueband.de The large, light rooms are comfortably furnished. In summer it is pleasant to eat lunch in the patio restaurant. 1 ▭ ⚡ ▯ ▤ ⬚ ⬚ P ⬚	701	●	■		■
FURTHER AFIELD: *Hecker's Hotel* (DM)(DM)(DM) Grolmannstr. 35, 10 623. Map 2 A4. ((030) 889 00. FAX (030) 889 02 60. W www.heckers-hotel.com Located right by the Kurfürstendamm, this hotel has tastefully furnished interiors with unpretentious furniture, lighting by famous designers and contemporary works of art. 1 ▭ ⚡ ⬚ ⬚ P ⬚	71	●			■

For key to symbols see back flap

Price categories for a twin room with bathroom or shower, and including breakfast, service and tax (in Deutsch Marks and Euros):
(DM) up to DM150 (up to (€)77)
(DM)(DM) DM150–250 ((€)77–128)
(DM)(DM)(DM) DM250–350 ((€)128–179)
(DM)(DM)(DM)(DM) DM350–450 ((€)179–230)
(DM)(DM)(DM)(DM)(DM) above DM450 (above (€)230).

RESTAURANT
The hotel has a restaurant that is open to non-residents as well as hotel guests.
GARDEN OR TERRACE
The hotel is set in a garden or has an outside terrace or courtyard, often with tables for eating outside.
SWIMMING POOL
The hotel has a swimming pool.
AIR CONDITIONING
All rooms are air-conditioned.

	NUMBER OF ROOMS	RESTAURANT	GARDEN OR TERRACE	SWIMMING POOL	AIR CONDITIONING
FURTHER AFIELD: *The Ritz-Carlton Schlosshotel Berlin* (DM)(DM)(DM)(DM)(DM) Brahmsstr. 10, 14 193 Berlin-Wilmersdorf. **[** (030) 89 58 40. **FAX** (030) 89 58 48 00. **w** www.ritzcarlton.com The most exclusive hotel in Berlin, with furnishings and interior decor by Karl Lagerfeld. The restaurant is renowned. 1 🛏 ⚡ 🍴 🛎 📶 **P** 🅰	54	●		●	■
BRANDENBURG					
BRANDENBURG: *Hotel Lindenhof* (DM) Chaussestr. 21, 14 774. **Map** E3. **[** (03381) 40 35 11. **FAX** (03381) 40 43 33. The hotel is housed within an attractive Art Nouveau building, with comfortable modern rooms. The restaurant serves regional and classic food. Hotel bar and beer garden. 1 🛏 📶 **P** 🅰	15	●	■		
CHORIN: *Haus Chorin* (DM) Neue Klosterallee 10, 16 230. **Map** E2. **[** (033366) 500. **FAX** (033366) 326. **w** www.haus-chorin.de Housed in a beautiful 100-year-old villa located by a lake, the hotel has a pleasant garden and comfortably furnished rooms. 1 🛏 📶 **P** 🅰	63	●	■		
COTTBUS: *Radisson SAS Hotel Cottbus* (DM)(DM) Vetschauer Str. 12, 03 048. **Map** F3. **[** (0355) 476 10. **FAX** (0355) 476 19 00. **w** www.radissonsas.com Located in the centre of town in the Pücklerpassage complex. Comfortable rooms, restaurant and piano bar. 1 ⚡ 🛏 📶 **P** 🍴 🅰	241	●	■	●	
JÜTERBOG: *Zum Goldenen Stern* (DM) Markt 14, 14 913. **Map** E3. **[** (03372) 40 14 76. **FAX** (03372) 40 16 14. **w** www.hotel-goldener-stern.de Comfortable, modern rooms within a traditional old house. Bicycles can be hired and function rooms are available. 1 🛏 **P** 🅰	25	●	■		
LEHNIN: *Markgraf* (DM) Friedensstr. 13, 14 797. **Map** E3. **[** (03382) 76 50. **FAX** (03382) 76 54 30. Recently restored hotel with pleasantly furnished rooms. The restaurant offers tasty regional dishes. 1 🛎 ⚡ 🛏 📶 **P** 🅰	43	●	■		
NEURUPPIN: *Altes Kasino am See* (DM) Seeufer 11, 16 816. **Map** E2. **[** (03391) 30 59. **FAX** (03391) 35 86 84. **w** www.hotel-altescasino.de Located at the edge of a lake, this hotel has pleasant and modern rooms, a good restaurant and a café on the terrace. 1 🛎 🛏 **P** 🅰	20	●	■		
POTSDAM: *art'otel Potsdam Design Hotel* (DM)(DM) Zeppelinstr. 136, 14 471. **Map** E3. **[** (0331) 981 50. **FAX** (0331) 981 55 55. **w** www.artotel.de This luxury hotel for art lovers displays an interesting architectural approach in linking the new section with the old part, which is housed in a 19th-century granary. The leading English designer Jasper Morrison was responsible for the innovative design. 🛏 📶 **P** 🛎 ⚡ 🅰	123	●	■		
POTSDAM: *Mercure Potsdam* (DM)(DM) Lange Brücke, 14 467. **Map** E3. **[** (0331) 27 22. **FAX** (0331) 29 34 96. **w** www.mercure.com Modern hotel situated in the centre of the town, directly by the river Havel. Hotel bar and restaurant with terrace. 1 🛏 📶 **P** ⚡ 🛎 🅰	214	●	■		
POTSDAM: *Relexa Schlosshotel Cecilienhof* (DM)(DM)(DM)(DM) Neuer Garten, 14 469. **Map** E3. **[** (0331) 370 50. **FAX** (0331) 29 24 98. **w** www.castle-cecilienhof.com Formerly owned by the Hohenzollern family, this is the castle in which the Potsdam treaty was signed in 1945. Stylishly decorated rooms, elegant restaurant and salon with an open fire. 1 🛎 🛏 📶 🅰	42	●	■		

WITTSTOCK: *Stadt Hamburg* ⓓⓜ ⓓⓜ 44 ●
Röbelerstr. 25, 16 909. **Map** E2. **[** and **FAX** (03394) 44 45 66.
Recently renovated hotel located fairly close to the old town. Cosy rooms
and a good restaurant. ① 🛏 🔃 P 🗐

SAXONY-ANHALT

BERNBURG: *Parkhotel Parforce-Haus* ⓓⓜ ⓓⓜ 103 ● ■
Aderstedter Str. 1, 06 406. **Map** E3. **[** (03471) 36 20. **FAX** (03471) 36 21 11.
Ⓦ www.parkhotelbernburg.webfind.de
Housed in a Baroque building, this hotel has comfortable rooms, bar,
garden and excellent restaurant. ① 🛏 🔃🎟 P 🗐 🖼 ⓖ 🗐

DESSAU: *Astron* ⓓⓜ ⓓⓜ 153 ●
Zerbster Str. 29, 06 844. **Map** E3. **[** (0340) 251 40. **FAX** (0340) 251 41 00.
Ⓦ www.astronhotel.com
This hotel in the Bauhaus style is near Dessau's historic town hall. Rooms
are comfortable and there is a good restaurant. ① 🛏 🔃 P 🖼 ⓖ 🗐

HALBERSTADT: *Parkhotel Unter den Linden* ⓓⓜ ⓓⓜ 45 ● ■
Klamrothstr. 2, 38 820. **Map** D3. **[** (03941) 625 40. **FAX** (03941) 625 44 44.
Ⓦ www.pudl.de
This hotel is housed in an attractive 100-year-old villa in the centre of
town. It features stylish, comfortable rooms and a high standard of
cuisine in the elegant restaurant. ① 🛏 🔃 P ⓖ 🗐

MAGDEBURG: *Herrenkrug Parkhotel* ⓓⓜ ⓓⓜ ⓓⓜ 155 ●
Herrenkrug 3, 39 114 Magdeburg-Ausserhalb. **Map** D3. **[** (0391) 850 80.
FAX (0391) 850 85 01. Ⓦ www.herrenkrug.de
The hotel is beautifully located in a vast park between the river Elbe and
the racecourse. Spacious and luxuriously furnished rooms, many in Art
Nouveau style. Several restaurants, pleasant café and hotel bar. Bicycles
and tennis courts for hire. ① 🛏 🎟 🔃 P🎟 🖼 ⓖ 🗐

MERSEBURG: *Radisson SAS* ⓓⓜ ⓓⓜ ⓓⓜ 138 ● ■
Oberaltenburg 4, 06 217. **Map** D4. **[** (03461) 452 00. **FAX** (03461) 45 21 00.
Ⓦ www.radissonsas.com
The hotel is housed within a small, refurbished, Baroque palace. It has
superbly furnished rooms, several restaurants, café with a terrace and
hotel bar. ① 🛏 🔃 P 🖼 ⓖ 🗐

NAUMBURG: *Zur alten Schmiede* ⓓⓜ 41 ●
Lindenring 36–37, 06 618. **Map** D4. **[** (03445) 243 60. **FAX** (03445) 24 36 66.
This hotel with tastefully furnished rooms is housed in a former forge.
① 🛏 🔃 P 🗐

QUEDLINBURG: *Romantik Hotel Am Brühl* ⓓⓜ ⓓⓜ 47 ●
Billungstr. 11, 06 484. **Map** D4. **[** (03946) 961 80. **FAX** (03946) 961 82 46.
Ⓦ www.hotelambruehl.de
A small, romantic, family-run hotel with tastefully furnished rooms.
A good dinner is served in the intimate wine bar. ① 🛏 🔃 P 🖼 🗐

STENDAL: *Altstadt-Hotel* ⓓⓜ ⓓⓜ 27 ●
Breite Str. 60, 39 576. **Map** D3. **[** (03931) 698 90. **FAX** (03931) 69 89 39.
Nice rooms in city-centre hotel with fax facility available. ① 🛏 🖼 🗐

TANGERMÜNDE: *Ringhotel Schwarzer Adler* ⓓⓜ 60 ● ■ ●
Lange Str. 52, 39 590. **Map** D3. **[** (039322) 23 91. **FAX** (039322) 36 42.
Ⓦ www.schwarzer-adler-tangermuende.de
A hotel that has been family-run for generations. The rooms are furnished
in a modern style and the restaurant offers home cooking. Sauna,
solarium and swimming pool are available. ①🎟 🛏 P ⓖ 🗐

WERNIGERODE: *Ringhotel Weisser Hirsch* ⓓⓜ ⓓⓜ 55 ●
Marktplatz 5, 38 855. **Map** D3. **[** (03943) 60 20 20. **FAX** (03943) 63 31 39.
Ⓦ www.hotel-weisser-hirsch.de
Recently restored and modernized, this family-run, 18th-century hotel is
the oldest hotel in town. Regional and international cuisine are available
in the restaurant. ① 🛏 🔃 P 🖼 ⓖ 🗐

WITTENBERG: *Park Plaza Wittenberg* ⓓⓜ ⓓⓜ 170 ● ■
Neustr. 7–10, 06 886. **Map** E3. **[** (03491) 46 10. **FAX** (03491) 46 12 00.
Ⓦ www.parkplazaww.com
Comfortable rooms, intimate bar, café with terrace and restaurant serving
international and regional cuisine. ① 🖼 🛏 🔃 P ⓖ 🗐

For key to symbols *see back flap*

Price categories for a twin room with bathroom or shower, and including breakfast, service and tax (in Deutsch Marks and Euros):
(DM) up to DM150 (up to (€)77)
(DM)(DM) DM150–250 ((€)77–128)
(DM)(DM)(DM) DM250–350 ((€)128–179)
(DM)(DM)(DM)(DM) DM350–450 ((€)179–230)
(DM)(DM)(DM)(DM)(DM) above DM450 (above (€)230).

RESTAURANT
The hotel has a restaurant that is open to non-residents as well as to hotel guests.
GARDEN OR TERRACE
The hotel is set in a garden or has an outside terrace or courtyard, often with tables for eating outside.
SWIMMING POOL
The hotel has a swimming pool.
AIR CONDITIONING
All rooms are air-conditioned.

	NUMBER OF ROOMS	RESTAURANT	GARDEN OR TERRACE	SWIMMING POOL	AIR CONDITIONING
WÖRLITZ: *Wörlitzer Hof* (DM)(DM) Markt 69, 06 786. **Map** E3. (*(034905) 41 10.* FAX *(034905) 411 22.* W www.woerlitzer-hof.de Newly built hotel near the main entrance to the park. Sunny and pleasant rooms. The restaurant serves home cooking. 1 🛏 🔁 P 🏊 🛎 🖥	52	●			
SAXONY					
BAUTZEN: *Goldener Adler* (DM)(DM) Hauptmarkt 4, 02 625. **Map** F4. (*(03591) 48 660.* FAX *(03591) 48 66 20.* Recently opened hotel within a 16th-century building. Each room is individually decorated. The restaurant serves regional and international cuisine. Bar and winebar. 1 🛏 🔁 P 🖥	30	●			
CHEMNITZ: *Ringhotel Schlosshotel Klaffenbach* (DM)(DM) Wasserschlossweg 6, 09 123 Chemnitz-Klaffenbach. **Map** E4. (*(0371) 261 10.* FAX *(0371) 261 11 00.* W www.schlosshotel-klaffenbach.de The hotel is located in a 17th-century moated castle, which is classified as a protected monument. The hotel restaurant has Gothic vaulting. 1 🛏 🔁 P 🏊 🛎 🖥	53	●			
DRESDEN: *Am Blauen Wunder* (DM)(DM) Loschwitzer Str. 48, 01 309 Dresden-Blasewitz. **Map** E4. (*(0351) 336 60.* FAX *(0351) 33 66 299.* Comfortably furnished hotel near the renowned "Blue Miracle" bridge. The restaurant serves Italian cuisine. 1 🛏 🔁 P 🏊 🛎 🖥	38	●	■		
DRESDEN: *art'otel Dresden Design Hotel* (DM)(DM)(DM) Ostra-Allee 33, 01 067. **Map** E4. (*(0351) 492 20.* FAX *(0351) 492 27 77.* W www.artotel.de Newly built, interestingly designed hotel, which is located near the renowned Zwinger gallery. Its comfortable rooms feature paintings by well-known artists, while exhibitions are held in the art gallery. The restaurant serves Californian cuisine. Excellent recreational facilities include a sauna. 1 📺 🛏 🔁 P 🏊 🛎 🖥	174	●		●	
DRESDEN: *Romantik Hotel Pattis* (DM)(DM)(DM) Merbitzer Str. 53, 01 157 Dresden-Briesnitz. **Map** E4. (*(0351) 425 50.* FAX *(0351) 425 52 55.* W www.pattis.net The hotel is located within a former 16th-century mill, set in a beautiful park. The restaurant's renowned chef prepares dishes according to recipes from the royal Saxon court. A particularly attractive offer is a two-night stay in the hotel, including a magnificent dinner served on Meissen porcelain and a visit to the nearby Meissen porcelain factory. 1 🛏 🔁 P 🛎 🖥	47	●			■
DRESDEN: *Kempinski Hotel Taschenbergpalais Dresden* (DM)(DM)(DM)(DM)(DM) Taschenberg 3, 01 067. **Map** E4. (*(0351) 491 20.* FAX *(0351) 491 28 12.* W www.kempinski-dresden.de Now one of the world's leading hotels, this recently restored building has been used to accommodate guests from the time of Augustus the Strong. The hotel's restaurants serve dishes from many countries. First-class facilities include a large ballroom and a business centre. 1 🛎 📺 🛏 🔁 P 🏊 🖥	213	●	■	●	■
FREIBERG: *Silberhof* (DM)(DM) Silberhofstr. 1, 09 599. **Map** E4. (*(03731) 239 70.* FAX *(03731) 26 88 78.* W www.silberhof.de Comfortable hotel in the centre of Freiberg. Rooms are comfortably equipped with top-quality furniture and furnishings. Buffet breakfast. 1 🛏 🛎 🔁 P 🖥	30	●			

GÖRLITZ: *Sorat Hotel Görlitz* (DM)(DM) 46
Struvestr. 1, 02 826. **Map** F4. **(** *(03581) 40 65 77.* **FAX** *(03581) 40 65 79.*
Based in a former merchant's house, this hotel has rooms furnished
in a modern style. Its Am Goldenen Strauss restaurant serves delicious
fare. 1 🛏 🕃 🗲 🛢 🖉

KAMENZ: *Goldner Hirsch* (DM)(DM) 40
Markt 10, 019 17. **Map** F4. **(** *(03578) 30 12 21.*
FAX *(03578) 30 44 97.* W www.goldner-hirsch.de
This city-centre hotel is located in a historic house dating from 1550. It
has recently been restored and rooms are elegantly furnished. Facilities
include free car parking and restaurants. 1 🛏 🕃 P 🛢 🖉

LEIPZIG: *Holiday Inn* (DM)(DM) 142
Wasserturmstr. 33, 04 299 Leipzig-Stötteritz. **Map** E4. **(** *(0341) 867 90.*
FAX *(0341) 867 94 44.* W www.holiday-inn-hotel.de
The hotel is based in an interesting Art Nouveau building with elegant
rooms. The restaurant serves international cuisine. 1 🛏 🕃 🗲 🛢 🍴 🖉

LEIPZIG: *Leipzig Marriott Hotel* (DM)(DM) 231
Am Hallischen Tor 1, 04 109. **Map** E4. **(** *(0341) 965 30.* **FAX** *(0341) 965 39 99.*
W www.marriott.com
city-centre hotel, opposite the railway station. Rooms are furnished in a
modern style, with exclusive suites for VIPs. The hotel also offers a
business centre with extensive facilities. 1 🛏 🕃 P 🍴 🗲 🛢 🖉

LEIPZIG: *Hotel Fürstenhof Leipzig* (DM)(DM)(DM)(DM) 92
Tröndlinring 8, 04 105. **Map** E4. **(** *(0341) 14 00.* **FAX** *(0341) 140 37 00.*
W www.arabellasheraton.com
This long-standing hotel features elegant rooms, marble floors and
interesting ceilings. 1 🗲 🛢 🛏 🕃 P 🍴 🖉

MEISSEN: *Ross* (DM)(DM) 40
Grossenhainer Str. 9, 01 662. **Map** E4. **(** *(03521) 75 10.* **FAX** *(03521) 75 19 99.*
W www.meiland.de/partnerhotels/ross
This hotel occupies a 100-year-old building. Facilities include a sauna,
solarium, restaurant and café with a terrace. 1 🛏 🕃 P 🗲 🛢 🖉

MORITZBURG: *Landhaus* (DM)(DM) 20
Schlossallee 37, 01 468. **Map** E4. **(** *(035207) 816 02/03.* **FAX** *(035207) 816 04.*
Hotel with spacious rooms, located near the castle. The elegant restaurant
serves both light and classic cuisine. Other features include an intimate
wine bar and a garden. 1 🛏 P 🗲 🖉

PIRNA: *Romantik Hotel Deutsches Haus* (DM)(DM) 40
Niedere Burgstr. 1, 01 796. **Map** F4. **(** *(03501) 44 34 40.*
FAX *(03501) 52 81 04.* W www.romantikhotels.com/pirna
Located in a beautiful Renaissance building, this hotel has a long tradition
of hospitality. Its rooms are furnished in a variety of styles, so that every
guest can feel at home. Bicycles are available for hire. The hotel offers an
attractive "gourmet weekend", which comprises three nights' accommodation with breakfast and dinner, plus a ticket for a musical event.
1 🗲 🛏 🛢 P 🖉

ZITTAU: *Schwarzer Bär* (DM) 208
Ottokar-Platz 12, 02 763. **Map** F4. **(** *(03583) 55 10.*
FAX *(03583) 55 11 11.*
Hotel with a tradition dating back over 300 years. Rooms furnished in
contemporary style. Good, unpretentious cooking. 1 🛏 🕃 P 🖉

ZWICKAU: *Achat* (DM) 18
Leipziger Str. 180, 08 058. **Map** E4. **(** *(0375) 87 20.* **FAX** *(0375) 87 29 99.*
W www.achat-hotel.de
This recently opened hotel has comfortable rooms and apartments with
small kitchens. 🖉 1 🛢 🗲 🛏 🕃 P

THURINGIA

ALTENBURG: *Best Western Parkhotel* (DM)(DM) 67
August-Bebel-Str. 16, 04 600. **Map** E4. **(** *(03447) 58 30.*
FAX *(03447) 58 34 44.* W www.parkhotel-altenburg.bestwestern.de
The hotel occupies a recently restored Neo-Classical building on the edge
of town and features newly equipped conference halls. The restaurant
serves classic and regional cuisine. 1 🛏 🕃 P 🗲 🛢 🖉

For key to symbols see back flap

Price categories for a twin room with bathroom or shower, and including breakfast, service and tax (in Deutsch Marks and Euros):
(DM) up to DM150 (up to (€)77)
(DM)(DM) DM150–250 ((€)77–128)
(DM)(DM)(DM) DM250–350 ((€)128–179)
(DM)(DM)(DM)(DM) DM350–450 ((€)179–230)
(DM)(DM)(DM)(DM)(DM) above DM450 (above (€)230).

RESTAURANT
The hotel has a restaurant that is open to non-residents as well as to hotel guests.
GARDEN OR TERRACE
The hotel is set in a garden or has an outside terrace or courtyard, often with tables for eating outside.
SWIMMING POOL
The hotel has a swimming pool.
AIR CONDITIONING
All rooms are air-conditioned.

	NUMBER OF ROOMS	RESTAURANT	GARDEN OR TERRACE	SWIMMING POOL	AIR CONDITIONING
EISENACH: *Kaiserhof Romantik Hotel* (DM)(DM)	64	●			

Wartburgallee 2, 99 817. **Map** D4. (03691) 21 35 13. FAX (03691) 20 36 53.
W www.romantikhotelkaiserhof.de
Housed in a beautiful Renaissance building, this hotel offers a Thuringian weekend package, which includes two nights with breakfast and dinner, a welcome cocktail, a city sightseeing tour and a visit to the Lutherhaus – a museum devoted to the Restoration.

ERFURT-APFELSTADT: *Country Inn by Carlson* (DM)	100	●			

Riedweg 1, 99 192. **Map** D4. (036202) 850. FAX (036202) 854 10.
W www.countryinns.de
This hotel is located beyond the city limits and offers a wonderful view of several medieval castles. Rooms are tastefully furnished, and the hotel has an elegant restaurant, café and hotel bar.

ERFURT: *ZumNorde* (DM)(DM)	50		■		

Anger 50, 99 084. **Map** D4. (0361) 568 00. FAX (0361) 568 04 00.
W www.hotel.zumnorde.de
The ZumNorde has beautifully furnished rooms, an intimate hotel bar and a spacious roof terrace.

GERA: *Comfort Inn* (DM)	70	●			

Hoferstr. 12d, 07 548 Gera-Dürrenebersdorf. **Map** D4. (0365) 821 50.
FAX (0365) 82 152 00. W www.comfort-inn-gera.de
Recently built hotel on the edge of a forest. Pleasant rooms and apartments with kitchens. A full breakfast is served in the morning, while light snacks are available in the evening.

GOTHA: *Toscana* (DM)	20	●			

Pfortenwallgasse 1, 99 867. **Map** D4. (03621) 295 93.
FAX (03621) 295 96.
Located in the city centre, the Toscana has elegantly furnished rooms and a restaurant serving mainly Italian cuisine.

GREIZ: *Schlossberg Hotel* (DM)	33	●			

Marienstr. 1–5. **Map** E4. (03661) 62 21 23.
FAX (03661) 62 21 66. W www.schlossberghotel-greiz.de
Situated at the foot of the castle hill, in the centre of the old town, this hotel is quiet and tranquil yet close to everything. Every room is brightly decorated. The hotel offers a large business centre and conference halls. The restaurant serves regional cuisine and an excellent breakfast buffet is available.

JENA: *Jembo Park* (DM)	48	●			

Rudolstädter Str. 93, 07 745 Jena-Göschwitz. **Map** D4. (03641) 68 50.
FAX (03641) 68 52 99. W www.jembo.de
Recently built motel complex located within the grounds of a large park. As well as hotel rooms, 22 bungalows are available. Within the complex is a bowling alley and a variety of other sports facilities.

MÜHLHAUSEN: *Mirage* (DM)(DM)	74	●			

Karl-Marx-Str. 9, 99 974. **Map** D4. (03601) 43 90.
FAX (03601) 43 91 00. W www.mirage-hotel.de
Situated in the centre of the city, the Mirage has attractively decorated rooms and a number of elegant suites.

WEIMAR: *Kempinski Hotel Elephant* (DM)(DM)(DM)	102	●	■		

Markt 19, 99 423. **Map** D4. (03643) 80 20. FAX (03643) 80 26 10.
W www.arabellasheraton.com
Guests, including many celebrities, have been received here since the 16th century. Very comfortable rooms and two restaurants, which include Thuringian dishes in their repertoire.

MUNICH

Cosmopolitan Hotel   (DM)(DM)   71
Hohenzollernstr. 5, 80 801. **Map** D7. [(089) 38 38 10. FAX (089) 38 38 11 11.
W www.cosmopolitan-hotel.de
Located in the centre of the Schwabing district, the hotel has comfortable,
modern rooms. The hotel bar is a popular meeting place in the evenings.
1 🚪 🔁 P 🔆 ⚡ ✎

Romantik Hotel Insel Mühle   (DM)(DM)   37 ● ■
Von-Kahr-Str. 87, 80 999 München-Untermenzing. **Map** D7. [(089) 810 10.
FAX (089) 812 05 71. W www.romantik.de/münchen
One of the most beautiful hotels in Munich. Most of its stylish rooms
have balconies. The restaurant is highly recommended. 1 🚪 P 🔆 ✎

Bayerischer Hof   (DM)(DM)(DM)(DM)(DM)   396 ● ■ ● ■
Promenadeplatz 2–6, 80 333. **Map** D7. [(089) 212 00.
FAX (089) 212 09 06. W www.bayerischerhof.de
Situated in the centre of the city, this is an internationally renowned
hotel. It offers elegantly furnished rooms, a choice of restaurants, a
winter garden, tropical bar, bar with live music, night club, roof-top
swimming pool, designer boutiques and a business centre.
1 ⚡ 🔆 🚪 🔁 P ✎

Kempinski Hotel Vier Jahreszeiten München   (DM)(DM)(DM)(DM)(DM)   316 ● ■ ● ■
Maximilianstr. 17, 80 539. **Map** D7. [(089) 212 50.
FAX (089) 21 25 20 00. W www.kempinski-vierjahreszeiten.de
Situated on one of the most architecturally beautiful streets in the world,
this hotel is renowned for excellent service and its elegant restaurant.
1 🚪 🔁 P ✎

BAVARIA

ALTÖTTING: *Zur Post*   (DM)(DM)(DM)   102 ● ■ ●
Kapellplatz 2, 84 503. **Map** E7. [(08671) 50 40. FAX (08671) 62 14.
Renowned hotel features stylishly furnished rooms equipped with
minibars. The elegant restaurant serves both Bavarian and international
cuisine. Bicycles can be hired at the hotel, which also has a large
swimming pool. 1 🚪 🔁 P 🔆 ⚡ ✎

ANSBACH: *Bürger-Palais*   (DM)(DM)   12 ● ■
Neustadt 48, 91 522. **Map** D6. [(0981) 951 31. FAX (0981) 956 00.
The Bürger-Palais is located in a Baroque building in the centre of the
town. Elegant rooms include bathrooms finished with marble. There is a
café with a terrace, while the hotel's Bratwurststüble restaurant serves
both Franconian and international specialities. 1 🚪 🔆 ✎

ASCHAFFENBURG: *Wilder Mann*   (DM)(DM)   70 ●
Loeherstr. 51, 63 739. **Map** C5. [(06021) 30 20. FAX (06021) 30 22 34.
W www.hotel-wilder-mann.de
This hotel is based in a 16th-century building in the heart of the old
town. The hotel's comfortably furnished rooms will please the most
demanding of guests. 1 🚪 🔁 P 🔆 ✎

AUGSBURG: *Dom-Hotel*   (DM)(DM)   52   ●
Frauentorstr. 8, 86 152. **Map** D6. [(0821) 34 39 30. FAX (0821) 34 39 32 00.
W www.domhotel-augsburg.de
This hotel is located near the cathedral, in a recently restored historic
building. Facilities include a swimming pool, sauna and solarium, and
even a golf course. 1 🚪 🔁 P 🔆 ⚡ ✎

AUGSBURG: *Romantik Hotel Augsburger Hof*   (DM)(DM)   36 ●
Auf dem Kreuz 2, 86 152. **Map** D6. [(0821) 34 30 50. FAX (0821) 34 30 50.
W www.augsburger-hof.de
One of a chain that specializes in hotels based in beautiful historic
buildings. Located near Mozart's house, the hotel has a stylish restaurant
offering exquisitely prepared dishes. 1 🚪 🔁 P ✎

AUGSBURG: *Steigenberger Drei Mohren*   (DM)(DM)(DM)   107 ● ■
Maximilianstr. 40, 86 150. **Map** D6. [(0821) 503 60.
FAX (0821) 15 78 64. W www.augsburg.steigenberger.de
Although this comfortable hotel is situated near the city's main street, the
rooms are completely quiet. The hotel offers a choice of restaurants,
including a fish restaurant, and a dance hall. 1 🚪 🔁 P 🔆 ⚡ ✎

Price categories for a twin room with bathroom or shower, and including breakfast, service and tax (in Deutsch Marks and Euros):

(DM) up to DM150 (up to €77)
(DM)(DM) DM150–250 (€77–128)
(DM)(DM)(DM) DM250–350 (€128–179)
(DM)(DM)(DM)(DM) DM350–450 (€179–230)
(DM)(DM)(DM)(DM)(DM) above DM450 (above €230).

RESTAURANT
The hotel has a restaurant that is open to non-residents as well as to hotel guests.

GARDEN OR TERRACE
The hotel is set in a garden or has an outside terrace or courtyard, often with tables for eating outside.

SWIMMING POOL
The hotel has a swimming pool.

AIR CONDITIONING
All rooms are air-conditioned.

		NUMBER OF ROOMS	RESTAURANT	GARDEN OR TERRACE	SWIMMING POOL	AIR CONDITIONING
BAMBERG: *Alt Ringlein*	(DM)(DM)	55	●			
Dominikanerstr. 9, 96 049. **Map** D5. (0951) 953 20. FAX (0951) 953 25 00. [W] www.alt-ringlein.com Based in a 14th-century building, this well-known establishment offers all the virtues of a modern hotel. [1] 🍴 ↕ **P** 🌐						
BAMBERG: *Romantik Hotel Weinhaus Messerschmitt*	(DM)(DM)	17		■		
Lange Str. 47, 96 047. **Map** D5. (0951) 278 66. FAX (0951) 261 41. [W] www.hotel-messerschmitt.de This hotel has been owned by the same family for many years. Cosy atmosphere and classic regional cuisine. [1] 🍴 **P** 🔒 🚫 🌐						
BAMBERG: *Residenzschloss*	(DM)(DM)(DM)	185	●	■		
Untere Sandstr. 32, 96 049. **Map** D5. (0951) 609 10. FAX (0951) 609 17 01. [W] www.hotel-residenzschloss.de Beautifully located by a river, this hotel is a charming complex of skilfully combined new and historic buildings. Facilities include an elegant restaurant and café with a terrace. [1] 🍴 ↕ **P** 🔒 🚫 🌐						
BAYREUTH: *Treff Hotel Rheingold*	(DM)(DM)	146	●	■	●	
Austasse 2/Unteres Tor, 95 445. **Map** D5. (0921) 756 50. FAX (0921) 756 58 01. [W] www.treff-hotel-bayreuth.de This new hotel is located in a supremely beautiful area. An English-style pub, café with a terrace, as well as a magnificent swimming pool, gym, sauna, solarium and golf course provide ideal opportunities for recreation. [1] 🍴 ↕ **P** 🖥 🔒 🚫 🌐						
BAYREUTH: *Lohmühle*	(DM)(DM)(DM)	42	●			
Badstr. 37, 95 444. **Map** D5. (0921) 530 60. FAX (0921) 530 64 69. [W] www.hotel-lohmuehle.de Although the hotel is constructed in traditional Franconian style, the rooms are equipped with every modern convenience. The restaurant offers both Franconian and international cuisine. [1] 🍴 ↕ **P** 🔒 🌐						
BAYREUTH: *Bayerischer Hof*	(DM)(DM)(DM)	49	●	■	●	
Bahnhofstr. 14, 95 444. **Map** D5. (0921) 786 00. FAX (0921) 786 05 60. A popular, comfortable hotel with interestingly furnished rooms. Facilities include a restaurant, bar and wine bar. [1] 🍴 ↕ **P** 🔒 🚫 🌐						
BURGHAUSEN: *Glöcklhofer*	(DM)(DM)	56	●	■	●	
Ludwigsberg 4, 84 489. **Map** E7. (08677) 961 70. FAX (08677) 655 00. [W] www.euroring.com In a beautiful location by the entrance to the castle, this hotel belongs to the EuroRing chain. Facilities include a large swimming pool, bicycle hire, tennis courts and pleasant gardens. [1] 🏊 🍴 ↕ **P** 🔒 🌐						
COBURG: *Festungshof*	(DM)(DM)	14	●	■		
Festungsberg 1, 96 450. **Map** D5. (09561) 802 90. FAX (09561) 80 29 33. [W] www.festungshof.de Small hotel, beautifully located opposite the castle. It was built 100 years ago, but has been modernized. [1] 🍴 **P** 🔒 🌐						
COBURG: *Romantik Hotel Goldene Traube*	(DM)(DM)	74	●	■		
Am Viktoriabrunnen 2, 96 450. **Map** D5. (09561) 87 60. FAX (09561) 87 62 22. [W] www.romantikhotels.com/coburg Hotel with comfortably furnished rooms, offering an excellent breakfast buffet and restaurant serving sophisticated cuisine. [1] 🍴 ↕ **P** 🔒 🚫 🌐						
DACHAU: *Fischer*	(DM)(DM)	26	●	■		
Bahnhofstr. 4, 85 221. **Map** D6. (08131) 782 05. FAX (08131) 785 08. A comfortable hotel situated opposite the railway station. Rooms are furnished in contemporary style and the restaurant serves regional and international cuisine. [1] 🍴 ↕ **P** 🚫 🌐						

DINKELSBÜHL: *Deutsches Haus*   (DM)(DM)   10
Weinmarkt 3, 91 550. **Map** D6. (*(09851) 60 58.* FAX *(09851) 79 11.*
W www.deutsches-haus-dkb.de
The comfortable rooms in this hotel are furnished with antique furniture.
The renowned restaurant is highly recommended. 1 🔒 🔃 **P** 🗲

EICHSTÄTT: *Adler garni*   (DM)   15
Marktplatz 22–24, 85 072. **Map** D6. (*(08421) 67 67.* FAX *(08421) 82 83.*
Based in a recently restored building dating from the 17th century, this
hotel has stylishly decorated, intimate rooms. The extensive breakfast
buffet includes "healthy eating" options. 1 🔒 🔃 **P** 🗲 🗲

FREISING: *Isar-Hotel*   (DM)(DM)   55
Isarstr. 4, 85 356. **Map** D6. (*(08161) 86 50.* FAX *(08161) 86 55 55.*
W www.isarhotel.de
This recently built hotel is located in the city centre. The rooms are
pleasantly furnished. Bicycles can be hired. 1 🔒 🔃 **P** 🗝 🗲 🗲

FÜSSEN: *Alpenblick*   (DM)(DM)   66
Uferstr. 10, 87 629 Füssen-Hopfen am See. **Map** D7. (*(08362) 505 70.*
FAX *(08362) 50 57 73.*
Attractive rooms and luxurious suites offer fine views of the Alps and the
Hopfensee. Evenings can be spent by an open fire. 1 🔒 🔃 **P** 🗲

GARMISCH-PARTENKIRCHEN: *Garmischer Hof*   (DM)(DM)   48
Chamonixstr. 10, 82 467. **Map** D7. (*(08821) 91 10.*
FAX *(08821) 514 40.* W www.garmischerhof.de
Beautifully located hotel with rooms decorated in the Alpine style.
Convenient for rail access to the Zugspitze mountain. 1 🔒 🔃 **P** 🗲

GARMISCH-PARTENKIRCHEN: *Posthotel-Partenkirchen*   (DM)(DM)   60
Ludwigstr. 49, 82 467. **Map** D7. (*(08821) 936 30.* FAX *(08821) 93 63 22 22.*
W www.post-hotel.de
This hotel is decorated in typical Bavarian style, with wooden features,
stylized furniture and comfortable rooms. 1 🔒 🔃 **P** 🗲

INGOLSTADT: *Ara Hotel*   (DM)   95
Schollstr. 10A, 85 055. **Map** D6. (*(0841) 954 30.* FAX *(0841) 954 34 44.*
Newly built hotel with Italian-style furnishings. Italian specialities are
served in the restaurant. Pleasant café with terrace. 1 🔒 🔃 **P** 🗲

KEMPTEN: *Bayerischer Hof*   (DM)(DM)   52
Füssener Str. 96, 87 437. **Map** C7. (*(0831) 571 80.*
FAX *(0831) 571 81 00.* W www.bayerischerhof-kempten.de
Conveniently located hotel in the centre of the city with rooms furnished
in a modern style, a pleasant bar and Chinese restaurant. 1 🔒 🔃 **P** 🗲

LANDSHUT: *Romantik Hotel Fürstenhof*   (DM)(DM)   24
Stethaimer Str. 3, 84 034. **Map** E6. (*(0871) 925 50.* FAX *(0871) 92 55 44.*
W www.romantikhotels.com/landshut
This hotel is based in a beautiful villa near the town centre. Two
restaurants offer a wide selection of dishes, including regional cuisine.
Lovers of tennis and golf will also enjoy staying here. 1 🔒 🔃 **P** 🗲

LINDAU: *Reutemann Seegarten*   (DM)(DM)(DM)   64
Seepromenade, 88 131. **Map** C7. (*(08382) 91 50.* FAX *(08382) 91 55 91.*
W www.bayrischerhof-lindau.de
The hotel is situated by a lake, with a beautiful view of the Swiss and
Austrian Alps. Bicycles can be hired. 1 🔒 **P** 🗲

NEU-ULM: *Römer Villa*   (DM)(DM)   23
Parkstr. 1, 89 231. **Map** C6. (*(0731) 80 00 40.* FAX *(0731) 800 04 50.*
W www.roemer-villa.de
Elegant rooms are a feature of this hotel, which occupies a beautiful Art
Nouveau building. Facilities include a restaurant, lounge with an open
fire, wine bar and winter garden. 1 🔒 🔃 **P** 🗝 🗲

NEUBURG AN DER DONAU: *Zum Klosterbräu*   (DM)   27
Kirchplatz 1, 86 633 Neuburg a.d. Donau-Bergen. **Map** D6. (*(08431) 677 50.*
FAX *(08431) 411 20.*
At this historic, modernized hotel, there are good facilities for taking part
in various sports, including tennis. The restaurant serves regional cuisine,
specializing in game dishes and fish from the local lakes.
1 🗝 🔒 🔃 **P** 🗲

For key to symbols *see back flap*

Price categories for a twin room with bathroom or shower, and including breakfast, service and tax (in Deutsch Marks and Euros):

- (DM) up to DM150 (up to (€)77)
- (DM)(DM) DM150–250 (€)77–128)
- (DM)(DM)(DM) DM250–350 (€)128–179)
- (DM)(DM)(DM)(DM) DM350–450 (€)179–230)
- (DM)(DM)(DM)(DM)(DM) above DM450 (above (€)230).

RESTAURANT
The hotel has a restaurant that is open to non-residents as well as to hotel guests.

GARDEN OR TERRACE
The hotel is set in a garden or has an outside terrace or courtyard, often with tables for eating outside.

SWIMMING POOL
The hotel has a swimming pool.

AIR CONDITIONING
All rooms are air-conditioned.

	NUMBER OF ROOMS	RESTAURANT	GARDEN OR TERRACE	SWIMMING POOL	AIR CONDITIONING
NÜRNBERG (NUREMBERG): *Burghotel-Grosses Haus* (DM)(DM)(DM) Lammsgasse 3, 90 403. **Map** D6. ((0911) 23 88 90. FAX (0911) 23 88 91 00. W www.altstadthotels-nürnberg.de From this hotel you can enjoy a beautiful view of the old town. Facilities include a swimming pool, sauna and a rustic bar. 1 ⟡ ⟡ P ⟡	57	●		●	
NÜRNBERG (NUREMBERG): *Romantik Hotel Am Josephsplatz* (DM)(DM) Josephsplatz 30/32, 90 403. **Map** D6. ((0911) 21 44 70. FAX (0911) 21 44 72 00. W www.romantikhotels.com/Nuernberg This splendid hotel lies in the heart of Nürnberg's old town. Some of the elegant rooms open onto a flower-filled courtyard. 1 ⟡ ⟡ ⟡ P ⟡ ⟡	36	●	▦		
NÜRNBERG (NUREMBERG): *Maritim* (DM)(DM)(DM)(DM) Frauentorgraben 11, 90 443. **Map** D6. ((0911) 236 30. FAX (0911) 236 38 36. W www.maritim.de A hotel of international standard, close to the railway station. Rooms are elegant and there are numerous dining options. 1 ⟡ ⟡ ⟡ ⟡ ⟡ P ⟡	316	●	▦	●	▦
OBERAMMERGAU: *Turmwirt* (DM) Ettalerstr. 2, 82 487. **Map** D7. ((08822) 926 00. FAX (08822) 14 37. A typical Bavarian hotel, with carefully chosen furnishings. Facilities include a restaurant, café and patisserie. 1 ⟡ ⟡ P ⟡ ⟡ ⟡	22	●			
OBERSTDORF: *Kappeler Haus* (DM) Am Seeler 2, 87 561. **Map** C7. ((08322) 968 60. FAX (08322) 96 86 13. This hotel has a pleasant family atmosphere. Facilities include a swimming pool and attractive café with terrace. 1 ⟡ ⟡ P ⟡	60	●	▦	●	
PASSAU: *Passauer Wolf* (DM)(DM) Rindermarkt 6, 94 032. **Map** E6. ((0851) 931 51 10. FAX (0851) 931 51 50. W www.passauerwolf.de Beautifully located in a historic building between the old town and the Danube. Modern rooms and excellent cuisine. 1 ⟡ ⟡ ⟡ ⟡	40	●			
REGENSBURG: *Bischofshof* (DM)(DM) Krauterer Markt 3, 93 047. **Map** D6. ((0941) 584 60. FAX (0941) 584 61 46. W www.hotel-bischofshof.de Located opposite the cathedral, the Bischofshof's rooms have been refurbished in rustic style. Elegant restaurant. 1 ⟡ ⟡ ⟡ ⟡ P ⟡	55	●			
ROTHENBURG OB DER TAUBER: *Prinzhotel* (DM)(DM)(DM) An der Hofstatt 3, 91 541. **Map** C6. ((09861) 97 50. FAX (09861) 975 75. W www.prinzhotel.rothenburg.de This hotel is located in the old city, near the Riderturm. All the rooms are attractively furnished in a modern style. 1 ⟡ ⟡ P ⟡	52	●	▦		
ROTHENBURG OB DER TAUBER: *Markusturm Romantik Hotel* (DM)(DM)(DM) Rödergasse 1, 91 541. **Map** C6. ((09861) 942 80. FAX (09861) 26 92. W www.markusturm.de Housed in a building dating from 1264, this hotel has rooms furnished with valuable antique furniture. 1 ⟡ ⟡ P ⟡	25	●			
WÜRZBURG: *Alter Kranen* (DM) Kärrmergasse 11, 97 070. **Map** C5. ((0931) 351 80. FAX (0931) 500 10. W www.hotel-alterkranen.de This middle-range hotel has a beautiful location on the bank of the river Main. A buffet breakfast is served. 1 ⟡ ⟡ P ⟡	14				
BADEN-WÜRTTEMBERG					
BADEN-BADEN: *Tannenhof* (DM)(DM) Hans-Bredow-Str. 20, 76 530. **Map** B6. ((07221) 30 09 90. FAX (07221) 300 99 51. Good hotel with attractively decorated, spacious rooms. North Italian cuisine is a speciality of the hotel restaurant. 1 ⟡ P ⟡ ⟡	28	●			

BADEN-BADEN: *Romantik Hotel Der Kleine Prinz* ⓓⓂⓓⓂⓓⓂⓓⓂ 40
Lichtentaler Str. 36, 76 530. **Map** B6. **(** *(07221) 346 60 04.*
FAX *(07221) 346 60 59.* **W** www.derkleineprinz.de
Based in a beautifully furnished and decorated villa, the hotel is named
after the children's novel *The Little Prince* by Antoine Saint-Exupéry.
1 🛏 **P** 🛒 🛎 🐕 🔞 ✉

BADEN-BADEN: *Steigenberger Badischer Hof* ⓓⓂⓓⓂⓓⓂⓓⓂ 139
Lange Str. 47, 76 530. **Map** B6. **(** *(07221) 93 40.*
FAX *(07221) 93 44 70.* **W** www.badischer-hof.steigenberger.de
This hotel is housed in a former monastery, which has been tastefully
refurbished to the highest international standards. **1** 🛏 **P** 🛒 🔞 🛎

BAD MERGENTHEIM: *Hotel Gästehaus Altemünze* ⓓⓂ 31
Münzgasse 12, 97 980. **Map** C5. **(** *(07931) 56 60.* **FAX** *(07931) 56 62 22.*
Opened in 1993, this hotel is situated in a central yet tranquil location
near the Knight's Castle. **1** 🛏 **P** 🛒 🛎 ✉

BAD MERGENTHEIM: *Victoria l'Art de Vivre-Residenz* ⓓⓂⓓⓂⓓⓂ 78
Poststr. 2, 97 980. **Map** C5. **(** *(07931) 59 30.* **FAX** *(07931) 59 35 00.*
W www.victoria-hotel.de
An intimate spa hotel with excellently equipped rooms, sauna and solarium.
Very highly regarded among connoisseurs. **1** 🛏 **P** 🛒 🛎 🔞 ✉

BAD WIMPFEN: *Am Rosengarten* ⓓⓂⓓⓂ 60
Osterbergstr. 16, 74 206. **Map** C6. **(** *(07063) 99 10.* **FAX** *(07063) 991 80 08.*
W www.rosengarten-hotel.com
Beautifully located on the edge of the old town. Pleasant hotel bar, café
with terrace and fitness studio. **1** 🛏 🛒 **P** 🛎 🔞 🍽 ✉

BRUCHSAL: *Ritter* ⓓⓂⓓⓂ 98
Au in den Buchen 72 & 83 & 92, 76 646. **Map** C6. **(** *(07257) 880.* **FAX** *(07257) 881 11.*
A hotel with a long tradition, the Ritter has luxurious rooms, two
restaurants and a beer garden. **1** 🛏 🛒 **P** 🔞 ✉

ESSLINGEN: *Am Schelztor garni* ⓓⓂⓓⓂ 33
Schelztorstr. 5, 73 728. **Map** C6. **(** *(0711) 396 96 40.* **FAX** *(0711) 35 98 87.*
The hotel is housed in a recently renovated period building within the
historic town centre. Breakfast only is served. **1** 🛏 🛒 **P** 🔞 ✉

FREIBURG IM BREISGAU: *Zum Roten Bären* ⓓⓂⓓⓂⓓⓂ 25
Oberlinden 12, 79 098. **Map** B7. **(** *(0761) 38 78 70.* **FAX** *(0761) 387 87 17.*
W www.roten-baeren.de
This is one of the oldest hotel buildings in Germany. Its traditions date
back to the 14th century and even to the 12th century in parts. It is
comfortably furnished in a modern manner. **1** 🛏 🛒 **P** 🔞 ✉

FREIBURG IM BREISGAU: *Colombi-Hotel* ⓓⓂⓓⓂⓓⓂⓓⓂ 120
Rotteckring 16, 79 098. **Map** B7. **(** *(0761) 210 60.*
FAX *(0761) 314 10.*
Quiet, centrally situated hotel with impeccable service and luxurious rooms
furnished in the Schwarzwald style. Facilities include swimming pool,
sauna, gym and excellent restaurant. **1** 🛏 🛒 **P** 🛎 🍽 ✉

HEIDELBERG: *Heidelberg Marriott Hotel garni* ⓓⓂⓓⓂⓓⓂⓓⓂ 254
Vangerowstr. 16, 69 115. **Map** C6. **(** *(06221) 90 80.*
FAX *(06221) 90 86 08.* **W** www.marriott.com
Located by the river Neckar, this modern hotel has a private jetty as well
as a well-equipped conference hall, bar and wine bar. From the café
there is a beautiful view along the river. **1** 🛏 🛒 **P** 🔞 🛎 ✉

HEIDELBERG: *Holländer Hof garni* ⓓⓂⓓⓂⓓⓂ 39
Neckarstaden 66, 69 117. **Map** C6. **(** *(06221) 605 00.* **FAX** *(06221) 60 50 60.*
W www.hollaender-hof.de
Beautifully located within the environs of the old town and with a view
of the famous castle, this hotel has a long tradition of hospitality. It is
very conveniently situated for sightseeing.
1 🛏 🛒 🛎 🔞 ✉

HEILBRONN: *Ringhotel Burkhardt* ⓓⓂⓓⓂ 82
Lohtorstr. 7, 74 072. **Map** C6. **(** *(07131) 622 40.*
FAX *(07131) 62 78 28.* **W** www.burkhardt-ringhotel.de
This old-established hotel is conveniently located in the centre of town,
near the river Neckar. It has a pleasant restaurant. **1** 🛏 🛒 **P** 🔞 ✉

For key to symbols *see back flap*

<table>
<tr><td colspan="2">

Price categories for a twin room with bathroom or shower, and including breakfast, service and tax (in Deutsch Marks and Euros):

(DM) up to DM150 (up to (€)77)
(DM)(DM) DM150–250 ((€)77–128)
(DM)(DM)(DM) DM250–350 ((€)128–179)
(DM)(DM)(DM)(DM) DM350–450 ((€)179–230)
(DM)(DM)(DM)(DM)(DM) above DM450 (above (€)230).

</td><td>

RESTAURANT
The hotel has a restaurant that is open to non-residents as well as to hotel guests.

GARDEN OR TERRACE
The hotel is set in a garden or has an outside terrace or courtyard, often with tables for eating outside.

SWIMMING POOL
The hotel has a swimming pool.

AIR CONDITIONING
All rooms are air-conditioned.

</td></tr>
</table>

	NUMBER OF ROOMS	RESTAURANT	GARDEN OR TERRACE	SWIMMING POOL	AIR CONDITIONING
KARLSRUHE: *Alfa garni* (DM)(DM) Bürgerstr. 4, 76 133. **Map** B6. **(** *(0721) 299 26.* **FAX** *(0721) 299 29.* W www.karlsrühe-hotel.de Situated in the centre of Karlsruhe, this hotel has attractively furnished rooms and a restaurant run by the Mövenpick chain. ① 📶 🔽 P 🌐	40	●			
KARLSRUHE: *Renaissance* (DM)(DM)(DM) Mendelssohnplatz, 76 131. **Map** B6. **(** *(0721) 371 70.* **FAX** *(0721) 37 71 56.* W www.renaissancehotels.com This hotel, near the Congress Centre, has several conference halls. The restaurant serves regional and international dishes. ① 📶 🔽 P 🌐 🌐	215	●			
KONSTANZ: *Steigenberger Inselhotel* (DM)(DM)(DM)(DM) Auf der Insel 1, 78 462. **Map** C7. **(** *(07531) 12 50.* **FAX** *(07531) 264 02.* W www.steigenberger.de Based in a former monastery building, this comfortable hotel has a sauna and solarium as well as private access to the lake. 📶 🔽 P 🌐 🌐 🌐	102	●	■	●	■
LUDWIGSBURG: *Nestor* (DM)(DM)(DM) Stuttgarter Str. 35, 71 638. **Map** C6. **(** *(07141) 96 70.* **FAX** *(07141) 96 71 13.* W www.nestor-hotels.de This elegant hotel occupies two 18th-century buildings. Regional and international dishes are served in the restaurant. ① 📶 🔽 P 🌐 🌐 🌐	150	●	■		
LUDWIGSBURG: *Schlosshotel Monrepos* (DM)(DM)(DM) Schloss Monrepos 22, 71 634. **Map** C6. **(** *(07141) 30 20.* **FAX** *(07141) 30 22 00.* W www.schlosshotel-monrepos.de Beautifully located by the lake near Prince Ludwig's palace Monrepos. There is an attractive café nearby. ① 🔽 P 🌐 🌐	80	●	■	●	
MANNHEIM: *Maritim Parkhotel* (DM)(DM)(DM) Friedrichsplatz 2, 68 165. **Map** B5. **(** *(0621) 158 80.* **FAX** *(0621) 158 88 00.* W www.maritim.de This elegant hotel offers beautiful interiors, excellent service and a restaurant serving regional cuisine. ① 📶 🔽 P 🌐 🌐 🌐	190	●		●	
MARBACH: *Parkhotel* (DM)(DM) Schillerhöhe 14, 71 672. **Map** C6. **(** *(07144) 90 50.* **FAX** *(07144) 905 88.* Located on Schillerhöhe, this hotel has pleasantly furnished, comfortable rooms. A buffet breakfast is served. ① 📶 🔽 P 🌐 🌐	43	●			
RAVENSBURG: *Waldhorn* (DM)(DM)(DM) Marienplatz 15, 88 212. **Map** C7. **(** *(0751) 361 20.* **FAX** *(0751) 361 21 00.* W www.waldhorn.de Well known for its excellent food, the Waldhorn's restaurant serves French cuisine, specializing in game and fish. ① 📶 🔽 P 🌐 🌐 🌐	38	●	■		
ROTTWEIL: *Haus zum Sternen* (DM)(DM) Hauptstr. 60, 78 628. **Map** C7. **(** *(0741) 533 00.* **FAX** *(0741) 53 30 30.* W www.romantikhotels.com Based in a 13th-century building but with modern facilities, this hotel overlooks the Neckar valley. ① 📶 P 🌐 🌐	11	●	■		
SALEM: *Reck* (DM) Bahnhofstr. 111, 88 682. **Map** C7. **(** *(07553) 201.* **FAX** *(07553) 202.* Hotel with a family atmosphere and rooms in various categories. The pleasant restaurant offers a large choice of wines. ① 📶 🔽 P 🌐	20	●	■		
SCHWÄBISCH GMÜND: *Einhorn* (DM) Rinderbachergasse 10, 73 525. **Map** C6. **(** *(07171) 630 23.* **FAX** *(07171) 616 80.* W www.hoteleinhorn.de City-centre hotel with pleasant rooms. Located in a 12th-century cellar, the restaurant serves international cuisine. ① 📶 🔽 P 🌐 🌐	18	●			

SCHWÄBISCH HALL: *Der Adelshof* (DM)(DM) 47
Am Markt 12–13, 74 523. **Map** C6. (*(0791) 758 90.* FAX *(0791) 60 36.*
W www.hotel-adelshof.de
In a beautiful location near the market. Excellent breakfast buffet, exclusive restaurant and pleasant bar.

STUTTGART: *Kronen-Hotel* (DM)(DM)(DM) 84
Kronenstr. 48, 70 174. **Map** C6. (*(0711) 225 10.* FAX *(0711) 225 14 04.*
W www.vch.de
Situated in a tranquil part of the city centre, not far from the railway station. Excellent breakfast. Garden with terrace.

STUTTGART: *Inter-Continental* (DM)(DM)(DM)(DM) 276
Willy-Brandt-Str. 30, 70 173. **Map** C6. (*(0711) 202 00.* FAX *(0711) 20 20 20 20.*
W www.interconti.de
Located opposite the castle park, the hotel's facilities include a business centre with internet access, gym and golf course.

TÜBINGEN: *Krone* (DM)(DM)(DM) 48
Uhlandstr. 1, 72 072. **Map** C6. (*(07071) 133 10.* FAX *(07071) 13 31 32.*
W www.krone-tuebingen.de
Regarded as one of the best hotels in the city, the Krone has elegantly furnished rooms and a renowned restaurant.

ULM: *Engel* (DM)(DM) 46
Loher Str. 35, 89 081 Ulm-Lehr. **Map** C6. (*(0731) 14 04 00.* FAX *(0731) 14 04 00.*
W www.hotel-engel-ulm.de
A well-known inn was converted into this modern, comfortable hotel. Pleasant rooms are furnished with wooden furniture.

WEINGARTEN: *Walk'sches Haus* (DM)(DM) 27
Marktplatz 7, 76 356. **Map** B6. (*(07244) 70 37 00.* FAX *(07244) 70 37 40.*
W www.walksches-haus.de
Beautifully located in a 16th century building near the market. A pleasant restaurant in the garden offers French cuisine.

RHINELAND-PALATINATE AND SAARLAND

KOBLENZ: *Top Hotel Krämer garni* (DM)(DM) 22
Kardinal-Krementz-Str. 12, 56 073. **Map** B5. (*(0261) 40 62 00.* FAX *(0261) 413 40.*
W www.tophotelkraemer.de
A family-run hotel in a quiet area of the city centre, providing a warm, comfortable atmosphere.

KOBLENZ: *Mercure* (DM)(DM)(DM) 169
Julius-Wegeler-Str. 6, 56 068. **Map** B5. (*(0261) 13 60.* FAX *(0261) 136 11 99.*
W www.mercure.com
The Mercure has a vast, mirrored façade and elegant restaurant. Rooms are comfortable and well furnished.

MARIA LAACH: *Seehotel Maria Laach* (DM)(DM)(DM) 66
Ortsteil Maria Laach, 56 653 Glees-Maria Laach. **Map** B5. (*(02652) 58 40.*
FAX *(02652) 58 45 22.* W www.maria-laach.de
Tranquil hotel with comfortable rooms. Popular with tourists visiting the nearby Benedictine monastery. Good restaurant and café with a terrace.

MAINZ: *Günnewig Bristol Hotel* (DM)(DM)(DM) 75
Friedrich-Ebert-Str. 20, 55 130 Mainz-Weisenau. **Map** B5. (*(06131) 80 60.*
FAX *(06131) 80 61 00.* W www.guennewig.de
Popular with business travellers, this conveniently located hotel has air-conditioned rooms and a good restaurant.

MAINZ: *Dorint Hotel Mainz* (DM)(DM)(DM)(DM) 217
Augustusstr. 6, 55 131. **Map** B5. (*(06131) 95 40.*
FAX *(06131) 95 41 00.* W www.dorint.de
Baroque cellars dating from the 17th century have been integrated into this unique hotel building. The Bajazzo restaurant offers international and regional dishes.

SAARBRÜCKEN: *La Residence* (DM)(DM) 142
Faktoreistr. 2, 66 111. **Map** B6. (*(0681) 388 20.* FAX *(0681) 388 21 85.*
W www.la-residence.net
Well located in the city centre, this hotel has comfortable rooms. A buffet breakfast is served in the winter garden.

Price categories for a twin room with bathroom or shower, and including breakfast, service and tax (in Deutsch Marks and Euros):

(DM) up to DM150 (up to (€)77):
(DM)(DM) DM150–250 ((€)77–128)
(DM)(DM)(DM) DM250–350 ((€)128–179)
(DM)(DM)(DM)(DM) DM350–450 ((€)179–230)
(DM)(DM)(DM)(DM)(DM) above DM450 (above (€)230).

RESTAURANT
The hotel has a restaurant that is open to non-residents as well as to hotel guests.

GARDEN OR TERRACE
The hotel is set in a garden or has an outside terrace or courtyard, often with tables for eating outside.

SWIMMING POOL
The hotel has a swimming pool.

AIR CONDITIONING
All rooms are air-conditioned.

		NUMBER OF ROOMS	RESTAURANT	GARDEN OR TERRACE	SWIMMING POOL	AIR CONDITIONING
SAARBRÜCKEN: *Mercure Kongress* Hafenstr. 8, 66 111. **Map** B6. (*(0681) 389 00.* FAX *(0861) 389 09 89.* W www.mercure.de Situated by the Congress Centre and urban motorway, this hotel has spacious, comfortably furnished rooms. 1 🛏 ↻ P ⇄ 🛎 ✉	(DM)(DM)	150	●			
SPEYER: *Domhof* Bauhof 3, 67 346. **Map** B6. (*(06232) 132 90.* FAX *(06232) 13 29 90.* W www.domhof.de Newly opened stylish hotel in a historic building near the Dom. 1 🛏 ↻ P ⇄ 🛎 ✉	(DM)(DM)	49				
SPEYER: *Binshof* Binshof 1, 67 346 Speyer-Binshof. **Map** B6. (*(06232) 64 70.* FAX *(06232) 64 71 99.* W www.binshof.de Located in a landscaped park some distance from the city is this excellent hotel. Features include a huge swimming-pool complex. 1 🛏 ↻ P ⇄ 🛎 ✉	(DM)(DM)(DM)(DM)	67	●	■	●	■
TRIER: *Römischer Kaiser* Porta-Nigra-Platz 6, 54 292. **Map** A5. (*(0651) 977 00.* FAX *(0651) 97 70 99.* W www.hotels-trier.de A modern hotel, with an elegant restaurant, has been created within the walls of a historic building. 1 🛏 ↻ P ✉	(DM)(DM)	43	●	■		
TRIER: *Dorint Hotel Porta Nigra* Porta-Nigra-Platz 1, 54 292. **Map** A5. (*(0651) 270 10.* FAX *(0651) 270 11 70.* W www.dorint.de One of the finest hotels in Trier, with rooms providing a high degree of comfort and a restaurant to satisfy gourmets. 1 🛏 ↻ P ⇄ 🛎 ✉	(DM)(DM)(DM)	106	●			
HESSE						
ALSFELD: *Zum Schwalbennest* Pfarrwiesenweg 12–14, 36 304. **Map** C4. (*(06631) 50 61.* FAX *(06631) 710 81.* A modern hotel with intimate rooms and a rustic restaurant. There is also a wine bar and a bar with a dance floor. 1 🛏 ↻ P ⇄ ✉	(DM)	65	●	■		
BAD HOMBURG: *Parkhotel* Kaiser-Friedrich-Promenade 53–55, 61 348. **Map** C5. (*(06172) 80 10.* FAX *(06172) 80 14 00.* W www.parkhotel-bad-homburg.de Located near the spa park, close to the Taunus baths and the casino. Large recreation room and several restaurants. 1 🛏 ↻ P 🛎 ⇄ 🍴 ✉	(DM)(DM)(DM)(DM)	122	●			
DARMSTADT: *Jagdschloss Kranichstein* Kranichsteiner Str. 261, 64 289 Darmstadt-Kranichstein. **Map** C5. (*(06151) 977 90.* FAX *(06151) 97 79 20.* W www.hotel-jagdschloss-kranichstein.de This hotel occupies one of Germany's most beautiful Renaissance castles. Comfortably furnished rooms and several restaurants. 1 🛏 ↻ P 🛎 ✉	(DM)(DM)(DM)	15	●	■		
ELTVILLE AM RHEIN: *Kronenschlösschen* Rheinallee, 65 347 Eltville-Hattenheim. **Map** B5. (*(06723) 640.* FAX *(06723) 76 73.* W www.kronenschloesschen.de Housed in a beautiful villa, this recently restored and modernized hotel is located close to the Rhine. Features include an elegant restaurant, bistro, wine bar, hotel bar and a restaurant in the garden. 1 🛎 🛏 P ✉	(DM)(DM)(DM)	18	●	■		
FRANKFURT AM MAIN: *Borger garni* Triebstr. 51, 60 388 Frankfurt-Bergen-Enkheim. **Map** C5. (*(06109) 309 00.* FAX *(06109) 30 90 30.* This hotel with a long family tradition is located in a historic area of Frankfurt. The rooms are comfortable and the area has good transport connections to the city centre. 1 🛏 P ✉	(DM)(DM)	34	●	■		

FRANKFURT AM MAIN: *Best Western Alexander am Zoo garni* ⓄⓄⓄ 59
Waldschmidtstr. 59–61, 60 316. **Map** C5. **(** (069) 94 96 00. **FAX** (069) 94 96 07 20.
W www.bestwestern.de
Italian-style hotel near the zoo, with modern, comfortably furnished
rooms. Pleasant hotel bar and varied breakfast buffet. Ideal venue for
businessmen. 🔲 🛏 ⬆ P 🍴 🛁 ⚡ ✉

FRANKFURT AM MAIN: *Frankfurt Hotel Savoy* ⓄⓄⓄ 144
Wiesenhüttenstr. 42, 60 329. **Map** C5. **(** (069) 27 39 60.
FAX (069) 27 39 67 95. W www.savoyhotel.de
High-class hotel with rooms decorated in a Swedish style and a roof-top
recreational centre. 🔲 🛏 ⬆ 🍴 ⚡ 🛁 ✉

FRANKFURT AM MAIN: *Steigenberger Frankfurter Hof* ⓄⓄⓄⓄ 332
Kaiserplatz, 60 311. **Map** C5. **(** (069) 215 02. **FAX** (069) 21 59 00.
W www.steigenberger.de
A flagship of the Steigenberger-Hotels chain. Rooms, including the vast
presidential suite, are luxurious. Several well-equipped function rooms
and a number of excellent restaurants. 🔲 🛏 ⬆ P ⚡ 🛁 ✉

FULDA: *Romantik Hotel Goldener Karpfen* ⓄⓄⓄ 50
Simpliziusbrunnen 1, 36 037. **Map** C5. **(** (0661) 868 00.
FAX (0661) 868 01 00. W www.hotel-goldener-karpfen.com
In perfect harmony with its Baroque surroundings, this hotel is located in
the city centre, near historic monuments and the most interesting shops.
Guests can relax in the hotel bar or intimate wine bar, and enjoy the
highly recommended cuisine. 🔲 🛏 ⬆ P 🍴 🛁 ⚡ ✉

KASSEL: *Residenz Domus* ⓄⓄ 54
Erzberger Str. 1–5, 34 117. **Map** C4. **(** (0561) 729 60. **FAX** (0561) 729 64 98.
Beyond the Art Nouveau façade lies a comfortable hotel with elegant
rooms and a winter garden with glass roof. 🔲 🛏 ⬆ P ⚡ 🛁 ✉

KASSEL: *Schlosshotel Wilhelmshöhe* ⓄⓄ 106
Schlosspark 8, 34 131 Kassel-Wilhelmshöhe. **Map** C4. **(** (0561) 308 80.
FAX (0561) 308 84 28. W www.schlosshotel.com
Beautifully located in the most exclusive part of the city, with pleasant,
comfortably furnished rooms. 🔲 🛏 ⬆ P 🍴 🛁 ✉

LIMBURG: *Romantik Hotel Zimmermann* ⓄⓄ 30
Blumenröder Str. 1, 65 549. **Map** B5. **(** (06431) 46 11. **FAX** (06431) 413 14.
W www.romantikhotels.com
Celebrities stay at this hotel whose motto is "Our guests are also our
friends." The hotel is elegantly furnished with various eye-catching and
interesting architectural features, including marble bathrooms.
🔲 🛏 P 🛁 ⚡ ✉

MARBURG: *Sorat Hotel Marburg* ⓄⓄ 146
Pilgrimstein 29, 35 037. **Map** C4. **(** (06421) 91 80. **FAX** (06421) 91 84 44.
W www.sorat-hotels.com
New hotel in the heart of the city, with attractively furnished rooms.
Facilities include a sauna, solarium and gym. 🔲 ⬆ P 🍴 ⚡ 🛏 ✉

MARBURG: *Waldecker Hof garni* ⓄⓄ 40
Bahnhofstr. 23, 35 037. **Map** C4. **(** (06421) 600 90.
FAX (06421) 60 09 59. W www.waldecker-hof-marburg.de
This family-run hotel with comfortable rooms is conveniently situated
close to the railway station. 🔲 🛁 ⚡ 🛏 ⬆ P 🍴 ✉

RÜDESHEIM AM RHEIN: *Jagdschloss Niederwald* ⓄⓄⓄ 52
Auf dem Niederwald, 65 385. **Map** B5. **(** (06722) 710 60. **FAX** (06722) 710 66 66.
W www.jagdschlossniederwald.de
Housed in a former hunting lodge/castle and beautifully located in the
midst of a forest above the Rhine. Stylized interiors create a unique
atmosphere. The panoramic restaurant serves fish and game dishes,
accompanied by a wide choice of wines. There is a small zoo near the
hotel. 🔲 🛏 ⬆ P ✉

WEILBURG: *Schlosshotel* ⓄⓄⓄ 33
Langgasse 25, 35 781. **Map** B5. **(** (06471) 390 96.
FAX (06471) 391 99. W www.schlosshotel-weilburg.de
This comfortable hotel is located within the administrative buildings of a
former Renaissance castle. Among its attractions are a good choice of
dishes in the restaurant and café with a terrace. 🔲 🛏 ⬆ P ⚡ 🛁 ✉

For key to symbols *see back flap*

Price categories for a twin room with bathroom or shower, and including breakfast, service and tax (in Deutsch Marks and Euros):
(DM) up to DM150 (up to €77)
(DM)(DM) DM150–250 (€77–128)
(DM)(DM)(DM) DM250–350 (€128–179)
(DM)(DM)(DM)(DM) DM350–450 (€179–230)
(DM)(DM)(DM)(DM)(DM) above DM450 (above €230).

RESTAURANT
The hotel has a restaurant that is open to non-residents as well as to hotel guests.
GARDEN OR TERRACE
The hotel is set in a garden or has an outside terrace or courtyard, often with tables for eating outside.
SWIMMING POOL
The hotel has a swimming pool.
AIR CONDITIONING
All rooms are air-conditioned.

	NUMBER OF ROOMS	RESTAURANT	GARDEN OR TERRACE	SWIMMING POOL	AIR CONDITIONING
WETZLAR: *Landhotel Naunheimer Mühle* (DM)(DM) An der Mühle 2, 35 584. **Map** C5. **(** *(06441) 935 30.* **FAX** *(06441) 93 53 93.* W www.naunheimer-muehle.de This modern hotel occupies a converted water mill on the bank of the river Lan. Facilities include tennis courts. [1] 🛏 🔼 **P** 🔒 🚭	32	●			
WIESBADEN: *Klee am Park* (DM)(DM)(DM) Parkstr. 4, 65 189. **Map** B5. **(** *(0611) 900 10.* **FAX** *(0611) 900 13 10.* W www.klee-am-park.de Excellent location close to theatres, park and spa buildings. Comfortable rooms. [1] 🛏 🔼 **P** 🚭 🔒 🍽	54	●			
WIESBADEN: *Nassauer Hof* (DM)(DM)(DM)(DM)(DM) Kaiser-Friedrich-Platz 3, 65 183. **Map** B5. **(** *(0611) 13 30.* **FAX** *(0611) 13 36 32.* www.nassauer-hof.de This long-established hotel has a beautiful Baroque façade and distinguished interiors. A particular attraction is the pool, which features water from the hotel's own spring. Other facilities include a luxurious beauty salon and good restaurant. [1] 🛏 🔼 **P** 🔒 🚭 🍽 🍽	198	●	▦	●	▦

NORTH RHINE-WESTPHALIA

	NUMBER OF ROOMS	RESTAURANT	GARDEN OR TERRACE	SWIMMING POOL	AIR CONDITIONING
AACHEN: *Best Western Hotel Royal garni* (DM)(DM)(DM) Jülicher Str. 1, 52 070. **Map** A4. **(** *(0241) 18 22 80.* **FAX** *(0241) 18 22 86 99.* www.royal.bestwestern.de Located in a recently refurbished historic building dating from the 18th century. Guests can relax in the wine bar or enjoy innovative dishes served in the hotel's elegant restaurant. [1] 🛏 🔼 **P** 🔒 🚭 🍽	35				▦
AACHEN: *Dorint Select Hotel Quellenhof* (DM)(DM)(DM)(DM) Monheimsallee 52, 52 062. **Map** A4. **(** *(0241) 913 20.* **FAX** *(0241) 913 21 00.* www.dorint.com This hotel recently re-opened following extensive refurbishment of the highest standard. Every technological facility is available, as well as a swimming pool and 12 tennis courts. [1] 🛏 🔼 🍽	174	●		●	
BIELEFELD: *Brenner Hotel Diekmann* (DM)(DM) Otto-Brenner-Str. 133, 33 607. **Map** C3. **(** *(0521) 299 90.* **FAX** *(0521) 299 92 20.* www.brenner-hotel.de Family-run hotel with attractive, spacious rooms. Facilities include a bowling alley, hotel bar and conference halls. [1] 🛏 🔼 🔒 **P** 🍽	68	●			
BONN: *Schlosshotel Kommende Ramersdorf* (DM)(DM) Oberkasslerstr. 10, 53 227 Bonn-Beuel. **Map** B4. **(** *(0228) 44 07 34.* **FAX** *(0228) 44 44 00.* This establishment, which belongs to a chain of castle hotels, is housed within the imposing Teutonic Knights Castle. Former meeting halls have been converted into a restaurant and function rooms. [1] 🛏 🔼 **P** 🍽	18	●			
BONN: *Best Western Domicil* (DM)(DM)(DM)(DM) Thomas-Mann-Str. 24, 53 111. **Map** B4. **(** *(0228) 72 90 90.* **FAX** *(0228) 69 12 07.* www.privathotel-domicil.de A hotel complex consisting of a number of buildings that have been carefully integrated. Features include a pleasant bar, a winter garden and a restaurant serving international cuisine. [1] 🛏 🔼 **P** 🔒 🍽	44	●	▦		
BONN: *Kaiser Karl* (DM)(DM)(DM)(DM) Vorgebirgsstr. 56, 53 119. **Map** B4. **(** *(0228) 98 55 70.* **FAX** *(0228) 985 57 77.* www.kaiser-karl-hotel-bonn.de Comfort and good service are guaranteed in this exclusive hotel. Rooms are elegantly furnished and decorated, and each one is equipped with a safe. Breakfast is served in the lounge or garden, and there is a pub-style bar. [1] 🛏 🔼 **P** 🔒 🍽	42	●	▦		

DETMOLD: *Lippischer Hof* (DM)(DM) 27
Willy-Brandt-Platz 1, 32 756. **Map** C3. [(05231) 93 60. FAX (05231) 244 70.
Housed in a historic 18th-century building; facilities include a bar, wine
bar, and an elegant restaurant serving innovative dishes.

DÜSSELDORF: *Ibis Hauptbahnhof* (DM)(DM) 166
Konrad-Adenauer-Platz 14, 40 210. **Map** B4. [(0211) 167 20. FAX (0211) 167 21 01.
W www.ibishotel.com
Located behind the historic façade of the railway station, this hotel has
been built around an atrium, so that guests' windows open onto a
courtyard filled with greenery.

DÜSSELDORF: *Madison I* (DM)(DM)(DM) 100
Graf-Adolf-Str. 94, 40 210. **Map** B4. [(0211) 168 50. FAX (0211) 168 53 28.
W www.madisonl.de
Attractively furnished rooms with pine furniture. The hotel complex
includes a sports club.

DÜSSELDORF: *Nikko* (DM)(DM)(DM)(DM) 301
Immermannstr. 41, 40 210. **Map** B4. [(0211) 83 40. FAX (0211) 16 12 16.
W www.nikko-hotel.de
This hotel complex is reminiscent of a small village with charming
architecture and modern technology. The Benkay restaurant specializes
in Japanese cuisine.

ESSEN: *Schlosshotel Hugenpoet* (DM)(DM)(DM)(DM) 25
August-Thyssen-Str. 51, 45 219 Essen-Kettwig. **Map** B4.
[(02054) 120 40. FAX (02054) 12 04 50. W www.hugenpoet.de
Housed within a former castle, this hotel is elegantly furnished with
stylish furniture and marble stairways. Some rooms feature original pieces
of furniture from the 16th century. Renowned restaurant in the park has a
large choice of wines and delicacies.

HÖXTER: *Ringhotel Niedersachsen* (DM)(DM) 82
Möllinger-Str. 4, 37 671. **Map** C3. [(05271) 68 80. FAX (05271) 68 84 44.
W www.hotelniedersachsen.de
This hotel is renowned for its hospitality, with comfortable rooms and an
intimate hotel bar for guests. The restaurant serves both regional and
international dishes.

KÖLN (COLOGNE): *Rheinblick garni* (DM) 27
Uferstr. 20, 50 996 Köln-Rodenkirchen. **Map** B4. [(0221) 39 12 82.
FAX (0221) 39 21 39.
The hotel is attractively located overlooking the Rhine. Rooms are
attractively furnished and breakfast is served in the winter garden, which
offers a beautiful view of the river.

KÖLN (COLOGNE): *Coellner Hof* (DM)(DM)(DM) 79
Hansaring 100, 50 670. **Map** B4. [(0221) 166 60.
FAX (0221) 166 61 66.
A well-known, beautifully furnished hotel with excellent service. Facilities
include a good restaurant and hotel inn with an extensive choice of drinks.

KÖLN (COLOGNE): *Im Wasserturm* (DM)(DM)(DM) 88
Kaygasse 2, 50 676. **Map** B4. [(0221) 200 80.
FAX (0221) 200 88 88. W www.hotel-im-wasserturm.de
Housed in a 19th-century former water tower, this hotel has an excellent
location in a park, just a few minutes from the old town. The wonderful
interiors were designed by a well-known Parisian artist and architect.
Sophisticated service and a panoramic restaurant on the 11th floor add to
guests' enjoyment of their stay here.

KÖLN (COLOGNE): *Hyatt Regency* (DM)(DM)(DM)(DM) 305
Kennedy-Ufer 2a, 50 679. **Map** B4. [(0221) 828 12 34.
FAX (0221) 828 13 70. W www.cologne.hyatt.com
With beautiful greenery and fountains gracing even the entrance hall, this
hotel has the feel of a botanical garden.

LEMGO: *Im Borke* (DM) 37
Salzufler Str. 132, 32 657 Lemgo-Kirchheide. **Map** C3. [(05266) 16 91.
FAX (05266) 12 31. W www.hotel-im-borke.de
Pleasant family hotel set in a garden. Guests can spend their time pleasantly
in the stylish restaurant, bowling alley or sauna.

For key to symbols *see back flap*

Price categories for a twin room with bathroom or shower, and including breakfast, service and tax (in Deutsch Marks and Euros):
(DM) up to DM150 (up to (€)77):
(DM)(DM) DM150–250 ((€)77–128)
(DM)(DM)(DM) DM250–350 ((€)128–179)
(DM)(DM)(DM)(DM) DM350–450 ((€)179–230)
(DM)(DM)(DM)(DM)(DM) above DM450 (above (€)230).

RESTAURANT
The hotel has a restaurant that is open to non-residents as well as to hotel guests.
GARDEN OR TERRACE
The hotel is set in a garden or has an outside terrace or courtyard, often with tables for eating outside.
SWIMMING POOL
The hotel has a swimming pool.
AIR CONDITIONING
All rooms are air-conditioned.

	NUMBER OF ROOMS	RESTAURANT	GARDEN OR TERRACE	SWIMMING POOL	AIR CONDITIONING
MÜNSTER: *Romantik Hotel Hof zur Linde* (DM)(DM) Handorfer Werseufer 1, 48 157 Münster-Handorf. **Map** B3. **(** *(0251) 327 50.* FAX *(0251) 32 82 09.* W www.hof-zur-linde.de This hotel was converted from a former 17th-century farm. The restaurant has an open fireplace and antique furniture. 1 🏊 🔒 🛏 🔼 P 🍽 🐾	48	●			
MÜNSTER: *Schloss Wilkinghege* (DM)(DM)(DM) Steinfurter Str. 374, 48 159 Münster-Ausserhalb. **Map** B3. **(** *(0251) 21 30 45.* FAX *(0251) 21 28 98.* W www.schloss-wilkinghege.de Modern, elegantly furnished rooms within the 16th-century walls. The highly recommended restaurant specializes in regional dishes. Other features include a knights' hall, golf course and a charming lounge with an open fireplace in the hotel's basement. 1 🛏 P 🐾	36	●			
SIEGEN: *Best Western Parkhotel Siegen* (DM)(DM) Koblenzer Str. 135, 57 072. **Map** B4. **(** *(0271) 338 10.* FAX *(0271) 338 14 50.* W www.bestwestern.de This modern hotel has spacious rooms and elegantly furnished suites as well as several fully equipped conference halls. 1 🛏 🔼 P 🏊 🐾	88	●	■		
WINTERBERG: *Steymann* (DM)(DM) Schneilstr. 4, 59 955. **Map** C4. **(** *(02981) 70 05.* FAX *(02981) 36 19.* W www.hotel-steymann.de A spa hotel, which also features a sauna and solarium. The restaurant offers various specialist dishes, at reasonable prices. 1 🛏 🔼 P 🐾	37	●	■	●	
WUPPERTAL: *Lindner Golfhotel Juliana* (DM)(DM)(DM) Mollenkotten 195, 42 279. **Map** B4. **(** *(0202) 647 50.* FAX *(0202) 647 57 77.* W www.lindner.de Comfortably furnished suites and rooms as well as conference halls and a swimming pool. 1 🛏 🔼 P 🏊 🐾	132	●	■		

LOWER SAXONY, HAMBURG AND BREMEN

	NUMBER OF ROOMS	RESTAURANT	GARDEN OR TERRACE	SWIMMING POOL	AIR CONDITIONING
BRAUNSCHWEIG (BRUNSWICK): *Ritter St. Georg* (DM)(DM)(DM) Alte Knochenhauerstr. 13, 38 100. **Map** D3. **(** *(0531) 130 30.* FAX *(0531) 130 38.* W www.ritter-st-georg-bs.de This hotel occupies a recently restored 500-year-old building. Rooms are comfortable and there is an atmospheric, rustic restaurant. 🛏 1 🐾	22	●			
BREMEN: *Lichtsinn garni* (DM)(DM) Rembertistr. 11, 28 203. **Map** C2. **(** *(0421) 36 80 70.* FAX *(0421) 32 72 87.* W www.hotel-lichtsinn.de Ten suites with small kitchens as well as individual rooms are available in this family-run hotel in the city centre. 1 🛏 🔼 🏊 P 🐾	50				
BREMEN: *Schaper-Siedenburg garni* (DM)(DM) Bahnhofstr. 8, 28 195. **Map** C2. **(** *(0421) 308 70.* FAX *(0421) 30 87 88.* This well-known, long-established hotel is conveniently located near the main railway station. 1 🛏 🔼 🏊 🐾	88				
BREMEN: *Best Western Zur Post* (DM)(DM)(DM) Bahnhofsplatz 11, 28 195. **Map** C2. **(** *(0421) 305 90.* FAX *(0421) 305 95 91.* W www.bestwestern.de On the sixth floor of this super deluxe establishment, the L'Orchidée restaurant offers panoramic views of the city. 1 🛏 🔼 P 🏊 🐾	183	●	■		
BREMEN: *Park Hotel* (DM)(DM)(DM)(DM)(DM) Im Bürgerpark, 28 209. **Map** C2. **(** *(0421) 340 80.* FAX *(0421) 340 86 02.* W www.park-hotel-bremen.de A luxurious hotel, renowned for its family atmosphere, excellent service, comfortable rooms and well-equipped conference halls. The restaurant specializes in fish, poultry and game dishes. 1 🛏 🔼 P 🍽 🐾	149	●	■	●	■

BÜCKEBURG: *Grosse Klus* (DM)(DM) 25
Am Klusbrink 19, 31 675. **Map** C3. **(** (05722) 951 20. **FAX** (05722) 95 12 50.
W www.klus.de
This hotel occupies two buildings, one dating from the 18th century.
Rooms are furnished in a modern manner and the cuisine includes
regional and classical dishes. Bicycles can be hired. 1 🛏 P 🔁 🛢 ⬛

CELLE: *Celler Hof garni* (DM)(DM) 49
Stechbahn 11, 29 221. **Map** C3. **(** (05141) 91 19 60. **FAX** (05141) 911 96 44.
W www.residenzhotels.de
Very high standard hotel with wonderful service. Features include a bar
in the winter garden, café with terrace and a highly recommended
restaurant. Other facilities include a gym, sauna and nearby golf course.
1 🛏 🔽 🛢 🍽 P ⬛

CLOPPENBURG: *Park Hotel* (DM)(DM) 51
Burgstr. 8, 49 661. **Map** B2. **(** (04471) 66 14. **FAX** (04471) 66 17.
W www.parkhotel.cloppenburg.de
Recently built hotel, with comfortably furnished rooms and a pleasant
location in a park, close to the civic hall. Facilities for playing golf and
skittles are available. 1 🛏 🔽 P 🔁 🛢 ⬛

DUDERSTADT: *Zum Löwen* (DM)(DM)(DM) 42
Marktstr. 30, 37 115. **Map** D4. **(** (05527) 30 72. **FAX** (05527) 726 30.
W www.hotelzumloewen.de
Housed in a 16th-century building with a Neo-Classical façade, this hotel
has been modernized to a very high standard. It features pleasant rooms
and a number of dining venues. 1 🛏 🔽 P 🔁 🛢 ⬛

EINBECK: *Der Schwan* (DM) 12
Tiedexerstr. 1, 37 574. **Map** C3. **(** (05561) 46 09. **FAX** (05561) 723 66.
This hotel is based in an Art Nouveau building with intimate rooms. The
elegant restaurant serves both classical and light cuisine. 1 🛏 P 🔁 ⬛

GOSLAR: *Der Achtermann* (DM)(DM)(DM) 152
Rosentorstr. 20, 38 640. **Map** D3. **(** (05321) 700 00. **FAX** (05321) 700 09 99.
W www.der-achtermann.de
Rooms in this hotel are furnished in a modern manner, while the
Altdeutsche Stuben restaurant specializes in typical German cooking.
1 🛏 🔽 P ⬛

GOSLAR: *Treff Hotel Das Brusttuch* (DM)(DM)(DM) 13
Hoher Weg 1, 38 640. **Map** D3. **(** (05321) 346 00. **FAX** (05321) 34 60 99.
A well-maintained late Gothic building has been converted into this
modern hotel. The restaurant serves international specialities.
1 🛏 🔽 P ⬛

GÖTTINGEN: *Gebhards Hotel* (DM)(DM)(DM) 63
Goetheallee 22, 37 073. **Map** C4. **(** (0551) 496 80. **FAX** (0551) 496 81 10.
W www.gebhards-hotel.de
Conveniently located opposite the railway station, this long-established
hotel is housed in a historic building. Facilities include an elegant
restaurant, hotel bar and several function rooms. 1 🛏 🔽 P 🔁 🛢 ⬛

HAMBURG: *Best Western Raphael Hotel Altona* (DM)(DM) 39
Präsident-Krahn-Str. 13, 22 765. **Map** C2. **(** (040) 38 02 40. **FAX** (040) 38 02 44 44.
W www.bestwestern.com
This hotel is conveniently located between the port and the business
centre, near the Altona railway station. Facilities include modern rooms
with safes and double-glazed windows, breakfast buffet and bar.
1 🔁 🛏 ⬛

HAMBURG: *Hafen Hamburg* (DM)(DM) 230
Seewartenstr. 9, 20 459. **Map** C2. **(** (040) 31 11 30. **FAX** (040) 31 11 37 55.
W www.hotel-hamburg.de
Formerly a mariner's house, this building has been extended and
refurbished as a hotel with large comfortable rooms. From the restaurant
a panoramic view of the port can be enjoyed. 1 🛏 🔽 P 🛢 ⬛

HAMBURG: *Europäischer Hof* (DM)(DM)(DM) 320
Kirchenallee 45, 20 099. **Map** C2. **(** (040) 24 82 48. **FAX** (040) 24 82 47 99.
W www.Europaeischer-hof.de
Modern, luxurious interiors, excellent service, a good restaurant and a
hotel bar with music. The hotel also issues guests with a card entitling
them to three days' free travel by public transport. 1 🛏 🔽 P 🔁 🛢 ⬛

For key to symbols *see back flap*

Price categories for a twin room with bathroom or shower, and including breakfast, service and tax (in Deutsch Marks and Euros):

(DM) up to DM150 (up to (€)77)
(DM)(DM) DM150–250 ((€)77–128)
(DM)(DM)(DM) DM250–350 ((€)128–179)
(DM)(DM)(DM)(DM) DM350–450 ((€)179–230)
(DM)(DM)(DM)(DM)(DM) above DM450 (above (€)230).

RESTAURANT
The hotel has a restaurant that is open to non-residents as well as to hotel guests.

GARDEN OR TERRACE
The hotel is set in a garden or has an outside terrace or courtyard, often with tables for eating outside.

SWIMMING POOL
The hotel has a swimming pool.

AIR CONDITIONING
All rooms are air-conditioned.

	NUMBER OF ROOMS	RESTAURANT	GARDEN OR TERRACE	SWIMMING POOL	AIR CONDITIONING
HAMBURG: *Kempinski Hotel Atlantic Hamburg* (DM)(DM)(DM)(DM) An der Alster 72, 20 099. **Map** C2. **[** *(040) 288 80.* **FAX** *(040) 24 71 29.* **W** www.kempinskiatlantic.de This long-established hotel has beautifully furnished rooms and excellent service. The restaurant serves sophisticated dishes.	254	●	▨	●	▨
HAMBURG: *Vier Jahreszeiten* (DM)(DM)(DM)(DM)(DM) Neuer Jungfernstieg 9, 20 354. **Map** C2. **[** *(040) 349 40.* **FAX** *(040) 34 94 26 00.* **W** www.hvj.de A luxury-class hotel with stylized interiors, decorated with precious woods, valuable rugs and antiques. The restaurant, well-stocked wine bar and excellent patisserie are very popular.	154	●	▨		▨
HANNOVER: *Best Western Parkhotel Kronsberg* (DM)(DM) Gut Kronsberg 1. 18, 30 539. **Map** C3. **[** *(0511) 874 00.* **FAX** *(0511) 86 71 12.* **W** www.kronsberg.bestwestern.de Situated opposite the Hannover trade fair area, this modern hotel is surrounded by beautiful greenery.	200	●	▨	●	
HANNOVER: *Grand Hotel Mussmann garni* (DM)(DM)(DM) Ernst-August-Platz 7, 30 159. **Map** C3. **[** *(0511) 365 60.* **FAX** *(0511) 365 61 45.* **W** www.grandhotel.de Well-maintained hotel in the city centre, opposite the railway station. Comfortable rooms and excellent service.	140				
HANNOVER: *Romantik Hotel Georgenhof* (DM)(DM)(DM) Herrenhäuser Kirchweg 20, 30 167. **Map** C3. **[** *(0511) 70 22 44.* **FAX** *(0511) 70 85 59.* **W** www.romantikhotels.com Set in a park, this hotel is near the city centre. The restaurant is one of the best in the country, and there is a wide choice of wines.	14	●	▨		
HILDESHEIM: *Parkhotel Berghölzchen* (DM)(DM) Am Berghölzchen 1, 31 139. **Map** C3. **[** *(05121) 97 90.* **FAX** *(05121) 97 94 00.* **W** www.berghoelzchen.de Beautifully located within a landscaped park, this hotel has traditions dating back to the 18th century.	80	●			
KÖNIGSLUTTER: *Avalon Hotelpark Königshof* (DM)(DM) Braunschweigerstr. 21A, 38 154. **Map** D3. **[** *(05353) 50 30.* **FAX** *(05353) 50 32 44.* **W** www.avalon-hotels.com Large hotel complex with comfortably furnished rooms and excellent sports facilities. Other features include several restaurants, café, beer garden and various banqueting halls.	185	●	▨	●	
LÜNEBURG: *Bremer Hof* (DM)(DM) Lüner Str. 12, 21 335. **Map** D2. **[** *(04131) 22 40.* **FAX** *(04131) 22 42 24.* **W** www.bremer-hof.de This hotel has traditions going back to the 16th century. Features include intimate rooms and regional cuisine.	55	●			
OLDENBURG: *Heide* (DM)(DM) Melkbrink 49–51, 26 121. **Map** B2. **[** *(0441) 80 40.* **FAX** *(0441) 88 40 60.* Occupying a modern building with every comfort, this hotel has well-equipped conference rooms and recreational areas. Two restaurants serve local specialities.	100	●	▨	●	
OSNABRÜCK: *Walhalla* (DM)(DM) Bierstr. 24, 49 074. **Map** B3. **[** *(0541) 349 10.* **FAX** *(0541) 349 11 44.* **W** www.hotel-walhalla.de This long-established hotel, with an elegant restaurant, has recently been modernized. Guests can enjoy the sauna and solarium, and there is a golf course available nearby.	65	●			

STADTHAGEN: *Gerber Hotel La Tannerie* ⓓⓂ 20 ●
Echternstr. 14, 31 655. **Map** C3. ☎ *(05721) 98 60.* ⒻⒶⓍ *(05721) 986 66.*
ⓌWWW.gerber-hotel.de
Conveniently located in the city centre, this hotel has pleasant,
individually decorated rooms. An excellent breakfast buffet is served.
🔢 📶 **P** 🔀 📶 🅴

WOLFENBÜTTEL: *Parkhotel Altes Kaffeehaus* ⓓⓂ 75 ●
Harztorwall 18, 38 300. **Map** D3. ☎ *(05331) 88 80.* ⒻⒶⓍ *(05331) 88 81 00.*
ⓌWWW.parkhotel-wolfenbuettel.de
A recently modernized hotel housed in a historic building. The restaurant
menu includes a variety of international dishes. 🔢 📶 📶 **P** 🔀 📶 📶 🅴

WOLFSBURG: *Brackstedter Mühle* ⓓⓂ 51 ●
Zum Kühlen Grunde 2, 38 448 Wolfsburg-Brackstedt. **Map** D3. ☎ *(05366) 900.*
ⒻⒶⓍ *(05366) 90 50.*
This comfortable hotel is located in a converted 17th-century building
with a water mill. The restaurant serves regional cuisine as well as
exquisitely innovative dishes. 🔢 📶 🔀 🅴

SCHLESWIG-HOLSTEIN

BAD MALENTE: *Admiralsholm* ⓓ 21 ●
Schweizer Str. 60, 23 714. **Map** D1. ☎ *(04523) 400 30.*
ⒻⒶⓍ *(04523) 40 03 31.* ⓌWWW.admiralsholm-malente.de
Once an admiral's residence, this hotel is located by the lake in a
beautiful park. Rooms are comfortably furnished. 🔢 📶 📶 **P** 🅴

FLENSBURG: *Am Wasserturm* ⓓⓂ 36 ● ■ ●
Blasberg 13, 24 943 Flensburg-Mürwik. **Map** C1. ☎ *(0461) 315 06 00.*
ⒻⒶⓍ *(0461) 31 22 87.* ⓌWWW.hotel-restaurant-am-wasserturm.de
Located in a tranquil spot, this hotel has rooms furnished in a modern
style. There is a café with a terrace. 🔢 📶 **P** 🔀 🅴

HELGOLAND: *Atoll* ⓓⓂⓂ 50 ● ●
Lung Wai, 27 498. **Map** B1. ☎ *(04725) 80 00.* ⒻⒶⓍ *(04725) 80 04 44.*
ⓌWWW.atoll.de
This super-modern hotel is constructed from glass and chrome, but some
of the rooms are furnished in a traditional manner. The restaurant serves
excellent cuisine, particularly fish and crab dishes. 🔢 📶 📶 🔀 🅴

KIEL: *Berliner Hof garni* ⓓⓂ 103
Ringstr. 6, 24 103. **Map** C1. ☎ *(0431) 663 40.* ⒻⒶⓍ *(0431) 663 43 45.*
Convenient located in the city centre near the railway station. Rooms are
attractively decorated and a buffet breakfast is served. 🔢 📶 📶 **P** 🔀 🅴

KIEL: *Kieler Yacht-Club* ⓓⓂⓂ 58 ●
Am Hindenburgufer 70, 24 105. **Map** C1. ☎ *(0431) 881 30.* ⒻⒶⓍ *(0431) 881 34 44.*
ⓌWWW.yachtclub.bestwestern.de
A hotel with elegantly furnished, modernized rooms, offering beautiful
views of the Baltic and Kiel fjord. The restaurant serves various regional
and international specialities and the bar is popular with yachtsmen.
🔢 📶 📶 🔀 📶 🅴

LÜBECK: *Alter Speicher garni* ⓓⓂ 45
Beckergrube 91–93, 23 552. **Map** D2. ☎ *(0451) 710 45.*
ⒻⒶⓍ *(0451) 70 48 04.*
Built in the style of a traditional granary, this hotel has comfortably furnished
rooms and a sauna and solarium for the benefit of guests. 🔢 📶 📶 🔀 📶 🅴

LÜBECK: *Kaiserhof garni* ⓓⓂ 60 ● ■ ●
Kronsforder Allee 11–13, 23 560. **Map** D2. ☎ *(0451) 70 33 01.*
ⒻⒶⓍ *(0451) 79 50 83.* ⓌWWW.kaiserhof-luebeck.de
A modern hotel has been created within two beautiful bourgeois houses,
which have been restored and linked together. All the rooms are
exquisitely furnished and the hotel has a terrace and a charming lounge
with an open fireplace. 🔢 📶 📶 **P** 📶 📶 🅴

LÜBECK: *Radisson SAS Senator Hotel Lübeck* ⓓⓂⓂ 224 ● ● ■
Willy-Brandt-Allee 6, 23 554. **Map** D2. ☎ *(0451) 14 20.* ⒻⒶⓍ *(0451) 142 22 22.*
ⓌWWW.radissonSAS.de
Beautifully located on the river Trave, this hotel has been harmoniously
integrated with the surrounding architecture. The hotel houses a well-
known restaurant, rustic wine bar and bar. 🔢 📶 📶 **P** 📶 🔀 📶 🅴

Price categories for a twin room with bathroom or shower, and including breakfast, service and tax (in Deutsch Marks and Euros):
(DM) up to DM150 (up to (€)77)
(DM)(DM) DM150–250 ((€)77–128)
(DM)(DM)(DM) DM250–350 ((€)128–179)
(DM)(DM)(DM)(DM) DM350–450 ((€)179–230)
(DM)(DM)(DM)(DM)(DM) above DM450 (above (€)230).

RESTAURANT
The hotel has a restaurant that is open to non-residents as well as to hotel guests.
GARDEN OR TERRACE
The hotel is set in a garden or has an outside terrace or courtyard, often with tables for eating outside.
SWIMMING POOL
The hotel has a swimming pool.
AIR CONDITIONING
All rooms are air-conditioned.

	NUMBER OF ROOMS	RESTAURANT	GARDEN OR TERRACE	SWIMMING POOL	AIR CONDITIONING
OEVERSEE: *Historischer Krug Romantik Hotel* (DM)(DM) Grazer Platz 1, 24 988. **Map** C1. **(** *(04630) 94 00.* **FAX** *(04630) 780.* W www.romantikhotels.com Located 9 km (5 miles) south of Flensburg, this hotel dates back to the 16th century; it was being run by the same family for almost 200 years. There is a good restaurant, a café with a terrace, hotel bar and garden. ① 🛏 P 📶 🍴 ✉	40	●	■	●	
RATZEBURG: *Der Seehof* (DM)(DM) Lüneburger Damm 1–3, 23 909. **Map** D2. **(** *(04541) 86 01 00.* **FAX** *(04541) 86 01 02.* W www.derseehof.de A comfortable hotel perched on pillars above the lake. As well as tastefully furnished rooms and a number of cafés and restaurants, the hotel has its own jetty, a beach and a swimming pool. ① 🛏 📶 P ✉	45	●			
SCHLESWIG: *Waldschlösschen* (DM)(DM) Kolonnenweg 152, 24 837. **Map** C1. **(** *(04621) 38 32 83.* **FAX** *(04621) 38 31 05.* Standing on the edge of the forest, this hotel has rooms furnished in a variety of styles. There are good facilities for taking part in sporting activities and bicycles can be hired. ① 🛏 📶 P 📶 🍴 ✉	117	●	■	●	
SYLT: *Benen-Diken-Hof* (DM)(DM)(DM)(DM) Süderstr. 3, 25 980 Keitum. **Map** B1. **(** *(04651) 938 30.* **FAX** *(04651) 938 31 83.* W www.benen-diken-hof.de A charming hotel in a quiet area. Rooms are comfortable, service is courteous and an abundant breakfast buffet is provided. There is a golf course nearby. ① 🛏 P ✉	40	●		●	
SYLT: *Miramar* (DM)(DM)(DM)(DM) Friedrichstr. 43, 25 980 Westerland. **Map** B1. **(** *(04651) 85 50.* **FAX** *(04651) 85 52 22.* W www.miramar.de Service is impeccable in this hotel by the sea. Fine views can be enjoyed from the terrace. ① 🛏 📶 P 🍴 🎬 ✉	93	●	■	●	
MECKLENBURG-LOWER POMERANIA					
ANKLAM: *Am Stadtwall* (DM) Demminer Str. 5, 17 389. **Map** E2. **(** *(03971) 83 31 36.* **FAX** *(03971) 83 31 37.* Recently built hotel with pleasant rooms and a restaurant, in which a hearty breakfast is served. ① 🛏 P ✉	18	●			
BAD DOBERAN: *Kurhotel* (DM)(DM)(DM) Am Kamp, 18 209. **Map** D1. **(** *(038203) 630 36.* **FAX** *(038203) 621 26.* W www.romantikhotels.com One of the oldest hotels on the Baltic sea and one of the finest in Germany, this hotel has been recently modernized. An excellent restaurant serves Mecklenburg specialities, and there is also a café and bistro. ① 🛏 📶 P ✉	45	●			
DARGUN: *Am Klostersee* (DM) Am Klosterdamm, 17 159. **Map** E2. **(** *(039959) 25 20.* **FAX** *(039959) 252 28.* This hotel is situated in a quiet, tranquil spot, on the edge of the forest and near the lake. Some of the pleasant rooms have balconies with a view of the lake. Other features include a lounge with an open fireplace and a beer garden. The restaurant serves regional cuisine. ① 🛏 ✉	27	●	■		
GREIFSWALD: *Parkhotel Greifswald* (DM) Pappelallee 1, 17 489. **Map** E1. **(** *(03834) 87 40.* **FAX** *(03834) 87 45 55.* W parkhotel.greifswald.de Set amidst greenery, this city-centre hotel has well-furnished rooms. The restaurant serves regional cuisine and a good breakfast buffet. ① 🛏 📶 P 📶 🍴 ✉	71	●			

GÜSTROW: *Am Güstrower Schloss* ⓓⓜ ⓒⓜ | 47
Schlossberg 1, 18 273. **Map** D2. ☎ *(03843) 76 70.*
FAX *(03843) 76 71 00.* W www.schlosshotel-guestrow.de
This modern hotel is housed within a former prison building opposite the castle. 🔲 🛏 🛁 P 📺 🎱 ♨ �‍

NEUBRANDENBURG: *Handicap-Hotel Ikarus* ⓓⓜ ⓒⓜ | 13
Oelmühlenstr. 29, 17 033. **Map** E2. ☎ *(0395) 58 17 70.*
FAX *(0395) 581 77 77.* W www.ikarushotel.de
A new hotel situated in a tranquil spot on the edge of the Teulensee.
Rooms are furnished in a comfortable, attractive manner. Bicycles can be hired. 🔲 🛏 🛁 P �‍

ROSTOCK: *Godewind* ⓓⓜ ⓒⓜ | 59
Warnemünder Str. 5, 18 146 Rostock-Markgrafenheide. **Map** D1. ☎ *(0381) 60 95 70.*
FAX *(0381) 60 95 71 11.* W www.hotel-godewind.de
Recently opened hotel with comfortable rooms, close to the Baltic Sea.
🔲 🛏 🛁 P ♨ 🎱 📺 �‍

ROSTOCK: *Courtyard by Marriott* ⓓⓜ ⓒⓜ | 150
Kröpeliner/Schwaansche Str. 6, 18 055. **Map** D1. ☎ *(0381) 497.00.*
FAX *(0381) 497 07 00.*
Rooms are comfortable in this hotel close to the city centre and the old harbour. There is a good restaurant and bar. 🔲 🛏 🛁 P ♨ 🎱 �‍

RÜGEN: *Landhotel Herrenhaus* ⓓⓜ | 20
Dorfstr. 6. **Map** E1. ☎ *(038391) 770.* FAX *(038391) 702 80.*
This family-run hotel is housed in what was once an aristocratic residence. Facilities include a pleasant restaurant and a lounge with an open fireplace. 🔲 🛏 P ♨ �‍

RÜGEN: *Kurhotel Sassnitz* ⓓⓜ ⓒⓜ | 83
Hauptstr. 1, 18 546 Sassnitz. **Map** E1. ☎ *(038392) 530.* FAX *(038392) 533 33.*
W www.rugen-hotel.de
This elegant spa hotel is housed in a former mariner's house, which has recently been restored. Rooms are spacious and regional cuisine is served. 🔲 🛏 🛁 📺 ♨ �‍

SCHWERIN: *Arte Schwerin* ⓓⓜ ⓒⓜ | 40
Dorfstr. 6, 19 061 Schwerin-Krebsförden. **Map** D2. ☎ *(0385) 634 50.*
FAX *(0385) 634 51 00.* W www.ringhotel-arte-schwerin.m-up.de
Housed within a former country inn dating from the 19th century, this recently modernized hotel has retained many interesting features.
Seasonal cuisine and an abundant breakfast buffet are served.
🔲 🛏 🛁 P ♨ 🎱 �‍

SCHWERIN: *Best Western Plaza Schwerin* ⓓⓜ ⓒⓜ | 76
Am Grünen Tal, 19 063 Schwerin-Grosser Dreesch. **Map** D2.
☎ *(0385) 399 20.* FAX *(0385) 399 21 88.* W www.bestwestern.com
This hotel, with sumptuously furnished rooms and a modern recreational centre, belongs to the Best Western hotel group. The elegant Primavera restaurant serves Italian delicacies. 🔲 🛏 🛁 P 📺 ♨ 🎱 �‍

STRALSUND: *Royal Hotel am Bahnhof* ⓓⓜ ⓒⓜ | 60
Tribseer Damm 4, 18 437. **Map** E1. ☎ *(03831) 29 52 68.*
FAX *(03831) 29 26 50.* W www.royal-hotel.de
An excellent starting point for seeing Stralsund on foot, this hotel has a beautiful Art Nouveau façade. The restaurant serves both international and regional cuisine. 🔲 🛏 🛁 P ♨ 📺 �‍

USEDOM: *Residenz Waldoase* ⓓⓜ ⓓⓜⓒⓜ | 68
Dünenstr.1, 17 419 Ahlbeck. **Map** E2. ☎ *(038378) 500.*
FAX *(038378) 502 99.*
This charmingly located modern hotel is based in a refurbished former holiday home. Also available are self-catering bungalows that are serviced by the hotel. Within the hotel grounds there are several dining venues, offering interesting dishes throughout the day.
🔲 🛏 🛁 P ♨ 🎱 �‍

WISMAR: *Altes Brauhaus garni* ⓓⓜ | 16
Lübschestr. 37, 23 966. **Map** D2. ☎ *(03841) 21 14 16.*
FAX *(03841) 28 32 23.*
Housed within a 16th-century building, this recently restored hotel has pleasantly furnished rooms. 🔲 🛏 �‍

For key to symbols *see back flap*

WHERE TO EAT

GERMAN CUISINE does not enjoy the same reputation as that of, say, France, but nevertheless you can eat very well here. There are many establishments that specialize in regional cuisine, which, although somewhat heavy, is always very appetizing. It is also easy to find good restaurants serving ethnic cuisine, such as Italian, Greek, Indian, Chinese, Thai or Turkish. In the past few years, some

The crest of the Forsthaus Paulsborn restaurant in Berlin

fine restaurants have opened. Run by renowned master chefs, they serve excellent cuisine of the very highest European standards.

From the many thousands of restaurants throughout Germany, we have chosen the finest for inclusion in this guidebook, with a view to catering for a variety of budgets. Detailed information on the selected restaurants can be found on pp504–527.

TYPES OF RESTAURANTS

THE TERM *Restaurant* is used to define both restaurants offering exquisite cuisine and excellent service, at steep prices, and popular local establishments with affordable prices. The word *Gasthaus* usually indicates a traditional style of inn that specializes in straightforward regional cuisine. In many towns, there is a *Ratskeller* established in the cellar of the town hall. These are usually good, not overly expensive restaurants serving dishes that represent the regional cuisine. They usually have atmospheric, stylized interiors that are well adapted to the vaulted, dark spaces of the historic cellars. A *Weinstube* is a wine bar, where good, usually local, wine is served. Often decent

Altdeutsche Weinstube in Dörrenbach

food is also available here. A *Bierstube* is similar in style, except that the beverage is beer. The term *Café* has a variety of connotations in Germany. This is a place that serves an excellent breakfast with various options in the mornings, while from noon they offer lunch dishes. The choice is usually somewhat heavy, though varied. In addition, at any time of the day and evening, customers can have a coffee here, eat some ice cream or a cake, drink beer or some other alcoholic beverage. In the evenings there is often music.

A typical venue in which you can spend an evening is a *Kneipe*. In terms of its atmosphere, this is somewhat reminiscent of an English pub. Patrons generally come here to have a drink, but there are usually a few hot dishes on offer to appease their hunger. Self-service venues offering snacks are known as *Imbiss*. These can have a very varied character, from a stall serving baked sausages and cans of drink, to elegant kiosks offering a large choice of salads and fast food. These kiosks are often run by immigrants. In fact in most large German towns there are numerous kiosks serving Arabic, Turkish, Chinese and American food. If shoppers feel the need for a snack, they might like to take

advantage of the restaurant or cafeteria facilities in department stores. These are usually self-service establishments known as *Stehcafé*, which means "Stand Up Café".

Entrance to a *Gasthaus* near the cathedral in Cologne

WHAT AND WHEN TO EAT

BREAKFAST IS USUALLY a hearty affair with various types of bread accompanied by cheese, sausages and marmalade. On Sundays brunch is served in most places until 2pm: this is a combination of breakfast and lunch, in the form of a Swedish buffet. During the lunch period (between noon and 2pm) most establishments serve an excellent salad or a bowl of filling soup, while many restaurants offer a special fixed-price menu that is significantly cheaper than in the evenings. Restaurants start to fill up in the evenings between 6 and 7pm, although dinner is most usually eaten after 8pm.

Wine festival in Alter Hof in Freiburg im Breisgau

OPENING HOURS

CAFÉS GENERALLY open from 9am, while restaurants are open from noon, sometimes with a break from 3 to 6pm. The most expensive places do not open until dinner time and are frequently closed for one day during the week.

A street stall serving snacks of freshly cooked sausages

MENU

IN MOST GOOD restaurants the menu is written in German and English, and sometimes also in French. In cafés and less expensive restaurants, the menu may be handwritten, in which case the staff may be able to help with a translation. In many of the less expensive places there is, in addition to the regular menu, a daily menu with attractive seasonal dishes. Sometimes the chef's special offers are written on a blackboard. In all restaurants and cafés, a menu showing prices will be displayed outside the establishment.

RESERVATIONS

MAKING A PRIOR reservation is essential in all the best restaurants while in most good and medium standard restaurants it is advisable to do so, particularly on a Friday or Saturday night. If you wish not made a reservation, try one of the popular restaurant complexes where you can usually get a table.

PRICES AND TIPS

THE COST OF restaurant meals in Germany is unusually diverse. A three-course meal without alcohol can be found for around DM 20–25 (€10–13), but in the centre of larger cities a minimum of DM 35–45 (€18–22) would be more usual. In a luxury restaurant, the bill for a six-course meal, without drinks, can cost in excess of DM150 (€76). The price of alcoholic drinks also varies, but beer is the cheapest drink.

Prices include service and tax, but it is usual to leave a tip – generally around 10 per cent of the total bill. When paying for a meal by credit card, the tip can be added to the total. Restaurants and cafés that accept credit cards usually display the logos of acceptable cards near the entrance. Before ordering, it is best to find out whether a minimum charge is applied to customers who wish to pay their bill by credit card.

DRESS CODE

GERMANS USUALLY prefer to dress comfortably, casually and practically, preferring a sporty style to more formal attire. When going out in the evenings, many women – regardless of their age – wear trousers and comfortable low-heeled shoes, though some prefer elegant dresses. Men generally wear jackets and ties only during office hours.

Going to a restaurant does not require any particular preparation unless you wish to go to a luxurious, gourmet restaurant, for which you will probably have to book up to two months in advance.

Interior of the Bamberger Reiter restaurant in Berlin

CHILDREN

RESTAURANTS usually provide high chairs for toddlers and, particularly during the lunch period, there will be light dishes for children – or you can order small portions.

VEGETARIANS

INCREASINGLY, Germans are turning to vegetarianism, although the number of vegetarian restaurants is still limited. However, a few vegetarian dishes can usually be found on most menus. If necessary, choose a restaurant that serves a national cuisine in which there is no shortage of vegetarian dishes – for example Indian or Thai.

DISABLED VISITORS

IF A TABLE WITH wheelchair access is required, it is best to specify this when making the reservation. At the same time, check whether toilets are easily accessible.

Picnicking – a popular form of relaxation in Germany

What to Eat

Bavarian dessert

GERMAN CUISINE IS very varied, good value and of a generally high standard. In the north, delicious fish dishes can be found while, throughout the country, wonderful, hearty meat dishes in thick sauces are served. Germany is renowned not just for sausages *(Wurst)* but also for excellently prepared pork knuckle, roast beef and pork, poultry dishes, as well as various types of dumpling, delicious bread and cakes.

Matjestopf
Young, salted herrings with onion and cream are often served with jacket potatoes.

Sweet mustard

Tomato sauce

Weisswurst (white sausage)

A beer pretzel

Reibekuchen
Otherwise known as Kartoffelpuffer, *these potato pancakes are served either savoury or sweet.*

Maultaschen
These square dumplings with a savoury (usually meat) filling are typical of Schwabian cuisine.

Pieces of meat

Leek

Potatoes

String beans

Sliced carrots

Pichelsteiner
This is a typical Eintopf, *a one-pot dish that replaces soup and the main course. It comprises meat, potatoes and various vegetables stewed in an aromatic sauce.*

Kartoffelsalat
This delicious potato salad is flavoured with piquant marinated cucumbers, onion and mayonnaise.

Kartoffelsuppe
Flavoured with marjoram, this creamy potato soup is served with slices of sausage.

Linsensuppe
When served with sausages, this lentil soup provides a satisfying lunch.

Leberknödelsuppe
A speciality of Bavaria, this clear consommé is served with liver dumplings.

Oven-baked goose with crunchy skin

Stuffing of chestnuts and diced apple

Martinsgans
Traditionally served on St Martin's Day (November 11, see p38), the goose is stuffed with chestnuts and apples before being roasted in the oven.

Eisbein mit Erbspüree
A dish of baked pork knuckle is served with puréed peas and cabbage cooked in champagne.

Sweet and sour sauce

Potato dumplings

Apple purée

Sliced roast meat

Kartoffelklösse
Often prepared from a mixture of raw and cooked potatoes, dumplings may accompany main courses.

Sauerbraten mit Kartoffelklössen und Apfelmus
Roast beef marinated in vinegar is served here with apple purée and dumplings prepared from cooked potatoes.

Karpfen
Carp, a popular freshwater fish, is prepared in different ways in different parts of the country. Here it is served with a smooth tomato sauce.

KAFFEE UND KUCHEN
A mouth-watering selection of cakes is generally offered with afternoon coffee. Germany is renowned for its light fruit tarts, apple charlottes, cheesecake and plum or cherry cakes.

Schwartenbraten
Roast pork is here served with sauerkraut and bread dumplings.

This almond-flavoured gingerbead is known as Weisse Nürnberger Lebkuchen

Rote Grütze
A thick, jellied dessert made from fruit juice and wine, with the addition of fruit.

Yeast doughnuts, deep-fried in fat, are known as Berliners

Schwarzwälder Kirschtorte
Chocolate gateau filled with cherries and cream is a speciality of the Black Forest.

What to Drink

T HROUGHOUT GERMANY, beer is undoubtedly the
most popular drink, and each region has its
own beer-brewing traditions. However, the country
is also renowned for excellent wines, which are
produced in the south. The most well known are
Mosel and Rhine wines, although these are not
necessarily better than Franconian wines. Stronger
spirits and liqueurs are also available, as are some
very pleasant non-alcoholic cold drinks.

**Shop in Eberbach stocked with wine
from the adjoining monastery**

HOT DRINKS

I N GERMAN ESTABLISHMENTS there is no difficulty in
getting a cup of tea *(Tee)*, but don't be surprised if
the waiter asks whether you mean mint tea *(Pfeffer-
minztee)* or camomile *(Kamillentee)*, since herbal
infusions are popular in Germany. To be sure of
being served Indian tea, it is advisable to specify
Schwarztee when placing the order.

Coffee is another popular drink. In general, filter
coffee, which is fairly mild, is served. For
customers who prefer a stronger coffee, it
is best to order an espresso.

**Herbal infusions include
mint and camomile tea**

NON-ALCOHOLIC COLD DRINKS

V ARIOUS TYPES of carbonated drinks and fruit
juices – ubiquitous throughout Europe and
the US – are popular, and an extensive choice is
available in every café and restaurant in
Germany. A refreshing non-alcoholic drink is
Apfel-Schorle, which is apple juice mixed with
equal proportions of sparkling mineral water.
(The alcoholic version is *Wein-Schorle*, which is
wine mixed with mineral water.) Another
popular non-alcoholic drink is *Spezi*, which is a
mixture of cola and Fanta.

Although tap water is generally
safe to drink, it is not usually served
with restaurant meals. To order a
bottle of mineral water, ask for
Mineralwasser, adding the phrase
"ohne gas" if still water is preferred.

Apfel-Schorle

**Limonade
(Lemonade)**

**Mineralwasser
(Mineral water)**

SPIRITS AND LIQUEURS

S TRONG SPIRITS are often drunk after heavy meals,
particularly pork dishes. It is best to order one
of the popular drinks distilled from rye or wheat,
such as *Doppel Korn*. Brandy (known as *Wein-
brand)* is also produced in Germany. Liqueurs are
also popular, as is a spirit flavoured with herbs
and roots (known as bitters). Among the most
popular are *Kümmerling* and *Jägermeister* while,
in Berlin, *Kaulzdorfer Kräuter Likör* is served. In
many restaurants various kinds of whisky can be
ordered, including well-known Scottish and Irish
brands and popular American bourbons, but
connoisseurs may miss their personal favourites.
Italian restaurants often serve grappa, a grape
spirit, after a meal, while in Greek restaurants
ouzo – an aniseed spirit – may be offered.

**Bitter-sweet
spirit,
Jägermeister**

**Herbal/root-
flavour spirit,
Kümmerling**

**Weizen Doppel
Korn (rye
spirit)**

WINES

Mainstockheimer Hofstück Spätburgunder

Spätburgunder from the Rheingau region

Germany is renowned for its excellent white wines, particularly those made from the Riesling grape. Among the most highly prized wines are those from the Rheingau region. Lovers of red wine might like to try Assmannshausen Spätburgunder wine, which is produced from the Pinot Noir grape.

Germany has a system of classifying wines into three groups according to their quality: the lowest quality is *Tafelwein*, then *Qualitätswein* and the highest quality *Qualitätswein mit Prädikat*. The latter includes wines produced from appropriately selected grapes, which is always confirmed on the bottle label. The term *Trocken* indicates a dry style, *Halbtrocken*, semi-dry and *Süss* means sweet. Very good sparkling wines, known as *Sekt*, are also produced in Germany

Riesling Schloss Vollrads

BEERS

Beermat with brewery logo

Each region of Germany has its own beer-brewing tradition: the most popular breweries in the north are Jever in Freesia and Beck's in Bremen, along with Bitburger, Warsteiner and Karlsberg. In the Rhine region, the biggest producers are DAB from Dortmund and König in Duisburg. In Berlin, Schultheiss, Berliner Kindl and Engelhardt compete for the primary position, while in Dresden the principal beers are produced by a brewery in Radeberg. However, Bavaria is by far the major brewing centre – the names of the breweries Löwenbräu, Hofbräu and Paulaner are known to every beer lover around the world. The most commonly drunk beer is Pils, a bottom-fermented lager of the pilsner type. Brown ales are also popular, particularly in the south. Schwarzbier, a top-fermented brown ale of over 4 per cent alcohol, is increasingly popular. Weizenbier, a bitter top-fermented beer, also has many fans, as has Bock, which is strong, at around 6 per cent alcohol.

Löwenbräu beer

König Ludwig Dunkel beer

Schultheiss beer

Wheat beer mixed with fruit juice, Berliner Weisse mit Schuss – speciality of Berlin

Franziskaner Hefe Weissbier beer

A tankard of beer with the essential head of foam

Choosing a Restaurant

THE RESTAURANTS in this guide have been selected because of their good food and interesting location. Venues are listed state by state, beginning with Berlin. The colour-coded thumb tabs on the side of the page correspond to the relevant pages in the book. A map of Berlin can be found on pages 104–9, and the road map for Germany is at the back of the book.

CREDIT CARDS   GARDEN OR TERRACE   GERMAN WINES   VEGETARIAN DISHES

BERLIN

BERLIN – EASTERN CENTRE: *Reinhard's*
Poststr. 28, 10 178. **City map** 5 E2. 【 *(030) 242 52 95.*
A captivating restaurant with a stylish interior themed as the Roaring Twenties, serving an excellent selection of dishes from various countries. The speciality is *Das Geheimnis aus dem Kaiserhof* (the secret from the emperor's court) – a succulent steak served with a sauce, apparently created for Max Liebermann.

BERLIN – EASTERN CENTRE: *Zum Nussbaum*
Am Nussbaum 3, 10 178. **Map** 5 E2. 【 *(030) 242 30 95.*
This inn, based in one of the lanes of Nikolaiviertel, is one of the most popular places in town. The cuisine is traditional Berlin style – both pork knuckle and herrings feature on the menu.

BERLIN – EASTERN CENTRE: *Borchardt*
Französische Str. 47, 10 117. **Map** 1 C5, 4 C2. 【 *(030) 20 38 71 10.*
FAX *(030) 20 38 71 50.*
One of a small number of restaurants that have retained their original interior in early 20th-century style, with marble columns, mosaics and parquet floors. Prices are reasonable, and the Italian food is very good. A favourite venue with German politicians.

BERLIN – EASTERN CENTRE: *Ermeler Haus*
Märkisches Ufer 10, 10 179. **Map** 5 E3. 【 *(030) 24 06 20.* FAX *(030) 24 06 22 72.*
Good regional cuisine, with a light, modern touch. The restaurant is lcoated within a gastronomic complex, Art'otel, in the unique room of an 18th-century palace with an ornamental Rococo ceiling. ● *Mon & Sun.*

BERLIN – EASTERN CENTRE: *L'Etoile*
Unter den Linden 77, 10 117. **Map** 1 B4, 4 B2. 【 *(030) 226 10.*
FAX *(030) 22 61 22 22.*
The restaurant lives up to the name of the famous Adlon Hotel, in which it is based. Thanks to the culinary art of the chef, Karlheinz Hauser, L'Etoile is easily one of the best restaurants in town.

BERLIN – WESTERN CENTRE: *Ottenthal*
Kantstr. 153, 10 623. **Map** 2 B4. 【 *(030) 313 31 62.*
Almost opposite the Theater des Westens, the modest interior of this restaurant is decorated with the mechanism of a church clock from the eponymous village of Ottenthal in Austria. Good Austrian food and an excellent selection of Austrian wines, accompanied by tunes from Mozart. Reservation is advisable.

BERLIN – WESTERN CENTRE: *Die Quadriga*
Eislebener Str. 14, 10 789. **Map** 2 B5. 【 *(030) 21 40 50.*
FAX *(030) 21 40 51 00.*
This gourmet restaurant is based in the Brandenburger Hof Hotel, which has long been one of Berlin's finest. The relatively small dining room is well equipped with furniture designed by Frank Lloyd Wright. Impeccable service complements the sophisticated French cuisine. Reservation is required. P ● *Sat & Sun.*

BERLIN – WESTERN CENTRE: *First Floor*
Budapester Str. 42, 10 789. **Map** 2 C4. 【 *(030) 25 02 10 20.*
FAX *(030) 25 02 11 60.*
Elegant restaurant of the highest calibre. The menu includes traditional German fare, such as pork knuckle with cabbage, as well as sophisticated creations with fish, crab and aromatic truffles. Lunchtime set menus are significantly lower in price. Reservation is necessary. ● *Sat until 6pm.*

Prices of a three course meal without drinks, including cover charge, tax and service in Deutschmarks (and in Euros): (DM) up to 40 DM (up to 20 €) (DM)(DM) 40–60 DM (20–29 €) (DM)(DM)(DM) 60–80 DM (30–39 €) (DM)(DM)(DM)(DM) 80–100 DM (40–49 €) (DM)(DM)(DM)(DM)(DM) over 100 DM (over 50 €)	**CREDIT CARDS** Credit cards are accepted. **GARDEN OR TERRACE** Weather permitting, it is possible to eat *al fresco*. **GERMAN WINES** A good selection of German wines. **VEGETARIAN DISHES** The restaurant offers a good selection of meat free and vegetarian dishes.			

	CREDIT CARDS	GARDEN OR TERRACE	GERMAN WINES	VEGETARIAN DISHES

FURTHER AFIELD: *Oren* — (DM) — ● ■ ● ■
Oranienburger Str. 28, 10 117. ((030) 282 82 28.
This restaurant, near the synagogue and the Centrum Judaicum, specializes in Jewish and Arabic vegetarian dishes for groups of 10 people or more. The menu includes such delicacies as falafels, tofu-stuffed peppers and excellent aubergine dishes. Wines from Israel. &

FURTHER AFIELD: *Am Karlsbad* — (DM)(DM)(DM) — ● ■ ● ■
Am Karlsbad 11, 10 785. **Map** 3 F4. ((030) 264 53 49. FAX (030) 264 42 40.
Hidden in the courtyard of an office block, this bistro-style restaurant is part of a modern, glass-fronted hotel. The interior is well designed, making use of granite, wood and chrome. Excellent, light Italian cuisine with seasonal specialities. The lunch menu is significantly less expensive. ● Mon, Sat until 7 pm, Sun.

FURTHER AFIELD: *Mare Bê* — (DM)(DM)(DM) — ● ■ ● ■
Rosenthaler Str. 46–48, 10 178. **Map** 5 D1. ((030) 283 65 45.
An excellent address for lovers of southern French, Italian and Spanish cooking, with a hint of the Middle East. It is worth eating here on a Tuesday, when the house speciality – oysters – are served. The courtyard has a peaceful garden. ⚡

FURTHER AFIELD: *Ana e Bruno* — (DM)(DM)(DM)(DM) — ● ■
Sophie-Charlotten Str. 101, 14 059. ((030) 325 71 10. FAX (030) 322 68 95.
Quite definitely the finest Italian restaurant in town. The elegant pastel interior and soft Italian melodies create an ideal setting for the delicious specialities created by the chef. ● Mon & Sun.

FURTHER AFIELD: *Bamberger Reiter* — (DM)(DM)(DM)(DM) — ● ■ ● ■
Regensburger Str. 7, 10 777. ((030) 218 42 82. FAX (030) 21 47 99.
One of Berlin's best establishments, this restaurant represents the crowning achievement of master chef Franz Raneburger. The small dining rooms are furnished in rustic style, and the intimate atmosphere is complemented by perfect service. Booking well in advance is essential. Similar fare is also served at the Bistro Bamberger Reiter next door, at lower prices. ● Mon & Sun. ⚡

FURTHER AFIELD: *Harlekin* — (DM)(DM)(DM)(DM)(DM) — ● ■ ● ■
Lützowufer 15, 10 785. **Map** 3 D4. ((030) 25 47 88 58. FAX (030) 265 11 71.
The Duma Grand Hotel Esplanade has one of the finest restaurants in the city. Guests can observe the chefs at work in the open kitchen. The exceptional menu lists European, including many Italian, and Asian dishes, which are served in an impeccable manner. A reservation is essential. P ● Mon & Sun. & ⚡

BRANDENBURG

BRANDENBURG: *Sorat* — (DM) — ● ■ ■
Altstädtischer Markt 1, 14 770. **Road map** E3. ((03381) 59 70. FAX (03381) 59 74 44.
This restaurant belongs to a hotel in the old town market square. A very pleasant venue, serving tasty and varied food, including a selection of dishes which are typical for different German regions. & ⚡

CHORIN: *Haus Chorin* — (DM) — ● ■ ● ■
Neue Klosterallee 10, 16 230 Chorin. **Road map** E2. ((033366) 500. FAX (033366) 326.
This hotel–restaurant is based in a stylish Art Nouveau villa situated on the shores of a lake. The regional fish and game dishes are particularly highly recommended. ● Wed in winter. & ⚡

COTTBUS: *Branitz–Fürst Pückler* — (DM) — ● ■ ■
Heinrich-Zille-Str., 03 042. **Road map** F3. ((0355) 751 00. FAX (0355) 71 31 72.
This elegant restaurant with open fireplace is based in the Best Western Branitz Hotel. & ⚡

Prices of a three course meal without drinks, including cover charge, tax and service in Deutschmarks (and in Euros):
- DM up to 40 DM (up to 20 €)
- DM DM 40–60 DM (20–29 €)
- DM DM DM 60–80 DM (30–39 €)
- DM DM DM DM 80–100 DM (40–49 €)
- DM DM DM DM DM over 100 DM (over 50 €)

CREDIT CARDS
Credit cards are accepted.
GARDEN OR TERRACE
Weather permitting, it is possible to eat *al fresco.*
GERMAN WINES
A good selection of German wines.
VEGETARIAN DISHES
The restaurant offers a good selection of meat free and vegetarian dishes.

LEHNIN: *Markgraf*   DM DM   ● ■ ● ■
Friedensstr. 13, 14 797. **Road map** E3. 🍴 *(03382) 76 50.* **FAX** *(03382) 76 54 30.*
Elegant yet unpretentious restaurant in the Markgraf Hotel, serving regional cuisine. After the meal, coffee can be taken on the terrace. 🔧 🔧

NEURUPPIN: *Altes Kasino am See*   DM DM   ●   ● ■
Seeufer 11, 16 816. **Road map** E2. 🍴 *(03391) 30 59.* **FAX** *(03391) 35 86 84.*
This hotel–restaurant serves delicious, no-nonsense food reminiscent of home cooking. Good selection of fish and game dishes. 🔧 🔧 🎵

ORANIENBURG: *Galerie*   DM DM DM   ● ■ ● ■
Andre-Pican-Str. 23, 16 515. **Road map** E3. 🍴 *(03301) 69 00.* **FAX** *(03301) 69 09 99.*
This new restaurant, part of the Stadthotel Oranienburg, is in the centre of town. The interior is presented like an art gallery, and there is also a bar. Excellent regional dishes and French cuisine. 🔧

POTSDAM: *Hofgarten*   DM   ● ■ ● ■
Friedrich-Ebert-Str. 88, 14 467. **Road map** E3. 🍴 *(0331) 231 70.*
FAX *(0331) 231 71 00.*
Modern restaurant in the Voltaire Hotel, serving mainly dishes of the day. Regional cuisine predominates. 🔧 🔧

POTSDAM: *Speckers Gaststätte zur Ratswaage*   DM DM DM   ● ■ ● ■
Am neuen Markt 10, 14 467. **Road map** E3. 🍴 *(0331) 280 43 11.* **FAX** *(0331) 280 43 19.*
Unpretentious, modern, family-run restaurant. Exquisite and original creations, mainly French-influenced, are prepared from locally grown produce. Excellent service. ● *Mon, Sun until 3pm.* 🔧 🔧

WITTSTOCK: *Stadt Hamburg*   DM   ● ■
Röbelerstr. 25, 16 909. **Road map** E2. 🍴 and **FAX** *(03394) 44 45 66.*
This restaurant, based in the Hotel Stadt Hamburg, is situated close to the old town of Wittstock. The interior is pleasant, and the menu is characterized by regional dishes. 🔧 🔧

SAXONY–ANHALT

BERNBURG: *Kartoffelhaus*   DM   ●   ● ■
Breite Str. 2–3, 06 406. **Road map** D3. 🍴 *(03471) 35 40.* **FAX** *(03471) 35 41 35.*
This restaurant, based in the Askania Hotel, serves regional food. Tasty dishes prepared with potatoes are house specialities. 🔧 🔧

DESSAU: *Fürst Leopold*   DM   ● ■ ● ■
Friedensplatz, 06 844. **Road map** E3. 🍴 *(0340) 251 50.* **FAX** *(0340) 251 51 77.*
This restaurant, part of the Steigenberger Seminar & Konferenzhotel, was built to cater especially for the needs of business people attending conferences and seminars, but other guests are equally welcome. The restaurant serves a large number of interesting and delicious German dishes. There is also a small bistro and a bar. 🔧 🔧 🎵

HALLE: *Dorint Hotel Charlottenhof*   DM DM   ●   ● ■
Dorotheenstr. 12, 06 108. **Road map** D4. 🍴 *(0345) 292 30.* **FAX** *(0345) 292 31 00.*
The restaurant belongs to the Dorint Hotel Charlottenhof, which is located in the city centre. Guests can watch their food being prepared while in the restaurant. The food is generally very tasty, the service friendly. Pleasant hotel bar. 🔧 🔧

MAGDEBURG: *Alt Prester*   DM   ● ■
Alt Prester 102, 39 114 Magdeburg-Prester. **Road map** D3. 🍴 *(0391) 819 30.*
FAX *(0391) 819 31 18.*
This restaurant, in the Alt Prester Hotel, is in a beautiful location on the banks of the Elbe river. It specializes mainly in traditional German cooking. Beer garden.

MERSEBURG: *Belle Epoque*
Oberaltenburg 4, 06 217. **Road map** D4. [(03461) 452 00.
FAX *(03461) 45 21 00.*
Exquisite restaurant, based in the Radisson SAS Hotel, specializing in
Scandinavian and German cuisine. Interesting decor and very good
service. There is also a café with terrace and a bar.

NAUMBURG: *Zum Alten Stadtgefängnis*
Mühlgasse 18, 06 618. **Road map** D4. [(03445) 20 09 40. FAX (03445) 70 87 20.
This establishment won the prize as the best of Saxony-Anhalt's
restaurants. Romantic, rustic furnishings. Generous portions.

QUEDLINBURG: *Theophano*
Markt 13–14, 06 484. **Road map** D4. [(03946) 963 00. FAX (03946) 96 30 36.
This restaurant, in one of the Romantik Hotels, is based in an almost 400-
year-old renovated building. Tasty dishes are served in a beautiful vaulted
cellar. It is particularly worth trying the game dishes. ● *Sun.*

STENDAL: *Altstadt-Hotel*
Breite Str. 60, 39 576. **Road map** D3. [(03931) 698 90. FAX (03931) 69 89 39.
Very pleasant, tastefully furnished hotel–restaurant, situated in the city
centre, serving regional and international dishes.

TANGERMÜNDE: *Kutscherstübchen*
Lange Str. 52, 39 590. **Road map** D3. [(039322) 23 91. FAX (039322) 36 42.
Part of the Schwarzer Adler Hotel, this is a family-friendly restaurant. It is
pleasantly furnished, and serves generous portions. Try the *Altmärkische
Hochzeitssuppe* – wedding soup from the Altmark. Small hotel bar.

WERNIGERODE: *Gothisches Haus*
Am Markt, 38 855. **Road map** D3. [(03943) 67 50. FAX (03943) 67 55 37.
Restaurant and hotel are housed in the oldest building in town. The
selection of dishes is extensive, and the service friendly. Apart from the
restaurant there is also a café with conservatory, a wine bar and a small
country inn, serving tasty, inexpensive food.

WITTENBERG: *Carré*
Braunsdorfer Str. 19, 06 886 Wittenberg-Apollensdorf. **Road map** E3.
[(03491) 64 00. FAX (03491) 64 06 40.
Based in the Sorat Hotel, this intimate restaurant is well known for its
regional and international cooking. One of the highlights is a menu,
which changes weekly, featuring dishes from different regions and
countries. There is also a café with a terrace.

SAXONY

AUGUSTUSBURG: *Waldhaus*
Am Kurplatz 7, 09 573. **Road map** E4. [(037291) 203 17. FAX (037291) 203 17.
This restaurant, based in the hotel of the same name, has recently been
renovated. It is pleasant, albeit modest, and serves excellent German
food.

BAD MUSKAU: *Am Schlossbrunnen*
Köbelner Str. 68, 02 953 Bad Muskau. **Road map** F4. [(035771) 52 30.
FAX *(035771) 523 50.*
Family-run restaurant on the edge of town with good views. Pleasing
interior. Regional and international food is served, specializing in fish
caught locally in the heathland lakes and steak dishes. It is worth trying
the excellent Fürst-Pückler ice-cream, a local speciality.

BAUTZEN: *Husarenhof*
Käthe-Kollwitz-Platz 1, 02 625. **Road map** F4. [(03591) 53 02 05.
FAX *(03591) 53 03 30.*
This restaurant, in the Husarenhof Hotel, is tastefully furnished and
serves a varied selection of dishes, gleaned from both regional and
international cuisines. P

CHEMNITZ: *Glashaus*
Salzstr. 56, 09 131. **Road map** E4. [(0371) 334 10. FAX (0371) 334 17 77.
Based in the Renaissance Hotel and surrounded by lush greenery, this
restaurant offers great views of the old town and the restaurant pond.
International dishes are served in this pleasant, modern venue, which
seems almost like a botanical garden. There is also an attractive terrace,
and various seasonal attractions are available to guests.

<table>
<tr><td colspan="2">

Prices of a three course meal without drinks, including cover charge, tax and service in Deutschmarks (and in Euros):

Ⓓ up to 40 DM (up to 20 €)
ⓄⓄ 40–60 DM (20–29 €)
ⓄⓄⓄ 60–80 DM (30–39 €)
ⓄⓄⓄⓄ 80–100 DM (40–49 €)
ⓄⓄⓄⓄⓄ over 100 DM (over 50 €)

</td></tr>
</table>

CREDIT CARDS
Credit cards are accepted.
GARDEN OR TERRACE
Weather permitting, it is possible to eat *al fresco*.
GERMAN WINES
A good selection of German wines.
VEGETARIAN DISHES
The restaurant offers a good selection of meat free and vegetarian dishes.

	CREDIT CARDS	GARDEN OR TERRACE	GERMAN WINES	VEGETARIAN DISHES
DRESDEN: *Fischgalerie* ⒹⒹ	●	■	●	■
Maxstr. 2, 01 067. **Road map** E4. 【 (0351) 490 35 06. FAX (0351) 490 35 08. This restaurant, decorated in avant-garde style, specializes in fish and seafood dishes. Guests can see how the dishes are prepared, just like at home. ● *Mon morning, Sat evening, Sun.*				
DRESDEN: *Villa Emma* Ⓓ	●	■	●	
Stechgrundstr. 2, Dresden-Weißer Hirsch. **Road map** E4. 【 (0351) 264 81–0. Gentle, soft music and original tableware produced by the famous German Bauhaus School provide the perfect ambience for the sophisticated dishes served in this beautiful Art Nouveau villa. P				
DRESDEN: *Das Caroussel* ⒹⒹⒹⒹ	●	■	●	■
Rähnitzgasse 19, Dresden-Neustadt. **Road map** E4. 【 (0351) 800 30. FAX (0351) 800 31 00. The hotel and restaurant are based within a recently restored Baroque palace in the historic city centre, dating from the 18th century. In culinary terms, this is one of the best addresses in Saxony. Only open in the evenings. French cuisine. & ⌘				
GÖRLITZ: *Zum Klötzelmönch* Ⓓ	●		●	■
Fleischerstr. 3, 02 826. **Road map** F4. 【 (03581) 475 80. FAX (03581) 47 58 20. The restaurant belongs to a hotel, based in a recently restored Baroque palace. Fragments of the historic architecture have been incorporated. This is an excellent place to spend a pleasant evening, while enjoying the local cuisine served in the restaurant. ● *Mon.* ⌘				
KAMENZ: *Goldener Hirsch* Ⓓ	●	■	●	■
Markt 10, 01 917. **Road map** F4. 【 (03578) 30 12 21. FAX (03578) 30 44 97. A beautifully situated restaurant, part of a hotel right on the market square, with traditions dating back to the 16th century. The elegant establishment serves exquisite Italian dishes. The rustic Ratskeller, serving traditional German fare, is also recommended. ⌘				
LEIPZIG: *Kaiser Maximilian* ⒹⒹⒹ	●	■	●	■
Neumarkt 9–19, 04 109. **Road map** E4. 【 (0341) 998 69 00. FAX (0341) 998 69 01. A bright restaurant, pleasantly decorated in well-chosen colours, with small recesses for the tables. There is a large selection of Italian dishes, and the menu changes every other week. & ⌘ ♫				
LEIPZIG: *Yamato* ⒹⒹ	●		●	■
Gerberstr. 15, 04 105. **Road map** E4. 【 (0341) 988 10 88. FAX (0341) 477 12 50. This restaurant is very popular with diners who enjoy Japanese food, and it is therefore best to reserve a table. The majority of dishes are prepared in front of diners. The service is courteous – guests are, for example, given small aprons and hot towels. &				
MEISSEN: *Parkhotel Pannonia* Ⓓ	●	■	●	■
Hafenstr. 27–31, 01 662. **Road map** E4. 【 (03521) 722 50. FAX (03521) 72 29 04. This classy hotel–restaurant, based in a large Art Nouveau villa on the banks of the Elbe river, serves regional and international food, including a wide selection of fish dishes. Guests can also dine in the café, which has a terrace, or in the intimate hotel bar. P ⌘				
MORITZBURG: *Waldschänke* Ⓓ	●	■	●	■
Große Fasanenstr., 01 468. **Road map** E4. 【 (035207) 86 00. FAX (035207) 860 93. This restaurant, in the Waldschänke Hotel and near a former pheasantry, serves regional German and international food, with a good choice of game dishes. There is also a winebar and café with a terrace. P & ⌘				
PIRNA: *Deutsches Haus* Ⓓ	●	■	●	■
Niedere Burgstr. 1, 01 796. **Road map** E4. 【 (03501) 52 80 30. FAX (03501) 52 81 04. The restaurant, part of a hotel belonging to the chain of Romantik Hotels, is highly rated in the area. & ⌘ ♫				

TORGAU: *Central-Hotel*   ⓓⓓ ● ●▪
Friedrichplatz 8, 04 860. **Road map** E4. ☎ *(03421) 732 80.* FAX *(03421) 73 28 50.*
Pleasant, modest hotel–restaurant, serving specialities from Baden.

ZWICKAU: *Restaurant Orangerie Holiday Inn*   ⓓⓓⓓ ● ▪ ● ▪
Kornmarkt 9, 08 056. **Road map** E4. ☎ *(0375) 279 20.* FAX *(0375) 71 00 27.*
The Holiday Inn hotel, located within the centre of the old town, has
several restaurants, a small bistro, serving well-prepared, uncomplicated
and inexpensive fare, as well as a hotel bar and a café with terrace. The
service is friendly.

ZITTAU: *Riedel*   ⓓⓓ ● ▪
Friedensstr. 23, 02 763. **Road map** F4. ☎ *(03583) 68 60.* FAX *(03583) 68 61 00.*
The restaurant in the Riedel Hotel serves typical German food. There is
also a small Bavarian pub and a garden.

THURINGIA

ALTENBURG: *Altenburger Hof*   ⓓⓓ ● ● ▪
Schmöllnsche Landstr. 8, 04 600. **Road map** E4. ☎ *(03447) 58 40.* FAX *(03447) 58 44 99.*
The Altenburger Hof Hotel has a restaurant, a café and a day-time bar – in
Germany hotel bars often close at night. 🚫 🏃 🎵

EISENACH: *Hellgrafenhof*   ⓓ ● ▪ ● ▪
Katharinenstr., 99 817. **Road map** D4. ☎ *(03691) 293 90.* FAX *(03691) 29 39 26.*
Modern restaurant and pizzeria in the Hellgrafenhof Hotel, which
specializes in German and Italian dishes. A good selection of fish and
pasta dishes. There is also a pleasant hotel bar, a disco and a café with
terrace. 🚫 🏃 🎵

ERFURT: *Castell*   ⓓⓓⓓ ● ▪ ● ▪
Kleine Arche 4, 99 084. **Road map** D4. ☎ *(0361) 644 22 22.* FAX *(0361) 644 22 22.*
Restaurant, wine bar and Baroque café belong to the same complex,
located in one of the most beautiful parts of the city. Sophisticated dishes
and a good selection of wines are served. ● *Sun evening.* 🚫 🏃

ERFURT: *Zum alten Schwan*   ⓓⓓ ● ▪ ● ▪
Gotthardtstr. 27, 99 084. **Road map** D4. ☎ *(0361) 674 00.* FAX *(0361) 674 04 44.*
The restaurant is housed in the Sorat Hotel situated in a historic part of
the city. The cooking is of a very high standard, and there is a wide
selection of dishes on offer. ● *Sun, Mon morning.* 🚫 🏃

GERA: *Piazzetta*   ⓓ ● ▪ ● ▪
Gutenbergstr. 2a, 07 548. **Road map** D4. ☎ *(0365) 290 94 14.* FAX *(0365) 290 91 00.*
The restaurant is based in the well-located Ramada Hotel. One of its
main attractions is that the diner can see the dishes being prepared from
start to finish. Foods in season are highlighted by special events, such as
"asparagus week" or "game week". The hotel also has a pleasant pub, a
bar and a garden restaurant. Pleasant and friendly service. 🚫 🏃

GOTHA: *Hotel am Schlosspark*   ⓓ ● ▪ ● ▪
Lindenauallee 20–24, 99 867. **Road map** D4. ☎ *(03621) 44 20.* FAX *(03621) 44 24 52.*
A nice, sunny hotel restaurant, with a wealth of plants, offering both
international and local dishes. Pleasant hotel bar. The restaurant is
situated at the end of the castle park. 🚫 🏃

JENA: *Steigenberger Maxx Hotel Jena*   ⓓ ● ▪ ● ▪
Stauffenbergstr. 59, 07 747 Jena-Lobeda. **Road map** D4. ☎ *(03641) 30 00.*
FAX *(03641) 30 08 88.*
Part of the Steigenberger Maxx Hotel, this restaurant specializes in local
dishes. Restaurant and hotel are both themed and decorated to evoke the
style of America in the years 1930–50. There is a beer garden, a hotel bar
and a terrace. The restaurant is relatively inexpensive. 🎵 🚫 🏃

MÜHLHAUSEN: *Brauhaus Zum Löwen*   ⓓ ● ▪ ● ▪
Kornmarkt 3, 99 974. **Road map** D4. ☎ *(03601) 47 10.* FAX *(03601) 44 07 59.*
A rustic hotel–restaurant and pub, serving beer that has been brewed on
the premises as well as traditional German food. 🚫 🏃 🎵

SAALFELD: *Obstgut Gehlen*   ⓓⓓ ● ● ▪
Hohe Str. 1, 07 318. **Road map** D4. ☎ *and* FAX *(03671) 20 27.*
Restaurant and hotel are based in a beautiful Art Nouveau building,
located some distance outside the town. A range of dishes are prepared
in the intimate restaurant, including food from France and Germany's
regions. ● *Jan.* 🏃

	CREDIT CARDS	GARDEN OR TERRACE	GERMAN WINES	VEGETARIAN DISHES

Prices of a three course meal without drinks, including cover charge, tax and service in Deutschmarks (and in Euros):
(DM) up to 40 DM (up to 20 €)
(DM)(DM) 40–60 DM (20–29 €)
(DM)(DM)(DM) 60–80 DM (30–39 €)
(DM)(DM)(DM)(DM) 80–100 DM (40–49 €)
(DM)(DM)(DM)(DM)(DM) over 100 DM (over 50 €)

CREDIT CARDS
Credit cards are accepted.
GARDEN OR TERRACE
Weather permitting, it is possible to eat *al fresco.*
GERMAN WINES
A good selection of German wines.
VEGETARIAN DISHES
The restaurant offers a good selection of meat free and vegetarian dishes.

	CC	G/T	GW	VD
WEIMAR: *Alt Weimar* Prellerstr. 2, 99 423. **Road map** D4. **(** and **FAX** *(03643) 861 90.* A hundred years ago, this restaurant was a popular meeting place for actors from the nearby theatre. Its cooking, consisting mainly of Italian dishes, is renowned throughout the region.	(DM)(DM)	●	■	●	
WEIMAR: *Wolff's Art Hotel & Restaurant* Freiherr-vom-Stein-Allee 3a/b, 99 425. **Road map** D4. **(** *(03643) 540 60.* **FAX** *(03643) 54 06 99.* Both the Art Hotel and its restaurant are furnished in the style created by the Bauhaus School. The menu includes international as well as German dishes. ● *Sun.* 🚻	(DM)	●	■	●	■
WEIMAR: *Anna Amalia* Markt 19, 99 423. **Road map** D4. **(** *(03643) 80 26 50.* **FAX** *(03643) 80 26 14.* This restaurant has a venerable tradition – famous celebrities, including Richard Wagner and Thomas Mann, have dined here, and it has remained very popular to this day. The finest Italian cooking in all of Thuringia is served in the restaurant, with a new menu to choose from every day. The interior is decorated in Art-Deco style. 🚻	(DM)(DM)(DM)	●	■	●	■

MUNICH

	CC	G/T	GW	VD
Austernkeller Stollbergstr. 11, 80 539. **Map** D7. **(** *(089) 29 87 87.* **FAX** *(089) 22 31 66.* This restaurant serves mainly dishes of the day. Seafood, including the *Austern* (oysters) of its name, is a speciality. 🚻	(DM)(DM)(DM)	●		●	■
Bistro Terrine Amalienstr. 89, 80 799 München-Schwabing. **Map** D7. **(** *(089) 28 17 80.* **FAX** *(089) 280 93 16.* The former chef of the Tantris, one of the best restaurants in Germany, now cooks here, preparing delicious, low-calorie dishes, particularly with lamb and fish. Try, for example, ray with artichokes or *zander* in a herb sauce, and for dessert the exquisite crème brûlée. The restaurant has a romantic ambience. ● *Sun.* 🚻	(DM)(DM)(DM)	●	■	●	■
Dallmayr Dienerstr. 14, 80 331. **Map** D7. **(** *(089) 213 51 00.* **FAX** *(089) 213 51 67.* This exceptionally elegant restaurant is popular with locals and visitors alike, just like the famous coffee of the same name. Traditional German and international dishes are served here. ● *Sat until 4 pm & Sun.*	(DM)(DM)(DM)	●		●	■
Käferschänke Prinzregentenstr. 73, 81 675. **Map** D7. **(** *(089) 416 82 47.* **FAX** *(089) 416 86 23.* Serving French and Italian food, this restaurant is one of the finest in Munich. Next door is a delicatessen counter run by the same company, selling regional delicacies. ● *Sun.* 🚻	(DM)(DM)(DM)(DM)	●	■	●	■
Königshof Karlsplatz 25, 80 335. **Map** D7. **(** *(089) 55 13 61 42.* **FAX** *(089) 55 13 61 13.* Elegantly furnished restaurant in the centre of the old town, very highly esteemed by gourmets. Wine lovers will be astonished by the vast selection: 1,000 different drinks are on offer.	(DM)(DM)(DM)(DM)(DM)	●		●	■
Tantris Johann-Fichte-Str. 7, 80 805 München-Schwabing. **Map** D7. **(** *(089) 361 95 90.* **FAX** *(089) 361 84 69.* One of the very best restaurants in Germany, the Tantris will satisfy even the jaded palate of a seasoned gourmet. It is luxuriously furnished, and the service is of a very high standard. Additional attractions include a terrace and a garden that is large enough to cater for 100 people. Reservation is recommended. ● *Mon & Sun.*	(DM)(DM)(DM)(DM)(DM)	●	■	●	■

BAVARIA

ANSBACH: *Drechsels-Stuben*
Am Drechselsgarten 1, 91 522. **Road map** D6. ((0981) 890 20. FAX (0981) 890 26 05.
This restaurant, in the Best Western Hotel Am Drechelsgarten, serves
French and international specialities. You can also while your time away
in the bar or the café which has a terrace. From the restaurant, the diner
will have magnificent views of the surrounding area.

ASCHAFFENBURG: *Post*
Goldbacher Str. 19, 63 739. **Road map** C5. ((06021) 33 40.
FAX (06021) 13 483.
The smartly furnished restaurant, based in the Post Hotel, has received
several awards for its cooking. Diners praise the traditional Bavarian
dishes, including *Wiener Schnitzel*. Special dishes on request.

AUGSBURG: *Die Ecke*
Elias-Holl-Platz 2, 86 150. **Road map** D6. ((0821) 51 06 00. FAX (0821) 31 19 92.
This restaurant, housed in a 16th-century building and traditionally
furnished, has an excellent atmosphere. Many celebrities have dined
here, including Brecht, Diesel and Mozart. One of the best restaurants in
town, it also has a beautiful garden.

AUGSBURG: *Wirthaus im Zuckerhof*
Pfärrle 14, 86 152. **Road map** D6. ((0821) 34 58 30. FAX (0821) 34 58 395.
Modern and pleasant restaurant which has long been run by the same
family. The food is delicious and sophisticated – try the excellent trout
coated in sesame seeds or the vegetable dumplings with a herb sauce.
The restaurant is small, and reservation is recommended. ● Sun.

BAMBERG: *St Nepomuk*
Obere Mühlbrücke 9, 96 049. **Road map** D5. ((0951) 98 42–0. FAX (0951) 984 21 00.
A good restaurant with beautiful views over the surrounding area,
specializing in fish and game dishes.

BAYREUTH: *Eremitage-Cuvée*
Eremitage 6, 95 448. **Road map** D5. ((0921) 79 99 7–0. FAX (0921) 79 99 7–11.
Cosima Wagner, the composer's wife, used to dine in this beautifully
furnished restaurant, one of the finest gastronomic establishments in
town. The excellent cooking is much revered by diners. ● Mon & Sun.

BAYREUTH: *Schloss Thiergarten*
Oberthiergärtner Str. 36, 95 448. **Road map** D5. ((09209) 98 40.
FAX (09209) 984 29.
There are two restaurants in the castle, the elegantly furnished Schloss-
Restaurant, and the less expensive Jagdstübchen, in a former hunting
lodge, which specializes in game dishes.

BURGHAUSEN: *Bayerische Alm*
Robert-Koch-Str. 211, 84 489. **Road map** E7. ((08677) 98 20. FAX (08677) 98 22 00.
Traditional Bavarian hospitality rules in this restaurant, based in the hotel
of the same name. It serves regional specialities, and many are prepared
right in front of the diners.

COBURG: *Kräutergarten*
Rosenauer Str. 30, 96 450. **Road map** D5. ((09561) 64 43 00.
FAX (09561) 75 674.
There are two restaurants in the Blankenburg Hotel, one serving
exquisite gourmet food, the other specializing in local Franconian dishes.
Elegant interiors and friendly service.

DINKELSBÜHL: *Zum kleinen Obristen*
Martin-Luther-Str.1, 91 550. **Road map** D6. ((09851) 577 00. FAX (09851) 57 70 70.
This connoisseurs' restaurant in the Eisenkrug Hotel is superbly furnished
and has a pleasant atmosphere. The menu includes the finest dishes from
the Franconian and Schwabian cuisines as well as international dishes.
The hotel also has a wine bar with a very attractive ceiling. Wine lovers
will enjoy the large selection of wines on offer.

EICHSTÄTT: *Klosterstuben*
Pedettistr. 24–26, 85 072. **Road map** D6. ((08421) 35 00. FAX (08421) 39 00.
This rustic restaurant in the Klosterstuben Hotel is situated in the old
town. The restaurant is small, and the chef prepares the food, mainly
Bavarian dishes, himself.

Prices of a three course meal without drinks, including cover charge, tax and service in Deutschmarks (and in Euros):

(DM) up to 40 DM (up to 20 €)
(DM)(DM) 40–60 DM (20–29 €)
(DM)(DM)(DM) 60–80 DM (30–39 €)
(DM)(DM)(DM)(DM) 80–100 DM (40–49 €)
(DM)(DM)(DM)(DM)(DM) over 100 DM (over 50 €)

CREDIT CARDS
Credit cards are accepted.
GARDEN OR TERRACE
Weather permitting, it is possible to eat al fresco.
GERMAN WINES
A good selection of German wines.
VEGETARIAN DISHES
The restaurant offers a good selection of meat free and vegetarian dishes.

	CREDIT CARDS	GARDEN OR TERRACE	GERMAN WINES	VEGETARIAN DISHES
FREISING: *Zur alten Schießstätte* (DM)(DM)	●	■	●	■

FREISING: *Zur alten Schießstätte*
Drs-von-Daller-Str. 3–5, 85 356. **Road map** D6. ((08161) 53 24 41.
FAX (08161) 53 21 00.
This restaurant, in the Dorint Hotel, serves superbly prepared international dishes, as well as Bavarian specialities. Its reputation for excellent cooking is well deserved.

FÜSSEN: *Geiger* (DM)
Uferstr. 18, Füssen-Hopfen am See. **Road map** D7. ((08362) 70 74.
FAX (08362) 388 38.
An attractive restaurant with a beautiful view of the lake, based in the Geiger Hotel.

GARMISCH-PARTENKIRCHEN: *Reindl's Restaurant* (DM)(DM)
Bahnhofstr. 15, 82 467. **Road map** D7. ((08821) 580 25. FAX (08821) 734 01.
The restaurant is part of the Reindl's Partenkirchner Hof Hotel. Its chef, who previously worked in other well-known establishments around Europe, has received many accolades for his cooking. The cuisine is international, mainly French, one of the specialities being crab cocktail. On request, the restaurant caters for guests who are on a special diet or wish to lose weight. A large selection of wines is available in the restaurant and the bar. **P ●** *Mid-Nov to mid-Dec.* **&** **†**

INGOLSTADT: *Hummel* (DM)(DM)
Feldkirchener Str. 69, 85 055. **Road map** D6. ((0841) 95 45 30. FAX (0841) 592 11.
Pleasant restaurant in the Domizil Hummel Hotel, serving German and Italian dishes. The hotel also has a café with a terrace, a bar and a pub.
● *Sun.* **&** **†**

KEMPTEN: *Peterhof* (DM)(DM)
Salzstr. 1, 87 435. **Road map** C7. ((0831) 524 40. FAX (0831) 52 44 20.
Friendly restaurant in the Peterhof Hotel, serving international food, including Greek dishes, pizzas and regional specialities. **&** **†**

LANDSHUT: *Schloss Schönbrunn* (DM)
Schönbrunn 1, 84 036 Landshut-Schönbrunn. **Road map** E6. ((0871) 952 20.
FAX (0871) 952 22 22.
The restaurant, part of the Schloss Schönbrunn Hotel, is based in the castle. It is furnished in rustic style, and a friendly family atmosphere prevails. Bavarian and international food is served, including excellent poultry and game dishes. **●** *Tue.* **&** **†**

LINDAU: *Bayerischer Hof* (DM)(DM)(DM)
Seepromenade, 88 131. **Road map** C7. ((08382) 91 50. FAX (08382) 91 55 91.
This restaurant, part of the Bayerischer Hof Hotel and situated right on the shores of Bodensee (Lake Constance), is renowned for its excellent service. A variety of fare, including much liked and highly prized trout dishes, is served in stylish surroundings. **&** **†**

NEU-ULM: *Landhof Meinl* (DM)(DM)
Marbacher Str. 4, 89 233 Neu-Ulm–Reutti. **Road map** C6. ((0731) 705 20.
FAX (0731) 705 22 22.
This restaurant belongs to the Silence Hotels chain, a group of hotels situated in particularly quiet and tranquil surroundings. The elegant and rustic restaurant, 7 km (4 miles) south of Neu-Ulm, serves dishes prepared from historical recipes. **●** *Sun.* **&** **†**

NEUBURG AN DER DONAU: *Zum Klosterbräu* (DM)(DM)
Kirchplatz 1, 86 633 Neuburg an der Donau-Bergen. **Road map** D6.
((08431) 677 50. FAX (08431) 411 20.
A restaurant with a long family tradition, specializing in regional food, with a predominance of game and fish dishes. Friendly service. **●** *Sun evening, Mon until 5pm.* **&** **†**

NÜRNBERG (NUREMBERG): *Seewald* (DM)(DM)(DM)
Bucher Hauptstr. 63, 90 427 Nürnberg-Buch. **Road map** D6.
☎ (0911) 38 13 03. FAX (0911) 34 63 13.
This restaurant has a cosy atmosphere. It is adorned with many pictures
and features a traditional tiled stove. Courteous staff serve appetizing
dishes, mainly Italian and German. P ⚅ 🕇 ♫

NÜRNBERG (NUREMBERG): *Essigbrätlein* (DM)(DM)(DM)(DM)(DM)
Weinmarkt 3, 90 403. **Road map** D6. ☎ and FAX (0911) 22 51 31.
Small and cosy restaurant, excellent cooking and elegant table settings.
Booking is recommended. Lunch menu is considerably less expensive.

NÜRNBERG (NUREMBERG): *Schelhorn* (DM)(DM)(DM)
Am Schlosspark 2, 90 475 Nürnberg-Fischbach. **Road map** D6. ☎ (0911) 83 24 24.
This elegant restaurant is popular in the area. Service is courteous and
professional. ● Mon. 🕇

OBERAMMERGAU: *Böld* (DM)(DM)(DM)
König-Ludwig-Str. 10, 82 487. **Road map** D7. ☎ (08822) 91 20. FAX (08822) 71 02.
The restaurant is part of the Böld Hotel, which also has a pub. In summer it is
possible to eat in the garden, which is set out in Bavarian style. ♫ ⚅ 🕇

OBERSTDORF: *Exquisit* (DM)(DM)(DM)
Prinzenstr. 17, 87 561. **Road map** C7. ☎ (08322) 963 30. FAX (08322) 96 33 60.
The restaurant of the Exquisit Hotel provides excellent service, starting
from the moment you enter. The staff are concerned that guests should
feel happy throughout their stay. ● Tue. ♫ ⚅ 🕇

PASSAU: *Heilig-Geist-Stift Schenke/Stiftskeller* (DM)
Heiliggeistgasse 4, 94 032. **Road map** E6. ☎ (0851) 26 07. FAX (0851) 353 87.
Rustic restaurant and wine bar, specializing in Bavarian food, including
fish dishes and delicious Austrian cakes. Open until late. ● Wed. 🕇

PASSAU: *Wilder Mann* (DM)(DM)
Am Rathausplatz, 94 032. **Road map** E6. ☎ (0851) 350 71. FAX (0851) 317 12.
Situated in a good spot, right in the city centre, this restaurant draws
diners with its good cooking and stylish surroundings. ⚅ 🕇

REGENSBURG: *Zum Neuen Gänsbauer* (DM)(DM)
Kepler Str. 10, 93 047. **Road map** D6. ☎ (0941) 578 58. FAX (0941) 56 53 71.
A rustic restaurant with a charming courtyard. Try one of the many exotic
specials of the day, or one of the duck or fish dishes. ⚅ 🕇

REGENSBURG: *David* (DM)(DM)(DM)(DM)
Watmarkt 5, 93 047. **Road map** D6. ☎ (0941) 56 18 58. FAX (0941) 516 18.
This restaurant, in an historical tower near the cathedral, offers quality
regional and international food. There are great views over the charming
old town from the large roof garden. ● Aug. ⚅ 🕇

ROTHENBURG OB DER TAUBER: *Eisenhut* (DM)(DM)
Herrngasse 3–7, 91 541. **Road map** C6. ☎ (09861) 70 50. FAX (09861) 705 45.
The restaurant, in the hotel of the same name, has a pleasingly stylish
interior. Sophisticated dishes, friendly service. There is also a garden
restaurant, a café with terrace and a hotel bar. ● 3 Jan–28 Mar. ♫ 🕇

WÜRZBURG: *Nikolaushof* (DM)(DM)
Johannisweg, 97 082. **Road map** C5. ☎ (0931) 79 75 00. FAX (0931) 797 50 22.
This restaurant is situated on top of a hill, right next to the famous
Baroque chapel. It serves international and Franconian dishes. ● Mon.

WÜRZBURG: *Schloss Steinburg* (DM)(DM)(DM)
Auf dem Steinburg, 97 080 Würzburg-Unterdürrbach. **Road map** C5.
☎ (0931) 970 20. FAX (0931) 971 21.
This restaurant, part of a hotel and based in a castle, boasts attractive and
exclusive furnishings. German cuisine is its speciality, and it is open late
at night. Excellent service. ● 24 Dec. 🕇

BADEN-WÜRTTEMBERG

BADEN-BADEN: *Rebstock* (DM)(DM)
Schlossackerweg 3, 76 534 Baden-Baden–Neuweier. **Road map** B6.
☎ (07223) 572 40.
This restaurant made the French saying "it is better to eat well than to
dress well" its motto. The decor is rustic, and the food includes both
regional and classic dishes. ● Mon, Tue. 🕇

Prices of a three course meal without drinks, including cover charge, tax and service in Deutschmarks (and in Euros):
(DM) up to 40 DM (up to 20 €)
(DM)(DM) 40–60 DM (20–29 €)
(DM)(DM)(DM) 60–80 DM (30–39 €)
(DM)(DM)(DM)(DM) 80–100 DM (40–49 €)
(DM)(DM)(DM)(DM)(DM) over 100 DM (over 50 €)

CREDIT CARDS
Credit cards are accepted.
GARDEN OR TERRACE
Weather permitting, it is possible to eat *al fresco*.
GERMAN WINES
A good selection of German wines.
VEGETARIAN DISHES
The restaurant offers a good selection of meat free and vegetarian dishes.

	CREDIT CARDS	GARDEN OR TERRACE	GERMAN WINES	VEGETARIAN DISHES

BADEN-BADEN: *Weblauers Papalangi*   (DM)(DM)
Lichtentaler Str. 13, 76 534. **Road map** B6. ((07221) 316 16. FAX (07221) 327 88.
This restaurant, one of the best in the area, is run by a couple who do their utmost to make diners feel comfortable. Try the lamb with courgettes or one of the fish dishes. Good selection of wines. Reasonable prices and high standard of quality. 🛉 ● *Sun, Mon.* 🛉

| | ● | ▦ | ● | ▦ |

BADEN-BADEN: *Stahlbad*   (DM)(DM)
Augustaplatz 2, 76 530. **Road map** B6. ((07221) 245 69.
FAX (07221) 390 22.
Elegant, romantic restaurant with a terrace, specializing in the most diverse range of casseroles, including many potato and fish dishes. Another attraction on the menu is the venison medallions served with chestnuts. ● *Mon.* 🛉

| | ● | ▦ | ● | ▦ |

BADEN-BADEN: *Zum Alde Gott*   (DM)(DM)(DM)(DM)(DM)
Weinstr. 10, 76 534 Baden-Baden–Neuweier. **Road map** B6.
((07223) 55 13. FAX (07223) 606 24.
Beautifully located restaurant with a terrace, from where the diner has a magnificent view of the surrounding Baden vineyards. The family-run restaurant serves regional specialities – diners are particularly fond of the home-cooked goose and the selection of local fish and game dishes. The restaurant ranks as one of the best in Germany. ● *Wed, Thu, 3 weeks in Jan.* 🛉

| | ● | ▦ | ● | ▦ |

BRAUNSBACH: *Schloss Döttingen*   (DM)(DM)(DM)
Hubertusstr. 2, 74 542 Braunsbach-Döttingen. **Road map** C6.
((07906) 10 10. FAX (07906) 101 10.
This restaurant, which is part of the Schloss Döttingen Hotel, is situated 16 km (10 miles) north of Schwäbisch Hall. Based in a former hunting lodge dating from the 12th century, it serves international cuisine. There is also a wine bar, a café with a terrace and a pleasant drawing room with an open fireplace. The restaurant only accepts pre-booked organized groups. ● *Sun.* 🛉

| | ● | ▦ | ● | ▦ |

FREIBURG IM BREISGAU: *Enoteca*   (DM)(DM)
Gerberau 21, 79 098. **Road map** B7. ((0761) 389 91 30.
FAX (0761) 38 99 13 24.
Modern, elegantly and stylishly furnished restaurant, located in the old town and beautifully set amid period buildings. The restaurant specializes in light Italian cuisine.

| | ● | | | |

HEIDELBERG: *Schlossweinstube Schönmehls*   (DM)(DM)(DM)
Im Schlosshof, 69 117. **Road map** B7. ((06221) 979 70.
FAX (06221) 16 79 69.
Modern and elegantly furnished restaurant, housed in a castle. When the weather permits, tables are set out on the terrace. Among the many dishes on the menu, the roast duck with all the trimmings is outstanding. ● *Wed, early Jan–early Feb.*

| | ● | ▦ | | |

HEIDELBERG: *Simplicissimus*   (DM)(DM)(DM)
Ingrimstr. 16, 69 117. **Road map** C6. ((06221) 18 33 36. FAX (06221) 18 19 80.
This restaurant, in the old town, is as popular with tourists as with the locals. The service is excellent. French cuisine predominates; even the simplest dishes are very tasty. The selection of wines includes German as well as Portuguese and Italian wines. Booking is recommended.
● *Tue.* 🛉

| | ● | | ● | |

HEILBRONN: *Grüner Kranz*   (DM)(DM)
Lohtorstr. 9, 74 072 Heilbronn-Neckar. **Road map** C6. ((07131) 96 17 77.
FAX (07131) 96 17 55.
Modern and elegant restaurant, specializing in traditional beef dishes. Try, for example, the roast beef with onion. ● *Mon, 3 weeks in Aug.* 🛉

| | ● | ▦ | ● | |

KARLSRUHE: *Ketterer*
Bahnhofplatz 14, 76 137. **Road map** B6. **[** (0721) 371 50. **FAX** (0721) 371 51 13.
The restaurant is based in the Residenz Hotel, which is part of the
Ringhotel chain. The specialities include tripe in a soured sauce, served
with potatoes and salad, pork medallions with *Spätzle* (a type of small
dumpling) and trout. **&** **†**

KARLSRUHE: *Oberländer Weinstube*
Akademiestr. 7, 76 133. **Road map** B6. **[** (0721) 250 66. **FAX** (0721) 211 57.
This restaurant has a beautiful interior, reminiscent of the 1920s, and a
courtyard in the garden. Huge selection of wines and dishes from around
the world. Excellent service; a pleasant time is usually had by all diners
and the food is excellent. **●** *Sun, 2 weeks in summer.*

KARLSRUHE: *Zum Ochsen*
Pfinzstr. 64, 76 227 Karlsruhe-Durlach. **Road map** B6. **[** (0721) 94 38 60.
FAX (0721) 943 86 43.
The very helpful staff will assist even the most indecisive person in
choosing the right meal and drink. The frequently changing menu is
dominated by French dishes. Try the green salad with oranges. One of
the longest wine lists in Germany. **●** *Mon, Tue.* **&** **†**

KONSTANZ: *Siber*
Seestr. 25, 78 464. **Road map** C7. **[** (07531) 630 44/45.
FAX (07531) 648 13.
Elegantly furnished restaurant, filled with flowers, based in the Seehotel.
Superb classic French cuisine, a good selection of wines and excellent
service. After the meal, the adjacent casinos may tempt diners. **♫** **†**

LUDWIGSBURG: *Stahl*
Dorfstr. 4, 71 636 Ludwigsburg-Pflugfelden. **Road map** C6. **[** (07141) 441 10.
FAX (07141) 44 11 42.
This stylishly furnished restaurant is based in a small hotel of the same
name. The menu is varied – the Schwabian dishes, particularly the roast
meat with onions, are especially worth trying. **&** **†**

MANNHEIM: *Wartburg*
68 159 Mannheim. **Road map** B5. **[** (0621) 12 00 90.
FAX (0621) 12 00 94 44.
This restaurant is located in a hotel of the same name, offering many
sophisticated dishes from around the world, and a large choice of fine
wines. Service is excellent, and the interior elegant.

MARBACH: *Schillerhöhe*
Schillerhöhe 14, 71 672. **Road map** C6. **[** (07144) 855 90.
FAX (07144) 905 88.
The restaurant, based in the Parkhotel, has an extensive menu which
offers dishes to suit every taste.

RAVENSBURG: *Goldene Uhr*
Saarlandstr. 44, 88 212. **Road map** C7. **[** (0751) 362 90.
FAX (0751) 36 29 256.
A pleasant restaurant in the Goldene Uhr Hotel, specializing mainly in
fish and game dishes. **●** *Thu.*

ROTTWEIL: *Haus zum Sternen*
Haupstr. 60, 78 628. **Road map** C7. **[** (0741) 533 00. **FAX** (0741) 53 30 30.
This smart restaurant and historic winebar, in the Haus zum Sternen
Hotel, tries to satisfy all its customers' culinary desires, however
sophisticated. The menu, which changes every 2–3 weeks, includes a
good selection of vegetarian dishes. From the terrace diners have good
views of the Neckar valley. **●** *Mon.* **†**

SALEM: *Reck*
Bahnhofstr. 111, 88 682. **Road map** C7. **[** (07553) 201. **FAX** (07553) 202.
A showcase restaurant in the hotel of the same name, serving very tasty
regional cuisine and offering a good choice of wines. During the summer
visitors can dine in the garden. **●** *Wed evening, Thu.* **†**

SCHWÄBISCH GMÜND: *Gmünder Geigerle*
Türlensteg 9, 73 525. **Road map** C6. **[** (07171) 35 90. **FAX** (07171) 35 93 59.
The restaurant is based in the Rühle City Hotel Pelikan in the old town.
The menu is characterized by dishes drawn from international cuisines.
● *Sat half day, Sun evening.* **&** **†**

For key to symbols *see back flap*

Prices of a three course meal without drinks, including cover charge, tax and service in Deutschmarks (and in Euros):

(DM) up to 40 DM (up to 20 €)
(DM)(DM) 40–60 DM (20–29 €)
(DM)(DM)(DM) 60–80 DM (30–39 €)
(DM)(DM)(DM)(DM) 80–100 DM (40–49 €)
(DM)(DM)(DM)(DM)(DM) over 100 DM (over 50 €)

CREDIT CARDS
Credit cards are accepted.
GARDEN OR TERRACE
Weather permitting, it is possible to eat al fresco.
GERMAN WINES
A good selection of German wines.
VEGETARIAN DISHES
The restaurant offers a good selection of meat free and vegetarian dishes.

	CREDIT CARDS	GARDEN OR TERRACE	GERMAN WINES	VEGETARIAN DISHES

STUTTGART: *Ecco* — (DM)
Plieninger Str. 100, 70 567. **Road map** C6. **(** (0711) 900 72 72. **FAX** (0711) 900 72 73.
Bistro with modern decor. The speciality of this restaurant is international food; try for example the liver with spinach, highly rated by regulars. 🔥 🏃

●	◼		◼

STUTTGART: *Weber's Gourmet im Turm* — (DM)(DM)(DM)
Jahnstr. 120, 70 597 Stuttgart-Degerloch. **Road map** C6. **(** (0711) 24 89 96 10.
FAX (0711) 24 89 96 27.
This restaurant is in a fantastic position, in a television tower, from where diners have stunning views over the town. The table settings are also exceptionally pretty and worth mentioning. All the dishes, mainly Italian and French cuisine, are tastefully prepared, and the service is highly professional. ● *Mon, Sun.* 🔥

●	◼	●	

STUTTGART: *Schloss Solitude* — (DM)(DM)(DM)(DM)(DM)
Kavaliersbau Haus 2, 70 197 Stuttgart. **Road map** C6.
((0711) 69 20 25. **FAX** (0711) 699 07 71.
The breathtakingly beautiful castle chambers and the regal cuisine ensure a culinary as well as an aesthetic experience. Receptions are held in the castle banqueting halls. **P** ● *Mon, Sun evening.* 🏃

●	◼		◼

TÜBINGEN: *Carat* — (DM)(DM)
Wöhrdstr. 5–9, 72 072. **Road map** C6. **(** (07071) 13 91 00.
FAX (07071) 13 92 50.
This restaurant, in the Domizil Hotel, serves especially light veal, beef and fish dishes. There is also a wide selection of pasta dishes. ● *Sun.*
🔥 🏃

			◼

WEINGARTEN: *Altdorfer Hof* — (DM)(DM)
Burachstr. 12, 88 250. **Road map** B6. **(** (0751) 500 90. **FAX** (0751) 50 09 70.
The restaurant, in the Altdorfer Hotel, serves exquisite Schwabian specialities. ● *Mon, Sun evening.* 🏃 🎵

●	◼	●	◼

RHINELAND–PALATINATE & SAARLAND

KOBLENZ: *Loup de mer* — (DM)(DM)
Neustadt 12, 56 068. **Road map** B5. **(** (0261) 161 38.
FAX (0261) 911 45 46.
This restaurant is one of the best in town, serving mainly seafood and fish dishes. ● *Sun.* 🏃

●	◼	●	◼

MAINZ: *Drei Lilien* — (DM)(DM)
Ballplatz 2, 55 116. **Road map** B5. **(** (06131) 22 50 68.
FAX (06131) 23 77 23.
Rustic restaurant serving traditional regional food. Booking is advisable. ● *Mon, Sun, 2 weeks in the summer.*

●	◼		

MAINZ: *Der Halbe Mond* — (DM)(DM)(DM)(DM)
In der Witz 12, 55 252 Mainz-Kastel. **Road map** B5.
((06134) 239 13.
The restaurant, located on the Hesse side of the Rhine, serves local specialities from the Rhineland–Palatine region. The venue is tastefully furnished, and the service is good.

●		●	

MARIA LAACH: *Seehotel Maria Laach* — (DM)(DM)
Ortsteil Maria Laach, 56 653 Glees-Maria Laach. **Road map** B5.
((02652) 58 40. **FAX** (02652) 58 45 22.
This well-known restaurant, situated in quiet and tranquil surroundings right next to the famous Benedictine monastery, specializes in fish dishes. Its delicious eel and salmon are particularly highly recommended. There is also a café with a terrace. 🔥 🏃

	◼	●	◼

SAARBRÜCKEN: *Schloss Halberg*
Am Halberg, 66 121 Saarbrücken outskirts. **Road map** B6. **(** (0681) 631 81.
FAX *(0681) 63 86 55.*
Beautifully situated inside Halberg castle, from where there is an
excellent view of the park and surroundings. Elegant service, French
cuisine. **P** ● *Sat morning, Sun.*

SAARBRÜCKEN: *Winzerstube/Restaurant Quack*
Deutschherrnstr. 3, 66 117. **Road map** B6. **(** (0681) 521 53.
FAX *(0681) 584 99 10.*
This comfortably furnished restaurant is well known in the area. The
dishes are presented in a tasteful and stylish way. Try the goose prepared
in the French style. Very courteous service. **P** ● *Mon, Sat morning, Sun
evening, 3 weeks in Jul.*

SPEYER: *Zweierlei*
Johannesstr. 1, 67 346. **Road map** B6. **(** (06232) 611 10. FAX *(06232) 611 29.*
Modern restaurant serving good food, mainly German.

SPEYER: *Backmulde*
Karmeliterstr. 11–13, 67 346. **Road map** B6. **(** (06232) 715 77.
FAX *(06232) 62 94 74.*
Very cosy restaurant; tasty French-influenced food. ● *Mon, Sun.*

TRIER: *Römischer Kaiser-Taverne*
Porta-Nigra-Platz 6, 54 292. **Road map** A5. **(** (0651) 977 00. FAX *(0651) 97 70 99.*
A split-level restaurant, situated in Trier's main square, a fact that has
guaranteed a never-ending stream of diners for the past 100 years. A
romantic setting, stylish furniture and plenty of light wood in the decor.
The food is German and international. **P**

TRIER: *Pfeffermühle*
Zurlaubener Ufer 76, 54 292 Trier-Zurlauben. **Road map** A5. **(** (0651) 261 33.
The restaurant is in a former fishermen's house dating from the 18th
century, beautifully situated on the banks of the Mosel River. Furnished
with numerous antiques and etchings. Classic and regional cuisine;
among the specialities are game, lamb and goose dishes. Booking is
recommended. **P** ● *Mon morning, Sun.*

WORMS: *Rôtisserie Dubs*
Kirchstr. 6, 67 550 Worms-Rheindürkheim. **Road map** B5.
((06242) 20 23. FAX *(06242) 20 24.*
Although situated in a less interesting area of Worms, it is well worth
visiting this very elegant and glamorously furnished restaurant, which
specializes in sophisticated dishes, revealing a French influence. The
manageress will be delighted to recommend a suitable wine. Booking is
advisable. ● *Tue, Sun morning.*

HESSE

ALSFELD: *Krone*
Schellengasse 2, 36 304. **Road map** C4. **(** (06631) 40 41–42.
FAX *(06631) 40 43.*
Both the restaurant and the Krone Hotel are known for their excellent
service. Among the house specialities are game dishes from its own
hunts. The menu features frequent variations. ● *Sun.*

BAD HOMBURG: *Charlys Bistro*
Kaiser-Friedrich-Promenade 69–75, 61 348. **Road map** C5. **(** (06172) 18 10.
FAX *(06172) 18 16 30.*
In the romantic restaurant of the Steigenberger Bad Homburg Hotel,
diners are seated at beautifully set tables, and attended by professional
and courteous staff who serve delicacies originating from America as well
as international cuisine. Interesting combination of dishes. The wine list
comprises around 130 wines from all over the world.

DARMSTADT: *Weinstuben*
Schleiermacherstr. 10, 64 283. **Road map** C5. **(** (06151) 290 80.
FAX *(06151) 235 92.*
Excellent restaurant in the Weinmichel Hotel, in the city centre. Its warm,
pastel interior is nicely fitted out with stylish furniture and comprises
some interesting interlinked seating areas. The speciality of the house is
salmon in saffron. The wine list, which is fairly extensive, includes
principally German and French wines.

For key to symbols *see back flap*

Prices of a three course meal without drinks,
including cover charge, tax and service in
Deutschmarks (and in Euros):
(DM) up to 40 DM (up to 20 €)
(DM)(DM) 40–60 DM (20–29 €)
(DM)(DM)(DM) 60–80 DM (30–39 €)
(DM)(DM)(DM)(DM) 80–100 DM (40–49 €)
(DM)(DM)(DM)(DM)(DM) over 100 DM (over 50 €)

CREDIT CARDS
Credit cards are accepted.
GARDEN OR TERRACE
Weather permitting, it is possible to eat
al fresco.
GERMAN WINES
A good selection of German wines.
VEGETARIAN DISHES
The restaurant offers a good selection of
meat free and vegetarian dishes.

	CREDIT CARDS	GARDEN OR TERRACE	GERMAN WINES	VEGETARIAN DISHES
ELTVILLE AM RHEIN: *Marcobrunn* (DM)(DM)(DM)(DM)(DM) Hauptstr. 43, 65 346 Eltville-Erbach. **Road map** B5. [(06123) 67 60. FAX (06123) 67 64 00. The Schloss Reinhartshausen Hotel complex, surrounded by a park and beautifully situated at the foot of vineyards, has several restaurants. Marcobrunn, an elegant establishment for gourmets, serves international cuisine, including Austrian dishes. The Schlosskeller restaurant serves mainly regional food. The wine list includes many wines produced in the restaurant's vineyards. ● *Mon.* 🅰 🅰 🎵	●	▨	●	▨
FRANKFURT AM MAIN: *Maaschanz* (DM)(DM) Färberstr. 75, 60 594 Frankfurt-Sachsenhausen. **Road map** C5. [(069) 62 28 86. FAX (069) 62 28 86. This restaurant, situated in one of the main tourist districts of Frankfurt, specializes in fish dishes. *Apfelwein,* the local cider, is available here as everywhere. ● *Mon.*	●			
FRANKFURT AM MAIN: *Zum Schwarzen Stern* (DM)(DM) Römerberg 6, 60 311. **Road map** C5. [(069) 29 19 79. FAX (069) 28 05 01. Modern, elegant restaurant in the old town, conveniently located right next to the cathedral. Regional cuisine of a high standard. 🅰 🅰	●		●	▨
FRANKFURT AM MAIN: *Bistro 77* (DM)(DM)(DM) Ziegelhüttenweg 1, 60 598 Frankfurt-Sachsenhausen. **Road map** C5. [(069) 61 40 40. The restaurant, which takes a German saying as its motto – "A good cook is the best doctor", is run by two brothers from Alsace, who serve French food. Try the truffles. ● *Sat morning, Sun.* 🅰 🅰	●			▨
FRANKFURT AM MAIN: *Tigerpalast* (DM)(DM)(DM) Heiligenkreuzgasse 20, 60 313. **Road map** C5. [(069) 92 00 22 25. FAX (069) 92 00 22 17. This venue is unusual among German restaurants, presenting a variety show in an elegant restaurant. It is easy to spend a pleasant evening here while watching the excellent show, which includes circus artists and other performers. Excellent service. A large selection of wines and many interesting Italian dishes. ● *Mon, Sun.* 🅰	●		●	▨
FRANKFURT AM MAIN: *L'Artichoc* (DM)(DM)(DM)(DM) Bockenheimer Landstr. 89–91, 60 325. **Road map** C5. [(069) 90 74 87 71. FAX (069) 90 74 87 72. This restaurant, located in the basement of the Palmenhof Hotel, is a popular tourist attraction just like the neighbouring botanical gardens. Traditional German and Asian food is served here. ● *Sun.* 🅰	●		●	▨
FRANKFURT AM MAIN: *Ente* (DM)(DM)(DM)(DM)(DM) Konrad-Adenauer-str. 7, 60 313. **Road map** C5. [(069) 298 10. FAX (069) 298 18 16. The most elegant of Frankfurt's restaurants, based in the Arabella Sheraton Grand Hotel, is frequented by many well-known celebrities. The service and cuisine are of a very high standard. [P]	●			
FULDA: *Zum Stiftskämmerer* (DM) Kämmerzeller Str. 10, 36 041 Fulda-Kämmerzell. **Road map** C5. [(0661) 523 69. FAX (0661) 595 45. This cosy and comfortable restaurant with rustic decor offers a variety of delicious dishes such as leg of lamb with a herb crust.	●	▨		
FULDA: *Dachsbau* (DM)(DM) Pfandhausstr. 8, 36 037. **Road map** C5. [(0661) 741 12. FAX (0661) 741 10. Beautifully situated split-level restaurant, in a road known as "the street for the hungry", with unusual furniture and decor, such as a huge wine barrel. Excellent selection of dishes and wines. ● *Mon morning.*	●	▨	●	

GIESSEN: *Köbler*
Westanlage 35, 35 390. **Road map** C4. ((0641) 760 86. FAX (0641) 760 88.
The Köhler Hotel and restaurant have been run by the same family for
many years, and the atmosphere is relaxed throughout. The menu has a
large selection of dishes, including German, Italian, French and
occasionally Hungarian food, and there is also a pleasant wine bar.

KASSEL: *Zum Steinernen Schweinchen*
Konrad-Adenauer-Str. 117, 34 132 Kassel-Wilhelmshöhe. **Road map** C4.
((0561) 61 94 04 80. FAX (0561) 40 58 54.
The complex comprises a restaurant, a hotel and a small brewery, which
can be visited. The dining room has an open fireplace and leads out to
the beer garden. The cooking is excellent.

LIMBURG: *Wirtshaus Obermühle*
Am Huttig 3, 65 549. **Road map** B5. (*and* FAX (06431) 279 27.
This lovely restaurant, situated in the old town near the cathedral and
right by the Lahn river, is housed in a 12th-century mill, renovated in the
traditional style. Seasonal, regional and international food, and bar.

MARBURG: *Das kleine Restaurant*
Barfüßertor 25, 35 037. **Road map** C4. ((06421) 222 93. FAX (06421) 514 95.
This restaurant, furnished like a French boudoir, serves appetizing French
food. ● *Mon.*

MICHELSTADT: *Drei Hasen*
Braunstr. 5, 64 720. **Road map** C5. ((06061) 710 17. FAX (06061) 725 96.
This well-run restaurant, in the hotel of the same name, is situated right
on the historic market square. Rustic furnishings and cuisine to match,
majoring on game dishes. Beer garden. ● *Mon.*

RÜDESHEIM AM RHEIN: *Krone*
Rheinuferstr. 10, 65 385 Rüdesheim-Assmannshausen. **Road map** B5.
((06722) 40 30. FAX (06722) 30 49.
The traditions of this restaurant, in the Krone Hotel, go back 400 years.
The interior, with its beautiful wooden features, is like a small museum.
Exquisite fish and game dishes, such as lobster in a champagne sauce or
venison with nuts. Wide selection of wines.

WEILBURG: *Alte Reitschule*
Langgasse 25, 35 781. **Road map** B5. ((06471) 390 96. FAX (06471) 391 99.
This restaurant, in the Schlosshotel, is based in former riding stables. The
pleasantly furnished venue serves international food – the lamb comes
highly recommended. The hotel also has a café with terrace.

WETZLAR: *Der Postreiter*
Konrad-Adenauer-Promenade 20, 35 578. **Road map** C5. ((06441) 90 30, 428 01.
FAX (06441) 90 31 00.
There are several restaurants in the Bürgerhof Hotel, among them the
Jägerstübchen and the Königlich-Preußisches Grenz-Post-Amt (royal
Prussian border post office), where regional and international dishes are
on offer. Large selection of wines. Very friendly service. ● *Thu.*

WIESBADEN: *Domäne*
65 205 Wiesbaden-Erbenheim outskirts. **Road map** B5. ((0611) 73 74 60.
FAX (0611) 73 74 79.
A vast complex, including a café, a restaurant, a patisserie, a wine bar
and more, situated on a farm a few kilometers from the centre of town.
The establishment is known throughout the region, in part because of its
excellent cuisine.

WIESBADEN: *Käfer's Bistro*
Kurhausplatz 1, 65 189. **Road map** B5. ((0611) 53 62 00. FAX (0611) 53 62 22.
Pleasant bistro in a spa building with garden and all-day piano music.
The restaurant is open late. The food is traditional German, although the
furnishings are more reminiscent of a French bistro.

NORTH RHINE–WESTPHALIA

AACHEN: *Schloss Schönau*
Schönauer Allee 20, 52 072 Aachen. **Road map** A4. (*and* FAX (0241) 17 35 77.
This excellent gourmet restaurant, about 5 km (3 miles) from the centre
of Aachen, is based in an 11th-century castle. French nouvelle cuisine is
served in a nostalgic and elegant ambience. There is also a bistro, with a
more rustic atmosphere. ● *Mon, 2 weeks early Jul.*

For key to symbols *see back flap*

Prices of a three course meal without drinks, including cover charge, tax and service in Deutschmarks (and in Euros):
(DM) up to 40 DM (up to 20 €)
(DM)(DM) 40–60 DM (20–29 €)
(DM)(DM)(DM) 60–80 DM (30–39 €)
(DM)(DM)(DM)(DM) 80–100 DM (40–49 €)
(DM)(DM)(DM)(DM)(DM) over 100 DM (over 50 €)

CREDIT CARDS
Credit cards are accepted.
GARDEN OR TERRACE
Weather permitting, it is possible to eat *al fresco*.
GERMAN WINES
A good selection of German wines.
VEGETARIAN DISHES
The restaurant offers a good selection of meat free and vegetarian dishes.

AACHEN: *St Benedikt*
Benediktusplatz 12, 52 076. **Road map** A4. ☎ (02408) 28 88. FAX (02408) 28 77.
Diners tend to feel at home in this restaurant, which has beautiful, romantic and antique furnishings, and offers impeccable service. The menu is changed twice a week. ● *Mon, Sun.* ⚐

AACHEN: *Gala*
Monheimsallee 44, 52 062. **Road map** A4. ☎ (0241) 15 30 13. FAX (0241) 15 85 78.
This classy restaurant is located in a casino. Here everything is glamorous, not just the furnishings and silver tableware, but the food too. The chef is very fond of desserts; portions are large and imaginatively presented. ● *Mon, Sun, 3 weeks in summer.* ♿ ⚐

BAD HONNEF: *Alexanders Restaurant*
Alexander-von-Humboldt-Str. 20, 53 604. **Road map** B4. ☎ (02224) 77 10. FAX (02244) 77 15 55.
One of the restaurants in the Seminaris Hotel, situated 18 km (11 miles) southeast of Bonn. German and international food. 🅿

BIELEFELD: *Westfälische Hofstube*
Niedernholz 2, 33 699 Bielefeld-Oldentrup. **Road map** C3. ☎ (0521) 209 00. FAX (0521) 209 01 00.
The restaurant is part of the Oldentruper Hof Hotel which belongs to the Best Western hotel group. It is a favourite place in the town for meeting a friend. Stylish setting; delicious regional cooking. The Scheune restaurant is also part of the hotel.

BONN: *Zur Lindenwirtin Aennchen*
Aennchenplatz 2, 53 173 Bonn-Bad Godesberg. **Road map** B4.
☎ (0228) 31 20 51. FAX (0228) 531 73.
Romantic restaurant with original furnishings, known throughout the entire Rhineland for its fantastic selections of wines from around the world. The chef often uses wine to cook his elaborate dishes, featuring both German and international recipes. ● *Sun.*

BONN: *Ristorante Salvatore*
Thomas Mann Str. 18, 53 111. **Road map** B4. ☎ (0228) 63 22 55. FAX (0228) 63 83 75.
Special lunch menu, extensive salad buffet, fish dishes. The cuisine is predominantly Italian, and Italian wines are also on offer.

BONN: *Halbedel's Gasthaus*
Rheinallee 47, 53 173 Bonn-Bad Godesberg. **Road map** B4.
☎ (0228) 35 42 53. FAX (0228) 35 25 34.
A favourite haunt of politicians, this restaurant is housed in a beautiful Art Nouveau villa in an elegant part of the town. Diners will undoubtedly take away fond memories of their meal. Specialities include rabbit in French pastry. Gallant service, stylish tableware. ● *Mon.* ⚐

BRÜHL: *Seerose*
Römerstr. 1–7, 50 321. **Road map** B4. ☎ (02232) 20 40. FAX (02232) 20 45 23.
This restaurant, in the Treff-Hansa Hotel, located about half-way between Cologne and Bonn, is in a particularly pleasant spot, surrounded by extensive green spaces. The elegant establishment offers its diners the choice between a number of different cuisines, including American, French and Bavarian. The hotel also has a café with a garden and the Treff bar, which is a popular meeting place.

DETMOLD: *Opera*
Paulinenstr. 19, 32 756. **Road map** C3. ☎ (05231) 93 70. FAX (05231) 93 73 33.
A smart restaurant in the Residenz Hotel, part of the Best Western chain of hotels, situated not far from the castle. The menu includes both regional and international dishes. There is also a pleasant café, which evokes the atmosphere of a botanical garden, and a bar. 🅿 ♿ ⚐

	CREDIT CARDS	GARDEN OR TERRACE	GERMAN WINES	VEGETARIAN DISHES
St Benedikt (DM)(DM)(DM)	●	■	●	
Gala (DM)(DM)(DM)(DM)(DM)	●			■
Alexanders Restaurant (DM)(DM)	●	■		■
Westfälische Hofstube (DM)(DM)	●		●	■
Zur Lindenwirtin Aennchen (DM)(DM)	●	■	●	■
Ristorante Salvatore (DM)(DM)	●	■		■
Halbedel's Gasthaus (DM)(DM)(DM)(DM)	●	■	●	
Seerose (DM)(DM)	●	■	●	
Opera (DM)(DM)	●	■	●	■

DÜSSELDORF: *Libanon Restaurant*
Berger Str. 19–21, 40 213. **Road map** B4. (0211) 13 49 17.
FAX (0211) 13 49 97.
This romantic and elegant restaurant offers diners the chance, from
Wednesday to Saturday, to watch belly dancing, which is very popular
with Middle Eastern guests. Food and wines are Lebanese.

DÜSSELDORF: *Canonicus*
Neusser Tor 16, 40 625 Düsseldorf-Gerresheim. **Road map** B4.
(0211) 28 96 44. FAX (0211) 28 35 03.
The restaurant is on the first floor of a 400-year-old building. Although
small and compact, the venue is pleasant. The avant-garde cuisine serves
up numerous culinary surprises. ● *Sun evening.*

DÜSSELDORF: *Savini*
Stromstr. 47, 40 221 Düsseldorf-Hafen. **Road map** B4. (0211) 39 39 31.
FAX (0211) 39 17 19.
This modern restaurant and terrace sets its tables in innovative ways.
There is also a long bar, reminiscent of film sets. Many celebrities have
visited this establishment, which is situated in an interesting spot in the
Rhine harbour district, opposite the TV building (WDR). The restaurant is
always well frequented, and advance booking is definitely recommended.
Charming service. The wine list includes an extensive selection of Italian
wines. ● *Sun.*

DÜSSELDORF: *Im Schiffchen*
Kaiserswerther Markt 9, 40 489 Düsseldorf-Kaiserswerth. **Road map** B4.
(0211) 40 10 50. FAX (0211) 40 36 67.
This restaurant has gained the highest accolades from restaurant critics in
Germany, and so it is essential to reserve a table. The talented master
chef, Jean Claude Bourgeuil, works here together with his wife. Diners
can choose from countless exquisite dishes as well as 600 different
wines. ● *Mon, Sun, Easter week.*

ESSEN: *Résidence*
Auf der Forst 1, 45 219 Essen-Kettwig. **Road map** B4. (02054) 89 11.
FAX (02054) 825 01.
The Résidence Hotel, based in a beautiful villa, has two restaurants: one
specializing in classical German cuisine, and the second preparing light
French dishes. The service is very friendly, and staff will be happy to
help undecided diners to choose a meal and a suitable wine. **P**
● *Mon, Sun, 3 weeks in summer.*

HAGEN: *Felsengarten*
Wasserloses Tal 4, 58 093. **Road map** B4. (02331) 39 10.
FAX (02331) 39 11 53.
This modern restaurant, part of the Queens Hotel, serves a large number
of delicious dishes from around the world. Among some of the
specialities on the menu, the masterfully prepared goose is worth trying.
Pleasant and professional service.

HÖXTER: *Entenfang*
Godelheimer Str. 16, 37 671. **Road map** C3. (05271) 970 80.
FAX (05271) 97 08 88.
The restaurant in the Weserberghof Hotel is attractively situated, with
views of the Weser and Solling rivers. The restaurant has an intimate,
homely atmosphere. The chef of the stylish and elegant establishment
prepares classical international dishes, including Scandinavian specialities.
Set-price menus are available.

KAMP-LINTFORT: *Casino im Park*
Friedrich-Heinrich-Allee 54, 47 475. **Road map** A4. (02842) 963 40.
FAX (02842) 606 61.
Pleasant restaurant with an open fireplace, based in the hotel of the same
name, serving delicious regional fare. The hotel also has a pub and a
small café.

KÖLN (COLOGNE): *Restaurant Pöttgen*
Landmannstr.19, 50 825. **Road map** B4. (0221) 55 52 46.
FAX (0221) 559 54 50.
This traditional restaurant, based in an Art Nouveau house with typical
Rhineland interior, has been run by the same family for four generations.
It serves specialities from Cologne and the Rhineland, fresh from the
market. *Flammkuchen* is a house favourite. ● *Mon.*

Prices of a three course meal without drinks, including cover charge, tax and service in Deutschmarks (and in Euros):
(DM) up to 40 DM (up to 20 €)
(DM)(DM) 40–60 DM (20–29 €)
(DM)(DM)(DM) 60–80 DM (30–39 €)
(DM)(DM)(DM)(DM) 80–100 DM (40–49 €)
(DM)(DM)(DM)(DM)(DM) over 100 DM (over 50 €)

CREDIT CARDS
Credit cards are accepted.
GARDEN OR TERRACE
Weather permitting, it is possible to eat *al fresco*.
GERMAN WINES
A good selection of German wines.
VEGETARIAN DISHES
The restaurant offers a good selection of meat free and vegetarian dishes.

	CREDIT CARDS	GARDEN OR TERRACE	GERMAN WINES	VEGETARIAN DISHES
KÖLN (COLOGNE): *Börsen-Restaurant Köln* (DM)(DM)(DM) Unter Sachsenhausen 10, 50 667. **Road map** B4. (0221) 13 30 21. FAX *(0221) 13 30 40.* The stylish and elegant Maître restaurant has a wonderful menu, consisting of the most ingenious French dishes. It is characterized by a pleasant atmosphere and courteous service. Diners also have the option of visiting the Börsenstube at the same establishment, which serves traditional food. *Sat, Sun, 2 weeks for Easter, 4 weeks in summer.*	●	▪	●	
KÖLN (COLOGNE): *Fischers* (DM)(DM)(DM) Hohenstaufenring 53, 50 674. **Road map** B4. (0221) 310 84 70. FAX *(0221) 31 08 47 89.* This restaurant doubles as a wine bar, and the landlady is a connoisseur and one of the greatest authorities on wine. Accordingly, there is a large selection of wines on offer, which is matched by the food, with the menu featuring specialities from around the world. The restaurant has a pleasant courtyard.	●	▪	●	
KÖLN (COLOGNE): *Landhaus Kuckuck* (DM)(DM)(DM) Olympiaweg 2, 50 933, **Road map** B4. (0221) 491 23 23. FAX *(0221) 497 28 47.* The proprietor is renowned for his good taste. The restaurant is elegant and refined, specializing in poultry dishes, and serving delicious liver and roast goose.	●			
LEMGO: *Im Borke* (DM) Salzufler-Str. 132, 32 657 Lemgo-Kirchheide. **Road map** C3. (05266) 16 91. FAX *(05266) 12 31.* This rustic restaurant has a family atmosphere. The building is located in a small garden which resembles a park. *Wed, Thu.* ♿ ⚹ 🅿	●			▪
MONSCHAU: *Wiesenthal* (DM) Laufenstr. 82, 52 156. **Road map** A4. (02472) 860. FAX *(02472) 861 99.* Modern, recently built restaurant in the Carat Hotel, which will delight even the most demanding diners. In the evening, the Christofel-Bistro is a favourite meeting place. ♿ ⚹	●	▪	●	▪
MÜNSTER: *Landhaus Eggert* (DM)(DM) Zur Haskenau 81, 48 157 Münster-Handorf. **Road map** B3. (0251) 32 80 40. FAX *(0251) 328 04 59.* This hotel, restaurant and beer garden is set on a former gentleman's estate, amid charming meadows and forests. The large selection of dishes includes specialities from around the world. The professional staff will help diners to select one of the 100 wines on offer. There is live music on Tuesdays. ♿ ⚹ ♫	●	▪	●	▪
MÜNSTER: *Villa Medici* (DM)(DM)(DM) Ostmarkstr. 15, 48 145. **Road map** B3. (0251) 342 18. FAX *(0251) 39 30 94.* This attractively furnished restaurant is the best place for Italian food. The chef is very attentive to his customers' needs, and he also offers a wine tour of Italy. *Sun, 2 weeks in summer, 2 weeks in winter.* ⚹	●			
PADERBORN: *Balthasar* (DM)(DM) Warburger Str. 28, 33 098. **Road map** C3. (05251) 244 48. FAX *(05251) 244 58.* This modern and exclusive restaurant is a mecca for gourmets. The "wild" young chef serves everything that is "fun", a changing menu of freshly prepared dishes, often in surprising combinations. *Mon, Sat lunch.*	●	▪	●	▪
SIEGEN: *Mercure* (DM)(DM) Kampenstr. 83, 57 072. **Road map** B4. (0271) 501 10. FAX *(0271) 501 11 50.* Comfortably furnished restaurant in the Mercure Hotel, serving interesting international and regional dishes. Courteous service. ⚹	●		●	▪

SOEST: *Hansa Hotel*
Siegmund-Schultze-Weg 100, 59 494. **Road map** B4. (02921) 709 00.
FAX (02921) 70 90 75.
Modern hotel restaurant, located on the edge of town, serving dishes
drawn from an international repertoire. There is also a café with terrace
and a beer garden.

WINTERBERG: *Waldhaus*
Kiefernweg 12, 59 955. **Road map** C4. (02981) 20 42. FAX (02981) 36 70.
This restaurant, in the Waldhaus Hotel, is beautifully sited in the middle
of the forest, near a tobogganing run. Excellently chosen furnishings
recreate the interior of a castle. Fish dishes are the house speciality.

WUPPERTAL: *Scarpati*
Scheffelstr. 41, 42 327 Wuppertal-Vohwinkel. **Road map** B4. (0202) 78 40 74.
FAX (0202) 78 98 28.
This restaurant, in the hotel of the same name, is somewhat hidden, yet it
is definitely worth seeking it out. The interior is furnished in a very
original style. The restaurant serves many excellent, classic Italian dishes
and a large choice of Italian wines. Pleasant terrace. Mon.

XANTEN: *Hotel van Bebber*
Klever Str. 12, 46 509 Xanten. **Road map** B4. (02801) 66 23.
FAX (02801) 5914.
This historical four-star restaurant, situated in the centre of the city, serves
excellent regional cuisine. Famous visitors have included Queen Victoria
and Winston Churchill. Mon lunch.

LOWER SAXONY, HAMBURG & BREMEN

BRAUNSCHWEIG (BRUNSWICK): *Herrendorf*
Am Magnitor 1, 38 100. **Road map** D3. (0531) 471 30. FAX (0531) 471 34 99.
Stylish restaurant in the Stadthotel Magnitor, serving classic dishes and
regional fare. There is also a pleasant hotel bar, the Teatro, and a café
with a small garden.

BREMEN: *Meierei*
Im Bürgerpark, 28 209. **Road map** C2. (0421) 340 86 19.
FAX (0421) 21 99 86 81.
Smart restaurant with rustic furniture, beautifully situated in the middle of
a park. The restaurant's stone oven, used for baking bread and other
dishes, is a particularly interesting feature.

BREMEN: *L'Orchidée*
Bahnhofsplatz 11, 28 195. **Road map** C2. (0421) 305 98 88.
FAX (0421) 305 95 91.
The interior of this modern restaurant, located in the centre of the city
near the main railway station, is elegant and luxurious. Excellent French
and regional cuisine; the hotel has a bar. Mon, first half Jan & Apr.

BREMEN: *Westfalia-Bierlachs*
Langemarckstr. 38–42, 28 199. **Road map** C2. (0421) 590 20.
FAX (0421) 50 74 57.
This elegant restaurant specializes in exquisite fish dishes. Sun evening.

BÜCKEBURG: *Ambiente*
Herminenstr. 11, 31 675. **Road map** C3. (05722) 96 70. FAX (05722) 96 74 44.
The restaurant is based in a modern hotel building. Diners can also eat in
the grill room or the garden. Regional specialities.

CELLE: *Entenfang*
Hannoversche Str. 55–56, 29 221. **Road map** C3. (05141) 20 10.
FAX (05141) 20 11 20.
Restaurant in the Fürstenhof Celle, housed in a 17th-century palace. This
is one of the best venues in Celle, where diners can enjoy an excellent ·
meal in a superb setting. The restaurant is adorned with many valuable
paintings and stylish furniture. Service is exemplary, and the standard of
the French dishes excellent.

CLOPPENBURG: *Schäfers Hotel*
Lange Str. 66, 49 661. **Road map** B2. (04471) 24 84. FAX (04471) 94 77 14.
Pleasant, romantic hotel–restaurant serving a variety of delicious dishes.
1 week in summer.

Prices of a three course meal without drinks, including cover charge, tax and service in Deutschmarks (and in Euros):
(DM) up to 40 DM (up to 20 €)
(DM)(DM) 40–60 DM (20–29 €)
(DM)(DM)(DM) 60–80 DM (30–39 €)
(DM)(DM)(DM)(DM) 80–100 DM (40–49 €)
(DM)(DM)(DM)(DM)(DM) over 100 DM (over 50 €)

CREDIT CARDS
Credit cards are accepted.
GARDEN OR TERRACE
Weather permitting, it is possible to eat *al fresco*.
GERMAN WINES
A good selection of German wines.
VEGETARIAN DISHES
The restaurant offers a good selection of meat free and vegetarian dishes.

	CREDIT CARDS	GARDEN OR TERRACE	GERMAN WINES	VEGETARIAN DISHES

GÖTTINGEN: *Clarion Hotel* (DM)
Kasseler Landstr. 45, 37 081 Göttingen-Grone. **Road map** C4. ☎ *(0551) 90 20.*
FAX *(0551) 90 21 66.*
This attractively furnished restaurant is based in the hotel of the same name. The menu changes every 2–3 weeks, reflecting the seasons. The lamb and game dishes come highly recommended. ☒ ☒ ♫

| ● | ▦ | ● | ▦ |

HAMBURG: *La Fattoria* (DM)(DM)
Isestr. 16, 20 144. **Road map** C2. ☎ *(040) 420 02 55.* FAX *(040) 420 94 49.*
This nostalgically fitted restaurant not only serves excellent food, but also offers some of its furnishings for sale. Italian cuisine. ☒ ☒

| ● | | | ▦ |

HAMBURG: *Fischereihafen-Restaurant* (DM)(DM)
Große Elbstr. 143, 22 767 Hamburg-Altona. **Road map** C2. ☎ *(040) 38 18 16.*
FAX *(040) 389 30 21.*
The restaurant has elegant, modern furnishings. From the windows there are fantastic views of the harbour. Restaurant and bar have played host to many celebrities, and their autographs now adorn the walls of the restaurant. The service is of the "old school". The menu features international fare, including a large selection of fish dishes. German, Californian and Australian wines. ☒ ☒

| ● | ▦ | ● | ▦ |

HAMBURG: *Fischküche* (DM)(DM)
Kajen 12, 20 459. **Road map** C2. ☎ *(040) 36 56 31.*
A very popular restaurant, serving fresh fish dishes. The decor has a maritime theme. ● *Sun, public holidays.* ☒ ☒

| ● | ▦ | ● | ▦ |

HAMBURG: *Fischmarkt* (DM)(DM)
Ditmar-Koel-Str. 1, 20 459. **Road map** C2. ☎ *(040) 36 38 09.* FAX *(040) 37 69 61 64.*
This restaurant is situated right on the Fish Market, which is a popular destination for virtually every visitor to Hamburg.

| ● | ▦ | ● | ▦ |

HAMBURG: *Jacobs Restaurant* (DM)(DM)(DM)(DM)
Elbchaussee 401–403, 22 609 Hamburg-Nienstedten. **Road map** C2.
☎ *(040) 82 25 50.* FAX *(040) 82 25 54 44.*
The Louis C. Jacob Hotel and its elegant restaurant are known well beyond Hamburg. The master chef is amazingly imaginative and very skilled in his craft. He serves light French cuisine with Italian accents as well as German dishes. The wine list has 900 different wines. ☒ ☒

| ● | ▦ | ● | ▦ |

HAMBURG: *La Mer* (DM)(DM)(DM)(DM)
An der Alster 9, 20 099. **Road map** C2. ☎ *(040) 24 83 40 40.*
The restaurant in the Prem Hotel is beautifully situated on the edge of the Alster river. In its pleasant setting the diner can enjoy imaginative dishes. Professional service. 🅿 ● *Sat, Sun morning.* ☒ ☒ ♫

| ● | ▦ | ● | ▦ |

HAMBURG: *L'Auberge Française* (DM)(DM)(DM)
Rutschbahn 34, 20 146. **Road map** C2. ☎ *(040) 410 25 32.* FAX *(040) 459 59 15.*
Although the interior is modest, the French food is excellent. Try the goose liver or the lobster with lemon. ● *Sun.* ☒

| ● | ▦ | | ▦ |

HAMBURG: *Tafelhaus* (DM)(DM)(DM)
Holstenkamp 71, 22 525 Hamburg-Bahrenfeld. **Road map** C2. ☎ *(040) 89 27 60.*
Bistro-style restaurant with original furnishings. The handwritten menu features international fare. Courteous service. ● *Mon, Sun.* ☒ ☒

| ● | ▦ | ● | ▦ |

HANNOVER: *Die Insel* (DM)(DM)(DM)
Rudolf-von-Bennigsen-Ufer 81, 30 519. **Road map** C3. ☎ *(0511) 83 12 14.*
FAX *(0511) 83 13 22.*
Modern restaurant, bar and café are combined in one gastronomic complex that attracts many guests. The restaurant windows give great views of the Masch lake. The menu includes interesting Asian specialities and game dishes; lunch is less expensive. 🅿 ● *Mon.* ☒ ☒

| ● | ▦ | ● | ▦ |

HANNOVER: *Gallo Nero*
Kirchweg 72b, 30 655 Hannover–Groß-Buchholz. **Road map** C3.
(*(0511) 546 34 34.* **FAX** *(0511) 54 82 83.*
The furnishings in the "black cockerel" are elegant, and the service
excellent. The menu includes Italian dishes and there is a large selection
of wines. **P** **●** *Sun, 4 weeks in summer.*

HANNOVER: *Hindenburg Klassik*
Gneisenaustr. 55, 30 175. **Road map** C3. **(** *(0511) 85 85 88.* **FAX** *(0511) 81 92 13.*
A classy restaurant, serving Italian food, including pasta. The menu
changes daily. The restaurant also has an art exhibition. **●** *Sun.*

HANNOVER: *Le Chalet*
Isernhagener Str. 21, 30 161 Hannover-List. **Road map** C3.
(*(0511) 31 95 88.* **FAX** *(0511) 31 33 54.*
"Klein aber fein" (small but good) is an appropriate epithet for this
restaurant. The chef is very experienced, and the restaurant specializes in
French cuisine. **●** *Mon.*

HILDESHEIM: *Kupferschmiede*
Am Steinberg 6, 31 139 Hildesheim-Ochtersum. **Road map** C3.
(*(05121) 26 30 25.* **FAX** *(05121) 26 30 70.*
Well hidden in the middle of a forest, this restaurant offers 48 different
types of champagne – the chef's favourite drink. Nouvelle cuisine is
served here as well as traditional German dishes; the prices reflect the
high quality of the cooking. Booking is advisable. **P** **●** *Mon, Sun.*

KÖNIGSLUTTER: *La Trevise*
Braunschweigerstr. 21 A, 38 154. **Road map** D3. **(** *(05353) 50 30.*
FAX *(05353) 50 32 44.*
There are several restaurants in the Königshof Hotel, ranging from a basic
restaurant offering a quick service, to La Trevise, a restaurant for
gourmets. **●** *Mon, Sun, 2 weeks in Jan, Aug.*

OLDENBURG: *Kiebitz-Stube*
Europaplatz 4–6, 26 123. **Road map** B2. **(** *(0441) 80 80.* **FAX** *(0441) 80 81 00.*
Within the City-Club-Hotel is the elegant restaurant Kiebitz-Stube, serving
international cuisine.

OSNABRÜCK: *Villa Real*
Natruper-Tor-Wall 1, 49 076. **Road map** B3. **(** *(0541) 60 96 27.*
FAX *(0541) 609 66 00.*
Pleasant restaurant in the Remarque Hotel, situated not far from the old
town, serving a large choice of Italian dishes. **●** *Mon, Sun.*

STADTHAGEN: *Gasthaus Oelkrug*
Waldstr. 2, 31 655 Stadthagen-Obernwöhren. **Road map** C3. **(** *(05721) 80 25 25.*
FAX *(05721) 80 25 50.*
This restaurant, in an inn about 4 km (2 miles) south of Stadthagen,
offers an abundance of dishes on its menu; the trout is especially worth
trying. During the summer guests may dine in the garden.
● *Mon, Tue–Thu lunchtimes.*

WOLFENBÜTTEL: *Parkhotel Altes Kaffeehaus*
Harztorwall 18, 38 300. **Road map** D3. **(** *(05331) 88 80.* **FAX** *(05331) 88 81 00.*
This hotel–restaurant is housed in a 19th-century building. The hotel is
elegantly furnished, serving traditional German specialities. The historic
grotto, which houses a wine bar, is also worth a visit.

WOLFSBURG: *La Fontaine*
Gifhorner Str. 25, 38 442 Wolfsburg-Fallersleben. **Road map** D3.
(*(05362) 94 00.* **FAX** *(05362) 94 04 00.*
The restaurant, in the Ludwig im Park Hotel, is superbly furnished with
valuable pieces. It is acclaimed by gourmets and professional food critics
alike. Many sophisticated dishes drawn from traditional German cuisine
are served here, complemented by suitable wines. The terrace is open
during the summer. Booking is advisable, as the restaurant only has 10
tables and 36 covers. **●** *Sun.*

SCHLESWIG-HOLSTEIN

BAD MALENTE: *Gartenhotel Weisser Hof*
Vossstr. 45, 23 714. **Road map** D1. **(** *(04523) 992 50.* **FAX** *(04523) 68 99.*
This hotel–restaurant is beautifully sited amid greenery. The stylishly
furnished restaurant has been run by the same family for many years.
Among its specialities are fish and game dishes.

For key to symbols *see back flap*

Prices of a three course meal without drinks, including cover charge, tax and service in Deutschmarks (and in Euros):
ⓓⓜ up to 40 DM (up to 20 €)
ⓓⓜⓓⓜ 40–60 DM (20–29 €)
ⓓⓜⓓⓜⓓⓜ 60–80 DM (30–39 €)
ⓓⓜⓓⓜⓓⓜⓓⓜ 80–100 DM (40–49 €)
ⓓⓜⓓⓜⓓⓜⓓⓜⓓⓜ over 100 DM (over 50 €)

CREDIT CARDS
Credit cards are accepted.
GARDEN OR TERRACE
Weather permitting, it is possible to eat *al fresco.*
GERMAN WINES
A good selection of German wines.
VEGETARIAN DISHES
The restaurant offers a good selection of meat free and vegetarian dishes.

	CREDIT CARDS	GARDEN OR TERRACE	GERMAN WINES	VEGETARIAN DISHES
FLENSBURG: *Rôtisserie* 24 955 Flensburg-Harrislee, Kupfermühle border crossing. **Road map** C1. 📞 *(0461) 70 20.* FAX *(0461) 70 27 02.* The restaurant is based in the Hotel des Nordens, which is right next to the German–Danish border. The pleasant venue, serving German and international dishes, affords beautiful views of the surroundings. The hotel also boasts a swimming pool and other recreational facilities. ♿ 👶 ⓓⓜ	●	▦	●	▦
KIEL: *Im Park* Niemannsweg 102, 24 105. **Road map** C1. 📞 *(0431) 881 10.* FAX *(0431) 881 11 35.* The elegant restaurant of the Parkhotel Kieler Kaufmann is located in a villa that was formerly the home of a banker. Its beautiful location gives fantastic views of the sea. The food – imaginative regional and international dishes – is highly rated in the area. There is also a good selection of wines. Charming lounge with an open fireplace. ⓓⓜⓓⓜⓓⓜ	●	▦	●	▦
LÜBECK: *Das kleine Restaurant* An der Untertrave 39, 23 552. **Road map** D2. 📞 and FAX *(0451) 70 59 59.* This unique little restaurant offers almost its entire repertoire, ten courses, at affordable prices. The portions are small enough to manage, and diners are sure to remember an evening here for a long time. ● *Sun.* ⓓⓜⓓⓜ	●		●	▦
LÜBECK: *Haus der Schiffergesellschaft* Breite Str. 2, 23 552. **Road map** D2. 📞 *(0451) 767 76.* FAX *(0451) 732 79.* This well-known historic restaurant, dating from the 16th century, is adorned with mementoes of Lübeck's yachtsmen. Booking is advisable as the venue is very popular. Many fish dishes and excellent lamb. ♿ ⓓⓜⓓⓜ	●		●	▦
LÜBECK: *Wullenwever* Beckergrube 71, 23 552. **Road map** D2. 📞 *(0451) 70 43 33.* FAX *(0451) 706 36 07.* A restaurant for connoisseurs, in a 16th-century building. Captivating decor and excellent service as well as cuisine. Large selection of wines. ● *Sun, Mon.* 👶 ⓓⓜⓓⓜⓓⓜⓓⓜ	●			
RATZEBURG: *Hansa Hotel* Schrangenstr. 25, 23 909. **Road map** D2. 📞 *(04541) 20 94.* FAX *(04541) 86 41 41.* This restaurant, in a hotel picturesquely situated by a lake, has attractive decor. The menu includes regional and international dishes. The hotel bar is also open to diners. ● *Mon.* ♿ 👶 🎵 ⓓⓜ	●		●	▦
SCHLESWIG: *Strandhalle* Am Yachthafen, 24 837. **Road map** C1. 📞 *(04621) 90 90.* FAX *(04621) 90 91 00.* This hotel–restaurant, in a charming location on the banks of the Schlei river, has for many years been run by the same family. Famous in the area, the cuisine is particularly renowned for its seafood dishes. Wine lovers will find a large choice of styles from different regions to choose from. There is a café with terrace, serving delicious iced coffee. 👶 ⓓⓜ	●	▦	●	▦
SYLT: *Fährhaus* Heefwai 1, 25 980 Sylt–Ost-Munkmarsch. **Road map** B1. 📞 *(04651) 939 70.* FAX *(04651) 93 97 10.* This gourmet restaurant, the best-known one on the island, has a beautiful view of the yachting marina. A large choice of fish and seafood. There is also a less expensive restaurant, the Käpt'n Selmer. 🅿 ● *Mon.* 👶 ⓓⓜⓓⓜⓓⓜⓓⓜ	●	▦	●	▦
SYLT: *Stadt Hamburg* Strandstr. 2, 25 980 Westerland. **Road map** B1. 📞 *(04651) 85 80.* FAX *(04651) 85 82 20.* The elegant restaurant for connoisseurs, in the Stadt Hamburg Hotel, is furnished with beautiful English furniture and floral decorations. The chef specializes in fish dishes, and there is a large selection of wines to accompany the meal. The bistro – also modern and elegantly furnished – offers light, tasty and significantly less expensive dishes. 🅿 ♿ 👶 ⓓⓜⓓⓜ	●	▦	●	▦

MECKLENBURG–LOWER POMERANIA

BAD DOBERAN: *Residenz*
Prof.-Dr.-Vogel-Str. 16, 18 209 Bad Doberan-Heiligendamm. **Road map** D1.
((038203) 46 20. FAX (038203) 46 248.
Comfortable restaurant in the Residenz Hotel, which is part of the chain of Romantik hotels. The extensive menu includes dishes from regional and international cuisine. Café with terrace. ● *Mon.*

DARGUN: *Am Klostersee*
Am Klosterdamm, 17 159. **Road map** E2. **(** (039959) 25 20. FAX (039959) 252 28.
The restaurant, in the Hotel Am Klostersee, is situated on the outskirts of the town, on the shores of a lake, right by the edge of the forest. Simple furnishings. Delicious regional food, including excellent fish and game dishes. Lounge with an open fireplace and beer garden.

GREIFSWALD: *Am Gorzberg*
Am Gorzberg, 17 489. **Road map** E1. **(** (03834) 54 40. FAX (03834) 54 44 44.
The hotel, in which the restaurant is located, is an excellent starting point for exploring the area, with excursions to the islands of Rügen and Usedom. The elegant restaurant serves German cuisine.

GÜSTROW: *Stadt Güstrow*
Pferdemarkt 58, 18 273 Güstrow. **Road map** D2. **(** (03843) 78 00. FAX (03843) 78 01 00.
The Stadt Güstrow Hotel, which has a long tradition, has several restaurants and cafés, as well as a friendly bar. Regional fare. ● *Sun.*

NEUBRANDENBURG: *St Georg*
Rostocker Str., 17 033. **Road map** E2. **(** (0395) 544 37 88. FAX (0395) 560 70 50.
The restaurant of the St Georg Hotel is conveniently situated on the edge of town, towards Rostock, next to the Treptow gate. The visitor can sample dishes from the region here. Beer garden.

ROSTOCK: *Il Ristorante Atlantic*
Am Strom 107/108, 18 119 Rostock-Warnemünde. **Road map** D1.
((0381) 526 74. FAX (0381) 526 05.
This modern restaurant, in the part of town which functions as a summer resort, affords great views. The food and service are of a high standard. Steak and fish dishes are particularly worth trying.

RÜGEN: *Poseidon*
Lottumstr. 1, 18 609 Binz. **Road map** E1. **(** (038393) 26 69. FAX (038393) 337 12.
This spacious restaurant with terrace serves delicious Italian and regional dishes.

RÜGEN: *Le Gourmet*
Zeppelinstr. 8, 18 609 Binz. **Road map** E1. **(** (038393) 500. FAX (038393) 504 30.
Small, elegant restaurant, specializing in traditional fish dishes, served in varying styles. This is a popular venue, and booking is advisable.

SCHWERIN: *Weinhaus Uhle*
Schusterstr. 13–15, 19 055. **Road map** D2. **(** (0385) 56 29 56. FAX (0385) 557 40 93.
This traditional restaurant, the best in town, is situated near the castle, theatre and cathedral. Excellent regional and French dishes are served in the elegant restaurant, the knights' hall and the wine bar. The Mecklenburger Zander (pike-perch) is worth trying.

USEDOM: *Villa Auguste Viktoria*
Bismarckstr. 1–2, 17 419 Ahlbeck. **Road map** E2. **(** (038378) 24 10.
FAX (038378) 241 44.
The restaurant is based in a hotel, and reminds one of an orangery. Pleasant service – the staff are happy to recommend one of the exquisite fish dishes or other specials.

USEDOM: *Kräutergarten*
Puschkinstr. 10, 17 424 Heringsdorf. **Road map** E2. **(** (038378) 26 50.
FAX (038378) 265 99.
The elegant restaurant is part of the Oasis Hotel, which also features a café with terrace and a bistro. Beach chairs are for hire, too.

WISMAR: *Stadt Hamburg*
Am Markt 24, 23 966. **Road map** D2. **(** (03841) 23 90. FAX (03841) 23 92 39.
Hotel–restaurant conveniently located near the market square, serving nourishing German dishes, as well as light Mediterranean food. The terrace gives a beautiful view of the city.

For key to symbols *see back flap*

SURVIVAL
GUIDE

PRACTICAL INFORMATION

GERMANY IS A country that is particularly well prepared to receive visitors. Every town, large and small, has a helpful tourist information centre that can offer help with finding accommodation and providing information about local restaurants, attractions and activities. Virtually all the larger cities also have Internet web sites where up-to-date information on hotels, restaurants, museums and historic monuments can be readily

Posters advertising future events

accessed. The country is served by an excellent public transport system and a first-rate network of roads and motorways, which makes getting around quick and easy. There is a plentiful supply of comfortable, affordable tourist accommodation in Germany, but it is worth bearing in mind that hotels can become booked up quickly during the festivals and fairs that occur throughout the year in different parts of the country.

WHEN TO VISIT

IN GERMANY, a pleasant and relaxing vacation can be enjoyed at any time of the year. When planning to visit cities and historic monuments, however, it is best to come in the spring or early autumn, particularly in the south of the country where it can be very warm. July and August are the ideal months for spending a restful holiday by the sea, in the lake districts or in the mountains. Arriving in Bavaria during the second half of September provides the opportunity to take part in the Oktoberfest. In December everybody is preoccupied with frantic Christmas shopping, while, in the winter, skiing is a popular pursuit in the Black Forest, the Alps and the Harz Mountains.

Increased traffic on the roads depends on the dates of school holidays, which are set independently in each

Typical information plaques on historic buildings

state. It can also be quite busy at the start of the "long weekends" that occur at Easter, Whitsun and around other national public holidays.

VISA REGULATIONS

CITIZENS OF countries that are members of the European Union, the US, Canada, Australia, and New Zealand do not require a visa to visit Germany, so long as their stay does not exceed three months duration. Visitors from South Africa will need a visa. In addition, citizens of many EU countries do not require a passport to enter Germany, though a national ID card is necessary.

CUSTOMS REGULATIONS

GERMAN REGULATIONS totally prohibit the importation of drugs, animals and exotic plants that are under special protection. There are also

regulations that restrict the importation of cigarettes. An adult may bring in 200 cigarettes or 100 cigars, and 250g (9oz) of tobacco, as well as one litre of spirits and two litres of wine. You can also import up to 5kg (11lb) of foodstuffs. Beyond these limits, goods are considered to be commercial imports and must be cleared by Customs when entering the country.

Tourist information office in Rottweil, Baden-Württemberg

TOURIST INFORMATION

A VERY WELL-DEVELOPED network of tourist information centres exists in Germany. These are generally run by the city or regional tourist authorities, *Verkehrsamt*. They provide information on accommodation, addresses and opening hours of historic monuments and museums, cruises, organized excursions and city tours, as well as brochures covering the most important tourist information.

Tourists on an excursion with a guide

◁ **Beer tankards from Heidelberg**

They sell useful guide books, maps and postcards and may be able to find and book you a hotel room.

OPENING HOURS

OPENING hours of shops, offices and other businesses depend to a great extent on the size of the town. In larger cities, the usual office opening hours are from around 9am until 6pm. Banks operate much shorter hours (see p536). In smaller towns, however, nothing tends to open until 10am, and many businesses close from 1–2pm for lunch. Visitors must also bear in mind that there is a compulsory and virtually total ban on trading on Saturday afternoons, Sundays and on public holidays. Restrictions also limit the opening hours of shops (see p540).

MUSEUMS AND HISTORIC MONUMENTS

MUSEUMS IN Germany are generally open from 9am until 6pm, and in smaller places from 10am until 5pm or even 4pm. Some museums, however, do close at lunchtime. Once a week, usually on Wednesdays or Thursdays, some museums may be open somewhat longer, while on Mondays they may be closed. Larger churches in major cities are accessible to tourists throughout the whole day. In smaller places, visiting may only be possible after making prior arrangements. There may be a notice on the door of the church advising visitors whom to contact in order to obtain the key.

Publications providing information on cultural events

ADMISSION TICKET PRICES

THE PRICE OF admission to museums and historic monuments can be high. For example, entrance to a small regional museum may cost DM2–3 (€1–1.5), to a large state-run museum around DM5–6 (€2.5–3), while a private or residential venue may charge DM10 (€5). Admission to churches is usually free but a fee may be charged in certain cathedrals and monastic churches. There may also be a fee to see the treasury, where the most valuable exhibits are displayed.

High fees are charged at large entertainment complexes: for example, you may have to pay DM20–30 (€10–15) for a tour of a film studio.

EMBASSIES AND CONSULATES

THE EMBASSIES of several countries, including the UK and US, are located in Berlin. Consulates are also based in other major German cities.

Illustrated admission tickets for tourist attractions

Practical Information

A kiosk selling newspapers and cigarettes

DISABLED VISITORS

GERMANY IS A country that is relatively well prepared to receive disabled travellers. Large museums and important historic monuments have special ramps or lifts for people who are confined to wheelchairs. Offices and banks are also accessible to wheelchair users, and there are usually lifts at railway stations and larger underground stations. A large proportion of public transport vehicles have been adapted to take wheelchair passengers. Most hotels, especially the higher grades, offer suitably equipped bedrooms. For visitors who use wheelchairs, there are usually specially designed toilet facilities within public toilets in car parks, railway stations and airports. A handicapped person may, however, still have problems in gaining access to small museums, certain historic monuments and to toilets in restaurants, which are often located in the cellar. **Contact Touristik Union International (TUI)** for further useful information.

RELIGION

IN A COUNTRY with profound historical influences, the dominant religion varies from area to area and from state to state, depending on which faith was chosen by local rulers in the past. Today, the southern states are predominantly Catholic while, in the north, Protestantism is more common. However, with a migrating population, this historical division has begun to change. The 20th century brought a huge influx of people of other faiths: the Muslim population now numbers several millions. Where large communities of ethnic minorities exist, services are held in their languages, while in most large cities there are some churches where extra services are held in English and in French.

Sign for public toilets, including facilities for disabled visitors

EVERYDAY CUSTOMS

GERMANS, and particularly the older generation, attach great importance to courteous behaviour. You constantly hear "*Guten Tag*" when entering a shop, and "*Auf Wiedersehen*" – or the more youthful "*Tschüss*" when leaving. Germans are also very punctual and consider even a small delay to be very impolite. Arriving somewhat earlier than arranged for an engagement is regarded as courteous.
It is also important to adapt to German regulations. It is a violation, for example, to cross the road when there is a red light showing, even if the road is clear, and can result in an official reprimand.
Among younger Germans, however, shifts in traditional ideas of politeness can be observed. Older people and women are no longer treated with such respect and are no longer automatically offered seats on public transport by younger passengers. Another notable change is the huge tolerance now shown towards even the most unruly children by parents and other adults.

LANGUAGE

ALTHOUGH ALL Germans can speak German, many of them continue to use dialects that are virtually incomprehensible, even to those from neighbouring regions. The most difficult dialects to understand are considered to be those of southern Germany, particularly Bavarian and Schwabian, but Frisian and Saxon dialects are also likely to cause severe communication problems for visitors.
Travellers can usually be understood in Germany by speaking English, particularly in larger cities and in places that are frequented by foreign tourists and holidaymakers.

NEWSPAPERS

PUBLICATIONS can be bought not only in kiosks, but also in automatic vending machines. In the evenings, papers are distributed in bars

Two of the most popular German newspapers

and restaurants by news-vendors. Current newspapers are usually available in cafés. Every state has its own titles. In Berlin the most popular newspapers are *Berliner Zeitung*, *Der Tagesspiegel* and *Die Tageszeitung*. In southern Germany it is *Süddeutsche Zeitung*. Highly respected throughout Germany is the *Frankfurter Allgemeine Zeitung*, while the most widely read is *Bild*. You can buy foreign language publications at railway stations and airports, as well as in more expensive hotels.

Information sign

Slot for coins

Pull lever to obtain newspaper after inserting coins

Automatic newspaper vending machine

INFORMATION FOR YOUNG PEOPLE

DURING A STAY in Germany it is worth carrying an International Student Identity Card (ISIC), which entitles holders to a 50 per cent discount in certain museums and reductions when buying certain theatre tickets. It also allows students to get useful discounts on air tickets.

Similar benefits can be obtained using the "GO25" and "Euro<26" cards, both of which entitle holders to a variety of reductions. These cards provide up to 300,000 different discounts.

Phantasialand, Brühl, a popular children's entertainment park

TRAVELLING WITH CHILDREN

TRAVELLING WITH children is common in Germany and consequently their needs are well catered for. Restaurants can usually provide a high chair for a toddler and offer a special *Kindermenu* with small portions. Public toilets at railway stations, airports and in motorway service stations, as well as in many museums and stores, usually offer a separate facility for mothers and babies. The majority of hotels and guest houses offer discounts for children *(see p473)*. Discounts or even free travel for the youngest children are available on various forms of transport and there are similar concessions in most museums. In many German cities it is possible to purchase family tickets that provide substantial discounts on fares and admission fees.

WOMEN TRAVELLING ALONE

A WOMAN TRAVELLING on her own will not surprise anyone in Germany and only the usual safety precautions need be taken, particularly in large cities at night. However, it is best to avoid certain areas in

Euro<26 and International Student Identity Cards

towns where there is a lively nightlife – for example the *Reeperbahn* in Hamburg. Hitchhiking is quite popular in Germany, but a better option for single women may be to use the services of *Mitfahrzentrale (see p549)*.

WEIGHTS AND MEASURES

THE METRIC system of measurement is used in Germany. Note that half a kilogram is expressed by the word *pfund*. In contrast to UK usage, decimals are indicated by a comma and thousands by a point: thus 10,000.50 (UK) = 10.000,50.

TIME

GERMANY uses Central European Time (GMT plus one hour). Clocks move forward one hour on the last Sunday in March and back on the last Sunday in October.

ELECTRICITY

THE ELECTRICAL system in Germany provides 220V, 50 Hz AC, except in some hotel bathrooms where a lower current is provided as a standard safety measure. UK 220V appliances can be plugged into German sockets with an adaptor. However US 110V appliances will have to be used with a transformer.

DIRECTORY

INFORMATION FOR DISABLED VISITORS

Directions Unlimited
720 N Bedford Road,
Bedford Hills,
NY 10507, USA.
(800) 533 53 43.

Mobility International
228 Borough High Street,
London SE1 1JX, England.
(020) 7403 5688.

Touristik Union International (TUI)
Karl Wichert Allee 23,
30625 Hannover 61.
(0511) 56 70.
FAX (0511) 567 1301.

Security and Health

Pharmacy sign

As IN OTHER COUNTRIES, visitors are far safer in small towns and villages in Germany than in big cities, where extra vigilance must be taken against pickpockets – particularly when travelling on public transport during rush hour. It is worth using a money belt or other means of concealing your money and documents. Taking out medical insurance cover is always advisable when travelling abroad, but for minor health problems that do not require the services of a doctor, pharmacists are a good and easily accessible source of assistance.

Characteristically coloured white and green police van

POLICE

GREEN IS THE predominant colour of German police uniforms and signs. Motorized police units, *Verkehrspolizei*, which look after safety on the streets, roads and motorways, are distinguished by their white caps, while uniformed policemen patrolling city streets have a cap that is the same colour as their uniform. However, the police who are responsible for criminal offences, *Kriminalpolizei*, are generally dressed in plain clothes. They will produce their identification and insignia as necessary.

In towns, urban police in navy-blue uniforms are in evidence. Their role is, above all, to catch motorists who have parked illegally or have failed to pay the appropriate parking fee. Such traffic offences may incur on-the-spot fines and rigorous checking of documents.

PERSONAL PROPERTY

THE MOST SERIOUS threat for a tourist is always the pickpocket. This type of thief tends to prowl in crowded places, such as railway platforms, in the carriages of trains and on buses. They also frequent popular tourist sights and any events where large groups of people are likely to gather. When setting off on an excursion it is best to leave valuable items and documents in the hotel safe.

Policeman and policewoman

Police sign

Conceal valuable items, such as cameras and audio equipment, under clothing and carry cash in a money belt. Park your car in the hotel car park whenever possible and never leave valuable items in the vehicle, especially if it has to be left in the street overnight.

ACCIDENTS AND EMERGENCIES

IF AN ACCIDENT or a serious breakdown occurs on the motorway, it is best to use one of the special telephones that are set out at regular intervals along the hard shoulder (*see p548*). Throughout the whole of Germany there is a special emergency number, *112*, which will be answered by an operator who is an experienced member of a rescue team. Among their responsibilities are informing the appropriate emergency services. Every telephone, including mobile phones, will allow callers to connect free of charge to this number.

Thefts and burglaries must be reported immediately to the criminal police. If a crime is committed on the platform of the S-Bahn or the U-Bahn, the appropriate emergency alarm button can be used to summon assistance. Special alarm buttons, within small red boxes, also provide a direct connection with the fire brigade (*Feuerwehr*). These alarm buttons are usually located in prominent positions on the streets and in large department stores.

In the case of more serious problems, such as loss of passport, visitors should turn to their Consulate (*see p531*). Officials in a consulate are available to help travellers in case they need to acquire a replacement passport, obtain legal advice, hire the services of a translator or assistance in contacting their family. In some circumstances, they may even be able to arrange for financial loans to finance the purchase of a ticket home.

Ambulance of the paramedic rescue services

LOST AND STOLEN PROPERTY

BEFORE LEAVING home it is advisable to take out an insurance policy to cover property against loss or theft. Theft must be reported to the police immediately and a certificate obtained to confirm that the loss has been reported; this is needed if an insurance claim is submitted.

If property has been lost, it is worth asking at a lost property office (Fundbüro). These exist in every German city. The railway network has its own lost property offices – Fundbüro der Deutschen Bahn AG – as do the urban transport systems in individual towns.

MEDICAL ASSISTANCE

CITIZENS OF COUNTRIES within the European Union do not have to take out medical insurance in order to obtain free medical care in Germany. In order to avail themselves

Entrance to a pharmacy in Heidelberg

of these reciprocal arrangements, however, visitors must obtain form E111 from a main post office before leaving home. However, it is still advisable to take out some form of health insurance. If plans include taking part in any sporting activities, particularly dangerous sports, make sure that the policy has a clause guaranteeing the refund of costs if rescue services are involved – for example mountain rescue services. This type of insurance is usually much more expensive.

In case of serious illness, it is necessary to call an ambulance who will take the patient to the nearest hospital out-patient clinic. In large hotels you can count on medical care being provided on the premises. For minor accidents it is best to turn for advice to a pharmacy (Apotheke).

Alarm button for the fire brigade

HEALTH

GERMANY POSES no health hazards for the traveller. The country is well served with hospitals and there are no prevalent diseases. No vaccinations are required when entering the country.

Visitors who require pre-scribed medication should ensure that they take enough to cover their stay, as it may not be available locally.

Throughout the whole of Germany, tap water is safe to drink. In department stores, pharmacies and large banks there are water tanks with plastic cups, which can be used free of charge.

PHARMACIES

PHARMACIES in Germany are indicated by a stylized letter "A" (Apotheke) and are usually open from 8am–6pm; in small towns they may close from 1–3pm. In larger towns there is always a rota and this is displayed in the window of each pharmacy with a note of addresses. Information on rota pharmacies may also be obtained from tourist offices.

PUBLIC CONVENIENCES

IN LARGE CITIES, public toilets (often automatic cubicles) can usually be found without much difficulty. Instructions on how to use these facilities are given in several languages on the doors of the cubicles. Public toilets can also usually be found in museums, cafés, restaurants and department stores. Men's toilets are marked Herren and ladies' Damen or Frauen.

DIRECTORY

EMERGENCY SERVICES

Fire Brigade and Ambulance
112.

Police
110.

Airborne Rescue Club (Deutsche Rettungsflugwacht)
(0711) 70 10 70.

Emergency Poison Help Line
(0761) 192 40.

LOST PROPERTY

Fundbüro der Deutschen Bahn AG
(01805) 99 05 99.

Zentrales Fundbüro Berlin
Platz der Luftbrücke 6, Berlin.
(030) 69 95.

Banks and Local Currency

Logo of the ReiseBank

U NTIL RECENTLY some credit cards, including Visa, were not quite as popular in Germany as in other countries. This has now changed, however, and tourists should have no problems. In cities and towns cash can be obtained from automatic cash points (ATMs) and foreign currency exchanged at a bank and currency exchange point.

Wechselstube – a currency exchange bureau in Berlin

CHANGING CURRENCY

T HERE ARE NO limits on the amount of foreign currency that can be brought into the country. Travellers generally use travellers' cheques or credit cards, both of which minimize problems in case of loss or theft.

Foreign currency can be exchanged in a bank or exchange bureau, *Wechselstube*. Both offer a similar rate of exchange, but they usually charge a commission. It is best to check this before undertaking a transaction in order to confirm how much you will have to pay. Most banks have quite inconvenient opening hours: they are open Monday–Friday, from 9am–3:30pm, with a break for lunch between noon and 1pm. Once a week (usually on a Thursday) they are open until 6pm. Opening hours may be a little longer in larger cities. It is advisable to take advantage of the services offered by a branch of the ReiseBank as soon as you arrive – these are

located in airports and railway stations. Currency exchange counters are usually located near railway stations or in places frequented by tourists. These have longer opening hours than banks, but may have less favourable exchange and commission rates.

Foreign currency can be exchanged at special automatic cash points, which can generally be found at larger airports, railway stations and in city centres that are visited by tourists. Cash can also always be exchanged at hotel reception desks, but check the exchange rate before going ahead as the rate may be quite low.

Automatic cash machine

TRAVELLERS' CHEQUES

T RAVELLERS' CHEQUES can be used to pay for goods and services, or to settle hotel bills, but it is often better to pay by cash. Cheques can be cashed in banks and currency exchange bureaux, but it should be remembered that

it is most advantageous to exchange them for local currency. It is a good idea to purchase travellers' cheques in Deutschmarks (DM) or Euro denominations.

Deutsche Bank

Logo of Deutsche Bank, one of the biggest banks in Germany

CREDIT CARDS

C REDIT CARDS can be used to pay bills in most hotels and restaurants, in all department stores and in most shops – a fact that is always confirmed by a sticker with the credit card logo on the door or by the cash till. Sometimes, especially in restaurants and cafés, there is a compulsory minimum limit that can be paid by credit card. It is advisable, therefore, to check the situation before ordering just a drink or snack, since it may not be possible to pay for small amounts by credit card.

In busy parts of town and in commercial centres, it is easy to find a cash point that accepts credit cards, but note that some of these accept only EuroCard-

The Bayerische Vereinsbank in Munich

MasterCard. Lost credit cards or travellers' cheques should be reported immediately to a bank or the issuing organization.

CURRENCY

THE DEUTSCHMARK will remain the sole German currency until 2002. On 1 January 2002, the Euro, common currency of the European Union, will be introduced into general circulation. (It is already quoted in non-cash transactions.) During the transition period, both currencies will be used. The Euro will initially be issued in 11 EU countries: Austria, Belgium, Finland, France, Germany, Holland, Ireland, Italy, Luxembourg, Portugal and Spain. The Deutschmark is scheduled to remain legal tender until 1 March 2002.

Euro Banknotes
Euro banknotes are distinguished from each other by differences in size and colour. The smallest, which reflects its value, is a note worth 5 Euros (grey); the largest is worth 500 Euros (purple). On all banknotes the stars of the European Union are displayed, together with various architectural details.

5-Euro note

10-Euro note

20-Euro note

50-Euro note

100-Euro note

200-Euro note

500-Euro note

2 Euro coin

1 Euro

50 Eurocent

20 Eurocent

10 Eurocent

Coins
Euro coins are issued in the following denominations, 1 and 2 Euro, and 1, 2, 5, 10, 20 and 50 Eurocents. The 1 and 2 Euro coins are dual-coloured, silver-gold, while the 1, 2 and 5 Eurocent coins are bronze. The 10, 20 and 50 Eurocent coins are a gold colour.

5 Eurocent

2 Eurocent

1 Eurocent

Communications

A rare, antique mail-box

THE POSTAL and telecommunications services in Germany work very efficiently. Though it may be necessary to queue for a few minutes in the post office, letters and postcards are usually delivered within the country in 24 hours. There are no problems using the telephone. Call boxes can be found on every street corner, in U- and S-Bahn stations, and in virtually every restaurant and café. The distinctive yellow mail-boxes are also a common sight.

USING THE TELEPHONE

GERMANY'S PUBLIC telephones are serviced by *Deutsche Telekom*. The oldest types are coin-operated and require the deposit of a minimum of 30 pfennigs, which is the cost of a single local call. Coins below 10 pfennigs are not accepted. Unused coins are returned, but no change is given. It is far more convenient to use a telephone card, which can be purchased at post offices, priced DM 6, 12 and 50 (€3, 6 and 25.5). Alternatively, travellers may

Deutsche Telekom sign

purchase an international phone card before leaving home. While using a phone card in a public phone, an illuminated display will show the amount of credit (in deutschmarks) still remaining on the card. Card-operated public phones can be found in many busy areas of towns and cities. In order to use them it is necessary to dial in a personal pin number.

Many phone boxes have their own telephone number. This means that they can receive incoming calls, so that a caller can be called back if

his money or card runs out. Every public phone should be equipped with a set of telephone directories, but these often go missing.

Telephone boxes marked with the word "*National*" can only be used to ring numbers with German dialling codes, but overseas calls can be made from other phones.

Telephone calls can be made from hotel rooms, but the cost of these will be much greater than those made from public telephone boxes.

Telephone calls can also be made at post offices: there, calls are booked at a window marked "*Fremdgespräche*".

TARIFFS

DEPENDING ON the time and day, different tariffs apply to local telephone calls, as well as to intercity and international calls. The most expensive period to make a call is between 7am and 6pm. Calls cost less between 6pm and 9pm, and, later in the evening, they are even cheaper. Likewise, telephone calls are cheaper at weekends than on weekdays.

USING A COIN-OPERATED TELEPHONE

1 Lift the handset and wait for the dial tone.

2 Insert coins into the slot.

3 Dial number and wait to be connected.

4 Add more coins when signal is given.

5 When you have finished your call, replace the handset. For the return of unused coins, press the button above the slot where you inserted the coins.

USING A CARD-OPERATED TELEPHONE

1 Lift the handset and wait for the dial tone.

2 Choose the appropriate language.

3 Insert the card as instructed. The illuminated display will show the amount of credit remaining.

4 Dial the number and wait to be connected.

5 After finishing the call replace the handset. Withdraw the card by pressing the green button.

Colourful chip telephone card (back and front) with instructions on how to use it.

MOBILE TELEPHONES

A MOBILE (CELLULAR) telephone can prove invaluable on holiday, especially for phoning ahead to book hotel rooms or when taking part in mountain sports or travelling in remote areas. Before leaving home, travellers should discuss their requirements with their network provider, including which countries are to be visited. The different options can be explained and the most suitable tariff selected. Charges vary according to the facilities and coverage offered.

Deutsche Post ✪

The logo of the German postal service

POSTAL SERVICES

JUST AS IN OTHER countries, registered mail, telegrams and parcels can be sent from post offices. As well as stamps, post offices also sell phone cards, postcards, envelopes and cartons in which to send items by post. Letters sent *Poste Restante* are usually issued from post offices near railway stations. Such correspondance should be marked with the words "*Postlagernde Briefe/Sendungen*". In order to collect mail, a passport or other form of identification will have to be produced.

SENDING A LETTER

STAMPS FOR LETTERS and postcards can be bought at a post office, and sometimes they are sold along with postcards. Stamps can also be

Information plaque indicating the collection times

Opening for local letters

Opening for long-distance mail

The most typical style of mail-box seen in Germany

bought from automatic stamp machines. Before posting a letter in a mail-box, check what is written on the box. Some mail-boxes have two slots – one marked for local post only, the other for other destinations. Also shown on the box are collection times and the name of the town in which it is located.

POST OFFICES

POST OFFICES in Germany are indicated by the word "*Post*", while mail-boxes and the official *Deutsche Post* logo are a distinctive yellow colour. In large towns, post offices are usually open from 8am until 6pm, and from 8am until noon on Saturdays. Branches with longer opening hours, and which are often also open on Sundays, can be found at most airports and large railway stations.

POSTAL ADDRESSES

IN GERMANY, the postal code of five digits is an important part of the address, allowing a more precise location than simply the street name and house number. In cities, for example, different sections of long streets will have different

Operating instructions

Buttons for different kinds of stamps

Slot for collecting stamps

Street vending machine selling postage stamps and telephone cards

Entrance to one of the post offices in Bonn

postal codes. In multiple-occupancy buildings, the number of individual apartments is not given in the address. Instead, mail is delivered according to the name cards at the entrance to the building. Consequently, in order to send mail to a person who is staying in someone else's house, it is necessary to write at the top of the envelope the name of the main occupant, preceded by the letters "c/o" (care of).

THE INTERNET AND E-MAIL

THE INTERNET and e-mail have become increasingly popular and essential as a means of communication, and they can be especially useful for people who are abroad on holiday or business. As a result, many hotels now offer guests access to the Internet and e-mail facilities. Internet cafés, where online access can be obtained for a small fee, can be found in most towns and cities, while computers can often be hired by the hour in commercial centres.

USEFUL TELEPHONE NUMBERS

- Directory enquiries, national numbers: 11 833.
- Directory enquiries, international numbers: 11 834.
- International calls: Dial 00, wait for dialling tone, then dial country code, area code + number, omitting first 0.
- Country codes: UK 44; Eire 353; Canada and US 1; Australia 61; South Africa 27; New Zealand 64.

Shopping in Germany

Decorative herbal wreath

GERMANS ARE RENOWNED for reliability and hard work, and manufactured goods produced here are of excellent quality. At the same time, the tradition of handicrafts and various types of folk art continue in different parts of the country. For elegantly produced, well-designed items, visitors should try one of the vast shopping centres that are to be found in every large city. However, visiting a market is an ideal opportunity to purchase a souvenir that is a regional speciality.

Souvenirs in the Wendt & Kühn shop in Meiningen

OPENING HOURS

DAYS AND OPENING hours of shops in Germany are governed by quite rigorous regulations. Apart from bakeries and pharmacies, which open on a rota system, very few shops are open on Sundays or in the evenings. From Monday to Friday shops are open from 9 or 10am and remain open until 7 or 8pm. However on Saturdays they cease trading at 3 or 4pm at the latest. On a Sunday the only shops open are those in petrol stations, railway stations or airports – but even then some of these shops close. Sunday- and late-night shopping is only really possible during December, when some department stores and shopping centres have extended opening hours.

MARKETS

A WEEKLY MARKET, known as *Wochenmarkt*, is held in many towns throughout Germany. In smaller towns, the stalls are set up in the market square, while in larger towns and cities the market is held in specially designated squares in different neighbourhoods. At these markets, fresh fruit and vegetables, cheeses, delicatessen items and cured meats, as well as many useful, everyday items, can be bought. Specialist fairs are often held at weekends – for example *Blumenmärkte*, at which flowers are sold, or *Kunstmärkte*, at which artists and craftsmen display their work for sale.

Black Forest cuckoo clock

Every large town also has its *Flohmarkt* (fleamarket) where, among the masses of cheap and damaged items, antique items or perhaps some rare or unusual curio can sometimes be found to take home as a unique souvenir.

VAT REFUNDS

EXCEPT FOR citizens of other EU countries, visitors to Germany are entitled to a VAT refund (*Mehrwertsteuer*) on any non-edible goods that are bought in German shops. Individual shops differ on the minimum taxable amount, but it is usually around DM 100 (€51). On entering a shop displaying a Tax-Free sign, visitors should ask for a special form or Tax-Free cheque. When going through Customs on leaving Germany, the form must be stamped. Visitors may be asked to show the goods, which must still be in their original packaging, unopened and unused. The tax is either refunded at the border or will be sent to the address on the envelope containing the cheque. Ensure that the correct information is given on the envelope, since chasing old VAT refund claims is a time-consuming amd often fruitless task.

SEASONAL DISCOUNTS

ALL SHOPS IN Germany hold vast sales (*Schlussverkauf*) twice a year. During the winter sales, *Winterschlussverkauf*, which begin in the last week of January, shops divest themselves of unsold autumn and winter clothing. The summer sale, *Sommer-schlussverkauf*, begins in the final week of July.

During these huge shopping festivals, which last for two weeks, it is easy to come across great bargains, as the prices may be reduced by 30, 50 or even 70 per cent.

In addition to these major, twice-yearly events, there are usually other shopping offers or reductions throughout the year, but there are not many other genuine sales where customers can save such significant amounts of money.

Stall at a weekly market in Goslar

How to Pay

THE MOST POPULAR credit card in Germany, **Eurocard**, is accepted virtually everywhere, while somewhat less popular is **VISA**. This card can be used in department stores and in larger shops, but it is rather less useful when shopping in smaller shops, where cash is preferred. A sign on the door of restaurants and shops will tell you which cards are accepted.

Ceramics and Glass

THE FIRST porcelain factory in Europe was established in Saxony, following the discovery in the early 18th century of the formula for this fine china. Fragile artifacts produced by Meissen are among the most sought-after in the world. Factories in Berlin, Nymphenburg and elsewhere produce china of similarly exquisite quality.

A souvenir beer tankard

German glass tableware is also renowned. Even now old glassworks in Saxony and Bavaria produce a range of artifacts made by traditional techniques: for example, beautifully cut and polished crystal tableware and ruby-coloured glassware.

Porcelain and glassware factories operate retail outlets in large towns. Visitors can arrange to have purchases sent to their home address.

Regional Specialities

VIRTUALLY EVERY state in Germany produces its own regional speciality. For example, Lübeck is known for marzipan, while Nürnberg is synonymous with gingerbread. In the region of Spreewald, cucumbers are pickled in various ways, while excellent cherry jam and confiture are produced in the area of the Black Forest.

In the north, it is worth buying a jar of marinated herrings and some of the excellent cheeses produced, for example, in Friesland or Schleswig. Westphalian hams also have a well-deserved reputation, as do sausages from Brunswick, while equally delicious are the cured meats that are produced, for instance, in Regensburg or Nürnberg.

Alcoholic Drinks

RENOWNED German beers *(see pp32–3 and 503)* are best drunk straight from the barrel, but it is also worth trying a few bottles of beers that are rarely seen outside Germany. German wines are worth trying, especially those from vineyards in the Mosel and Rhine valleys. Excellent wines are produced in Bavaria and Baden-Wurttemberg, while wines from Saxony have recently regained popularity.

Local specialities providing souvenirs for gourmets

In Germany, there is large-scale production of various types of spirits, as well as herbal and root-flavoured liqueurs and bitters.

A unique souvenir from a holiday in Germany would be a bottle of a herbal infusion or liqueur produced at one of the country's monasteries according to their traditional centuries-old recipes.

Dolls in folk costumes

Handicrafts and Folk Art

DESPITE GERMANY's high level of industrialization, local traditions have not vanished. Occasions such as holy days and festivals, which are held in the streets of towns in Bavaria and Schwarzwald, are still celebrated by men and women in folk costumes, while the shops stock folk costumes modelled on the local folklore. In mountain regions visitors can purchase items made from leather and wool. It is also worth looking at the traditional toys that are still crafted in some regions, such as miniature towns and dolls' houses together with their entire scaled-down furnishings. Nürnberg has a long tradition of toy manufacture, including colourful tin toys and wooden dolls.

A Berlin porcelain factory's retail outlet

Activity Holidays

GERMANY IS A COUNTRY that offers numerous opportunities for activity holidays. In the mountains visitors can climb and hike or go skiing in the winter, while the lake districts and coastal shores provide ideal conditions for sailing and water sports. Interesting areas for cycling tours can be found everywhere. Detailed information and advice on the availability of local sports activities and activity holidays can be obtained from regional tourist information offices.

A keen young hiker

Well-earned relaxation after an arduous cycle ride

For visitors planning a cycle tour, **Bund Deutscher Radfahrer** can supply maps, guidebooks and advice.

LANGUAGE COURSES

A POPULAR WAY of spending a holiday in Germany and at the same time improving language skills is to take a summer language course. Popular with young people, these courses are often linked to the possibility of taking part in sporting activities. Many options are available, but courses organized by the **Goethe Institute** are of the very highest standard.

WALKING EXCURSIONS

HIKING IS virtually a national sport in Germany. Visitors can hike just about anywhere, but it is best in the mountains. The most demanding walkers can choose Alpine trails, but excursions in the Erzgebirge, Thuringian Forest, Harz Mountains, Franconian Switzerland or the ever-popular Schwarzwald are equally exhilarating.

Before setting off on an expedition it is worth getting maps showing walking trails in the chosen region. These are generally available from local tourist offices. More detailed information can be obtained from the **Verband Deutscher Gebirgs-und Wandervereine e.V.** For those who prefer to ramble through the Alps, the **Deutscher Alpenverein (DAV)** provides information on trails and hostels, as well as advice on safety and the protection of nature and wildlife. Guided walking excursions can also be organized through local tourist offices.

CYCLING TOURS

THE BICYCLE is a popular and environmentally friendly means of transport that allows visitors to combine the joys of sightseeing with a sporting activity. In larger towns and in particularly popular tourist areas bicycles can usually be hired for just a few days or for a week or more. A bike can easily be transported on the trains and on the U-Bahn or S-Bahn in towns. In most towns and also in large villages there are separate cycling lanes, and there are usually bicycle stands in front of offices, shops and cafés.

GOLF AND TENNIS

MOST LARGE German towns have tennis courts that can be hired for a few hours. There are also many excellent golf courses throughout the country. For more information, or to make a booking, contact regional associations through the **Deutscher Tennis Bund** and the **Deutscher Golf Verband e.V.**

A relaxing afternoon sailing on the calm waters of a lake

WATER SPORTS

WATER SPORTS are very popular in Germany. Canoe trips can be undertaken on many rivers – from calm and picturesque stretches of water and the canals of the Spreewald to exhilarating adventures in rapidly flowing Alpine streams that demand professional skills. Windsurfing and waterskiing are also extremely popular. There are excellent conditions for sailing in the lake districts of Mecklenburg, the coastal region and Brandenburg, as well as by the sea.

Hikers on a bridge over a ravine in the mountains

CRUISING

CRUISES are available from April to October on rivers and lakes in many parts of Germany. An interesting excursion, from Dresden to Saxonian Switzerland, can be made on the Elbe, while many trips can also be made on the Rhine and Danube.

From a cruise ship, visitors may enjoy a leisurely look at Berlin or marvel at the Frisian Islands, while a cruise around the Bodensee islands or on the Chiemsee (Bavaria's largest lake) is always popular.

HORSE RIDING

GERMANS LOVE horses and riding and there are equestrian centres in many areas where visitors can ride under supervision or head off for a ride on their own. More information can be obtained from **Deutsche Reiterliche Vereinigung**.

SKIING

THE MOST POPULAR skiing centres are in the Alps, while the most renowned centre (having hosted the 1936 Winter Olympics) is Garmisch-Partenkirchen.

A beach volleyball match played on a square in Essen

However, it is also possible to ski in other regions – for example in Schwarzwald, in the Thuringian Forest or Erzgebirge. Throughout these areas are well-prepared skiing trails and an extensive network of ski-lifts and cable cars. Cross-country skiing is a popular winter sport in Germany, and there are many well-prepared and specially signed routes. Information and advice on this subject can be obtained from local tourist information offices. Visitors can also contact the **Freunde Des Skisports e.V.**

Deutscher Alpen-verein logo

MOUNTAIN SPORTS

THE MOUNTAIN regions of Germany provide ideal conditions for climbers. Interesting rock formations that provide memorable challenges are not only to be found in the Alps, but also in Franconian Switzerland and in Saxony. Professional climbers who specialize in climbing without the use of safety harness undertake specialist training here.

Alpine mountain strips are excellent locations for taking off on flights in hang-gliders and para-gliders.

DIRECTORY

GENERAL INFORMATION

Deutscher Sportbund
Otto-Fleck-Schneise 12,
Frankfurt am Main.
((069) 67 00 257.
FAX (069) 67 02 317.

LANGUAGE COURSES

Goethe-Institut e.V.
Helene-Weber-Allee 1,
80 637 Munich.
((089) 15 92 10.
FAX (089) 15 92 14 50.
W www.goethe.de

Goethe Institute
50 Princes Gate,
Exhibition Road,
London SW7 2PH.

((020) 7596 4000.
FAX (089) 7594 0240.

HIKING TOURS

DAV Summit Club
Am Perlacher Forst 186
81545 München
((089) 64 24 00.
FAX (089) 64 24 01 00.

Potsdamer Wanderbung e.V.
c/o Dietrich Kern,
Paul-Neumann-Str. 77
14482 Potsdam.
((0331) 748 04 88.

Verband Deutscher Gebirgs- und Wandervereine e.V.
Wilhelmshöher Allee 157–159
34 121 Kassel.
((0561) 93 87 30.
FAX (0561) 93 87 310.

CYCLING TOURS

Bund Deutscher Radfahrer
Otto-Fleck-Schneise 4,
60 528 Frankfurt am Main.
((069) 96 78 000.
FAX (069) 96 78 008.

GOLF & TENNIS

Deutscher Golf Verband e. V.
Viktoriastrasse 16,
65 189 Wiesbaden.
((0611) 99 02 00.
FAX (0611) 99 02 040.
W www.golf.de

Deutscher Tennis Bund
Hallerstrasse 89,
20 149 Hamburg.
((040) 41 17 80.
FAX (040) 41 17 82 22.
W www.dtb-tennis.de

WATER SPORTS

Deutsche Segler-Verband
Gründgensstraße 18,
22 309 Hamburg.
((040) 63 20 090.
FAX 040) 63 20 09 28.

HORSE RIDING

Deutsche Reiterliche Vereinigung
Frhr.-von-Langen-Str. 13,
48 231 Warendorf.
((02 581) 63 620.
FAX (02 581) 62 144.

SKIING

Freunde Des Skisports e.V.
Im Deutschen Skiverband.
((089) 85 79 00.
W www.ski-online.de

TRAVEL INFORMATION

TRAVELLING IN Germany is very quick and easy. In every large city there is an airport, most of which offer international connections. The whole of Germany is linked by a dense network of motorways, while main roads are of a high standard and are well signposted. Rail travel throughout the country is comfortable

Lufthansa plane

and reliable; for longer journeys it is worth taking advantage of the fast connections offered by InterCity Express (ICE). Buses are also comfortable and efficient and are particularly useful in rural areas not served by rail. In German cities, trams, buses and sometimes underground rail systems provide useful services.

ARRIVING BY AIR

GERMANY'S MOST important airports are Frankfurt am Main, Munich and Düsseldorf, from where connecting flights can be made to other German cities. The country's national carrier is Lufthansa, which operates regular, scheduled flights to most of the world's major destinations. British Airways also offers regular, scheduled flights to Germany from London (Heathrow and Gatwick) as well as from several regional airports in the United Kingdom.

The US is well served with flights to German cities, particularly to Berlin and to Frankfurt, which is Germany's largest airport and one of the busiest in Europe. Direct flights are usually available from major US cities, including New York (JFK), Washington DC, Boston, Chicago, San Francisco and Los Angeles.

Although Canada does not have many direct flights to Germany, AirCanada operates a regular flight from Toronto to Frankfurt while Canadian offers a direct flight from Vancouver to Frankfurt.

DOMESTIC FLIGHTS

IN ADDITION to Lufthansa, there are a number of other smaller carriers in Germany. These include Deutsche BA, which is a subsidiary of British Airways. These carriers often offer cheaper fares than Lufthansa on internal routes, as well as providing air links with small airports, such as Augsburg, Dortmund and Erfurt, that would not be economically viable for Lufthansa to operate.

AIR FARES

THE COST OF scheduled airfares can vary considerably, so it is always worth checking whether any carriers are offering special promotional fares. When buying a ticket it is worth finding out about any price reductions for children, young people and elderly passengers. Students and passengers under the age of 26 are often eligible for discounts. If the journey is going to be undertaken by a larger group, then it would be worth checking whether

Control tower at Munich's international airport

this qualifies for a group discount on the fare or a free ticket for the group leader.

It should also be borne in mind that fares vary depending on whether travellers are able to confirm their return date when buying the ticket. The cheapest scheduled ticket is an APEX, which requires booking well in advance, staying over a Saturday night,

Car park and airport building at Tegel airport, Berlin

View of runway and airport buildings at Frankfurt airport

and a fixed return date. Once booked, these tickets cannot be altered or cancelled, so it is wise to take out insurance to cover the loss if travel plans have to be changed.

The cheapest fares are often those offered by the new low-cost, no-frills airlines, or by discount agents. The latter are usually for seats on charter or scheduled flights.

INTERNATIONAL AIRPORTS

THE LARGEST German airports are Frankfurt am Main and Munich. The gigantic airport in Frankfurt comprises two huge terminals, which are connected by a fast over-ground railway. Both terminals are comprehensively equipped with everything that a traveller could possibly require. If you do have some free time it is worth watching the planes as they take off and land, and which form long queues at peak times.

The airport in Munich is somewhat smaller and less comfortable. The terminal extends along one axis, with the result that if you have to change planes, you have to take a long walk along a corridor to make the transfer.

Among the busiest airports are Düsseldorf, Cologne-Bonn and Berlin, which actually has three airports, Tempelhof, Tegel and Schönefeld.

AIRPORT	☎ INFORMATION	DISTANCE FROM CENTRE	JOURNEY TIME TO CENTRE BY TAXI	JOURNEY TIME TO CENTRE BY PUBLIC TRANSPORT
Berlin Tegel	(0180) 500 01 86	8 km (5 miles)	25 min	Bus: 25 min
Berlin Tempelhof	(0180) 500 01 86	5 km (3 miles)	20 min	U-Bahn: 15 min
Berlin Schönefeld	(0180) 500 01 86	20 km (12 miles)	45 min	S-Bahn: 35 min
Bremen-Neuenland	(0421) 559 50	3.5 km (2 miles)	15 min	Tram: 17 min
Dresden	(0351) 88 10	9 km (5.5miles)	25 min	Bus: 30 min
Düsseldorf	(0211) 42 10	8 km (5 miles)	25 min	S-Bahn: 13 min
Frankfurt am Main	(069) 69 03 05 11	10 km (6 miles)	20 min	Train: 11 min S-Bahn: 10 min
Hamburg	(040) 507 50	13 km (8 miles)	30 min	Bus: 30 min
Hannover	(01803) 80 38 03	12 km (7.5 miles)	20 min	S-Bahn: 13 min
Cologne-Bonn	(02203) 400	Bonn: 28 km (17.5 miles) Cologne: 17 km (10.5 miles)	Bonn: 15 min Cologne: 20 min	Bus to Bonn: 35 min Bus to Cologne: 45 min
Leipzig	(0341) 224 11 55	18 km (11 miles)	30 min	Bus: 30 min
Munich	(089) 97 52 13 13	40 km (25 miles)	45 min	S-Bahn: 40 min Bus: 45 min
Nürnberg	(0911) 937 12 00	6 km (4 miles)	20 min	Bus: 45 min U-Bahn: 12 min
Stuttgart	(0711) 94 80	18 km (11 miles)	25 min	S-Bahn: 30 min

Travelling by Train, Ferry and Ship

DB

Logo of German railways (Deutsche Bahn)

TRAVELLING AROUND Germany by train is not the cheapest form of transport, but it is undoubtedly one of the most comfortable. German trains are renowned for their punctuality, safety and cleanliness, though in high season visitors may feel that these are a little overrated. The fastest are InterCity-Express (ICE) trains. Germany is also well served by ports to which ferries and passenger ships operate.

Narrow-gauge tourist railway service in the Harz mountains

GETTING TO GERMANY BY TRAIN

TRAVELLING by train from the UK generally costs more than flying, as well as taking longer. Main routes are via Dover to Ostend or Harwich to Hook of Holland. From either of these ports, connections to Berlin, Frankfurt and other German cities are made. An alternative is to travel to Brussels by Eurostar and pick up an onward connection there.

Deutsche Bahn railway workers

GERMAN TRAINS

THE FASTEST TRAINS, InterCity Express (ICE), are aerodynamically designed, painted white, with air-conditioning in coaches and airline-style seats. Unfortunately, there is not much room for luggage. They can travel at more than 200 kph (125 mph), which means that a journey from Hamburg to Munich takes only a few hours. ICE trains operate on just a few routes linking the country's largest cities. Somewhat slower and less expensive are the InterCity (IC) trains, which stop only at

certain stations, and offer an express service. When travelling over shorter distances it is best to take the Regional-Express (RE) trains.

TICKETS

TRAIN FARES are quite expensive in Germany and in express trains there is a compulsory surcharge, *Zuschlag*. It is not essential to reserve seats, but in the high season it is a good idea to do so and charges are not exorbitant. One way to travel more cheaply is to buy a *BahnCard*, which gives a 50 per cent discount. The cost of this card is recouped the second time a longer train journey is undertaken.

When planning a lengthy stay in Germany and travelling around the country, it is worth acquiring an InterRail card, which is available to every European citizen, regardless of age. Every year the variety of discounted fares to which this card entitles the bearer is extended, so that it is worth checking out the full range. The price of the card depends on the age of the

traveller. Schoolchildren and students are entitled to a reduced rate. The cost also depends on which countries are to be visited. An InterRail card that is valid for travel in Germany is also valid for Austria, Switzerland and Denmark. InterRail cards can be obtained from Rail Europe or from some travel agents.

During the summer season in Germany, various discounts and special offers are introduced – for example, weekend tickets, family, group and so on, so it is worth making enquiries about these before setting off on a train journey.

RESERVATIONS

TRAIN TICKETS CAN be bought and reservations made in travel agents or at the railway station at the *Reisezentrum*, which at the same time acts as an information centre. Tickets can also be reserved by telephone or through the Internet, where a detailed timetable can be viewed. Using this facility, it is simple to plan the appropriate routes for your journey yourself.

RAILWAY STATIONS

IN GERMANY, many railway stations are magnificent, historic buildings with vast halls covering the platforms. Among the most beautiful is

The fastest and most comfortable German train – InterCity Express

TRAIN ROUTES IN GERMANY

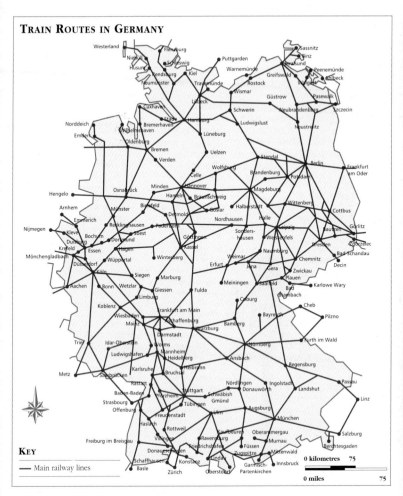

KEY

— Main railway lines

0 kilometres 75

0 miles 75

the main station in Leipzig. In large towns, railway stations are generally located in the centre. They include dozens of shops (often open on Sundays), car rental firms, hotel reservation bureaux, and other services, such as cash points, left luggage provision and public toilets with shower facilities.

TRAVELLING BY FERRY AND SHIP

VISITORS TRAVELLING TO Germany by car from the UK will have to decide which crossing to use (unless using the Channel Tunnel). This will depend to some extent on which part of Germany is to be visited. The crossings

from Dover to Ostend, in Belgium, or to Calais, in France, are the shortest, while the Harwich to Hook of Holland route is useful for those travelling from further north. There are also two ferry services to Hamburg, operated by Scandinavian Seaways – one from Harwich and one from North Shields, near Newcastle-upon-Tyne.

There are also many links between German ports and other countries. Color Line runs a service from Oslo (Norway) to Kiel; Scandlines runs two ferries from Sweden: Trelleborg to Rostock and Trelleborg to Sassnitz; Scandline also runs three ferries from Denmark: Gedser to Rostock, Rødby to Puttgarden and Rønne (Bornholm) to Sassnitz.

Ship taking passengers to Helgoland

Travelling by Car and Bus

Sign for parking ticket machine

THE FASTEST AND MOST comfortable way of travelling around Germany is to use the motorways. The excellent network of toll-free routes guarantees fast progress over longer distances, while a well-maintained system of main roads enables you to reach interesting places throughout the country. Motorways have the advantage of regularly sited service stations, where travellers can stop for fuel and something to eat. On lesser roads and in remote areas, petrol stations may be few and far between.

A selection of traffic signs on German roads

ARRIVING BY CAR

THERE ARE MANY border crossings into Germany and providing that you carry the necessary documents and your car does not look disreputable, you should experience a minimum of delay and formalities. EU citizens do not have to make a Customs declaration on arrival, but there are limits on the amount of duty-free goods that can be brought in *(see p530)*.

WHAT TO TAKE

VISITORS travelling by car in Germany must carry a valid driving licence as well as their vehicle's registration document and insurance policy. Before leaving home check with your insurance company whether your policy will cover you while you are in Germany. If it may be necessary to obtain a Green Card to extend the cover for the duration of your stay.

The car must carry a plate indicating country of origin, and it must also be equipped with a red warning triangle for use in case of breakdown.

Seatbelts are compulsory and children under 12 must sit in the back, with babies and toddlers in child-seats.

ROADS AND MOTORWAYS

THE GERMAN motorway network is extensive. They are all toll-free and have regularly spaced petrol stations, as well as parking facilities with toilets, restaurants and motels. Ranging along the hard shoulder are yellow poles with emergency buttons, which can be used to call for help in the event of a breakdown or accident. An *Autobahn* (motorway) is indicated by the letter "A" followed by a number – some also have a letter "E" and a number, denoting that the road crosses the German border. A *Bundesstraße* (main road) is indicated by the letter "B" and a number.

Motorway telephone

ADDITIONAL ROAD SIGNS

IN ADDITION to internationally understood road signs on German roads, there are also written signs that clarify the meaning of the sign above.

On motorways, for example, a yellow triangular warning sign with a row of cars is a warning about the possibility of traffic jams, which may be accompanied by the word *"Stau"*. On mountain roads, a warning sign showing a car tyre wrapped in a chain will be accompanied by the word *"Schnee"*, which warns against driving without chains when there is snow.

A diversion is indicated by the colour yellow and the word *"Umleitung"*, while the diversion route is indicated by the letter "U" followed by the number of the road. A sign with the slogan *"Baustelle"* (meaning "refurbishment") always precedes the stretch that is being renovated.

A sign showing a horizontal blue arrow with the word *"Einbahnstrasse"* indicates a one-way street.

RULES OF THE ROAD

GERMANS on the whole drive in accordance with the regulations. They are generally courteous, but they can be a little aggressive, particularly on motorways. German drivers hurtle along the outside lane at very great speed and get very annoyed if they have to slow down because of other drivers. Visitors should be particularly careful when first starting to drive in Germany, especially if they are unused to driving on the right. Bear in mind that being caught exceeding the speed limit incurs a large fine.

In the event of an accident on the motorway, or if a traffic jam necessitates an abrupt reduction in speed, drivers should turn on their flashing emergency lights to warn drivers behind of the impending danger.

Petrol station at a motorway service area

Parking-ticket Machine

Automatic parking-ticket machines like this issue receipts that are placed on the inside of the windscreen. There are also parking meters with a timer, which allow parking for up to 2 hours.

Clock indicating date and time

Slot for inserting coins

Information in different languages

Ticket is dispensed from here

DRIVING IN TOWNS

FINDING A PLACE in which to park is not easy: it is often best to use a multi-storey car park, which is indicated by "*Parkhaus*"; the word "*Frei*" indicates that parking spaces are available. It is never worth leaving your car in a prohibited area – a traffic warden will arrive immediately, impose a fine and arrange for the car to be towed away. Retrieving an impounded car is expensive and difficult.

Cars left in a controlled parking zone must either display a parking ticket or be parked validly at a meter.

ROAD TRAFFIC REGULATIONS

IN GERMANY, the same road traffic regulations apply as in most European countries. For example, all passengers must wear a seat-belt and children under the age of 12 must travel in the back seats. Driving after drinking a small amount of alcohol is allowed, but if you cause an accident, the consequences will be more severe if a breathalyzer shows the presence of alcohol in your blood. In built-up areas the speed limit is 50 km/h (31 mph); beyond this it

is 100 km/h (62 mph), and on motorways the limit is 130 km/h (81 mph). In practice, many drivers drive at speeds exceeding 200 km/h (125 mph). When travelling with a caravan or camping trailer outside built-up areas, drivers should not exceed 70 km/h (44 mph), and on motorways 100 km/h (62 mph). Road traffic police are strict about imposing fines for breaches of speed restrictions.

Drivers can incur fines for driving too close to the vehicle in front and for parking in prohibited areas as well as for breaking the speed limits.

HIRING A CAR

REPRESENTATIVES of car-hire firms can be found at airports, railway stations and in more expensive hotels. In order to hire a car, drivers need to produce their passport and driving licence and to be over 18. In some cases, they may be required to have an international driving licence.

HITCH-HIKING

HITCH-HIKING is a popular way of travelling, particularly among young people. A safer method of finding a lift or a travelling companion is

to make use of the services of Mitfahrzentralen, a contact agency for drivers who offer spare seats on a journey for an agreed fee. Check addresses and telephone numbers in local telephone directories.

ARRIVING BY COACH

TRAVELLING TO GERMANY by coach from the UK is not a very attractive option as the journey is long and fares are not particularly cheap. Routes are operated by Eurolines.

TRAVELLING BY COACH

THERE IS A GOOD network of inter-city coach services in Germany, though journeys are generally no cheaper than travelling by train. Most towns have a *Zentraler Omnibus Bahnhof* (ZOB) close to the train station. It is here that most bus services originate and where service timetables can be obtained and tickets purchased. Many local coach services also operate from the central bus station, although suburban areas have their own services to the centre of town. It is best to ask at the tourist information centre for information about getting to your destination.

Comfortable, long-distance, double-decker coach

Transport in Cities

GETTING AROUND huge cities is not easy and the historic centres are best visited on foot. Large towns often suffer from traffic congestion and it can be difficult to find vacant parking places. It is advisable to leave your car in a car park on the outskirts and travel around using the fast railway (S-Bahn),

The S-Bahn logo

underground (U-Bahn), trams or city buses. The latter operate frequent, timetabled services and can usually avoid traffic jams as they have the advantage of travelling along specially designated traffic lanes.

The city rail line, Schwebebahn, in Wuppertal

TAXIS

TAXIS OFFER A comfortable though expensive way of getting around towns and cities. If several people share a cab, however, this can work out cheaper than using the bus or train. Every taxi vehicle, regardless of make, is a cream colour and has a "TAXI" sign on the roof; this will be illuminated if the taxi is free. Cabs can be hailed on the street or booked by telephone. They can also be picked up at a taxi rank, though these are rare. If the rank is empty, a cab can be called for from the telephone there.

The fare is calculated by an illuminated meter on the dashboard. The lowest rates apply during the week, for journeys within the city limits. At nights and at weekends the rates are higher.

Telephone at a taxi rank

TRAVELLING ON THE U-BAHN AND S-BAHN

ALL THE BIG German cities have a network of fast connections by underground railway (U-Bahn) and by rail (S-Bahn). The U-Bahn offers frequent services – in peak hours every 3–5 minutes – and individual stations are situated quite close to each other. The S-Bahn offers less frequent services, every 10 or 20 minutes, while the stations are quite markedly apart. Generally the S- and U-Bahn use the same tickets, as do buses and trams. Various

types of ticket can be bought from ticket machines located by the entrance to stations; the tickets must be punched in the red punching machine situated nearby. On German railway stations there are no regulatory measures, such as ticket-operated barriers, so it is easy for unscrupulous passengers to get onto a train without a ticket. However it is not worth trying to do this as trains are patrolled by ticket inspectors, often dressed in civilian clothes, who start checking tickets once a train has left the station. Fines for travelling without a ticket are very high.

U-Bahn stations are indicated by square signs with a white "U" on a dark blue background, while S-Bahn stations have round signs with a white "S" on a green background. On maps of the network, each line of the U- and S-Bahn is marked in a different colour and has its own number. The direction of

the route is indicated by the name of the station at which the route terminates. On every station platform a display shows the destination of the next incoming train. A white circle or oval on the map indicates an interchange station. On every station you will find town maps and maps of the transport network displayed in prominent positions. Maps are also displayed in carriages.

Carriage doors on U- and S-Bahn trains are operated manually, but they close automatically. At major stations a member of staff gives the signal for trains to leave the station. Passengers are not allowed to board the train after his cry of "*Zurückbleiben!*" – which means that the doors are about to close. Throughout the journey, the names of the next stations are announced, while in modern trains these are usually also indicated on illuminated displays in the carriages.

Automatic Ticket Machine

To use this machine, select the appropriate ticket by pressing a button. Insert the amount of money indicated by the display. Your ticket and change will then be delivered.

A map of the U-Bahn and S-Bahn system

Slot for coins

Slot for bank notes

Buttons for selecting different types of ticket

Opening, from which tickets and change are delivered

Tram and Bus Stop Sign

At every stop, a board displays the numbers and destinations of trams and buses that stop there. Timetables and maps of the public transport system are also displayed.

Tram stop stymbol: Haltestelle

S-Bhf Oranienburger Str.

=1 Heinersdorf — **Bus numbers and names of destinations**

=13 Hohenschönhausen Zingster Str.

A map of the transport network

Timetable of individual routes

BUSES

Bus ROUTES HAVE individual timetables, which are displayed on boards at bus stops. Maps showing each stage of the route are also displayed there. As well as a route number, buses also have a sign indicating where their particular journey ends. This is useful as some buses operate on shorter routes outside peak hours.

During the journey, the bus driver generally announces the name of the bus stop that the bus is approaching. In the centre of town, this is not so important, as in heavy traffic the bus stops at every bus stop as a matter of course. However, further away from the city centre or in periods where the traffic is not so heavy, you have to listen out for these announcements.

At many bus stops, the driver will pull in only on request, so passengers must press the "Halt" button in plenty of time to warn the driver that they wish to alight.

TRAMS

Trams ARE a comfortable means of urban transport, with the advantage that they do not get stuck in traffic jams. The same tickets as for buses and S-Bahn can be used.

TICKETS

For THE PURPOSE of public transport charges, large cities are generally divided into zones, with the cost of a ticket depending on which zones are travelled through during a journey.

In many cities a single-use ticket is valid for two hours, and during this time you can use all the modes of transport available, including the S- and U-Bahn, even changing routes several times. However, using this type of ticket is the most expensive way to travel. In addition to these standard tickets *(Normltarif)*, there are also cheaper tickets available *(Kurzstrecke)*, which limit you to short distances. In many German cities you can also buy tickets in the form of a strip, which has to be punched according to the length of the journey.

Children who have not reached the age of 14 are eligible for a reduced rate *(Ermässigunstarif)*, while toddlers up to the age of six travel free. Children's push-chairs and dogs will often be carried on public transport without any extra charge.

A modern type of tram that operates in German cities

There are many other types of tickets and travelcards – for example a one-day ticket *(Tageskarte)*, a one-day group ticket *(Gruppentageskarte)*, and a weekly ticket *(7-Tage-Karte)*. Some towns issue a *WelcomeCard* that allows for three days' travel around town as well as giving many discounts in museums.

Bicycles parked near the entrance to the Hofgarten in Munich

BICYCLES

Bicycles ARE a popular form of transport in Germany. There are numerous cycle lanes and many junctions have special lights for cyclists. In front of virtually every office, bank and school there is a bicycle stand, although these should be used only for a short period and, of course, the bicycle still needs to be secured against theft. Bicycles can be transported on the S-Bahn, although owners will need to get on the train at the appropriate door and stand their vehicle in the designated place. Bicycles can be hired at the station or other hire places *(Fahrradverleih)*.

A city bus in Munich

Index

Acknowledgements

DORLING KINDERSLEY AND WIEDZA I ŻYCIE would like to thank the following people for their help in preparing this guide:

ADDITIONAL TEXT
Michał Jaranowski
Barbara Sudnik-Wójcicka
Grażyna Winiarska
Konrad Gruda
Bożena Steinborn

ADDITIONAL PHOTOGRAPHS
Maciej Bronarski
Witold Danilkiewicz
Grzegorz Kłosowski
Renata and Marek Kosińscy
Sergiusz Michalski
Nils Meyer
Andrzej Zygmuntowicz and Ireneusz Winnicki
Władysław Wisławski

PUBLISHING MANAGER
Helen Townsend

MANAGING ART EDITOR
Kate Poole

CONSULTANT
Gerhard Bruschke

FACTCHECKER
Barbara Sobeck

DIRECTOR OF PUBLISHING
Gillian Allan

EDITORIAL AND DESIGN ASSISTANCE
Sam Atkinson, Hilary Bird, Arwen Burnett, Jo Cowen, Marcus Hardy, Lucinda Hawksley, Jacky Jackson, Claire Marsden, Ferdie McDonald, Casper Morris, Dave Pugh, Andrew Szudek, Stewart J. Wild

The publisher would also like to thank all the people and institutions who allowed photographs belonging to them to be reproduced, as well as granting permission to use photographs from their archives:

Archäologische Staatssammlung in Munich; Arthothek (Jürgen Hinrichsowi); Bawaria Filmstadt; Bayerisches Nationalmuseum in Munich; Bildarchiv Preussischer Kulturbesitz in Berlin (Heidrun Klein); Bildvorlagen Römerschatz – Gäubodenmuseum Straubing (Dr. Prammer); Bischöfliches Dom- und Diözesanmuseum Mainz (Dr. Hansowi-Jurgenowi Kotzurowi); Brecht-Weigel-Gedenkstätte in Berlin (Elke Pfeil); Bridgeman Art Library; Bröhan-Museum in Berlin (Ingrid Jagr and Frau Betzker); Brücke-Museum in Berlin; Brüder-Grimm-Museum in Kassel; Corbis; Das Domkapitel (Gertraut Mockel, Büro Dr Georg Minkenberg); Deutsche Apothekenmuseum in Heidelberg; Deutsche Historisches in Berlin (Kathi Rumlow); Deutsche Press Agentur (dpa) in Berlin (Tanija Teichmann); Deutsches Museum in Munich (Sigrid Schneider and Marlene Schwarz); Deutsches Schiffahrtsmuseum in Bremerhaven (Hansowi-Walterowi Kewelohowi); Deutsches Tapetenmuseum Kassel (Sabine Thümmler); Deutsches Technikmuseum Berlin (Renate Förster); Diözesanmuseum in Bamberg (Birgit Kandora); Dombauverwaltung des Metropolitankapitels Köln (Birgit Lambert); Dresden Museum für Geschichte der Stadt Dresden (Dr. Christel Wünsch); Flash Press Media (Sylwii Wilgockiej); Forschung- und Gedenkstätte Normannenstraße (Stasi-Museum) in Berlin (Andrei Holland-Moritz); Fürstlich Hohenzollernsche Schlossverwaltung in Sigmaringen (Heldze Boban); Gemäldegalerie Alte Meister (Steffi Reh); Gemäldegalerie Neue Meister (Gisela Mehnert); Germanisches Nationalmuseum in Nuremberg (Hermanowi Maué); Hamburger Bahnhof in Berlin; Hamburger Kunsthalle; Hessisches Landesmuseum Kassel; Käthe-Kollwitz-Museum in Berlin (A. Ingrid Findell); Komische Oper Berlin (Gaby Hofmann); Kunstmuseum Düsseldorf (Anne-Marie Katins); Kunstsammlungen Paula Modersohn in Bremen (Hubertusowi Morgenthalowi); Kunstsammlungen zu Weimar (Angelice Goder); Kunstverlag Maria Laach (Helmutowi Keipowi); Kurdirektion des Berchtesgadener Landes (Vroni Aigner, Birgit Tica); Landesmuseum Trier (Margot Redwanz); LBB Photo Archives (Dyrektorowi Christophowi Kalischowi); Linden-Museum Stuttgart, Staatliches Museum für Völkerkunde (Dr. Doris Kurelli); Lutherstube in Wittenberg (Jutcie Strehle); Markgrafliches Operhaus in Bayreuth; Mercedes-Benz-Museum in Stuttgart; Museum am Ostwall in Dortmund; Museum der Bildenden Künste in Leipzig (Roswitha Engel); Museum Folkwang in Essen, Stadt Essen (Mr Hildebrandowi); Museum of the City of Berlin; Porzelansammlung (Ulrike Maltschew); Rheinisches Landesmuseum Bonn (Dr Gerhard Bauchhenß); Rüstkammer (Yvonne Brandt); Schlösserverwaltung in Munich (Frau Gerum); Seebul Ada und Emil Nolde (Dr Andreasowi Fluckowi); Staatliche Graphische Sammlung in Munich (Wiebke Tomaschek); Staatliche Kunstsammlungen Dresden, Albertinum, Grünes Gewölbe; Staatliche Porzellan-Manufaktur Meißen GMBH (Christine Mangold); Staatliche Schlösser und Gärten, Pfarzheim (Herr Braunowi); Staatsarchiv Hamburg (Kathrin Berger); Staatsgalerie Stuttgart (Frau Fönnauer); Städelsches Kunstinstitut in Frankfurt am Main (Elisabeth Heinemann); Stadt Köln, Wallraf-Richartz-Museum in Cologne (Dr Roswitha Neu-Kock and Dr Mai); Stadtmuseum in Munich; Stiftung Luthergedenkstätten in Sachsen-Anhalt; Stiftung Preussische Schlösser und Gärten Berlin (Carli Kamarze); Superstock Polska Sp. z.o.o. (Elżbiecie Gajewskiej); Von der Heydt-Museum Wuppertal (Margarecie Janz); Wartburg-Stiftung in Eisenach (Petrze Wilke); Zefa (Ewie Kozłowskiej)

The publisher would also like to thank the following for their assistance on the guide:

Joanna Minz for coordinating information, Tamara and Jacek Draber for their help with correspondence and telephone contacts, Jürgen Christoffer of Deutscher Wetterdienst for meteorological information.

Picture Credits

t = top; tl = top left; tlb = top left below; tc = top centre; tcb = top centre below; tr = top right; tra = top right above; trb = top right below; cl = centre left; cla = centre left above; clb = centre left below; c = centre; ca = centre above; cb = centre below; cr = centre right; cra = centre right above; cbr = centre bottom right; crb = centre right below; bl = bottom left; blb = bottom left below; bc = bottom centre; br = bottom right; bra = bottom right above; brb = bottom right below; b = bottom

Aachener Dom (Copyright: Domkapitel Aachen – photo. Ann Münchow) 382t, 382ca, 382cb, 382t (Skarbiec), 383ca, 383cb, 383br, 383bl
Albertinum (Dresden) 162t
Archäologische Staatssammlung (Munich) 209d
Arthothek 26t, 26b, 27cla, 27blb, 50t, 166ca, 166cb, 166b, 167t, 167ca, 167cb, 167b, 165cb, 212cb, 247b, 422t, 422b, 423t, 423cb, 423b, 430t; Joachim Blauel 27bra, 46t, 212t, 212b, 213cb, 246t, 280cr; Blauel/Gnamm 208t, 212ca, 213t, 213ca, 245tr; Bayer d'Mitko 213d; Sophie-R. Gnamm 216; Alexander Koch 27trb; Christoph Sandig 456d; G. Westermann 418b, 423t

Bavaria Filmstadt 217t
Brecht-Weigel-Gedenkstätte (Berlin) 97c
Bridgeman Art Library 30br, 99t
Bronarski Maciej 320t, 336t, 336c, 336b, 337t, 337ca, 337cb, 337b
Bröhan-Museum (Berlin) 92t
Brüder-Grimm-Museum (Kassel) 350tr, 354tr (© Staatliche Museum Kassel)
Corbis 25tr, 25bra, 25blb, 432–433 (©Bob Krist/Corbis), 440 (© Nilk Wheeler/Corbis)

Danilkiewicz Witold 411b, 452, 460t
Deutsche Apothekenmuseum (Heidelberg) 284tr
Deutsche Techikmuseum Berlin 77b
Deutsches Historisches Museum Berlin (Zeughaus) 22b, 24c, 30ca, 30cla, 30clb, 30crb, 30br, 31cla, 31tlb, 31tr, 31clb, 31cb, 31crb, 31cbr (Holz & Kunststoff), 32 cla, 42, 48tl (R. Bemke), 48tr (Jurgen Liepe), 48c, 48b (A.C. Theil), 49t (R. Boemke), 50b, 51t, 51cla, 52cl, 56b, 57bl, 116tr, 116b, 117t
Deutsches Museum (Munich) 218t, 218cra, 218clb, 218b, 219t, 219cra, 219crb, 219cl, 219b
Deutsches Schiffahrtsmuseum Bremerhaven 46d
Diözesanmuseum (Bamberg) 237t
dpa 22tra, 23tl, 23tr, 23cra, 23crb, 23br, 23bl, 24tl, 24tr, 31cla, 31cra, 31bl, 32tr, 39t, 56ca, 129t, 103t, 195tl, 279t, 447t; Jens Büttner 57t; Claus Felix 39b; Matthias Hiekel 36b; Peter Förster 36t; Wulf Hirschberger 37b; Ralf Hirschberger 34b; Peer Grimm 18tr; Frank Leonhardt 35t; Wolfgang Kluge 24b; Wolfgang Kumm 57br; Kay Nietfeld 34t, 35t; Frank Mächler 37t; Carsten Rehder 34t; Wulf Pfeiffer 37d; Martin Schutt 38t, 171d; Roland Scheidemann 39t; Ingo Wagner 57t; Heinz Wieseler 38b
Dresden Museum für Geschichte der Stadt Dresden 51crb

Eisenach-Wartburg 176t, 176tl, 176tr, 177t

Gäubodenmuseum Straubing 43bl
Germanisches Nationalmuseum (Nuremberg) 246cra, 246cla, 246bl, 247t, 247c, 247b
Grünes Gewölbe (Dresden) 162t

Hamburger Bahnhof (Berlin) 89bl
Hamburger Kunsthalle (Hamburg) 26cla, 422t
Hessisches Landesmuseum Kassel 350tl, 350b (© Staatliche Museum Kassel Deutsches Tapetenmuseum)

Käthe-Kollwitz-Museum (Berlin) 83t
Klosowski Grzegorz 20cra
Kloster Maulbronn 288t, 288b, 289cla, 289crb, 289b
Kölner Dom 388tl, 388c, 388b, 389t, 389ca, 389cb, 389bl, 389br (© Dombauarchiv Köln, Matz und Schenk)
Komische Oper (Berlin) Rittershaus Monika 102b
Kosińscy, Renata and Marek 20clb, 20bra, 20blb, 21cla, 21tlb, 21blb, 194tl, 195ca, 195tr, 195cl, 195cr, 195br
Kunstmuseum Düsseldorf 26clb
Kunstsammlungen Paula Modersohn 419tl
Kunstverlag Maria Laach 320b, 344tl, 344tr, 344ca, 345t, 345ca, 345cb, 345b
Kurdirektion des Berchtesgadener Landes Storto, Leonberg 262b

Landesmuseum Trier Thomas Zühmer 328t
Linden Museum für Völkerkunde (Stuttgart) 296tlb
Ludwigsburg – Schloss 292ca, 292cb, 292b, 293t
Lutherstube (Wittenberg) 117t

Mainz – Dom 321b (© M. Hankel-Studio)
Mercedes-Benz-Museum (Stuttgart) 296tra
Meyer Nils 56cb
Michalski Sergiusz 16t
Mittelalterliches Museum (Rothenburg ob der Tauber) 248br
Museum der bildenden Künste (Leipzig) 49t (MdbK,

Gerstenberger 1994)
Museum Folkwang (Essen) 27t
Museum für Naturkunde (Berlin) 89br
Museum am Ostwall (Dortmund) 376t
Musikinstrumenten-Museum (Berlin) 81ca

Nationalmuseum (Munich) 209t

Opernhaus (Bayreuth) 238t

Philharmonie (Berlin) 81t

Rheinisches Landesmuseum Bonn 394t

Schauspielhaus (Konzerthaus Berlin) 68d
Schloss Sigmaringen 301b
Schlösserverwaltung (Munich) 232ca, 233t, 233ca, 233cb, 233b, 268t, 268ca, 268cb, 268b
Staatarchiv Hamburg 46–47
Staatliche Museen Preußischer Kulturbesitz (Berlin) 44c, 51br, 52–53, 53tl, 53br, 54t, 54cra, 54clb, 54b, 55t, 55bl, 55br, 56t, 60br, 61cra, 71t, 72ca, 73t, 85t, 86cb, 87clb, 94cla, 95crb, 100t, 114tl, 115brb; Hans-Joachim Bartsch 45c, 45b, 51bl; Jorg P. Anders 80c, 80b, 84b, 86tr, 86tl, 86ca, 86b, 87t, 87cra, 87d; Grammes 44br; Klaus Göken 52b, 55c, 72b, 73d; Erich Lessing 70clb, 72t, 73cb; Jurgen Liepe 71c, 72cb, 92d; Georg Niedermeister 73ca; Arne Psille 43br, 44tr, 44bl; Steinkopf 80tr
Staatliche Porzellan-Manufaktur Meißen GMBH 30cra, 114tr, 114cra, 114clb, 114b, 115t, 115bra
Klaus Tänzer 115cra
Staatsgalerie Stuttgart 298tra, 298tlb, 298t, 298b, 299t, 299ca, 299cb, 299b
Städelsches Kunstinstitut (Frankfurt am Main) 364t, 364c, 364ab, 365t, 365ca, 365cb, 365b
Stadtmuseum Berlin 65c, 67t; Hans-Joachim Bartsch 49bl
Stadtmuseum (Munich) 65c, 204tl; Hans-Joachim Bartsch 5t; Sudnik 21crb
Stasi-Museum (Berlin) 98b
Stiftung Preussische Schlösser und Gärten Berlin 50c, 94cl, 95ca, 95b, 125cr, 126b, 129b
Superstock Polska Sp. zo.o. 310t

Tourist Office – Altötting 256t, 256b

Wallraf-Richartz-Museum (Cologne) 390t, 390ca, 390cb, 390b, 391t, 391c, 391br, 391bl (© Rheinisches Bildarchiv)

Zefa 21cl, 192–193c, 373b, 398–399, 408bra, 408t, 409b, 419b, 436t, 436c, 437tl, 437tr, 437b, 439b, 464t; Bloemendal 5t; Damm 17b, 384b, 274, 380b, 437tra, 453d; Eckstein 19b, 409tl, 409tr, 463b; Freytag 15b, 194tr, 313t; Haenel 1, 29tcb, 442b, 455t, 467t; Kehrer 21cr; Kinne 392t, 392b; Kohlhas 395t; Leidorf 11t, 11b; Rossenbach 8–9, 308–309, 384c, 396b, 397t, 398–399, 445b, 456t; Rose 397t; Steeger 409t; Streichan 338–339, 349t, 369b; Svenja-Foto 380t, 389cra; Waldkirch 436t; M. Winkel 388tr
Zwinger (Dresden) 164t, 164cb, 165b
Gemäldegalerie Alte Meister 166t

All other images ©Dorling Kindersley.
For further information see: www.dkimages.com

DORLING KINDERSLEY SPECIAL EDITIONS

Dorling Kindersley books can be purchased in bulk quantities at discounted prices for use in promotions or as premiums. We are also able to offer special editions and personalized jackets, corporate imprints, and excerpts from all of our books, tailored specifically to meet your own needs.

To find out more, please contact:
(in the United Kingdom) – SPECIAL SALES, DORLING KINDERSLEY LIMITED, 80 STRAND, LONDON WC2R 0RL.
(in the United States) – SPECIAL MARKETS DEPARTMENT, DORLING KINDERSLEY, INC., 95 MADISON AVENUE, NEW YORK, NY 10016.

Phrasebook

In an Emergency

Where is the telephone?	Wo ist das Telefon?	voh ist duss tel-e-fone?
Help!	Hilfe!	hilf-uh
Please call a doctor	Bitte rufen Sie einen Arzt	bitt-uh roof'n zee ine-en artst
Please call the police	Bitte rufen Sie die Polizei	bitt-uh roof'n zee dee poli-tsy
Please call the fire brigade	Bitte rufen Sie die Feuerwehr	bitt-uh roof'n zee dee foyer-vayr
Stop!	Halt!	hult

Communication Essentials

Yes	Ja	yah
No	Nein	nine
Please	Bitte	bitt-uh
Thank you	Danke	dunk-uh
Excuse me	Verzeihung	fair-tsy-hoong
Hello (good day)	Guten Tag	goot-en tahk
Goodbye	Auf Wiedersehen	owf-veed-er-zay-ern
Good evening	Guten Abend	goot'n ahb'nt
Good night	Gute Nacht	goot-uh nukht
Until tomorrow	Bis morgen	biss morg'n
See you	Tschüss	chooss
What is that?	Was ist das?	voss ist duss
Why?	Warum?	var-room
Where?	Wo?	voh
When?	Wann?	vunn
today	heute	hoyt-uh
tomorrow	morgen	morg'n
month	Monat	mohn-aht
night	Nacht	nukht
afternoon	Nachmittag	nahkh-mit-tahk
morning	Morgen	morg'n
year	Jahr	yar
there	dort	dort
here	hier	hear
week	Woche	vokh-uh
yesterday	gestern	gest'n
evening	Abend	ahb'nt

Useful Phrases

How are you? (informal)	Wie geht's?	vee gayts
Fine, thanks	Danke, es geht mir gut	dunk-uh, es gayt meer goot
Until later	Bis später	biss shpay-ter
Where is/are?	Wo ist/sind...?	voh ist/sind
How far is it to...?	Wie weit ist es...?	vee vite ist ess
Do you speak English?	Sprechen Sie Englisch?	shpresh'n zee eng-glish
I don't understand	Ich verstehe nicht	ish fair-shtay-uh nisht
Could you speak more slowly?	Könnten Sie langsamer sprechen?	kurnt-en zee lung-zam-er shpresh'n

Useful Words

large	gross	grohss
small	klein	kline
hot	heiss	hyce
cold	kalt	kult
good	gut	goot
bad	böse/schlecht	burss-uh/shlesht
open	geöffnet	g'urff-nett
closed	geschlossen	g'shloss'n
left	links	links
right	rechts	reshts
straight ahead	geradeaus	g'rah-der-owss

Making a Telephone Call

I would like to make a phone call	Ich möchte telefonieren	ish mer-shtuh tel-e-fon-eer'n
I'll try again later	Ich versuche noch ein mal später	ish fair-zookh-uh nokh ine-mull shpay-ter
Can I leave a message?	Kann ich eine Nachricht hinterlassen?	kan ish ine-uh nakh-risht hint-er-lahss-en
answer phone	Anrufbeantworter	an-roof-be-ahnt-vort-er
telephone card	Telefonkarte	tel-e-fohn-kart-uh
receiver	Hörer	hur-er
mobile	Handi	han-dee
engaged (busy)	besetzt	b'zetst
wrong number	Falsche Verbindung	falsh-uh fair-bin-doong

Sightseeing

library	Bibliothek	bib-leo-tek
entrance ticket	Eintrittskarte	ine-tritz-kart-uh
cemetery	Friedhof	freed-hofe
train station	Bahnhof	barn-hofe
gallery	Galerie	gall-er-ree
information	Auskunft	owss-koonft
church	Kirche	keersh-uh
garden	Garten	gart'n
palace/castle	Palast/Schloss	pallast/shloss
place (square)	Platz	plats
bus stop	Haltestelle	hal-te-shtel-uh
national holiday	Nationalfeiertag	nats-yon-ahl-fire-tahk
theatre	Theater	tay-aht-er
free admission	Eintritt frei	ine-tritt fry

Shopping

Do you have/ Is there...?	Gibt es...?	geept ess
How much does it cost?	Was kostet das?	voss kost't duss?
When do you open/ close?	Wann öffnen Sie/ schliessen Sie?	vunn off'n zee shlees'n zee
this	das	duss
expensive	teuer	toy-er
cheap	preiswert	price-vurt
size	Grösse	gruhs-uh
number	Nummer	noom-er
colour	Farbe	farb-uh
brown	braun	brown
black	schwarz	shvarts
red	rot	roht
blue	blau	blau
green	grün	groon
yellow	gelb	gelp

Types of Shop

antique shop	Antiquariat	antik-var-yat
chemist (pharmacy)	Apotheke	appo-tay-kuh
bank	Bank	bunk
market	Markt	markt
travel agency	Reisebüro	rye-zer-boo-roe
department store	Warenhaus	vahr'n-hows
chemist's, drugstore	Drogerie	droog-er-ree
hairdresser	Friseur	freezz-er
newspaper kiosk	Zeitungskiosk	tsytoongs-kee-osk
bookshop	Buchhandlung	bookh-hant-loong

bakery	Bäckerei	beck-er-**eye**
post office	Post	posst
shop/store	Geschäft/Laden	gush-**eft**/**lard**'n
film processing shop	Photogeschäft	fo-to-gush-**eft**
self-service shop	Selbstbedienungs-laden	selpst-bed-**ee**-nungs-lard'n
shoe shop	Schuhladen	shoo-lard'n
clothes shop	Kleiderladen, Boutique	klyder-lard'n boo-**teek**-uh
food shop	Lebensmittel-geschäft	**lay**-bens-mittel-gush-eft
glass, porcelain	Glas, Porzellan	**glars**, Port-**sellahn**

STAYING IN A HOTEL

Do you have any vacancies?	Haben Sie noch Zimmer frei?	harb'n zee nokh **tsimm**-er-fry
with twin beds?	mit zwei Betten?	mitt tsvy bett'n
with a double bed?	mit einem Doppelbett?	mitt ine'm **dopp**'l-bet
with a bath?	mit Bad?	mitt **bart**
with a shower?	mit Dusche?	mitt **doosh**-uh
I have a reservation	Ich habe eine Reservierung	ish **harb**-uh ine-uh rez-er-**veer**-oong
key	Schlüssel	shlooss'l
porter	Pförtner	**pfert**-ner

EATING OUT

Do you have a table for...?	Haben Sie einen Tisch für...?	harb'n zee tish foor
I would like to reserve a table	Ich möchte eine Reservierung machen	ish **mer**-shtuh ine-uh rezer-**veer**-oong makh'n
I'm a vegetarian	Ich bin Vegetarier	ish bin vegg-er-**tah**-ree-er
Waiter!	Herr Ober!	hair **oh**-bare!
The bill (check), please	Die Rechnung, bitte	dee **resh**-noong bitt-uh
breakfast	Frühstück	**froo**-shtock
lunch	Mittagessen	**mit**-targ-ess'n
dinner	Abendessen	**arb**'nt-ess'n
bottle	Flasche	**flush**-uh
dish of the day	Tagesgericht	**tahg**-es-gur-isht
main dish	Hauptgericht	**howpt**-gur-isht
dessert	Nachtisch	**nahkh**-tish
cup	Tasse	**tass**-uh
wine list	Weinkarte	vine-kart-uh
tankard	Krug	khroog
glass	Glas	**glars**
spoon	Löffel	**lerff**'l
teaspoon	Teelöffel	tay-lerff'l
tip	Trinkgeld	**trink**-gelt
knife	Messer	**mess**-er
starter (appetizer)	Vorspeise	**for**-shpize-uh
the bill	Rechnung	**resh**-noong
plate	Teller	**tell**-er
fork	Gabel	**gahb**'l

MENU DECODER

Aal	**arl**	eel
Apfel	**upf**'l	apple
Apfelschorle	**upf**'l-shoorl-uh	apple juice with sparkling mineral water
Apfelsine	**upf**'l-seen-uh	orange
Aprikose	upri-**kawz**-uh	apricot
Artischocke	arti-**shokh**-uh-or-ber-jeen-uh	artichoke
Aubergine (eggplant)		aubergine
Banane	bar-**narn**-uh	banana
Beefsteack	**beef**-stayk	steak
Bier	beer	beer

Bockwurst	**bokh**-voorst	a type of sausage
Bohnensuppe	burn-en-zoop-uh	bean soup
Branntwein	brant-vine	spirits
Bratkartoffeln	brat-kar-toff'ln	fried potatoes
Bratwurst	brat-voorst	fried sausage
Brötchen	bret-tchen	bread roll
Brot	brot	bread
Brühe	bruh-uh	broth
Butter	**boot**-ter	butter
Champignon	**shum**-pin-yong	mushroom
Currywurst	**kha**-ree-voorst	sausage with curry sauce
Dill	**dill**	dill
Ei	**eye**	egg
Eis	**ice**	ice/ ice cream
Ente	**ent**-uh	duck
Erdbeeren	ayrt-**beer**'n	strawberries
Fisch	**fish**	fish
Forelle	for-**ell**-uh	trout
Frikadelle	Frika-dayl-uh	rissole/hamburger
Gans	ganns	goose
Garnele	**gar**-nayl-uh	prawn/shrimp
gebraten	g'**braat**'n	fried
gegrillt	g'**grilt**	grilled
gekocht	g'**kokht**	boiled
geräuchert	g'**rowk**-ert	smoked
Geflügel	g'**floog**'l	poultry
Gemüse	g'**mooz**-uh	vegetables
Grütze	**grurt**-ser	groats, gruel
Gulasch	**goo**-lush	goulash
Gurke	**goork**-uh	gherkin
Hammelbraten	hamm'l-**braat**'n	roast mutton
Hähnchen	haynsh'n	chicken
Hering	**hair**-ing	herring
Himbeeren	him-beer'n	raspberries
Honig	**hoe**-nikh	honey
Kaffee	kaf-**fay**	coffee
Kalbfleisch	kalp-flysh	veal
Kaninchen	ka-**neensh**'n	rabbit
Karpfen	**karpf**'n	carp
Kartoffelpüree	kar-toff'l-poor-ay	mashed potatoes
Käse	**kayz**-uh	cheese
Kaviar	**kar**-vee-ar	caviar
Knoblauch	k'**nob**-lowkh	garlic
Knödel	k'**nerd**'l	noodle
Kohl	**koal**	cabbage
Kopfsalat	**kopf**-zal-aat	lettuce
Krebs	**krayps**	crab
Kuchen	**kookh**'n	cake
Lachs	**lahkhs**	salmon
Leber	**lay**-ber	liver
mariniert	mari-neert	marinated
Marmelade	marmer-**lard**-uh	marmalade, jam
Meerrettich	may-re-tish	horseradish
Milch	**milsh**	milk
Mineralwasser	minn-er-**arl**-vuss-er	mineral water
Möhre	**mer**-uh	carrot
Nuss	**nooss**	nut
Öl	**erl**	oil
Olive	o-**leev**-uh	olive
Petersilie	payt-er-**zee**-li-uh	parsley
Pfeffer	**pfeff**-er	pepper
Pfirsich	**pfir**-zish	peach
Pflaumen	**pflow**-men	plum
Pommes frites	pomm-**fritt**	chips/ French fries
Quark	kvark	soft cheese
Radieschen	ra-**deesh**'n	radish
Rinderbraten	**rind**-er-brat'n	joint of beef
Rinderroulade	**rind**-er-roo-lard-uh	beef olive
Rindfleisch	**rint**-flysh	beef
Rippchen	**rip**-sh'n	cured pork rib
Rotkohl	roht-koal	red cabbage
Rüben	rhoob'n	turnip
Rührei	**rhoo**-er-eye	scrambled eggs
Saft	**zuft**	juice
Salat	zal-aat	salad

Salz	**zults**	salt
Salzkartoffeln	zults-kar-toff'l	boiled potatoes
Sauerkirschen	zow-er-**keersh**'n	cherries
Sauerkraut	zow-er-krowt	sauerkraut
Sekt	**zekt**	sparkling wine
Senf	**zenf**	mustard
scharf	sharf	spicy
Schaschlik	shash-lik	kebab
Schlagsahne	shlahgg-zarn-uh	whipped cream
Schnittlauch	shnit-lowhkh	chives
Schnitzel	**shnitz**'l	veal or pork cutlet
Schweinefleisch	**shvine**-flysh	pork
Spargel	**shparg**'l	asparagus
Spiegelei	shpeeg'l-eye	fried egg
Spinat	shpin-art	spinach
Tee	**tay**	tea
Tomate	tom-art-uh	tomato
Wassermelone	vuss-er-me-lohn-uh	watermelon
Wein	**vine**	wine
Weintrauben	vine-trowb'n	grapes
Wiener Würstchen	veen-er voorst-sh'n	frankfurter
Zander	**tsan**-der	pike-perch
Zitrone	tsi-trohn-uh	lemon
Zucker	**tsook**-er	sugar
Zwieback	tsvee-bak	rusk
Zwiebel	**tsveeb**'l	onion

NUMBERS

0	null	**nool**
1	eins	**eye'ns**
2	zwei	**tsvy**
3	drei	**dry**
4	vier	**feer**
5	fünf	**foonf**
6	sechs	**zex**
7	sieben	**zeeb**'n
8	acht	**uhkht**
9	neun	**noyn**
10	zehn	**tsayn**
11	elf	**elf**
12	zwölf	**tserlf**
13	dreizehn	**dry**-tsayn
14	vierzehn	**feer**-tsayn
15	fünfzehn	**foonf**-tsayn
16	sechzehn	**zex**-tsayn
17	siebzehn	**zeep**-tsayn
18	achtzehn	**uhkht**-tsayn
19	neunzehn	**noyn**-tsayn
20	zwanzig	**tsvunn**-tsig
21	einundzwanzig	**ine**-oont-tsvunn-tsig
30	dreissig	**dry**-sig
40	vierzig	**feer**-sig
50	fünfzig	**foonf**-tsig
60	sechzig	**zex**-tsig
70	siebzig	**zeep**-tsig
80	achtzig	**uhkht**-tsig
90	neunzig	**noyn**-tsig
100	hundert	**hoond**'t
1000	tausend	**towz**'nt
1 000 000	eine Million	**ine**-uh **mill**-yon

TIME

one minute	eine Minute	**ine**-uh min-**oot**-uh
one hour	eine Stunde	**ine**-uh **shtoond**-uh
half an hour	eine halbe Stunde	**ine**-uh hullb-uh **shtoond**-uh
Monday	Montag	**mohn**-targ
Tuesday	Dienstag	**deens**-targ
Wednesday	Mittwoch	**mitt**-vokh
Thursday	Donnerstag	**donn**-ers-targ
Friday	Freitag	**fry**-targ
Saturday	Samstag/ Sonnabend	**zums**-targ **zonn**-ah-bent
Sunday	Sonntag	**zon**-targ
January	Januar	**yan**-ooar
February	Februar	**fay**-brooar
March	März	**mairts**
April	April	**april**
May	Mai	**my**
June	Juni	**yoo**-ni
July	Juli	**yoo**-lee
August	August	ow-**goost**
September	September	zep-**tem**-ber
October	Oktober	ok-toh-ber
November	November	no-**vem**-ber
December	Dezember	day-**tsem**-ber
spring	Frühling	**froo**-ling
summer	Sommer	**zomm**-er
autumn (fall)	Herbst	**hairpst**
winter	Winter	**vint**-er

Road Map of Germany